Seeds of Something Different

Volume II

Seeds of Something Different

An Oral History of the University of California, Santa Cruz

Volume II

Irene Reti, Cameron Vanderscoff, and Sarah Rabkin

Science & Engineering Library, 2016

Photo by Irene Reti

Regional History Project, Special Collections & Archives
University Library, University of California, Santa Cruz
Santa Cruz, California

Seeds of Something Different: An Oral History of the University of California, Santa Cruz. Copyright © 2020 by the Regents of the University of California. Volume II.

ISBN: 978-0-97-233439-6

Printed in the United States of America by Integrated Books International.

Library of Congress Control Number: 2019911562

To contact the Regional History Project:
speccoll@library.ucsc.edu
Regional History Project
McHenry Library, Special Collections & Archives
UC Santa Cruz
Santa Cruz, CA 95064
Phone: 831-459-2547

Cover design by Sandy Bell.

For the companion website to this printed book, which contains digitized archival images and documents not found in these volumes, as well as audio clips of oral histories, and links to other resources see: https://exhibits.library.ucsc.edu/exhibits/show/seeds.

Cover photo by Ansel Adams. Campus meadow with wooden fence. November 1962. Courtesy Special Collections, UCSC Library. MS 002: Ansel Adams Photographs: ms0002_pho_0138.tif.

Back cover photo: Banana slug weathervane by Ken Jensen at West Coast Weather Vanes. Photo by Matt Fitt. Photo copyright by UC Regents. Communications & Marketing Department, UC Santa Cruz.

Contents

Volume II

Part III: Reorganization and Redefinition

Part IV: A Research University with Experimental Roots

Coda

Appendices

Students in front of McHenry
Library, 2018

Photo by Irene Reti

Part III:

Reorganization and Redefinition

Students rally against the grade option, 1981

Photo by Mike Kay

Photo by UCSC Public Information Office

Chancellor Sinsheimer's
inauguration, October 1978,
with demonstrators in the
background

Photo by Carol Foote

Chapter 19

Cutting the Gordian Knot

Chancellor Sinsheimer and the "Reorganization" of the Experiment

Chancellor Sinsheimer's announced transformations were breathtaking in their radical foundations, their scope, and their direct implications for the future.

—*Don Rothman*

Facing the Enrollment Crisis

Angus Taylor: President David Saxon had asked me privately if there were any people on the campus whom I thought might be candidates for the chancellorship. I wrote in my journal that I thought there were only a very few possibilities. There was one man who came to UCSC, whom I thought was an interesting possibility, and that was Kai Erikson, the son of the famous psychologist Erik Erikson.[1]

Herman Blake: I was able to bring another person that everybody got excited about, Kai Erikson, who'd been master of Trumbull College at Yale. The faculty decided Kai was too nice. What was needed was somebody who would run the place with a firm hand. And somewhere in this process Bob Sinsheimer emerged. His daughter had been a student at Santa Cruz. She graduated from Cowell College: Kathy Sinsheimer. People were quite excited about having somebody from Caltech [California Institute of Technology].

Pavel Machotka: Sinsheimer was one of two final candidates for the chancellorship. The other was Kai Erikson, the son of Erik Erikson, the psychoanalyst. The Council of Provosts interviewed them both, and put forth a collective opinion, a very cautious one, I thought, essentially praising Sinsheimer just somewhat more than Kai Erikson. And Sinsheimer got the position. I had favored Erikson at the time. But Sinsheimer had a number of virtues. He really did his work well. He read everything that he had to read, and so on. He was not a person inspiring intimacy or confidence, and I think that was a problem in the long run for him.

Ed Landesman: When we interviewed Robert Sinsheimer, he was by far the best candidate for chancellor of UC Santa Cruz. He was likely a candidate for a Nobel Prize for the research he was doing in biology. He arrived, looked at the campus, at the college system, at how the research

414 SEEDS OF SOMETHING DIFFERENT

was proceeding, and did not find any of it too favorable, especially based on his experience at Caltech, a very traditional college producing top-notch research in science. He saw our research as being weak. And he had the burden of turning things around, or this campus might not survive.

Todd Newberry: I share a sense that Sinsheimer almost was brought in to put us in our place. In reading over that part of his memoirs that have to do with UCSC, I think he sees it that way too. He's a perfectly good man. That's not the issue. It's not a personal thing at all. But it was a totally inappropriate appointment.

Robert Sinsheimer: It became clear that UCSC's image was really very bad. It was not thought of as a serious school. It was thought of as a hippie school with students flaking out under the redwoods and smoking pot. The college system left students with a very inadequate education. I'm not saying how much of this is true. I'm just saying that that was the image.

Santa Cruz Sentinel: Saving the world was only one of the items on our lists of things to do before we grew up. We had to end the war, upend the middle class, exorcise racism, educate our parents and catch the Jefferson Airplane the next time they played at the Fillmore Auditorium. For the first students, those of us dubbed "the pioneers," UCSC in the '60s was a wonderful movie. It was a youthful romance, unfolding in a sensual redwood forest, where the mist turned everything into a backdrop for a fairy tale, and the Monterey Peninsula floated on the horizon like something out of *Gulliver's Travels*. It was a folk-rock musical, orchestrated to the visionary lyrics, the newfound conscience, and the blazing electricity of our poet-prophets. It was a political adventure,

we thought, of ideals and courage. And it was, ultimately, an escapist fantasy.[2]

Los Angeles Times: "Ten years ago, Santa Cruz was turning people down, forcing them to go to Harvard," says Bob Walsh, a senior in politics from Santa Monica. "Now it's definitely a buyer's market. Santa Cruz has the image of a 'hippie school'—a leftover from the '60s, a place where you can feed a deer on the way to class. Students now are more concerned over how they're going to make it in the real world. There are no overwhelming causes. Vietnam's over. Racism has diminished. Students are more worried these days over stories they hear about PhDs ending up driving trucks."[3]

Robert Sinsheimer: Freshman applications had been falling off since 1971. For a time, that had little effect on the enrollment growth, because they'd had a surplus in 1971, and they had significantly increased the numbers of transfer students over the years.

San Francisco Chronicle: Today, Santa Cruz is having a hard time attracting enough students to fill its $100 million worth of splendid buildings. What went wrong? The foremost reason appears to be the swing of the pendulum. In its formative years, the Vietnam War was in full force and many Santa Cruz students were worried most about finding a haven where they could evade the draft. The new generation of undergraduates is chiefly concerned with economics—the personal kind.[4]

George Blumenthal: Narrative evaluations started becoming controversial in the seventies because the seventies became kind of the Me Generation. Whereas in the sixties, everybody wanted to come to Santa Cruz, by the seventies, nobody wanted to come to Santa Cruz. Part of the reason was the fear that this would destroy your future. You couldn't get into medical school, the myth went, if you went to Santa Cruz, because we didn't give grades. Well in fact, as I understand it, the evidence, the actual real evidence, was quite to the contrary. Our students did remarkably well getting into things like medical school. But that was the myth that was out there.

I have to admit, there were some unfortunate aspects to the narrative evaluation system. For example, my wife is a professor at Hastings College of the Law. And what she told me was that at Hastings when they got an application from UCSC, what they would do is they would have a clerk go through all of the narrative evaluations and assign a grade point average based upon reading the narrative evaluations. And then they would proceed only from that assigned GPA in terms of their admissions decision, so nobody making a decision actually read the evaluations and they had consigned this to a clerk of some sort. It is scary. We would say in Santa Cruz that was an abrogation of responsibility. They might say we don't have the time for this. This isn't a right or wrong thing; it's simply an observation.

Robert Sinsheimer: The enrollment had not actually begun to decline until 1978. But the numbers of freshmen applications had been falling precipitously. It was down to less than a quarter of what it had been in 1971. Obviously, something had to be done. The problem was that the campus had been so oversubscribed from day one, in the early years, that they never bothered to develop any significant outreach program.

William Adams, Writer: In 1973, after eight years of steady increases, applications to Santa

Cruz finally stabilized. In 1976, they fell abruptly. Worse still, Santa Cruz was suddenly unable to hold on to the students it did accept and enrollments started to fall. The economy was steadily shrinking, the general application pool grew smaller and smaller, and the cultural and political radicalism of the sixties was being rapidly displaced by professional and vocational anxieties. On top of all of that, California's entire university system was forced to begin severe budget cutbacks. As a consequence of these austerity measures, David Saxon, president of the statewide university system, threatened Santa Cruz with staff and faculty reductions if enrollments did not increase. There were less definite, but more ominous rumors that Santa Cruz might be shut down for good."[5]

Robert Sinsheimer: My education was to be a problem solver. I went to MIT, and one thing you learn at MIT is to solve problems. They give you the impression that all problems are solvable. When I perceived that there was a crucial enrollment problem, I set out to solve it, although it took longer than I would have liked.

George Von der Muhll: In the opening years of this campus, we had been turning four student applicants out of five away. Even though they were qualified to come here as part of the top 12.5 percent of the California student body, we had been sending them to places like Berkeley and Davis. Those we accepted seemed generally and genuinely attracted by the distinctive qualities of this campus. But now, we were urgently searching for the students whom Berkeley, UCLA, and UC San Diego could not accommodate. We were having to undergo the unfamiliar and unwelcome experience of having to adapt to the needs and preferences of more conventionally minded students, who had not wanted to come here in the first place.

Robert Sinsheimer: In general, one of the things you learn in the UC system is how long it takes to get anything done. I really had no idea of the UC system, of the extent to which the campus is simply a small part of a huge public institution and is constrained by the policies, goodwill, and whatever else you want, of the central administration. I learned what a difference it made. It made all the difference in the world to the UC system and to the state if your enrollment went down. Somehow that was interpreted as you were doing a lousy job.

Angus Taylor: In 1920, the regents gave the faculty of the University of California tremendous autonomy. No administrative officer can tell the faculty what courses to teach. A dean can have influence on the curriculum if he's clever, but he can't issue orders. It's very different from other institutions of higher education. Every chancellor who is appointed from outside the University of California experiences a great shock of awareness that he has to get accustomed to.

Sinsheimer didn't have as broad an experience with the UC system as I had had when I went to UCSC. He had been the head of biology at Caltech and was a very distinguished scientist. He'd made a big reputation at Iowa before going to Caltech. But they don't have an academic senate at Caltech.

Michael Cowan: During Chancellor Robert Sinsheimer's first year at Santa Cruz, he faced a faculty that was highly concerned about the future of the campus, how to solve these enrollment problems, and the turnover in administration. I think they were less concerned about the campus's survival. There were some

rumors that the campus might be closed down and sold to Mormons, but I don't think many of us took much stock in that. I think there was a much greater concern that the campus would just limp along for the foreseeable future, as a kind of weak sister in the system, again linked with UC Riverside, which was having a lot of problems, and not able to compete successfully for students from other campuses, and not able to realize a lot of the dreams of the original founding of the campus.

Dan McFadden: My doomsday model is that the state comes down along the coast—there's been a couple of state and federal purchases of property in there—to tie that into a park, come up through the campus and down into Henry Cowell State park and tie that all together. They change the sign at the entrance to the campus to "KOA" and make this another Asilomar.[6]

People keep saying we're not in a UC Riverside situation because they're in trouble with enrollments in the south. But in this region we are competing with UC Berkeley and Davis.

Robert Sinsheimer: I came here and fell into all these structural problems. Then I found out, to my astonishment, that the Santa Cruz community was unhappy with the campus being here. Then I came to realize that in the central UC administration, not at the presidential level, but I'd say at the second and third level, there was no sympathy for this campus, at all. They thought it was an aberration, a mistake, probably doomed to fail. After all, most of the people at central administration are the products of UC. They'd naturally think of a conventional UC as a great place. So why would you want to change it? If it should, for heaven's sake, turn out that Santa Cruz was a great improvement, that would, in a way, diminish the other campuses.

Kenneth Thimann: We never have had many resources. This has always been a terribly impecunious campus—more so, I think, than any of the other UC campuses. The regents have never felt for what we did. Remember that McHenry had to sell the regents on the idea by assuring them that the college system wouldn't cost any more than an ordinary campus. That's asking for trouble. Because it does, of course, inevitably.

Robert Sinsheimer: To my knowledge, the central administration never seriously considered closing Santa Cruz. But the rumors existed. And the rumors were deadly. Who wants to come to a campus that might be closed? Who wants to give any money to a campus that might be closed?

George Blumenthal: I knew the rumor about UC Santa Cruz closing was serious enough that I followed the discussion that was taking place at a systemwide level. There was a big debate at the time about whether tenure was departmental, campuswide or systemwide. President David Saxon was arguing that tenure resided within a department and certainly resided within a campus. So this was a clear message that if that became the rule of the land and the Santa Cruz campus closed, all of us who were tenured faculty were out on our ear. At the end of the day, before Saxon left office, he abandoned the question and said he wasn't going to rule on it and he was just going to let the matter sit without resolution.

Michael Cowan: So there was strong faculty pressure on Sinsheimer to do something. There was pressure coming from the campus, from the faculty, but also pressure coming from the Office of the President. We needed to reverse the enrollment losses. We needed to get the campus budget, and therefore the campus, growing again. We needed to mount a strong effort to repair and

to strengthen our slightly frayed reputation, particularly elsewhere in the UC system and at the Office of the President.

Angus Taylor: Some people felt enrollment at Santa Cruz had dropped back, slowed down, because of the lack of a grading system. That's always been a question that's hard to decide. The record shows that Santa Cruz graduates, on the whole, do well in getting into professional schools and graduate schools. Chancellor Sinsheimer hired a man to study the enrollment problem, Richard Moll.[7] He focused on that and tried to persuade the campus to go back to a regular grading system. He ran into a buzz saw.

William Adams: The university hired Richard Moll, former head of admissions at Bowdoin and Vassar. Moll had great success in shaping new images for these institutions, but the image problem at Santa Cruz was especially severe. The campus had, in his words, a nearly unshakable reputation for being "flaky" and "touchy-feely," residues of the culture of the sixties.[8]

Richard Moll, Director of Admissions: The campus was planned to be an undergraduate utopia—in program, in tone, and even in appearance. But the majesty of that "new era" of alternative education was short-lived. At about the turn of the 1973-74 school year, America suddenly shied from such noble experiments. Almost overnight, Santa Cruz, along with a handful of other '60s stylists, was forced into a defensive posture. A series of ghastly murders of undergraduate women (by one deranged off-campus visitor) seemed the final blow. *Time* magazine called Santa Cruz the "murder capital of America" just as America itself turned its back on the campus's educational style and tone.[9]

Elizabeth Calciano: My husband had the phone by his bedside because he was a doctor and he'd get called at any time of the night or day. One morning he picked up the phone, and he went, "No. Oh, no, no, no, no. What's happened?" Well, our friends, the Ohtas, Dr. Victor Ohta and his wife, had been brutally murdered along with their housekeeper and two of their four children. That was just horrendous. My family had gone to a Christmas party there the year before.[10]

Jean Rose: Santa Cruz for a time was thought to be the Murder Capital of California. There were about four or five murders. It was terrifying, because actually the sister of the murderer used to babysit for our children—she was all right, but her brother was the criminal. I think Professor of Psychology David Marlowe[11] had to interview him when he was jailed. He said he was completely sane and just completely cold.

This man killed one or two students hitchhiking. The students would hitchhike onto campus. And this man would pick them up and he'd lock the door, so that they couldn't open the doors. And he would murder them. I think about four students were murdered. Students were forbidden to hitchhike.

Katie King: When I first arrived in 1970, we did not have buses taking us up and down to town. So it was pretty hard to get up and down to town and we did hitchhike. We were told, "Oh, well it's probably safer, if you do hitchhike, if you only get in cars with people that have stickers to show they are UCSC employees in some way." So I would hitchhike back and forth and many of my friends did too.

It was very scary when it turned out that Edmund Kemper was targeting young women. One of my friends was a victim of Kemper. She had hitchhiked. The sticker issue turned out to be not good advice because Kemper was living with his mom, who was a staff member. I did quite a bit of hitchhiking in the area and I had amazingly good luck. On the other hand, one time was all that Rosalind Thorpe needed to not have good luck. So that was pretty terrifying.

I don't remember exactly how long it was afterwards, but I was called in for jury duty. I went down to the Courthouse and walked in— this was very first time I had ever done jury duty, so I had no idea what it was about or how it worked—I walked in and I realized that the person who was sitting there in orange, in chains, was Kemper. I was completely dumbfounded and scared. Almost the very first thing happened that the judge said, "If anyone has a reason not be here, what is it?" I said, "Well, I was friends with one of the women who was killed." He said, "You're excused."

The campus wasn't that large. Santa Cruz was still a bit of a seedy old beach town, although it was changing a little bit. Hitchhiking was part of what made it feel like a neighborhood, in fact. The feeling of small town safety was being shifted. My mother had been so pleased I was in Santa Cruz, and had said so to her friends. Then one of her friends said, "Well, see. You sent her there and that's where these murders are taking place." So there was this way in which Santa Cruz was both a very safe place and then a place where these murders were going on.

Jasper Rose: There were the possibilities of murders. And they haunted on and haunted on.

De Clarke: Santa Cruz had a reputation because of the multiple murder cases. When I came to Santa Cruz in the mid-1970s it was a sort of pop-culture byword: "Oh, Santa Cruz! That's where those murders happened. Be careful!"

Figure 1

Richard (Dick) Moll, Dean
of Admissions, at the Cook
House, 1981

Photo by Don Fukuda

There was a certain amount of fear in the atmosphere.

George Von der Muhll: In 1973, *Newsweek* proclaimed on its cover that Santa Cruz had become the murder capital of the United States. We had three mass murderers on the prowl in one year.

Robert Sinsheimer: Some people thought that the murders could have been a factor in declining enrollments because of people not wanting to send their children here.

Richard Moll: UCSC was ushered from the winner's circle almost as quickly as it had stepped in. But its pride would not be compromised. It remembered the fame, the super-selectivity of the student body and faculty. The mid-to-late '70s, however, brought lonely times and a dramatic drop in freshman and transfer applications.[12]

William Adams: Moll embarked on a remarkable strategy. If Santa Cruz could not completely shake its liberal, innovative image, then it would have to turn vice into virtue. The selling of Santa Cruz has provoked controversy within the institution. The new image, critics charge, is a cheap, unprincipled hustle. It also betrays the original intentions of the institution.[13]

Robert Sinsheimer: You can't be an oddball in the UC system. There was a little bit of an attitude here that I would almost call precious: we can forget the rest of the world and build this city on a hill. UCSC could just select faculty who spent their lives in the colleges teaching. But the obvious consequence of that would be you'd have no academic reputation. People expect a certain academic status. We didn't have it. Students wouldn't come and they weren't coming. By 1977, they weren't coming in droves, you might say.

George Von der Muhll: UCSC was frantically scrambling to attract students. And that is why we became so ready to accept transfer students.

Robert Sinsheimer: We made an arrangement with UC Berkeley Chancellor Mike Heyman. Berkeley was always being oversubscribed. So we worked out an arrangement whereby two hundred freshmen whom they could not accept would be referred to Santa Cruz. This was the "re-direct program," in which these students were guaranteed that if they did well here for two years they could go back to Berkeley as juniors. That worked quite well, and helped us during the period we were turning it around. It was interesting because actually, as you might imagine, about half of them, after the two years, would choose to stay here. They'd make friends and liked it here.

George Von der Muhll: But transfer students came at a cost. UC Santa Cruz had been originally planned as a campus for four-year students who would spend their first two years taking college courses inside their colleges before selecting a discipline to major in. Transfer students, on the other hand, had no reason to take any particular interest in college themes, college core courses, or anything like that. They came here to spend two years taking courses in their disciplinary major to prepare themselves for the outside world and its demands. In fact, some of them rather resented four-year students with a thematic attachment to a particular college because they were left to feel that they were outsiders with no real home except for the courses they took, whereas some of the other students, who had been here from the outset of their undergraduate years, had lived

Figure 2

Enrollment recruitment poster,
early 1980s

on campus longer and had developed friendships growing out of those years. I think it's fair to say that, though not immediately recognized at the time, UCSC's growing dependence on transfer students signaled the end of the original Kerr-McHenry vision for this campus.

Robert Sinsheimer: There was this fundamental structural problem: How do you reconcile the idea of colleges as centers of academic life with the idea of being a University of California campus with its research orientation and its professional motivations? The problem was never thought through. Clark Kerr never thought it through. Clark Kerr somehow had the notion—I hate to say it, it's just so simplistic—of a set of Swarthmores dotted around, but each college without the resources of a Swarthmore. I mean, Swarthmore runs on a student/faculty ratio of 9 or 10 to 1. I don't know what we started at, but by the time I came here it was more like 20 to 1. You just can't do it.

William Adams: It is clear that the architects of adaptation, administrators like Sinsheimer and Moll, are unmoved by the ideals of the old Santa Cruz. For them, the innovative side of the institution was excessive, infantile, and, most important, lacking in standards.[14]

Robert Sinsheimer: My first year here I spent trying to understand all these problems and how the campus stood in relation to the whole system. I noticed, in reading the oral history interviews with Ken Thimann, for whom I have immense regard, that he never understood that. Because he wouldn't. There's no reason he should have. He never understood how the system operated and how the campus could not be exempt from the strictures and ethos of the UC system. Clark Kerr may have thought that as president of the

system, he could make it exempt. But he wasn't president for long after the campus was started. None of the other presidents was interested in making this campus exempt from the whole pattern of the UC system. So here was this oddball campus.

Kenneth Thimann: Robert Sinsheimer has done many things very well. He's made some good senior appointments. But he came from a background, MIT and Caltech, that had nothing in common with a Swarthmore kind of idea. So he had no reason to think that Clark Kerr had an important piece of vision in designing a university along these lines.

Robert Sinsheimer: Proposition 13 came along; the budget was cut repeatedly and everything was negative.[15] We had to get the colleges to solve this stalemate over appointments and promotions. I had wanted to get the colleges out of the promotion business because, quite frankly, it seemed to me that, in terms of academic quality, the boards had the right idea and the colleges didn't. The colleges had become, in a sense, clubs. Now, this doesn't mean that I didn't think teaching should be valued. But I couldn't see promoting people who were doing no scholarly research at all, which many of the colleges were willing to do. In part, maybe that's my scientific bias, because as a scientist I think if you are not engaged in scholarly activity, you are going to be hopelessly obsolete in ten years. This college/board conflict had produced a stalemate on the campus, a stagnation.

Helene Moglen: When I was dean of humanities, I came to realize that the faculty at UCSC, uniquely in the country, had the ability to vote two ways, which utterly fulfilled their sometimes contradictory desires and needs as professional academics and as people. They could vote in their colleges for a colleague whom they loved and admired and respected. They could vote against that same person in their department, if they happened to be in their department, on the basis of their inadequate scholarship. This was done again and again.

Robert Sinsheimer: So these split recommendations would come up through the channels and they would go to the Academic Senate Committee on Privilege and Tenure. They would likewise be confused about the criteria, and they would often come up with a split vote, so it would end up in the chancellor's office. Then the

chancellor would somehow have to decide the tenure decision, leaving one group or the other very unhappy.

Helene Moglen: So many of the personnel decisions on this campus had been kicked up to the administration because the faculty had the ability to undermine their own votes.

Figure 3

Brochure created during enrollment crisis by Richard Moll during the late 1970s

Renewal or Betrayal:
The Painful Debate Over Reorganization

Robert Sinsheimer: The campus had to be re-organized. UCSC was part of the University of California. We're not all the same as Berkeley, but we're supposed to be pretty good. UC is considered one of the best public universities. People expect a certain academic status. We didn't have it.

There was really only one way to go within the UC system with the resources available. That was to go toward a more discipline-oriented campus, of the kind that the other UC campuses are, and for which the whole reward system within UC is structured, and preserve as much of the college concept as you could. That was all you could do, unless somehow you could get other resources.

It seemed like an enormous task because the campus was sliding downhill fast. The enrollments were falling. It was going to be very hard to get other resources.

Michael Cowan: In the late fall of 1978, Sinsheimer announced a two-part reorganization. One was that he was going to take away faculty FTE-holding power from the colleges and locate it entirely in boards, or in divisions. That was a very important—and of course very controversial—piece. Most faculty on campus supported that. But the older colleges, particularly Stevenson and Cowell, were resistant.

Sinsheimer also wanted to move the faculty around, to in effect continue that re-clustering of faculty that had begun in a more modest form in reaggregation in the mid-seventies, and to create significant support clusters of faculty within particular disciplines in particular colleges. But he was also interested in creating cross-disciplinary clusters, so he was very supportive of not just having a single board in a college, as was attempted during the earlier reaggregation program, but having parts of several boards together in the college. He didn't work out the details of that. He was leaving that to the deans of the divisions to work on.

Interestingly enough, he exempted two colleges from that a bit. One was College Eight, which had become the home of environmental studies. The provost of College Eight was going to be also chair of environmental studies, and so their appointments would be together. The other was Oakes, which was somewhat left alone; they were still allowed to maintain some joint appointments. But otherwise, Sinsheimer wanted to get rid of the joint appointments between colleges and boards. The other proposal was to reduce the number of courses offered by the college, to basically divisionalize the curriculum. That was also very controversial.

There were some other things, though, that he wanted to do that I think were not fully appreciated at the time, or enough, in the swirl of the controversy about the colleges. He wanted to strengthen the liberal arts and general education on campus. And he did want to strengthen the interdisciplinary research, as well as teaching on campus.

George Blumenthal: Sinsheimer proposed a realignment of the roles of the colleges and the boards. He laid a stake in the ground that he thought we needed to reorganize, that we needed to complete reorganization. And he set up a committee to implement it, and as near as I can tell, the committee did a good job. It was efficient and effective.

Robert Sinsheimer: Reorganization did away with college courses, except the core courses. I was astonished that when I came there were only two core courses left, only Cowell and Stevenson. Cowell was down to a one-quarter course. They were thinking of abolishing that. I thought that the core courses were really valuable. They provided a broad interdisciplinary introduction to some theme. They had a socializing effect; all the freshmen in the college take the same course. It gives them something to talk about to each other, something to think about with each other. The core course should introduce them to the level of a university education.

Part of the reorganization was my insistence that every college should offer a core course. I believe a college can be an exciting intellectual and cultural place without being a place that is trying to offer academic courses. I did allow for a college to sponsor certain kinds of small interdisciplinary programs which simply didn't fit elsewhere. For instance, Stevenson College had its program on nuclear proliferation. They offered a couple of courses and I provided funding for that.

George Blumenthal: Reorganization did affect Oakes College because teaching two courses in Oakes was not going to be a welcome strategy anymore. I went and talked to Herman about it, and said that I was still committed to the college and I would give it some energy, but I wasn't prepared to continue to teach in the college. And if that was unacceptable, he just needed to tell me that, but I was at a point in my career where I needed to do that. I had just gotten tenure but I really felt that to continue my development and my relationship with my department, I needed to devote more of my time to my department.

Herman was fine with that and there were no ill feelings. But reorganization had a devastating effect on Oakes College because there were far fewer courses that could be offered. I think that was ultimately the death knell of the Oakes Science Program. We kept it going for a number of years, both from getting some faculty to teach in the science program and from some private money that Herman devoted toward keeping the program going. He hired a lecturer and there was somebody in chemistry who also did some lecturing at Oakes in those days. So we kept it going for a while. But in a sense, it was an unsustainable thing to do under those circumstances within the campus.

Michael Cowan: Sinsheimer was a controversial chancellor in many ways. He was somewhat awkward socially, uncomfortable with idle chit-chat. He tended to think very carefully and then come forward with proposals. But he was a very systematic and deep thinker. He was an extraordinarily good writer. He was very articulate in those contexts. And a lot of what he moved toward proposing was because he was under pressure from the faculty to do something. It wasn't merely that President David Saxon had said you've got to reorganize and so forth. The faculty themselves, at least a considerable body of faculty, was telling him to do something. It's just that faculty were divided as to what they wanted him to do.

Robert Sinsheimer: It was a difficult time for me. I felt under an immense amount of pressure, because in the end, of course, the faculty had to approve reorganization or it wouldn't go. In the end they did. The final faculty vote was 75 or 80 percent in favor, which was very good, but that also meant that there was 20 or 25 percent who were dead set against it.

John Dizikes: UCSC's problems were wildly exaggerated, and Sinsheimer took advantage of that to impose the changes he always wanted to make. He was not happy with the collegiate system. He did not really believe in it. He recognized that he had to put up with it because so many of the faculty were still associated with it.

They were not going to close UCSC. We could have said, "What we need to do to restore our popularity is to reinvigorate the college system. We can never compete with the bigger campuses in traditional terms. But what we could do is to reestablish ourselves as a modest alternative, while being within the university system."

I remember how shocked I was to find out that when new faculty who were hired came, Sinsheimer had organized an orientation program in Asilomar in Pacific Grove. All new faculty went to be oriented, and colleges were prohibited from having any representation there, saying anything about it. All the new faculty were brought in to understand that they were coming to a traditional place. It was their board that would really determine their future.

John Isbister, Professor: I came to Santa Cruz in 1968. I was one of the founding members of Merrill College. I came because I believed in the dream. I had a couple of other offers; I could have gone a couple of other places, standard universities. Phil Bell, who was the provost of Merrill College, told me about this college and the interdisciplinary approach to studying the Third World. It sounded marvelous. It was where I wanted to be.

So I came. I believed deeply in the thing and I really worked hard for, I would say, seven or eight years in that college, to try to create this dream. And a lot of us did; a lot of people at Merrill devoted the best part of their lives, for seven or eight years, to trying to make this thing work. The problem was that it didn't work, not because we didn't try. But at the end, if we had

looked at the thing in 1973 or 1974—what had we accomplished after all that work? Well, we had a core course. We had the beginnings of a Latin American studies major, nothing much at that point. (It's become quite fine since then.) And we had a lot of ulcers, a lot of late nights and a lot of raw nerves, personal relationships that were very strained because we had fought so hard and intimately with each other.

So we backed off. There was a burnout and we backed off. And when the final decision was made to back off from this college system, it had already happened three or four years before at Merrill, in truth, because we had so burned out over trying to create this thing, and we had accomplished so little, we had just accomplished so little, for all the work that we had put into it.[16]

Kenneth Thimann: One of the things that Sinsheimer has done is to say all the science faculty should be associated with Crown College. Well, that's absurd. I mean, you've got seventy-five science faculty or something. You don't want that many. As a result, most of them never come. They have no stake in the college and no interest in it. There's something equally silly about all the artists being in College Five. So the whole idea of the interaction between faculty of different interests is lost.

John Isbister: Actually, we're doing much better now [in 1987, post reorganization]. We've got a college that functions just fine as far as a residential unit goes, as far as an extracurricular unit goes. The faculty gets along well with each other; they work with each other. We don't have a curriculum, except for the core course. What we don't have, and what we imagined we would have at the beginning, was a curriculum. We never got it. So I'm much happier now in terms of my working life, whether I'm provost of Merrill or on faculty, than I was then, because I can be productive in ways that are really useful and not drive myself nuts.

Kenneth Thimann: I used to have lunch with economists and historians and a very good man in Greek history. We had wonderful times. That's what you get at the colleges. Of course, you get the same in the Oxford and Cambridge colleges. I'm sure that was in Clark Kerr's thinking. That's all going out the window, very sadly. As we took in more and more people, the balance of people who see the point, to put it crudely, and those who didn't, has gradually increased in favor of those with no investment in the college system. So, in a way, it was sort of doomed after the first half-dozen years. It began to slide. Then when Sinsheimer came, he completed the destruction.

George Blumenthal: Reorganization took place relatively quickly. The colleges lost the power to influence hiring and tenure decisions. I think that it still was the case that the colleges could express an opinion and that the opinion needed to be heard, but they didn't wield the kind of equal power that had been the case before.

In a way, thinking back on it, in a way, that's kind of sad because Santa Cruz had adopted a very different kind of model for the organization of academia. It was a model that worked remarkably well during the first years of the campus. Some marvelous things happened here. But that model was not sustainable in a state university facing funding cuts on a regular, ongoing basis. It was simply not going to be sustainable because the colleges as academic units were not the most efficient way of spending your money for academia. I'm not sure if people knew that we were going to face this long road of decline of state support for public higher education.

Jasper Rose: It was a total disaster. People who wanted to *expand* the educational possibilities of the curriculum and make use of the intercommunication of variegated fields felt squish-squashed out. But it also felt that, in fact, the whole thing was being squish-squashed out, in essence. There wasn't any longer any interest in the development of a university which was new and full of gushing interaction. It was just a place where people quickly got a job—and got some money and got a position—and then went on to the next place. I mean, it was very much a businessman's point of view.

But the other point of view was never very strong, really, the whole notion of a campus devoted to reorganizing the way in which we looked at education, and the way we looked at human beings and so on so forth. The prevailing attitude became "No, no, no. That's jejune, and that belongs to the sixties. And it isn't really what we're after."

Don Rothman: Sinsheimer's announced transformations were breathtaking in their radical foundations, scope, and direct implications for the future of the UCSC faculty. They clearly spelled the end of the college-centered system on which the campus had been founded, and the innovative interdisciplinary courses they had engendered, and eliminated the grounds for the continued conflict between colleges and boards that had polarized and paralyzed the campus.

Carolyn Martin Shaw: I was in the senate when the reorganization vote passed. I have never heard such thunderous applause, ever, in any other place.

Don Rothman: What was equally surprising was how little resistance our new chancellor encountered to his proclaimed "reorganization." By this point, a large, if hitherto largely silent, majority had lost the enthusiasm its members had once shown for the opportunities the college system had opened up. By now, they seemed ready to side with the chancellor in wishing to jettison the "soft" courses, the duplicative courses, and the inauthentic majors the college system had spawned. They were no longer willing to bear the burden of dual college-board committees, the dubious criteria employed in college personnel proceedings, the strained efforts to give the colleges a nominal thematic identity, and the resultant marginalization and isolation many faculty felt they had experienced as a consequence. Many shared Chancellor Sinsheimer's view that the colleges had not demonstrated that their promotion of interdisciplinary contact had stimulated more imaginative, more widely received, more well-received research. Most of all, perhaps, a substantial majority of the faculty now appeared increasingly eager to get on with the teaching and research projects for which their graduate schools had prepared them. For them, the experimental college system had run its course.

Jasper Rose: People wanted to be more traditional because they could get better jobs. They could leave the campus, and it wasn't just an isolated experiment. They could join other institutions, so they felt more secure when it was changed.

Ronnie Gruhn: A lot of faculty believed reorganization was a good idea: You should put departments together. You should stop doing the wishy-washy things the colleges were doing. While I agreed that the colleges should get out of the businesses of independently hiring and promotion cases, I did think the colleges should stay in the business of offering lower-division course work and remedial work and things like that.

Robert Sinsheimer: The faculty were expected to provide courses in the colleges. My impression, frankly is that, with time, these courses kind of deteriorated. People felt they were obliged to give them, so they would give a chemistry course focusing on the chemistry of wine making. Now that's somewhat interesting, but hardly a major academic subject, except maybe in the oenology department.[17] There were even courses given in chess, or things of that kind. This meant that the faculty weren't teaching as much in their discipline. This meant that the disciplinary education was recognizably thin. In other words, the students weren't able to get all the courses they should be getting; the offerings were weak, too limited. There was an increasing resentment on the part of the people who thought about the boards of studies, about the time that they had to spend teaching what they regarded increasingly as Mickey Mouse courses in the colleges. This was another source of constant tug of war.

William Rose: Sinsheimer represented the power and coercion of the sciences. The founders, like my father, Jasper Rose, were mostly humanists, more concerned with literature, history, art: Renaissance culture. I think that sense of Cowell College being ebullient with culture, that was what the founders were interested in. Page Smith wrote about the chicken—but he made it history and science. They lost all of that with Sinsheimer.

Robert Sinsheimer: By the time I came, some faculty simply refused to teach any college courses. They felt it wasn't worth their time and that they were needed in the disciplines. And I honestly believe that we destroyed some younger faculty by putting them out in a college, where they had no contact with other people in their discipline, no mentoring from senior members of the discipline. They floundered.

Helene Moglen: I came a year later than Bob Sinsheimer did and he reorganized the campus in my first year [1978-79]. That was a major change for faculty who had been here for many years. My impressions of the campus were that it had been wonderfully theorized, wonderfully architected, and that the vision was very inadequate, and that it wasn't surprising that it was undone.

There was significant tension between the vision of the colleges as centers of experimental education and the importance—however secondary—of the academic divisions, where traditional forms of institutional power resided. I think the tension marked the administration's failure of courage to fully commit to innovation, and that failure of courage was also related to UCSC's intention to be a graduate, as well as an undergraduate institution. How you build a graduate institution without strong departments was a major question. There needed to be something that looked like departments, even if they weren't called departments, in order to support graduate education, if it was going to be worth anything in the outside world. That was where the conflict was, right from the beginning.

Leta Miller, Professor: After reorganization, the music curriculum became a lot more focused. Before, there had also been the problem of independent majors. People got majors in unusual things, such as sound art or aesthetics, which were partly music and partly something else. What did they do with those majors? If they wanted to go on to get a job, or go on to graduate school, they would be asked, what did that major mean? And when they would say that they had a few courses in music, and they had a few courses in art, and they had a few courses in this and that, it was difficult for some of those students to move forward and be accepted in other

programs, or to be accepted in jobs, because they didn't have in-depth training in one area.

William Adams: The student conception of relevance was dramatically, and ironically, shifting. What now seemed relevant, both inside and outside the university, was not the innovative potential of the institution but the seriousness with which it pursued a conventional curriculum, and how well that curriculum prepared the vocationally anxious for advanced professional training. Like so many institutions, Santa Cruz began its own long, mutinous march back to the familiar lines of academic respectability.[18]

Leta Miller: The early experimentation of the UCSC curriculum had positives, but also had negatives. The reorganization focused the programs. On the other hand, it made UCSC more like everybody else.

Jasper Rose: Robert Sinsheimer was exactly the dear, old formal way of running things which had happened in the 1940s, 1950s, and 1960s. It was a very, very sticky and stuffy and dull way of dealing with things, and I had no place in it. I had no place in it whatsoever. He took one look at me and said, "Well, there's somebody whom I've got to get rid of." Why on earth would I bother myself sticking around a place where there was no interest in students?

John Lynch: Reorganization was not done in the most sensitive way. Faculty were yanked from places that they had built themselves, that they had put a lot of themselves into. When you build a structure, you don't like to hear, "Okay, we're going to take you over to a structure that someone else built and plonk you down there because you belong there." That underestimates values like loyalty and the amounts of your own soul and personal being that you put into a place.

Ruth Solomon: Everybody got segregated into their little departments. The Performing Arts building became a little enclave and we no longer were in proximity with the scientists or the physics people, who were our friends. All of a sudden, I wasn't seeing them anymore. Those were people that fed me ideas and nurtured my growth.

Ronnie Gruhn: I think some reorganization was necessary. But they went too far. What they did was to undermine the possibility of the architectural structure of this campus allowing for more direct contact between students and faculty. We had the colleges, and they were meant for a purpose. They were not going to work like Cambridge and Oxford, and they weren't even going to work the way McHenry thought they should work, but they could be made to work for *something*. They threw out the baby with the bathwater.

Helene Moglen: I was seen by people who were advocates for the colleges as not being pro-college. That wasn't true. But this was a very interesting campus, in the way you had to be all or nothing for all kinds of things. There were very few people who were up for compromises. There were very few people who supported Bob's reorganization, but were also up for supporting the colleges in a different incarnation.

Ronnie Gruhn: I was not one of these extreme people who said, "Let's not have any change here." I thought that things could be rescued. No one was even willing to discuss it.

Helene Moglen: I wanted to strengthen the college system. I didn't want to keep it as it was, but I loved the early vision of Santa Cruz. I did come to see the ways in which it wasn't working. The failure had been built in from the beginning.

Ronnie Gruhn: Reorganization is a sad chapter in Santa Cruz history, and a chapter that needs to be revisited in the future.

Herman Blake: Reorganization destroyed us. It had a very negative impact in terms of the whole gestalt. Robert Sinsheimer was one of the worst, absolutely worst, people we could have ever brought in for the college system, and in my opinion, for UC Santa Cruz and everything else.

Santa Cruz Sentinel: Dean McHenry, the man who helped birth Santa Cruz, got tears in his eyes Monday evening as he talked about the way his university has grown into adulthood. The first chancellor likened how he feels about what has happened to UCSC to the words of a saddened King Arthur watching his dream fall apart in "Camelot."[19]

Michael Cowan: Reorganization left a lot of bad feelings that lingered for some time, although most of the faculty on campus, not just the natural scientists, ended up supporting it—to a certain extent out of desperation, but also because they thought it made sense. Bob Sinsheimer was not trying to destroy general education and liberal education. He really believed, and I think a lot of faculty came to agree with him, that this would be a way of further strengthening that. But all of this was happening at once. I think part of the problem was that these various complex streams got confused, and some of the streams kind of got lost in the later folklore of what happened during this period.

Robert Sinsheimer: UC Santa Cruz was betrayed in three ways. It was betrayed by Kerr and McHenry because they didn't think it through; they had this great vision and they simply did not think through how they could do this within the University of California. They had an idea, and they hadn't thought it through. People are going to invest years of their life in it. You can't launch that kind of an experiment without having thought it through. In an experimental lab, the *E. coli* aren't going to complain if there is a fault in the experiment and they are wasted. But people are.

Secondly, UCSC was betrayed by the community which invited it here and then turned on them. And thirdly, it got betrayed by the UC system, in that after Kerr left it seems clear nobody in the system felt any obligation to foster this experiment.

Julia Armstrong-Zwart, Assistant Chancellor for Human Resources: Chancellor Sinsheimer was controversial because of how he came in. He was sent to change the campus. He was sent to bring the campus structure more in line with the University of California. That was what he was asked to do and that is what he did. At the same time, I saw him at regents' meetings, and I knew from being privy to his correspondence that he was a fierce fighter for resources for this campus.

Angus Taylor: The campus never really accepted him. But that was partly because Sinsheimer was trying to make Santa Cruz like Caltech, a great research institution to the exclusion of most everything else.

Julia Armstrong-Zwart: Bob Sinsheimer was a quiet man, almost shy, very reserved—but what I noticed at the regents' meetings was that the other chancellors, like Mike Heyman from UC Berkeley or Chuck Young from UCLA, would go over and consult with Bob. The other chancellors really respected him and his opinion. I'm not sure that the campus ever realized that he was well respected among his peers.

He came back, maybe two or three years after he had retired, to give a talk and he was given a standing ovation. I think people, at that point, realized what Bob had done for UCSC. We were not on life support when he arrived, but we were in a very shaky position. Bob came in and really did shelter the campus, in part because of his relationship with President Saxon—they had a very good relationship—the fact that he was respected, and the fact that he was willing to make some difficult, unpopular decisions. He wasn't always right. Like all of us, he made mistakes. We all make bad decisions sometimes. But on the whole, he worked for the benefit of this campus. I respected him and became very fond of him as a person.

Angus Taylor: Robert Sinsheimer, in his book, said the Master Plan for Higher Education designated the University of California as the chief research arm of the state. That defines how Sinsheimer perceived UCSC's mission as a UC campus.

Ed Landesman: There's some validity to that view of a UC campus. However, I believe that it went to an extreme, where it changed, to a great extent, the direction of what the campus had been. Yes, you could do things to make it a better place for research. Great. But at the same time, let's not forget how the campus was meant to be, why it started the way it was, why it was supposed to be different than the other UC campuses.

Angus Taylor: But that view of a UC campus's mission is a narrowing of the University of California's responsibility. It's much more than that. It's to educate people to be good citizens; to be moral and sensitive human beings.

The college concept at Santa Cruz could further this. You have a small community of students and faculty, who see each other regularly. Students eat and meet together every day. They meet with certain members of the faculty once a month maybe, in some kind of a formal occasion. They're civilizing themselves. They're educating themselves in ways that have nothing to do with being lectured to. They're using their minds and bodies and souls. That's what the colleges should be for. So a certain share of the resources, perhaps only a small share in terms of hours, should be in the colleges.

Robert Sinsheimer: Some felt reorganization was a betrayal of the original idea. The only answer to that would be that the original idea was impractical in real terms. I remember saying at the time, "Look, you did an experiment. Not every experiment works. All scientists know that." But people who aren't scientists don't know that. It seems to me that when you do an experiment you have to evaluate it and see if it works or not. If it didn't work, what do we keep; what do we throw out? But nonscientists don't think that way.

A lot of these people had invested five or ten years of their life in this and worked very, very hard at it. When you've done that, it's very, very hard to admit that you made all that effort for something that wasn't worth it.

Herman Blake: Experiments are expedient. I never felt that what the college system was and what we were doing at Oakes College—which was, in my opinion, manifesting to a greater degree of fulfillment the plans and dreams of Dean McHenry and Clark Kerr—I didn't see that as an experiment. The data were long in about the effectiveness of that approach to education. We added to it by opening that quality of excellence to a different set of clients, but we never altered the principles, or the content, or the values of liberal education. But we were in a research university, and the mission of the research university was to do something very different from what we were doing. But I didn't feel we were, in any way, going away from that mission. I thought we were enhancing it.

I use the words: *The experience.* Not *experiment,* but *the experience,* the experience of people who love teaching and learning, sitting down with people who sought to learn, along with others who sought to support that effort, and it becoming a fantastic educational experience like Clark Kerr imagined and Dean McHenry began to implement. Clark Kerr said to me on more than one occasion he thought that Oakes came closest to being what he envisioned for Santa Cruz. And Sinsheimer just couldn't figure out Oakes College. One time we were having a conversation with him, the faculty and others, and we were talking about developing student values. He said, "Well, I wouldn't want them to have the values of Harlem." He said that. He said that to the faculty.

Michael Cowan: What Clark Kerr and Dean McHenry wanted to do was to bring a liberal arts ethos, a living-learning ethos, to a large public university, or a university that was going to be very large. That was the innovative part: to reach the whole person, not merely the students' minds, to take the individual students seriously, to broaden the students' horizons by interacting with lots of different people. And by providing them with a general education that involved their learning something, they would be gaining an appreciation for fields other than the ones they were going to focus on, and gain a bigger sense of the richness and complexity of the world as a whole—standard and important goals of liberal education.

Also, of course, to close the gap between the student and the teacher through close, supportive interaction. And then, to bind all of those elements together in a mutually supportive civil community that might model the kind of communities they would want to help build and nurture and protect when they moved on out into the world. It was a kind of practice for living; it was both a living experiment, and a practice for future living. The term *human scale* was often used in some of those early planning documents to capture that. Both taking the individual seriously, but also taking the community seriously, bringing the body and the mind and the feelings together.

Herman Blake: It was very different in 1972 when we were building on a sense of hope. We not only anticipated administrative support; we got it. And resources were flowing. By reorganization, resources were declining, and the central administration was hostile to Oakes College. We were fighting a rearguard action, just holding on. Sort of like Reconstruction, where you had the Compromise of 1877, and the development of the society go backwards.[20]

Michael Cowan: One of the questions that the campus didn't fully raise at the outset, in their focus on the colleges, was why those goals applied primarily, or only, to the college, and not to the campus as a whole. What if at the outset one had said: every board of study, every department should be trying to create a humane learning environment for its students, both for its majors, but also for the students who are taking their courses as part of a general education. What if every board said: we want to honor a student's bill of rights and make sure that they have an opportunity, in the course of their education, to interact closely with at least a couple of our faculty members? What if individual departments had said: much of what we do involves, not only strict work within some sort of narrow, disciplinary framework, but because of our own curiosity as scholars, it makes sense for us as scholars to make contact with people outside our own disciplines?

What would have happened at the outset if we had been saying: we want to make sure that all parts of this campus respect the liberal-arts ethos in their teaching and in their research? And what if the central administration had said: we are going to make our allocations of resources to boards, to divisions based in part on whether they are manifesting their commitment to undergraduate teaching as well as research, including effective lower-division teaching, their commitment to providing a humane experience and to encouraging students to ask, not just specialized questions, but larger questions. That was a set of questions that perhaps could have been raised.

The college system was a noble dream and achieved many important things. I can personally testify to that in the life of my own work and that of many of my colleagues. But there were some tensions and problems. If they had been looked at more directly at the outset, if they had been addressed more directly, or worked to be solved more directly, then some of the things that finally happened in the college structure might not have happened.

Endnotes

1. German-American developmental psychologist and psychoanalyst Erik Erikson was known for his theory on psychological development and for coining the phrase "identity crisis." He died in 1994. His son, Kai Erikson, is a renowned sociologist.

2. Rick Chatenever quoted in "A Youthful Romance Under the Redwoods," *Santa Cruz Sentinel*, Volume 129, Number 251, 24 October 1985.

3. *San Francisco Chronicle*, February 5, 1979.

4. *San Francisco Chronicle*, February 5, 1979.

5. William Adams, "Getting Real: Santa Cruz and the Crisis of Liberal Education," *Change* Magazine, May/June 1984.

6. Asilomar State Beach and Conference Grounds in Pacific Grove, was established as a YWCA camp in 1913 and transferred to the California State Park System in 1956.

7. Richard Moll worked as an admissions officer at Yale University, and as the director of admissions at UCSC, Bowdoin College, and Vassar College.

8. William Adams, *Change* Magazine.

9. Richard W. Moll, "A Flower Child Grows Up: Responding to Changing Times at UC Santa Cruz," *Case Currents*, November/December 1983.

10. On October 19, 1970, firefighters responded to a fire at a home in the Santa Cruz Mountains and discovered the bodies of Dr. Victor Ohta, a Japanese-American 45-year-old eye surgeon; his wife, Virginia, 43; their sons, Derrick, 12, and Taggart, 11; and Victor Ohta's secretary, Dorothy Cadwallader, 38. Under the windshield wiper of the family Rolls-Royce they found a typewritten rant against "persons who misuse the natural environment." It was signed with Tarot symbols. Police asked anyone with information to come forward, and soon several locals called in tips about a man named John Linley Frazier. Four days after the Ohta murders, police arrested Frazier, who lived in a shack in the mountains near the Ohta residence. Frazier was imprisoned for life and committed suicide in prison in 2009.

11. David Marlowe came to UCSC in 1966 as a fellow of Stevenson College and a founder of the psychology board. He died in 1990.

12. Richard W. Moll, 1983.

13. William Adams, *Change* Magazine.

14. William Adams, *Change* Magazine.

15. On June 6, 1978, California's voters passed Proposition 13, reducing property tax rates on homes, businesses and farms, and freezing them at the 1976 assessed value. Proposition 13 also limited tax increases on any given property to no more than 2 percent per year, as long as the property was not sold. Voters backed Proposition 13 in large part because they felt that older Californians should not be priced out of their homes through high taxes. This proposition marked a turning point in California's economic history, as markedly less money now flowed into public schools and governmental agencies.

16. John Isbister made these remarks on the panel: "College Night Panel Discussion: The Middle Years."

17. UCSC has never had an oenology course.

18. William Adams, *Change* Magazine.

19. "UCSC—A Dream Begins to Fade," *Santa Cruz Sentinel*, Volume 134, Number 274, November 6, 1990.

20. Reconstruction (1863 to 1877) began after the Civil War, when newly freed slaves became citizens with civil rights apparently guaranteed by three new Constitutional amendments and when attempts were made to address the political, social, and economic legacy of slavery in the Southern states that had seceded during the war. A politically mobilized black community joined with white allies to bring the Republican Party (then liberal) to power. This period ended with the Compromise of 1877 during a disputed presidential election when "Only South Carolina, Florida, and Louisiana remained under Republican control. The outcome of that year's presidential contest between Republican Rutherford B. Hayes and Democrat Samuel J. Tilden hinged on disputed returns from these states. Negotiations between Southern political leaders and representatives of Hayes produced a bargain: Hayes would recognize Democratic control of the remaining Southern states, and Democrats would not block the certification of his election by Congress. Hayes was inaugurated; federal troops returned to their barracks; and as an era when the federal government accepted the responsibility for protecting the rights of the former slaves, Reconstruction came to an end." See: https://www.britannica.com/event/Reconstruction-United-States-history.

Illustrations

Figure 1. Richard (Dick) Moll, Dean of Admissions, at the Cook House, 1981. Photo by Don Fukuda. Courtesy Special Collections, University Library, University of California, Santa Cruz. UA 50: UCSC Photography Services: ua0050_neg_0198-2461_05a.tif.

Figure 2. Enrollment recruitment poster, early 1980s. Courtesy Special Collections, University Library, University of California, Santa Cruz. UA100: Chancellor's Office Records: ua100_010_0001.

Figure 3. "An Ideal Becoming Real." Brochure created during enrollment crisis by Richard Moll during the late 1970s. Courtesy Special Collections, University Library, University of California Santa Cruz: UA 100: Chancellor's Office Records: ua100_010_0001.

Figure 4. Courtyard behind Bookshop Santa Cruz, 1978. Santa Cruz. Photo by Mark Zemelman. Courtesy Special Collections, University Library, University of California, Santa Cruz: UA128: Public Information Records: ua0128_022_0018.

Figure 5. Campus meadow with fence and the city of Santa Cruz in the distance. Photo by Ansel Adams, 1960s. Courtesy Special Collections, University Library, University of California, Santa Cruz: MS 002: Ansel Adams Photographs: ms0002_pho_0065.tif.

Figure 4

Courtyard behind Bookshop Santa Cruz, 1978

Photo by Mark Zemelman

Figure 5

Campus meadow with fence and the city of Santa Cruz in the distance, 1960s

Photo by Ansel Adams

Chapter 20

A Growing UCSC in the Community

Universities are terrible neighbors.

—John Dizikes

Campus Growth, Town-Gown Tensions, and Dramatic Shifts in Local Politics

Robert Sinsheimer: By the mid-1980s, the campus had turned the corner and was growing. One could project that we would exceed 10,000 students and we could reach 15,000 in a foreseeable time.

Michael Cowan: There was renewed campus, as well as University of California growth, in the early eighties. The demographic projectors who said that fewer students would be coming to the university hadn't proved to be quite accurate. It was universitywide. There were a lot of reasons for that that the demographers and universitywide officials hadn't fully seen. One, for a variety of reasons, the University of California started getting a higher proportion of high school students applying to the university. Secondly, there were groups like Asian-American students who began to apply to UC in much higher proportions and coming to UC in higher proportions. And those were two dynamics that simply hadn't been anticipated.

So all the campuses were beginning to grow. This campus was—partly because it was doing more effective, more active recruiting of students—getting its enrollments back. It had that decline and had been told by David Saxon that it would lose positions if it didn't get its enrollments back up to about 6,300 or so by the start of 1984-1985. Well, it reached that point by 1982, as a result of the recruitments, and in fact by 1983, when I became dean, it was up to around 6,700 students. It was partly the Berkeley Redirect Program. And about half of those students ended up staying in Santa Cruz. So Santa Cruz got some benefit from that.

So what we thought was not something we were going to top out with until the 1990s, we were already there in the mid-1980s. That was a big boost to campus morale, and it did quiet not all, but some of the concerns and strife that had happened during reorganization and bringing in Richard Moll as a director of admissions. He left about that time, but the campus's outreach structure was much more firmly in place by then. Campus enrollments were growing steadily through the 1980s. We were continuing to grow by about 300 students a year. It was still an uncertain time, and we knew that we couldn't be complacent, but there was that sense that we were on the move again.

Robert Sinsheimer: I went down and talked to Mayor Mardi Wormhoudt.[1] I thought I ought to apprise her that this was a real opportunity for this town, that Santa Cruz could become something absolutely unique in California, which was a real university town, like Cambridge, like Oxford, like Princeton.

Well, she was noncommittal. Then I said the same thing to Supervisor Gary Patton.[2] It soon became clear that they were mightily unhappy about the university growing. They didn't want any more people here. This struck me as perverse, because their biggest supporters were the students. If they had more students, they'd have more voters. But they had this anti-growth ideology; they had on total blinders. Then they started using the Long Range Development Plan and the environmental impact report as threats; they would sue if we didn't provide enough mitigation.

Michael Cowan: The campus was isolated from the town, more than the initial planners had envisioned. Town-gown relations were complicated from the start, in part, but not only because of that.

Robert Sinsheimer: In fact, that attitude goes back a long ways. When there were just two colleges, they were opposed to building Crown and Merrill, and that's continued. It's an extremely selfish position: now that we're here, nobody else should come. Of course, they believe in democracy

and, of course, they want more minority students and so forth, but they don't want to have any more students. It's not a consistent attitude.

Page Smith: I am by no means as innocent about co-relations between town and gown, because now that I'm in the town and look up at the hill I understand some of the feelings that exist in the town about the university. That feeling has been exacerbated by the student upheavals, by the students' right to vote, and their mixing in county and city politics. But I think, quite apart from those issues—as important as they have been or as much of a role as they've played in inflaming or increasing tension—the university is not really much interested in the town. At least the town perceives that the university is not really much interested in the problems and issues of the town, except as the students come down and meddle in or vote in elections, and faculty and the university's condescending attitude toward the community, feeling itself in some way superior to the community.

I think that perception is right: I think the university—even with the best of intentions, and putting aside Dean's very active public relations program which was largely a personal matter—has never understood this.

Paul Niebanck: I don't think there's an inherent difficulty between town and gown. There's an enormous physical separation and our being on the hill makes it inherently difficult. We should have built near High Street.

Page Smith: I *do* think the physical distance makes the difference. Since space in Santa Cruz is limited, I don't know whether, practically, you could do it, but the model of the great universities of Europe—they're all right in the middle. If the university's attitude toward the community was different, the fact that it was a distance away and up on the hill, wouldn't matter. But since its attitude towards the community is basically a condescending one, that distance is reinforced.

Daniel McFadden: When I first came out for an interview, we had a discussion up at the house. There was McHenry, and Vice Chancellor Hal Hyde, and Gurden Mooser,[3] and we were talking about community relations. I said, "Well, you really have to establish roots in the community, because poor community relations can hurt you in a lot of different ways and you can't tell when. People will lay back and if they see you're vulnerable, if you want something, they can deny it; they're going to deny it to you." McHenry said, "We're a state university. We're not a community college. We really can't be involved with the community that much." He felt that it was necessary to keep the community pacified so you could do your own thing, but not really open up the institution, which was a terribly elitist institution.

Dean McHenry: Faculty people have not mixed in the town very much except for Karl Lamb[4] and Manny Shaffer[5] and a few others—a few faculty wives. A very few of us are carrying the load of relationships. It's very difficult to carry on a proper relationship when there're so few points of contact.

I've been looked upon by the town with a good deal of suspicion for harboring so many longhairs and weirdos and strange people up here. With the Malcolm X college proposal, as I've had to take a position in opposition, I've suddenly become a kind of a semi-hero in town. I'm embarrassed when I go to the Chamber of Commerce and service clubs now at the ovation I get. Men who I suspect of being near-John-Birchers will say, "We're right with you 100 percent."[6] And just as I'm alarmed at the hostility that I felt, now I'm alarmed at this acclaim that I've got in the community. It's awfully hard to strike a balance.

Daniel McFadden: I said to McHenry, "Well, I'm sure it's going to break. You're going to need something and they're going to be able to deny it to you because the feelings are so bad." I knew Santa Cruz City Manager David Koester, and you could just pick it up from the community people here.

Well, then College Eight came up for an appropriations hearing and Republican Assemblyman Frank Murphy appeared and pleaded for it not to go through unless there was housing with it, and that killed College Eight. So I felt there was some prophecy in what I was saying at that point.

George Blumenthal: I moved here in the spring of 1972. I knew very little about the city of Santa Cruz when I arrived here. I knew nothing about the local politics. I knew that when Bill and Cynthia Mathews moved up here, one of Cynthia's first acts was to open a Planned Parenthood office across the street from the high school, which I thought was such a cool idea.[7]

So I was actually somewhat surprised to discover how conservative the community of Santa Cruz was when I first arrived here. Within six to nine months of coming to Santa Cruz, I moved to Live Oak. Not long after I moved in, there was an election for county supervisor. One day I was at home and this guy, Phil Baldwin, came by. He was campaigning. I chatted with him for a few minutes. Turns out he was a teacher and he seemed like a very reasonable guy. So when the election came, I happily voted for him. And it turned out he was elected, to everyone's shock and surprise, but he was really detested by some of the powers-that-be in county politics. So they organized a recall election and removed him from office. So far as I can recall, there was no cause. It's not like he did something wrong, other than carrying a liberal brand. But these were really contentious times, and some of the county folks that were in power were remarkably conservative. The county was dominated by conservative political forces and when Baldwin got elected, that was a shock to their system.

Hal Hyde, Vice Chancellor for Business and Finance: Students had the vote in Santa Cruz and in Berkeley. That became their official residence. With radical faculty leadership locally and in the Vietnam crisis, the council make-up rapidly changed in Santa Cruz with this large student vote.[8]

George Blumenthal: Things really began to change once we got into the seventies. When I got here, there were maybe three or four thousand students on campus, so there weren't a lot of students, and most of them wouldn't have voted anyway. But when students did get the right to vote,[9] they started voting. Even if it was in small numbers, that made a big difference in a place like Santa Cruz, which in those days had maybe thirty thousand total residents and maybe a voting population, I'm guessing, of ten thousand. So adding a couple thousand students could make a huge difference in that kind of politics, particularly within the city. The student vote, coupled with the fact that so many alums in those days were staying in Santa Cruz, caused a tremendous change in the local politics.

The county was much slower to change, however. There were lawsuits within Santa Cruz challenging the validity of student voting, arguing that eighteen-year-olds may have the right to vote, but one didn't have the right to vote on a campus. Those lawsuits took a while to resolve. So it was contentious locally. I think change is always hard, but in Santa Cruz, that was not an easy change. Change didn't come easily here. There was a lot of bitterness: bitterness toward the university, bitterness toward students among some of the local population.

John Laird: I was the first UCSC graduate ever elected to the city council, who was an undergraduate for four years. Mike Rotkin had been a graduate student, and had gotten there a couple of years earlier. I was also the first openly gay mayor to be elected in the United States.

George Blumenthal: The city council fairly quickly became more moderate and more divided, with real liberal factions. I remember one year when a group of people ran for council on a feminist platform. I think virtually all of them won. Mike Rotkin was one.

John Laird: A substantial number of people in town hated the university. They said, "We've lived here forever. They are changing our way of life. They are yahoos. We're more stable townies who stay here forever." There was this pronounced split.

Mike Rotkin, Lecturer: Bill Friedland was the official teacher of a community studies student-directed seminar I taught on highways and widening Highway 17. They were trying to build freeways everywhere in Santa Cruz and we were trying to stop them. So, our students did a survey.[10]

Bill Friedland: They wanted me to design a community studies program which would require full-time field study. I set out the basic orientation, the three basic parts. I set out the notion that students will choose their own field study. It's their responsibility. There are two limitations: it couldn't be on any campus, and it couldn't be illegal. And then, the other element was we want to emphasize students going to communities that the UC has pretty much overlooked, which meant poor people, racial minorities. Getting community studies started occupied me for several years.

We were the first interdisciplinary department at UCSC.

Michael Cowan: Bill Friedland was working with a group of students on looking at transportation, an attitude study. It was a hot topic in the early campus history, whether we should have ring roads and so forth. Bill got some funds from the Office of the President and I agreed to form a group of students, mainly community studies majors, to do a survey of housing conditions and attitudes in Santa Cruz. I had never had any experience in doing this kind of a study, but I thought it would be a useful contribution.

Community studies also had a very strong fieldwork program—it was built in from the very outset—where students would take some introductory courses, a field preparation course, then spend six months full time in the field, come back and write a senior thesis.

Mike Rotkin: We surveyed Santa Cruz and found that the majority of people didn't like any of the five freeway choices they were being offered, and they didn't want *any* freeway—and we killed the freeway through Santa Cruz.

The city council took us out of the freeway system, based on that survey that our students did. During the "freeway mania" period of the early seventies we didn't have a freeway through town. Otherwise we might have had a double-decked Mission Street, or a freeway through what's now the Pogonip and University Terrace, and down through what's now Wilder Ranch State Park, if we hadn't stopped it. The options included double-decking Mission Street, or making King Street and California into one-way loops of the freeway.

Michael Cowan: Another attitude that came out in the survey was that people were opposed to skip-out, suburban sprawl development. They wanted to preserve the North Coast. There had been a big proposal from a major firm that wanted to build a large housing development up the coast, about halfway between here and Davenport. It was just on the other side of the Wilder Ranch property. People were very much opposed to that.

Mike Rotkin: Plus, a nuclear power plant at Davenport;[11] ten thousand homes for the wealthy on the North Coast, and two twelve-story towers on Frederick Street—all of which got killed. That was the beginning of serious environmental stuff in Santa Cruz, in 1970, '71.

John Daly: There was this growing no-growth attitude coming out of the university, and among citizens too. Many of our new citizens of Santa Cruz had come from metropolitan areas like New York, Boston, Philadelphia, and/or they came up from Los Angeles, and had seen what happened to growth after World War II in cities. And so they're very anti-growth. People who come here from metropolitan areas say, "Oh no, no. Jeez, we don't want this place to grow. We witnessed that."

Michael Cowan: The other major conclusion of the survey was that the vast majority of the Santa Cruz population was very much opposed to the 1964 city and county long-range plans, which called for the university of 27,000 and for an urban area of about 200,000 by 1990. This was built into that initial plan, which was very much led by the business community. It was quite clear that the residents of Santa Cruz—and you have to remember there were a lot of elderly too, on fixed incomes, but others too—did not want that to happen. This university was beginning to come also to the understanding that there were all sorts of reasons that it was going to be impractical for them to build to that scale.

John Daly: The no-growth people have kept this town squashed down. Before they started coming forward, nobody ever said, "Hey, wait a minute! Wait a minute! Wait a minute! You're going to wreck some of the ecostructure." (I guess that is what they call it.) "Oh, you're going to wreck this. You're going to disturb some of the animals, or some of the bugs." Nobody worried about that in those days.

George Blumenthal: When I got here in 1972, the first local issue that I found interesting concerned Lighthouse Field. There was a proposal before the city council and the planning commission to convert Lighthouse Field into two things: a condominium complex and a big shopping center. It was very controversial in Santa Cruz, so the planning commission held public hearings. I attended a few of those and I was kind of appalled at the planning that was going into this.[12]

I read the report of the traffic consultants because traffic was something I understand. It's just numbers. I looked at their numbers for total traffic and was kind of shocked by it. Lighthouse Field is accessible only through residential streets. There are no thoroughfares to Lighthouse Field. And they were talking about a number of car visits per day. When you actually looked at it, it was equal to the number of seconds in a day. So there would be like one car per second averaged over a day (assuming it was uniform) to Lighthouse Field. It was ridiculous. And so I pointed out how, in some ways, ridiculous some of the traffic assessments were for Lighthouse Field. It simply wouldn't have worked, given the infrastructure within the city.

John Daly: Gary Patton gained his fame from carrying the banner against development of Lighthouse Field. I knew Gary quite well because his father and mother were close social friends of my wife and I. Gary Patton was an attorney, Stanford grad, and a no-growther. The man has never changed. He and his disciples kept a clamp on Santa Cruz.

George Blumenthal: Ultimately, the Lighthouse Field development was rejected. I think that was a good thing. This was one of Gary Patton's first major forays into local politics. He was one of the leaders to stop Lighthouse Field, and I think it is to his credit that it succeeded. Ultimately, Lighthouse Field was made into a park, which was a completely appropriate and good choice for that land. So it ended up having a happy ending, but it was not an easy pathway. Can you imagine what Santa Cruz would have been like had that succeeded?

Michael Cowan: So already you had that anti-growth attitude here that was then going to be an ongoing theme in university-community relations.

John Laird: I campaigned on the basis that I was going to try to bring us together as one community. But the term I was mayor was begun by a ballot measure that was anti-university growth, that when I was elected mayor, I was charged with implementing.[13] That was very difficult. Then we sued the university the second time I was mayor. They were unwilling to compromise. They were unwilling to look for common ground. It was like, "We are exempt from local land use. We are exempt from laws under the state constitution. Basically, we're going to do what we're going to do." That was the attitude.

Angus Taylor, Chancellor: There were several potential sore points with some members of the Santa Cruz community. One was the traffic situation; the traffic on Mission Street was noticeably more congested as a result of the university presence. The university had originally had a negotiated agreement with the county and the city to build what they called the Eastern Access Road. It was to come up into the campus without going up onto Mission Street at all. But there were people there who were determined that they didn't want that to happen, for two different reasons. One was cost. The university agreement was binding that that was going to happen. But it wasn't guaranteed to happen right away; it was in the indefinite future. Well, the time really had come by that time. But the county was backing down, to some extent.

Some people believed that the road up through Pogonip would be a scar, would be a very unpleasant thing to see. The idea that I pushed, and got some sympathy for, was to route the traffic up Highway 9 a short distance and then turn around and start climbing the hillside and come into the campus just at the very upper end of where the road along that side of the campus turns to go over by the garden beneath Merrill College. And then turn around and bring the road up through the trees where you couldn't see it. Well, no action ever occurred on that but that seemed to me a reasonable way to do it. There was a young fellow, Gary Patton, who was a county supervisor. Patton was a squeaky wheel. He didn't want anything to happen to Pogonip.

Robert Sinsheimer: When I first came here in 1977, I learned about the promise by the county to build the Eastern Access Road. The county originally promised it would build a six-lane road to the junction of Highway 9 and River Street. It's in writing. At that time, relations with the community and the county and everything were so happy they never put a date; they didn't say when they would build it. Obviously, they should have said it would be built by 19-X. But they never did.

I discussed this with the UC General Counsel's Office. In theory, the university could take the county to court, but it's not going to do that, for political reasons.

Lou Fackler, Engineer: During the early engineering design for the campus, I would call the county director of public works quite often. Sometimes I'd get Vince Locatelli. Vince Locatelli was also a county supervisor. We got into a little conversation about some of these roads. On one call he said, "Ah! All that stuff we signed. Those were the honeymoon papers! Those don't mean anything." That was entirely unofficial, but that's what the man said.

Robert Sinsheimer: Santa Cruz was purchased by the regents to be a campus, not to be a state park. There is a huge state park, Wilder Ranch State Park, right next door. That ought to provide enough natural reserve and whatever hiking trails people want. The campus doesn't have to be preserved as a park. That doesn't mean you can bulldoze it, pave the whole thing over, but you do use it for a campus as sensibly as you can.

By 1982, we'd been through four years of post-Proposition 13, with budgets being cut every year, and things didn't look as if they were going to get any better. How could we get some money? What could the campus do? The one asset the campus had was land. Could we use that land for something useful? You could see what Stanford did with their research park. Could we make use of the land in such a way as to do something worthwhile, generate income for the campus and also solve the isolation? We were in a recession. Unemployment was around 12, 15 percent in Santa Cruz.

Well, all of these things coalesced in this idea for a research and development park. While it would require some initial investment, that would all be recouped, and after a period of time it looked like it could generate for the campus a few million dollars a year. For the community, it would provide—I think we estimated—2,000 jobs. It would bring in about 750 scientists and technically trained people into the area. Even though it was on university ground, it was understood that this would be what we call inclusionary, so it would be a tax base for the community. It would not be a smoke-stack industry. Clean industry.

George Blumenthal: I was at home one day when Harry Berger called me and said there was going to be a gathering at Chancellor Sinsheimer's house that night. He wanted me to be there to represent astronomy. The issue at hand was Sinsheimer's idea of a research park on campus.

One of Sinsheimer's big problems was the lack of money to fund operations. Sinsheimer was thinking well, okay, we need more money, how do we get more money? Well, maybe one way of getting more money is to use one of our biggest resources, which is land. We have lots of land on campus. So maybe we should put aside some land, sort of like Stanford did, and have a research park on the campus. We'd have companies come in. They would also employ our students. They'd interact with our faculty. We would get a double benefit. And we'd get the benefit of the revenue of our land. So that was Sinsheimer's big idea.

Robert Sinsheimer: I thought the prospects of jobs and tax base and so on would be attractive. But, of course, to people like Gary Patton and so on, it was a threat. I was naive. It was an eye-opener. I remember having a discussion at University House with Gary Patton. It became very clear to me, and he said it in so many words, that what he didn't like about it was that he didn't think the scientists and engineers who would come and work at the research and development

park would vote for him. It was that blunt: they weren't his kind of people, but they would be in his district.

John Laird: Robert Sinsheimer was the chancellor for most of the time I was on the city council. He wanted to build a research and development park that was on university land on an area that the city considered a greenbelt, and using the contracts that the city had with the university. People were pretty outraged about it in town because the city was actually going to pay for a lot of the infrastructure for this research and development park that was going to be oriented to the university. The private company was going to benefit from this public subsidy and the university land.

George Blumenthal: It was not the most popular idea on our campus. We discussed it within my department. I was one of the dissenters. I thought it was a bad idea. Number one, I wasn't all that anxious to get involved with the industrial complex of the country. And number two, I didn't think that the infrastructure of the campus could withstand it. We have only one road going up to campus. There's only one school nearby, Westlake, and I didn't think they could handle a huge influx of students. I just didn't think it was a good idea. I told that to Harry Berger when he called. I said, "You may not want me to be the one that represents my department because probably if you took a vote, it would be 60/40 the other way." He said, "That's okay." He said it didn't matter. He wanted a diversity of opinions for Sinsheimer to hear.

Robert Sinsheimer: I'd have to have the UC president's or the regents' approval for the research and development park, with the likelihood of legal action against the university by the city of Santa Cruz. I raised the issue with President Gardner,

Figure 1

Flyer protesting proposed Research and Development Park, 1980s

who had replaced Saxon. Well, Gardner wasn't enthused at all. When I pursued it further with him, and in particular raised the issue of the community concern, I told him that I would have to have the university's backing in this, if it came to a lawsuit and so on. He simply discouraged going ahead with it.

George Blumenthal: So I said fine and I went to this thing. It was actually a very good meeting that Harry had orchestrated. There were a wide diversity of opinions. I was hardly the most outspoken person there. But I did make one really solid point. I said to Sinsheimer, "Look, you promised at the beginning that you would bring this to a vote of the faculty, and you would abide by a vote of the faculty. So let's leave aside all of the issues of the merits. It is my impression that right now you would get about 50 percent of the vote in the science division and you'd get about 3 percent of the vote in humanities and social sciences and arts. So I don't see how you have a pathway to getting this approved by the faculty. And since you've committed to seeking that approval, it seems to me that this is DOA."

He took it seriously. He said we need to be more specific about what it would mean, what it would look like, and then maybe people will support it. I mean, he wasn't ready to give up. But after that, his efforts were much more half-hearted. I think he saw the handwriting on the wall.

John Laird: The chancellor would like to portray it as the anti-university town. So I went up to debate him, and I would open up the debate by saying, "This is the time of the annual fund drive for the university. The UCSC Foundation needs your money for scholarships (or whatever). Here's the address of the UCSC Foundation." Then I'd talk about the issues, and make him crazy, because he was trying to make the point that we

were anti-UCSC, that we didn't like it here. I was trying to make the point that that wasn't the issue.

Robert Sinsheimer: People don't understand the structure of governments in the state. There is the state, then the counties, cities, and then there's the University of California. There are many other state institutions as well. And since they are state entities they are not subordinate to local entities. UCSC is not Santa Cruz City College. It's the University of California and it doesn't serve the Santa Cruz community in the same way that Cabrillo College does. It serves the people of the state. It seems to me, quite properly, not subject to local ordinances.

John Laird: The university is behind the times sometimes. When we sent Mardi Wormhoudt to the Long Range Development Committee meetings as the city representative in 1988 or 1989, when she first served on it I think there were twenty-six people on the committee and she was the only woman! They did some changes. They managed to get four or five women on it. The university is such an insulated institution, insulated from trends, the public, politics, in certain ways. But university towns tend to be places where there's organizing, where there's been progress.

John Dizikes: Universities are terrible neighbors. They really are, everywhere, in England, in America, wherever. They're devastatingly self-centered and selfish. And enough of the innumerable chancellors would say to people in the town, "Well yes we're located in Santa Cruz, but we're actually a statewide institution. We're not just Santa Cruz." Yes, but you're located in Santa Cruz and you impact this local community.

"Everybody Breathes Together":
Shakespeare Santa Cruz as a Bridge Between Campus and Community

Robert Sinsheimer: I really tried to generate things for Santa Cruz, to make the art programs more accessible and have more of them in the community. I think a number of people here thought when the university came that there would be big football games and so on. There's no question that that is an attraction at other campuses.

I arranged that the conductor of the Santa Cruz Symphony would have an appointment on the campus so that we could put together a much better package and get a better person. I think the relationship between music and the campus has improved town/gown relations. Things like that, to some extent, can mitigate the unhappiness that I know part of the community felt with the university.

Audrey Stanley, Co-founder, Shakespeare Santa Cruz: I wanted to do some serious theater. I set up Shakespeare Santa Cruz[14] here in Santa Cruz. C.L. ["Joe"] Barber was one of our three Shakespearean professors and was also dean of humanities and arts. When he died in 1980, somewhat unexpectedly, Dane Archer from the social sciences wrote a letter to the chancellor to say, would we not honor C.L. Barber by setting up a Shakespeare festival, with town and gown meetings to see if this was a possibility? He said in the letter, "I've not yet talked with Audrey Stanley, but obviously she should be involved." And that's when the townspeople said, "Well, let's have our own festival." It was the townspeople who, in one sense, pushed this, and the townspeople who provided the board of directors to set it up.

We had a gathering in Bargetto's Winery and some of our Royal Shakespeare Company actors read some sonnets. It was the first event of Shakespeare Santa Cruz. We applied for money from Chancellor Sinsheimer, who donated ten thousand dollars. The chancellor had married Karen Sinsheimer, who had worked in Twentieth Century Fox. So I invited myself to tea.

Karen Sinsheimer, Co-Founder, Shakespeare Santa Cruz: In 1981, theater arts professor Audrey Stanley came to me and said, "Could we have tea? I have an idea for a little Shakespeare festival." So we had tea and the subtly persuasive Stanley said, "Would you be able to get a group, a few community people, involved to support a small festival?"

Audrey Stanley: Karen Sinsheimer was absolutely splendid in setting this up. I always declared that we were like two war horses taking a chariot that was a runaway chariot, or the runaway horses, and each of us were one of the two horses running side by side, we were so busy trying to set up this festival.

In the beginning we had to do so many jobs. I did an awful lot of PR and came up with the idea of having Shakespeare arrive in Jack O'Neill's wonderful yacht.[15] He was rowed ashore at the Beach Boardwalk, and the press was lined up. The waves threw him into the water, so he came out a shivering Shakespeare. He was a young student, but he performed Shakespeare brilliantly, quipping jokes at the Boardwalk. The newspapers had wonderful shots of him falling into the waves. So that was a good start to the publicity. It was Karen Sinsheimer who persuaded O'Neill to loan his boat for the occasion.

Karen Sinsheimer: I started to organize a small group of community people, including Cleo Barber, wife of the Shakespearean scholar Joe

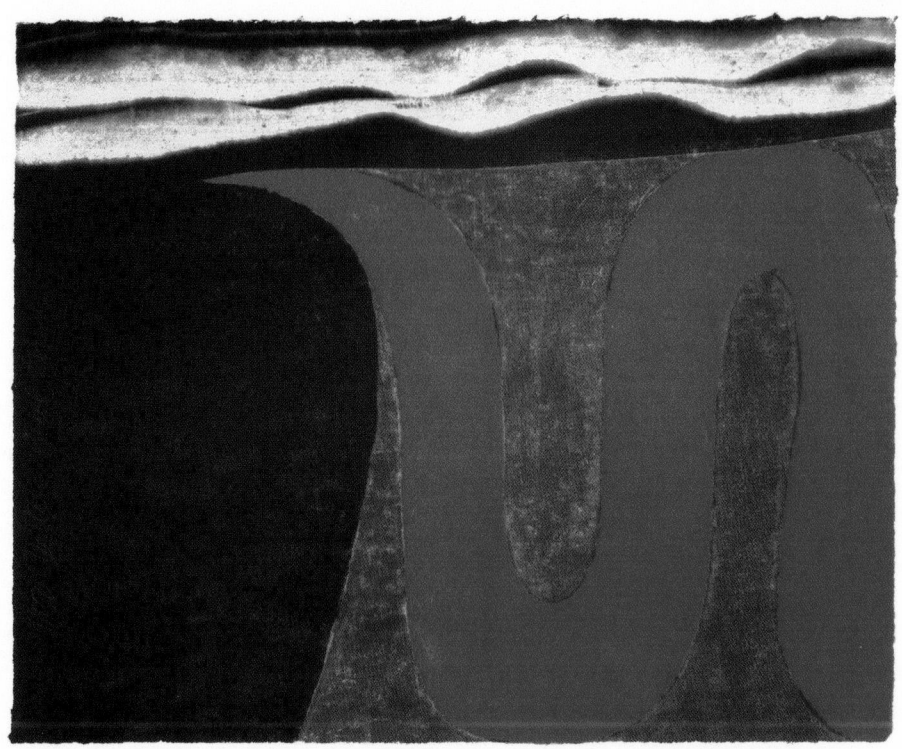

SHAKESPEARE / SANTA CRUZ

July 14 - August 14, 1983

The Merry Wives of Windsor · Macbeth

Performing Arts Complex, University of California, Santa Cruz

Figure 2

Shakespeare Santa Cruz program, 1983 festival season

Barber.[16] There were about five of us. We set about raising money; with Audrey as the "force majeure" we went forward. Audrey had a way of making us feel it was all quite manageable. We devoted huge numbers of hours and effort during those first years, Audrey Stanley most of all.

Audrey Stanley: Shakespeare Santa Cruz achieved mention amongst the top-ten most influential Shakespeare festivals in the country. People like English actors Patrick Stewart and Tony Church came to this campus. It brought people onto the campus to explore and enjoy what it has to offer. It was the townspeople who filled the board and helped to raise the money to pay for the festival.

John Daly: I was a Shakespeare fan. They brought Shakespeare to town. I thought, "Oh boy. This is wonderful." My wife and I were very supportive. We bought the season tickets and we had some of the players to the house for cocktails to meet our friends. But then we began going to plays. And for some reason, the director and then his followers got off into this modern approach to Shakespeare.

I'll never forget. I went to see *Henry V*. I think it was the second or third year. And here these guys come out in this black leather, and they ride onto the stage in the glen on motorcycles. I thought, "What in the hell is this?" They recited the Shakespeare lines, but compared to the Shakespeare I had seen in the past it was just weird, to say the least. And then we went to see another play the following year with our daughter, and again—they had this jester in it who played an important role. It was a comedy. Well, the bottom line was this ghoul came out holding his penis and waving it around. I mean, it was a long penis. I thought, "My God!" And then even in the curtain call, I'll be damned if he didn't come out and here he is with his penis, waving it. That was

the Shakespeare that we were getting exposed to. I lost interest. I said, "Uh-oh. That's too much."

Audrey Stanley: I think these plays take us into places that perhaps we might not otherwise experience.

Michael Warren: Santa Cruz in the summer is quite amazing. It has the Cabrillo Music Festival.[17] It has the Cabrillo College musical theater productions. And then it has Shakespeare Santa Cruz.

Audrey Stanley: I'll never forget watching *Macbeth* with the fog creeping in. It seemed so appropriate to the play. And then a lovely production of *Titus Andronicus*, in which Lavinia's being taken into the woods and cruelly dealt with there. It was eerie, and the fact that the trees were there made it even darker as a play, more ominous, because of the reality of the trees. And then, just simply the whole glen itself, with the references to the sun and the moon. And there it is—you can have the sun in the afternoon matinees and you have the moon sometimes in the evening shows.

It's one of the most beautiful sites in North America to perform Shakespeare. It's both intimate and vast, because the trees are so tall and the glen appears to go on for a long stretch.

Shakespeare is so very relevant to living our lives, and encourages us to take risks, to try things. You get to a point, when if the acting is right, the text is right, and the audience is right: everybody breathes together. It's a magical moment. It's something that only live theater can do.

Learning to Be of Service:
Expanding Community Activism and Advocacy

Reggie Knox, Student: The community studies major at UCSC set me off in a career working in community organizations. I was a classic community studies student in terms of the path that I took and the way that it influenced me. One of my initial contacts in the agriculture community was Mark Lipson at CCOF [California Certified Organic Farmers]. I did a community studies internship with him in 1987, in my last year of college. And then the CCOF internship developed into a job. I eventually ended up working on national organic standards development.

Amy Katzenstein-Escobar, Student: I was in community studies, and I was working with migrant kids in Watsonville. I saw that there was a Ford Foundation education project that you could apply for. There was a group of people who had an idea that we wanted to teach the migrants year-round. When they went back to Mexico after the strawberry season, which ends in October, we would follow our migrant students down to Mexico and we would teach them there, so that we could understand what was going on for six months of their lives and be better teachers, and they could continue their English, so they wouldn't forget everything. So I wrote a grant, and it was accepted.

Pedro Castillo, Professor: I started working with students to do oral histories. This came out of a seminar on race, gender, and class in California history. I told the students, "We're going to focus locally on Watsonville, and we're going to focus on oral histories, and look at different social, cultural, political organizations in Watsonville, or individuals in Watsonville."

Amy Katzenstein-Escobar: I'm, like, twenty years old, maybe nineteen then. I did my student teaching at Freedom Elementary School, which was the feeder school for Buena Vista Migrant Camp. So I knew the kids from my student teaching. I left before them to go down—so I was down there for August and September before they arrived in October. It's the state of Michoacán, about three hours south of Guadalajara. In Watsonville in the late seventies, early eighties, most of the people, migrants, came from Michoacán because it has a very similar climate, and therefore grows similar crops. I have pictures of Michoacán where I lived that look exactly like Watsonville. So that's where I lived, in a small village named Tangancicuaro. I worked at Gomez Farms, about six kilometers up the road. I became very close to a lot of my students. The experience made me a much better teacher because I understood their culture and life in Mexico.

Pedro Castillo: We did a walking tour of Watsonville, the downtown area, the neighborhoods. We got maps and found out where the different communities are, where different people live—the more middle class, the more working class, the more upper class. We spent five hours or so doing that. Then I usually would take them to a restaurant and we'd have dinner or something like that. That was cool. There was nothing really on Watsonville except what Sandy Lydon had done. He was doing work on the Chinese and the Japanese of Monterey Bay.[18]

Then the class assignment was to do an oral history, either of an organization or of an individual. In the winter we worked on refining, going back, doing the oral interviews, and transcribing most of the interview. Some of them said, "Well, what are going to do with this?" I said, "Why don't we publish it in a book?"[19]

Ed Landesman: I started the Monterey Bay Area Math Project in 1985, and that was one of the seventeen California Math Projects. I brought in twenty or thirty teachers every summer, who taught math at all levels, from elementary to high school. Often, we chose teachers who came from underrepresented areas, such as Pajaro, Salinas, and Watsonville, and we worked on upgrading their math skills, so that they would do better as far as getting their students interested in mathematics. And then, when I started doing research in math education with Ron Henderson, we went out into the schools, and we also worked in Pajaro, in Watsonville, in Salinas.

I became more and more interested in how students learn math and what we could do to improve math learning and teaching and get students to be more proficient prior to coming to the university, and to get teachers to be more knowledgeable in the subject matter. All of this was something that could help the university. If you get students who are more prepared when they arrive, you're better off and they're better off.

Herman Blake: I always believed that the university should serve the community. There was a guy at UC Santa Cruz who was in charge of what I would call Extended Education. His name was Carl Tjerandsen.[20] He was the most mild, pleasant, middle-class, Midwest white man that you'd ever want to meet, just as mild as they come. I met Carl Tjerandsen, but didn't really know anything about him. He didn't know anything about me.

But one day after I had been here a year at Santa Cruz, I was sitting in my office in Cowell College and Carl Tjerandsen walked into my office and said that he was the executive secretary for the Emil Schwarzhaupt Foundation. This

was a foundation started by a Polish immigrant in Chicago years ago. He'd come to Chicago as a poor person, became very successful, and left his money to a foundation to help immigrants make the transition to American society, like he did. Carl Tjerandsen was the executive secretary here at Santa Cruz of a foundation in Chicago.

Well, what had happened was, over time, as the immigrant population declined and the Schwarzhaupt Foundation still had money, they started putting their money into projects to help other groups who were on the periphery of American society come to the center. And in that capacity they had funded Saul Alinsky's work in Chicago.[21] In addition to funding Saul Alinsky, they had funded Myles Horton and the Highlander Folk School to work with people in the Sea Islands of South Carolina, specifically Johns Island, to develop strategies for helping them to become part of the larger society.

So this white man in Santa Cruz was, through a foundation in Chicago, funding operations in Chicago; Lackawanna, New York; Buffalo, New York; and Johns Island, South Carolina to bring people into the mainstream of American society. And he said to me they were looking for someone to go and do an evaluation of the work of Saul Alinsky and his work in Chicago, and of Myles Horton[22] and Septima Clark's work on Johns Island, South Carolina. He wondered if I might be interested, whereupon I pointed out to him that I had family in South Carolina, specifically on Johns Island. My family history on Johns Island went back into the days of slavery. He could not believe it. I happened to have two wedding invitations from two cousins on Johns Island sitting on my desk with a Johns Island postmark, and I showed them to him. He couldn't believe that he'd walked into my office and all of these connections.

Michael James, Student: Herman Blake had a great big impact on all of us, not just black students, but all students. He was, in a sense, the model of the 21st century scholar. Herman was already postmodern.

Herman Blake: Long story short, they commissioned me to go and spend a summer in Chicago with Saul Alinsky and his organization, at Highlander Folk School with Myles Horton, and from Highlander to Johns Island, South Carolina, where I would work with Septima Clark and Esau Jenkins,[23] to get an understanding of the long-term consequences of their work. That's how I got started and that's how I made the link. That's how I met Myles Horton. That's how I met Septima Clark. And since I came representing the foundation that had funded them, that's how it all got started.

I got a profound education from Myles Horton. Myles Horton had this belief that people from the grassroots had the knowledge to resolve the challenges and issues facing them, but they did not have the level of confidence, did not have confidence *in* their knowledge, and very often did not have the skills to deal with the larger society. And sitting there with him at Highlander Folk School, at the time in Monteagle, Tennessee, on the porch of his house, feeding sunflower seeds to the cardinals—he loved to feed sunflower seeds to cardinals and they came, beautiful birds—we talked about these things.

From there I made my way to Johns Island, where I stayed with my family, stayed at my aunt's house, because she was just down the road, and I made contact with Septima Clark, Bernice Robinson,[24] and Esau Jenkins, and through them into a wide range of grassroots people. So I was home, as a person who was linked to the community, but I was also from the outside, as a scholar who brought a different perspective.

I developed a profound respect, indeed love, for Septima Clark. And she for me. We began to work together in a variety of ways. First of all, as I listened to her talk about her successes, I asked a question which was at the center of my thinking. Sometimes you can learn more about success through failure. And that came through my studies of the poverty programs in California, where I'd dealt with a number of Latino-based programs that were headed by people who talked about the Cursillo [Christian service] Movement that they'd been involved in and the two key leaders in that were people who had been utter failures in their original program, but they grew from their failures. So I said to Septima, "Have you ever failed?" And she said, "Yes. Daufuskie Island." So I had to go see Daufuskie Island.[25]

George Blumenthal: I went on a trip to South Carolina with Herman Blake. We went to Daufuskie Island. Daufuskie was, at the time, completely undeveloped, the original Gullah people living there. It was very poor, very rural. They were very close, connected to each other.

I understood, being there, why Herman wanted, as a sociologist, to study the island. This was a way station, so people would be dropped off there and then later picked up and brought to the mainland and sold as slaves. But when slavery ended, and the Civil War ended, there were these people left on the island. They became the residents of the island. So they all descended from more or less the same time. They weren't necessarily related to each other originally. Many of them left the island. Joe Frazier, who Ali lost a fight to, came from the island. The Thrilla in Manila.[26]

Herman Blake: Page Smith was talking about getting some students doing work in communities. But Page had a different idea from mine. Page had been through the Civilian Conservation Corps in

Figure 3

Professor Herman
Blake, 1976

Photo by UCSC
Photography Services

the thirties and he talked about his experiences learning from being in that setting. He thought the students could learn from the same kind of a setting. But his idea was you send the students off into the community, turn them loose, they gather data and come back and write reports and stuff. My question was, "Well, what does the community get out of it?" Page never addressed that question. "You turn the students loose in the community." Well, in my opinion, that was nothing more than middle-class voyeurism.

So, I objected to Page's idea. Vocally, and in faculty meetings I argued against turning students loose in the community.

Instead, I came up with the idea: Let's figure out ways students can live in the community, and serve the community, and in the process of *living* they will get an education—and *serving*. And that way the community will get a benefit and the student will get a benefit. The university should stay involved in humankind, where the path from the university to the community and the community to the university are open paths.

George Blumenthal: Herman had bought a house there because he wanted to be there to study and be a part of that community. There were several of us traveling together. It was Bill Doyle and me, and by then we had picked up a couple of students from Oakes College. You had to go by boat to the island. Herman placed us all in different houses. So I stayed with Miss Hamilton, who was kind of an elderly woman. Maybe in her sixties. I was twenty-six, twenty-seven, so anyone over forty seemed old to me. I felt really warm being there. I enjoyed talking with her.

Herman Blake: That's when I came up with the idea of sending students to Daufuskie to live in the homes of the people on Daufuskie and work on projects. They built outhouses and did other

things. People thought it was awful. You got California students going all the way across the country to build outhouses for blacks who sit and watch them. No, they weren't going to build outhouses. They were going to live in the home of Frances Jones, or live in the home of Ervin Simmons, or others like this, with sometimes dirt floors. They were learning but they were providing service.

George Blumenthal: The next morning, Herman was off doing something. There was a dirt road that ran the length of the island. We were told that at the end of the island there were these tabby huts[27] where slaves were kept. They were kept in those tabby huts when they were dropped off on the island.

So Bill and I and the students thought we'd walk down to the end of the island and see the tabby huts, although we'd also heard there were a lot of rattlesnakes down there. So we were a little bit concerned about that.

So we're walking down the road quite happily. There were people out. We were still in the residential area and there were kids playing in the street. We came to a bunch of kids and they said to us, "What are you doing?" I said, "Well, we're walking down to the tabby huts." And they said, "Oh, yeah, we play down there all the time." And then one of the women students said, "Well, do you worry about the snakes?" I'll never forget what the kid said. He said, "No, we don't worry about the snakes. They only bite white people."

Michael James: Herman had this field study project in the Sea Islands, Daufuskie Island. The Sea Islands were one of the last places on the continent where the African community was able to have some autonomy and maintain some of the African dialects. It's a fishing area. He would have students come from Santa Cruz and go do field study and work and live out there and re-ground ourselves in the larger African American narrative.

Herman Blake: The students' experience of learning was living in the community. You didn't live in separate housing, like a hostel, where the students could come together and do student stuff. No, you lived in the community. They learned to cook the cuisine. They learned the religion. One young lady said she heard a lady talking on the phone, saying, "My daughter's in the kitchen, doing something or other." She looked and realized, "Oh, that's me."

Sheila Coonerty: There had never been females that went to Daufuskie. Herman originally sent guys to fix houses and electricity and sewer systems. He purposely just sent guys so that there wouldn't be any difficulties with female relationships, or relationships between the guys and the girls, or anything like that. We were the experiment. He sent six of us. All of us were older. I had already graduated by that point and was teaching. We were trying to start a summer school program and a preschool. Daufuskie used to be a slave island and the slave huts were still there—they were made of oyster shells—on one end of the island. It was very overgrown. It was the closest thing to a jungle that I ever went to.

There I was, on this island. We got mail twice a week by boat and we got supplies by boat. It took three hours to ride a boat back to the mainland. We were out in the middle of nowhere.

Herman had very high standards for all of us and everybody that he took in. He also had this great heart—not only a great heart, but he was smart. He brought a couple of the kids, who were no longer kids from Daufuskie, to go to UCSC. It was a big stretch for them. He figured out how to get them the help that they needed. They didn't all make it, but if they didn't make it, he helped them figure out what else they wanted to do. He offered the support.

Herman Blake: I wanted to provide resources to people in these communities, but the only resource I had was education. So it was important for me to try and open avenues of educational opportunity, and when people came *into* the academy, to develop strategies that they might succeed. That was at Oakes College. That was serving the community. That's always been my motivation. That's always been my goal.

Figure 4

Brochure for extramural education community programs, Daufuskie Island youth, circa 1970

Endnotes

1. Mardi Wormhoudt was first elected to the Santa Cruz County Board of Supervisors in 1994; from 1981 to 1990, she sat on the Santa Cruz City Council and was elected mayor three times, serving as mayor during the very difficult period after the 1989 Loma Prieta earthquake.

2. Gary Patton was a Santa Cruz County supervisor from 1975 to 1995. An environmental attorney practicing in Santa Cruz County, he has been a major figure in the Santa Cruz progressive community. See the Gary Patton Political Papers at the UCSC Library's Special Collections: MS 81: https://oac.cdlib.org/findaid/ark:/13030/tf1489n8d2/entire_text/.

3. Dean McHenry appointed Gurden Mooser to the position of assistant chancellor for university relations in 1965. By the time Mooser retired in 1978, he had helped attract a series of major gifts that established UCSC's college system and provided support to many other academic and administrative programs. As part of that effort, Mooser formed the UC Santa Cruz Foundation in 1974. Mooser died in 1999.

4. Karl Lamb helped plan the campus and then became a professor of government. He is another key UCSC figure who came from Oxford University.

5. Manfred Shaffer was a professor of geography and came to UCSC in 1965.

6. The John Birch Society is a right-wing conservative advocacy group supporting limits on government and opposing communism.

7. Cynthia Mathews was the founder and executive director of Planned Parenthood of Santa Cruz County; she has served six times on the Santa Cruz City Council, including four times as mayor.

8. For a detailed history of the transformation of the city of Santa Cruz from a conservative to a progressive town, see Richard Gendron and G. William Domhoff's *The Leftmost City: Power and Politics in Santa Cruz* (Routledge, 2009). Also see the accompanying website curated by Domhoff at: https://whorulesamerica.ucsc.edu/santacruz/.

9. Eighteen-year-old US citizens won the right to vote in 1971 and could cast ballots in their city of residence. This meant that UCSC students could vote in Santa Cruz elections. In 1973, UCSC students helped elect the first progressive, pro-environment city council in Santa Cruz. According to Randy Shaw, writing on the Leftmost City website: "In those 1973 local contests, the three progressive

candidates swept into power after each won over 90% of the campus vote. 74% of eligible student voters cast ballots, and their impact was so great that only one of the three would have won but for the student turnout." http://beyondchron.org/santa-cruz-where-the-left-and-no-growth-politics-meet/.

10. Between 1964 and 1970, the State Division of Highways considered several freeway corridors through Santa Cruz. Routes 1 and 2 were outlined in the Santa Cruz General Plan of 1964. Route 1 would cut through the Westside north of Mission Street, while Route 2 was south of Mission Street. Route 4, proposed in 1967, would have passed through the Pogonip open space, the southern edge of UCSC, and the Westlake District. A fourth corridor would have constructed an expressway from Highway 17 to the beach area. There was widespread opposition from neighborhood activists; in August 1968, 1000 people came to the Santa Cruz Civic Auditorium for a public hearing. A majority favored Route 4, which was adopted in 1970 by the State Highway Commission—but the plan was scrapped by the state in 1975 due to cutbacks in highway funds. See Frank Perry, "An Alternative History of Santa Cruz County," in Elizabeth Schilling, ed. *LandScapes: Activism that Shaped Santa Cruz County, 1955-2005* (Santa Cruz Museum of Art and History, *Santa Cruz County History Journal* Number 9, 2018), 157-158.

11. On April 9, 1970, Pacific Gas & Electric Company announced that they planned to buy the Coast Dairies property just north of Davenport and build a large nuclear power plant there. On June 23, 1970, a public forum was held in the Santa Cruz Civic Auditorium on the pros and cons of nuclear power and this proposal. 1300 people attended the forum, most of them opposed to the plant. In April of 1973, UCSC earth sciences graduate student Jerry Weber released data mapping the San Gregorio Fault Zone. He had discovered that an active earthquake fault lay within 2000 feet of the proposed plant site. It is unclear whether Weber's research constituted the killing blow for the project, but on April 8, 1985, PG&E dropped its option to buy the Coast Dairies property. For more see Celia and Peter Scott, "Grassroots Activism: A Crucial Factor in the Preservation of the North Coast," in Elizabeth Schilling, ed. *LandScapes: Activism that Shaped Santa Cruz County, 1955-2005* (Santa Cruz Museum of Art and History, *Santa Cruz County History Journal* Number 9, 2018), 49.

12. For more on the environmental battle over Lighthouse Field, a turning point in Santa Cruz politics, see Gary A. Patton, "Saving Lighthouse Field," in Elizabeth Schilling, ed. *LandScapes: Activism that Shaped Santa Cruz County, 1955-2005* (Santa Cruz Museum of Art and History, *Santa Cruz*

County History Journal Number 9, 2018), 8-17.

13. Laird is referring to Measure J, a growth management initiative that voters in Santa Cruz County passed in 1978. The measure set out six policies, including an annual growth rate and the delineation of boundaries for urban services such as sewer, water, and fire services. The measure also required that 15 percent of all newly developed housing be affordable by people of average and below-average income, and preserved certain areas such as the Pogonip as greenbelt land. See Nick Ibarra, "Q and A on Growth Management: An Interview with Andy Schiffrin," in Elizabeth Schilling, ed. *LandScapes: Activism that Shaped Santa Cruz County, 1955-2005* (Santa Cruz Museum of Art and History, *Santa Cruz County History Journal* Number 9, 2018).

14. See the UCSC Library digital exhibit on Shakespeare Santa Cruz at http://exhibits.library.ucsc.edu/exhibits/show/ssc/ssc-home and UCSC's Shakespeare Santa Cruz records (UA 41): https://oac.cdlib.org/findaid/ark:/13030/kt938nd6h4/?query=shakespeare+santa+cruz.

15. Jack O'Neill was a pioneer in surfing and innovator of the wetsuit. He became a supporter of marine conservation through his nonprofit O'Neill Sea Odyssey program, which takes schoolchildren on marine education trips on the Monterey Bay. He died in 2017. For an oral history of Jack O. Neill see *Ocean Odysseys: Jack O'Neill, Dan Haifley, and the Monterey Bay National Marine Sanctuary* (Regional History Project, UCSC Library, 2012).

16. Cesar L. "Joe" Barber was a renowned Shakespeare scholar who taught literature at UCSC and also served as the vice chancellor for the humanities division in the early 1970s. He was a fellow of College Five. He died in 1980.

17. For recordings from the Cabrillo Music Festival see the Other Minds Archive (MS 414) at: https://oac.cdlib.org/findaid/ark:/13030/c8wq0984/admin/.

18. Sandy Lydon is known in Santa Cruz as "the History Dude." He taught Asian history and Santa Cruz history for several decades at Cabrillo College, until his retirement in 2000. Since then he has continued leading history tours both locally and internationally, writing, and hosting television shows. See: http://www.sandylydon.com/. He is the author of *Chinese Gold: the Chinese in the Monterey Bay Region* (Capitola, CA: Capitola Book Co., 1985) and *The Japanese in the Monterey Bay Region: a Brief History* (Capitola, CA: Capitola Book Co., 1997).

19. *Watsonville: I Would Have Told It, if I Had a Chance: A Collection of Oral Histories of Ethnic Peoples* (Watsonville, CA, 1978) and *The Other Side of Main Street: A Collection of Oral Histories of Ethnic Peoples,* (Watsonville, California, 1979).

20. Carl Tjerandsen was hired to establish Extension Services at UCSC in 1965, where he served as dean until his retirement in 1977. Dr. Tjerandsen also worked as executive secretary of the philanthropic Emil Schwarzhaupt Foundation from 1953 until 1980. Among the Foundation's many initiatives, it supported Saul Alinsky's community organizing and the Highlander School in Tennessee which played a vital role in the civil rights movement.

21. Community organizer, labor activist, and writer Saul David Alinsky is generally considered to be the founder of modern community organizing.

22. Myles Horton was an educator, socialist and cofounder of the Highlander Folk School, famous for its role in the Civil Rights Movement, where activists like Martin Luther King, Jr., John Lewis, and Rosa Parks were trained in nonviolent civil disobedience.

23. Esau Jenkins was an African American human rights leader, businessman, and community organizer born on Johns Island in South Carolina. In 1948, through the aid of Citizenship Schools, to which he was introduced at Highlander Folk Center in Tennessee, Jenkins founded the Progressive Club, which encouraged local African Americans to register to vote.

24. Bernice Robinson was a civil rights movement activist who helped establish adult citizenship schools in South Carolina and became field supervisor for the Southern Christian Leadership Conference, teaching adult literacy and political education workshops all over the south.

25. For more on Professor Blake's work bringing UCSC students to Daufuskie Island see: Herman Blake and Ervin R. Simmons, "A Daufuskie Island Lad in an Academic Community: An Extraordinary Journey of Personal Transformation," *Journal of College and Character*, 10:1, 2008. Also see Herman Blake's oral history.

26. Blumenthal is referring to the third and final boxing match between Frazier and Ali, on October 1st, 1975.

27. Tabby is a construction material made from a mixture of ground oyster shells, sand, and water. This material was used to build the huts in which slaves were kept on Daufuskie Island.

Illustrations

Figure 1. An Ideal Becoming Real Estate." Flyer protesting proposed Research and Development Park at UCSC. 1980s. Courtesy Special Collections, University Library, University of California, Santa Cruz. UA 70: UCSC Ephemera Collection: ua070-0040.

Figure 2. Shakespeare Santa Cruz program. 1983 festival season. Courtesy Special Collections, University Library, University of California, Santa Cruz. UA41: Shakespeare Santa Cruz records: Production files: ua_0041_gra_0003.

Figure 3. Herman Blake, professor of sociology, founding provost of Oakes College. 1976. Courtesy Special Collections, University Library, University of California, Santa Cruz. UA50: UCSC Photography Services: ua0050_neg_sc6410a_15.tif.

Figure 4. Cover of brochure for Extramural Education Community Programs. Daufuskie Island Youth. Courtesy Special Collections, University Library, University of California Santa Cruz. UA 70: UCSC Ephemera Collection: ua070-0057.

Figure 5. Student climbing over fence between UCSC and Pogonip, 1966. Photo by Eric Thiermann. Courtesy Special Collections, University Library, University of California Santa Cruz. MS290: Eric Thiermann photographs of the University of California, Santa Cruz: ms0290_neg_0139_25.

Figure 6. Black Commencement Program, 1975. Courtesy Special Collections, University Library, University of California Santa Cruz. UA 70: UCSC Ephemera Collection: ua070-0115.

Figure 7. Chicano Commencement Program, 1984. Courtesy Special Collections, University Library, University of California, Santa Cruz. UA 70: UCSC Ephemera Collection: ua070-0112.

Figure 5

Student climbing fence between UCSC
and Pogonip, 1966

Photo by Eric Thiermann

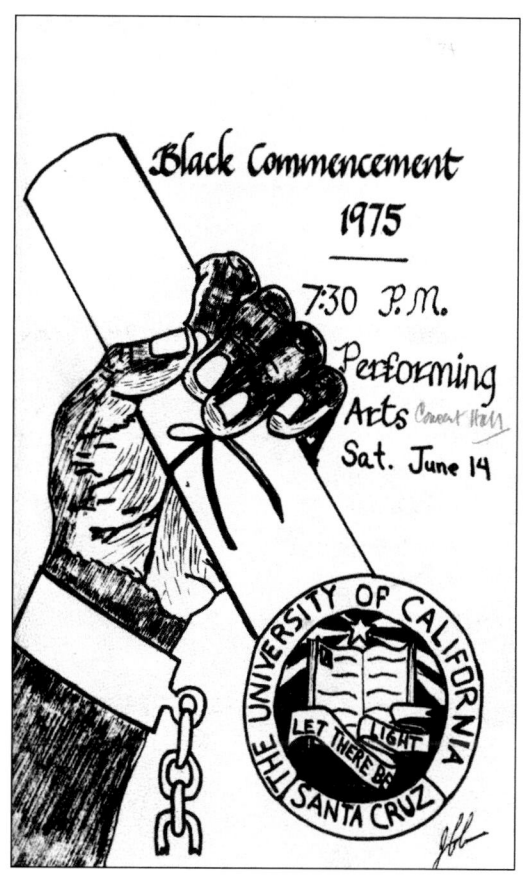

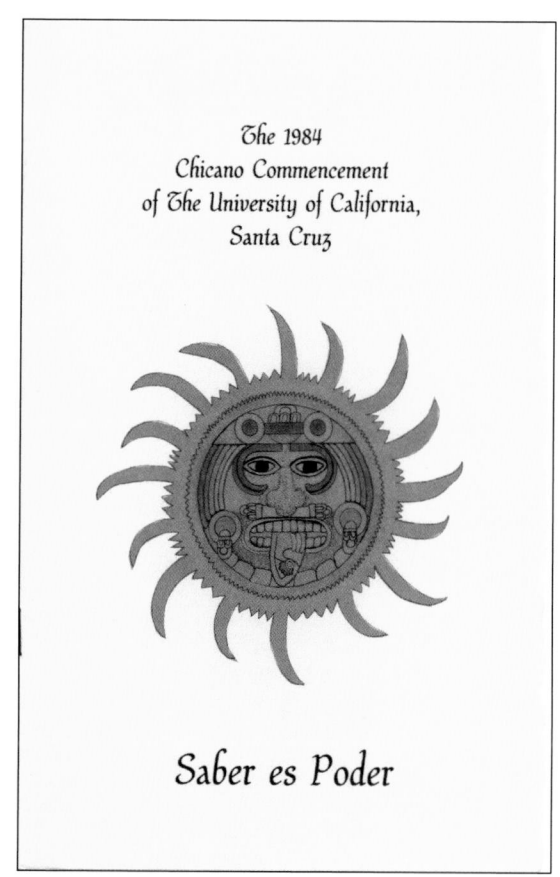

Figures 6 and 7

Left: Black Commencement Program, 1975

Right: Chicano Commencement Program, 1984

Chapter 21

"Open the Door"

Finding a Place on a "Very White Campus"

We were doing subversive work. [The administration] probably just thought, oh, yeah, they're teaching their language courses for Spanish speakers over here. They did not know we were arming students with knowledge, self-knowledge, which is to me the most valuable of all.

—Elba Sánchez

"We're Wondering about the Conscience of the Campus"

Don Rothman, Lecturer: Oakes faculty have plunged ahead, perhaps recklessly, making a commitment to working with students, and discovered that many of the institutional rewards that they thought existed, in fact don't. The rewards are mostly what you see happening to your students, but not in terms of your own career. They've felt betrayed; they've gotten fired, and they've lost their jobs. I think they felt, in some ways, that the other faculty on campus who played it safe may be laughing at our naiveté and saying, "Well, of course we didn't do this. We knew damn well that publishing was going to count."

Roberto Crespi, Professor: The faculty at Oakes is demoralized and tired. Oakes made a very crucial error in thinking that this administration was going to let us do what we had originally set out to do. For the first five years, it was easy. We were all junior faculty. There were no negative tenure decisions. We weren't coming up for tenure for five or six years. We were building this college. No one had slapped us in the face yet. No one had fired us. We didn't even think the threat existed, because we thought the administration was supportive of what we were doing.

But as soon as we had the realization that Oakes College was being attacked, and people started being bumped off one by one, the demoralization happened very quickly.

Don Rothman: But we're also wondering about the conscience of the campus. I am. In talking about Oakes and the role we've played on campus, I confront the issue of the conscience of the campus. Can the campus look at what's happened to Oakes faculty—people who are not getting tenure, who aren't getting merit increases, whose promotions are being delayed indefinitely, it appears—can the rest

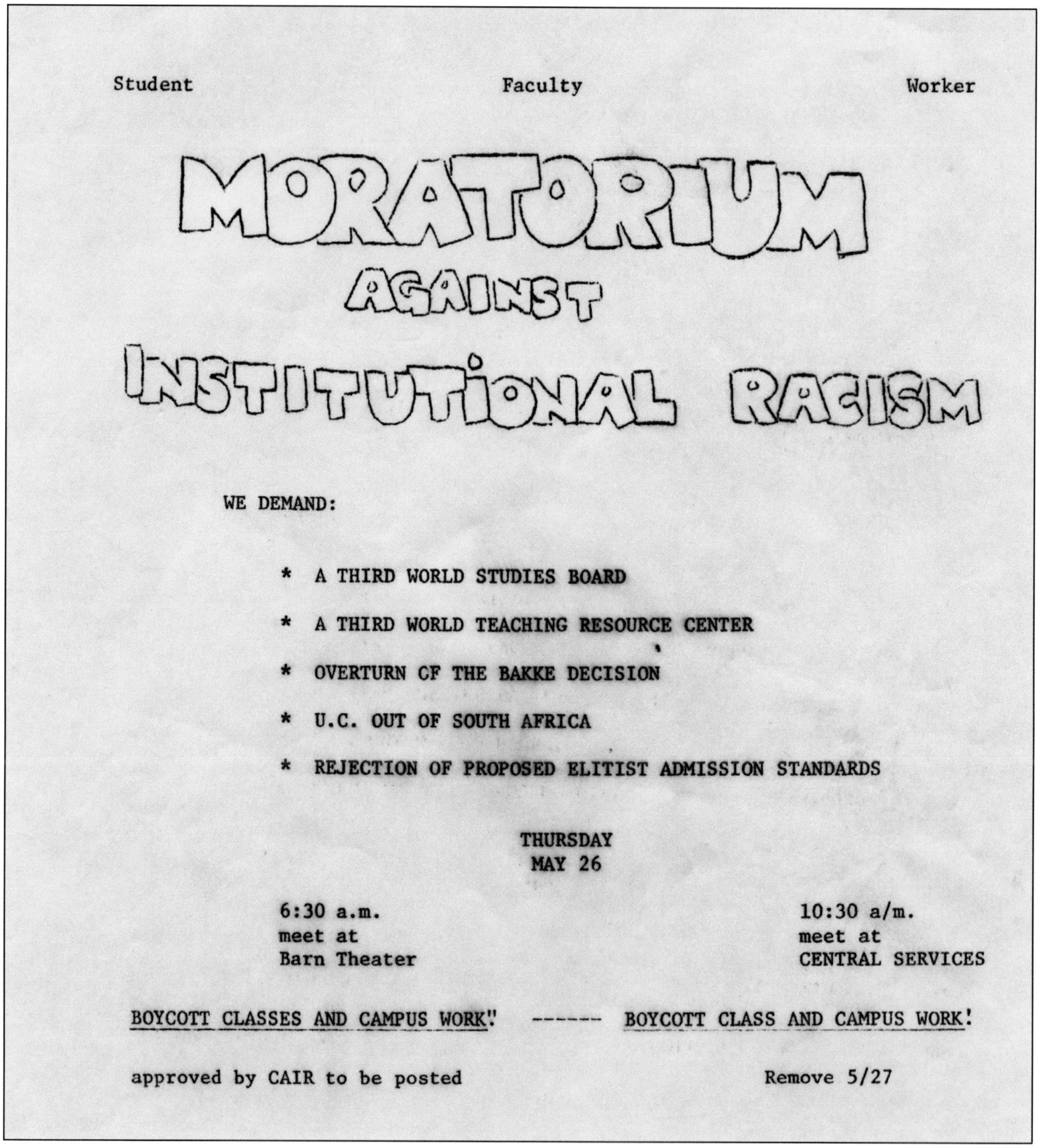

Student Faculty Worker

MORATORIUM AGAINST INSTITUTIONAL RACISM

WE DEMAND:

* A THIRD WORLD STUDIES BOARD
* A THIRD WORLD TEACHING RESOURCE CENTER
* OVERTURN CF THE BAKKE DECISION
* U.C. OUT OF SOUTH AFRICA
* REJECTION OF PROPOSED ELITIST ADMISSION STANDARDS

THURSDAY
MAY 26

6:30 a.m.
meet at
Barn Theater

10:30 a/m.
meet at
CENTRAL SERVICES

BOYCOTT CLASSES AND CAMPUS WORK! ------ BOYCOTT CLASS AND CAMPUS WORK!

approved by CAIR to be posted Remove 5/27

Figure 1

Moratorium Against Institutional Racism poster

Late 1970s

of the campus look upon all of this without taking some of the responsibility?

Michael Cowan: Santa Cruz was still a very white campus, especially compared to other UC campuses. Students and faculty shared that awareness; certainly my colleagues in Merrill did. It was also the case that there were a growing number of high school students of color in the California system at that time, especially Chicano and Asian-American students. Our campus was not attracting what was thought to be its appropriate share of such students.

Robert Sinsheimer: Putting out statements saying affirmative action is important, putting out statements saying the campus has got to employ affirmative action in its appointments, even verbally going around and making this kind of statement had limited effect. Therefore, in order to improve the situation, we had to develop—install—what you might crudely call the carrot and the stick, both. The carrot that the faculty would have is the Target of Opportunity program, whereby we specifically would make a certain number of faculty positions available, undesignated as to field, to departments, boards, or whatever, that would come up with able minority candidates.

So we had to set up procedures where they had to advertise; we developed lists of other institutions that were more likely to produce minority applicants that had to be solicited. We had to have checklists to make sure they had done this. Then when they got down to their short lists, these had to be surveyed, and if there were no women or minorities on them, why not? In the final selection if there was not a woman or a minority, and there didn't have to be, then they had to provide a written justification. You had to monitor what they did. We had to have somebody in charge of all that. Julia Armstrong [Zwart] was brought in

to do that. She was a great find because she did an excellent job.

Julia Armstrong-Zwart: When I came to campus, in 1981, I went around to meet all of the provosts, the deans, the department chairs, in my role as ombudsman. I thought that was a really good way of introducing myself in a positive way rather than coming in as—"I'm Ms. Affirmative Action and I'm here to knock you upside the head to make you do right."

When I came, there was money for affirmative action. We had funding for postdoc fellowships for recent PhDs who were women or minorities. There was money for doing junior-faculty development. There was an assistant vice president of affirmative action in the Office of the President, and there was a whole affirmative action apparatus at the Office of the President as well. After talking to the chancellor, the decision was made to focus on faculty affirmative action first, feeling that if faculty attitudes can be changed, the institution will change. The capacity for change in the institution is much greater if you have the faculty behind it.

Don Rothman: We have at Oakes College, in many ways, served the campus by putting ourselves in an area that very few people know anything about.[1] We've taken the risks; we've put the time in to work with nontraditional students; and we're getting picked off one by one for it. We're living at a time, it appears, when to even talk about the conscience of the campus seems almost anachronistic. What will this campus do with its responsibility for working with nontraditional students?

Rosa M. Plaza, Student: I was born in Mexico and I was brought to the US when I was eight years old. I grew up near Fresno. My friend and I came to visit UC Santa Cruz. I fell in love with the environment: the fact that you can see the ocean, the

Figure 2

Julia Armstrong-Zwart, 1981

Photo by UCSC Photography Services

fact that it was on a hill, and the trees. And then we went to Oakes. We're walking through the dorms and we're hearing rap music coming out of Casa Huerta.[2] We said to each other, "We're going to live there." That's how we decided to come here. We came here together. I felt at home at Oakes the minute I stepped onto campus. It wasn't just the excitement. It was knowing that I was accomplishing something that not anybody got to do, at least in my family.

But I had absolutely no clue what college was. I didn't know what a syllabus was. I didn't know that you didn't go to classes, like you did in high school, that you had a schedule for a couple of hours and the rest of the time you had to study. I didn't know that! I learned it the hard way, but I learned it.

The college system makes for very intimate experience, even in a large campus. I think that is what I most appreciated about this system, the fact that I felt safe in a large university and that I felt like I belonged. Being at Oakes, I was with a bunch of people who understood me. I had found a family. I could be myself. The idea of Oakes is very revolutionary. It gave us a home. By "us" I mean the students that otherwise wouldn't have a place at a university campus.

Ekua Omosupe, Student: I was born in 1951 on a plantation in Yazoo County, Mississippi. So it was a very long journey from sharecropping and poverty to a PhD from the University of California, Santa Cruz. I came from a family that valued education; however, it did not have a lot of access. Since I'm African American, we can figure out numerous reasons as to why there was no access.

My mother always impressed upon us the importance of education. She said if you have an education, it is something that *they*—meaning the white power structure, the white people—would not be able to take away from you, and it would definitely improve your chances. At least, that

certainly is what we all believe. Here in the United States, we are sold that dream: get an education and work hard and you can be anyone you want to be. You don't have to spend your life impoverished. Of course, we find that that's not wholly true.

Antoinette Gonzalez, Student: I grew up in a single-parent, working-class family. We moved a lot. We didn't follow the crops; we weren't migrant workers. We followed the rent, whatever the lowest rent was.

Ekua Omosupe: UCSC was my first choice of three colleges that I applied to for graduate work. I was looking for a college that had a strong reputation for American literature and freedom in study. I was also looking to study with teachers who were of African-American descent, in this kind of a setting.

I saw a brochure that they sent to me. It had Nate Mackey [faculty in literature] on it. I thought, this is great. I assumed that if there was one black person, there were others. But I made a wrong assumption, which is something my mother would always warn me about when I was growing up. Don't assume. There wasn't a whole bunch. There was just Nate Mackey. And the brochure made promises about the beauty of the town. You got the impression that the beauty was not only in the landscape but possibly in the people who lived here. So it was a combination of naiveté, idealism, and really believing what I saw on the brochure.

Antoinette Gonzalez: It was hard being in Santa Cruz, coming from Fresno. Crown was the whitest college at the time. It's all relative, because Santa Cruz is pretty white—but it was the whitest, and I felt really alienated. I had another roommate who was Chicana, and we were all going through hard times the first year.

Figure 3

Cover of *Revista Mujeres*

Elba Sánchez, Director, Spanish for Spanish Speakers: The experience up at UCSC is so foreign. Most of my students in Spanish for Spanish Speakers were from Los Angeles, urban kids, kids from *barrios* where they had helicopters flying overhead at all kinds of hours of the day and night. They would tell me, "I can't sleep at night. It's too quiet. I need to hear the traffic. I need to hear the helicopters. I need to hear the sirens." This is what they grew up in. Most of the population that they were recruiting from was from the LA area, Southern California. This campus was such a foreign place to them. It was like a country club.

Hayden White, Professor: I remember talking to the president of the university one year. He said, "Our aim is to mainstream all of these people." I said, "Why don't you provide enough money to allow the entire faculty of the University of California to take a year off and study Spanish, so the whole faculty would be able to speak Spanish, you know, at a minimal level at least. We've got this huge population of Spanish-speaking people." He said, "No. Our aim is to mainstream." Turn them into, you know, straight, white—as the feminist movement said, "I was given an education to turn me into a white, Anglo-Saxon gentleman of the nineteenth century."

Ekua Omosupe: When I got to UCSC, my kids and I were living in our car because I didn't know that the rents were so exorbitant. I didn't know that I needed to apply for Family Student Housing. I thought I could have found a place near the school, and close enough so the children would be able to get back and forth to their elementary school or junior high, and be able to take care of my business. It wasn't like that, though. It was not like that. We ended up living in our car and being harassed by the police because you're not supposed to park. We didn't know that either. They'd knock on the car window: "You can't park here. You have to get up. You have to leave." So we'd just drive around. At first, I was able to amuse the children by saying we were on a long camping trip. But pretty soon they got tired: "I want to go home. Where is home? I'm tired of barbecuing dinner every day."

Elba Sánchez: In the late 1970s and early 1980s in Santa Cruz, there still were not a lot of Chicano/Latino students. [The organization] Las Mujeres was a way for us to connect, no matter who we were on campus, to be witnesses to our community. Las Mujeres always had a welcome reception at the beginning of the year. It was a way to break down some of the walls and give us an opportunity to know each other and extend our hands to each other, to create community. Las Mujeres was crucial, a life-saver.[3]

As mujeres, we had major issues. A lot of us had to really struggle to get to UCSC. The natural leaders within Las Mujeres organization started working to try and get the creative writing journal *Revista Mujeres* going. We saw *Revista* as an extension, in terms of the communication and creating community.

The first couple of issues of *Revista Mujeres*, and really pretty much all of them, were a struggle. We had to go around to different colleges to ask for money. At that time, the provosts had discretionary funds. Since our students came from all over the campus, we tried to hit each provost. We told them, "We want to do an issue. We will distribute it free to all of the Chicano/Latino students, faculty, and staff on campus. It's for building community. It's for bringing up issues that are important to us. It's for giving graduate students an opportunity to publish. We need it! We need it."

Olga Nájera-Ramírez, Student: I came here as a Merrill student. I had a very good friend who was a Merrill student, Anglo, and he invited me to go see him dance in Los Mejicas. It was a Merrill College Night in the spring. I remember the group coming out and I thought oh, my God, they're all Mexicanos, practically. They were so full of energy. It was contagious. And at the end of the show they said that it was open, that you didn't have to have any experience to join, and please come back in the fall. I thought, I'm there.

So my second year I started working with Los Mejicas. It made a big impact. We performed. We would go back to people's home communities, like Visalia, and wherever the kids went to school. They'd go to their former high school and we'd do a noontime assembly. Then we would use that opportunity to encourage kids to go to school. So we were doing outreach: "You should think about going to college." We would do a lot of recruitment. And then internally, it was a retention thing, because we were bonding with each other and surviving through our different majors.

It was a uniting experience—working collectively, with meager resources, but a lot of enthusiasm, a lot of passion. And we were able to be very politically active. We would go to all of the rallies, the farmworker rallies. Of course, you have to have your dance group and mariachi, mural painting and stuff like that. There was a lot of collaboration with other artists. It was a lot of fun.

Elba Sánchez: We wanted students to feel pride in their work. When you're a writer, when you're a poet, when you're an academic, the most important thing is to get your work out. But nobody in administration really saw the importance of *Revista Mujeres*. They never *once* saw the value of what we were doing or acknowledged it. It was individual provosts or deans that were giving us $500 or whatever. But all the work was volunteer.

There was nothing in the whole state that was like this—produced by a collective of women, not just staff or faculty. We had undergraduates, graduates, a wonderful, organic mix of women.

Revista Mujeres was one of various journals seeking work by Chicana/Latina writers and artists. There was this effervescence of culture and cultural events, all kinds of things popping. It was a beautiful time. There was so much happening, so much cultural flowering. We were making the space, creating the space. It makes a difference for a young poet to see their stuff published. It makes a difference for a young artist to see their work on the cover of a journal. We wanted to encourage people to do more writing, to do more artistic, visual stuff, to take us—in our minds, in our imagination—someplace else. To write poetry. To sing, dance, whatever your passion. There was this cultural flowering, this constant effervescence of activity that was reaffirming and encouraging at the same time. You could feel it simmer.

Alison Kim, Student: I was born in 1955 in Honolulu. My mom is Chinese and my dad is Korean. California is my home. I grew up in the Monterey Bay area, outside and on the ex-military base, Fort Ord. Moving from Marina to go to Santa Cruz was, for me, moving to the big city.

I did the double major of art and women's studies. Santa Cruz has such a strong focus on writing. It didn't matter if you took the astronomy class, which I did as one of my core classes; you still have to write a paper. Or statistics, women's studies, anthropology. I got to really learn a lot.

In the house where I lived, there were no other Asian lesbians. I put an ad in *Matrix Women's Newsmagazine,* and a notice up in Bookshop Santa Cruz, at Café Pergolesi, and up on campus, saying that I was forming an Asian lesbian group, so anyone please contact me. The first person who contacted me was Kaweah Lemeshewsky. Kaweah is Japanese and Native American, so she was involved in a lot of Native American things,

BETWEEN THE LINES

**An Anthology by Pacific/Asian Lesbians
of Santa Cruz, California**

editors
C. Chung, A. Kim, A.K. Lemeshewsky

Figure 4

Cover of *Between the Lines*, published in 1987

but she also wanted to connect with Asian lesbians. I met Cristy Chung at Bookshop Santa Cruz. So my second year at UC we said, "Well, let's form a writing group, so we can start getting together." So we started putting up flyers, and did a benefit saying we wanted money because we want to put an Asian lesbian book together.

It was not until 1987 that we got the grants from the university to write the book *Between the Lines*.[4] I also got the President's Undergraduate Fellowship to do the research. The research money was for me to go to different archives and then to go cross-country and interview people. That year, with the fellowship, Cristy and I went cross-country. We went to Los Angeles, to one of the archives. We met women along the way. All along the way, we had our book. People ate it up with eagerness. I never really understood how isolated so many of us did feel, or how much there was lacking in print and a sense of community. So by the time we got to Washington, D.C., we were walking across this huge field and this woman went up to Cristy and said, "You're in that book, aren't you!" We were like, "How could this be?"

We got a lot of support from everybody—from teachers, from staff, from the library, our friends. Of course, the bookstores in Santa Cruz carried them. But even small bookstores where we had no clue what the Asian population was, they would say, "This is great." It started in Santa Cruz, and it carried us the whole way coming back. The support was there. We never could have done the book without the financial, academic, and emotional support. That was the thing about UCSC. That's why I always recommend Santa Cruz to everybody.

Ekua Omosupe: In my second year, suddenly there wasn't enough financial aid for me. I have three kids and I live in Family Student Housing. I am a poor woman. I went to Marta Morello-Frosch.[5] She was there for me. I went to Marta and I told

her that I did not have enough money. I also told Literature Board Advisor Claire Braz-Valentine.[6] I said, "They told me at Financial Aid to get a job at McDonald's to help support my family, because they did not have enough financial aid for me. Not only did that hurt me, it completely insulted me! I don't have time to work at McDonald's. I am a graduate student." I also thought that it was very racist for whoever it was to say that to me. I told Martha and I told Claire, "I feel as if they are trying to drive me out and drive me away. I don't want that to happen. Surely there is money. Nobody told me when I came here that financial aid was going to be an issue. Everybody knew that I have three children and I'm supporting them on my own."

I don't know what Marta and Claire did, but I know they acted in good faith on my behalf and got money for me. After that, I never had another problem with my financial aid.

Antoinette Gonzalez: It was in MEChA that I developed my community, and grew up here in Santa Cruz, and became comfortable with who I am, and explored who I am, as a woman of color, as a Chicana. I learned a lot of history, just learned so much, looking at my experiences, my family's experiences, and putting them in perspective, seeing the connection of the history of oppression, and feeling really empowered, as we were doing different campaigns on campus with other ethnic groups, and being part of a statewide group.

In a year or so, I was part of the leadership. It was mostly women. And we were freaks. We did so much. We were going through our hardships being in Santa Cruz, going through our own personal hardships. Some of us were dealing with abusive relationships; some of us were dealing with abortion. You know, just coming to our own sexualities, in different ways. I had an attraction with another Mechista. That's how we came out. At the time, in MEChA, being gay, lesbian, bisexuality, wasn't heard of. The language of bisexuality wasn't a common thing, much less transgendered or inter-sexed. So we were rocking the boat not only for MeCHA, but for ourselves.

Ekua Omosupe: I had met an African-American woman in Nate Mackey's[7] *Harlem Renaissance Literature* class, a beautiful black woman. Since she was a lesbian, she already had connections with the lesbian communities. So she would introduce me to people, or I'd meet somebody at a party. Then I'd end up meeting people who lived in Oakland, or in San Francisco. But I didn't meet many African-American lesbians over here in Santa Cruz. For a long time, aside from her, I wasn't sure if there was another African-American lesbian around.

Robert Sinsheimer: There is no black community in Santa Cruz. There's nobody to relate to. At least there are Hispanics here, but no black commu-nity. It's very isolating. We think the redwoods are great, but if you've been raised in an urban ghetto, they're kind of forbidding probably, quite alien. Maybe not at all comforting. In a sense, it's a crit-ical mass problem; if you've got enough minorities on campus they can form their own communities.

Elaine Kihara, Staff, Oakes College: I am Japanese American, third generation. Most of my father's family was interned during World War II and most of my mother's side too. I have a BS from UC Davis in international agricultural development, with an emphasis in community development. I came to UCSC to work as a provost's assistant to Provost Victor Rocha at Oakes College.

I think some students at UCSC had the feeling that they were bailing out. They were leaving a dif-ficult situation behind and coming to this beautiful place in the woods. They felt like they did not so much belong here. But as they stayed here longer, they didn't so much fit in at home the way they

used to either. Their world view changed. They were living a whole different experience. That was something that was on a lot of people's minds at that time—how to create support for students to be here and be able to stay connected to home, but also have community here.

Rosie Cabrera, EOP Counselor: I think EOP [Educational Opportunity Program] was the one place on campus that race, class, gender, sexuality mattered, and the one place that there was excite-ment about collegially working with each other to figure out how do we best serve these students? Class background was diverse. We would have students that were middle class; we would have students that were super-low income. Engagement and tension sometimes would arise as a result of that class dif-ference. How do you create common ground, so that those markers were not part of something that differentiated you, but could be utilized to bring the community together?

Richard Vasquez, EOP Counselor: In November of 1978, I started my tenure as a counselor with EOP. EOP was housed at Merrill College A-Dorm. Staff and faculty could live at the university with students. They were called residential preceptors. I became the first person of color, the first EOP counselor to live in Merrill, at 4th floor B-Dorm. And my office was in the 4th floor, A Dorm.

Rosie Cabrera: When I worked for the Educational Opportunity Program, I coordinated the Summer BRIDGE Program.[8] My introduction to SAA/EOP [Student Affirmative Action/Educational Opportunity Program] programming was with a cohort of about forty-two students and teaching staff. I lived in the dorms with students. I hadn't had that level of intimacy with the students, and it was really exciting. SAA/EOP used to have an orienta-tion program that was a week long. So there were

Figure 5

Rosie Cabrera, Circa 2000s

Photo by Jim MacKenzie

structures that tried to help students understand, not only the transition of coming to a UC system, but the whys. There was a level of consciousness around trying to ensure that students understood they were walking into a campus that, for all practical purposes, was a predominantly white campus. EOP was responsible for not only BRIDGE, but the Orientation Program, and then, a few years later, starting the Faculty Mentor Program. So there was this focus on trying to develop curriculum that would be responsive to students of color, with this acknowledgement that the exposure to the material may not have been there.

Julia Armstrong-Zwart: In 1981, there were twenty-three women on the tenure track and twenty-three faculty of color.[9] That includes women of color and foreign faculty, any non-white faculty member. And women of color, of course, were double counted, so there weren't even as many as that. There were probably around thirty-five, all told. It was fortunate that at that time Dick Wasserstrom chaired the Academic Senate Affirmative Action Committee. He was, has been, is still, such a staunch supporter of affirmative action and equal employment opportunity, and he was a well-respected senior faculty member. It couldn't have been a better circumstance for trying to do something in the area of faculty affirmative action.

And you also had the fact that the campus was young. The faculty were in two groups when they were first hired. The campus hired the senior eminences in their fields, who were attracted to the idea of this new institution, and if they weren't attracted to the reality of the campus, they left. And then you had a big gulf and all of these newly minted PhDs who had come up through the time of the troubles, the sixties, so they had a mindset which was less traditional. What you didn't have was that middle stratum of associate and full professors, who usually are the ones who maintain

traditional values and structures of the institution. Also, although the college reorganization had taken place, the departmental structure was very weak; there were still the boards of studies. In my experience, the academic department is the basic, fundamental building block of a traditional university, the political building block, and because there was a weak board structure, you didn't have the entrenched political bulwark of traditional academic departments. That also helped.

Things were more fluid here, politically. There weren't as many windmills to tilt against. It felt more fluid and flexible. There was also an egalitarianism on this campus. The role of staff was valued. More faculty seemed to be involved in committee structures and devoted to the maintenance and development of the institution. There was a different feel to UCSC. I have to say, I fell in love with UCSC. There was something about the idealism, the egalitarianism. It felt that things were possible here.

Arlyn Osborne: Other than Beatriz Lopez-Flores, there was no other director for years among the UC women's centers, or among many national women's centers, who was a woman of color. If we hadn't had Beatriz as a director, there're a lot of alliances we never could have made.[10] That was one of the things we discussed at the meeting of all UC Women's Centers. Having a woman of color as a director in the position of power and then the white women as the support staff, is something you might want to look at, even as a statement. And so, when you're doing a director search and looking for candidates, definitely don't get token candidates. Get somebody who knows what they're doing.

Lan Dyson, University Librarian: The library had probably the best-intentioned white people of any library anywhere. And we did all the right things in terms of what we thought were the right things, in terms of recruitment. But I noticed that the only minority librarian who was here when I got here was retiring. And you have a sense as to who [students of color] is not using the library. Even if you're not walking down the McHenry Library spiral staircase noticing it, you get this kind of subconscious impression.

Donald Clark: As a child, my whole upbringing was that one should not be prejudiced. I must say in my family life, when I was growing up, I certainly was not aware of prejudices against race, religion, color, or anything else. To be absolutely told that I had to make a body count of minorities and make a statistical count of how many blacks, etc. we had in the library was distasteful. It went against my whole upbringing.

Arlyn Osborne: Affirmative action has a long history and was done very poorly in many areas, but it was discussed at the Women's Center, because we saw women hired on campus, again and again, who were token hirings, giving a nod to affirmative action, and then were never given the support they needed as an employee to do the position they were chosen to do. Then they were expected to represent all women of color, all women of their ethnicity. It happened with faculty. It happened with staff. It happened with students, over and over and over again. The tokenizing of people.

Sig Puknat, Professor: I do not believe in discrimination on the basis of the unusual. Therefore I am not in sympathy with the apparent situation at present, where a white, Anglo-Saxon male has difficulty getting into certain institutions. I do not believe in the quota system. In fact, if we use the quota system, what would happen if we identified Jews as an ethnic group? If we did, then we would have to cut down the number of Jews. I think it's a

dreadful thing. America has discriminated against minorities; we have discriminated against women. But now, in order to make up for the crimes of the past, are we going to commit a different kind of injustice? I read in *Newsweek* or *Time* that about a third of Harvard is Jewish. I bring this up because I am a teacher of German literature and I'm very much interested in German culture and my background is German. Of course, I'm very sensitive to that great tragedy of the 20th century, the period from especially 1933 to 1945. I'm against quotas.

If you're going to increase the number of minority students and you have a fixed target figure, that means you disqualify certain others. I think a person should be admitted on the basis of criteria that are set up. Now it can be argued, as many people who were very strong in affirmative action do argue, that lots of people have been disadvantaged at early years. Well, of course we've got the junior colleges, as I've said. And if they're disadvantaged financially, I'm very much in favor of financial support for a student who is admissible.

But I can't quite see the justification for the admission of students who are going to find the competition a great struggle if they do not qualify academically. After all, we do have the state college system, and the junior colleges they can attend and adjust to, and then transfer into the University of California. I don't really know whether it's doing them a favor, and I'm sure it's not doing the faculty or the other students of the university a favor. I mean, if they're able to do it, fine.

Donald Clark: There were some things that made it easier for me to retire early. The thing that got to me was the change in personnel policies that was foisted upon the university by the Department of Health, Education and Welfare, for example, new changes that were created by the social, economic changes going on in America. I'm talking about affirmative action.

Ideologically, I can understand the history of affirmative action, the fact that the minorities had been deprived of opportunities. They certainly may well have been under my administration, but I was not cognizant of being party to restrictions.

Robert Sinsheimer: Caltech is an ultra-elitist institution. Caltech chooses its students on the basis of merit and merit alone. UC does not, and cannot. As a public institution, UC has to represent the populace of the state. If it doesn't, it's going to lose its political support; it's going to lose its funding; it's going to lose the whole ball of wax.

I perfectly well understand that minority students want to have some minority role models on the faculty. How are you going to get them? It's a difficult problem. You know, you can question the whole philosophy of affirmative action. Why do we have affirmative action? Affirmative action is discrimination. As far as I'm concerned it is. It gets you into some really complicated contradictions. You can justify it, certainly for blacks, on the basis that you are trying to remedy what were the early centuries of discrimination against blacks. We did discriminate. There's no question about it. We were enslaving people, for God's sake. Even if they weren't enslaved, they were discriminated against, and still are in many sectors. So you can justify affirmative action as a compensation. But then you get into inevitable snarls, because, okay you are going to favor the blacks, and maybe the Chicanos and then the Asians say, "Well you are discriminating against us, and we didn't discriminate against the blacks, so why are we being penalized?" So you kind of have to say, well, what's the lesser evil?

Rosie Cabrera: People were engaging diversity in weird ways. They were either really against it, or feeling like the students shouldn't be here if they couldn't do the work. Or they were like, "Well, they can't help it," and then inflating their grade. Is

that not an act of racism? Our students are tough. They're resilient. They can handle it. But if you don't believe they can handle it, you don't give the feedback and the critique that's needed.

Sometimes we would find white faculty had inflated a grade because they were scared. I'll never forget this one student that submitted this one paper, and we had to talk with her about it. She had gotten an A in sociology. We read the paper to consider it for publication in the journal *Revista Mujeres* and it was so flawed. Then we were confronted with, we can't publish it the way it is. How do we talk with the student about this and yet not make the student feel less-than? She was furious, furious. It made her question the viability of what she had learned so far. She rewrote the paper. She rewrote it and it was beautiful, but she ended up confronting the faculty member about it.

Herman Blake: I accuse many of the minority and majority people for distorting the concept of affirmative action. By "distort," I mean they kept saying affirmative action was essentially a pattern to make you hire people who might not cut the mustard: people who were minority. So they'd say, "We're going to do an affirmative action hire." "What are you talking about?" "Well, that means we're going to hire a minority." That was not *my* concept of affirmative action. Affirmative action wasn't saying you appointed or admitted. Affirmative action said you open the door so that people might come through. But they had to measure up. The way they talked about it, "Oh, these people who can't make it—so we're going to do affirmative action."

George Blumenthal: One of the things I learned quickly about Herman Blake was that he was no soft touch. Herman had high expectations of students. He was no pushover. If students didn't meet his expectations, he let them know about it. He had no compunctions about that. That actually surprised me, because I just assumed, naively, that someone who was steeped in the social sciences and really wanted to create this new set of opportunities for students would be much more tolerant of failure or bad behavior. Herman wasn't. Herman felt that—and I learned so much from him in this regard—that it's just as fair to have high expectations of students from different backgrounds as it is to have high expectations of students from wealthier, or more white, or more traditional backgrounds. That was part of the life he lived, and who he was. And it was really important for our students.

Lan Dyson: One day, there had been one of the usual outbreaks of concern with regards to minority studies on the campus. There was to be a meeting in Classroom Unit 2 where kids were going to meet with the campus administration and ask questions. It wasn't like riots were being threatened, but loud noises were being made. So I thought, oh, I should go to that.

I walked in the door and I looked around. This classroom, one of the largest lecture halls on campus, was packed, people standing. And it was 98 percent minority kids. Five seconds after I walked in, I got it. The important thing happened in the first five seconds. I said, I've never seen any of these kids in my library. *I've never seen any of them.* If you had asked me, I wouldn't even have believed that there were this many minority kids on this campus. Of course, there are thousands, but I'd never seen any of those kids in the library. And that shook me. This flashbulb went off in my face.

I came back. We were, at that point, in the middle of recruiting for our first librarian that had a business studies background. There was a lot of community interest and there were more and more courses and departments on campus that were edging near applied economics and things like that. The professional staff was saying, "Especially on the weekends, we get all these questions, and we

don't have an expert to refer them to." So I came back, and I said "Unh uh. There's something really wrong here. I mean, it may be nice that we want to hire a business librarian that can help out on the weekends, when we have all these other people from off the campus coming, but we've got this enormous constituency that is *our* constituency, that isn't being served." There were other key people who had had the same reaction, so it wasn't just me trying to convince people about some weird thing that had happened to me.

In a very short period of time, we decided that we had to create an atmosphere in the library that was more welcoming to these folks, that we had to educate ourselves and reach out, and that the best way to do that was to hire somebody that was going to come in and shake us up. So we aborted the recruitment for the business librarian, which was getting close to the final stages. This wasn't something that was in theory. We'd already received the applications. We created the position of Multicultural Outreach Librarian.

Elba Sánchez: Identity, culture, and history were a part of everything that we were teaching in the Spanish for Spanish Speakers Program. Aside from teaching, we *were* instigators, cultural instigators. We were encouraging our students to write poetry, to publish, and read their poetry. We were always having poetry readings, cultural nights. We had a gallery. We had all these visual artists in our classes, so we had a gala night where we did an exhibition of the artist's work. We were promoting and supporting so much creative expression. We were doing subversive work. Our program was a subversive program. The administration probably just thought, oh, yeah, they're teaching their language courses for Spanish speakers over here. They did not know we were arming students with knowledge, self-knowledge, which is to me the most valuable of all.

"Women's Issues Don't Stop Anywhere": The Nancy (Stoller) Shaw Tenure Battle, the Founding of the Women's Center, and the Flowering of Campus Feminism

Nancy Stoller, Professor: My tenure battle was a fight between two forces of that period. On one side were the forces that were opposed to feminism, the real meaning of feminism in research. And they were aligned with those who thought that being a lesbian or a gay man was a personal sexual practice, and that it was perverted or inappropriate to make it public, and therefore the person was inappropriate as a teacher in the university. If that person could somehow keep it a secret, maybe it was okay for them to be there. But better yet, it should be so much of a secret that not even the faculty knew. If you felt you had to talk about it, it was like you were talking about your bathroom habits. You just weren't appropriate.

Robert Sinsheimer: My role in the Nancy Stoller (Shaw) tenure case was simple. It came to me as a tenure case; it came with a divided opinion, both from the board of studies and from the community it represented. I went over it. I read about everything she'd written. I concluded that this was not work of the caliber that merited tenure. I think I remember saying somewhere that I thought any skilled investigative reporter could have done this work. And I still think it's true. I didn't see anything that required much scholarship, that required a PhD, which we ask of all our faculty, that tied in what she found to broader themes in social science. I just felt it wasn't qualified for tenure.

Nancy Stoller: Some of the criticisms that were made of me by the chancellor when he turned me down for tenure were that I was, "more concerned with social amelioration rather than sociological theory." He accused me of being a journalist. So one of the things we did in organizing our defense for court was to get some really well-known journalists

to explain that I was not a journalist. English journalist Jessica Mitford wrote a letter for me saying, "I've read her books and her stuff might be good but it's not journalism. Journalism is this." Lots of academics wrote letters supporting my work as ethnography.

Robert Sinsheimer: She appealed to the Committee on Privilege and Tenure. This was one of the sorrier episodes of my term. I felt the committee acted in a very unprofessional way. They clearly had an ax to grind. They, in effect, claimed that I had acted on political grounds. They raised several issues in their final report which they had never raised during the hearing, and therefore we had never had any opportunity to respond to, which I thought was outrageous. Well, to resolve this I refused to accept their conclusion.

But then she filed suit. That's another whole aspect of affirmative action, the legal aspect, which is outrageous. She claimed that she was being denied tenure on the grounds that she was a woman.

Nancy Stoller: Many academics treated my tenure denial as an attack on feminist research. One aspect of my research was I gave weight to the voices of women in prison. I argued that they knew as much from their own point of view, their situation as prisoners seeking health care, as the doctors and nurses who served them. One of the things that Sinsheimer said was: "She asserts that male patients who go to clinics in prison are given more serious diagnoses and therefore more treatment for the same illnesses that women prisoner patients have." In other words, that they get better treatment. He said, "I'm sure if she did further research she'd come up with a different answer." Now this was not anything that any of the scholars who read my work asserted or anything like that. But he didn't like the results of my research, and he thought my work was an attack on the medical profession, so he just dissed my work, and asserted that that was another reason why I shouldn't become a permanent faculty member. And he said in his letter that I didn't have the proper quality of mind to be a faculty member at the University of California. This is all in the documents.

Robert Sinsheimer: The subject matter was appropriate to her field. No, that wasn't the problem. It was the level of the investigation and the level of inquiry, the level of analysis, the extent to which you would tie in these conclusions to broader issues in sociology, broader theories. There was no theoretical framework. It was like a reporter from the *Santa Cruz Sentinel* who could go out and collect some statistics and that was about it. There was a lot of brouhaha about it because it had to do with women's issues, and lower-class economic issues. I understand that some groups feel that these issues were not being given enough attention by academics, and that therefore this was very meritorious, simply because she looked at them. But we had the right to expect a higher quality of research from somebody we were going to give tenure to.

Nancy Stoller: I think there was a struggle between those people who thought that, and other people who thought there are new ways of doing research; there are new ways of thinking. They were aligned with those who believe that we are a world in which these strict views about sexuality and the right of people to have their personal lives and their affectional lives has changed. This is a different world, and we want it to be a different world, because if we constrain our faculty, we are really denying ourselves and the university the opportunity to have people who are operating at their fullest capacity. If it's the other way, people are not able to think, to

act, to research, to teach, to be honest. If you create an environment where people have to lie about who they are, that's totally contrary to what a university is supposed to be like. As long as the people who we are talking about aren't harming other people, then they should be full participants in the community.

Robert Sinsheimer: I have to tell you, in all honesty, I did not know until long after the decision that Nancy Shaw was lesbian. I didn't know that; there was no reason I should know that.

Nancy Stoller: Beatriz Lopez-Flores, who was an early director of the Women's Center, always maintained that the fact they were able to get the Women's Center was directly related to the tenure fight. That happened a year or two before, during the time when I was not actually on campus [because of the lawsuit Stoller was pursuing against UCSC after her tenure was denied]. But one of the things that women argued then, in support of the Center, was that my tenure case showed the depth of discrimination against women on campus. During the period of my lawsuit, a number of faculty on campus came out, including some untenured faculty who later got tenure: Bettina Aptheker, for example. Prior to my case there had never been anybody who was out as an untenured faculty person, who made it through.

George Blumenthal: Nancy Stoller was denied tenure by Chancellor Sinsheimer after unanimous recommendations from both her department and her dean, as well as from two separate ad hoc committees. And Sinsheimer decided no.

So she filed an appeal with the Committee on Privilege and Tenure of the senate. The Committee on Privilege and Tenure found in her favor. Privilege and Tenure cannot look at substantive issues, like should she have gotten tenure. What they can look at whether or not there were procedural errors in

Figures 6 and 7

Left: Downtown benefit for Nancy Shaw's tenure battle, early 1980s

Below: Postcard requesting that Chancellor Sinsheimer grant Nancy Shaw tenure, early 1980s

Dear Chancellor Sinsheimer,

I strongly urge you to grant Nancy Shaw tenure. In view of her community service, significant research and excellent teaching I feel she is an invaluable part of the UCSC faculty.

_____

_____

_____

_____
(signed)

_____
(address)

the processing of her case, which they found there were. Their report goes to the chancellor, but the chancellor, since he was the one being complained about, kicked it up to the president of the university for a decision. It was David Saxon, and Saxon rejected the appeal, after which Nancy hired an attorney and pursued a court case challenging the denial of tenure. At that point in history, never in the history of the University of California had a case of tenure denial ever been overturned.

Nancy's case ultimately settled with an agreement that there would be a de novo tenure review with three people making the decision. Ultimately, that troika decided to grant her tenure, and that's how she got tenure.

Oakes College had strongly supported her tenure. There were questions that were raised, but there was almost nothing that Oakes could do. Ultimately the decision of tenure and non-tenure is a decision to be made by the chancellor. It's as simple as that.

What made her case unusual was that Sinsheimer applied his own judgment to her file. Chancellors only can work realistically, in my view, with the recommendations that they get from others. Sinsheimer, for whatever reason, decided not to do that, and that led him to that decision.

The procedural errors that Privilege and Tenure had identified were threefold. One was that he had had two ad hoc committees, rather than one, presumably because he didn't like the results of the first one. To be honest with you, I'm not sure that's a procedural error. I mean, if he was disinclined to give tenure and wanted more information, it doesn't strike me as a bad thing to get more information. The second one was that he had written some letters to a third party about her case. It astonishes me that he would do that. That seems so silly. It's not that he said anything bad, particularly, but he was accused of it. It just was a bad idea to do that. The third one, though, was completely legitimate, and

that is he used information from her earlier review as a part of the decision making in this review. She had not been apprised of that. She didn't have an opportunity to rebut it. That *was* a legitimate complaint about the procedure and I think it was a fatal complaint about the procedure. So she actually was right in the end. Even if I didn't agree with all three reasons, I certainly agreed with that one.

Valerie Jean Chase: There were a lot of out women professors, people like Nancy Stoller, Josette Mondanaro,[11] and Karlene Faith.[12] So there were real role models on campus. Soon afterwards, Bettina Aptheker came.

Bettina Aptheker, Professor: I arrived in Santa Cruz in the fall of 1979 to begin my graduate studies in the History of Consciousness Program. I had two young children, and I was finalizing a divorce from my husband of thirteen years. I was also struggling to claim my lesbian identity. Brutalized by the police and FBI because of my Communist affiliation and radical activism in the 1960s and 1970s, 'coming out' for me was at once traumatic and exhilarating.

Having completed a Master's degree at San Jose State University, I had been teaching African-American and women's studies on that campus for several years. When I arrived in Santa Cruz, I was invited to teach in UCSC's Women's Studies Program. In the winter of 1980, I taught my first *Introduction to Feminism* class as a seminar with thirty-five students. Embraced by students in that class, and in succeeding years, I grew into my feminist consciousness and my lesbian life. I met my life partner, Kate Miller, at a Holly Near concert at Santa Cruz's Civic Auditorium in October 1979. We came together in November, and merged households the following June, beginning a lesbian family with three children and two cats. It sounds like a 'case study' out of a sociological text, but it is exactly what happened. With its staunch feminist organizing and large, visible lesbian community, the Santa Cruz campus and community have provided me with an extraordinary haven.[13]

Arlyn Osborne: The scuttlebutt is that we got the Women's Center as a bone thrown to women who were agitating, and strident voices on campus, and a pain in the butt to a chancellor at the time of the Nancy Stoller (then Nancy Shaw) tenure struggle and lawsuit against the campus. Certain women's issues were not considered worthy of scholarly study: Women in the prisons. Women and HIV. Women who were prostitutes. Women in the sex trades. Women and work. It just goes on and on. Women themselves, in any way, shape, or form, for a long time were not considered worthy of a doctoral dissertation, of that kind of study. Money shouldn't go into it! Time should not go into it. You know, it's the old Evans-Pritchard thing with anthropology: "I've been studying people in Africa for this many months and I've learned nothing. There's no one here but women and children. The men are out on a hunt." Okay. That was a mindset for a long time.

Shane Snowdon: It would be tough to keep the Women's Center vital without Bettina Aptheker's introductory women's studies class *Introduction to Feminism*, which is full, year in, year out. It helped many young women feel their power and speak the truth of their lives, and led them to want to be part of the Women's Center, want to try a program, want to join the staff, want to volunteer, want to take a chance.

Valerie Jean Chase: There were a whole host of women, and also gay men like David Thomas. It was a climate that made you feel like you were going to find yourself. I still remember that poster

that admissions did, "Coming to Santa Cruz is a Good Idea." *City on a Hill Press* took that poster and recreated it as, "Coming Out at Santa Cruz is a Good Idea." It was an environment where you discovered who you were, and had the space to rethink where you were going, and what you were going to do.

Linda Rosewood, Student: I graduated from College Eight in 1984. I came here from Fresno City College in 1981. I came here for a Preview Day, and somebody had saved some copies of *City on a Hill* for me. I saw that cover and I thought, oh yes, I bet I could meet some lesbians if I came to that school.

Donna Haraway, Professor: I began teaching here in the fall of 1980 in history of consciousness. I was beginning to publish in the context of feminist theory on animal-human relations and the relations of biologies and anthropologies and politics, and so forth. Those articles got some attention, and the people here really liked them. So they invited me to interview.

I really, seriously wanted this job. I had been picked up from the airport by two women: Mischa Adams, a history of consciousness graduate student, and Katie King, her friend—they were both Santa Cruz graduates of Cowell. They picked me up from the airport and dropped me off at the Dream Inn, that hotel down there on the ocean, a beautiful spot. They said they were sorry they couldn't stay and socialize and whatnot, but they had to get off to a ceremony in the Santa Cruz Mountains to celebrate a home birth. Absolutely classic. They were going to be able to make the job talk, but they were going to be late to the dinner.

So they went off to the birth ceremony. It was a lay midwife-mediated birth. The point was to consume the placenta. That was going to be part of the birthing ceremony, to celebrate the birth. The

Figure 8

Bettina Aptheker, 1993

Photo by Don Harris, UCSC Photography Services

placenta had been saved. The placenta was to be shared by everyone who came, to be eaten. Now, being a lapsed Catholic, I understood immediately what it was like to eat the flesh. I thought this was a good thing. The sign and the flesh come together. Consuming the placenta is serious. They thought that, too, so they were heading off.

But then it turned out that the husband of the placenta had cooked it, or the father, or whatever his relationship to the placenta was. The placenta was cooked and served. Then that completely changed the semiotics as far as I was concerned. It made it rather yuppie. What in the world does a *cooked* placenta signify? Well, that's a mystery. And is it easier or harder to eat it? And for whom?

So anyway, Katie and Mischa get to—we were at India Joze, an important Santa Cruz restaurant of the period for lapsed histcon students and everybody else—Katie and Mischa show up at dinner and talk about the ceremony to celebrate the birth. And immediately ensues this fabulous conversation about who *could* eat the placenta, who *would* eat the placenta, and who *must* eat the placenta. It was a Friday. So the question of whether you could eat it on a Friday if you were a pre-Vatican II Catholic also came into this discussion.

Professor of Anthropology Adrienne Zihlman[14] was hard line: "This is meat. It's animal protein. If you are a Catholic of that period, you can't eat it because it's meat." That was Adrienne's position. Others are saying you should eat it—it doesn't matter whether it's cooked or raw or whatever else, you have accepted the obligation to share in the ceremony and so good manners alone, if not dedication to the cause, prevail. Others maintained the position that cooking the placenta is a violation of all of the relevant symbolism, and you must not, no matter if the poor person who cooked it was doing his best and had his feelings deeply hurt. Every imaginable position on the placenta appeared in this fabulous, very funny, very smart discussion

about politics and semiotics and disgust and rationality. I decided that night that this had to be my community. This was definitely my place.

I gave a kind of crazy job talk that had Jack Schaar[15] running from the room in horror, and Norman O. Brown jumping up and down in pleasure. It had the kind of messy mix of things that my work has always had, that characterized "A Cyborg Manifesto,"[16] that characterizes, for better and for worse, who I am. For better and for worse, I have the kind of mind and soul that makes connections fast.

It was flaming crazy and it was fun! And it got people excited. The search committee, which was made up of Adrienne Zihlman, and Barbara Epstein,[17] and Helene Moglen, and Bettina Aptheker, and Jim Clifford and Hayden White, liked it. So they ended up hiring me. I think they deliberately hired someone who was unpredictable in some interesting ways. I think that had a lot to do with the kind of craziness that Hayden White had, and liked—a kind of fundamental hatred of being bored. It was an historical moment in the history of scholarship, in the women's movement, in the kinds of risks universities would and wouldn't take.

History of consciousness was the first department in the United States to hire a person in feminist theory. There were plenty of other people who were doing feminist theory at that time. And feminist theory was not canonized as this Thing yet, thank God. It was highly diverse, located in many domains of practice in and out of the university, and understood to be this highly diverse activity. For history of consciousness to ask for, and get, a faculty line in feminist theory was innovative, not just in this institution, but nationally. It would make sense that UCSC and history of consciousness would do that. It grew out of the history of feminist work on this campus.

Helene Moglen, Professor: When I said I would chair the Women's Studies Program, I wanted to do three different things. I wanted to get women's studies established as a strong department with FTE of its own. I wanted to start a feminist research group—which we did: the Feminist Studies FRA [Focused Research Activity]. And I wanted to have a women's center, which would both allow women's studies to begin to grow as an academic unit, and provide us with a place, a space for feminist activism between the campus and the community.

So I sold a group of faculty on our need for all three things, and Bob Sinsheimer—who certainly didn't know from feminism, but had hired me and was very supportive of me—I was able to persuade him that we needed a women's center.[18] I think he was very concerned also to build university-community relations, which were not in good shape.

I thought if the Women's Center was going to be an original place that could initiate, could imagine itself, could conceptualize itself in whatever ways it wanted to, it needed to be free of Student Affairs, and we needed therefore to have a governing board that was not only university-connected. And that's when I asked Mayor Mardi Wormhoudt if she would co-chair the steering committee with me. We would bring in community people who had weight—like Ciel Benedetto, who was really major in building the health movement at that time. We would be bringing people in from the community who would have a vision of this as a university-community activity. We would work together to plan it. Mardi really showed up, despite the fact that she was the mayor of Santa Cruz and she was on the city council. She was absolutely engaged in trying to make the center work. Having Mardi co-directing was a stroke, if I may say so, of

genius, since there was no more important woman in Santa Cruz than the mayor.

Kathie Olsen, Assistant Director, Women's Center: We got the keys to Cardiff House, which was empty. At that time, there was almost nothing around Cardiff House. There were lemon groves around. It was a beautiful, bucolic space. We had a working fireplace. We saw the house as an extraordinary asset, something that could be used as a way to make people from town feel comfortable, people from the county feel comfortable there. I had images of being able to raise money (and we actually did a little bit of this), by having people use it for weddings and anniversaries and parties and pay rent for it. Community groups could use it for free meetings and for their fundraisers. We had a very little budget. We bought most of the furnishings used because the university didn't have any for us, really. But we wanted it to look beautiful, and we wanted it to look like a home for the women of UCSC and for the women of Santa Cruz. So, we went zooming around and furnished it more like a home than like an office.

There were a lot of community women. The wonderful poet Maude Meehan[19] came up; if we had writers reading, she would come to cheer them on. When Adrienne Rich moved to Santa Cruz, she'd come to events to say, "Good for you," show her woman-to-woman support.[20]

Arlyn Osborne: People in community studies often found field studies through the Women's Center, and went to various women's organizations in town, like Programa para las Niñas at La Familia Center in Beach Flats. We were all talking about: how do we have students contribute, and the university contribute to the community, work *with* the community, and benefit students, and benefit faculty? Everybody benefits from what's going on, and from the monies that are community monies and university monies and state funding and donors' funding. How do you make it all work? The Women's Center was the hub of that, because women's issues don't stop anywhere.

Valerie Jean Chase: I came to UCSC in 1979. I graduated from College Five in the last graduating class of the era when Porter College was still called College Five, which was 1981. I hung out afterwards and became a staff member. I must say, I was really clueless. I was the last person to realize I was a lesbian. When I came here, one of my gay friends in Santa Barbara said, "Oh, you'll love UCSC. It's crawling with lesbians!" It just passed over my head. 1979 was that period where women had short hair and wore flannel shirts, and everyone was very butch. You couldn't go anywhere without seeing this big lesbian presence. I think that became the influence for that article in *Ms.* Magazine which said Santa Cruz was the feminist utopia of the United States.[21] The climate was very out and very proud and very feminist.

De Clarke, Lick Observatory Staff: The Take Back the Night march was something that us undergraduate feminists decided that we wanted to do. It was the first time that it happened in Santa Cruz. There had been Take Back the Night marches in larger cities with more feminists in them—New York, San Francisco. But this was the first time it had happened in Santa Cruz. And this was my first experience of political organizing, of the process of making a political event happen. It was my very first experience of having to work with other people at all, as a team, as a collective with consensus decision-making. It was a very exciting experience to have a Take Back the Night march, to have all of these women marching through campus after dark, feeling totally safe because we were in this big mob, chanting these chants, which of course now that we're old and jaded strike us

as terribly cliché and boring, but at the time they were pretty darned empowering. To be marching through these dorms where we had been, some of us, intimidated by male party animals, and been whistled at and so forth, and marching there and yelling, "What do we want? NO RAPE! When do we want it? NOW!" The walls were echoing.

Helene Moglen: The extent of sexual harassment on the campus at that time was unbelievable. The worst of it was in the sciences.

I was the only woman administrator, I was asked to take on thing, after thing, after thing. The university needed a sexual harassment committee. Sinsheimer asked me if I would chair and put together the committee, which I did.[22] And we took it very seriously. I think the fact that we existed, and that students could come and talk to us was very important. We did work behind the scenes. We did talk to faculty, and if it came to it, we would force confrontations. There were faculty who were accused of sexual harassment and there were some faculty who were forced to take time off for some time.

But the most effective work was not done by my committee. It was done by students. There was a group of women who worked with us, in the sciences. They would go around to people's labs and they would insist that somebody come out into the corridor. Then they would read him a statement about what the harassment consisted of. These were undergraduates. Graduate students were too dependent; they were too embroiled in the system.

Julia Armstrong-Zwart: The campus was established in the sixties amid everything that was going on in the sixties. Everybody was feeling sexually liberated. Women were supposed to be as sexually liberated as men. But it seemed to work better for men than for eighteen-year-old women.

Helene Moglen: It was amazing. I would get calls from a faculty member: "Helene, these women are— You've got to get them out of here!" "Well, what are they doing?" Well, they would read what faculty members had done: "You took so-and-so out for dinner and you did this and that." Or, "This is what you wanted in exchange for this grade." That was what they were telling them. The students were publicly reading about their experiences, and they were telling the faculty members what it meant to women that they had done this. And it was scary for these guys.

A lot of the men just saw it as their prerogative. There were guys who, when they were showing men around to whom they were planning to offer jobs, would sort of let them know, "Well, there are this sort of women here in this college—" It was awful! There were a number of men, and some very distinguished scholars on campus, who just saw it as their prerogative to have sex with students.

Julia Armstrong-Zwart: I think part of the problem at UCSC was that certain boundaries which seemed to exist in other, older institutions didn't seem to exist here. There was a degree of fraternization between faculty and staff, faculty and faculty, and faculty and students that just seemed to be part of the campus culture, and that I had never witnessed before. It was a shock for me. The line not to be crossed with students didn't seem to be as well defined. I think that some of the male faculty thought sexual relationships with students were one of the perks of the job.

Helene Moglen: There were substantial boundary issues in the early days of this campus. Faculty and students worked together, and staff, and everybody got together. And stuff happened. I think there were a certain number of faculty who wanted to act as though they didn't have power, that they could give their power to everyone else, so everyone was in it

together. I think that was what often fueled these situations. And then the pain that there would be for students, and the incredulity. There were a number of students I saw, over the years, who dropped out because of sexual harassment, because their advisor was harassing them and they didn't know how to deal with it. They didn't finish. There were many really sad stories. But it was endemic to the culture. As women came into the university, there was very little sense of what it meant to treat them like equals.

Julia Armstrong-Zwart: The issue of sexual harassment emerged as a public issue as part of women finding a public voice, as a result of the latest iteration of the women's movement. It's something that women always knew existed and may have talked about to each other sub rosa, but we never put it out there in the public square.

It was an even greater challenge for this campus to understand the concept of sexual harassment and the fact that it was not just against university policy, but it also was a violation of federal law, and that both the institution and the faculty member—whether it was a faculty member or a supervisor or whoever—were actually liable in a legal way. It took a while to educate the campus. The work that was done by the first Committee on Sexual Harassment, chaired by Helene Moglen, did the campus an amazing service by raising the issue, talking about it, naming it, explaining what it was.

Marge Frantz, Lecturer: One of the big things we did when I was on the women's studies executive board was Helene Moglen's campaign to educate Chancellor Sinsheimer about sexual harassment. We had a meeting about sexual harassment. He came late and stood in the back. You could read his face. He was astonished to hear these stories of sexual harassment. He didn't know what was going on. You could see his mouth drop.

Julia Armstrong-Zwart: A few years later two faculty members came to see me, Wendy Mink and Bob Meister, who were serving on a new committee on sexual harassment. Both were faculty in politics. They believed that the sexual harassment policy should not only deal with unwelcome sexual attention. They were also concerned about seemingly consensual relationships between a faculty member and a student in his/her class.

I can remember Bob Meister saying to me with great earnestness, "We get to screw with their minds. We have to leave their bodies alone."[23] I thought that captured it. The faculty-student relationship, the student is so vulnerable in so many ways, emotionally, intellectually. There's almost the same transference that goes on between a therapist and a patient. The faculty member simply has to be made aware of the power that he or she has in relation to a student, and therefore, students cannot really fully and freely consent.

Arlyn Osborne: There was a sexual harassment task force that was looking at: are we following the sexual harassment grievance procedures on campus? Those procedures had been set up by the earlier committee chaired by Helene Moglen, but they were not being followed. That was a real problem on campus. And Wendy Mink, tenured faculty, was very clear that this needed to be dealt with. She worked on that for years. She went at it from every direction, over and over and over.[24]

Wendy Mink created more change and pushed for more advancement of women on campus than almost anyone, besides maybe Helene. I watched her do it over and over and over. She was not going to let things ride. Often, things would get brought up on campus about pay levels, or diversity, or affirmative action issues of various kinds, about how many women were in what positions, about glass ceilings, about sexual harassment of graduate students.

Helene Moglen: Graduate students were utterly stuck. The undergraduates could move, but the graduate student, by the time she was connected with a guy— There were some departments that were just infamous, infamous! And infamous among staff. Staff had to put up with a kind of gender harassment that was horrible.

Julia Armstrong-Zwart: Graduate students had so much on the line. For a graduate student, in either instance, whether she willingly entered into the relationship or rebuffed an advance, her whole career was at risk. There was no way to level that playing field. I think that the Resolution on Romantic Relationships was something that needed to be spelled out and discussed. To the senate's credit, it passed that resolution. I'm not sure if that would have happened on any other campus within the University of California at that time.[25]

Endnotes

1. Rothman is speaking from the Oakes College perspective amid the pressures of the reorganization period, while Armstrong-Zwart is speaking from the perspective of the central administration and the Sinsheimer administration's support for affirmative action.

2. Casa Huerta, named after Chicana activist and United Farm Workers (UFW) vice president Dolores Huerta, is part of multicultural theme housing at Oakes College. In 1975, Huerta pushed for legislation granting amnesty to farm workers who had lived, worked, and paid taxes in the United States for many years but were not extended the privileges of citizenship. Her efforts resulted in the Immigration Act of 1985, in which 1.4 million farm workers received amnesty. She was awarded the Presidential Medal of Freedom by President Barack Obama in 2012.

3. A small collection related to the publishing of *Revista Mujeres* and to the UCSC organization Las Mujeres is available in the UCSC Library's Special Collections Department.

4. C. Chung, A. Kim, and A.K. Lemeshewsky, eds. *Between the Lines: An Anthology by Pacific/Asian Lesbians of Santa Cruz, California* (Dancing Bird Press, 1987) is available in full text online at: https://library.ucsc.edu/sites/default/files/betweenthelines_0.pdf. Also see the Asian Pacific Islander Lesbian Collection curated by Alison Kim at UCSC Library Special Collections: http://pdf.oac.cdlib.org/pdf/ucsc/spcoll/ms40.pdf.

5. Marta Morello-Frosch was a member of the literature board from July 1, 1974 to June 30, 1994. Her research and teaching focused on Latin American literature. She died in 2010.

6. In addition to having served for many years as the staff advisor for the literature board, Claire Braz-Valentine is a poet, a freelance writer of both children's and adult fiction and nonfiction, and an award-winning playwright. As part of the California Arts in Corrections Program, she has worked with youth at risk and with incarcerated adults.

7. Nate Mackey came to UCSC as a professor of literature in 1979. A poet, novelist, editor, and critic, he won the National Book Award in 2006. Mackey left UCSC in 2010 and now teaches literature at Duke University.

8. The EOP Summer BRIDGE Program supported and guided first-generation college students making the transition to university life.

9. The editors were not able to obtain statistics on the number of faculty members at UCSC in 1981, but according to *Santa Cruz Plans for the 80s: Long-Range Academic Planning Statement: 1980-1985, February 8, 1980* (available in Special Collections), in 1980 the campus employed a total of 225 tenured faculty members.

10. Beatriz Lopez-Flores was hired as the Women's Center director in September 1986 and held that position until 1994. Her previous experience included activism with organizations such as the United Farm Workers of America, as well as a background in media. Immediately before assuming the Women's Center directorship, Lopez-Flores had worked as an outreach counselor for UCSC's Educational Opportunity Program (EOP).

11. Physician Josette Mondanaro directed drug-abuse services for California during the early 1970s. Later in that decade, she opened Wingspread, a Santa Cruz medical clinic dedicated to serving low-income patients, especially those fighting drug addiction. She also taught a course at UCSC entitled *Female Physiology and Gynecology*. Mondanaro died in 2003. See https://www.ncbi.nlm.nih.gov/pmc/articles/PMC1448441/.

12. Feminist activist Karlene Faith came to UCSC as an anthropology student in 1966, earning her BA in 1970; she returned to complete a PhD in history of consciousness in 1981. Faith began working with women in prison while she was an undergraduate, and as a graduate student taught courses on women in prison. She played a large role in developing the Santa Cruz Women's Prison Project in 1972. She died in 2017.

13. This excerpt is from Aptheker's narrative in the Out in the Redwoods project: https://library.ucsc.edu/reg-hist/oir.exhibit/bettina_aptheker. Also see Aptheker's memoir: *Intimate Politics: How I Grew up Red, Fought for Free Speech, and Became a Feminist Rebel* (Emeryville, CA: Seal Press, 2006) and the Bettina Aptheker Papers (MS 157) at UCSC Library Special Collections: http://pdf.oac.cdlib.org/pdf/ucsc/spcoll/ms157.pdf. Earlier in her life, Bettina Aptheker was one of the leaders of the Free Speech Movement at UC Berkeley and a leader of the movement to free Angela Davis from prison in the early 1970s. She came to UCSC in fall 1979 as a PhD student in History of Consciousness and in 1980 began working as a lecturer in women's studies. She earned her doctorate in 1983. In 1987, she became the women's studies board's first ladder rank faculty member. Aptheker's now-legendary *Introduction to Feminisms* course is often described as "life-changing"; her lectures for that course

have been filmed and are available at the UCSC Library. From 2012-2015, Aptheker and literature professor Karen Yamashita held the University of California Presidential Chair in Feminist Critical Race and Ethnic Studies.

14. Adrienne Zihlman's "work on comparative anatomy has yielded paradigm-changing insights about locomotion and the search for the common ape-human ancestor." She joined the anthropology board in 1967, becoming one of very few women faculty members at the time." https://news.ucsc.edu/2018/11/zihlman-lecture.html.

15. Jack Schaar "came to UCSC in 1970, arriving as one of the earliest members of the Politics Department. Not only did he help to shape the campus's founding ethos, his courses were as influential beyond the campus. Before coming to Santa Cruz, Jack was active in the political and intellectual controversies at UC Berkeley, where he taught in the 1960s. He was involved in the free speech movement and contributed to debates regarding the application of social science methods to things political." https://news.ucsc.edu/2012/01/jack-schaar-memoriam.html.

16. Donna Haraway, "A Cyborg Manifesto: Science, Technology and Socialist--Feminism in the Late Twentieth Century," in D. Bell and B.M. Kennedy (eds), *The Cybercultures Reader*, (London: Routledge, 2000), 291–324. See also Donna Haraway's papers available at UCSC Library Special Collections (UA 42).

17. Barbara Epstein was a professor in the History of Consciousness Department specializing in the history of social movements. She retired recently.

18. See the oral histories about the UCSC Women's Center in: Irene Reti, Interviewer and Editor, *Crossing Borders: The UCSC Women's Center, 1985-2005.* https://library.ucsc.edu/reg-hist/crossing-borders-the-ucsc-womens-center-1985-2005.

19. Maude Meehan was a poet and political activist.

20. Adrienne Rich is one of the most widely read and influential poets of the second half of the twentieth century. Rich won the National Book Award and a MacArthur Fellowship, among many other awards. She lived in Santa Cruz from the 1980s until her death in 2012. Rich was active with the UCSC Women's Center and Jewish progressive organizations in Santa Cruz.

21. Grace Lichtenstein, "Should You Move to Santa Cruz? A Tough Look at a 'Feminist Utopia,'" *Ms.* Magazine, December 1983.

22. See Patricia L. Maes and Susan Brutschy, *Sexual Harassment at U.C. Santa Cruz: an Exploratory Study*, 1983. Available at UCSC Library Special Collections.

23. Politics professor Robert Meister taught political and social thought and history of consciousness at UCSC for over forty years. See the interview with him, which includes his thoughts on the history of UCSC, on Full Stop at http://www.full-stop.net/2014/09/03/interviews/michael-schapira/robert-meister-pt-2/.

24. Gwendolyn Mink taught US equality law, poverty policy, gender issues, and American politics at UCSC from 1980-2001. Her mother, Representative Patsy Mink (D-Hawaii), in 1964 became the first woman of color elected to the US House of Representatives, and served twelve terms.

25. It is a violation of the Faculty Code of Conduct for a faculty member to engage "in a romantic or sexual relationship with a student for whom he or she has or should expect to have in the future, academic instructional, evaluative or supervisory responsibility." The Title IX Office is committed to fostering a campus climate in which members of the campus community are protected from all forms of sex discrimination, including sexual harassment, sexual violence, and gender-based harassment and discrimination. See: https://titleix.ucsc.edu/.

Illustrations

Figure 1. Moratorium Against Institutional Racism poster. Late 1970s. Courtesy Special Collections, University Library, University of California, Santa Cruz. UA70: UCSC Ephemera Collection: UA70_00_0052.tif.

Figure 2. Julia Armstrong [Zwart], Special Assistant to the Chancellor, 1981. Courtesy Special Collections, University Library, University of California, Santa Cruz. UA 50: UCSC Photography Services: ua0050_neg_0023-8096b_05.tif.

Figure 3. Cover of *Revista Mujeres.* Courtesy Special Collections, University Library, University of California Santa Cruz.

Figure 4. Cover of *Between the Lines: An Anthology by Pacific/Asian Lesbians of Santa Cruz, California.* 1987. Courtesy Special Collections, University Library, University of California, Santa Cruz. UA 27: Out in the Redwoods Collection.

Figure 5. Rosie Cabrera. Circa 2000s. Photo by Jim MacKenzie. Circa 1990s. Courtesy Special Collections, University Library, University of California, Santa Cruz. UA 38: Regional History Project Records.

Figure 6. Downtown Benefit for Nancy Shaw's tenure battle, early 1980s. Courtesy Special Collections, University Library, University of California, Santa Cruz. UA 97: Feminist Studies Department Records: ua097_016_0002.

Figure 7. Postcard requesting that Chancellor Sinsheimer grant Nancy Shaw tenure. Early 1980s. Courtesy Special Collections, University Library, University of California, Santa Cruz. UA 97: Feminist Studies Department Records: ua097_011_0011.

Figure 8. Bettina Aptheker. 1993. Photo by Don Harris. Courtesy Special Collections, University Library, University of California, Santa Cruz. UA 50: UCSC Photography Services: ua0050_neg_1030-3824b_16.tif.

Figure 9. Banana slug. Campus Photo Archive. Communications and Marketing Department, UCSC. Copyright UC Regents.

Figure 10. Banana Slug Spring Fair: students in banana slug costume with Chancellor Robert Sinsheimer, on the East Field. Photo by Don Fukuda. 1986. Courtesy Special Collections, University Library, University of California, Santa Cruz. UA 50: UCSC Photography Services: ua0050_neg_0308-4387c_22a.tif.

Figure 9

Banana slug, Campus
Photo Archive

Figure 1

Banana Slug Spring Fair: students in banana slug costume with Chancellor Robert Sinsheimer, on the East Field, 1986

Photo by Don Fukuda

Chapter 22

The Sinsheimer Era's Final Years

Students knew what they were doing when they adopted the slug. If other colleges used fierce mammals to hype their football teams, then UCSC, which had no football team, would take up the cause of a slow-moving, slimy creature that had no spine or shell and could mate for eight hours at a time.

—UCSC News Center

Divest Now:

Students Protest South African Apartheid

Jim Burns, Public Information Officer: In July 1986, anti-apartheid protests all over our country were occurring, related to companies and, in our case, universities that were doing business with South Africa. There were numerous protests throughout the UC system aimed at the regents for the university's investment in companies doing business there.

It was UC Santa Cruz's turn to host the regents' meeting. The board was scheduled to vote—with the governor, Governor Deukmejian at the time, in attendance—about whether or not to have UC divest of its holdings in companies that do business in South Africa.

Cowell College became the epicenter for the press who descended on UC Santa Cruz for that summertime meeting, during a time of year when it normally would be very quiet on campus.

We had reporters come from all over the country. The Office of the President was staffing the press center, and they asked the members of [the Public Information] office if we could help them do that. For me, it was helpful exposure to a large protest at UC Santa Cruz: how such protests did or did not move the needle, and the amazing amount of logistics that were required to enable a protest of that scale to occur, and to help reporters cover a story with that degree of local, statewide, and national interest. Irrespective of our personal views, or the soundness of the protest, the members of our office had an obligation to make it as easy as possible for reporters to do their work.

The protestors lined up to get arrested. There were dozens of people arrested during the penultimate day of the regents meeting.

Figure 2

Students demonstrating for divestment from South African apartheid regime, UC Regents' meeting, Cowell College, July 17-18, 1986

Photo by UCSC Photography Services

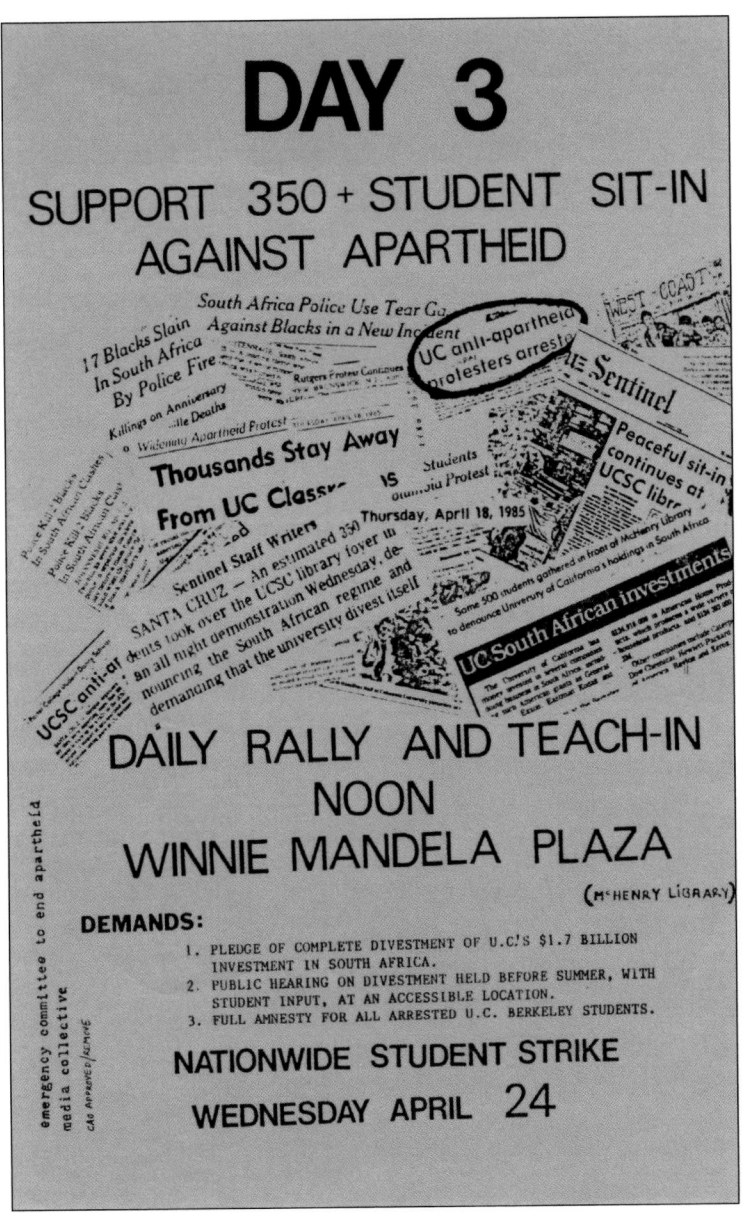

Figure 3

Anti-apartheid protest, Day 3 flyer, April 1985

Robert Sinsheimer: The divestiture issue was a difficult one for me because, in principle, I was in favor of divestiture, personally. But it's not my decision. It's the regents' decision. The students were sitting in and, I don't know, I guess they thought somehow through me they would be putting pressure on the regents, but I didn't have any pressure to put on the regents.

Julia Armstrong-Zwart: The chancellor's office was occupied several times. Sinsheimer would always come out and talk to the students. He would say, "There are people here working. You can't disturb them. But I'll come out and I'll talk to you. Then I'll have to go back." Students would hand the chief of police a list of the students who were going to be arrested. When the students occupied the foyer of the library over divestment—the regents divesting themselves of stock in South Africa—the chancellor said he wasn't going to call the police out; he wasn't going to have them forcibly removed. So they stayed there for it seemed like forever.

Robert Sinsheimer: The sit-in in McHenry Library got really out of hand. It just went on and on. Part of the problem was that the student leadership kept changing. We would meet with the leadership and come to an agreement. They'd agree to end the sit-in in a given period, and by that time there was new leadership. This happened about three or four times, every time we worked out an arrangement. I have to say I was about ready to have them arrested when they finally did move out, I mean, just to get them out of there. It couldn't go on forever. It was by far the most protracted sit-in. At that point, I was kind of locked into a pattern of not having students arrested. But it was inconvenient and highly unsanitary. They did not block the entrance to the library; they did not block the entrance to the

chancellor's office, which occupied a wing of the library building.[1] They knew that was off-limits. They could not interfere with what other students were doing.

I didn't feel the sit-in was a very intellectual way of dealing with the problem. It was a purely emotional response. It doesn't really get the problem discussed. I'm not particularly sympathetic with that form of student activism. Students certainly have the right to express their opinions and have rallies and speeches and discussion and what have you, but I don't think it should take the form of what is actually trespassing.

I did have open office hours. I started them when I came here and I continued them. To be honest, I found I was a little disappointed with them. I thought students might come in and want to discuss divestiture, or something like that.

Jim Burns: The thing that I most remember was how organized the protest was—and ultimately how successful it was. Perhaps the regents, because of mounting political pressure based in part on the sheer number of protests, would have done the right thing anyway. But the protestors were very focused and didn't turn the protest into a battle with UCSC police.

In fact, at that particular protest, they partnered with the police, let the police know that this was an important enough issue to them that they were prepared to be arrested. A large number of them filed onto a bus at the base of campus and were driven downtown, where they were booked. The protestors that day were nonviolent, worked with the campus to ensure that the arrests were conducted without force, and in the process, drew a lot of media attention to this historically important vote and this historically important meeting at UC Santa Cruz.

The Slug Versus the Sea Lion:
A Mascot Battle Embroils the Campus and the Chancellor

UCSC News Center: Soon after UCSC opened its doors in 1965, the students started taking hikes through the redwoods. It didn't take them long to notice the giant, banana-yellow organisms hanging around the ferns and the underbrush. Native to Western North America, these creatures are the second-largest land slugs in the world. They descended from marine snails who tried their luck on land 400 million years ago. Students knew what they were doing when they adopted the slug. If other colleges used fierce mammals to hype their football teams, then UCSC, which had no football team, would take up the cause of a slow-moving, slimy creature that had no spine or shell and could mate for eight hours at a time.[2]

Robert Sinsheimer: Santa Cruz has always had a low-key approach to athletics and I was quite satisfied to continue in a similar vein. I did not want to become involved in the corrupting programs of big-time athletics, with recruiting, athletic scholarships, under-the-table bribes, and the exploitation of "student athletes" with inadequate academic preparation. I believed in strictly amateur athletics for those students who played simply because they enjoyed sport. I brought the campus into the NCAA Class III Division to play other schools of like mind.

This approach to athletics had several consequences. For one, it alienated one sector of the local community, which had hoped the university would provide them with athletic spectacles. And it is true that the provision of sports events can provide a bond between university and town, as I have observed elsewhere, and which we thus lacked at Santa Cruz. Also, because of its limited program, Santa Cruz tended to attract students who had little interest in or experience with athletics, and thus had never learned the lessons of sports—the concepts of fair play, the value of team play, the ideas that "you win some, you lose some" and "nobody bats a thousand."[3]

UCSC News Center: "The slug just suited the campus so well—its symbiotic relationship with the redwoods and its nonviolent Gandhi-an characteristics," said Marc Ratner (Cowell '87, linguistics) [who designed an iconic slug image that appeared on t-shirts, mugs, and posters].[4]

Bill Domhoff: I was on the OPERS [Office of Physical Education, Recreation and Sports] advisory committee. I had a bird's-eye view of the banana slug story. It's a hilarious story. And it's also a story about administrators and the lack of democracy when you claim that you have a democratic process.

For some reason, Sinsheimer got it in his head—I don't know from where—maybe because he wanted to see us have a little more organized sports, still at Division Three level, that we needed a mascot name. The students had informally often called their teams whatever they wanted. Usually they'd use "banana slug."

Robert Sinsheimer: The low-key attitude toward sport also gave rise to an amusing episode. When we joined the NCAA, we needed a team mascot. Some of the athletic "clubs" that preceded the NCAA teams had used the banana slug—a yellow, rather sickly looking gastropod found among the redwoods on the campus—to symbolize the campus's low regard for competitive athletics. The members of the teams, however, did not want to compete with such a mascot. A competition

Figure 4

Sluggo's, Porter College Cafe menu, 1990s (left)

Figure 5

Sammy the Safe Sex Slug. Created by Jenny Wardrip Keller of the Graphic Services Department for the Cowell Health Center, 1990s

Figure 6

"Fey" Slug. Designed by UCSC students Pablo Beck and Helen Cole, early 2000s

for mascot was held and a straw vote among the athletes selected the sea lion, a sizable mammal indigenous to the nearby California coast.[5]

Bill Domhoff: He also put out a statement to all the colleges saying, "What should be the name of the team?" Sinsheimer got back unanimous, or at least nearly unanimous, advice to name the teams The Banana Slugs. He didn't like that.

Los Angeles Times: Chancellor Robert L. Sinsheimer, who for years has been trying to change the university's image as an easygoing place that has never left the '60s, ignored overwhelming student sentiment for the slimy creature and decreed that the school mascot would henceforth be the sea lion.[6]

Bill Domhoff: He thought that that was kind of demeaning to sports, and made our teams look laughable. And he took what was either a distant second choice, or what people had maybe suggested to him, given where we're located, and he wanted to name us the Sea Lions.

So I gave him this advice, on which I never heard back and which he didn't follow. I said, "Why don't you just decide that you're going to leave things the way they are? Every team can name themselves what they want to, because that's the Santa Cruz way." I don't even know whether he received it, read it, but of course he named them the Sea Lions.

And therein started his trouble. It was hilarious: from that point forward, the name Sea Lions *never* appeared in anything written by any student. There were the sea slugs, the banana lions; there was sea kelp; there were the sea cucumbers. On and on and on with the mockery.

Los Angeles Times: The students have been slow to drop the idea, however, popularizing the cheers of "Go, Slugs" and "Slime 'em, Slugs" at basketball games. "The banana slug is sort of a symbol of Santa Cruz's uniqueness, rather than something more conventional like the Fighting Tigers," said student government leader Eric Satzman.[7]

Audubon Magazine: To understand how and why the University of California Santa Cruz officially allied itself with *Ariolimax [dolichophallus,* the banana slug] last spring, one must first comprehend the nature of both the student body and the banana slug. In a sense, the two are in the same league. Or, at least, so felt the young scholars who overwhelmingly voted for Banana Slugs over Sea Lions in a referendum on the university's mascot.

Santa Cruz has, from its beginnings, consciously developed an oddball reputation. Like the other schools in the University of California system, including Berkeley, Davis, and Los Angeles, it skims the academic cream from the state's high schools. Residents need a 3.0 grade point average for acceptance, while out-of-state applicants must pack a GPA of 3.5 or better. However, as founding faculty member Todd Newberry explains, the school was born "in frank opposition to the university system of the fifties and early sixties. We set up against a system that fostered an almost industrial approach to education." "Santa Cruz," he adds, "has been raised on improbabilities; peculiar arrangements like our colleges (there are eight of them under the UCSC umbrella), strange procedures like narrative evaluations, odd absences like no football, weird dances like the waltz."[8]

Bill Domhoff: He'd asked for student opinion; they'd given this strong opinion that reflected the campus mentality—and he'd ignored it, and he'd made them the sea lions. And he's got himself a fight. He had no sense of the student involvement in the campus and their willingness to rise up, so to speak. There was still that whole mentality here from the sixties and early seventies.

Robert Sinsheimer: When the student body learned of this, it was indignant. They scheduled a referendum on the issue of the mascot.[9]

Bill Domhoff: Then a wonderful student did a logo of "No grades, please," with Plato on it.[10] I think he had little glasses on the banana slug. He was holding Plato, this student banana slug. It was wonderful. It reflected the campus. Students loved it. Sold them like crazy.

John Lynch, Professor: Pete Blackshaw, who was probably the leader in the "banana slug" campaign, says in a *City on a Hill Press* letter that the sitting that I did for Marc Ratner was the basis of the slug emblem, the guy reading Plato with the glasses, the look, was supposed to be me. Whether Pete was teasing me, whether he was making a joke or that's true, I don't know. I've never gotten any royalties for being the model of the slug. Sometimes I see the resemblance. It goes beyond the glasses and the Plato. It was also the sluggishness. I was known for a slow and deliberate way of going about things.

UCSC News Center: In 1986, the newly formed Student Union Assembly voted to put the mascot issue on a campuswide ballot measure. It was a non-binding resolution. The administration, not the students, had the final say about the mascot issue.[11]

Los Angeles Times: Students at the Santa Cruz campus of the University of California are voting this week on a proposal to readopt the banana slug, a snail-like creature found in the damp forests of the Santa Cruz Mountains, as the school mascot.[12]

UCSC News Center: In conjunction with the SUA measure, a number of students rallied for the cause. Students formed a rock group, Bobby and the Slugtones, which released a single called "The Slugs Are Back." The "Bobby" part of their name was a winking reference to Chancellor Sinsheimer. The song resonated. A major radio station in San Francisco played it. The song's popularity, and the national publicity surrounding the slug-versus-sea lion debate, galvanized the campus. Radio stations across the country weighed in. So did national newspapers and magazines, from *People* to *Audubon*. Meanwhile, at UCSC, the slug continued to grow in popularity. Alumni sent letters supporting the slug. The results of the student vote were clear: A five-to-one majority favored the banana slug.[13]

Robert Sinsheimer: Of course, the banana slug won the referendum by a five-to-one margin.[14]

Los Angeles Times: Sinsheimer remains opposed to the idea. "As a symbol of our athletic ambitions," he pleaded in a recent letter to the campus newspaper, "consider that the banana slug is: spineless (ipso facto), yellow (cowardly), sluggish (slow of foot) and slimy (enough said)."

Economics professor David Kaun replied that the chancellor was overlooking the slug's "flexible, golden and deliberate" qualities. He said the campaign to readopt the slug shows that students want to keep sports in perspective as just being "fun" or "play" compared to their studies.[15]

Bill Domhoff: The chancellor stood his ground. One of his statements was, "Well, look, the basketball team would be embarrassed by this. I'm not going to embarrass them. They're NCAA Division III." And then *they* said, "Oh, we love it." So he now was kind of trapped. And he capitulated.

Robert Sinsheimer: Acknowledging the inevitable, I accepted the outcome of the referendum. The students are entitled to a mascot they desire and with which they can empathize.[16]

Michael Cowan: Budweiser used to give posters to campuses that would allow them to advertise their sporting events. And so, very shortly after it had been officially adopted as our mascot, Budweiser came out with a poster which showed a slug looking like Rambo. A backbone, big muscles. Here was a notion of not banana slug, but Slug, with all its other connotations, slug and slime, and a more aggressive, more assertive, more competitive kind of thing.

Bill Domhoff: And then *Sports Illustrated* picked the banana slug as the mascot of the year, the most interesting mascot. It appeared in the newspapers, and, of course, got us publicity. And they interviewed Sinsheimer and so on. So, after resisting, he ended up a hero.[17]

Jenny Keller, Staff: I worked at Graphic Services. I was hired to do technical and illustrative illustrations for professors on campus, for whatever they needed. The university also wanted, at one point, the mascot to be promoting safe sex on campus. It was the Health Center that said, "Can you possibly do something that we can use to promote safe sex?" I thought of Sammy, the Safe Sex Slug. I think I was the one who said, "I think we can incorporate the slug in this." What I did was I drew a condom. Sammy was—you know, when you're doing a three-legged race and you've got a gunny sack? So, Sammy was kind of like in the gunny sack, sort of holding it up to his chest and scooching along, and it was jutting along behind him, with the little curvy marks that looked like something is sort of jiggling. And he's proudly holding it up like, "I practice safe sex." [The gunny sack, in this case, was a condom.] And they went for it. They thought it was great. And the students thought it was really fun too. It was done in a tasteful way.

Robert Sinsheimer: Therefore I designate the banana slug as the official mascot until such occasion as the students might wish to hold another election. I also suggest that it would be most desirable for our biological scientists to begin a program of genetic engineering research on the slug to improve the breed. The potential seems endless. Viva le (and/or la) slug." This last remark [of mine] was a nod to the fact that the slug is an hermaphrodite. And so at Santa Cruz athletic events there ring out stirring cries of "Go Slugs!"[18]

Figure 7

On a 1986 visit to the Long Marine Lab, Carl Sagan displaying the official UCSC Banana Slug t-shirt with design by Marc Ratner

Figure 8

Nancy Enomoto with sculpture of Banana Slug, in the sculpture studio, 1989

Photo by Don Fukuda, UCSC Photography Services

"It was Time to Go":

Chancellor Sinsheimer Retires (1987)

George Blumenthal: I had huge admiration for Sinsheimer. Stepping back for a minute, when Angus Taylor came in, his coming in was a moment of rationality. Taylor was a rational guy. Angus Taylor brought us back down to earth and made us realize that we can't just keep going down the pathway of craziness. We needed to be solid and rational. Sinsheimer was the ultimate rational guy. And he was very close to David Saxon. I don't know if they were friends, but he did tell me later that Saxon really twisted his arm to take on the chancellorship.

For him, the model of the university was Caltech. Of course, we're not Caltech and shouldn't be Caltech, but mixing a little dose of Caltech into the Santa Cruz experience was not a bad thing. It brought a level of academic rigor.

Sinsheimer was the one who came up with the idea of the genome project. He organized a conference at Santa Cruz during his chancellorship to conceive of the concept of mapping the human genome. The DNA molecule, the work of Watson and Crick, was done in the early- to mid-fifties. Nobody understood the coding of DNA for a long time. I think Sinsheimer proposed this as soon as it was realized that there was a coding. His idea was that there should be an international effort to actually map the human genome. That was the real point of this conference. He also did a lot of work on the ethics of genomics. He was one of the first people in the world to be thinking about issues of ethics and genomics. But in a very real sense, this concept of mapping the human genome originated at Santa Cruz.[19]

I'd go to the senate meetings to hear his updates. I used to joke that you could fall asleep between words in Sinsheimer's speeches. But still, he always had something to say. He deeply cared about the place and he deeply cared about scholarship. He brought a high level of respectability within the UC system because he was a man that deserved respect; his campus deserved that equally. I think ultimately that helped put to bed this discussion of potentially closing the Santa Cruz campus.

Sinsheimer married Karen. She did all this great work with Shakespeare Santa Cruz. She was a presence on campus. Bob and Karen entertained in a way that I don't think any chancellor has since. There would be annual parties. I remember one year Bob roasted a pig at University House, which I thought was kind of a strange thing to do. He enjoyed being chancellor and it came through. I think that also lent a spirit to the campus. I know that there were some people, and I even know some people today who you almost can't mention his name to because of reorganization, because of what he did to the colleges. But frankly, I think he had no choice. I viewed him as the savior of the campus. I rank chancellors by how did they leave the campus compared to how they got there. And by any measure, Bob left the campus in much better shape than when he arrived. He did it ethically; he did it warmly. He was a man of principle.

Herman Blake: Robert Sinsheimer was not the most engaging person individually. He might have been brilliant as a scholar, and did a lot of good things, I guess. I don't know. But I could not stand him and I knew I had to leave. What we stood for at Oakes College and what we were doing struck him as being antithetical to academic excellence. We pointed out when Oakes student Jim Willis graduated with honors—he'd come in with a D-minus average—had never read a book, and he accomplished so much. Well, to Sinsheimer it was criminal to have somebody who had never read a book come into your college. The fact that he comes out having read all of the books, and with honors, was not the point.

Helene Moglen: Sinsheimer was committed to social justice in the way that he understood it. He was a scientist; he was a very distinguished scientist, and he had spent his life in laboratories. I think feminism was not an issue that he had ever come across, but he was very fair and very just. And he was also a very decent administrator. I had been hired in this position as dean of humanities and he absolutely supported me. And he kind of got that it was not easy to be the first and only female administrator on the campus, and a feminist to boot.

Pavel Machotka: Sinsheimer struck me as someone who was dry and perhaps literal and not quite imaginative enough. But I did find him an absolutely honest worker in his position.

Jim Pepper: To this day, I think that Sinsheimer felt that environmental studies couldn't possibly have meritorious kinds of intellectual integrity.

Dan McFadden: I worked from August 1973 through the 1980s as the assistant for public affairs and planning to Chancellors McHenry, Christensen, Taylor, and Sinsheimer. It is difficult to overstate the contribution Chancellor Sinsheimer made to the campus. Being viewed as a "hippie school" was the least of its problems.

When I arrived on the campus, it was clear that UC Santa Cruz faced a number of major challenges—from the legislature; the community; the UC system; the campus itself; and the negative national, state, and local media coverage of the

mass murders in Santa Cruz. UC Santa Cruz—this gorgeous campus that had done so many things right—was struggling.

Only if one understands the depth of the challenge can one appreciate what Bob Sinsheimer accomplished. His appointment as chancellor was a significant lift for the campus. Through his exceptional intellect and integrity he not only saved the campus, but also laid the foundation for the outstanding institution UC Santa Cruz has become.[20]

Robert Sinsheimer: It was time to go. Ten years of administration were enough. The routine of the academic year—meeting the new freshmen, reporting to the Academic Senate, the fall UCSC Foundation meeting, the staff Christmas party at University House, the monthly Council of Chancellors' meetings, the monthly regents' meetings, the regular senate meetings, the spring Foundation meeting, the myriad annual receptions for Friends of—, the scholars' lunch, the athletic awards party, the staff awards picnic, the multiple commencements, the end-of-the-year faculty party, the annual budget sessions, all punctuated by student protests over some issue or other—had indeed become routine and begun to pall.

Old issues—never settled, only patched—began to recur: affirmative action, financial aid, childcare, ethnic studies, community unhappiness with campus growth, yet another provost for Kresge College, yet another dean for natural sciences, yet another furor in the music board. The freshmen seemed younger every year. The freshmen in 1986 had been born around 1968. To them the Kennedy assassination, the Vietnam War, and Watergate were as much ancient history as were World War II, the Great Depression, the American Revolution, and the Roman Empire.

Repetition breeds cynicism. Hearing the same time-worn complaints from each new crop of

Figure 9

Chancellor Robert Sinsheimer retirement reception poster, June 5, 1987

students, watching and bearing their patterned protests and antics, it became harder each year to muster an open mind, to remember that it was new to them, to respect their need for growth and expression. I had reviewed the arguments many times and come by then to firm conclusions. It thus became hard to enter into a true dialogue with students, to present a paternal rather than a dictatorial face. Having heard all of the arguments many times over, my mind tended to wander, to concentrate on the student personalities in lieu of the substance—callow but earnest, naive but impassioned, incredibly self-centered, incredibly arrogant, and convinced at their tender age of their superior wisdom.

My natural tendency is toward a "liberal" orientation. A liberal philosophy necessarily is based on a belief that people are basically good and well motivated and will, if left free, act for the common weal. Contact with succeeding generations of students, however, corrodes that belief and reminds one how much education is needed to achieve even a modest maturity. An ability to view this frothy scene with a sense of humor had been a saving grace, but even this had begun to ebb.

To be a chancellor is a baptism in a whirlpool spun ever faster by the conflicting forces of modern society, for these forces correctly focus on the university as the fountainhead of the future—and seek to influence its direction by acting on its titular head. But the chancellor cannot directly oblige any of them for, in fact, he or she has very limited power to alter its course. Who does? In truth, very often, no one. Inertia dominates.[21]

Endnotes

1. At the time, the chancellor's office was located in the McHenry Library building.

2. Dan White, The UCSC News Center: https://news.ucsc.edu/2011/06/banana-slug-25th-anniversary.html.

3. Robert L. Sinsheimer, *The Strands of a Life: The Science of DNA and the Art of Education.* (Berkeley: University of California, 1994), 237.

4. Dan White, The UCSC News Center. See UCSC's website on the Banana Slug mascot: https://www.ucsc.edu/about/mascot.html.

5. Robert L. Sinsheimer, *The Strands of a Life,* 237.

6. Jay Stuller, "Slugging It Out: UC Santa Cruz Students Try Again to Adopt Slimy Local Creature as Mascot," April 25, 1986. *Los Angeles Times.*

7. Jay Stuller, "Slugging It Out."

8. "Fight, Fight, Fight, Banana Slugs, Banana Slugs." *Audubon* Magazine, 1987.

9. Robert L. Sinsheimer, *The Strands of a Life,* p. 237.

10. The student was Marc Ratner. See https://porter.ucsc.edu/news-events/news/slug-mascot-history.html.

11. Dan White, The UCSC News Center.

12. Jay Stuller, "Slugging It Out."

13. Dan White, The UCSC News Center.

14. Jay Stuller, "Slugging It Out."

15. Robert L. Sinsheimer, *The Strands of a Life,* 237.

16. Robert L. Sinsheimer, *The Strands of a Life,* 237.

17. Robert L. Sinsheimer, *The Strands of a Life,* 237.

18. Robert L. Sinsheimer, *The Strands of a Life*, 237.

19. See the timeline of the Human Genome Project's History: https://ucscgenomics.soe.ucsc.edu/about/history/.

20. "https://magazine.ucsc.edu/2018/03/letters-from-fall-2017/ *UCSC Magazine*, Spring 2018.

21. Robert L. Sinsheimer, *The Strands of a Life*, 272.

Illustrations

Figure 1. Banana Slug Spring Fair: students in banana slug costume with Chancellor Robert Sinsheimer, on the East Field, 1986. Photo by Don Fukuda. University Library, University of California, Santa Cruz. UA 50: UCSC Photography Services: ua0050_neg_0308-4387c_23a.tif.

Figure 2. UC Regents' meeting, Cowell College, July 17-18, 1986. Students protesting apartheid in South Africa. Photo by Shmuel Thaler. Courtesy Special Collections, University Library, University of California, Santa Cruz. UA 50: UCSC Photography Services: ua0050_neg_0325-4512a_10.tif.

Figure 3. Anti-apartheid Protest. Day 3 Flyer. April 1985. Courtesy Special Collections, University Library, University of California, Santa Cruz. UA 70: UCSC Ephemera Collection: ua070-0093.

Figure 4. Sluggo's Porter College Cafe. Menu with Slug. Courtesy Special Collections, University Library, University of California, Santa Cruz. UA 79: UCSC Banana Slug Collection: ua079_001_0001.

Figure 5. Sammy the Safe Sex Slug. Created by UCSC Graphic Services for Cowell Health Center by Jenny Wardrip Keller, 1990s. Courtesy of Jenny Wardrip Keller personal archive.

Figure 6. "Fey" Slug. Designed by UCSC students Pablo Beck and Helen Cole, early 2000s. Courtesy Special Collections, University Library, University of California, Santa Cruz. UA 27: Out in the Redwoods Collection.

Figure 7. Carl Sagan holding up the UCSC Banana Slug T-shirt. 1986. Courtesy Special Collections, University Library, University of California, Santa Cruz. UA 79: UCSC Banana Slug Collection.

Figure 8. Nancy Enomoto (student) with sculpture of Banana Slug, in the sculpture studio, 1989. Photo by Don Fukuda. Courtesy Special Collections, University Library, University of California, Santa Cruz. UA50: UCSC Photography Services: ua0050_neg_0650-8382_05.tif.

Figure 9. Chancellor Robert Sinsheimer Retirement Reception poster, featuring Sea Lion and Slug. June 5, 1987. Courtesy Special Collections, University Library, University of California, Santa Cruz. UA 4: Chancellor Sinsheimer Records: ua004_001_0001.

Chapter 23

Earthquakes

The Stevens Years

The quake came at the end of a whole period of anti-university growth.

—Frank Zwart

The Arrival of Chancellor Robert Stevens
and the "Revitalization" of the College System

Robert Stevens: In the fall of 1986, I had been president at Haverford College for eight and a half years. I decided that I really wanted to think out the remainder of my life. So I let my name go forward in a couple of searches, including a general one at the University of California. I did not apply for this particular job. I knew virtually nothing about this campus, although I'm a historian of higher education. I thought I had been nominated for UC Santa Barbara.

My wife, Kathy, and I caught a plane to San Francisco Airport. The interview was conducted in the most remarkable secrecy. We registered under Kathy's name. I had an hour-and-a-half interview with the committee in one of the hotels at the airport. We were invited to come down to the campus. We met UC Vice President of Budget and University Relations Bill Baker and we were driven around the campus. It was all very mysterious. Bill Baker said I was to say I was his brother, so he wouldn't have to introduce me to anyone.

We drove around the campus, went into Oakes and around University House, but we didn't go in. I met no one on the campus. I was allowed to meet the three members of the committee, although Isebill (Ronnie) Gruhn was not in town. I met Hardy Frye,[1] and Charles Daniel, and the concession was made that I was allowed to meet Chancellor Robert Sinsheimer. But that was all.

I was certainly told about town-gown relations. That was seen by the regents as the most important problem facing the campus. I hadn't the faintest idea whether I would be any good at dealing with the city, because I had virtually no experience in that. At Haverford there was a little problem with the local community, but it was not quite the all-engaging sport it is in Santa Cruz.

Ronnie Gruhn: I was on the search committee and interviewed a number of candidates. I had a favorite candidate. It was not Robert Stevens. But I was persuadable, I suppose, by the committee.

Figure 1

Chancellor Robert Stevens, 1988

Photo by Don Fukuda

George Blumenthal: Stevens was a law professor at Yale; then he went to Haverford as the president of Haverford; and then he came here. He was a major figure in legal history. He had played a role in the Connecticut birth control case where the Supreme Court ruled that for a married couple to use birth control fell within the privacy rights.[2] So his reputation preceded him.

Robert Stevens: I'd never been in the public sector.[3] I liked what I heard about Santa Cruz's college system, what I knew about the liberal arts and science approach, attempting to inject the residential liberal arts college into the public sector. I was very interested in the graduate programs that were developing. I thought that was a tremendously interesting challenge. I care a great deal about access, and I was worried that in the private sector access was being increasingly restricted, and the private colleges were going to end up as preserves of the rich. So I accepted the job sometime in March or April and started in July 1987.

Ronnie Gruhn: Robert Stevens was selected. The majority of the committee was very taken with him. He was very affable, and quite funny, and quite warm and fuzzy.

George Blumenthal: Somebody in physics had checked with Haverford and they said, "Oh, yeah, Stevens is a great guy. He's been a good president of Haverford." So he had good reviews.

Robert Stevens: I came out here and met people. It was very hard to get a clear sense of what the main issues were, but certainly they were very clearly the issues that had come through in the interview. The relations with the city were obviously very, very serious. The conflict between teaching and research was more acute than I would

have imagined. I had assumed the faculty would be more research-oriented than it is, being part of the University of California. It's not easy getting to know an alien system. I think that the differences between the private sector and the public sector, I hadn't fully appreciated. And the college system was probably in worse shambles than had been reported to me.

UC President Gardner thinks colleges are wonderful, but he made it very clear to me when I got here that this was the last chance they had. He was not prepared to go on supporting the concept of the colleges unless the colleges got their act together.[4]

I wanted to reinvigorate the colleges. The colleges were reorganized in 1979 by Bob Sinsheimer and I think the decision was quite right to put the responsibility for academic programs in the boards. On the other hand, this campus was founded as a collegiate institution and it would have been a great loss not to have fulfilled that mission. I've spent my life in collegiate institutions and one has a great advantage, undoubtedly, by having colleges. But the colleges had totally lost their way.

Carol Freeman, Lecturer: The colleges, in the middle of the 1980s, had gone out of the business of really contributing to the academic curriculum, except in the core courses.

Robert Stevens: I tried to talk to people about the colleges, but any changes that I suggested in the colleges immediately got all kinds of people paranoid. The colleges were feeling wounded and threatened, and therefore any suggestion, even for strengthening them, was greeted with childish hostility.

I wanted to see the colleges playing a better academic role. And I knew that if we were to continue using the colleges, we were going to have to make certain that we could afford to use them. The colleges were rather expensive to run.

I asked the academic vice chancellor to ask the senate to form a committee. The chairman was Bill Friedland, who chose Carol Freeman of CEP [Committee on Educational Policy] to think about the educational side. Then I decided to appoint a committee of three academic deans and three vice chancellors to think about organizational resources.

Carol Freeman: Carolyn Martin Shaw, as chair of the Committee on Budget and Planning, and I co-chaired. We did a year-long program of consulting with everybody under the sun on the colleges, and ended up in, I think it was April of '91, coming up with this big report about what we thought should happen, about the role that the colleges should play.[5]

Carolyn Martin Shaw, Professor: I got together with Carol Freeman to do the "revitalization" of the role of the colleges. By this time, newly hired faculty members coming to campus didn't necessarily get assigned to a college. That was a surprise to me. I'd actually thought that we were still assigned to a college, even though you didn't have anything to do with the college. But that was one of the things I found out when I started calling around and trying to check on: where are the faculty members?

Patricia Dorsey Bassett: The following questions seem basic to any examination of the Santa Cruz structure if one assumes that any of the original goals and assumptions still stand: How can the focus on undergraduate teaching be maintained within the UC research-driven context? How can interdisciplinary education thrive within the discipline-oriented academic personnel system? How

can general education be promoted and preserved within the college locus?

Carolyn Martin Shaw: Carol and I tried to come up with a sense of what people felt was missing in what they were already doing on campus. What is it that faculty may actually want to have, or do, or say, or be involved with on campus? I wanted to go out there and find out what it is: how happy are people, now that they don't have this college affiliation, or now that they are in their department "silos," and not having any relations with others.

Carol Freeman: We looked at everything: we talked to students; we talked to faculty; we talked to the deans. This coincided with a lot of discussion among universities and theorists about undergraduate education, and about how faculty needed to be more involved in the education of undergraduates. Many people thought of UCSC as a place where this still existed. We were able to talk about the colleges from all those different perspectives, and make the point that a lot of what people said about them, both praise and criticism, was not true.

Carolyn Martin Shaw: What I found out was that a number of people would like greater interdisciplinary relationships with others. Some of them would care to be more directly involved with undergraduates if they could. But nobody wanted to do an overload. Nobody wanted to say, "I've got four classes for my department; now let me go and teach something else for my college."

The first thing that we did, besides going around talking to all these people and trying to get as wide a survey as possible, was to get together to talk about what a vision for the colleges could be. If it's not going to be everybody is sitting in the college and getting to know each other, what kinds of things could you come up with? We came up with quite a few. The one thing that seemed to work the best was to think about having everybody agree to teach one course for a college every third year.

Why did faculty come to UCSC in the first place? I'm sure that some people came to UCSC because there were great laboratories and they had just the equipment they wanted, or because of the ocean, or because there was some faculty member here that they felt like they needed to work with, or had influenced them. But some people came here because we offer a different structure. What we were trying to do is to try to revitalize that, and to see if we could get more folks interested in participating.

After talking to people about what they wanted, we presented a proposal to the Academic Senate. The proposal was to ask all ladder-rank faculty to teach one additional course every third year. And it passed! It passed! Again, with great acclaim. People liked it. That felt affirming. People felt that there's something the colleges offer. They were interested in the interdisciplinary and they were willing to work a little bit more.

Robert Stevens: The college committee made some very interesting suggestions. Far and away the most important was that the faculty should be mandated to teach a course each third year that would be taught in the colleges. This meant that the provost job became more important because it became a more academic job. Now the provosts will report to the academic vice chancellor, not on the day-to-day side of the colleges, but on the academic side. The colleges will be run by a redefined bursar as the college administrative officer, who will, for the most part, be dean of students there, and they will report to the vice chancellor of student affairs.

There is a quite dramatic change in the colleges, a very important change of direction. It will enable the colleges to renew themselves on the academic side. On the student services side, there will be some reductions in staff, because we have been putting far too much money into the colleges. This change of direction is going to provide integrated student services and a much more academic atmosphere in the colleges. I think that committee chaired by Carolyn Clark [Martin Shaw] and Carol Freeman did a first-rate job in working with people.

Carol Freeman: One of the times I had the most fun, of the whole time I spent as CEP chair, was in the senate meeting when we presented our resolutions. The report was pages and pages long, but the resolutions were: that "the senate approves, in principle, that the colleges are social and intellectual entities with responsibilities to mount courses taught by senate faculty; develop and administer an advising program; and plan and sponsor a wide range of extracurricular intellectual activities." Because a lot of people had been saying that the colleges should really just be residential, and there were claims that advising would be more efficient if it were set off in some central place.

Robert Stevens: I hope that this is a renewal of the colleges. I feel relatively optimistic. I have been worried because the colleges have complained bitterly that they don't have a real role, but have not been willing to discuss what a real role might be. They have been trying to protect what turf they have. I think what was achieved here was to open up enormously that process. The majority of students, the majority of college staff, the alumni, the faculty, are pleased with where it's going.

Patricia Dorsey Bassett: Can and should the campus remain committed to the collegiate structure as it moves into the future?[6]

"No Longer the Whitest Campus in the System": Voices from a Changing UCSC

Bill Domhoff: By 1985, 1986, the campus was going to grow. By then we—meaning people like me—were in charge of this campus. Not me, but particularly my buddy, John Isbister, had a fair amount of say, and others. There were some sensible things that could be done. We had to grow. The state was going to jam it on us anyhow. You have to be for the students of California. You can't become totally elitist. I remember my buddy, Tom Pettigrew,[7] a social psychologist and an antiracist—he was mad as hell at these anti-growthers for the campus, because if we don't have more spaces we're certainly not going to achieve more affirmative action. When times are tough, who gets screwed? It's the lower-income people and people of color. We understood that.

David Anthony, Professor: What is called diversity, the process of broadening the base and democratizing an institution, is never easy. It always involves a certain amount of struggle, and a number of people will resist it. The people who will resist it will express that in all kinds of ways. Some of them are faculty, and some of them are staff, and some of them are students. You had an environment by the late 1980s in which there were many conflicts over what the university is going to be like, what the student body was going to be like, what the faculty was going to be like. Some of those conflicts revolved around affirmative action, which was still a very alive issue in the late 1980s. There were all kinds of attempts to diversify, across the board, and that wasn't easy.

Robert Stevens: The vast majority of students of color are admitted onto the campus on exactly the same basis as the majority group. The vast majority

are in that top 12 percent. There are relatively few special admits.

Antoinette Gonzalez: That fact of being a special admit student: it killed me: "I don't belong here. I snuck in here. I don't fit in." I bought all those stereotypes that are out there about affirmative action. I was dealing with my ethnic identity, with being alienated in Santa Cruz, and then learning to understand that I wasn't stupid. That's how deep these myths, these stereotypes are. The idea of meritocracy. There's a certain breed of people who can enter any university, and you're not part of this breed. There's something wrong with you.

Robert Stevens: What is true is that we will admit underrepresented minorities who may be less well qualified than white students or Asian students. But we also give some kind of preference to students from remote areas, students from near Santa Cruz. We give some preference to students who are very musical, or very athletic, or have run the yearbook. We have adhered to the Bakke decision.[8] There's a relatively small hostility to our admissions policies. But the idea that we admit greatly unqualified black students is just not true.

Clearly, we need to do the very best we can to make this an attractive place for all people, whether they are from lower socioeconomic classes, whatever their sex, whatever their sexual preference, whatever their race. We do that by trying to sensitize people in the colleges. We do that by trying to sensitize staff, faculty, everyone who works here, all of us.

Antoinette Gonzalez: I remember grieving in EOP, and moaning about my identity, and having a hard time, and Rosie Cabrera connected me with a staff person in Financial Aid, a lesbian Chicana, who opened my eyes. In conversations, we talked, and it was just similar backgrounds. It was like— oh, you mean it's not unique?

Gwendolyn Morgan: I moved to Santa Cruz in January of 1989. I was a re-entry student. I came in as a transfer junior. I heard UCSC had a really good classics and literature department, so I applied. It's funny, being the first person in your nuclear family to go to college. I struggled to get that application together. I was living in a furnished trailer. I would sit up and look at that application. You had to write a statement of purpose. I had no clue of how to write that statement of purpose. I typed and typed, and re-typed. Finally, I had to turn it in because there was a deadline. There is an art to writing a statement of purpose. Nobody had ever taught me anything like that! Writing a statement of purpose? You just say, "I want to go to school." This is it! "And I need financial aid, by the way."

So I wrote it and I went in under the Educational Opportunity Program [EOP]. I was an EOP student. But I was actually a good student. I think I came in with a 3.7 or a 3.8 grade point average. So it really didn't matter, EOP or not. But I thought that would help me. I checked EOP on the application. I thought that would help me get in the door.

I got into Santa Cruz. I came up, quit my job with a smile. I had no clue. I could never visit the campus because I was working, and I was trying to work up until the last day so I could get all my money, so I could have a nest egg to go to school.

I came up. I looked around. I paid my first quarter's registration fees, and that left me with six hundred dollars. It was crazy. I had six hundred dollars left to find a place to live, to buy my books. It was really gutsy of me to do it that way.

But I did. I enrolled. I took classical music with Leta Miller. It was a basic class. I needed an "H" requirement, or something like that. At the time, I was homeless. I was living in my car, because I had paid for my registration fees, I had bought my books, and I didn't have enough money to find a place to live. I must have been loony to do it this way. I figured I could study in the library. I could stay warm in the library. I could eat at the Whole Earth Restaurant, or at the residence halls, if I could afford it. I would park my car and I would sleep.

Robert Stevens: We cannot solve the problems of the world. We do not exist in a vacuum. To expect it to be a perfect place is unrealistic. I think that we are better than most campuses in terms of making this an attractive place for all students.

Gwendolyn Morgan: That was the best quarter I ever had. I was homeless. It was amazing. I made friends in my classes, and I put out the word to various women to let them know—do you know of anybody who has a cheap, cheap place? But I was homeless for six weeks during the winter quarter. It rained just about every single day. Actually, it was a blessing that it rained, because I could park my car, and there weren't too many people out walking around in the rain when I was sleeping. So I was pretty safe. Because it was just pouring and pouring, I stayed at the library until they closed. I stayed and I studied and I took a little nap.

I found a place to live with a woman who had a garage with this room that had a loft. I stayed there for three years. Even after I graduated, I was still there. I graduated in 1991. I studied classics, with an emphasis on Greek, Roman, and Egyptian history. I took several Latin classes, although I was not a Latin minor. I did pretty well. I studied all the time. I was always on time, never missed a

SEEDS OF SOMETHING DIFFERENT

class. I figured this was going to be my only time that I could do this. So I was dead serious in my classes, and studying, trying to get halfway decent grades. I'm not a scholar, but I applied myself.

Teresa Antonia Broccoli, Student: As a young adult, I often dreamed of attaining an education. My thirst for knowledge, diverse culture, literature, and art carried me into college. Attending UCSC was like an unattainable utopian dream come true. I'm a second-generation Italian/Latin American. My family believed I should secure a good, stable long-term job and a marriage. Anything beyond that was a luxury. Therefore, pursuing my education was something I did on my own. My budding adulthood did not come with a college fund.

I was accepted into the literature undergraduate program at UCSC. UCSC came with a package deal: secure and affordable housing at Family Student Housing. I chose literature because UCSC had a good reputation for their comparative literature program. The literature program is diverse and multicultural in international, English, and American literature. My focus was on Latin and Italian women writers, early nineteenth-century literature, particularly African-American women writers, and slave narratives. I also collect oral histories/herstories by Italian American women.

Arlyn Osborne: "Celebrating Women: Twenty Years of Victory" was a panel at the Civic Auditorium in 1989. Adrienne Rich; Sharon Maeda, who worked with Pacifica Radio; Lucille Clifton;[9] Gloria Anzaldúa;[10] Grace Paley;[11] and Paula Gunn Allen[12]—what a group of women! When this happened, it was the first time the Civic Auditorium had been a sell-out crowd in years. This group of women coming together and talking about what their lives were, what they had tried to do in their lives, what got in their ways, and what

empowered them, and about the women's movements. It was a big statement, that it was not one women's movement. There were movements.

Teresa Antonia Broccoli: Each class I took was on the cutting edge of innovative thoughts, theories, of literature, world cultures, arts, and multicultural representation. These were the best three years of my educational career. I was single-by-choice during my studies at UCSC. I was committed to my schoolwork and raising my son through his middle and high-school years. During the first two years of my work at UCSC, I also was enrolled in the extension program and received an advanced certificate in alcohol and drug studies. This enabled me to work as a chemical dependency educator and counselor/lay social worker. I graduated with a B.A. in comparative American and English literature from Kresge College. I am the first and only person in my immediate family to complete a higher college education.

Jessica Delgado, Student: I remember going to Chicano/Latino graduation.[13] There's this tradition of wearing your country's flag's colors on this little sash. Some people would have the Mexican flag. I wanted to wear the Colombian flag on one side, and the Mexican flag on the other, and I did. Then I had a rainbow flag on top. So I had three. It was fine. I don't think there were very many other students in the graduation who had that, but I was comfortable doing that.

Robert Stevens: California is becoming the most multicultural state, possibly with the exception of Hawaii. If we do not change, the University of California will become increasingly irrelevant to the needs of the state, and that's disastrous for a public institution.

Figure 2

Gloria Anzaldúa

Photo by Annie Valva, circa late
1980s

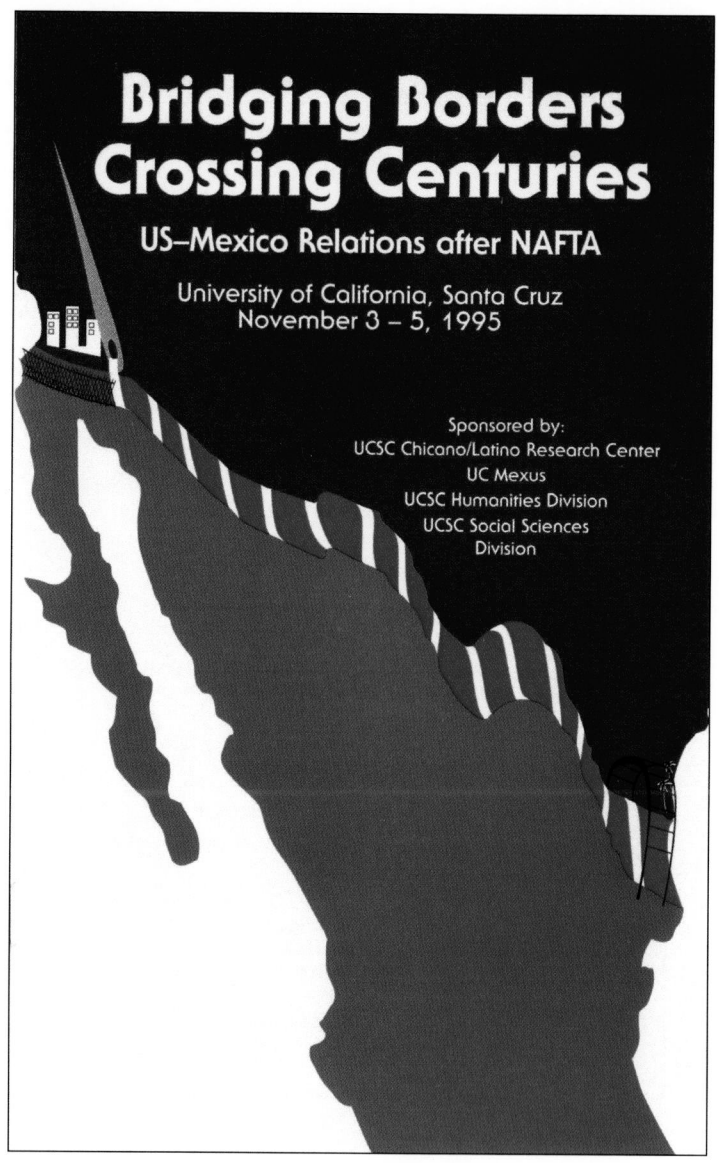

Figure 3

Bridging Borders poster

1995

Pedro Castillo: In 1993, [Professor of Literature] Norma Klahn[14] and I found out that there was money that came from the Office of the President that was supposed to be used for faculty research. So Norma and I got the Chicano/Latino faculty together and said, "We'd like to start a Chicano/Latino Research Center that would look at, not only the Chicano/Latino population in the US, but would link up and would look at Latin America as well. It would be interdisciplinary and it would be comparative."[15] Because you can't look at Puerto Ricans in New York without looking at Puerto Rico. You can't look at Cuban Americans in Florida without looking at Cuba. You can't understand Central Americans or Mexican Americans without looking at Central America and Mexico. We wanted to not just make it "Chicano/Latino studies or Latin American studies," but to combine that. That increased the number of people who were interested, not just people focusing on Chicano/Latino studies but people focusing on Latin American history: interdisciplinary.

We had mini grants for graduate students. We had mini grants for faculty to sponsor their research. We brought in people—we had a colloquium series—to give their talks, people who were going through we invited: "Why don't you come here and give a talk on your research?" We had conferences. We had publications. The Chicano Latino Research Center [CLRC] really began to develop.

Patricia Zavella, Professor: I know firsthand of faculty who got outside offers, who decided they wanted to stay at UCSC. The Chicano Latino Research Center was a piece of that. It was like: here's my intellectual and social community.

Robert Stevens: Next fall, of 1991, the UCSC student body will be 45 percent minority. We are no longer the whitest campus in the system.[16]

Elba Sánchez: Spanish for Spanish Speakers' pedagogy, curriculum, was pioneering. There was no other program in the state at the university level trying to do what we were trying to do.[17] We wanted to do language, but we also wanted to do literature; we wanted to do history; we wanted to do current events and developments. We decided to divide the yearlong, intermediate level into three, interrelated grammar-focused and thematic links. It was to the students' benefit to stay with us for the whole year. Students felt they belonged: they had a place, a home, where they felt good and they could grow.

We wanted students to come away with critical thinking skills, confidence in writing, confidence in their own speaking abilities, and feeling good about their own language and culture. We wanted them to gain knowledge, historical knowledge, self-knowledge, and community, Latina knowledge. We hoped what we were doing in the classroom was going to be a part of their professional and personal lives.

It was a golden chapter in my professional and personal development. It helped me to grow tremendously as an instructor, as a teacher, a counselor—because I was a little bit of all of those. My students were also my teachers.

Patricia Zavella: On other campuses, I'm finding out the culture is: nobody goes to talks, or if they do go, you sort of lay into the speaker. You do these scathing-critique kind of questions. You don't see that happen at Santa Cruz. It's always: thank you for your talk, and now what about this? People will be critical, but in a very supportive, constructive way. I really appreciate that we have that space here.

The "Asian Food Affair"

Julia Armstrong-Zwart: And then in 1988, the Asian Food Affair blew up. It was a small mistake which mushroomed into a giant contretemps. It was like a spark in dry tinder, which became a forest fire that burned acres and acres of goodwill on campus, and everybody involved in it came away feeling dissatisfied with the resolution.

Robert Stevens: In December 1988, one of the colleges, Crown, refused to serve Asian food on Pearl Harbor day. This became known as the "Asian Food Affair." The food they were going to serve, as it turns out after more investigation, was Filipino food. It all strikes me as incredibly bizarre. Manila was bombed the same day as Pearl Harbor. The Philippines were on our side. The idea that one would not serve Asian food on the anniversary of Pearl Harbor still strikes me as insensitive.[18]

Julia Armstrong-Zwart: Crown College provost Peggy Musgrave felt that she was sort of keelhauled over something that was an innocent mistake.[19] John Isbister and the people at Merrill felt that the chancellor hadn't been harsh enough on Crown College. Part of this is, I think, was a longer-standing tension between Crown, as the college of the scientists, and Merrill, as the Third World college. So there was a history of tense relations even before I came to campus.

Robert Stevens: I think it's naive to expect that we're going to have massive sensitivity. We're all very insensitive, whether it's an issue of race, sex, or various other things. They clearly are difficult issues, and as this becomes a more diverse state and, one trusts, a much more diverse university, those problems are going to become more complex and not easier.

The "Asian Food Affair" does show how far we have to go. Crown College has manufactured a whole series of explanations of why they did it. Each one I find somewhat less convincing than the previous one.

Julia Armstrong Zwart: It became an issue of showing the lack of understanding and the hostility of this campus environment for people of color. One Saturday morning, I led a two-hour workshop for students. There were Merrill students there; there were Crown students there. The Merrill students overwhelmingly were students of color, although there were some white students. The Crown students were mostly white students, a lot of white male students.

It was an interesting discussion because there was honest communication, with a white student saying that he thought it was unfair that because of student affirmative action, students of color got spaces in the University of California that otherwise would have gone to white students whose academic records were better. I started to respond to that, and a young Chicano student said, "No, let me respond to that." He said, "Throughout high school, I worked between twenty and thirty-five hours a week because my family needed the money. The school that I went to had no AP courses." He laid out what his life had been as a high school student and said: "Those factors didn't mean that I didn't have the ability to go to the University of California, but if you only looked at the criteria that fit white suburban high schools, I would never have gotten in." It was a moment of understanding. I could see that the white students there had never thought about things from that angle. I thought this was a good thing that came out of a very, very painful, unnecessarily antagonistic incident.

Robert Stevens: I still thought it was a relatively minor error of judgment. I urged the provost to issue an apology because clearly reasonable students, reasonable Asian students and others, were very offended. I thought she did an excellent job of issuing an apology and I assumed the matter would be over. I urged her to sit down with the Asian students and that would be the end of the matter.

George Blumenthal: Stevens made what I think was a huge, huge blunder. He intervened. As chancellor, the right move would have been to not intervene or to intervene behind the scenes. But he intervened in a very public way, and made some comments about it without necessarily knowing all of the facts. He, as I heard it, called in Peggy Musgrave and sort of read the riot act to her about what had happened at Crown College. And the upshot of it is that Peggy resigned as provost and she was a popular provost at Crown. Don Van Den Berg was beaten up something awful over this. I didn't know him very well. It wasn't my college. But he didn't have a mean bone in his body, and I suspect he didn't have a racist bone in his body. He was motivated by good things. It may have been a huge mistake—I'm not saying it wasn't a big mistake—but I don't think he was ill-motivated, and I don't think he was motivated out of fundamental racism.

Robert Stevens: I issued a statement saying that we could all learn from this and we're all capable of doing equally stupid things, or probably more stupid things. It seemed to me one of those issues that could happen in any well-run society and I assumed it would be over in a week. But it has dragged on and on and on.

George Blumenthal: It hugely pissed off the faculty at Crown College. One day I was talking to Don Osterbrock. Don was a very solid man. He's a great scientist. Down to earth. I'd never seen him emotional. I had never in the years that I'd known him heard him utter a four-letter word. I was talking to Don about something, and somehow the issue of the Asian food affair came up, and Don started cursing. And it was so unlike Don; it was so un-Don to do that. I emerged from that discussion kind of shaken. I understood. He was in Crown College, he may have had relationships, etcetera. But I also realized as soon as I left the office that Stevens was doomed. I've said this to many people: there are a lot of faculty you can piss off on the left, on the right. But you don't do that to the great silent majority, the great center. And basically the Crown College faculty were the center. I think virtually all of the faculty at that point became extremely negative about Stevens.

Julia Armstrong-Zwart: A friend's father once said to me that academic arguments are always so vicious because the stakes are so low. I don't think the stakes, ultimately, in the Asian food affair were low at all.

Robert Stevens: The director of the UCSC budget, Victor Kimura, who is himself Asian [and was born in a Japanese American internment camp during World War II], wrote a very intemperate letter.[20] I understand why he did it. But it was a tremendously unfortunate letter. I tried to distance myself from it. I couldn't order him to rescind it because of his First Amendment rights. I was advised by general counsel. I did urge him to write a letter of apology. His letter of apology did almost as much damage. It was almost as insensitive as the original letter. So that certainly dragged on.

BURSAR VAN DEN BERG, Crown College
Re: Pilipino College Night

December 12, 1988

Dear Don,

I'm certain you've received your share of criticism for how Crown College rejected Pilipino College Night last Wednesday on the basis that it would be inappropriate to serve Asian food on December 7, the anniversary of the bombing of Pearl Harbor. Let me add my criticism.

As one of the few Asian administrators on campus, particularly of Japanese descent, I have to say to you and Peggy Musgrave that I am absolutely appalled and disgusted with your cancellation of Pilipino College Night. Your actions reinforce the view that Crown College is extremely racist, a growing campus view held by people of color and by enlightened faculty, staff, students, and campus administrators.

The very notion that you would attempt "to punish" our young Pilipino students for an unfortunate act of aggression which occurred 47 years ago by the Japanese government, demonstrates not only an incredible level of bigotry, but also a total ignorance of two of the most fundamental requirements of affirmative action: the need to recognize ethnic differences and the ability to not discriminate because of those differences.

Sadly, your unwillingness to recognize and even to admit a wrongdoing is the real tragedy. You and Peggy are perfect examples of what enlightened people of all ethnic and cultural backgrounds define as "racist" and "bigoted," and are at least responsible for severely impeding in a major way the campus' ability to mount a truly effective affirmative action program. The commitment to affirmative action starts at the top levels of institutions and, unfortunately, for the faculty, staff, and students of Crown College, stops at the level of provost and bursar.

A white friend of mine visited Hiroshima recently. As she stood in front of a memorial which acknowledged the names of thousands of Japanese people who died as a result of the atomic bomb dropped by the United States, she was overcome by the devastation and carnage that took place, and was ashamed at what Americans had done over 40 years ago. As tears were streaming down her face, an elderly Japanese man walked up to her and said, "You're not responsible for what happened here, just as our Japanese children are not responsible for what happened at Pearl Harbor. We must learn to forgive and to forget."

Although I remember little of the internment camp I was born in, I recall the stories of how hard the years of relocation were on my parents. Following our return from a series of different internment camps, I remember as a young child having rocks thrown through the windows of our house and listening to racial slurs and personal threats. I remember listening helplessly as my grandmother, who was one of the people in Hiroshima at the time of the bomb, coughed herself to death from radiation poisoning. Her badly disfigured and burned body was a constant reminder to my family of the destructive capability of a nuclear bomb, so powerful that it has been used as a weapon only twice in history (by the United States against Japan's cities of Hiroshima and Nagasaki). The point here is that many people of all ethnic backgrounds and cultures have suffered.

I would prefer that you and Peggy not respond either in writing, by person, or by telephone. I'm afraid the racist rhetoric and perverted excuses you and Peggy have been spouting will only make me more angry and more upset.

Sincerely, Victor (Kimura)

Los Angeles Times: "If you read that letter you would have thought he was in the Ku Klux Klan burning crosses on people's lawns," Lombardo [the attorney for Don Van Den Berg] said. "There was a certain element out for a witch hunt, and they found him even though he wasn't the witch." The letter said that in the view of a growing number of faculty, students and administrators, Crown College was 'extremely racist'—and blamed Van den Berg and Musgrave for 'seriously impeding' affirmative action on campus.

In the aftermath, Van Den Berg received death threats and his car was painted with racial epithets. Van Den Berg took a leave of absence and Musgrave resigned, citing lack of university backing against Kimura's charges.[21]

Rosie Cabrera: A libel lawsuit was filed against Victor Kimura that focused on defamation of character. A state court of appeals ruled to dismiss the libel suit against Kimura and held that such speech was constitutional. Victor Kimura spoke out and was reprimanded for speaking out. For many staff and faculty of color, this represented a significant confrontation with the lack of cultural competency on the campus. Personally, I am indebted to Victor for his courage to take a stand and to raise this as a community issue. These events highly impacted students of color, and the overall campus community.

Julia Armstrong-Zwart: I think that it was a teachable moment which we were able to take advantage of in some minimal way—but it was a wasted opportunity to have had a much broader-based discussion on campus of how there could be such different reactions to the same small decision.

"We Are Very Out": Queer Scholarship and Activism

Tchad Sanger, Student: In 1988, when I was doing tours of campuses, I came to Santa Cruz on a campus tour. Me and my mother and my father all drove up, and we had breakfast at the Whole Earth Restaurant. It was the quintessential Santa Cruz first experience—sprouts everywhere. A *Good Times* was there, the local Santa Cruz entertainment paper. I looked through it and there were classified ads. There was an ad that said: "Bi white male seeking similar." That's when it clicked. That's me! People identify like this. I could be here and be okay. It was funny. I was sitting at the Whole Earth Restaurant with my parents. And the exhilaration and the shame, such contradictory things. I felt dirty looking at it, but I was also totally exhilarated. So that's when I decided.

The late 1980s were a very interesting political time for queer sexuality. Borders were being tested and challenged. It hadn't quite really all the way sunk in, as far as admissions saying, we have the GLBT Center. We went by there on the tour. It was mentioned, but not explained. As a seventeen- or eighteen-year-old, I kind of needed that explanation. It was on a Friday. Right at five o'clock we were going through Porter College and people were coming out of everywhere. It could have been any college at five o'clock and it would have been the same thing, but it was the last college we went through, and it was Porter at five o'clock. It was just such a live environment. That's when I decided: it's Santa Cruz and it's Porter. That's how I came here.

Jacquelyn Marie, Librarian: A young, out lesbian librarian comes to UCSC. I realize I must be far more out than I have been to be a mentor and role model to her. Finally, the library has a coterie of GLB staff and it is more comfortable for all of us. We celebrate October as GLBT month and put together a workshop, panel, and exhibit. We are very out. Whenever I teach the students how to do library research, I use GLBT examples, as well as those of race, class, disability, age, and others. I talk about subject headings for books and articles which have changed through the years to be more accepting. In the past, lesbians and gays have been treated as other, such as, "homosexuals as doctors." Now you can see subjects such as "lesbian mothers," "gay soldiers," etc.

Tchad Sanger: That time was also Queer Nation[22] and ACT UP [AIDS Coalition to Unleash Power].[23] I did get harassing notes and threats on my door. There was also rallying around it. We did have inflammatory things spray-painted or chalked on the sidewalks—"Queers Die" or "Faggots Die."

With ACT UP and Queer Nation, we had the energy, the focus, and the anger to direct our community activism. I wasn't arrested, but groups of us were arrested for kissing in the Capitola Mall. It was very powerful. We had kiss-ins up on campus because at the time it was really important to be visible. A lot of what I did back then was to be visible, to make sure that the queer portion of my life existed with honesty and integrity. It was a unique experience in time—Porter College in the late-1980s and early-1990s.

Carter Wilson: AIDS education efforts have been startlingly good at UC Santa Cruz. The Condom Co-op and those things now are in the UCSC system.[24] I was the chancellor's representative to all of those groups for a long time. My partner was HIV-positive and I made it my business to be involved in that issue. At one point, in terms of public service or community service, AIDS work was the most popular thing that UC Santa Cruz

Figure 4

Wendy Chapkis, Queer Nation action at the Santa Cruz Boardwalk

Photo by Wilton Woods

Circa 1990

students did. If you were to go and try to write a history of AIDS in the state of California, you would find that some of the biggest movers and shakers, particularly in the Latino community, began as UCSC undergraduates. I could pick out ten people now working in statewide stuff who came out of UC Santa Cruz. UCSC students started both the Needle Exchange Program in Santa Cruz County and the Needle Exchange in Monterey County.[25] A lot of that came out of community studies. Knowing that I had an interest in AIDS, they came to me. So I was faculty adviser for all of those people.

Wendy Chapkis, Student: By the late-1980s, feminist sex radicalism had run head-on into feminist anti-porn, anti-prostitution, anti-sadomasochism (SM) activism. The Bulkhead Gallery[26] was positioned as a sex-radical organization. We had some of the big names—men and women who were known nationally and regionally as members of the "perv" community coming to Santa Cruz. We were hosting them, and broadcasting them on our radio show. That caused huge consternation among anti-SM feminists in town,[27] including, most notably, Ann Simonton, who runs Media Watch. The whole thing really exploded at the end of the 1980s.

1989 was also the year of the big earthquake and that was the thing that finally caused the Bulkhead Gallery to close. Our space was red-tagged. Anyway, that was the excuse the owners gave us. They said they weren't going to evict us because of the queer stuff that went on, even though Santa Cruz didn't have an anti-discrimination ordinance yet. They knew that would be politically unpopular. But they could throw us out because the building had been red-tagged and needed retrofitting after the earthquake.

Figure 5

Queer Nation sticker

Circa 1990s

5:04 p.m., October 17, 1989: The Loma Prieta Earthquake

Frank Zwart, Architect: The earthquake was a moment that nobody living in Santa Cruz at the time is going to forget, for lots and lots of reasons. It was 5:04 p.m., October 17, 1989.

George Blumenthal: That day I was very, very lazy. It was around five o'clock or so, and I was coming back from somewhere. I went to my office and I rode the elevator up to the third floor. So I was caught in the elevator when the Loma Prieta earthquake hit.[28]

Frank Zwart: I was in my office down in Barn G and I was meeting with one of our architects, Bill Taber. I had felt earthquakes before, but this was like a big hand had taken the end of our building and was shaking it back and forth.

George Blumenthal: I was alone. The power went off, so there were no lights in the elevator. Meanwhile, the building's klaxons were klaxoning, loud horns making all kinds of noise. There I was, inside of this thing. It was like being inside of a malted milk machine when it's going. I was a ragdoll in there, being thrown against the wall.

Steve Garvin, Student: I was in my room. I was sitting at my desk. The earthquake hits, and first I think it's just kind of a little one, because we have those all the time. But then it starts to get kind of big and I start realizing, ooh, this is a big earthquake! I start to kind of stress out. I get up out of my chair and I walk over to the door. And as I get to the door, and the door slams in front of me. The earthquake shakes it shut. I start grabbing on the door and it's locked. I'm kind of locked in my room, and then I turn to my left and watch my dresser with my stereo on top of it tumble to

the ground, and all this stuff go flying everywhere. My turntable gets destroyed.

Frank Zwart: I heard some glass breaking. Bill and I looked at each other and said, "Wow! What was that?" We and everybody else hustled outside. But as we walked through our building, we didn't see a whole lot of damage. I think the glass that I'd heard was a drinking glass, or a vase, or something falling off an upper shelf. There was a little bit of disorder, but nothing catastrophic at all. So I had no real sense of the extent of the damage.

Steve Garvin: So, I work the door open, and I stumble down the hallway, and then I go downstairs, and I get to the bottom of the stairs, and at the bottom of our stairs you end up in the kitchen. I see this big jug of soy sauce come tumbling out of the cupboard and explode on the floor. Our kitchen for the next like four and a half days was covered with soy sauce because no one wanted to clean anything up.

I stumble outside. And all of my neighbors, who I did not at that time know, were standing outside with us.

George Blumenthal: Well, the good news is that I don't suffer from claustrophobia. The bad news is, I was stuck in there alone. I was terrified that the cable in the elevator would break and I'd come crashing down. I was in that elevator trying to figure out if the cable broke, whether or not I would be better off standing, jumping, lying on my back, or lying on my stomach. I eliminated lying on my stomach as a reasonable alternative, but I couldn't quite decide whether I was better off standing, or lying on my back.

Figure 6

Ford's Department Store, Watsonville; damaged in the October 17, 1989 earthquake

December 1989

Photo by Vester Dick

At a certain point, I realized that there was a phone in the elevator. So I picked up the phone and it worked. Somebody on campus, some campus operator somewhere answered the phone. I was very grateful to be in touch with another human being. I said, "What the hell happened? Was that an earthquake?" Her response was, "Where have you been?" She said to me, "Just stay on the line." There wasn't much I could do.

Frank Zwart: I went out to my car and turned on the radio. My radio was tuned to the station that was broadcasting the World Series game at Candlestick Park in San Francisco. They were playing a Budweiser commercial. I thought to myself, well, gee, if they're doing the game and it's a Budweiser commercial it can't be too bad.

George Blumenthal: Then the first aftershock hit. The first aftershock was a 6.0 earthquake. Loma Prieta was about 7.0 or 7.1. The first aftershock was a 6.0, and that's pretty hefty as well. Meanwhile, the woman gets back on the phone. She says, "So, what's your name?" I told her. She said, "Are you listed in the phone directory?" I said yeah. And she said, "Okay, hang on." I realized that this was to notify my next of kin.

Steve Garvin: There are all these power lines nearby. I kind of live in the slum of Santa Cruz. I don't live in the best area. Some of the buildings are pretty old, and people were talking about stuff falling everywhere. And the house right next to ours, the kitchen just got wasted. I mean, everything came out.

George Blumenthal: So I just waited. About forty-five minutes later, suddenly the lights came up. And the klaxons were still klaxoning. I said, what the hell. I pushed 1. The elevator went down to

1 and the doors opened. I kind of thought there would be cheering crowds and bands playing. There was *nobody* there. Everybody had left the building. So I went back in the elevator, carefully holding the door open, and told the campus operator that I was fine and they could take me off their worry list.

Frank Zwart: That night my wife and I were scheduled to have dinner with friends in one of the faculty housing units right next to Barn G in the Cardiff Terrace development. People weren't carrying cell phones in those days, or texting, or any of that kind of stuff. We had agreed to meet at Professor Gary Lease[29] and Dorothea Ditchfield's house. I just walked over because it was a hundred yards away. Gary was cooking with gas and had candles. Somebody had a battery-powered radio and we were listening to reports of the Bay Bridge collapse and fires in the Marina.

Steve Garvin: So we're sitting out in front of the house, and this guy gets in his car and turns on the radio, because all the power's gone. And we hear the emergency broadcast signal, the little ooop. That was a little scary because I was always under the impression that it was solely for nuclear war warnings. I was thinking wow, you know—for a second. But then this guy gets on and he says that a major earthquake had hit the San Francisco Bay Area. Immediately I thought it was San Francisco, and I was convinced that San Francisco was absolutely wasted because we were in Santa Cruz an hour away and it was just crushed.

Anonymous, Student: I didn't know about deaths when the quake happened. But I looked over—the Santa Cruz Hotel is on Locust and Cedar and I was able to have a pretty clear vision of the part of the Pacific Garden Mall going from, say, Gottschalk's department store down to the Santa

Cruz Coffee Roasting Company. I couldn't see in the Mall but I was looking at large amounts of dust coming off the buildings. And in fact, right over where Gottschalk's was, I remember looking and thinking there was a fire. I saw this spiral going in the air. It was dust. When I realized that it was not a fire, not smoke, but that it was actually a dust plume going eighty feet into the air, that's when I knew this was really serious. Really serious.[30]

Steve Garvin: Highway 880 collapsed, which was horrifying. Forty-two lives were lost in the earthquake when a 1.25 mile section of the Cypress section of the Nimitz Freeway (I-880) collapsed.

Quinton Skinner: I went down Lincoln towards the Nickelodeon movie theater. That was one of the buildings in the national papers when President George H.W. Bush walked by it and said, "Look what an earthquake can do." There were people sitting outside and they were yelling inside, "Is anyone in there? Is anyone trapped?" Nothing. Silence. It just—if you've ever seen a brick building reduced to a pile of bricks. If there's anyone in it they are not alive.

Frank Zwart: At some point there was a phone call to Gary's that was tracking me down. They'd pulled into place the Emergency Response Center at the UCSC Campus Fire Department. So I went up there and wound up spending most of the night there. A lot of people spent the night in tents outside, and we went around inspecting various dorms.

Steve Garvin: The night of the earthquake we were hanging out at my house. It had become a link-up point, and there were about twelve of us here. I think it was pretty much what everyone did. The

college students banded together and slept up on campus, or in various houses. There were all these mass sleep-ins and mass sleeping togethers.

Ramona Noriega, Student: I lived in an apartment complex at Family Student Housing. All the residents who were evacuated were camping out outside of the building. I was with my children and another neighbor who had come with her kids and her baby to be with us. We slept outside for the first two nights, because everybody was afraid and did not want to go back in.

Steve Garvin: I drove up to my friend's house. We call him "Condo" because he lives in condoland near UCSC. I'm driving along and at almost all the gas stations I totally smelled gas. And there was no light, which was very eerie. You could see stars, though, more stars than you ever saw, because there was no orange light blocking them. There was perfect visibility. The astronomers did real well.

So we were up at the condo and there were about twelve of us. We had a big pillow fight and fell asleep. And in the middle of the night there's another earthquake and I had a dream. I didn't wake up, but in my dream there was a huge earthquake and I was running from falling stuff.

George Blumenthal: Then I went home. Kelly, my wife, was at home. We had two kids by then. She felt the earthquake. She said she took it seriously when she started hearing glass breaking. So she grabbed the kids and ran outside, and then realized that running outside was not the right thing to do. So she ran back inside and found a doorway to stand in, or something like that.

I walked in. I said, "Hey, Kelly, I have the best excuse ever for being late for dinner." And, you know, we were okay. We lost a chimney.

Figure 7

Professor Frank Drake's office in Natural Sciences II, with earthquake
damage, October 19, 1989

Photo by Jim MacKenzie

But our immediate problem was, we had two kids in diapers. We were almost out of diapers. So the next day they opened Safeway to like five customers at a time. There was a long line. It was blocks long. So I stood in that line for many, many hours. Everybody else in line was buying water and batteries. Those were the two big commodities. I didn't care about water. I didn't care about batteries. I wanted diapers. So I bought a bunch of diapers and brought them home.

Frank Zwart: Over the next few days, we had engineers and architects coming in from other campuses, and from throughout the state, to give clearance to all of the buildings. Hazmat [hazardous materials] teams came up from UC Santa Barbara. The protocol in the laboratory buildings was to shut them down, get everybody out, and not let anybody in until skilled Environmental Health and Safety Hazmat teams had gone through to make sure there weren't any hazards resulting from spilled chemicals. First, it was the Hazmat investigation, then it was the structural analysis, and then it was all clear. That took several days, to get those all back online.

Jim Burns: Under difficult circumstances, we did our best to handle the initial round of internal and external communications. What became a much more demanding job for us during the Loma Prieta Earthquake, was working with and supporting the many local, statewide, national, and even international print and broadcast reporters who were coming to Santa Cruz in droves. Downtown Santa Cruz was in shambles, as were other areas of Santa Cruz County. President Bush came to tour the downtown, what was called the Pacific Garden Mall at the time. By virtue of our proximity to the epicenter, and the sheer scale of the destruction and the number of deaths that occurred here, Santa Cruz was a magnet for the media.

But also, we had earthquake experts on our faculty. We had seismologists who could weigh in, and who provided important expertise in the days, weeks, and months of coverage that followed that quake. A crew from Japan that had flown into San Francisco from Tokyo, helicoptered down from San Francisco, and landed in the Great Meadow to cover the story, to interview our scientists, and to get our B roll of the destruction. The quake occurred at a time when the media had more resources to cover a story of that magnitude. Everybody who covered science was seemingly coming here to cover the quake, or at least everybody who covered earth sciences. Obviously, for many reasons, it was a big deal in campus history.

Frank Zwart: I remember a series of meetings at the conference room in the fire station where all of this stuff was being coordinated. I remember some people saying, "Oh boy, it's a good thing it wasn't any worse. We really would have been in chaos." But the simple fact is that you can't write a script to react to something like that. It was really a matter of improvisation. And what really got us through, is that because the campus was a relatively small campus community, people knew who could do what, and called on them. They did it. The campus didn't suffer very much damage. But Natural Sciences II was badly damaged.

George Blumenthal: Nat Sci II became uninhabitable. We now know that Nat Sci II came within seconds of completely collapsing.

Frank Zwart: In the aftermath of the Loma Prieta Earthquake, we had a protocol for going around and inspecting buildings. We closed off all of the buildings on Science Hill and were, as we inspected them, opening them back up for use. And as we looked in, there were areas of Natural Sciences II where there was a lot of glass on the ground floor. As we looked inside, there was a little bit of concrete on the floor, not very much. My first thought was, well, that doesn't look too bad. The quantity under each column was probably about half or less the size of a deck of cards. It was a very small amount of concrete.

But as we went through the building, we saw that where the concrete had fallen off was absolutely critical.

George Blumenthal: Nat Sci II became the poster child of how not to build a building in earthquake country. It was exacerbated by the fact that Nat Sci II was a very long, thin building and the axis of the earthquake, or the motion of the earthquake, was perpendicular to the building. So it was the worst possible orientation. The reason it was such a bad building is that it was concrete, and the concrete pillars supported concrete floors, but the concrete floors were just laid on the concrete pillars. During the earthquake, they shook back and forth. Concrete on concrete doesn't do well. There were huge rocks that fell off those pillars, where the floors connected to the pillars. Rocks of concrete. I think I even saved one. Somewhere I have one of those big chunks. I saved it as a souvenir.

Frank Zwart: The structure of the building is pre-cast [concrete] T-beams. These are long beams that are built in a factory, brought here on a truck and then erected. They were done in such a way that they would form the structural element plus the floor. So if you put a beam in, that created the floor surface of the floor above. And they sat on little shelves on, again, prefabricated columns. So they would have erected the columns, and at each floor level, or at each beam level there would be this little shelf. And the building had moved in such a way that the beams started rocking and spalled off some of the concrete from the shelf. So what might have been designed as a four or

five-inch bearing area had been reduced in some cases to two or three inches. Uh-oh. Engineer Bob Wildman said, "Keep that building closed until I get back to the office and give this some thought."

George Blumenthal: The building was uninhabitable. They wouldn't let us back in for literally weeks. They propped it up. They brought in people with chainsaws and chainsawed holes in the walls throughout the building. And they brought in these humongous four-by-four chunks of wood, which they pounded in place to prop up the floors. They did that in every office throughout the building. So they basically destroyed all the walls to put in those four-by-fours.

Frank Zwart: The engineers Wildman and Morris eventually came up with a scheme that allowed us to shore the building with heavy timbers and then re-open it. But all that would do would be to strengthen the building in a vertical way. Both earthquake loads (seismic loads) and wind loads are horizontal loads. Wildman and Morris started looking at ways to introduce lateral resistance. We got through it and I think the building was improved as a result of it.

George Blumenthal: They finally said we could go back into our offices for no more than twenty minutes to get material if we signed a waiver. I remember, I just didn't know what to do. So I called my wife, Kelly, who's after all a lawyer. I said, "What the hell should I do? With these waivers of liability, I'm saying the university won't be liable if a building falls on my head." And she said, "Don't worry about it, just sign it." She said, "Those waivers are not worth their weight in paper. They're not worth anything."

So I signed the waiver, went back in my office, and discovered that my office was flooded, because we had a problem with the roof—and it

Figure 8

McHenry Library stacks earthquake damage, October 19, 1989

Photo by Jim MacKenzie

had rained since then. Water was everywhere. It was awful, a complete wreck. Every book was off my shelves. My computer was sopping wet. I got what I could quickly salvage—I was mostly interested in my notes—and got out of there.

Frank Zwart: In addition to the damage at Natural Sciences II there was some concrete spalling [peeling or flaking] and concerns at some of the residence halls over at Stevenson. There was some pounding of concrete building parts at what was then the Applied Sciences Building. But given that we were only eight or ten miles from the epicenter, we did remarkably well. The biggest damage that I saw was to contents and furnishings. Some of the photographs of the shelving at McHenry Library where it buckled were quite frightening. There were photographs of some of the faculty offices in Kerr Hall, where pretty flimsy shelving had been attached to the wall and it came down in a heap. I think one of the most serious injuries was in a lecture hall in Kresge College where a ceiling-mounted light fixture came down and hit somebody in the wrist.

But all in all, the campus did remarkably well. It was a real tribute to the skill of the engineers who designed the buildings in the first place. And the campus had taken seismic safety quite seriously and had completed a series of retrofit projects.

Robert Stevens: I thought this campus handled the earthquake excellently. We could have done some things better, but we did have an emergency plan. It did work. We fed the students. We had six, seven million dollars worth of damage. But we closed for a minimum length of time, three or four days. It was altogether very impressive.

Frank Zwart: And we were fortunate because, while our sinkhole-ridden karst geology is awful, our soils are very good. We have very stiff soils.

We didn't suffer the kind of damage that downtown Santa Cruz had. Downtown Santa Cruz is on an old riverbed, and the unreinforced masonry buildings were subjected to shaking of low frequency, high amplitude. They moved slowly, but moved a long way. That led to more damage than high frequency, low amplitude, here where we had good stiff soils to build on. We had qualified engineers doing the work. Our inspectors did a good job of making sure things were built as designed. So we came through it pretty well.

Robert Stevens: The campus police we lent to the city because we didn't need them. We cooperated well with the city. My goal was not to make any demands on the city at all. So we didn't use their fire services; we didn't use their police; we tried to handle everything ourselves. I made it clear to the mayor that we would help in any way we could. As soon as it was over, when the mayor did eventually start asking for things, we lent them our cars—they needed city cars. When they started a redevelopment program, we lent them staff to run that program. Several months after the earthquake, we had a mortgage program which would help them redevelop the city. We certainly intended, as I tried in all things, to be good citizens.

Frank Zwart: In the immediate aftermath of the earthquake, the campus was seen by the community as a benefit. The quake came at the end of a whole period of anti-university growth, and oh, "we hate them," and so on. And in fact, afterwards, Jim Pepper, the environmental studies professor, put together a series of public sessions. He called on his resources at Berkeley's College of Environmental Design and so on to come down and talk about rebuilding after earthquakes. It was a real impetus to help the city and the county get back up and going again. That wouldn't have happened without the university here.

Michael Cowan: The rebuilding of downtown Santa Cruz after the earthquake in 1989 turned out to be significant for the campus. Among the things that it did was to highlight the university's more stabilizing presence in the economic recovery—in terms of money that people had to shop with, in terms of housing and lots of other things. At the same time, the rebuilding of the downtown made it a much more vibrant and attractive place, particularly for UCSC students. That probably added to the campus's attractiveness. Of course, the students themselves particularly were contributing to the liveliness of the downtown. And although there were ongoing town-gown tensions—that's a constant theme—it was a point where there was not only a certain amount of collaboration, but a certain amount of mutual benefit that came out of what was a very traumatic period.

Figure 9

Collapsed section of Struve Slough bridge, Highway 1, Watsonville, December 1989

Photo by Vester Dick

Figure 10

View of façades of Roberts, Shockley's Jewelry, and Lilly Marlene's on Pacific Avenue in Santa Cruz after the Loma Prieta Earthquake, October 17, 1989

Photo by Vester Dick

Endnotes

1. Hardy Frye worked as an organizer with the Student Nonviolent Coordinating Committee (SNCC) and was one of over a thousand students who were part of the 1964 Summer Voter Registration Project in Mississippi. He often collaborated with Dr. Martin Luther King and his organization, the Southern Christian Leadership Conference (SCLC). Frye taught sociology at UCSC from 1978 to 1999. His research and publications have dealt with issues of politics and power in African American and urban communities.

2. Griswold v. Connecticut, 381 US 479 (1965).

3. Both Robert Sinsheimer and Robert Stevens came from the private sector of higher education and had little knowledge of UCSC or the University of California system when they arrived. Stevens arrived in the fall of 1987 and served until July of 1991.

4. By "supporting the colleges" Gardner meant supporting UCSC in retaining a college system, not extra financial support.

5. See *The Colleges at UC Santa Cruz*, 1988, and Bassett, 3.

6. Bassett, 3.

7. Thomas (Tom) Pettigrew joined the psychology board in 1979 and retired in 1994. Pettigrew has been at the forefront of studies of racial prejudice for more than five decades. In 2009, Pettigrew won the University of California's Constantine Panunzio Distinguished Emeriti Award for research accomplishments since retirement.

8. Regents of the University of California vs. Bakke: June 28, 1978. In this case, the US Supreme Court found that the UC Davis Medical School acted illegally by disallowing a white applicant, Allan Bakke, from competing for a set number of places reserved for minority applicants. The court, however, validated the concept of affirmative action and stipulated that admissions policies could include race as one of the criteria for evaluating applicants. Also see: Sinsheimer, Robert., Cota-Robles, Eugene Henry, Tilley, David C., Blake, J. Herman., Randolph, Richard R., Niebanck, Paul L., Strong, Walter L., Morrison, Gary., Vasconcelles, John., and Torres, Art. [Bakke Case Forums, University of California, Santa Cruz], 2004. Available in Special Collections, UCSC Library.

9. Lucille Clifton was a poet, writer, and educator, Poet Laureate of Maryland and a finalist twice for the Pulitzer Prize for Poetry. Clifton traced her family's roots to the West

African Kingdom of Dahomey, now the Republic of Benin. From 1985 to 1989, Clifton was a professor of literature and creative writing at UCSC. She died in 2010.

10. Gloria Anzaldúa was an internationally renowned author, cultural theorist, and feminist philosopher. She earned her PhD in literature at UCSC and was a lecturer in women's studies, where taught the courses *Autohistorias* and *Women of Color in the United States*, before her death from diabetes in 2004. Anzaldúa drew inspiration from altars she created in her home near Lighthouse Point in Santa Cruz; her *altares* are now archived in McHenry Library's Special Collections. See: http://pdf.oac.cdlib.org/pdf/ucsc/spcoll/ms308.pdf. Her literary archive is housed at the Benson Latin American Library at the University of Texas, Austin. A study room in McHenry Library is also named in her honor.

11. Grace Paley was a short-story writer and social activist. Paley was among the first American writers to explore the daily lives of women—mostly secular Jewish New Yorkers.

12. Paula Gunn Allen was a Laguna Pueblo and Lebanese American lesbian poet, novelist, and nonfiction writer.

13. For more than forty years, the Chicano/a and Latino/a commencement has celebrated the academic and cultural successes of graduating seniors with live music, guest speakers, and refreshments.

14. Norma Klahn joined UCSC's literature department in 1989 and was a fellow of Merrill College. Her research and publications focus on the literatures and cultures of Latin America and Mexico and on Chicana/o and Latina/o expressions from a cross-border perspective.

15. The Research Center for the Americas (RCA)—previously the Chicano Latino Research Center (CLRC)—was founded in 1992 by Pedro Castillo and Norma Klahn, faculty members in the history and literature departments with ties to (what was then) the program in Latin American studies. The RCA's mission is to support Latin American, Latino, and migration studies at UCSC, drawing from the social sciences, humanities, and arts to explore the diversity of the Americas, with a focus on the mobility of people, ideas, and commodities. See the archive (UA 120) at UCSC Library Special Collections at: http://pdf.oac.cdlib.org/pdf/ucsc/uarc/UA120.pdf.

16. For statistics on the demographics of UCSC students see the Institutional Research Office's website: https://iraps.ucsc.edu/student-statistics/all-students.html These online statistics

only date back to 1994. The intrepid researcher can obtain figures from earlier eras at UCSC Special Collections.

17. "The Spanish for Spanish Speakers Program was developed by faculty and students who believe that there should be no reason for native, near-native, or comfortable speakers of Spanish to study Spanish as if it were a foreign language. The program also recognizes the language learning needs of those students who, although raised in Spanish-speaking communities or households, are not yet proficient in spoken Spanish. We therefore offer courses in beginning, intermediate, and advanced Spanish courses which take into account the direct and indirect experiences and influences of being raised in Spanish-speaking environments." This statement is from the 1990-91 *UCSC General Catalog*. The Spanish for Spanish Speakers Program continues today.

18. Pearl Harbor, a US naval base near Honolulu, Hawaii, was the scene of a devastating surprise attack by Japanese forces on December 7, 1941.

19. Peggy Musgrave joined the economics board at UCSC in 1979.

20. Victor Kimura was one of UCSC's first staff members, starting work in 1964 as a clerk at McHenry Library, and retiring as UCSC's budget director.

21. Philip Hager, "Appeals Court Voids College Official's Libel Suit Over Racism Charge: Constitution: An open letter accusing the man of being a bigot is an expression of opinion, justices rule." *Los Angeles Times*, June 1, 1991.

22. According to queer historian Susan Stryker, "Queer Nation erupted into being in the summer of 1990, when militant AIDS activists at New York's Gay Pride parade passed out to the assembled crowd a manifesto. Within days, Queer Nation chapters had sprung up in San Francisco and other major cities. Described by activist scholars Allan Bérubé and Jeffrey Escoffier as the first 'retro-future/postmodern' activist group to address gay, lesbian, bisexual, and transgender concerns, the short-lived organization (lasting only two years) made a lasting impact on sexual identity politics in the United States. To a significant degree, the relative frequency and acceptability of GLBTQ representation in mass culture in the1990s and early twenty-first century can be dated to the emergence of Queer Nation." See: http://www.glbtqarchive.com/ssh/queer_nation_S.pdf.

23. ACT UP [AIDS Coalition to Unleash Power] is an international organization founded in the US in 1987 to bring attention to the AIDS epidemic.

24. The Condom Co-op was founded at UCSC in 1985.

25. Needle and syringe programs (NSPs) are a type of harm reduction initiative that provide clean needles and syringes to people who inject drugs to reduce transmission of HIV and other blood borne viruses such as hepatitis B and C.

26. Bulkhead Gallery was an art and performance space located on Bulkhead Street in downtown Santa Cruz during the 1980s. It was founded by UCSC alumna and lecturer Wendy Chapkis and other sex radicals.

27. For more on this controversy see: Reti, Irene, Pat Parker, Kathy Miriam, Anna Livia, Jamie Lee Evans, Sharon Lim-Hing, and D. A. Clarke. 1993. *Unleashing Feminism: Critiquing Lesbian Sadomasochism in the Gay Nineties.* (Santa Cruz, CA (HerBooks, 1993). (Full disclosure: Irene Reti is also one of the editors and the publisher of this title, but *Unleashing Feminism* was not a UCSC publication.) For a contrasting perspective see Samois, *ed. Coming to Power: Writing and Graphics on Lesbian S/M* (Alyson Books, 1982).

28. On October 17, 1989, at 5:04 p.m. a 7.1 magnitude earthquake on the San Andreas Fault shook the Central Coast of California and lasted for fifteen seconds. The quake's epicenter lay somewhat near Loma Prieta Peak in the Santa Cruz Mountains, about ten miles northeast of the city of Santa Cruz, California. This earthquake killed sixty-three people, injured 3,757 others, and caused an estimated six billion dollars in property damage. It was the largest earthquake to occur on the San Andreas fault since the great San Francisco earthquake in April 1906.

29. Gary Lease was a professor in history of consciousness. He came to UCSC in 1973 and served as the chairperson of a number of different departments, including religious studies, environmental studies, the language program, as well as dean of humanities, and provost of Kresge College. He died in 2008.

30. This narrator chose anonymity due to the sensitive and confidential nature of the material discussed in the oral history, which included issues of substance abuse.

Illustrations

Figure 1. Chancellor Robert Stevens. Photo by Don Fukuda. Courtesy Special Collections, University Library, University of California, Santa Cruz. UA 50: UCSC Photography Services: ua0050_neg_0598-7684_22.tif.

Figure 2. Gloria Anzaldúa. 1980s. Photo by Annie Valva.

Figure 3. Bridging Borders Poster. 1995. Courtesy Special Collections, University Library, University of California, Santa Cruz. UA 120: Research Center for the Americas Records: ua120_007_0001.

Figure 4. Wendy Chapkis, Queer Nation action at the Santa Cruz Boardwalk. Photo by Wilton Woods. Circa 1990. Courtesy Special Collections, University Library, University of California Santa Cruz. UA 27: Out in the Redwoods Collection.

Figure 5. Queer Nation Sticker. Late 1990s. Courtesy Special Collections, University Library, University of California, Santa Cruz. UA 27: Out in the Redwoods Collection.

Figure 6. Ford's Department Store, Watsonville, damaged in the October 17 earthquake. December 1989. Courtesy Special Collections, University Library, University of California, Santa Cruz. Photo by Vester Dick: VD1.16.19.

Figure 7. Loma Prieta Earthquake: Professor Frank Drake's office in Natural Sciences II, with earthquake damage, October 19, 1989. Photo by Jim MacKenzie. Courtesy Special Collections, University Library, University of California, Santa Cruz. UA 128: Public Information Office Records: ua0128_sld_b15p21s16.

Figure 8. McHenry Library stacks earthquake damage, October 19, 1989. Photo by Jim MacKenzie. Courtesy Special Collections, University Library, University of California, Santa Cruz. UA 128: Public Information Office Records: ua0128_sld_b15p22s11.tiff.

Figure 9. Collapsed section of Struve Slough Bridge, Highway One, Watsonville, December 1989. Photo by Vester Dick. Courtesy Special Collections, University Library, University of California, Santa Cruz: vd1_16_12.tif.

Figure 10. View of façades of Roberts, Shockley's Jewelry, and Lilly Marlene's on Pacific Avenue in Santa Cruz after the Loma Prieta Earthquake. October 17, 1989. Courtesy Special Collections, University Library, University of California, Santa Cruz. Photo by Vester Dick: VD1.05.26.

Chapter 24

Growing Pains

A "Maturing" Campus Considers Its Direction

We are something of the elephant in the tent. There is no doubt that we will trample the grass from time to time.

—Robert Stevens

Budget Quakes:
Growth, Conflict, and Compromise in the Early Nineties

Frank Zwart: Shortly after the earthquake there was an economic setback, a slowdown.

Michael Cowan: The 1990s was the decade where the campus finally matured, or was seen to mature. The decade got off to a pretty rocky start.

Robert Stevens: We have had three budget cuts during a twelve-month period. There was a budget cut which specifically targeted research and administration and public services. Then there was the gigantic cut where we had 295 million dollars less than we thought we were going to get. There will be another cut of probably, in total, some 17 million dollars, when the budget is finally settled. It's been an enormously difficult year.

We had a series of budget hearings. Each of the vice chancellors and deans was asked to prioritize his interests, and say how he or she would handle cuts. The effects of the cuts are that the faculty are going to have to do more teaching with the same resources. The staff are going to have to do more work with the same resources. And nobody's going to get a pay increase. There will be gradual layoffs.

Lan Dyson, University Librarian: Over time, I came to realize something that wasn't stated when I got here, and that is that bad budget times run through California every ten years, like clockwork. Committees would be formed. Public hand-wringing would be done in front of the senate library committee, et cetera, et cetera. So you get through that, and then you come out the other side, and then you continue to build.

Robert Stevens: I do worry very much about the increase of 40 percent in tuition. The University of California, as a whole, has taken a position that there is no real impact on students because we've increased the amount of student aid. But there are enormous psychological barriers as you raise tuition. I worry that the increase will have a very real impact on those groups that we should be seeking to attract. At a time when we are trying in terms of admissions to make this a much more diverse campus, I worry a great deal when tuition is raised that amount.[1]

Henry Mello, California State Senator: I'm all in favor of providing a college education and providing access. I fought against the tuition increases. You have to have economic access and not price people out of it. Education is getting more and more expensive.

Todd Newberry: Whether it's the budget, or for whatever reasons, I think we're pulling in, losing our imagination, losing our willingness to push our best students hard. Education is, in a way, a very inefficient enterprise; that's why it's a non-profit institution, after all. And then, the budget shrinking. People try to streamline it. You can't streamline it. It's like pregnancy—teaching takes time. We ruin it if we rush it. Now we have huge classes where you don't get to know anybody. The sea of faces. You're administering a class, not teaching students.

Robert Stevens: The goals now attributed to this place when it began are not the goals that were then held by Dean McHenry and others, but a sort of rewriting of history about this being an undergraduate campus. If that had been the case it should have belonged in the state college system rather than in the University of California, if it was really intended to be an undergraduate place in the University of California. But of course it wasn't. The intention was that ten years out,

15 percent of the students would be graduate students and 20 percent of them would be professional students, so it's perfectly logical that the same standard was applied to us as the rest of the UC campuses. But because this original goal was never met, UCSC received short shrift from the University of California because of its heavy undergraduate orientation. So UCSC really needs to develop some more graduate programs, but more importantly, good professional schools. That doesn't mean it can't have a wonderful undergraduate program.

Santa Cruz Sentinel: Love, hate. Green, red. Yes, no. Grow, halt. The campus community, like the ambivalent town community, seems to suffer schizophrenia on university growth.[2]

Robert Stevens: When I arrived, the very real concern of the UC President's office, and especially perhaps of the regents, was what appeared to be the appalling relations between the city and the county on the one hand, and the university on the other. The university was regarded as high handed because it relied on its constitutional exemption.[3] But the chief difficulty was that the university wanted to grow, and the city and county did not want it to. Old-line conservatives didn't like having a university here, at least as the university had turned out. They regarded it as a university that was populated by dangerous left-wingers, people who essentially, under the guise of the environment, espoused a no-growth policy.

Clearly, the growth of the university had led to all sorts of problems. It did lead to problems of students displacing people in housing; the traffic had a deleterious effect on the Westside. The university was perceived as not being interested in the genuine impacts of growth.

The university having been put here, the question was: how does one ameliorate this without giving up the needs of the state? There are obligations that we have to the state. We are a rapidly growing state. One doesn't always realize that, sitting here in Santa Cruz, but we are a state that has grown by 23 percent in a ten-year period. We grow by almost a million people a year, and not all of them can be in Los Angeles. If the University of California is to fulfill its educational responsibilities and retain its political support, it has to grow, too. There are a limited number of places it can grow. Obviously in an ideal world one would have more campuses. But this had been planned originally as a campus of 27,500, and clearly this campus has to take its responsibility seriously, and to grow.[4]

Henry Mello: Chancellor Robert Stevens let me know how important it was to get started on the Music Building.

Robert Stevens: Two controversial things, recently, have been Meyer Drive[5] and the siting of the Music Building.[6] Meyer Drive has been in each Long Range Development Plan—1963, 1972, 1979—Meyer Drive, and the outer ring road has been there. It was part of the original intention of the campus that we would have this outer ring road, which would make it a pedestrian-friendly campus. If we shouldn't be doing it, then it shouldn't have been in the Long Range Development Plan, and we should have had a different plan for the campus.

Now, like everyone else I value the meadow. In fact, I probably am a more regular user of the meadow than many of the people who are most articulate about it. It is a beautiful, beautiful spot. That's one of the reasons why I recommended in the Long Range Development Plan, and the regents accepted it, closing Hagar Drive so that we would preserve more of the meadow.

I suspected we'd have a similar problem in terms of the siting of the music facilities. We had a series of public meetings for what is called the community access area, which is between University House and the Student Center. The idea there is that this will be the place where we reach out to the community with the music facilities—performing arts and those other things.

Henry Mello: Of course, I was also so happy to see the music center there. I was chairman of the state legislature's joint committee on the arts, and music has always been one of my highest priorities. I felt this would be a tremendous resource for the university.

Robert Stevens: So I set about to try and make us good citizens—in other words, to take the concerns of the responsible citizen seriously without being intimidated by the politicians who want to stop all growth. That's a very difficult line to draw.

As soon as I arrived on campus, there was an effort to stop the building of College Eight, and we had a long piece of litigation. The first few months here were really quite ugly in dealing with both the city and the county. It was an effort, I think, by the city and county politicians, especially Gary Patton, to prevent any growth in the university. It was an effort to intimidate the campus. It was an effort to prevent the Long Range Development Plan from going through. It was entirely illogical, because the university had made a commitment to try to accommodate more students, ultimately with a goal of 70 percent undergraduate and 30 percent graduate students, and to try to stop the building of College Eight was just irrational.

Bill Domhoff: I started a town-gown forum, where I met with former Santa Cruz mayor Norm Lezin. He brought a guy from town and I brought a guy from the campus. We were up to

Figure 1

Meyer Drive protest flyer, 1990

Figure 2

Great Meadow, 2016

Photo by Irene Reti

twenty-some people meeting, and we found we had a lot of agreements. I wrote an article in the *Santa Cruz Sentinel* talking about some of these things, and campus growth, and how it could be done if we put a lot of housing on the campus, which, of course, got me in trouble with the progressives. I said in the newspaper—relating to UCSC: "We'll grow, but we'll grow on campus." This really annoyed Gary Patton. They wanted to deny us every kind of water and timber permit. So even when we started to build housing, we needed a timber permit. And Peter Scott in physics, and Gary Patton—they were all fighting our timber permit even though we had kind of cut this deal. I was really annoyed with them.

Robert Stevens: We had a hearing before the judge in chambers. Mardi Wormhoudt represented the city, together with the city attorney. Mardi was very aggressive and unpleasant towards the university, but we eventually came to a sensible compromise, which was that College Eight would go through, but we would have an annual public meeting to discuss the university's growth.

What I really was striving to do was to have the university pay its fair share of infrastructure developments. Working with people on campus, I concluded that a university of 15,000 probably met all three needs: the needs of the state, the needs of the university, and the needs of the community. It seemed to me that if we paid our fair share of infrastructure we could support a university of 15,000 in this town and we certainly needed 15,000 in order to be a serious university. Certainly, the state needed at least 15,000 students here.[7]

Henry Mello: I said, I want to know how much money UCSC contributed to the local economy because every dollar will circulate seven or eight times in a community, as much as ten times. The

university gave the figure of all the salaries that are paid out. Salaries were something like seventy or eighty million. Then the goods and services purchased in Santa Cruz was a big number as well. And with other supplies and things that they purchased. UCSC's influence was about two or three hundred million a year.

Robert Stevens: I spent a disproportionate amount of my time during these first two years trying to make certain that we developed reasonable relations with the city and to try and convince the moderates. I knew I would never convince the more extreme groups that this was an appropriate way to go. This was a campaign to convince people that the university wasn't a big, bad wolf.

Getting the university to agree that we would be prepared to pay our fair share was an enormous battle. That had never been done, not only by anybody in the university, but by any state agency. There were a lot of negotiations with University Hall, and eventually President Gardner came out in favor of it. Some of my fellow chancellors were annoyed with me for having done it, because it put them in a more difficult position, but it was the right way to go, quite honestly. I'm very glad that David Gardner showed the statesmanship to support it. Trying to get the faculty to be supportive of 15,000 was not easy. There were a handful of faculty who didn't want any growth. But there were also a quite vocal group of faculty who didn't want any limits at all.[8]

The most difficult problem was dealing with the city and county. I think, in different ways, Supervisor Gary Patton, and Santa Cruz City Council members Mardi Wormhoudt and John Laird, all were interested in bringing the university to its knees.

Bill Domhoff: I thought this was really crazy. And then-Santa Cruz County supervisor Fred Keeley, he looked like he was going to go along with the anti-growth contingent. He had come up to talk at Stevenson College, and boy, did Tom Pettigrew and some others tell him what they thought. There's ways that progressives can sometimes get a little narrow. We have to grow this university, not for the sake of the downtown, but for the sake of students.

Robert Stevens: I was perfectly willing to be reasonable and to make certain the university behaved as a very responsible citizen. I was obviously not prepared to let the politicians control the university. I'd have to say that the work by State Senator Henry Mello and Assemblyman Sam Farr was very important. They came in and told the local politicians that I had gone further than I ought to have. They said I'd made a wonderful offer. They, in a sense, forced Mardi and John and Gary to back off and to let the university grow to 15,000, in exchange for getting university support for infrastructure costs.

San Jose Mercury News: A grudging peace appears to have broken out between Santa Cruz and UCSC in the war over campus growth. In a tentative agreement described as unprecedented, the city and the county have decided to accept university promises to share the cost of improving water facilities, sewers, and roads that will become overloaded as the campus grows from its enrollment of 9200 students to 15,000 by the turn of the century. The agreement was hammered out in meetings between city and county leaders on one side, and University of California, Santa Cruz officials on the other—with state Senator Henry Mello, D-Watsonville, and Assemblyman Sam Farr, D-Carmel, as mediators in the middle."[9]

Henry Mello: We did reach an agreement with the city of Santa Cruz to cap UCSC's growth at 15,000 [for the 1988 Long Range Development Plan which would guide campus growth until 2005]. I was trying to help negotiate that agreement.

I stressed several points. Number one, I stressed education. I said you can't deny people an education. I mean, it would be a shame if you lived in Santa Cruz, and a block away is the university and you can't attend it, even though you might have the fiscal means to attend it and the grades, because of some stated cap that says no, you have to stop growing now. It would hinder people's education. There're enough hindrances already.

Robert Stevens: So, in the spring of 1989, we took this agreement to the regents, who approved, in principle, a cap of 15,000, and that we would pay our fair share of an enumerated list of infrastructure costs. That certainly hasn't solved all the problems. But after that, it really distinguished between the no-growth people who would oppose the university whatever they did, and reasonable people in town who felt the university at least tried to behave honorably and tried to pay its fair share. I think we have had more support in town and in the county since then, and certainly relations are very much better. People understand the university is here to stay. At the same time, they understand the university is serious about being a good citizen. We are something of the elephant in the tent. There is no doubt that we will trample the grass from time to time.

Henry Mello: UCSC wanted to be a good neighbor, while still holding out for what they are constitutionally entitled to. That was their position. I think both sides came out okay. The city was happy. They felt, well, for the long term, we are looking at 15,000 students. But when we reach 15,000, we can sit down again and agree to raise it to 20,000. Fifteen thousand is a cap that was set by both sides, but legally it's an agreement between both sides as of that date, projecting what their growth is going to be. There were attorneys involved too. If UCSC wanted to increase that number, I think the university would have to say, "Well, we're up to our max now. We're at 15,000 and we're just bursting at the seams. People are applying and we're turning down people who really need an education. We've built UC Merced and it's filling up fast. We'd like to sit down and talk about another increment in growth, and share our plans with you, and show you what our needs are." Reasonable people would have to look at that. I think for them to lift the cap, the university would have to make a gesture of showing that there would be sufficient student housing available and other resources, so that it doesn't upset the balance in the community, cause rent increases for everybody in Santa Cruz and nearby areas, and be a drain on very limited resources.

Figure 3

Burrowing Owl in the
Great Meadow, 2018

Photo by Lee Jaffe

THE LONG RANGE DESTRUCTION PLAN

UCSC's new Long Range Development Plan calls for destroying 120 acres of beautiful redwood, chaparral, and mixed evergreen forests in the Upper Campus, home to hundreds of remarkable plant and animal species. Impacts to these sensitive habitats would extend far beyond the developed acreage, as sediment and polluted run-off are flushed in to creeks & caves, wildlife corridors are disrupted and natural water systems are impeded by concrete and pavement.

Alternatives exist. Learn more, and fight for the forest!

LONG RANGE RESISTANCE
lrdpresistance.org

Figure 4

Flyer protesting Long Range Development Plan, late 1980s

"Ungovernable": Robert Stevens Resigns

Robert Stevens: I have spent thirty years in the private or independent sector of higher education, and it was much more difficult to integrate myself into the public sector, where there is less of a sense of mission. That's perhaps not a very tactful way of putting it, or a very accurate way of putting it, but there are not the same shared goals you have in the private sector. I found that very frustrating. I probably didn't handle it very well. This is a campus where there are perhaps a disproportionate number of people who are still fighting their fathers as they reach their fifties. I'm not certain I handled them well. I suffer fools less gladly than I did a few years ago.

George Blumenthal: The first time I saw Robert Stevens, he was giving a speech to the Academic Senate. He was a very articulate speaker. Of course, having a British accent and speaking to the senate is not a bad thing. But just as I used to joke that you could fall asleep between the words of Bob Sinsheimer's speeches, Stevens was a complete contrast. So I was pleased with the appointment and how things were going.

But it went to hell really fast.

Bill Domhoff: When they asked to me to be senate chair in the early 1990s, I said, "Okay." The reason they asked me was that I had not been in any arguments with anybody, or had any disagreements with the chancellor. He was in a fix. He didn't fit. He was a British guy that didn't know the system. Furthermore, he'd been the president of a small college, Haverford. That's quite a difference from UC. He didn't understand that when some biologist in blue jeans and no tie walked into his office and said, "We ought to do X and Y," that he was talking to one of the most productive biologists in

the country. He had no sense of what his faculty was really like.

Robert Stevens: One of the problems that I inherited was that there was really no administration on this campus, in the accepted sense of a major university. The structure had been developed by Dean McHenry, who ran the campus out of his back pocket. There was no effective central administration. It was essentially Bob Sinsheimer and Wendell Brase,[10] who is extremely effective and sensible, who was a kind of executive vice chancellor. You can't run a university that way when you have 10,000 students.

Julia Armstrong-Zwart: Robert Stevens was fun to be around, but I think that he was temperamentally unsuited to be a chancellor at a public university. He wasn't prepared to deal with the kind of empowered faculty we have within the University of California, which is somewhat unique. The faculty senate has delegated powers, which certainly isn't true at private schools, and that are unique in higher education. He also had the misfortune to have a couple of crises arise—the "Asian Food Affair," for example—that he could have handled better and differently.

Michael Tanner, in his capacity as academic and then executive vice chancellor,[11] gave a stability that I think enabled Chancellor Stevens to last for an additional two years. But things with the faculty were getting out of hand.

George Blumenthal: The controversy over the Asian Food Affair didn't just go away. Stevens never recovered from that. When I was at Harvard on sabbatical years later, somehow the topic came up. I was with a bunch of people at Harvard and I was describing this event. They thought I was joking. They couldn't believe that this was going to lead to one of the big campus controversies of our time.

I held Stevens in higher regard than most faculty. I think he made a huge mistake on the "Asian food affair." It basically undermined his entire chancellorship. But in talking to him, and at least in my interactions with him, I believed he was a well-meaning person, and that he brought some skills to bear on the job of chancellor. So I was inclined to be more supportive and forgiving than many of my colleagues were.

On the other hand, I also recognize you can't be a chancellor of a campus if people don't support you. His entire tenure was in turmoil. I went off to Harvard on sabbatical for a year. During that year at Harvard, it was announced that Robert Stevens was stepping down.

Bill Domhoff: He was up for evaluation, and he was not well liked on the campus, and certainly not by the people who had always attacked authority figures, who had a history of it by then—I knew it well. I thought, if they're in on it, they're mongooses. They're going to kill that authority figure, which they had done to others.

I was at a distance from all this. They wanted me as somebody neutral to be faculty senate chair while he was going to be evaluated.

Julia Armstrong-Zwart: Midway through Chancellor Stevens' fourth year, things were getting worse and worse with the faculty. Dean of Humanities Gary Lease and I, and Stephanie Hauk, Special Assistant to the Chancellor, Community Relations travelled up to UCOP. Actually, Chancellor Stevens had arranged for us to meet with UC President David Gardner. I think at that point he wanted out. The three of us met with David Gardner. Gary and I—Stephanie didn't say much—but Gary and I, both of whom

were equally garrulous, were pretty honest about what the situation was.

David Gardner got angry. He didn't want to hear it. He had appointed Chancellor Stevens. He was a man who didn't normally swear, but he said, "Dammit, I can shut that campus down. I can park it"—in effect, saying, you better go back and shake people up. Gary and I said, "That's not going to solve the problem." Basically, things had come to a point where Chancellor Stevens really was ineffective. He couldn't function anymore.

Robert Stevens: I had told David Gardner when I came that I wouldn't stay beyond six years. I would do five or six years. I am now fifty-eight and I have done a little over four years. I actually offered to do four and a half, if he wanted to have a national search. So I am cutting it a little bit short on the time.

I have to confess, I am feeling tired. I'm now in my sixteenth year of trying to run a university. I know that time is running out on me. I feel I have one very different job left in me, so I need to make a move. I have a stunningly attractive offer. I'd been asked if I would be interested in joining this law firm several years ago and I said no. Actually, the offer came just as I arrived here. I thought, of course, I couldn't do that. But they have now opened a London office. They inquired whether I would be interested. The opportunity of living in London, working in Europe as the Common Market comes into full force, working in Europe over the next few years while Eastern Europe opens up, is very exciting. I've always had at the back of my mind that at some point I'd like to spend the last few years in England. So that's what I'm going to do.

Julia Armstrong-Zwart: David Gardner had a problem because Chancellor Stevens ran into difficulties and Chancellor Barbara Uehling at UC

Santa Barbara ran into difficulties.[12] He was not batting even five hundred with the chancellors he had appointed. They were bad matches for their campus, which said that he and the regents didn't understand the campuses.

Robert Stevens: I had less success at UCSC than I would have hoped, but I'm very pleased with many of the things that were accomplished. We do now have proper administration. We have intelligent budgeting. We have made enormous strides in developing graduate programs. We have a proper academic plan. We'll begin to see the establishment of an engineering school. I am very pleased that we were able to put into place a total renewal of the colleges.

We do have a public relations problem. The reputation of this campus inside of the state, but to some extent, nationally, is as a rather crazy place with crazy faculty and a wonderful climate. An impossible situation. Undoubtedly, it makes it very difficult to recruit deans from outside, and it makes it very difficult to recruit people at the vice chancelloral level who are really first rate. And there's no point in having a development person or a vice chancellor of an institution who isn't first rate.

I think the relationship with the city was evidence that things can be changed. We've done a lot in the last four years. A lot remains to be done.

Julia Armstrong-Zwart: So we came back. Chancellor Stevens didn't ask us what we had talked about. I think he pretty much knew. We didn't say anything we wouldn't have said to him. At the end of that year he stepped down.

Michael Cowan: There was a combination of significant budget cuts right at the start of the nineties, and then an abrupt and rather contentious turnover in the chancellor's office, with the departure of Robert Stevens. His leaving supposedly caused President David Gardner to remark that the campus once again seemed ungovernable.

George Blumenthal: I was told when I became chancellor that this was the ungovernable campus. I got a huge amount of credit for being able to quote "tame" the ungovernable campus. I heard it from two presidents of UC, Bob Dynes and Dick Atkinson, quite explicitly. Everyone believed Santa Cruz was ungovernable. We have a history of making it difficult for some of our leading administrators to succeed. On the other hand, those chancellors didn't make it necessarily easy, either. Did Christensen deserve the pushback that he got? Probably he did. He did not lead the campus well. Did Stevens deserve that pushback? Yeah. Stevens could have ended the Asian food affair business so easily. All he had to do was A, not intervene; or B, even after he intervened, come back and say he apologized, he wanted to clear the air, we need to come together as a university. Just those words would have meant a lot! But he didn't do it. He was perceived constantly as being on one side only.

I don't think the campus is ungovernable. I just think that it requires a person who has certain characteristics and a certain value system in order to successfully govern the campus: a commitment to shared governance; a willingness to be okay with having dissenting views and having people have very different opinions. I think that was hard for Stevens. It scarred him, too. He left and he became a barrister in London for many years.

Julia Armstrong-Zwart: It was all very unfortunate because when there are battles between the faculty and the chancellor, it leaves scars that take a long time to heal.

Endnotes

1. Until 1968, UC education was free to California residents. Governor Ronald Reagan imposed student registration fees in that year. By 1977, the fees stood at about $700 a year. In 1980, UC began to charge tuition; by 1988 tuition and fees totaled about $1500 a year. In 1990, tuition for a California resident was about $1800 a year; by 1996 it had risen to roughly $4000. In 2010 it was roughly $11,000 a year, having effectively doubled over the previous decade. In 2011, for the first time, the total amount UC students collectively paid in tuition exceeded the amount of funding the UC system received from the state. In the late 1980s and early 1990s, the state provided between 50 and 60 percent of UCSC's funding; by 2001, state funds accounted for less than 40 percent of the campus's budget. In 2015, just 25 percent of UCSC's funding came from the state of California. See the *UC Santa Cruz Budget: A Bird's Eye View, Office of Planning and Budget, 2015-16*. https://planning.ucsc.edu/budget/reports-overviews/pdfs-images/profile2015.pdf.

In 2015, under pressure from student activists, Governor Jerry Brown stated his opposition to tuition increases, which were frozen until 2017, when a 2.5 percent increase was implemented. In 2018, tuition is roughly $14,000 a year. This does not include the cost of housing, textbooks, student health insurance, and other expenses. Some of the cost is covered through financial aid, but there is still an increasing financial burden on students, who are going into debt. http://forbestadvice.com/Education/Articles/2011_0721_University_of_California_CAL_Tuition_Fee_History.html. Also see a table of historical tuition and fee increases since 1981 at UC from the UC Office of the President at: https://www.ucop.edu/operating-budget/_files/fees/201415/documents/Historical_Fee_Levels.pdf.

2. *Santa Cruz Sentinel,* May 29, 1988.

3. Under the 1879 California Constitution Article IX, Section 9, the University of California is exempt from local land-use regulations, including general plans and zoning. As a state agency, UC must abide by the California Environmental Quality Act (CEQA), which requires the preparation of environmental impact reports for proposed developments.

4. Enrollment was at about 8,000 students when Robert Stevens arrived and at almost 9,000 when he left. See: https://mediafiles.ucsc.edu/iraps/enrollment-history/2017-18/headcountenrollmenthistory.pdf.

5. The Meyer Drive Extension project, proposed in 1991, would have involved the extension of Meyer Drive from the Performing Arts parking lot eastward to Hagar Drive, with a bridge at Jordan Gulch and an intersection with the entrance to the East Remote parking lot. It would also have involved widening the existing segments of Meyer Drive, to result in a two-lane road between Heller Drive and Hagar Drive. This development would have had significant environmental impact on the Great Meadow and on mixed evergreen forest habitat in Jordan Gulch. The project met with considerable protest and was ultimately cancelled. See *Final Environmental Impact Report: Meyer Drive Extension, Phase I ,* Office of Campus Facilities, University of California, Santa Cruz, 1991. Available in UCSC Library Special Collections.

6. For a detailed discussion of the siting and design of the UCSC Music Recital Hall see the oral history *Growth and Stewardship: Frank Zwart's Four Decades at UC Santa Cruz* (Regional History Project, UCSC Library, 2011). https://escholarship.org/uc/item/3nf9m5pr. Much of the controversy about the Music Recital Hall centered on the visual impact of siting a building at the edge of the Great Meadow.

7. In, 1987, when Stevens arrived, there were 8786 students; 800 were graduate students.

8. The enrollment-ceiling figure of 15,000 that was agreed upon for the 1988 Long Range Development Plan was revised to 19,500 for the 2005 Long Range Development Plan, and is currently under revision again for the 2020 Long Range Development Plan, which is in process as of 2019. There have been several legal settlements concerning issues between the city of Santa Cruz and UC Santa Cruz, such as the 2005 settlement agreement over water use.

9. *San Jose Mercury News,* May 3, 1989.

10. Wendell Brase was vice chancellor for finance, planning, and administration for thirteen years.

11. R. Michael Tanner had a thirty-year career at UCSC, where he served as chair of the department of computer and information sciences and acting dean of natural sciences, before becoming academic vice chancellor for nine years. An oral history with EVC Tanner was conducted in 2019, as this book was going to press, and was not able to be included. Tanner's oral history provides many cogent insights into UCSC's history and can be found on the Regional History Project's website, as well as in the UCSC Library.

12. UCSB Chancellor Barbara Uehling was arrested on suspicion of drunk driving in 1988. She pled no contest to a reduced charge of reckless driving, paid a $400 fine and agreed to attend driving school. Her license was not suspended. See http://articles.latimes.com/1988-05-02/news/mn-1470_1_santa-barbara and http://articles.latimes.com/1988-06-30/news/mn-7851_1_reckless-driving.

Illustrations

Figure 1 "Save My Habitat": Meyer Drive protest flyer, 1990. Courtesy Special Collections, University Library, University of California, Santa Cruz. UA 70: UCSC Ephemera Collection: ua070-0044.

Figure 2. Great Meadow, 2016. Photo by Irene Reti.

Figure 3. Burrowing owl in the Great Meadow, 2018. Photo by Lee Jaffe.

Figure 4. Flyer protesting 1988 Long Range Development Plan. Late 1980s. Courtesy Special Collections, University Library, University of California, Santa Cruz. UA 70: UCSC Ephemera Collection: ua070-0046.

Part IV

A Research University with Experimental Roots

Biomedical Building, 2012

Photo by Steve Kurtz

Figure 1

Chancellor Pister with Student Union Assembly chair Brant Smith on tandem bicycle at McHenry Library (Chancellor's Office), 1992

Photo by Don Harris

Chapter 25

Chancellor Karl Pister

"Restoring the Balance"

We had a reputation for being "Ungovernable! Ungovernable! Ungovernable!" That was such a bad rap. The campus wasn't ungovernable. It just took somebody who was straight up to govern it.

—Julia Armstrong-Zwart

"To Calm Troubled Waters": The Arrival of Chancellor Karl Pister

Bill Domhoff: The joy was Stevens resigned and I didn't have to evaluate him. It was as simple as pie. They brought in this wonderful guy, Karl Pister, as the chancellor.

Karl Pister: Robert Stevens resigned in December 1990. I had a number of conversations with UC President David Gardner about accepting an interim appointment here. David said to me, "The Santa Cruz campus is in a chaotic state. The faculty are divided; the chancellor is in real trouble." He said there was no way that he could go out and recruit for a chancellor. He needed somebody to go down and do damage control and try to quiet down the campus. Because I'd had long experience in the University of California, he thought I could probably have the best chance of doing that.

Bill Domhoff: I was able to work closely with Pister and give him a sense of the campus, which wasn't hard because he had worked his way through the senate in Berkeley; he had been chair of the statewide Academic Senate. He was from an engineering school. He was raised in a rural area. He had picked apples in the Depression. He had a lot of heart in him.

George Blumenthal: So Pister came in. It was clear he was a really solid guy. He had been the dean of engineering at UC Berkeley for many years. He was somebody who had leadership skills, understood the politics of UC, and could move the campus forward. He had a seriousness about him that struck people well. So we figured if he could be the dean of engineering at Berkeley and be successful, he could be the chancellor here.

Karl Pister: The first person whom I called was former Acting Chancellor Angus Taylor. I said, "Angus, tell me, what do you think about my going to Santa Cruz?" "That's a great idea. You ought to do it. No question about your success in doing that." I called former UCSC Chancellor Robert Sinsheimer. "Bob, what do you think?" He said, "Why in the hell would you want to do that?" Or words to that effect. "Do you know what you're getting into?"

Then I had a wonderful two-hour lunch session with Clark Kerr, to ask Clark, and he encouraged me to come. He gave me a lot of good historical background about UC Santa Cruz. Little did I know that Clark, Angus, and David Gardner had had lunch at Berkeley to discuss the Santa Cruz situation and that they decided that I was the one who should be recommended. David had turned to both Clark and Angus because of their interest in UC Santa Cruz. I'm very honored that that triumvirate recommended me.

Hal Hyde: I was delighted to see Karl Pister's appointment and renew acquaintance with Karl. My acquaintance with him goes back to 1942 when he was in a sailor suit and I was a private first class at Berkeley, in an army suit. I met him at that time and I liked him. He made a great record at Berkeley as dean of engineering. He's an excellent administrator.

Karl Pister: I came down to the campus incognito with University of California Vice President Bill Baker. Bill knew the campus very well, and he drove me down and we drove all over the campus, sneaking around, and he said, well, if someone asks, sees me, we'll invent something. We did many drive-throughs all through the different paths. I remember getting out of the car. There were no students. It must have been spring break. I remember walking up and seeing Merrill

College. I had a chance to see, physically, what the campus looked like. And by the way, this is a chance to record my first impressions of the campus, which even are sustained today. *Where is the campus?* That was my first question to Bill. There's no campanile. There's no tower. There's no there there. That was my first orientation towards something that I've become accustomed to now, that the campus is everywhere at Santa Cruz. There is no center of the campus, really.

I had to bring my wife along, who had no great desire to leave our home in the East Bay in Lafayette. She had no plans to be even an interim chancellor's spouse. I remember a number of conversations with David Gardner in his office at UC's central administration headquarters in Oakland's Kaiser Center, during which he tried very hard to convince my wife—I was more interested in the idea than my wife—to take on this interim assignment at Santa Cruz. Ultimately, we made that decision. I think it was in March of 1991 that I agreed to have him recommend me to the regents. He did that, and I was confirmed.

Julia Armstrong-Zwart: With Karl Pister, you couldn't have had a better doctor to come in to heal the wounds. First of all, his demeanor was that of an elder statesman. He was calm. He was outgoing. He was firm. You name what you need to calm troubled waters, and up would pop Karl Pister's picture. I know that when he came here he didn't quite know what he was getting into.

Ed Landesman: Karl Pister had been in engineering and the dean of engineering at UC Berkeley. He was a highly rated civil/mechanical engineer. He was brought to UCSC as the chancellor. He was a strong advocate for the campus. He had a definite understanding of the major issues that are prevalent in education, prior to coming to UCSC. He was sympathetic with the goals of the campus, and he worked tirelessly to improve all aspects of the campus.

Bill Domhoff: He really made a difference on the campus. Pretty quickly, people were coming to me saying, "Bill, is he really good?" I'd say, "Yeah, he's great."

Karl Pister: I think President Gardner had made some public statements saying that the Santa Cruz campus was virtually ungovernable. I guess, in retrospect, I was sort of a fool to think that I could come to UCSC, when the president of the university said the campus was virtually ungovernable. It was a challenge that I simply couldn't pass up.

Julia Armstrong-Zwart: You always hear about the Santa Cruz campus. It had the reputation for being the place that killed chancellors, first Christensen— We had a reputation for being Ungovernable! Ungovernable! Ungovernable! That was such a bad rap. The campus wasn't ungovernable. It just took somebody who was straight up to govern it, to work with the faculty. The faculty, more than any place I've ever been, were integral to the running of this institution. They gave service. The faculty were engaged in ways that I'd never seen faculty engaged before, in terms of the running of the institution, and that's a good thing, a healthy thing, for an institution. But it means that you can't have an imperial chancellor; we expect our chancellors to be engaged constructively with the campus, especially the faculty. If there's any wobble in that engagement, then the wobble gets worse and worse, and the campus spins out of control.

Karl Pister: The thing that really attracted me here was problem-solving. Academics, and particularly engineers, I have to say, are problem-solvers.

I've spent all my life solving problems. In a sense the job at UCSC was a huge new problem: how to take my forty years of experience at Berkeley in the UC system and come down here and help this campus realize its potential.

I had a growing disaffection with the way in which the academic community insisted on dividing knowledge into boxes called departments. The tremendous autonomy and power of academic departments was often at the expense of the institution. I wrote an essay in 1979 about the importance of dual citizenship, that you needed to be a citizen of your department: that you needed to be a citizen of your campus as well. Growing out of that experience as dean, I saw the importance of getting out of this very narrow disciplinary focus, to try to restore a stronger sense of collegiality on the campus. Santa Cruz was founded on the basis of the college system, and I knew something of Dean McHenry's vision. Clark Kerr filled me in a great deal more on this matter. I saw an opportunity to join a campus where there was already a better sense of collegiality.

Leo Laporte, Professor: It's not surprising that we've done well under people like McHenry and Taylor and now Pister. They have a broader vision.

Karl Pister: Once I got here, some of the faculty said to me, "How can you espouse this restoration of balance and move away from this very clear and dominant model of a research university? How can you espouse that, when the faculty here are judged by their colleagues on other campuses, and they can't possibly call themselves different from their colleagues?" There was an underlying tension between the boards and the colleges here that I had overlooked in my zeal for the collegiate system.

I tried to restore the balance. I first articulated this in my remarks at my investiture, where I appealed to the campus to set up a model of a people-centered research university.[1] I prefaced that statement with the statement, "The nation doesn't need another research university." I was heartened to hear from the back, over to the right side behind me, in a stage whisper and a clap from Clark Kerr, "I agree with that." Later on, when I sent him a copy of my remarks, he wrote back one of his beautiful little one-line notes in green ink—the letters are about an eighth of an inch or a sixteenth of inch high. In my speech I talked about four dreams. He said, "I concur heartily with your four dreams." Among them was the idea of a people-centered research university. The point, as I was trying to make it, is that there needed to be more time spent in the development of human potential, and less time spent on the acquisition of knowledge. The two were not obviously mutually exclusive.

There's a kind of academic materialism that's measured by the quantity of work someone publishes, as opposed to a somewhat more spiritual content of a faculty member's proper work, as the personnel manual calls it, which involves much more intangible things like working with people in one's office, talking about the subject, talking about research, or talking about teaching, talking about life in general, and not just concentrating on this mad pursuit to find some new piece of knowledge. I had found myself and many of my colleagues engaged in the pursuit of triviality. Moving out of that kind of an environment was very appealing to me.

But yet interestingly enough, once I got here, and after I'd talked about this for a while, I began to get a backlash from the faculty.

George Blumenthal: His tenure didn't go that well at first, from the perspective of the science division. The feeling was that solid science was not being supported at the campus.

Karl Pister: I was perceived as a heretic by some members of the biology board, and more broadly, by some members of the division of natural sciences. It was less clear that other people in the natural sciences division were as upset with me as the biologists were. So I attended a department meeting, and tried to explain to them that I wasn't against research, I didn't want them to give up their research, but that I thought there was room to achieve a better balance between time spent on research and teaching.

A perennial problem in any research university, or in any university that has a tradition of shared governance: there's always a perception on the part of the faculty that it's the administration that's holding them back from doing this or that. Since I spent thirty years as a faculty member before the last fifteen years as an academic administrator, I well understand the faculty perspective. For two thirds of my academic life, I served in the role of a faculty member critical of the administration. I did my share of dean- and chancellor-bashing as a faculty member. In fact, I once wrote a letter to the editor of the *Daily Californian* along with a group of faculty members who severely criticized Chancellor Roger Heyns for his mishandling of the Free Speech Movement. As a consequence of that, we said we're joining the AFT [American Federation of Teachers union] and we're going to fight you, basically. I was a red-hot. I grew a beard and I pounded the table as a faculty member at Berkeley. So I understand the faculty perspective.

Michael Cowan: There were ongoing debates during the nineties about the roles of the colleges, about the grading system and the narrative evaluation system, about general education, about all those long-standing issues. But I don't think that the way those debates took shape in the nineties was as polarizing. They didn't, for the most part, arouse the same degree of passion that they had in previous decades. There was almost a kind of ritualistic aspect of continuing to raise these issues.

Karl Pister: I got here to find that the college system had been pretty much dismantled. The power and authority had been taken away from the college provosts, and in 1990 or 1991, there was a substantial budget reduction as well. The last of the provosts' control in the academic area was removed. The loyalty of the faculty to the college had been severely or seriously changed or eroded. Indeed, I heard more than one faculty member say, "Well, I'm a member of such and such a college, but I've never been there since I've been on the campus."

So the idea that I was coming to a place where the colleges offered an alternative to Berkeley was quickly challenged. That didn't mean that I gave up on the idea. I worked with the Council of Provosts and others to try to find ways to reattach, or to rekindle, the spirit of faculty to work in the colleges. There were several attempts made to put together proposals to strengthen the colleges.

The role of the colleges is still undefined. There's an elusive goal that many would like to see attained. In the final analysis, I think the only way that will sustain any role for the colleges will be to make some academic resources available to the provosts again, without giving the provosts control over faculty appointment or promotion. The colleges are a main attraction. How that will change in the next few decades: that's an open question.

Figure 2

Long-tailed weasel, 2008

Photo by Lee Jaffe

Campus Development Controversies:
Meyer Drive, the Music Building, and the Great Meadow

Frank Zwart: Karl Pister arrived on campus in the early 1990s facing a major controversy about extending Meyer Drive, which was a roadway across the Great Meadow, and the way the Music Building was going to be sited.

Karl Pister: I started getting email from people in the Friends of the Great Meadow group in late May or June of 1991 concerning the Meyer Drive Extension. One of the people I remember sending me email was Professor of Physics Michael Nauenberg, whom I knew from previous system-wide Academic Senate work. We'd been on the same committee together back in the 1970s, so I knew Mike. He was lobbying me right away about protecting the Great Meadow and stopping Meyer Drive. And Professor of Physics Peter Scott was another one. I think he was one of the Friends of the Great Meadow Who Ride Bicycles, or something like that.

When the debate over Meyer Drive happened on campus, I was struck by one of the faculty getting up and reciting a sonnet that he had written in memory of the Great Meadow. The vote was narrowly in favor of extending the road through the Great Meadow. But there was a resolution passed at the same time offered by professors Ronald Ruby[2] and Jim Pepper. The Ruby-Pepper resolution said that this vote extending Meyer Drive through the Great Meadow ought to be conditional upon a satisfactory transportation and circulation plan being developed for the campus.

By the way, it didn't take me more than a couple of days to realize the stupidity, and in a sense the error, in trying to put Meyer Drive through the Great Meadow. That might have been a cost-effective way to move people across campus, but it would have done tremendous harm to that beautiful meadow. I started to walk through the Great Meadow every morning, and that's really what did it for me. I took six o'clock walks down and back up again. I said there is no way that I'm going to be the one that wrecks this meadow.

I used to then joke with people when we had affairs at University House and say, "Well, I'm not going to put a road through, but out there on the mound I'm going to put a ten-story tower." It evoked a certain amount of surprise. Of course, I had no intention of doing that, but it got people's attention.

Leta Miller: There was a lot of opposition to the new Music Building because it was going to be on the edge of the Great Meadow. There was a Long Range Development Plan which said, "Thou shalt not build anything on the meadow." Well, this was sort of on the meadow. It is on the edge of the meadow. When Project Executive Architect Antoine Predock came out, he spent a long time sitting in the meadow and looking at the site from that vantage point, from the bike path that comes up from the front of campus. He just looked at the site. And he put in this beautiful columned walkway that's nonfunctional, just really attractive. If you come up the bike path you see these lovely columns. But from the parking lot what you see is the blank walls of the recital hall. Well, you can't have windows in a recital hall. That lets noise in and out. You need quiet. We don't want to hear the cars coming. And our recital hall functions not only for concerts, but people doing recordings in there. It's a great place to record because you can't hear anything from outside. You can have a truck coming outside and you don't hear it. So you need a blank wall. I've often suggested, only half in jest, that we have the art students paint a slug orchestra on that wall, but no one seems to have taken me up on that idea.

So people debated that: "What are we going to see? We're going to see a blank wall, and it's going to be this tall, and it's not going to have any windows and it's on the edge of the meadow." We had students lying down in front of the trucks and somebody cut electrical wires at one point.

Karl Pister: When I arrived here in August, I arrived just after a meeting of the regents in July, in which the plans for the new music facility had been rejected by the board. The first design was characterized as a massive block of concrete and a travesty to Santa Cruz's sensibilities. So here I arrived in August with the problem of what we were going to do about the music facility. As a result of the vote of the regents, it went back to the architect for redesign; it went back to our architects here and the executive architect for the project, Antoine Predock. In addition to looking at the redesign, there were still very strong questionings about why that facility was located in the Great Meadow.

So I had to deal with that issue. During August and the first half of September, I had to get up to speed on the history of the siting of the music facility, the history of its design, because it was going back to the Board of Regents in September. If the facility, if the design were rejected once again, there was a very high probability that the campus would lose the funds entirely. This is typical of projects like this that come up on the five-year cycle. If you don't hold your place, you lose it.

Our campus architects worked feverishly with the architect to get a new design, to do some relocation, to move it back away from the edge of the meadow, lower it down. I remember attending a meeting of the campus Physical Planning Committee. I remember the strident opposition of the people whom I heard. I was sitting away from the table watching this meeting go on, because at that time the chancellor had nothing to do with this. It was an advisory council or committee. I remember Jim Pepper getting up and speaking against the design, and community studies faculty member Mike Rotkin was in the back of the room. Mike got up and said, "This is outrageous. This thing was done with no student input." And physics faculty member Peter Scott was there, the great opponent of anything except bicycles in the Great Meadow. All these people were dumping on the design.

I heard all those comments. I looked at the new design. In the meantime, we took the new design up to a meeting of the regents' Special Committee on Buildings. They were favorably impressed by the design and the relocation. I carefully read the environmental impact report on the siting of the building. I looked at all the alternatives that had been considered, and determined that, in fact, the siting of the building was the best among the five alternatives. I really did my homework.

So I took that music facility to the regents in September. There were a couple of very strident opponents who spoke at the meeting. At the regents' meeting in September of 1991, Regent Designate Paul Hall, who is an alumnus of UC Santa Cruz, was just starting his term as regent designate.[3] Paul was very upset with the siting of the building. I met Paul in the lobby of the Clift Hotel in San Francisco the morning of the regents meeting. I'd never met him before. We sat down and had breakfast together. I explained my position on the music facility, that I had reviewed it all—the EIR; I'd reviewed the new design—and I felt it was the right thing to do, to go ahead. So Paul said, "Fine." He understood my position. I presented the case to the regents, the Building and Grounds Committee. Paul supported it and the thing was approved.

Leta Miller: We had to lower the building down into the ground further than it was originally slated to be [so that the view of the ocean would not be obstructed by the building]. So we had to make compromises. We cut the lobby of the Recital Hall. The lobby is half the size it was supposed to be. We had to cut out the wall coverings and floor coverings within the attached classroom building. We had to fill in that proposed glass wall with concrete blocks. We had to make all these savings, in part to make up for lowering that building, in part to meet the university's budget.

Karl Pister: I drew a lesson out of that whole Music Building controversy. With anything that was built on the campus, there was a problem. At that point I said, "Look. There's not going to be any more building like this, any more discussion about siting until we've brought the campus master plan up to date." I made a commitment then that led ultimately to the creation of three new entities that have been absolutely critical to helping to stabilize the campus. It was clear that buildings, or anything to do with altering the environment, were such sensitive issues for so many people on this campus that we had to be very, very careful that we had a clear plan that the maximum number of people would be comfortable with for any future development of the campus. So I made that a public statement that we were going to develop an update of the 1963 Long Range Development Plan, which had never, in my view, been carefully and systematically updated to modify it for a 15,000-student campus instead of a 27,500 student campus.

People were sick and tired of these kinds of ad hoc additions to the campus without a sense that it was part of a larger plan. I became sensitized to that instantly because of what I saw on the Meyer Drive extension and the music facility. I said, we can't continue that way. The campus will never

settle down. So I brought in a consultant in the person of Richard Bender, a Berkeley colleague, who was dean of environmental design at Berkeley. He's an architect, and a person who's had substantial experience in campus planning. He had a major role in developing a master plan for UC San Diego. He worked for UC Davis in a similar capacity. So he was very experienced in campus planning and in addition to that had an international reputation as an architect and planner.

Frank Zwart: Up until then a lot of the planning had been handled in the office of Vice Chancellor for Finance, Planning, and Administration Wendell Brase. Pister heard the need to do this intermediate-level planning. And he brought in the past dean of the College of Environmental Design at Berkeley, an architect named Richard Bender, who, then associated with the San Francisco architecture firm Skidmore, Owings, and Merrill, undertook a two- or three-year process to put in place what was then called the LRDP Implementation Program: how the campus would implement the 1988 Long Range Development Plan in more levels of detail. They met with a lot of campus groups. They looked at particular areas of the campus, and they came up with a plan that has proved to be extremely useful and extremely helpful.

The campus has different "vegetation zones"—different kinds of physical characteristics—and buildings in each of them need to respond to that general characteristic. The meadows are the lower third or 40 percent of the campus; the forests are the upper 60 percent to two-thirds of the campus. Then there is what's called the ecotone, or the forest edge, where the two come together. And finally, deep ravines that carve their way north and south through the campus. Once you start looking at the campus as a combination of those kinds of land types or vegetation types, you start to see it in a very different way.

Then they went on to talk about the use of clusters within the forest, to leave pieces of that spectacular landscape effectively untouched, or at least less developed. The document talked about the desire to densify, rather than jump into the North Campus, to fill in before pioneering new land. And then it used the term "a ladder of roadways," mainly east-west roadways that would provide vehicular access from one side of the campus to another. And then, the term that people often continue to joke about: "a warped grid" of pedestrian paths that knit all of this stuff together.

Karl Pister: I think the Bender Report worked. We totally relocated the Meyer Drive extension.

Frank Zwart: It's been a good model to get a visual, mental image of the campus. The Implementation Plan made some recommendations for siting particular buildings and particular types of buildings. It took a look at some traffic and transportation alternatives and studies, both on and off campus, and got the campus thinking in a very serious way about alternative transportation, something that the campus has done a good job at.

It's not enough to have a physical plan for a campus. You also have to have a process in place, where planning decisions come to the surface, are evaluated, refined, and implemented. One very strong recommendation that Bender's report made was the creation of some of sort of design review body that would evaluate the designs of buildings for suitability for the site, conformance with the plan, potential for future expansion, and the like. Chancellor Pister decided that that was something he wanted to move forward with, and so we moved it forward. My interactions with the Design Advisory Board were one of the most pleasurable aspects of my job. The project managers didn't always like it, or the design architects didn't like it, because sometimes architects would have

to go back and rethink something. But, all in all, I think they have added an enormous amount.

Santa Cruz Sentinel: A new road map to ease UCSC into the 21st century works because it embraces the visions of its founders. Chancellor Karl Pister has molded consensus on important issues facing UC Santa Cruz by wielding a weapon that too many leaders forget to add to their arsenal: The art of listening. Really listening. The latest evidence of Pister's special ability to listen while he leads are the new guidelines for long-range growth at UCSC. Embraced by the faculty, the guidelines reflect the early, visionary plans for a campus that was to be as unique as its wooded hilltop setting and its alternative educational offerings. Environmental protection was an important element to the people whose dream for the city on a hill has been rekindled with these latest growth guidelines. Faculty leaders, who have given their stamp of approval to these guidelines, credit Pister's willingness to seek out and listen to staff, faculty and student concerns. High on the list of changes that set these guidelines apart from those embraced during Chancellor Robert Stevens's short, controversial tenure is the notion that the Great Meadow is to be preserved. That includes rerouting the hated Meyer Drive extension around the meadow rather than through it.[4]

SAVE ELFLAND!

YES, IT DOES EXIST, BUT NOT FOR LONG!

🍂 IF YOU CARE ABOUT THE FOREST

🍂 IF YOU WANT TO KEEP THE SPECIAL PLACES
FOR FUTURE GENERATIONS TO ENJOY

🍂 WHETHER OR NOT YOU BELIEVE IN ELVES

We need to take action now, in any way we can, including:

Write a letter to the Board of Regents, local newspapers,
the City Council, the Mayor, Environmental Organizations
and anyone else who can make a difference.

Attend any meetings or hearings and make your voice heard.
Get a pair of elf ears and wear them to show solidarity.

Use whatever official channels available to designate the site
as a community art project, an Indian burial site, a nature
preserve, a religious refuge, any pigeonhole that will give it
value in the eyes of the Regents and City Government.

call Edda at 427-9560

Do it now!

Figure 3

Elfland poster, 1991

Figure 4

Golden Eagle on a campus bus stop shelter, July 12, 2013

Photo by Lee Jaffe

"Immaculate Construction": the Elfland Controversy

Benjamin Weitzman and Colin Horn, with Jeff Arnett, Writers: Santa Cruz is one of the few college campuses to be built within a forest. The trees grow large and dense around many of the buildings, producing a campus within the trees, rather than a campus with trees. One of the most unique characteristics of the redwood is the growth of tree rings, also called cathedral rings, where the trees grow in a circle with an empty center. Students and visitors to the campus began to build structures and dens within the rings starting sometime in the 1960s.[5]

Vicky Peterson, Student: There was always a magical feeling in the air at Elfland. Whatever entrance you went in, you felt it along the way; the energy would change and you knew you had entered Elfland. My favorite moments were those when I would go up there between class, with no libations, and feel ultimately transported into a timeless place. Sometimes I would even study in those beautiful places, if the topic so agreed.[6]

New York Times: Students past and present call it Elfland, a wooded refuge on the University of California, Santa Cruz campus that is revered as a sanctuary and spiritual haven. Since the 1960's, students have erected totems, altars and "fairy rings"—circles of branches—among the towering redwoods. In one small altar, a hand-lettered scroll reads: "Lord of the gnomes and earth elements, let your kingdom of little people surround this area, forming a cordon to protect and defend it from interlopers, developers, realtors, construction, vandalism, ruin and assassination.[7]

Santa Cruz Sentinel: Dozens of people convened Saturday among the stumps of Elfland, chanting, praying and bearing flowers at what was billed as a healing ceremony for the area where 150 trees were cut to make room for two new colleges at UC Santa Cruz.[8]

Karl Pister: The last of the projects that I inherited was the problem of creating the sites for Colleges Nine and Ten. I remember well the pain of that December of 1991. My staff said, "Well, we have to get ready to do the logging so we can do the site preparation for Colleges Nine and Ten." Some people felt that we were invading what became known as Elfland.

Jim Burns: I don't remember a protest that became as violent as the Elfland protest. Elfland was sort of a spiritual web of pathways through the woods in an area that is now behind the site where Colleges Nine and Ten were built. UCSC was on a growth trajectory at the time, and long had plans to build its two newest colleges in an area that was pretty heavily wooded and was very popular among students because it was a fun area in which to take a walk, connect with nature, or do who knows what.

The campus, because of safety issues and to just make the job easier for the chainsaw crew, had identified in advance a number of trees that needed to be felled. As was the case with virtually every construction project I witnessed on campus over my thirty years, the planners had gone to great lengths to save as many trees as possible. But, to be fair, we weren't going to build two new colleges in that area of the campus without a large number of trees being removed.

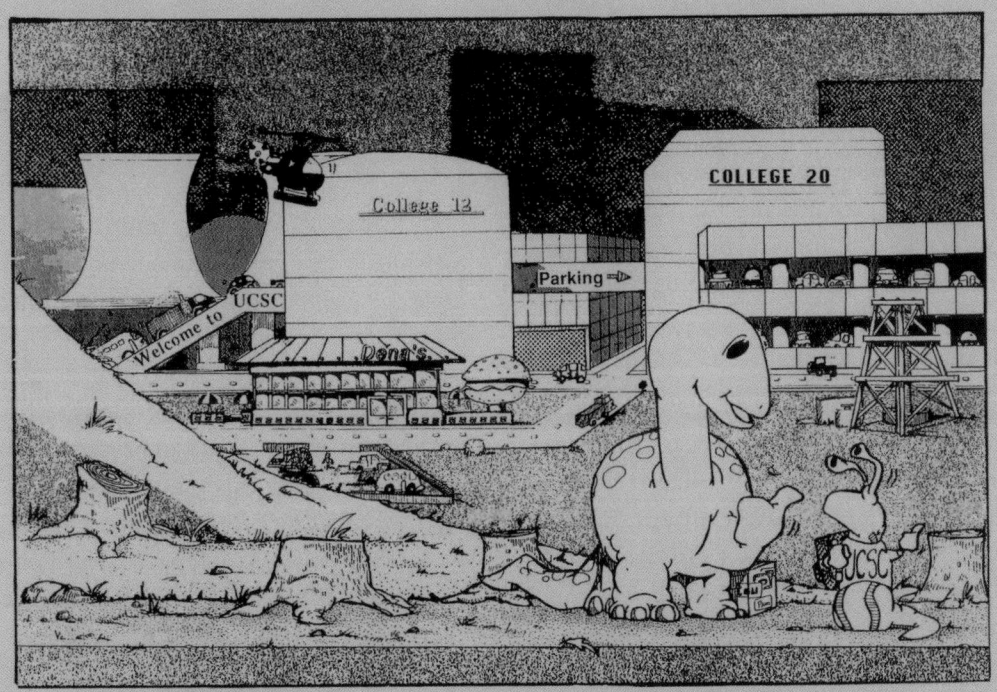

Figure 5

Flyer protesting development, 1996

Karl Pister: It was reinvented in a way that made it sound like that I was invading St. Peter's Square, or something like that, to destroy this place. It turns out there were fewer trees removed for Colleges Nine and Ten than in the construction of Kresge. That's not a way to win the war. We weren't really raping that part of the campus. There was a mystique and a history that was embellished by people who were opposed to any expansion of the campus. This happened so often that I invented a characterization of those who believed that existing buildings simply appeared with no prior site preparations. I called this belief in the principle of "Immaculate Construction." Some people call this the drawbridge phenomenon or mentality: we're here, let's pull the bridge up. Nobody else can come.

Jim Burns: From the campus's perspective, we're the University of California. We had to provide space for an increasing number of state students who were eligible for UC. It was pretty clear that UCSC, as one of the younger campuses, was going to have to take its share of these new students. And we were going to want to grow, to some extent, in order to continue a natural trajectory of academic development.

Karl Pister: So that painful December 1991, we started the logging. We had some unfortunate intruders who got in the way of the logging. I think there were thirty-eight or forty-four people. An attorney was arrested for walking through the police line and she got very, very upset. I think, ultimately, she was not prosecuted.

Jim Burns: It became clear to the people who were running the tree-cutting operation that this was going to be a challenge. The Earth First! group, which learned in advance that we were going to be cutting trees, was intent on disrupting the operation. Anticipating the potential for problems, the campus brought in a lot more police than I think it had originally planned. It was at the end of a quarter on our campus, and between semesters at UC Berkeley. Because of the proximity of Berkeley to Santa Cruz, the outside police that we brought in were mostly from that campus.

The whole event was awful—the TV footage was as bad as could be; the protestors were completely uncivil; the police response seemed very aggressive.

Karl Pister: A Berkeley campus police officer pushed a television cameraman and knocked him down. His camera was damaged and I had to pay the cost of fixing up the camera. The *Santa Cruz Sentinel* wrote a nasty editorial accusing me of not knowing the law and supporting the abridgment of the rights of journalists to be on the property. I remember turning this office into a press conference. I was sitting behind a table with my chief of the campus police, Jan Tepper. The room was full of reporters and bright lights and television cameras. It was the first time I had ever been through this. As a dean, I never had this kind of a problem. It was a very uncomfortable affair.

Jim Burns: On a personal note, one of the things that bothered me about that day, aside from the painful events I've already described, was that this happened very early in the tenure of Karl Pister, who was a chancellor who I greatly admired, and grew particularly close to. He had accepted the chancellor's position on an acting basis just weeks or months prior to the Elfland protest, and I think at least some of the planning for the tree-cutting operation preceded his arrival on campus. And here he was, kind of stuck with this mess.

Karl Pister: I remember one morning after the logging, opening my front door and there was a bag of garbage on my doorstep at University House. And a note on the door saying these were friends of Elfland, or something, saying, "Here, we picked this stuff up that your loggers left." Their lunches and stuff like that. Dumping it on my doorstep.

In another incident, my wife and I were in our apartment in University House on Saturday morning, and the doorbell rang. My wife went down. I was behind her and there was a person shouting. I said, "Don't open the door." There was a guy walking outside the front door with a long club, a big four-foot club of some kind. He was screaming, demanding to see me. I hit the panic alarm. I said "No, I am not going to talk to you."

Later on, I learned the identity of this person. It was someone who had come in and talked to me at one time, I realized. It was a person called Peat Moss. Peat Moss had been one of the guys that had put his arms around a tree and had gotten arrested, and he was coming up, brandishing this stick, to complain about it. Peat Moss, I remembered, came in to talk to me during my office hours and said, "This campus is all screwed up. The students and faculty and staff ought to grow their own food, make their own places to live on the campus, and raise hemp." Peat Moss, fortunately, disappeared from my life. I don't know where he is now. That was one of the last Elfland incidents.

Looking back, I don't know how we could have handled it differently at that stage of the history of the campus. It hurt because there were a lot of very critical people. The fact is that we were simply doing what had been on the books for some years. But I learned that people had strong feelings about the environment here and they were expressing them. They didn't like the way we did things.

Jeff Arnett, Writer: By 1990, Elfland's grim future had been confirmed, and in the summer of 1991, construction began and the destruction of Elfland was imminent. As logging continued through the fall, a large protest occurred in December of 1991, during which students chained themselves to trees and stood before bulldozers, leading to the arrest of 42 protestors. Before the logging was finished, a group of 50 students and community members began an nonviolent protest and an Ohlone religious ceremony was held in the nearby Crown Meadow to pay final respects to Elfland as a sacred place.

Today, Elfland is broken and scattered, replaced by College 9 and College 10 and an unending onslaught of new students who most likely will never know that Elfland or its natural beauty ever existed. It has been replaced by dorms and dining halls.[9]

Jim Burns: Chancellor Pister was, and is, a truly amazing person who had a great capacity to tackle difficult issues, including many very thorny land-use issues on campus. I think he did a particularly good job helping the campus think about what it was trying to do with respect to land use and growth and all of the tension that our growth created on campus and in the community. That he ended up having to be front and center at a post-protest press conference to explain why it was that a tree-cutting operation on his watch had gone a bit south—I felt like we all had let him down.

As a campus, we—and I include myself in that—learned a lot from Elfland. For one, we learned that we needed to have a much closer connection between the people who are running the operation—whether it be Physical Planning and Construction, or the police, or some other office— and the communications staff, if we expected there to be media coverage.

Karl Pister: I see some signs that there is some softening of the hard feelings about the university in the last four or five years. Having gone through an economic depression in the early 1990s,[10] the university remained the largest employer in Santa Cruz County at a time when many people were out on the streets.

I hope that our county supervisors and city council will continue to see the importance of the university. I don't mean in any way abrogating the very important and commendable commitment to preserving the things that are good about this county, but to understand that an absolutely no-growth, no-change mentality will not serve this region at all over the next century. There will, inevitably, have to be some accommodations made to continue to allow people to move into this area, to build a stronger economic base for the region. We'll clearly be a big part of it.

The LRDP settlement of 1988 requires an annual meeting between the city council and the campus. Each of us has a chance to put things on the agenda. We have to sit together and discuss these issues, and there's a comment period at the end. I was told that before I got here the meetings used to be in the Civic Auditorium, because there was so much acrimony, so many people wanted to be heard. Well, fortunately, we seemed to have gotten over that hurdle. We had meetings either downtown, in the library, or up here on the campus. We never had more than ten or fifteen people come to those meetings. The last two years when Katherine Beiers[11] was mayor, and later when Mike Rotkin was mayor, they've been virtual love feasts. Kathy Beiers and Mike, this last time, couldn't say enough good about the campus and about me. In fact, Mike gave me a proclamation. He created Chancellor Karl Pister Day in Santa Cruz, gave me a key to the city.

Figure 6

Annual joint meeting between the Santa Cruz city council and university officials at the Civic Auditorium: Mayor Michael Rotkin and Chancellor Karl Pister, 1996

Photo by Victor Schiffrin

From State-Supported to State-Assisted:
Waning Funds for Public Education

Michael Cowan: Another theme of the nineties was about how to reduce the campus's dependency on state funding, which was steadily declining. This campus had a higher proportion of its budget coming from state funds than did any other UC campus. So external fundraising became an increasingly important concern.

Karl Pister: I grew up in a University of California which had always been either, if not growing, at least sustaining itself. The only recollections I have of serious cuts at Berkeley were during the time when Governor Ronald Reagan cut faculty, or failed to give faculty or staff salary increases for a couple of years. But except for minor retrenchments that took place along the way, UC was relatively healthy.

In 1991, when I came to UCSC, the university was faced with a budget crisis of what Clark Kerr called "unprecedented magnitude." He felt that the crisis of the 1990s even exceeded the crisis that the university sustained during the Great Depression. All the economists in the state now agree [in 1996] that we're out of the bottom of the recession and we're in the recovery period. The optimists say that our recovery is going to be much faster than the rest of the nation. At least in the near term, the revenue picture looks very good. The University of California is beginning to be funded in a more reasonable way, but we've been cut back so badly that—limiting ourselves just to this campus—we have a great deal of catching up to do. The area of faculty and staff salaries needs a great deal of attention. We're not competitive with those institutions with whom we compete for the best faculty and staff. And deferred maintenance of our plant is woefully behind schedule.

There are some clear prospects for growth of the campus. With the budget turnaround, we are looking very seriously at the resurrection of the engineering school plan. The campus has almost reached the point of agreement between the faculty and administration as to the desirability of adding two new programs: electrical engineering and applied mathematics. The president's office is very supportive of our adding these programs. So I'm hopeful that before I leave we'll get some clear signs that will add these two new professional programs, which I think will be good for balance on this campus.

Hal Hyde: Chancellor Pister asked me to come back and be a member of the UC Santa Cruz Foundation. I was pleased to see him re-lay the groundwork for a UCSC school of engineering that Francis Clauser had originally started. He was the right person at the right time. His educational outreach has been outstanding.

Karl Pister: I've spent virtually my entire adult life in the University of California. I was able to get my education and find my career in the university because generations of people before me built that university. For a number of years, as a taxpayer in California, I continued to perpetuate that for my children. But clearly, there's a discontinuity occurring. It's going to be hitting us very, very quickly. We are already in the throes of that discontinuity. We are now paying the price and suffering the consequences of massive underinvestments in education in this state, at all levels, not just the university.

The statistics are extraordinary. I think it reflects very badly on the political leadership of our state that we can, as a state, be complacent about the fact that we have the worst class-size ratio of any state in the United States. We're 45th in K-12 textbook expenditures per pupil; we're 40th in total per pupil expenditures for K-12. We're in that position in the United States at a time when every industrialized society, or every society that's moving toward industrialization, like China, values education as the tool to bring them into the 21st century. Here we are, in this ridiculous position of saying—Californians can't afford to invest in education—but, by the way, because we're failing so many young people we're going to build more and more prisons to take care of all the failures because we haven't educated people to earn a living. I am very depressed by the incredible failure of public policy to address the root causes. The companion of underinvestment in education is the rising levels of poverty among our citizens, particularly the percentage of children living in poverty.

Robert Stevens: We have done very well in gifts but not nearly well enough. It's simply very probable within the long run what's going to make the difference on a campus like this is our ability to raise private funds as well as just relying on state funds.

Compared, for instance, with San Jose State, which does raise a lot of money in Silicon Valley, we are at a tremendous disadvantage in raising private money. People know very little about us. Highway 17 serves as a barrier to people knowing what's going on here, or wanting to know what's going on here. Each year we put in more and more energy to get people to know, but it is an uphill battle. So from the point of view of major gifts from Silicon Valley, which ought to be a logical place for us to get massive gifts, they tend to go to Stanford and to Berkeley, which are more visible and more accessible. People don't feel the psychological links to the university they would

if the university had been put where Governor Pat Brown wanted it—which was in the Almaden Valley.

Karl Pister: When I came to Santa Cruz, I'd just finished a capital campaign at Berkeley which raised tens of millions of dollars. I thought, with that experience, it would be a cinch to go to Santa Cruz: I know how to do fundraising, and we'll be able to really move UC Santa Cruz along.

Well, I received two rude shocks when I got here. The first was the realization that the age and tradition of a campus are enormously important when it comes to raising outside money. Berkeley was a century older than Santa Cruz, so it had a century more alumni. Furthermore, it had more than a dozen professional programs, in addition to its academic programs. Professional programs are traditionally more fruitful sources of outside support than academic programs. Engineering, business, law were the big players at Berkeley, and they were missing here.

Even at a place like engineering at Berkeley, I had a substantial challenge to get the faculty to understand that it was more important for me as dean to spend time trying to get outside funds, than to fight with the chancellor over state funds. So coming here, it was not that much of a surprise that the faculty felt: the state pays our bills—why waste time going out to get private money?

There was a culture that had to be changed. Public universities, and UC is a great example of that, are no longer state-supported. They are state-assisted. Overall, in the university, state funding represents about a quarter of our total funding now. This campus is higher because we have a higher percentage of state assistance. But that's because we have fewer graduate programs than other campuses. As we move ahead and expand, we're going to get a smaller and smaller percentage of state money.

Michael Cowan: The budgetary crisis in the nineties throughout the UC system had led to the establishment of the VERIP program between 1991 and 1994—an early retirement program in which a large number of faculty and staff, not only here but elsewhere, retired. By when the dust had settled on the VERIPs, over half of the campus faculty had arrived after the reorganization of the campus in 1979.[12] Therefore they weren't a part of the often-bitter debates and hard feelings that were left in the wake of reorganization. Many of the issues that had been fueled in those founding years simply didn't resonate with many of the new faculty.

Leo Laporte: Since I VERIPed, I told my board, "You can send me stuff, but the future belongs to the people who are there now. They're going to have to live with the place. I'm not. I'm not going to meddle at all because it's not appropriate. What's appropriate is those young people." Everybody's saying with the VERIP, all the work is going down to these middle-level professors. Well, that's where it should be. That's how we built a program here. I was a young full professor. We had good associate professors and assistant professors. We built a good program. That's where the energy and the vision comes from.

I think there's something about the gracefulness of letting go. It's natural. I mean, here is a universe that's fifteen billion years old. You're not here, then you're here, then you're not here. It's okay. I'm grateful that I was here for some part of that universe, and to be conscious of it. It's really important to be able to let go, and not be so tight and greedy. You have to manifest that in all sorts of ways, including letting go at retirement.

George Blumenthal: In astronomy, we lost a lot of people during the VERIP. We lost a lot of our most eminent faculty. But I think it was actually an opportunity, too. It provided an opportunity to hire junior people to replace some of the senior people. The hiring may not have been immediate, because we didn't have positions, but we knew it would come. Sometimes there is some advantage to having a housecleaning.

I think it was maybe, in some ways, a long-term benefit to the campus. But it was difficult at the time. The reason that they did the VERIPs is because the retirement system was so overfunded. The retirement system for UC, UCRS, was so overfunded that the university was in danger of getting in trouble with the IRS. It wasn't just funded at 100 percent. It was funded at like 150 or 175 percent. It's because they were conservative about contributions. They insisted that the university and the employees make generous contributions to the retirement system. And because the retirement system is a Defined Benefit plan, if you don't vest, then you lose all of the contributions made by the university on your behalf. So that money just stays in the retirement system.

And so what happened was that the regents decided to stop contributions to the retirement system. I think employees were asked to contribute a couple of percent to some Defined Benefit plan. But the retirement system got no money and that persisted for a long time, until just a few years ago. But in addition to doing that, which slowly degraded the fundedness of the retirement system, the university also did certain things which drained the retirement system, and VERIP was one of them. The only reason VERIP makes sense is you're taking these high-income people, the senior people, and you're taking them from the state money and putting them into retirement system money. They gave them extra years of service as well, which was an additional drain. So it was really using the retirement system as a way of making up for shortfalls in state funding, which I'm sure felt like a good short-term gain in terms

Figure 7

Cattle stile, Great
Meadow, 2016

Photo by Irene Reti

of policy, but long-term it was a very bad idea. And it was also a bad idea because in later downturns, many faculty and staff expected there to be VERIPs.

Todd Newberry: One in eight faculty is retiring at UCSC in these three years. It's what I call the gang of eighty-four. There's eighty-four of us, eighty-four faculty, let alone staff. Almost all the original faculty. To some observers, it cleans out the stables. Maybe it will turn out to be a good thing on this campus, a chance to start afresh. Each campus is facing its own consequences. Berkeley is truly alarmed. But maybe what Berkeley is losing is different from what we're losing. Maybe we are losing a lot of people who are simply worn out. It's hard to know.

The feeling many of us have felt, that our going really is a loss, has come mostly from our students. The administration seems almost gleeful—or indifferent. I can't speak for other departments, but there's been nothing so far in biology to mark the occasion at all. Not even an email. If anything, it vindicates the decisions that many of us made to go, if this is what we're leaving.

Figure 8

Gopher snake, Great Meadow

Photo by Lee Jaffe

Endnotes

1. See "The Ceremony of Investiture of Chancellor Karl Pister: University of California, Santa Cruz, October 9, 1992," (Santa Cruz, Calif.: Presentations Unit of Media Services, the University Library, University of California, Santa Cruz, 1992), and Karl Pister, "Four Dreams" Typescript, Oct. 9, 1992, Available at Special Collections.

2. "Ronald Ruby came to UC Santa Cruz in 1965. He conducted research in biophysics. He served as chair of the physics board, chair of the Academic Senate, and associate dean of natural sciences. Ruby retired from UCSC in 1991 and died in 2003." See: https://currents.ucsc.edu/03-04/11-10/inmemoriam.html.

3. The student regent designate is a voting member of the Regents of the University of California, attending all meetings of the board and its committees and serving a one-year term. All mandatory university fees and tuition are waived for the student regent during the academic years in which he or she serves and expenses of attending the meetings are covered.

4. "Karl Pister's Willingness to Listen Carries the Day," *Santa Cruz Sentinel*, March 8, 1994.

5. An extensive colorful history of Elfland and the Elfland protests, as well as a map of Elfland, can be found in Jeffrey Arnett, *An Unnatural History of UCSC* (Second edition) Santa Cruz, Calif.: Bay Tree Bookstore, 2008).

6. Quoted in Jeffrey Arnett, 2008.

7. "California, Santa Cruz; Redwood Haven Inspires Battle Over an Elfland," *New York Times*, January 12, 1992.

8. "Tree Mourners Convene at Elfland," *Santa Cruz Sentinel*, Sunday, January 12, 1992.

9. Arnett, 2008.

10. On October 19, 1987, the Dow Jones Industrial Average lost over 22 percent of its value. The American housing market presented another sign of weakness as a result of the bankruptcy of many savings-and-loan associations. The collapse of the S&L industry hurt American households and led to a government bailout that caused government deficits. The Federal Reserve raised interest rates; then the Iraq War exacerbated the downturn. By 1990, the United States and other world economies were in a recession which officially is considered to have lasted eight months, but job losses and unemployment continued to rise, peaking at 7.8 percent in June 1992. The economy bounced back by 1993, fueled by the internet boom, low interest rates, low energy prices, and a booming housing market.

11. Katherine Beiers has deep ties to both the city and UCSC. She served as the assistant university librarian at UCSC's University Library for more than two decades; she has also served on the Santa Cruz City Council and twice as the city's mayor (1994-95 and 1998-99).

12. UC offered three early retirement opportunities to faculty and staff in 1990. As senior faculty and staff retired, the university could recruit junior employees at lower salaries. This program was known as the Voluntary Early Retirement Incentive Program (VERIP). A large number (one in eight, or eighty-four in total) of UCSC's faculty retired, along with many experienced staff. Many of the faculty continued to teach part time or do research.

Illustrations

Figure 1. Chancellor Pister with Student Union Assembly chair Brant Smith on tandem bicycle at McHenry Library, 1992. Photo by Don Harris. Courtesy Special Collections, University Library, University of California, Santa Cruz. UA 50: UCSC Photography Services: ua0050_neg_0932-2226a_19.tif.

Figure 2. Long-tailed weasel, 2008. UCSC Great Meadow. Photo by Lee Jaffe.

Figure 3. Save Elfland poster, 1991. Courtesy Special Collections, University Library, University of California, Santa Cruz. UA 70: UCSC Ephemera Collection: ua070-0048.

Figure 4. Golden Eagle on a campus bus stop shelter. July 12, 2013. Photo by Lee Jaffe.

Figure 5. Flyer Protesting Development. 1996. Courtesy Special Collections, University Library, University of California, Santa Cruz. UA 60: UCSC Poster Collection: ua060_013_0043.

Figure 6. Annual joint meeting between the Santa Cruz city council and university officials at the Civic Auditorium: Mayor Michael Rotkin and Chancellor Karl Pister, 1996. Courtesy Special Collections, University Library, University of California, Santa Cruz. UA 50: UCSC Photography Services: ua0050_neg_1225-1066b_06.tif.

Figure 7. Cattle stile, Great Meadow. 2016. Photo by Irene Reti.

Figure 8. Gopher snake, Great Meadow. Photo by Lee Jaffe.

Chapter 26

Persistent and Mounting Pressures
Affirmative Action and Diversity in a Hostile Climate

If you were a student of color, or a first-generation college student, if you were working class, you felt under attack.

—Tera Martin

"We Are All Involved":
Backlash, Proposition 209, and Campus Coalitions for Social Justice

Michael Cowan: There was the press for greater campus diversity in faculty, students, staff, courses. That pressure was constant and continued to mount in the 1990s. It was fueled not only by student activism, but by concerned faculty and administrators. At the same time, the campus, and the UC system as a whole, in pursuing affirmative action goals, had to deal with countercurrents in SP1 and 2 and then Proposition 209.[1]

Karl Pister: When I came to Santa Cruz, I brought a commitment to make accessible to all Californians the benefits of a college education. When I got here, I found that the campus certainly lacked no commitment to that same set of goals, but there were some problems; there were internal discords. The responsibility for diversifying the campus for students was too diffuse. It wasn't well articulated in the administrative structure we had.

The press that talked about my coming here mentioned my commitment to affirmative action at Berkeley, and the success I had at Berkeley. It was very important that the campus knew that. At my investiture, when I was formally made chancellor of this campus, in October 1992, we chose the theme Unity with Diversity. At a press conference associated with that ceremony, I made the statement, because we were entering into the budget-cut era, that I would not cut budgets of programs that were explicitly directed toward affirmative action. I have kept that commitment.

Valerie Simmons, Director, Equal Opportunity/ Affirmative Action: I was putting together UCSC's affirmative action plan. There hadn't been strong support on campus. My boss, Julia

Armstrong, was wonderful. She was in the chancellor's office, so she did a lot to persuade people there what needed to be done. When we had a new chancellor, Karl Pister, he was a tremendous champion for affirmative action. He backed everything that we were wanting to do.

Karl Pister: Over most of the time I've been here, the SAA/EOP students as a group were not disrespectful. They were not dumping on me. But they were suspicious. They didn't trust a white chancellor, to put it very bluntly. That, in my view, has changed at the end of my tenure here. I had an interview with two students who were writing for the magazine that the SAA/EOP students put out. [*TWANAS*] The students conveyed to me gratitude and respect for the work I've done. Putting myself in their position, I understand. Their initial wariness is a perfectly human thing, and I'm certain I would feel the same way, were I in their shoes, if the roles were reversed. At any rate, I think the student affirmative action structure and the relationship among the different groups is vastly improved at this point.

Leo Laporte: Only now, in the last several years, has the student body at UCSC changed in character. It's looking more like the state of California. We're in an exciting period. If the University of California is going to remain a premier public institution of higher education, not only nationally but internationally, how will we respond to the complexion of the student body who are going to be educated? The potential student base is changing, from dominantly middle-class white Anglos, to many more Hispanics, certainly Asian Americans. I always liked what President Bill Clinton said about having the US government look like the rest of the US population. I think that the University of California has to look like the rest of the state. It's going to take time. But

you got to start. You have to get kids in the pipeline in the schools.

Jessica Delgado, Student: I was born in 1968 in Los Angeles. My father is undocumented. He's from Cartagena, Colombia. My mother's family comes from New Mexico, and many of them are still in Santa Fe. I came to Santa Cruz in 1991, and I've been on this coast ever since. I graduated from UCSC in 1995.

I chose to focus on welfare policy, and I did original research on public assistance in Santa Cruz County. There was a community-based group of leaders working in a loose coalition called the Central Coast Coalition for Immigrant Rights. I decided to try to make my academic work flow with what I was trying to do as an activist, and worked on welfare politics, public assistance, and immigrants. I had support and room to do that. I didn't feel restrained by anybody.

I was in the Faculty Mentorship Program and in the Chancellor's Undergraduate Intern Program. I had support from the politics department. I also had an economics professor who helped me with the research and coming up with all the graphs and charts that I did for my final work. And I had help from community-based organizations. Oh, and the librarians! Oh my God, the two government documents librarians: Pat Pfremmer and Joanne Nelson, especially. I lived in the library, and they had this whole little section for me, a little tray with all this research that they would put in as they would get it. They really took good care of me, and so I was free to do what I wanted, and perfectly supported. As a student, it was a good place, going to school here.

Pablo Reguerín, Student: I was born in La Paz, Bolivia, in 1972. We came here when I was two. I come from a very loving family and people who believe in education. I feel very fortunate.

Figure 1

Indigenous California Women's Conference sponsored by the UCSC Women's Center. Drawing by Linda Yamane. 1992

California was much more immigrant-friendly back then. The country was in a different place and that opened up opportunities for my parents.

Once I got into college prep courses, I was oftentimes one of the only Latinos or people of color in class. I remember becoming increasingly angry. Until I came to UCSC in the early 1990s, and Oakes College, and took my first Oakes Core course, I didn't always have the language and I didn't know how to articulate what I was feeling, but I knew something was wrong.

My sister went to UCSC. I remember coming to visit her. She lived at Oakes and I liked the community. She took me to a class. It was a Spanish for Spanish Speakers class. I walked into a classroom full of Latino students and I knew that UCSC was the place for me.

David Anthony: Oakes was the hub of insurgency. Oakes attracted activist faculty and activist students.

Pablo Reguerín: Oakes was where the people of color were. College Nine and College Ten did not exist back then, so themes of social justice and social change were much stronger at Oakes. Oakes was the place to be as an activist for racial and economic justice. It was regarded as a home away from home for students of color. The year prior to when I came, there were student protests to create ethnic-themed floored housing. Casa Kahlo and Casa Huerta had been named. My sister was an RA at Casa Huerta when Dolores Huerta came for the naming of the building.

My experience at UCSC was transformative. I developed into a whole different person. I got a work-study job in the EOP office doing early academic outreach. I would go out to high schools to help people fill out their FAFSA's [Free Application for Federal Student Aid], help them fill out their college applications. I loved it. My need for social

change and equity in our society was being met through this work-study job.

I was nominated and selected as the Herman Blake Fellow for my graduating class of 1994 at Oakes. And even though I didn't know him, I had heard about Herman Blake, who he was and the influence he had on people.

David Anthony: Oakes became a lightning rod for many diversity issues. What is talked about in the culture wars[2] was definitely being waged there, like other places. At Oakes, diversity was being practiced. It wasn't being forced. I could certainly see this from the time I was provost, by who came through my office. It was a whole world in microcosm. You had immigrant folks; you had people who were transplants from other states and cities. It was a tremendous amount of vitality and differences, in terms of ethnicity and social class and languages. You can see it in the College Nights. There were so many special parts of the Oakes experience that I was enriched by.

People were very aware of the Rodney King riots in 1992.[3] People were aware of it in different kinds of ways. I think the people that were most aware of it were the people who were in, or close to L.A. We have a critical-mass connection to people who are from Los Angeles. Therefore, that was a very local issue, in addition to being a statewide issue. It led to forums; it led to people integrating these issues into the classrooms, and then to rallies. It was a galvanizing moment.

Arlyn Osborne: In 1992, the Women's Center helped a group of students, staff, and community members organize the Indigenous California Women's Conference at UCSC. We stipulated, "This conference is by, for, and about the indigenous women of California, the Native women of California. You don't have to be Native American. You don't have to be a woman in order to come.

Figure 2

Black Women of Santa Cruz Speak. Anita Hill/Clarence Thomas hearings. 1992

However, we request that you let the Native California women be at the center."

The group of Native American students and staff who put this together were very clear that even though their tribes were from all over, they wanted this to be for the California Indian women. So when it came to planning what the various workshops were, planning how people would be cared for, or housed, all of that, the California Indian women were involved in all of that. The conference was not about anthropologists being experts on Indians or Native Americans. It was not about people who want to learn the Lakota spirituality in a day or two, or in a weekend, and then practice it and become "a medicine person," or rub shoulders with someone who is a Native American because they somehow are in awe of that. It wasn't about that kind of appropriation. It was about women taking power over their lives, and talking with each other. To get this many tribes together, to get this many women together, was groundbreaking, and from what we understood, had never happened before.

Karl Pister: This campus, among the nine UC campuses, has the highest percentage of women on its faculty, and the highest percentage of faculty of color of any of the nine campuses.[4] But that doesn't mean that things are over. In my experience, the problem that has to be solved in diversifying the faculty is at least two-fold. First of all, in many fields the pool of candidates is very small, so you've got people pulling in three thousand directions. There are some three thousand post-secondary institutions in the United States. That brings you back to the pipeline. We need to educate more young people to start with, so the pool is larger.

The second problem is that there is a very strong, lingering, male-dominated academic environment in our institution.

Leta Miller: I never used my kids as an excuse for not being able to attend a faculty meeting or whatever. I did try to set up my teaching schedule—if it would work—earlier in the day so that I could be available after 2:30 in the afternoon. I felt strongly that I should not use my children as an excuse because that would reinforce stereotypes against women and against women's advancement.

I did notice that many of my male colleagues would use their children as an excuse: "Oh, I'm sorry. I have to watch my kids that afternoon." They didn't worry about it. But I worried about it because I didn't want it to reflect on me as a woman. Maybe I was too concerned about it. But I made a strong point of avoiding that. I don't believe there was anything conscious there at all on the part of my colleagues, but I didn't want to reinforce that stereotype.

Arlyn Osborne: The women students coming in by about 1992, 1993, did not expect to be sexually harassed. They got angry! Which is a very different reaction from being intimidated, scared, going home, changing majors.

The Anita Hill hearings were a tough time for women.[5] People came to the Women's Center and watched the hearings live on television: Arlen Specter and the things he would say to Anita Hill, the questions he asked. And behind him were the interns, the senate interns. We would see the looks on their faces with some of the questions. They could sit there for a certain amount of time, but then all of a sudden a question would come up—the way the senators asked some of these things of the women, or of Clarence Thomas, or of any of these people who were witnesses, during the hearing—you could see this look of complete disbelief come over— Then the camera would pan away, and they'd come back to Arlen Specter again, and those people would be gone and there'd be a whole new set of interns behind him, because obviously their shocked expressions were not good publicity for what was going on in the senate, the way the hearings were going—to blame her for being sexually harassed.

Women were riveted to these hearings. We schemed and talked, and next thing you know, we decided to have a "Breaking the Silence" event about sexual harassment on campus. It was a very powerful, very powerful. We did it in Classroom Unit 2, that big classroom. We collected stories of graduate students who were currently, or had been, undergoing sexual harassment on campus, who would not talk about it publicly because they felt their ability to continue in their field would be affected. They wrote some of their stories. They were changed enough not to be identifiable. Then undergraduates would read them, what women were undergoing in their fields, just trying to stay in their disciplines.

Rosie Cabrera: Another major sexual harassment incident erupted about 1990. The men in one of the Chicano/Latino organizations lived back in the Crown/Merrill apartments; they would set up the younger women. They would have parties and have drinking games. One student shared that she had been raped in the apartments. And that's when we found out the guys would get the younger students really drunk and then tell them, "Oh, go and rest in the bedroom." Some of them—it even hurts to even articulate it this way—they were really taken advantage of.

So there were years that were really tense, because, as staff, we took a stand. Imagine, these were students we knew—they were activists on campus, the men—and then having to work with the student. The campus couldn't really deal with this. It was a difficult time.[6]

We didn't have a Title IX office. There was the campus Rape Prevention Program and a sexual harassment prevention effort, but there were

nuances of conflict that had to do with cultural issues, even tensions with Rape Prevention. That office did what it needed to do, but there was more that needed to happen. The bottom line is the university wasn't dealing with the reality of what was happening.

Arlyn Osborne: We made this task force to review the policies and make recommendations to the campus on what needed to be done. There were a lot of discussions; we interviewed a lot of people, came up with a lot of recommendations, including having a sexual harassment officer on campus, because that was required by law, and previously it had been just tacked on to people's job descriptions. It was called Title IX officer, and it was tacked on to a number of job descriptions, and sometimes over the years people didn't even know it was in their job description. So we made some very clear recommendations that there needed to be a separate office, a contract with an outside consultant, because we felt that over the years, over and over it had been shown that it was a conflict of interest for someone who was an employee of the university to try to resolve a dispute against the university.

Julia Armstrong-Zwart: Rita Walker,[7] who had been serving as a sexual harassment officer—she worked in the police department, but she had also been performing that role—was hired after a search, as the first Title IX officer that the campus has had. We couldn't have made a better choice. I used to tell her, "You're like Joe Friday. It's sort of 'Dragnet.' Just the facts, ma'am. Just the facts." I think that the campus, with the revised policy and the hiring of Rita Walker, took a giant step forward on this issue.

There was also a systemwide Committee on Sexual Harassment, and I did serve on it. Serving on systemwide committees was one of the ways we were able to take what we had accomplished on this campus and inject it into the system. It was very different dealing with faculty from other campuses. While we at UCSC might have had a very permissive culture, we also had a very permeable culture—that is, one which was amenable to change. The cultures at the more established campuses were not that amenable to change. The Office of the President and the Office of General Counsel took what we had developed on this campus and, via this committee, sort of shoehorned it into the other campuses.

I'm the youngest child of four in our family. I felt that UCSC was also one of the youngest, not the youngest, but we were definitely the little brother or the little sister campus, and it was a good feeling that we actually had a voice in the family, in family discussions. We were the younger sibling who didn't quite measure up to its older brother. So, for UCSC to be able to join a systemwide committee and have that kind of impact was a good feeling.

Karl Pister: No matter what people say, the language, the culture, of the academy is white-male dominant. We're trying to break out of that.

Julia Armstrong-Zwart: If you figure we started the Target of Opportunity Program, maybe in 1982 or 1983 and in 1995 it was chopped off, that was a relatively short period of time. But it really did transform the campus. When I took over that role as assistant vice chancellor for faculty relations, my role was to look at the academic personnel process, and identify those decision points throughout the process where the process could be reviewed, and the decisions made to that point, scrutinized. The person carrying out that review could say: "Yes, you made a good faith effort. Yes, the pool is diverse enough." Or, "No, you need to go out and reopen the search." The first reviewer

would be the chair, and then, before the department could invite people for interviews, the dean had would have to sign off on it.

At that point, the dean could say, "No, I've looked at your pool. It's not diverse enough. I've looked at what you've done, your efforts. They're not adequate. You need to go back and do it again." At the point of appointment, where the academic vice chancellor looks at the file, we have had instances where the vice chancellor has stopped the search and refused to approve an appointment because he or she didn't feel that the search process had done everything that it could. It's a rare occasion that a search has been stopped—I remember two or three instances—but the possibility that it could happen, the fact that everyone knew that somebody was scrutinizing what was going on, kept departments honest.

Karl Pister: I have seen over and over again in faculty recruitments, when a person who's different from the dominant culture is discussed, there's an implicit assumption that difference means "less than." That's what we're dealing with. There's an enormous problem of acceptance, that a person can be different and yet be of the same quality. And God help us on that. It's going to take generations.

Julia Armstrong-Zwart: I think that TOP and the modification of the academic personnel process were the two most significant things the campus did. It could not have been done without the chancellor, vice chancellor, the senate, the deans, the chairs, and the faculty. The willingness to change was extraordinary. For a long time this campus—I don't know if it's still true—had the most diverse faculty by percentages of all the UC campuses. We had the largest percentage of women and the largest percentage of minority faculty. I would go to systemwide meetings and

Right Now Polls Say That Proposition 184 and 187 Might Pass.

California's White Supremacist Movement Must Be Stopped!

Prop. 184

"3 Strikes Initiative"

Will result in a massive increase of police and prisons without looking at the conditions such as racism, sexism and poverty that motivate crime. Taking money from social services to build prisons will only increase crime.

NO!
Prop. 187

"Save Our State Initiave"

This is an illegal attack on the indigenous people of California and any people who **"look like" immigrants**. Undocumented people would be deprived of all social services such as education and health care, and face deportation. **NO!**

We cannot afford to be silent. Join the March and **FREEDOM SCHOOL, Wed. Nov. 2nd.** Meet at UCSC, base of campus @ 9:30am for a March to the Couthouse on Ocean St. Demonstration at **noon**.

Labor Donated

Figure 3

Proposition 184 and 187 protest flyer, 1996

I would have people ask me, "How did you do it?" I'd talk about what we did, and they'd say: "Well, we could never do that at"—fill in the blank. Their campus cultures were not as permeable. I think because of the hires made initially, of very senior people and very junior people, that the junior faculty, as they developed their careers here, had a different mindset than some of their older colleagues.

Karl Pister: If I look back thirty or forty years, I lived in a virtually white world. That has been forty years or so of my experience at UC. That has changed dramatically. I can look back and remember when that white world started to take on some colored hues, and the process of learning to accept that and to be comfortable with that. I'm just one person in millions. We all have to go through that. Some people are never able to accept that, to go into a room where there are different kinds of people present, and not see that. In my view, that's what we're trying to do: we're trying to remove that differentiating quality, or the qualities of difference that are really accidental and have nothing to do with people.

Valerie Simmons: Then things started tightening down. People were questioning affirmative action.

Rosie Cabrera: There were the starts of attacks on bilingual education and attacks on who was legal, who was not. The students were very vocal. MEChA had coalitions with other orgs. At one point, with Propositions 227 and 187,[8] they went off campus, and where you turn to get on Highway 1 to go over the hill to San Jose, they all were arm-in-arm and stopped traffic right under the bridge that goes by the church. It was dangerous. Somebody could have really gotten hurt, but I think they really felt like there was a necessity to express.

Tera Martin, Student: I started grad school in American studies in 1993. Pete Wilson was governor most of the nineties. The mid-nineties was politically a lot of turmoil, such as race-baiting happening statewide. Proposition 187 was passed, which denied undocumented immigrants any public services—access to healthcare, access to schools. It was a heated election issue, ugly. It was held up in courts and never implemented. But the fact that it passed statewide spoke a lot to the time.

At the same time, California Governor Pete Wilson[9] and a UC Regent named Ward Connerly[10] moved to abolish affirmative action policies at UC.

Karl Pister: Amidst great controversy, in July 1995, the Regents of the University of California voted 14-10 on a resolution proposed by Regent Ward Connerly, to ban the use of gender and ethnicity in student admissions, substituting instead, economic and social need. The policy took effect in January 1997. I worked very hard with my colleague chancellors, and urged them to not be silent on this issue. I wrote the first draft of the position statement that the chancellors and the president adopted, because I felt compelled to have the chancellors (and later the president decided to join us) make a public statement. It was subsequently modified. We passed the draft around and the other chancellors had a chance to take a shot at it. That, ultimately, was the document that was published. I was very pleased that we were able to show that kind of unanimous support.

Well, of course the rest is history. I still have memories of sitting through that infamous regents' meeting. I still see the actors on the stage. I have to say that it was a staged play. I have no personal doubt whatever that the whole thing was staged for the governor's campaign. That doesn't mean that there are not some regents whose ideologies are against affirmative action. I'm not sure that there were fourteen regents who felt that way, who voted for these resolutions. But certainly a substantial number are simply opposed to the idea for various reasons. I've had some very frank discussions with a couple of regents that I really respect. I simply feel that this kind of a law, or this kind of a policy, is not the right one.

There was such an obvious political motive to this. After the meeting, I remember talking to a *Los Angeles Times* reporter. I was quoted as saying, "In all my years at UC, this is the worst day of my life." I felt so low about the university and felt so disappointed. I thought of all the years that I'd been working for the university, to open it up to students, to help the state reach out to the people of the state—all the reasons why I believe in affirmative action, the social good that is produced as a result, the fact that affirmative action is not just for the people that it helps, but for the society as a whole. It's so bloody damn obvious to me you're not just helping some small group of people; you're making your society better by doing this. For all these reasons, I felt very low after that meeting.

I've since written a couple of pieces on this decision. One of the pieces I wrote for the *UC Santa Cruz Review* went to the regents. It caused Regent Ward Connerly to be very angry with me. He wrote to the president and said that he thought I was insubordinate to write such an article. He insisted some action be taken—and the president ignored the letter, as far as I know. He may have responded, but he said nothing to me about it. But I subsequently talked to Mr. Connerly about his letter because I felt that I owed that to him. I explained to him that if one looked carefully at what I wrote, I said simply that I continue to feel that the regents' decision was the wrong decision, but that we had to be guided by it. As a long-time naval reserve officer I understood the idea of insubordination and I simply said to him "I was not insubordinate, sir. I don't have to agree with

your position, but I have to do what you ask me to do."

Tera Martin: And then Proposition 209 was passed on a state level, which abolished affirmative action policies in hiring and school admissions to anywhere that received public money. A lot of students and staff and faculty here felt very conflicted. If you were a student of color, or a first-generation college student, if you were working class, you felt under attack.

Karl Pister: We're working hard now with new admissions strategies. I would say that the university, vis à vis student admissions, now is not in an impossible position, but it just makes our job a great deal more difficult. I can't overlook the symbolic impact of the regents' action on our admission pool. I am convinced that the symbolic act they took will influence the number of applications that we get this year. By concentrating our outreach efforts, by doing a better job of working with our high schools and K-12 schools that send students to Santa Cruz, or to the university, we can increase the eligibility pool to offset the problem of the regents' action. We are doing that vigorously.

Valerie Simmons: UCSC had a program called Target of Opportunity, in which the chancellor would make available some faculty positions and if somebody came up with an outstanding applicant of color, then the chancellor would give the position to the department that had it, so that they could hire that person. That went away. When Prop 209 and similar sorts of movements were beginning to happen, the university attorneys were trying to get us to tighten up more and more.

Julia Armstrong-Zwart: I've objected to the substitution of the terms "diversity" for "affirmative action" or "equal employment opportunity," because "affirmative action" and "equal employment opportunity" have legal underpinnings. "Diversity" doesn't. It doesn't mean that you shouldn't focus on diversity, because that's a broader concept, but it's not a substitute for affirmative action or equal employment opportunity. To the extent that we have substituted "diversity" for those two legally based concepts, we've lost the two legally based concepts. They've become blanded out. I think there's room for all three concepts.

Herman Blake: I don't like the word "diversity" because too many people use it as a bean-counting thing—you got so many of this, so many of that, so many of the other. Well, does that make you a different or transcendent society?

Karl Pister: What can the university do? We can continue to emphasize our outreach programs, to create larger pools of applicants in California. The fact that the population base of California itself is diversifying means that if we do a better job of reaching out into the K-12 system to get young people, to get students for a university-level education, that in itself is going to help diversify our student body. Certainly there are geographic areas in California that are crying out for intervention to help raise the quality of preparation of students.

Valerie Simmons: After Proposition 209, we put a whole lot of emphasis on how academic units that were hiring defined positions, and where they did outreach, and how they did outreach. When I met with the search committee, I would give a whole talk on how to evaluate people fairly. We were tied with UC Riverside for the most diverse faculty in the UC system, which wasn't saying much. The faculty wasn't that diverse, but among the campuses, we were right up there. I think it's because the majority of faculty and staff on campus were in favor of affirmative action.

Jessica Delgado: We formed LOCA [Lesbians of Color Alliance]. We came together because we didn't feel like we belonged in the mainstream community. There were women who were new to identifying themselves as women of color or lesbians of color, in particular, and then there were others who had been around a long time, and had been fighting the battle for quite some time. We stayed together for a while, and mostly we were just trying to be shit-disturbers.

Some of us were really active in the No on 187 campaign. We marched at the pride parade. Everybody seemed to be unanimous about that, to show our visibility.

Rosie Cabrera: We moved from protesting Proposition 187, to Proposition 209, and Ward Connerly raising the affirmative action attacks. The students were real involved. I have to give Bettina Aptheker and Judy Yung[11] total props. The two of them assumed leadership and did a lot to raise the question on the campus to the broader front. They organized with graduate students. They organized with undergrads. And they organized with staff; they made every effort to include all segments of the campus community. They organized lots of teach-ins. All of us were involved. It became the question of the day.

Karl Pister: Santa Cruz originally was the most selective campus. It outdid Berkeley and UCLA and everyone else. Then it went through that dark night, which was turned around. But like many things, even though an institution has changed, just like a person changes from one experience in life and one characterization to another, the perception or the image doesn't change. There's a lag. I think Santa Cruz still is suffering from that.

That's one of the reasons why we've created a task force to look at our image to the outside world. This isn't the first time that's happened. Professor Dane Archer[12] sent me a report he put out sometime in the early seventies addressing the same question. There's a continuing sense on the part of some people that the fact that we have a narrative evaluation system—which overlooks the fact that grades are optional in many areas if you want to get a grade—this immediately says to some people, "Oh they don't give grades. They can't be a serious place with any quality." We're trying to deal with that issue. Among the campuses, we still are not seen by many as a serious place.

In the five years that I've been here, this year was the first time where I've really seen the whole campus—the academic part of the house, the faculty, the divisions, the boards of studies, along with student affairs and the enrollment people, the staff—working together on our open house day on April 20. For the first time, open house was not seen as just something the admissions people do, or the colleges do, but as something the whole campus does. There was a dramatic increase in the number of top students that we acquired this year. We had a scholars day, and invited the top 600 applicants, out of whom we got 123, including more than a dozen regents' scholars.

The old timers would say this is déjà vu because this happened when Bob Sinsheimer was first chancellor and he brought in Richard Moll to turn around admissions. In this last year, we brought in J. Michael Thompson from Irvine, who is a very accomplished enrollment manager.[13] Even in his first year he's made a dramatic difference, and we'll continue to see that reflected, just as Dick Moll did fifteen years ago. We have a task force designed to look at all the issues that affect Santa Cruz's image—retention, recruitment, academic programs. We're looking at how we present ourselves to our different publics. How do we characterize Santa Cruz?

In the years ahead there will be a gradual move to add more graduate study here. I don't see how we can remain as part of the UC system without doing that. This campus has a great opportunity to do that without giving up its commitment to undergraduate education. In the natural sciences, although now there're dominant graduate programs, there's still a demonstrable commitment to undergraduate teaching. What I'm hoping is that the campus in its evolution will keep that in proper balance. The faculty will be encouraged and rewarded to continue to work with serious undergraduates, to keep their teaching at the level that it has been, and not give that up in adding graduate students. It's not impossible. It's just that in other sister campuses and across the country the whole thing has gotten out of balance, to the point where too often the case is that in a research university a great deal of the undergraduate instruction is done by temporary faculty.

There's a real opportunity for us to carve out our niche. I hope my successor will see that and I think she will be encouraged by the faculty to maintain that commitment to undergraduate teaching.

Clark Kerr, in something he wrote in the eighties, called attention to the fact that, of the institutions of our society that have survived since 1500, our universities are among them. There are very few institutions that have survived the last five hundred years, universities being one. My personal sense of this is that among all institutions of society, our universities, and our churches and synagogues are the stabilizing influences that have provided continuity to our civilization. They are the glue that holds us together.

"The Glue that Holds Us Together": Karl Pister's 1996 Retirement

George Blumenthal: I always liked Karl Pister. My view of Karl's chancellorship has evolved over time. I thought, when he stepped down, that he had not been a particularly good chancellor. I wouldn't have said he was bad, but I would have said he wasn't particularly good. I felt that he hadn't given us a vision. He delegated too much. His style with Executive Vice Chancellor Michael Tanner was kind of Mr. Inside/Mr. Outside, which is a football term. He would deal with the outside world and he left Michael to deal with the campus. And as time went on, it was clear that he was devoting most of his time and attention to issues outside of the university—fundraising, working within UC, working in Sacramento.

Today I would take a different view. I think he was a pretty good chancellor. He did some things that had long-term benefit for the campus. He started the Educational Partnership Center, which did outreach to underserved communities in Monterey and Santa Cruz and other areas around here.[14] He did many good things that, as a faculty member, I wasn't really all that aware of. I've come to appreciate his chancellorship much more. I would now say he was a good chancellor, maybe not the best chancellor we've had in our history, but certainly a very good one.

Michael Cowan: I thought a great deal of Karl Pister. An immensely fair, thoughtful, caring person, with wonderful interactive skills; he cared immensely about diversity—his initiatives in terms of outreach, concerns about working with K-12, his initiative to establish a leadership opportunity scholarship for students transferring from community colleges—many things he did, he put his actions where his mouth was on that. I think that on the whole, despite the various controversies he had to deal with, he played a very positive

role and left the campus in very good shape for his successor.

Todd Newberry: UC campus organization is almost like a military arrangement, with the central administration, the commissioned officers. And if we non-com professors had any ambition, we'd rise to be lieutenants and captains and colonels like them. But we don't. We do other things. Yet here at UCSC we do want—we once had—our voices heard and honored, one by one, our voices of UCSC experience—or at least our voices of passionate commitment. Angus Taylor, I think, was a great success. He's an old UC hand. And the same thing with Karl Pister. But through their years, we grew and grew, and grew apart—administration and faculty turning into management and labor. Pister was probably a terrific appointment, but it should have been made fifteen years ago.

Rosie Cabrera: We did have a chancellor, Chancellor Karl Pister, who was profound. He was chancellor when Propositions 227, 187 passed; he was here when César Chávez passed away.[15] He grew up in the Central Valley. He understood these issues. He personally asked us to host a meeting with the faculty. He came to the meeting and he told the faculty, "If you work with this Faculty Mentorship Program, when your paperwork for tenure or promotion comes before my desk, I will not forget that you contributed." And that has never happened since, in terms of a personal commitment. When it came to affirmative action, he understood this was a big issue. I always felt like the students didn't really appreciate him, what it took for a person in leadership like that to take those steps, to be on the front lines.

Endnotes

1. In July 1995, the Regents of the University of California passed two landmark resolutions, Standing Policy 1 (SP1) and Standing Policy 2 (SP2), prohibiting "preferential treatment" on the basis of race, ethnicity, sex, and national origin in admissions, employment, and contracting. These resolutions were followed by the passage of the 1996 voter initiative Proposition 209, which incorporated similar prohibitions into the California State Constitution, effective August 1998. After Proposition 209, SP1 and SP2, Student Affirmative Action was eliminated and SAA/EOP changed to EOP only.

2. The term *culture wars* refers to the conflict between classical liberal, or conservative values, and social democratic or progressive values. The term was popularized in the 1990s in the United States by James Davison Hunter in his 1991 book *Culture Wars: The Struggle to Define America.* Hunter described what he saw as a dramatic realignment and polarization that had transformed American politics and culture, particularly with regard to controversial issues such as abortion, gun control, women's rights, gay rights, and racial politics.

3. The Rodney King riots took place in Los Angeles County in April-May 1992 when a jury acquitted four white officers of the Los Angeles Police Department of the usage of excessive force in the March 1991 arrest and beating of African American man Rodney King.

4. The earliest online data for UCSC faculty by ethnicity and gender are from 1996: https://planning1.ucsc.edu/irps/facRosters/FacultyDemographicReports1996.pdf.

5. Anita Hill became a national figure in 1991 when she testified that US Supreme Court nominee Clarence Thomas, who was her supervisor at the US Department of Education and the Equal Employment Opportunity Commission, had sexually harassed her. She was one of the people the FBI talked to while vetting Thomas. Arlen Specter (R-PA) interrogated her during the hearings and was widely criticized for his treatment of Hill.

6. See: "Letter to Karl Pister, Chancellor, University of California, Santa Cruz, from John E. Palomino, Regional Civil Rights Director, Region IX, San Francisco, Office for Civil Rights, United States Department of Education, concerning sexual discrimination at the University of California, Santa Cruz." Available in Special Collections, UCSC Library.

7. Rita Walker was UCSC's founding Title IX officer for twenty-one years, until she retired in 2014.

8. California Proposition 187 (also known as the Save Our State [SOS] initiative) was a 1994 ballot initiative to establish a state-run citizenship screening system and prohibit undocumented immigrants from using health care, public education, and other social services in California. Passed by voters, it was challenged in several legal suits and ultimately ruled unconstitutional by a US district court. Proposition 227, also called the English Language in Public Schools Statute, was approved in 1998. The proposition claimed bilingual education was the culprit for the low academic achievement and high dropout rates of immigrant children and proposed that English Language Learners (ELLs) be "taught English as rapidly and effectively as possible." This undermined most bilingual education in California.

9. Pete Wilson was governor of California from 1991 to 1999.

10. Wardell Anthony "Ward" Connerly is an African-American political activist, businessman, and was a UC regent from 1993–2005. He founded the American Civil Rights Institute, a national non-profit organization opposing racial and gender preferences.

11. Judy Yung was a professor of American studies, and taught Asian American studies and oral history (among other subjects) from the early 1980s until she retired in 2004.

12. Professor Dane Archer joined the sociology board in 1972. An expert in verbal and nonverbal communication; violence, war, and peace; social psychology; cross-national research; and crime and law, he taught at UCSC until his death in 2007.

13. UCSC hired J. Michael Thompson in 1995 as associate vice chancellor of enrollment management and director of admissions.

14. Established in 1999, the Educational Partnership Center helps increase access to postsecondary education for students in the Monterey Bay and Silicon Valley regions and helps underserved students succeed in college. https://epc.ucsc.edu/.

15. César Chávez, who co-founded the United Farm Workers Union, died April 24, 1993.

Illustrations

Figure 1. Poster, Indigenous California Women's Conference: Visioning the Next 500 Years. February 20-22, 1992. Sponsored by the UCSC Women's Center. Drawing by Linda Yamane. Courtesy Special Collections, University Library, University of California Santa Cruz. UA60: UCSC Poster Collection: ua060_021_0040.

Figure 2. Black Women of Santa Cruz Speak. Anita Hill/ Clarence Thomas hearings. 1992. Courtesy Special Collections, University Library, University of California Santa Cruz. UA 70: UCSC Ephemera Collection: ua070-0119.

Figure 3. Proposition 184 and 187 Protest Flyer, 1996. Courtesy Special Collections, University Library, University of California Santa Cruz. UA 70: UCSC Ephemera Collection: ua070-0013.

Chapter 27

Shaping an Identity for the New Millennium

UCSC as a Leader in Scientific Research

The words "research university" have appeared again.

—Hal Hyde

"The Best Opportunity in the Country":
Chancellor M.R.C. Greenwood

Henry Mello, California State Senator: No one expected UCSC to turn out as it did. They thought it would be like when they were in college. I thought that we'd have our own football team here, and a stadium.

I have worked with every chancellor at UCSC in one way or another. Dean McHenry said very proudly that the campus here would have as its main emphasis the liberal arts and humanities. I thought, nothing wrong with that, but what I saw as a pressing need, and the community did also, was for professional schools: computer science, engineering, and so forth. I made a pitch to all the chancellors. I said we have to diversify more. A lot of people went to Berkeley and to UC Davis and UCLA because we were not offering the kind of professional curriculum that they wanted.

Under Karl Pister is when it began to change. Then M.R.C. Greenwood got some people like Jack Baskin and others who made contributions, and established the school of engineering.

Hal Hyde: I think M.R.C. Greenwood is great. The words "research university" have appeared again. She's a very competent, bright, charismatic, fearless leader. I cheer her on.

Henry Mello: M.R.C. is probably the most phenomenal of all the UCSC chancellors. She's so bright and involved in the sciences, and master of everything. She gets out and raises a tremendous amount of money for the programs and the school, and has good relationships with the students. Now they are on a track to fulfill the true greatness of the University of California.

M.R.C. Greenwood: If one thinks about what made me different from most of the other chancellors, the most obvious answer is that I'm a woman. And the second most obvious thing is that I had had a different path because of my experience in the White House. I had been graduate dean at

Davis for about five years when I was approached by the White House during President Clinton's first term to serve as associate director for science. It reports directly to the science advisor, who reports directly to the president. The White House experience shaped my perspective on higher education. Probably the most important lesson I learned was that political agendas are decipherable, that political agendas require compromise, that political agendas are predictable, and if you can establish a relationship you can actually work in that environment and get things done.

When UC President Dick Atkinson called and offered me the chancellorship of UCSC I thought, what a great idea. It's such a perfect match. I'd had UC experience, but I'd also been at a small liberal arts college and in private universities, and I understood those mentalities, and the positives and the negatives of different types of institutions. I have strong professional credentials. l think that it's very important for the chancellor at Santa Cruz, maybe even more so than on some other campuses, to have the level of academic credentialing that allows one to carry one's weight in the circle of chancellors, and to be a national spokesperson on your own terms, not just because you are the chancellor of UC Santa Cruz, but because people know you in some other context. I think that's very important, because on the smaller, growing campuses it's a little bit like being Avis rental car agency [vs. the other major competitor car rental company, Hertz]. You are always having to prove that you deserve being in the game.

Some very distinguished people at Berkeley came up to me about a month or so after I had been announced, saying, "Why did you do that? You could have done something else." I said, "I did it because it feels like the right match. It feels like the kind of campus that I can enjoy, that I can work with. I have some ideas of how to advance it. It's a nice, manageable size. It's not such an overgrown octopus that you can't ever figure out where the next tentacle is. It has lost focus, but it can get focus again. I think it's the best opportunity in the country, frankly."

The offer came around the end of March, or the very first week of April. I snuck into town. This was supposed to be hush-hush. Nobody was supposed to know. I called Karl Pister and said, "Can I come and see you tomorrow?" He knew by then and he said, "Of course you can."

It was Easter Sunday. All the cherry blossoms were in bloom. The campus was exquisite. And, of course, all the camellias. Nobody knew that camellias were my favorite flowers in the world, so walking up to the door to University House was an astonishing experience. Karl and Rita Pister showed me around the house, and I chatted with them and had a light lunch.

Then Karl and I sat down and he told me what things they tell you the day after you say yes. There were some issues. The UCSC budget had been more or less fully expended—virtually no reserve. But nonetheless, being the optimist that I am, I said, "Oh well, I said yes. Now we go on." In my view, we had the opportunity to jump forward. I knew the engineering school was ready to be approved. I saw the opportunities in Silicon Valley and began to figure out how we could start making those moves.

I liked development and I knew we were behind in raising money. It was time for us to start putting a professional development organization in place. We've been working hard on: what is the image of Santa Cruz? The one that's current right now, "Thinking at the Edge," I believe captures our essence. I actually had suggested "Santa Cruz: Where Innovation Is Tradition," and then San Diego used it first. Or maybe we had the same idea and they just got there first, but in any case, that's where I had wanted to be. "Thinking at the Edge" is a really good way to go, too.

Michael Cowan: There was a committee that M.R.C. had appointed on the campus image. The goal was to brand the campus, to find a slogan. I, at one point, proposed that we use the term "Santa Cruz: A Campus on the Edge." I thought, cutting edge. Executive Vice Chancellor David Kliger strongly objected. He said it made it sound like we were about ready to fall off.

M.R.C. Greenwood: We made a list of every important group that I should speak with. We went through all the chambers of commerce for about forty miles around, a lot of Kiwanis and Lions and Rotaries. We talked about getting to know the city council members and the city manager, developing relations in Silicon Valley, joining an important group over there, speaking at their chambers of commerce, talking at the Commonwealth Club, doing the things that you need to do to be visible over there. So we started a systematic process of changing the look and the content of everything we were doing.

Figure 1

Chancellor M.R.C. Greenwood, 1997

Photo by UCSC Photography Services

The Science Success Story

Lan Dyson, University Librarian: Denial had to be pretty heavy to not think of science as a substantial component of Santa Cruz. As Santa Cruz reached its adolescence, it was the program it could sell its maturity on. Things like the Lick Observatory existed and were world-renowned. And the kind of attention that Santa Cruz wanted, as being something other than kind of a flaky, late-sixties, early-seventies time-warp place, required that you be able to, as they say, "point with pride" at programs such as the science program here, primarily biology and astronomy/physics, as being the premier programs, although certainly others such as environmental studies and chemistry had grown to equal prominence.

M.R.C. Greenwood: Our astronomy and astrophysics program is probably the best known and one of the strongest in the country. They had creative ideas about adaptive optics that sounded really good to me. I encouraged them. I personally got involved in advising them, from the perspective of somebody who knew what science and technology centers had to have in order to be successful. I became an active participant in helping them figure out their strengths, and how to make the best case for the Center for Adaptive Optics. I went to the National Science Foundation site visit on campus and spent the entire day. We were able to make some commitments at the site visit that may have been critical in helping us win the competition.

The STEPS Institute for Innovation in Environmental Research, founded to integrate science, technology, engineering, policy, and the Center for Ocean Health, were also faculty-led proposals. The Center for Ocean Health successfully got the new facility. I helped get the funding from the Packard Foundation to build that facility. When I first arrived, the folks had been working for a long time trying to get what is now the Seymour Marine Discovery Center and they needed the additional research facility.[1]

Burney Le Boeuf, Professor: I remember Chancellor Dean McHenry saying in the early years, "If this place is going to be successful, you people who are coming in right now fresh and new will have to make names for yourselves. You will have to be successful if this place is going to succeed." I think we've done that. There are many people in biology who have had exemplary careers— e.g., Harry F. Noller. He started here, became a leader in his field, and he's still the same person he was then. There are many others who have achieved much in other fields as well. Chancellor McHenry was prophetic.

But Dean McHenry, early on, said, or quoted someone else saying, when they first saw this campus, they thought that it would be a great place to do humanities, and to write poems under the redwoods, but surely they weren't going to do science in this atmosphere.

Michael Nauenberg, Professor: Humanities was supposed to be the centerpiece of this campus, with sciences only as the frosting on the cake.

Burney Le Bouef: Well, it has turned out to be just the opposite. Physics, astronomy, biology, and chemistry have all been very successful. The field I'm in, marine biology, or at least marine mammals, marine vertebrates—there's no better place in the world than UCSC, in my opinion, that trains people to do this kind of work, and gives them access to these kinds of animals. We get the best applicants. Marine science has a very attractive future here at Santa Cruz.

Figure 2

Earth and Marine Sciences
Building, 2003

Photo by Alan Nyiri

With the Monterey Bay Marine Sanctuary, and the 1994 closing of former US army base Fort Ord, we have a great deal of visibility for doing research on marine vertebrates here.[2] We have MBARI, the Monterey Bay Aquarium Research Institute, which is a very powerful unit.[3] We have something like seventeen institutions in Monterey Bay that do marine-related research. There is coalescing, collaboration and integration among all of these units. Monterey Bay is being used as a model for studying the ocean—the ocean interface with the land; the nearshore, and the effects of human activities. Our campus is in the forefront of this effort.

Michael Warren: There's still a powerful progressive vision latent in the campus: the idea that if people were going to do research, it should be socially responsible, and it should benefit humankind. For example, with the Human Genome Project, that extraordinary study was made available to everybody.[4] They were in a race with a private company and they won and made it publicly available, free. That is really admirable. That's what state universities should do. They are public institutions. I like to think that the people of the sixties would have said, "Yes. That's what's it's about."

George Blumenthal: David Haussler and the biologist, Jim Kent, who was a graduate student in biology, completed the Human Genome Project. Labs all over the world were measuring pieces of the human genome, but no one had solved the problem of how to put the pieces of the puzzle together and there were literally millions and millions and millions of pieces to that puzzle. David and his colleague figured out how to put them together into one map of the human genome, which we published on our website.

Jim Burns: Sequencing the human genome came to fruition in July 2000, when David Haussler's group announced that he and his team had sequenced a draft of the human genome and published it on the UCSC website. The web hits continue through the roof on that project.

The seeds for that went back fifteen years earlier, when Robert Sinsheimer, when he was chancellor here—and he was an eminent biologist himself—convened a meeting at UC Santa Cruz in 1985. Out of this group came the very radical proposal—at least at the time—to launch a massive project to ultimately map the complete DNA sequence of the human genome. It was fabulous that the sequence ultimately was completed by David Haussler's group on our campus, and the publishing of the draft sequence put UC Santa Cruz on the map in the genomics world.[5] It really did begin here, with Robert Sinsheimer back in 1985.

Dave Kliger, Dean of Natural Sciences: People thought of this campus as a humanities campus. It was amazing to me how many times I would talk to people from off campus, especially in Silicon Valley, and when I would say I was from UCSC and I was the dean of natural sciences, they would be shocked that we had any natural science departments on the campus. So it became pretty obvious that we needed a lot of work to develop our reputation in the science area.

I think in the early years of the campus, because of the nature of the discussions about the emphasis of the campus, a lot of people thought that this was really a humanities, social sciences campus. I don't think it ever was that, but that's where the reputation was developed. The reputation of any university is often at least ten years out of date.

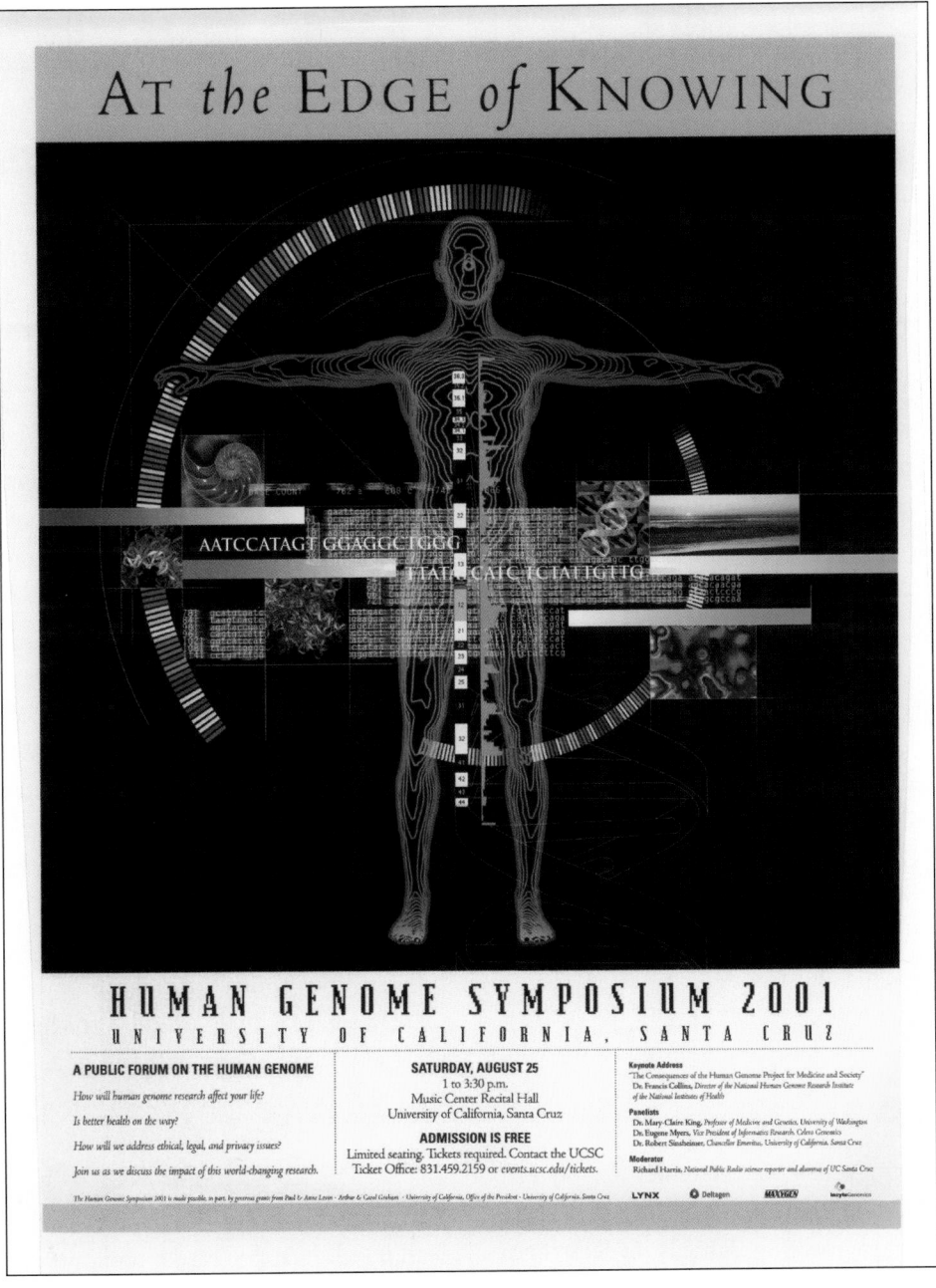

Figure 3

Human Genome Symposium
poster, 2001

"Finally Established":
Launching the Baskin School of Engineering After Thirty Years

Ed Landesman, Professor: I was put on the first engineering committee soon after I arrived at the campus in '66. That was the one where we were expected to—and McHenry certainly wanted this to happen—start a school of engineering. Francis Clauser, who had been hired from California Institute of Technology, was an engineer—and he was brought in to start an engineering school. There were two other faculty members from computer science who were also on that committee: Harry Huskey[6] and David Huffman.[7]

Kenneth Thimann: Francis Clauser was McHenry's vice chancellor. He's a physicist and was very helpful on the physics and math side. Clauser was a most useful, interesting, and delightful person. He was thinking all the time about an engineering school along some fresh lines. He and his wife were very charming too. Do you know what they had for a hobby? You would never think of it; you wouldn't believe it if I gave you a hundred guesses—deciphering Egyptian hieroglyphics. It requires a knowledge of history and linguistics and symbology and so forth— all kinds of things that have nothing to do with physics or engineering.

Ed Landesman: When we presented our plan, it was turned down. There was a feeling that there were enough engineering schools in Northern California, let alone in the state. Also, at that time, there weren't that many engineering jobs available. Stanford University had engineering; UC Berkeley had engineering. The very distinguished engineer, Frederick E. Terman, at Stanford—and others— came back with the recommendation that we do not start an engineering school at UCSC. That

took care of any prospects for engineering on the campus at that time.

Kenneth Thimann: Clauser was awfully disappointed when some feeble committee came in with the recommendation that we didn't need an engineering school. That's when he left and went to Caltech. It was a terrible disappointment. I know a number of us, including McHenry, were very, very disappointed. McHenry had envisioned an engineering school as the start of other professional schools at Santa Cruz, and that did not happen.[8]

Dean McHenry: A report came out that said California already had more engineering schools than it needed. It killed us. Charles Hitch was new as president of UC. He didn't stand up and fight. I've often regretted that I didn't threaten to resign. It was my greatest disappointment. We had good connections, but we didn't have punch.[9]

Clark Kerr: I think that was a great tragedy in the life of the campus. The campus developed a kind of soft image which would have been corrected with some professional schools, which would have started with the engineering school, which got cut out.

Ed Landesman: But the happier part of the story is that it did happen, but it took more than twenty years for it to occur. I was delighted to be selected to be on the "second" engineering committee in the early 1980s, and that was when we finally did begin to get engineering on the campus. At that time, what was most needed was computer engineering, both locally and in the state. There was a demand for highly qualified engineers with

Figure 4

Engineering 2 Building, 2008

Photo by Phil Carter

degrees in computer engineering. Pat Mantey[10] was brought in from private industry to start engineering on the campus. Pat and I collaborated by developing and instituting the first advanced math course, beyond calculus, for the engineering students.

M.R.C. Greenwood: Before I arrived, during Karl Pister's time, a committee had been put together by Pister, headed by theoretical chemist Eugene Switkes, that presented the case for moving forward with a school of engineering.[11] And it was probably the first decision that I had input into, actually before I was chancellor, because this had been approved and was moving forward to the Office of the President, and as Karl Pister was leaving it moved up to the Office of the President for presidential concurrence. President Atkinson called me at that point and said, did I know about the proposal? I said, yes, I had been informed about it in my briefings to become chancellor. And was I in favor of it? Was I ready to move forward with it? Of course, I had some trepidation, because I already knew enough about Santa Cruz to know that there was at least some opposition to the introduction of engineering, and that moving it forward was probably going to require some energy and some talent. I also, however, recognized that if I were to hesitate it probably would have been very difficult to implement it two or three years later. Something like that happens and it gets moving, and then if you end up stalling it for a couple of years, people start thinking about other things they'd like to see the university do. Then you lose the impact of the faculty committee's report and it can get effectively stalled.

I had read the report, and I thought they made a very compelling case. At the time, of course, there was no question that California needed more engineers, and that Santa Cruz was capable of producing them. We had quite a number of students who were transferring out of Santa Cruz to go someplace where they could get engineering degrees in something other than computer engineering.

So we established the school. We had a benefactor in the wings, Jack Baskin, who was interested in starting the school. I was a brand-new, naive chancellor. I went over and I just said, "Mr. Baskin, I think it's really important that we launch this school. We need your support. You've helped us so much, and I know this is what you see as your legacy." His wife, Peggy Downes Baskin,[12] said to him, "Jack, this is an opportunity for a legacy." And we were able to announce that we had the gift at my inauguration, which was really nice.

Ed Landesman: It was certainly exciting that finally engineering had been established on the campus. Pat Mantey was chair of computer engineering and became the founding dean of the Jack Baskin School of Engineering.

M.R.C. Greenwood: Then, having gotten the engineering school off the ground, it became clear to the faculty and also, I think, to the university and particularly to the Silicon Valley folks, that we were serious. I started talking about how we were going to be graduating as many undergraduate engineers as Stanford in a relatively short period of time, that we would be hiring first-rate faculty, UC-quality faculty, only in the really high-tech moving fields. We weren't going to be burdened with outdated departments. Some of the engineering schools that have such departments have no way of getting rid of them, and those faculty are still quite powerful professors, so they continue to influence the direction of the curriculum.

I talked with the deans of engineering at Berkeley and Stanford and Michigan and a couple of other places, and they all said to me, "You've got the best opportunity of anybody in the country, even though I'm sure you're starting it on a shoestring. But you can build a 21st-century engineering school, instead of trying to reshape a 20th-century engineering school. You've got some real opportunities here." And that was the approach we took. We took the approach that we wanted to make it an engineering school that would focus on what California and the nation needed for the future.

David Kliger: M.R.C. was very ambitious for the campus, was a cheerleader for the campus, and had tremendous energy. The National Science Foundation has these science and technology centers that are very big deals. It's very large grants for five years. It can be renewed for a total of ten years. We had never gotten one of these before, but the Center for Adaptive Optics was developed.[13] Certainly, that got approval because of a very strong proposal from the astronomy faculty, who partnered with other universities and came up with a great idea. But it wouldn't have happened without M.R.C. pushing and M.R.C. making commitments that she knew would be necessary in order to finalize the deal. M.R.C. was tuned into political issues and knew how to get things done that I have not seen any other chancellor be able to do.

Figure 5

Center for Adaptive Optics, 2011

Photo by Chenyue Jiang

"There Really Are Two Universities":
The Diminishing Space for Humanities

Jim Clifford: The humanities division has shrunk, withered. Looked at as a whole, it's catastrophic and frightening. It's becoming a miniature division, with small departments on the edge of dysfunction.[14] I suppose humanities may rebound eventually. But in the meantime, deep damage has been inflicted. I keep being reminded of Norman O. Brown's late collection of essays. Its title fit perfectly: *Apocalypse and/or Metamorphosis.*[15]

What is humanities, anyway? Humanities is something much bigger than an academic division. I have developed an idea of what I call the greater humanities. This is an attempt to resist the tendency to belittle the humanities—an ever-decreasing and less relevant sector under the corporate logic of the contemporary university. In the new context, if you don't bring in money and you don't produce outputs that can be shown to directly benefit the economy of the state of California, you hardly exist. You're kept on at sufferance.

The humanities are undergoing a process of relentless belittlement, turned into a kind of décor, or a garnish for the real meal at the university. You know, "Everyone needs a bit of Shakespeare. Everyone really should take an art history or a philosophy course, but let's not encourage students to major in these fields. They don't lead to careers, do they?" And so on and so forth. We know the relentless logic. The greater humanities, as I define it, is not small. It cannot be marginalized. It is a broad potential alliance and common perspective that includes segments of the social sciences, the qualitative social sciences and the historical social sciences, as well as the arts and a whole range of historical subjects.

Helene Moglen: The Writing Program has been cut way back. You can really talk about literacy problems, the gap between what students hear in lectures and what they need work in understanding and writing about. We've lost a lot of the soul of Santa Cruz—in the abandonment of later incarnations of the colleges, of interdisciplinary programs, of institutionalized opportunities for meaningful community work. When I came, there was a little publication called *Teacher on the Hill.*[16] People used to talk about pedagogy all the time. We have gifted teachers here. But they are so overworked. And you have a situation in the social sciences where mostly what students are doing is taking short answer exams. That's what they do. They're not writing papers in the social sciences, because—I don't know how many students are assigned to each TA, they can't read papers. They do these Scantron exams. This is UCSC! Scantron exams. There are a few programs, of course, in the humanities and a few in the humanistic social sciences where students are still writing.

Jim Clifford: The value of the greater humanities would be to break down the distinctions that result in blindness, like the inability to recognize humanities research as research—a whole set of assumptions that are in the air. I certainly don't want to pin these on individual scientists, especially not those at UCSC, many of whom have a very broad notion of the relation of natural science to other forms of knowledge production. But anything that could break down the structural, institutional, material forces that are hardening this boundary line now in all sorts of ways, that are absolutely inimical to what I used to think of as the arts and sciences university—where the

Figure 6

Jim Clifford, 1985

Photo by Shmuel Thaler

"and" in arts and sciences was a genuine "and," where there was no hierarchy built into that joining of two sides. The greater humanities—which I'm associating with the word "arts" in that phrase—the greater humanities were half the university. But now the humanities are at best a fifth of the university, when you start to break it down in the funding charts—actually less than a fifth in most places. I don't mean to reduce everything to funding. But you can't ignore it. There are intellectual consequences that are devastating the university.

Pavel Machotka, Professor: The humanities are, by nature, both deeply attentive and critical, indispensable to all critical thinking. But they are in retreat, here at UCSC as well, and it is they that are the most urgently needed by society, whether as disciplinary programs, or interdisciplinary ones like the aesthetic studies major at College Five. There may be pockets of humanities teaching, but they're like the monasteries of the past, oases of learning which managed to preserve ancient manuscripts for the future.

Jim Clifford: C.P. Snow wrote a book in the fifties about the two cultures, which is about the humanities/science split.[17] It was a controversial and scandalous book in its day. Lots of things can be said about the value and reality of that particular sharp line. But I think increasingly in the actual university, in the institutional university today—and this has to do with questions of resources and funding and things like that—there really are two cultures. There really are two universities. The line is drawn, and it falls roughly onto divisional categories. Now, with the addition of engineering to natural sciences—and we can probably throw economics into the bag—that's a sharp line. Very little substantive research and thinking and collegiality of the sort of thing that was part of the

dream of the colleges, very little of that crosses the boundary. Oh, there are small crossings, and a good deal of unfocused desire to make links. But the two cultures have hardened.

Figure 7

Angela Davis event poster, 2009

"I Learned the History":
Town-Gown Frictions and a Search for Common Ground

John Laird, Mayor of Santa Cruz: The university has matured. M.R.C. Greenwood is the most community-friendly chancellor there has been, with the possible exception of Dean McHenry, who brought the campus here. But the community has changed in thirty-five years. I think it's down now to where the more conservative or older part of the community can't be more than 10 or 15 percent of the community.

Rahne Alexander, Student: I've been working at the Santa Cruz Diner for the last six months or so. A couple of weeks ago, I had some hillbilly patrons come in, like gun-toting guys from out of town, in the middle of the night, really loud, really obnoxious. At the same time, there was a couple, UCSC students, definitely heterosexual and together. They were holding hands across the table and all this really cute stuff. These are my only patrons in the diner. And these guys come in, and one of them, after I serve them their food, asks me, "What gender are you?" Immediately, I'm on edge because these are guys who could do a lot of damage to me if they decided they were going to commit violence. A lot of these things come to mind. I think of Matthew Shepherd[18] and Brandon Teena[19] in those moments. I turned to him and I told him, "I'm femme."

He starts musing aloud about this. I don't remember exactly what all he was saying, but I walked away from him, and a moment later, I just turned and asked him, "So, what makes you think I'm female?" Which is like this really incredibly confrontational statement, right? I'm not letting this go. Clearly, I'm going to make him work some more. He starts musing aloud about this, about what he thinks sex and gender is, and how he figured this stuff out. And the male of this UCSC student cute couple pops his little head up and goes, "Gender is a social construct!" This guy, he just leans over his shoulder and goes, "No, it's not." And starts trying to figure out-loud how gender is not a social construct. Then the girl of the couple, she pipes up and goes, "Yes, gender is a social construct. Sex is a biological fact, but gender is a social thing." And suddenly this whole conversation is going on without me even being involved, between my patrons, about what sex and gender are.

I've initiated this, because something about my presentation was not necessarily normatively gendered. After this goes on for a little bit, I'm thinking, this is amazing; this is marvelous. Clearly there're some things that are going on through UCSC, and I don't know whether it's just because of the women's studies classes, or if these classes have informed other classes. But clearly, this is something that is being really filtered down.

John Laird: Now, the university is really part of the community. And if you look at the alumni numbers, I think over 8000 graduates of UCSC are still in the Monterey Bay area.

M.R.C. Greenwood: So, part of what I did that started repairing and working out relationships with the city council was to learn the history. When Dean McHenry rode into town, the tax laws in the state of California allowed for the city to get substantial real estate taxes, which they then promised to use to build infrastructure, including the eastern access to the campus, and other roads and bridges that were needed on the campus. Santa Cruz wanted the university. The county promised all sorts of things to try to beat out the competition in Almaden. The city had every expectation that it would be able to provide these services. Well, the 1986 tax laws,[20] Proposition 13, and other things changed the tax base that the city had to work with, which then changed the politics in terms of whether the university was seen as a boon or a drain to the local community.

I learned the history, not just who owed whom what, but what the terms of engagement were. What had changed? Why is it harder for the city to do this? Why do they really react, or overreact, when we do something? Why do they think that we should do different things on the campus? Why did Bob Sinsheimer get in trouble when he proposed a research park, and now the city wants one? What is considered acceptable in order to have a tax base to provide social services changes over decades?

What I've always tried to do, whether it's here or in Silicon Valley, is to try to understand what the local politicians are having to deal with. What is their constituency base? What are their main concerns? What levers do they have to get what they need to stay in office and to provide services? Then, how can the university try to play to those strengths, and not run up against them?

We did not have any obligation to have more city-university meetings after the last meeting associated with the College Eight lawsuit, which was settled in December 1987.[21] But instead of saying, "Okay, that's it. We're done," which is what I was advised by some to do, and what another chancellor might have done, I decided to continue the meetings. These had typically been annual "bash-the-university" meetings. One particular one was headed in that direction, in part because of UCSC's proposal to build the Core West parking garage.[22] I decided, I'm going to try to stop this bashing, so I asked the UCSC staff to find out how many parking garages the city had built. How many parking spaces does the city

have? Why is it that when they build a parking garage, it's not said to draw traffic? I'm going to have those numbers when this issue comes up at the meeting.

That was one of their first encounters with me. When one of the then-councilpersons started down that road, I let them go all the way down the road for a while. Then I said, "Well, now let me give you some perspective. From our point of view, you've done this and this, and I think you're about to build another parking garage. We propose to build a parking garage and it's going to draw traffic." I just used a little humor. I said, "So I've asked our physicists if they can help me explain why it is that the materials in our parking garage will draw traffic, while the materials in your parking garages apparently repel traffic, and we'll try to modify our building plans to include the repelling materials in the garage." They all cracked up. I mean, what can you do? Politicians are politicians. They know when they're playing politics and they know when their good case has been undermined.

Michael Cowan: One of the things I had to do when I was working as faculty advisor to M.R.C. Greenwood was to sit in a small negotiating group—it wasn't a formal negotiating group—but to talk with city leaders and county leaders, including Mardi Wormhoudt, about campus growth. And conscientiously trying to represent the university's position, I at one point indirectly accused Mardi Wormhoudt of having positions that were strangely close to those of people who wanted to block immigration into California. It was a kind of pull-up-the-drawbridge attitude. This campus also had a responsibility for diversifying its body and it had to do that by growing. It was not a happy confrontation. I was unusually undiplomatic. I'm usually better on such matters.

M.R.C. Greenwood: We're paying for part of the city water system. We are the best water users in the county. We're using only 5 more percent more water today than we were using when we had five thousand fewer students. Why is nobody else in the city held to these standards? Why is it that there's no penalty for using more than your fair share of water anyplace else in the city? We're not water hogs.

We are a stable—not likely to outsource overseas—source of employment for people who will, in fact, stay in the area and participate in the community. I recently did an analysis that showed that of the 1200 high-tech jobs they have lost on the Westside starting in about the year 2000, we've already replaced about 800, because we've gotten a laboratory for adaptive optics; we've gotten several major grants in the education area. We've got 250 more faculty members, and the ones that are in the sciences are already generating new grants. So, these create technical jobs. They create secretarial and support jobs. They create some new entry-level jobs in maintenance, etc. The jobs that you want to have here in Santa Cruz, some of them are generated by the university. When our faculty members get grants, 80 percent of that money, more or less, goes to pay for people's jobs, and benefits, and taxes in the county and city, when these individuals buy houses and shop in the community. So when you're talking about how is the city going to sustain itself, you need to be talking about how many more jobs of a certain type can we expect the university to generate? And are those jobs that will replace jobs we are losing in some other sector?

John Laird: This year, with the opening of the new colleges, and even though very controversial, the Holiday Inn, the Town Center, they are doing a lot of things to provide additional housing.[23]

Additional housing will help the housing crisis in the region.

Michael Cowan: I think that the campus quietly told the Office of the President that they wanted to have a higher bar than the 15,000 agreed to in the 1988 LRDP. The UC administration argued that we had a state mandate to absorb our share of the so-called Tidal Wave II[24] and that all the campuses had to do their job. It had been the rationale for establishing UC Merced[25] and the other campuses were supposed to do their share, including Santa Cruz.

M.R.C. Greenwood: The city fathers and city politicians will say, "The university can do whatever it wants to do. They're autonomous. They don't have to do what we want them to do." That is, in fact, a half-truth. We do have constitutional autonomy. We do not have to have their permission for every permit that we need. It is also, however, the case that we have to abide by CEQA rules and regulations, that we have to have a long range development plan, which, while the city doesn't get to approve, they can certainly influence.[26] We can't dig up a field; we can't build a building without going through an environmental impact statement.[27]

Yes, we get the students, and they are an economic positive impact, in that they buy stuff, and they eat in the restaurants, and their parents come to town, and their families come to town and stay in the hotels, particularly in the off-time of the season. All these factors exist. But then, there are the most important factors, like the real jobs that the university creates, which don't disappear when a dot-bomb bubble happens.

John Laird: I think the relationship between the city and the university has gotten closer, although there are still some tensions over a number of different things. It will never be easy.

Endnotes

1. The Center for Ocean Health at the Joseph M. Long Marine Laboratory opened in 2001 and serves as a focal point for scientific research, education, and policy programs that address ocean conservation and management issues. Two nonprofit conservation groups have offices at the Center for Ocean Health: the Nature Conservancy's Coastal Waters Program and the Island Conservation and Ecology Group. Also located nearby are the Seymour Marine Discovery Center, with a university teaching lab and public education programs; the National Marine Fisheries Service (NMFS) Santa Cruz Laboratory; and a marine wildlife center run by the California Department of Fish and Game (CDFG).

2. Fort Ord is a former United States Army post on forty-five square miles near Seaside, on the shore of Monterey Bay. It closed in 1994—one of the largest US military bases ever shut down, leaving behind an area the size of San Francisco—as a result of the Defense Base Closure and Realignment Act of 1990. Military use of the site dates back to 1917. For a detailed discussion on the closure and conversion of Fort Ord see the oral history *Congressmember Sam Farr: A Life of Public Service* (Regional History Project, UCSC Library, 2017). The Fort Ord Reuse Authority (FORA) is responsible for the oversight of Monterey Bay area economic recovery from the closure of and reuse planning of the former Fort Ord military base. The Fort Ord Dunes State Park and National Monument was established on part of the former Fort Ord in 2012 and UCSC also manages the Fort Ord Natural Reserve on the site.

3. Founded in 1987, the Monterey Bay Aquarium Research Institute (MBARI), in Moss Landing, California, is a world center for advanced research and education in ocean science and technology.

4. "On June 22, 2000, UCSC and the other members of the International Human Genome Project consortium completed the first working draft of the human genome assembly, forever ensuring free public access to the genome and the information it contains. A few weeks later, on July 7, 2000, the newly assembled genome was released on the web, along with the initial prototype of a graphical viewing tool, the UCSC Genome Browser. In the ensuing years, the website has grown to include a broad collection of vertebrate and model organism assemblies and annotations, along with a large suite of tools for viewing, analyzing and downloading data." See: http://genome.ucsc.edu/.

5. A Distinguished Professor of Biomolecular Engineering, David Haussler leads the Genome Bioinformatics Group at UC Santa Cruz, which assembled the first working draft of the human genome sequence and posted it on the web.

6. Harry Huskey was a pioneering computer scientist who worked on early computing systems and later helped universities around the world establish computer centers and computer science programs. Huskey came to UCSC in 1967 and became a founding faculty member of the computer and information science program. He set up the UCSC Computer Center and served as its director for over ten years. He retired in 1986 at the age of 70 and died in 2013 at age 101.

7. David Huffman came to UC Santa Cruz from MIT in 1967 as a founding faculty member of the computer science board. He played a major role in the development of the board's academic programs and the hiring of its faculty, and served as chair from 1970 to 1973. He retired in 1994, but remains active as an emeritus professor.

8. The Coordinating Council for Higher Education in California hired Frederick Terman as a consultant. He produced what became known as the 1968 Terman Report: "A Study of Engineering Education in California." See https://files.eric.ed.gov/fulltext/ED037199.pdf. This report resulted in the regents deciding not to support an engineering school at UCSC during its early years.

9. Don Miller, "Dean McHenry—Taking a Look at the Way Things Were," *Santa Cruz Sentinel*, October 24, 1985.

10. Patrick Mantey came to UCSC in 1984 from IBM. The founding dean of the Jack Baskin School of Engineering, he now directs the school's Information Technologies Institute.

11. Theoretical chemist Eugene Switkes is Professor Emeritus of Chemistry and Psychobiology.

12. In addition to her philanthropic work with her husband, Jack Baskin, Peggy Downes Baskin has been involved and active in the humanities at UCSC for many years as a lecturer and senior research associate in feminist studies. She helped create and fund UCSC's Girls in Engineering summer-school program, which is designed to encourage interest in engineering among seventh- and eighth-grade girls from Santa Cruz and Monterey counties. Before her tenure at UCSC, Peggy taught politics at Santa Clara University for eighteen years. In addition to her academic interests, Peggy is a writer and photographer.

13. The Center for Adaptive Optics is a Science and Technology Center that was funded for ten years by the National Science Foundation (NSF) and is now funded by

the University of California. The Center is headquartered at UC Santa Cruz, with members from eight other UC campuses and with many academic and industrial affiliates.

14. In 1997, UCSC officially began using the term "departments" instead of "boards of studies." Some longtime faculty and staff still use the term "boards of studies," either out of habit, or as a political statement in support of the early ideals of the campus.

15. Norman Oliver Brown, *Apocalypse And/or Metamorphosis* (Berkeley: University of California Press, 1991).

16. *Teacher on the Hill: Faculty Conversations About Teaching and Learning at UCSC.* (Santa Cruz, University of California, Santa Cruz). Available at UCSC Library Special Collections.

17. C.P. Snow, *The Two Cultures* (Canto edition. Cambridge, England: Cambridge University Press, 1993).

18. Matthew Shepherd was a gay student at the University of Wyoming who was beaten, tortured, and left to die near Laramie on the night of October 6, 1998. After Matthew's murder, members of the Tectonic Theater Project in New York City traveled to Laramie, Wyoming, to interview residents about how the attack on Matt had affected the town. These oral histories were transformed into the play *The Laramie Project.*

19. Brandon Teena was a trans man who was raped and murdered in Humboldt, Nebraska in 1993. His story was made into the film *Boys Don't Cry* and raised consciousness of hate crimes against the trans community.

20. In October 1986, under President Ronald Reagan, the US Congress passed the Tax Reform Act of 1986 (TRA) to simplify the income tax code, broaden the tax base and eliminate many tax shelters. The top tax rate for individuals for tax year 1987 was lowered from 50 percent to 38 percent.

21. In 1987, the city of Santa Cruz filed a lawsuit against UCSC for its plans to build a new $20.7 million college (College Eight). The suit sought to invalidate the UC Regents' approval for funding until university officials could prove that construction would comply with state and environmental requirements.

22. The Core West Parking Garage is often praised and recognized as architecturally innovative. See Frank Zwart's oral history for a detailed discussion of its design.

23. Laird is referring to a period from the mid-2000s to 2011, when UCSC housed some undergraduate students in the University (Holiday) Inn downtown on Ocean Street.

Other students were housed, as they are today, in a building on Pacific Avenue called the University Town Center. See https://housing.ucsc.edu/guest/ and https://housing.ucsc.edu/utc/.

24. Tidal Wave II is the name former UC president Clark Kerr gave to the enrollment swell that would be generated by children of the Baby Boom.

25. The history of UC Merced dates back to 1988, when the regents first authorized planning for at least one additional campus based on projections of long-range enrollment demand. In May 1995, after a long site-selection and environmental-review process, the UC Board of Regents selected a site in eastern Merced County for the 10th campus of the University of California, which opened in 2005.

26. The California Environmental Quality Act (CEQA) passed in 1970, instituting a statewide policy of environmental protection. CEQA does not directly regulate land uses, but instead requires state and local agencies within California to follow a protocol of analysis and public disclosure of environmental impacts of proposed projects and to adopt all feasible measures to mitigate those impacts. CEQA makes environmental protection a mandatory part of the development decisionmaking process of every California state and local (public) agency. It has also become the basis for numerous lawsuits concerning public and private projects.

27. Under the 1879 California Constitution Article IX, Section 9, the University of California is exempt from local land-use regulations, including general plans and zoning. UC still abides by the California Environmental Quality Act (CEQA). For more on UC's constitutional autonomy see: http://www.lib.berkeley.edu/uchistory/archives_exhibits/masterplan/law2.html.

Illustrations

Figure 1. Chancellor M.R.C. Greenwood. Courtesy Special Collections, University Library, University of California, Santa Cruz. UA 50: UCSC Photography Services: ua0050_neg_0097-2110e_12.jpg.

Figure 2. Earth and Marine Sciences Building: interior detail view of the atrium. Photograph © 2003 by Alan Nyiri, courtesy of the Atkinson Photographic Archive. UCSC_12_rf. Contact Special Collections and Archives for a high-resolution electronic file for University of California purposes. All other requests for permission to publish this image should be directed to Alan Nyiri, My College Image, LLC, 1129 East Main Street, Poultney, VT 05764. Email: anyiri@adelphia.net.

Figure 3. Human Genome Symposium poster, 2001. Courtesy Special Collections, University Library, University of California Santa Cruz. UA 60: UCSC Poster Collection: ua060_021_0042.

Figure 4. Engineering 2. Photo by Phil Carter. Campus photo archive, Communciations and Marketing Department, UC Santa Cruz. Copyright UC Regents, 2009.

Figure 5. Center for Adaptive Optics. Photo by Chenyue Jiang. 2011. Campus Photo Archive. Communications and Marketing Department, UCSC. Copyright UC Regents.

Figure 6. Jim Clifford. Photo by Shmuel Thaler. 1985. Courtesy Special Collections, University Library, University of California, Santa Cruz. UA 50: UCSC Photography Services: ua0050_neg_0248-3425a_01.tif.

Figure 7. Angela Davis event poster. 2009. Courtesy Special Collections, University Library, University of California, Santa Cruz. UA 97: UCSC Feminist Studies Department Records: ua097_016_0005.

Figure 8. Staircase, Sinsheimer Labs, 2019. Photo courtesy of Shmuel Thaler.

Figure 8

Sinsheimer Labs

Photo by Shmuel Thaler, 2019

Chapter 28

Sea Changes and Possibilities

Conventional Grading, Graduate Education, and New Priorities

We can't operate the way we were founded.

—*M.R.C. Greenwood*

"We Do Research":
The Debate Over Graduate Education

George Von der Muhll: Another factor in the early differentiation of the Santa Cruz campus from other UC campuses was that most of them had built up very powerful graduate departments. Throughout all of the USA, with the notable exception of independent liberal arts colleges like Oberlin, Swarthmore, Dartmouth, Williams, and Bryn Mawr, the reputation of an educational institution rests heavily on the reputation of its graduate departments. Here in California, it's notable that the state colleges are eager to start up PhD programs so that they can call themselves "universities" instead of "colleges."

But at UC Santa Cruz, the prospect of graduate programs evoked surprisingly mixed feelings that even Kerr and McHenry had shared, to some extent. Kerr understood very well that the malaise experienced in many of the undergraduate colleges within university campuses derived from a top-heavy graduate-school structure in which

the money and prestige flowed to the specialized graduate-school programs, even though most of the teaching was done in the large undergraduate classes. McHenry understood that we needed to have graduate programs pretty soon, if we were to gain the recognition typically accruing to graduate programs. When I went to meetings at other UC campuses, I encountered repeated comments based on the supposition that, whatever the quality of the undergraduate program, a campus worthy of being part of a California university system must have conspicuous graduate programs. Without them, a campus masquerading as part of the University of California was "just" a state college.

But there was another side to that issue, and it was one to which my politics board was particularly sensitive. Graduate schools thrive on a degree of specialization that is often productive of highly concentrated, intensive, heavily funded research at the frontiers of knowledge; but this kind of work is not necessarily well suited to designing courses introducing undergraduates to the interconnections among the subfields that make up a discipline.

The politics board adhered to the notion that its undergraduate courses in the early days would become unadventurous, less open to experimentation and the use of insights drawn from other disciplines, if it allowed its undergraduate curriculum to be set by the needs of a graduate politics program and viewed as only a service agency for that purpose.

And beyond that, the politics board didn't want a small, mediocre graduate program, simply to have a graduate program. We were both alert to the ways in which a graduate program could be too big and too powerful and too prestigious for the good of the undergraduates, but ironically—and maybe this is contradictory—we also felt that, with Stanford and Berkeley having absolutely first-class graduate programs that attract the best students, we didn't simply want to attract any graduate student we could get in order to have a graduate department.

The politics board was one of the very last to have a graduate program. We were the final custodians of the notion that our comparative advantage lay in first-class undergraduate education and preparation for the first-class graduate programs elsewhere in the country, which had different orientations.

M.R.C. Greenwood: Another problem at UCSC was not having enough graduate students. This means that you're not providing the unique role that the University of California serves, which is to provide research-ready students for the future. That's why we're different from the California State University (CSU) system, because we do research, and because we train advanced students. The undergraduate student body is educated by CSU, as well as by us. We think we do it especially well. We give undergraduate students more opportunities to engage in interesting research. In research universities, typically, students are taught by the people who are writing the textbooks, instead of being taught by the people teaching the textbooks. It's an important difference in approach.

Mike Rotkin: The University of California has always had a three-part goal, or mission—since it was founded 100-plus years ago—which is research, teaching, and public service. They're never exactly equal. I think it's fair to say that 95 percent of the focus of the university is on research, and the other two fall somewhere in the remaining 5 percent. And you measure that by the fact that people who can't teach their way out of a paper bag, but do great research, are destined to get tenure; people who are the best teachers you've ever had but don't necessarily have a stellar research record tend not to get tenured. It's publish or perish.

And, concomitant with that, you need graduate students to help the faculty with their research, to work as research assistants and work on faculty research projects, particularly in the natural sciences, where you can't run labs without post-docs and graduate students.

M.R.C. Greenwood: I thought that since Santa Cruz is focused on colleges, a graduate college could be very positive. One of things the graduate students told me is that they don't have an identity. They come in, and all the forms at UCSC say, "Check your college"—Cowell, whatever. Many of them felt like they were sort of an appendage to a department. We have many student services, but none of them were focused on graduate students.

There are places around the country where there is a graduate college. All the graduate students belong to the graduate college, and the graduate college has programs, resources. We need more housing anyhow, so why don't we build a graduate college, and have a focus there, and make the provost of the graduate college the dean of graduate education or graduate studies. And basically give our graduate students a feeling of community, and a feeling of place, a sense of importance that they don't feel right now. Santa Cruz's graduate population is still small. Any institution that decides that they can have a coherent set of services and programs for graduate students has some value added. Something needs to be done to make graduate education at Santa Cruz vital, and make those students feel that they're as important, or maybe even more important, in some ways, than the large numbers of undergraduates, as much as I love them.

Mike Rotkin: There's intense pressure in the UC system—probably in all higher educational institutions, but certainly at universities that have the right to offer PhDs and master's programs—to have such programs. They're valued much more highly by the outside world and by the funders within the university structure. Departments that don't have graduate programs are always looked at with suspicion, as being not serious academically. I think that's a fallout from the focus on research in research universities like the University of California, and the fact that research is valued much more highly than instruction and teaching, or public service.

M.R.C. Greenwood: But furthermore, some of the early faculty who were so loyal to McHenry felt that any deviation from the urban legend of McHenry's legacy amounted to an act of disloyalty to Dean. They believed that any faculty members who didn't appreciate the original model were really not "Santa Cruz" faculty members. For a lot of years, because the early faculty dominated the senate, people who had any new ideas of how one might take the current situation and the unique

residential and cocurricular environment, and make the most of it, were seen as traitors to the old model. That has prevented a hard-nosed look at the fundamental financial dilemma. We can't operate the way we were founded. When the model changed so that campuses that had more graduate students got more money, UCSC really suffered. We need to be smart enough to figure out what today's model is.

Dean and Clark Kerr came up with a concept which was a counterpoint to the mega-university, which was nonetheless going to be a very large institution. The original plan included 27,500 students: a medical school, a law school, a school of natural resources, an engineering school, and the twenty-plus colleges. Clark certainly, and Dean also, had the opportunity to argue for Santa Cruz as a counterpoint, for example, to UC San Diego, where the founding principle was in graduate education, and to say, at Santa Cruz we want to try this experiment where we're going to focus on the undergraduate component, and we want to try to build the graduate programs out of the undergraduate programs. San Diego adopted the other model, which is let's build first-rate graduate programs and develop the college system. We'll have great faculty and they'll figure out what the college system will be.

Dean McHenry and Clark Kerr said, "Graduate programs will come later. There will be a reserve to provide capacity to do that." It didn't happen. I think that Dean McHenry and Clark Kerr (and I told Clark this) share some responsibility for creating a model which they said in the initial stages was not going to cost more than the other models. And then they were not prepared to fight to the death to get a funding model that would allow the experiment to succeed. So after that, what every UCSC chancellor faced was a deficit and a growing divide. I had to face that there was a sentimental

618 SEEDS OF SOMETHING DIFFERENT

attachment to a model in the colleges that we had no feasible financial way to support.

Michael Cowan: The campus moved into saying: we're a campus that cares a great deal about undergraduate education but we also care about graduate growth, and we aspire to the 15 percent graduate students which we think we need for healthy balance. There was a gradual change in the language to say, "We are a major research university that pays particular attention to undergraduate education."

M.R.C. Greenwood: Times change. Funding models change. Early in the campus's history, we went into a phase where UC campuses were reimbursed for graduate students at almost three times the rate of undergraduate students. There was no Santa Cruz exception. Nobody argued that in order for Santa Cruz to be the experiment, then at least for a period of five or six, or eight, or ten years there should be a Santa Cruz subsidy—let's assume they are only at 10 percent graduate students, and give them the same weighted amount of money as San Diego and Irvine.

If you don't have a pretty healthy cadre of graduate students, you have trouble getting high-quality faculty members to come, because they aren't going to come if they cannot engage with very bright young people who are going to become the advanced scholars in the field. They like teaching undergraduate students, but they want students who are studying with them at the highest levels as well. This university has got to get up above 10 percent graduate students. It's really bad for us to be so low.

Leta Miller, Professor: We started a PhD in musicology. We called it cultural musicology, to incorporate both the Western musicologists and the ethnomusicologists. We made it an unusual program, in that the emphasis was on the interfaces between European-American music and world musics. We offer a course in rhythm systems, for instance, in which we cover rhythmic systems in Western music, and rhythm systems in Indonesian music, and in Indian music, etc. We do world comparisons of rhythmic systems. We have a similar course for pitch systems and tuning systems. So we're looking always on a global scale. All of our doctoral courses have this cross-cultural component.

It's hard to get these kinds of programs going, but my hope would be that we look at the possibilities and we explore the uniqueness of Santa Cruz. It's fine with me that we got out of narrative evaluations, which were so time consuming. But I don't want us to become just like everybody else. Let's highlight our multicultural heritage, maintain our openness to different points of view, and enhance our historical commitment to pluralism.

Carolyn Martin Shaw, Professor: The other thing about PhD programs is you take away from your undergraduates. You take time, you take energy, you take concern. And it happened with us: we got rid of the senior thesis. But lots of people got rid of the senior thesis: "We're not going to read students' senior theses at the time that we have graduate students. We're not going to spend the same amount of time working with our undergraduates that we would have before we had graduate students." That was the kind of loss to undergraduate education that I was concerned about.

Things went really well in the anthropology department until we decided to get a graduate program. I had some concerns about how graduate students are treated, and whether or not I really wanted to be a part of the kind of divisiveness and competition that is a part of graduate education. To my surprise, I have found great joy in working with graduate students, but I don't tend to teach them courses that have to do with my own thinking, or material that comes from my work. I teach them grant-writing, where I get a sense of what they're doing, and try to help them improve their arguments and such.

When we decided to go into a graduate program, we wanted to beef up our department and bring in big names from elsewhere. Bringing in those big names, you also brought in big egos. We brought in the division between the sociocultural component of the department and the scientific component—that's archaeology and physical anthropology. This happened right around the time when I was chair of the department. It was probably the worst year of my life. One of the people I liked very much there came to me and said, "We will oppose you." "We" is the new group of people who are coming in to build the graduate program. They will "oppose" me.

I still don't know exactly why I was opposed. I think partly it's because I was open to physical anthropology and archaeology. I felt that we [the sociocultural and scientific anthropologists] had something to say; we could talk to each other. At one point, when we got our graduate program, we only took sociocultural students, and we had them in a core course. One of my faculty members in my department said to physical and archaeology students who would be coming into another graduate program, "You cannot take this course. I don't want the issues, the questions that you raise to be raised in my classroom." It's that kind of division that was going on. It was really a difficult point in time.

I know from what I've seen in Britain and other places that faculty members use their graduate students to argue with each other. This graduate student is going off doing something directed by a faculty member with a particular theoretical bent. Instead of a faculty member saying to a colleague, "What you're saying is poppycock," that faculty member goes after the student.

So graduate students are working really hard, they're trying to please—and at the same time, they are losing something of themselves. They're subsuming something because of the power of the advisors. Anthropology is a pretty established discipline, and it will last forever, and it's great to have graduate students out there trying to influence the discipline. But I'm not sure that it's the highest calling that anybody could ever have, to be able to churn out more PhDs and have more graduate students.

John Wilkes, Director, Science Communication: I wanted to position our Science Communication Graduate Program outside of the usual real estate claimed by science writing programs. There were already a dozen full-blown science writing programs in the country, graduate programs, and many others in master's-in-journalism programs. You could take a science track through a standard master-of-journalism program, and they'd have one professor of science writing. I was competing with these programs.

But I wasn't ever sure that there was a need for more of the kind of science writer that was already out there. What I thought was needed is people who are trained in science, who understand the process of science and why it's done the way it's done, and when a story is a story, and when it's not yet ripe and may never be ripe. Those are all things that you are better prepared for deciding if you have had science training. It was really more important for me to be a mentor than to be a classroom teacher. I wanted people to succeed. I wanted people to get out there and make a living. I was very concerned about that. As far as I know, all of my students have done it. That's a great joy to me.

Ann Caudle, Science Illustration: There was a sense about the UCSC campus of being completely unique, and open to ideas, and loving nature,

Figure 1

Poster for graduate student science illustration exhibit, 1991

Figure 2

Poster for graduate student science illustration exhibit, 1997

and being stewards of the environment. The opportunity for John Wilkes to start this graduate certificate program in science writing and science illustration in this environment seems like such a natural fit. There we were in the forest, and could walk right outside of our classroom and be in nature, and wander out and look at the ocean from the campus.

When the Science Illustration Graduate Certificate Program came on board with Science Communication,[1] the science writing track had established both internships and established guest speakers. There was a budget for that. And as we started to build our program, the science illustration side, there wasn't much of a budget set up for bringing guest speakers. At some point, it became pretty obvious that we weren't going to go any further unless we started to raise our profile.

John Wilkes and I met and talked about it quite a bit. And he eventually said, "If you can show Dean David Kliger that you could bring some top-notch people in, then maybe he'll give us the money for that to happen. Choose people that are involved with publications that Dean Kliger gets in his mailbox." So, I went to the newsstand and bought every science magazine that I could find, including some of the big ones, and even *Ranger Rick*, which is a children's science magazine. And I started making cold calls. I called *Scientific American*, *National Geographic*, *Natural History* magazine, *Ranger Rick*. I went through the list. And all I could do was introduce this tiny little program in Santa Cruz and say, "If we could pay your way and your expenses and offer you a stipend of a hundred dollars, would you say yes? Would you come?" And they said, yes! They said yes. The first one was Ed Bell from *Scientific American*. We had *Scientific American*, *National Geographic*, *Ranger Rick*.

Ed from *Scientific American*—he is a person who wants to give back and is a natural mentor.

He had been mentored and he felt like this was a great opportunity to do that himself. Ed came and said, "I understand that there's internships, that you are doing internships." And up until now, the internships had been very small, local kinds of things, very practical: working with a researcher, etcetera. He said, "I'd like to take an intern." And so did Chris Sloan of *National Geographic* and so did Donna Miller of *Ranger Rick*. And so did our guest from American Museum of Natural History. Every one of them took interns. In the case of *Scientific American*, the intern that he took was hired, before she was finished with her internship, to become an assistant art director. That blew the whole thing open to a whole different level.

Scientific American continued to take interns for years. They ended up hiring so many of our graduates, it was amazing. And the same with *National Geographic*. In fact, that was the first internship they had ever had, so they started an internship program because it was so successful. And then, we had several people go to Cornell Lab of Ornithology. It's become a very, very sought-after internship, where people are there for three to six months, and they are paid, and it's extraordinary.

Donna Haraway, Professor: It was at Santa Cruz that I wrote "The Cyborg Manifesto" and "Teddy Bear Patriarchy" and "Situated Knowledges."[2] There is a body of papers that I wrote here that have had a life of their own. Those papers were the fruit of coming into this place, and getting permission to write through that kind of connectivity that those papers perform. I think graduate teaching was more formative for me in this regard than the undergraduate teaching was, although it's hardly either-or. It's because graduate students are more like colleagues than undergraduates are. They're older and they've got their own research projects. It's just different.

M.R.C. Greenwood: The other thing is that undergraduates make decisions about whether they want to pursue advanced careers based, at least in part, on their interaction with graduate students, as well as faculty members. And in a science laboratory, about which I know more than I do about how it's done in history, for example, there's always a structure. There's the professor, and there are sometimes postdocs, and graduate students, and undergraduate students. It's a vertically integrated team. The undergraduates, and the graduate students, the postdocs, the professor, all become, in many ways, a kind of family. They help each other. Certainly when I was going through it, I learned a lot from the graduate students. When I was working as a technician, and then when I was an undergraduate student, graduate students were always sitting around at midnight teaching undergraduates how to do something, how to interpret their data. You need that, or you can't create the intense activity that characterizes intellectual thought.

Mike Rotkin: The education piece, or the instruction piece, is really subservient to the research model. And for the most part (and I'm being harsh, but I'm not pulling back from this one iota), there are exceptions, but they're few and far between. When people fight for resources for programs, they're typically fighting for more research fellowships for their graduate students. They would much rather have fellowships for research than teaching assistantships, but they want to find *something* to allow them to support their graduate students, because having a graduate program, having the graduate students, having graduate students that are working directly with faculty members successfully, is the key evidence that you've got an academically sound program. And without a graduate program, you're always under suspicion that you're really frivolous and not a serious university institution. It's nothing less than that.

Figure 3

Digital Arts and New Media graduate program exhibit, 2010

Photo by Jim MacKenzie

Foundation Shift:
The Turn to Conventional Grading

Carol Freeman: Times were changing. More and more graduate and professional schools were looking at students only on the grades; their first screening was grade point.[3]

Pavel Machotka: Grades kept pushing in against the narrative evaluations. I resisted. Like Jasper Rose, I resisted quite passionately. But I came to realize, as I taught larger and larger courses, that if I were to continue with narrative evaluations I would have to cheat, to some degree. With three hundred students, I would have to write out an outline of the evaluation and fill in the words. And at that point it became quite meaningless, so even I had to admit that they had to go. Reluctantly and slowly, but ultimately yes.

Tilly Shaw: I found it very, very, very difficult to write narrative evaluations. It was wearing. There were people who didn't complete them. This was one of the problems of evaluations. Then people didn't have full records. They varied tremendously in type of evaluations, also. I mean, some of them were almost direct translations of grades.

John Dizikes: They came to be rather perfunctory. The reason they finally were abandoned was the faculty didn't have the time and energy to do them. The faculty abandoned them and betrayed the whole system. Students still wanted them, and the faculty couldn't go on doing them.

Michael Warren: The narrative evaluation system was labor intensive. People lost desire to do it. It was unwieldy. On one occasion, I found myself writing the evaluations with one TA. We wrote two hundred and fifty evaluations between us. It took me to about the fifth week of the next quarter.

John Lynch: I do think it failed. The system failed because it just doesn't work for large classes and there's no way we could live without large classes. There may have been some other way, some brilliant idea to handle large classes so the smaller classes could continue to have narratives.

Michael Cowan: As the number of students choosing the letter grade option grew, more and more students would come into my office wanting to argue, not about the comments I'd written on their papers, but about the grade I had given them.

George Blumenthal: In the spring of 2000, a special meeting of the senate was called to consider a motion to end the narrative evaluations and to adopt a pure grading system. Boy, did life become controversial. The alumni went crazy. A lot of faculty went crazy. This was all done in a rush and we had no idea what would ultimately happen.

Before the meeting, all faculty got many emails and letters from concerned alumni and students lobbying us to continue the system as it was. The meeting was in one of the large lecture halls on campus. A huge turnout from members of the senate. Lots of people were there, lots of emotion. As we started to discuss this, one member of the faculty got up and made a motion to table the issue. It was seconded. So the issue on the table was not whether to get rid of narratives. The issue was whether to table the issue.

Then people got up and spoke. There were long lines at the microphone. Some of my colleagues who rarely, if ever, came to senate meetings—I remember astrophysicist Sandy Faber was there, and she wanted to get rid of the narratives. It wasn't clear which way it was going to lean.

People marshalled their arguments. We were getting toward the end, because it was getting to be five o'clock, and I made a decision to stand up and go to the microphone. I think I ended up being the last speaker. It was kind of dramatic. I got up there and said that I wanted to begin by thanking Lincoln Taiz[4] and the others for bringing what I thought was a really important issue to the Academic Senate. I wanted to affirm that this was a senate issue, and we were the ones who were going to have to decide it, no matter how controversial or how close that decision would be. I also acknowledged that there was real merit to their proposal to eliminate narrative evaluations. By then it was becoming very difficult to do this in lecture classes. People were running computer programs to write narrative evaluations. Some of the spirit of the original idea behind narrative evaluations had been lost. And so, I said I had a lot of sympathy toward this idea.

And then I said, "However." As soon as I said "however," there was this cheer that went up from the alumni. I said, "However, I just don't think it's appropriate for us to resolve a matter that is so central to the campus and so important—for us to resolve this at an emergency meeting of the Academic Senate. I think it's something we need to think through carefully. We need to have a reasoned debate about the subject. I find myself in a position where I'm not sure how I'll vote on the ultimate motion. I could well imagine myself supporting it, reluctantly, but nevertheless supporting it. But I certainly cannot support having that vote now." I urged everyone to vote in favor of the tabling motion. I think I was the last person to speak.

[A few months later] the students came and chained the room shut that we were supposed to have the [next Academic Senate] meeting in. They

literally put chains there and they had students inside to defend it so that we couldn't have our meeting.

Chancellor M.R.C. Greenwood was there. It was really fascinating to watch M.R.C., because part of me thought, this is horrible. How can you keep the senate from acting? We're going to have to figure out a way that we can have the meeting. But there was almost no way to do that without bringing in lots of police and making it a really messy thing. I think M.R.C., quite correctly, didn't want to escalate it to that point. So they tried various other things, but the bottom line was the meeting didn't happen.

M.R.C. Greenwood: I had some faculty yelling in one ear, "Arrest these students. How dare they do this? You have to take some action, Chancellor. This is a violation of our academic freedom. You need to be decisive here!" I had other faculty saying, "Well now, the students have certainly let us know how they feel. We just need to move the senate meeting, and next time we need to find a way to be sure that they can't lock us out."

So I've got this going in this ear, and that going in the other ear, and people just screaming at each other. Of course, some of the students and faculty were yelling at each other fairly loudly, too.

The following senate meeting was moved to another facility, where we were able to ensure that we could keep the doors open, and that people could get in the building. There the faculty voted to make grades mandatory.

Carol Freeman: I was Chair of the Committee on Educational Policy in the Academic Senate and I had to do something about dealing with the impact of the senate's vote to make grades mandatory. So we did a lot of research. We were working within the rubric of the UC regulations on grades. I looked at all the different campuses, and what their grading systems were, because there was a lot of questioning about, well, should there be pluses and minuses? And you know, once you've opened this can of worms, there are lots of questions to deal with. Should the pluses and minuses be reflected in the grade point, and so on. There were many people supporting the continuation of the NES. But as chair of the Committee on Educational Planning, I had the last words, my proudest rhetorical moment in the senate. I had five minutes, and I gave a speech which resulted in a standing ovation and a vote to keep the NES.[5]

George Blumenthal: So we would continue to have evaluations but letter grades would now be mandatory.

M.R.C. Greenwood: My own personal view, but I never did express this at the time, is that there is value to both letter grades and narrative evaluations. If you could sustain grades and narratives, you would, in fact, be a leader nationally. Sustaining the narrative evaluations in certain areas, for example, arts and humanities, probably would be a sane thing to do, probably more meaningful. But it's probably not so meaningful in engineering and the sciences. People aren't going to read it. They want to know, did you make an A or a B?

I don't doubt for a second, though, that [grades] made us more attractive to lot of low-income and first generation kids. Those families understand grades. They don't understand anything else. They want their kids to go someplace where they can say what they did in what they consider to be normal terms.

I think that narrative evaluations are performance evaluations, and if we had said that early on it might have been easier for people to understand what we were doing, instead of, "Well, we don't give grades." If we had called them performance evaluations, that would have been much easier for people to understand than narrative evaluations. If you don't know education-ese, you wouldn't even be able to guess. But 'performance evaluation' you would understand, because it's a business term and people get it. They understand that their sons and daughters are getting a performance evaluation.

Murray Baumgarten: Narrative evaluations were much harder for students who did not come from an advantaged background. They didn't understand what it meant that we were thinking that they could do, as best they could—almost like the army motto: "Be All That You Can Be"—that the narrative evaluations were not competition against other students, but against what they could achieve. Instead, they wanted grades to keep them oriented to their working habits that they had learned in high school and community college.

Carol Freeman: The question was, what was the fate of the narrative evaluations now that grades were mandatory? [The 2000 vote] delayed the inevitable, but the inevitable came [in 2010]. Everybody kind of assumed that once you had grades, that it was no longer necessary to have narrative evaluations. And, of course, that's what, eventually, ten years later, has proven to be the case.

George Blumenthal: I was optimistic. I actually thought there was a real shot that narratives would continue in addition to grades. I thought that might be the best of all possible worlds.

M.R.C. Greenwood: The battle was cast as: for or against narrative evaluations. In fact, it was really not negative on the narrative evaluations. It was insisting on grades as well. Now, some will say, and it may turn out, that it will be the demise of the narrative evaluation system. While I was still there, that wasn't true.

Carol Freeman: Some people still do write some narratives. But I think the thing that killed it for people, even people who believed in it, was when the students stopped reading them. They were no longer mailed to students, so you had to log in to your MyUCSC account and read them. I myself, in my last year, discovered that none of the freshmen had even looked to see if they had any narratives. They didn't know about them. They didn't exist, in any meaningful way.

So—the culture changed. I think we just became too big for many things.

Audrey Stanley: The stupidity of grades in the arts was revealed completely for me when I returned to teach a class after retiring. How on earth do I grade these people? I wanted to grade them by the way in which they had progressed. All had worked very hard during the course. When I looked at how they had progressed and what they had learnt, I thought they all deserved an A grade. So I decided I would give A-minus, A, and one A-plus, which was differentiation enough, but it represented, for me, the chaos of trying to assess creative work alongside factual work. A lot of the sciences are based, obviously, on facts and it's much easier, and for them very important, I think, to have their grading, although philosophically I don't agree with it.

Frank Andrews: There have been countless experiments, countless studies of grades as prediction of success by any definition of success that you can come up with. Grades have proved to be fairly poor predictors.

John Wilkes: I never changed my dislike of grades. I do recognize that it's efficient, a bureaucratic convenience.

Audrey Stanley: Grades encourage you to play it safe, which is an attitude you don't do in theater. You play it as dangerously as you can to make as many discoveries as you can. You blow your top in order to find out where is the point where you shouldn't blow it—in acting, and directing, and doing the creative side of theater. For the arts, grades are killing.

Michael Warren: It was not deliberate, but symbolically appropriate that I retired in 2001, just when grades became mandatory. The change was a great transformation.

Endnotes

1. UCSC's Graduate Program in Science Communication was launched in 1981 by John Wilkes as a certificate-granting program. It has been lauded by *New Scientist* as the country's best academic training ground for science journalism; it was ranked by *Nature* as the best such program in the US, UK, and Western Europe. In June 2018, the program began granting a master's degree. UC Santa Cruz alumnae Jenny Keller and Ann Caudle have built, administered and taught in the Science Illustration Certificate Program since helping to establish it in the 1980s under the auspices of the Graduate Program in Science Communication. They presided over the illustration program's migration to UCSC Extension's classroom facility in downtown Santa Cruz, and later to their current institutional home: the College of Science at California State University, Monterey Bay. The year-long program involves a rigorous curriculum of classroom and studio work, guest presentations, and field trips, followed by ten or more weeks of internship. Graduates work as freelance and staff illustrators for zoos, aquaria, museums and botanical gardens, public and private research institutes and public agencies such as the US Fish and Wildlife Service, and publications such as *Scientific American* and *National Geographic*.

2. Donna Haraway, "A Cyborg Manifesto: Science, Technology and Socialist--Feminism in the Late Twentieth Century," in D. Bell and B.M. Kennedy (eds), *The Cybercultures Reader*, (London: Routledge, 2000), 291–324; Donna Haraway, "Teddy Bear Patriarchy: Taxidermy in the Garden of Eden, New York City, 1908-1936," *Social Text*, no. 11 (1984): 20-64; and Donna Haraway, "Situated Knowledges: The Science Question in Feminism and the Privilege of Partial Perspective," *Feminist Studies* 14, no. 3 (1988): 575-99. See also Donna Haraway's papers available at UCSC Library Special Collections (UA 42).

3. A brief history of UCSC's Narrative Evaluation System and Letter Grade Option: For the first decade and a half of UCSC's history, no letter grades were conferred; instructors reviewed all students' work by means of narrative evaluations: written reviews of student performance and participation, sometimes quite extensive, detailed, and nuanced, ranging in length from one to many paragraphs. The letter-grade option for upper-division courses was first voted in by the Academic Senate in 1981. In 1996, the senate voted to extend the grade option to lower-division classes, and an optional GPA was established. By 2000, UCSC adopted a revised student evaluation system that added mandatory letter grades (previously optional) to the existing evaluation system. In 2010, the faculty voted to make narrative evaluations optional. They are provided solely at the discretion of the instructor. A student may request an evaluation, but very few do (within a couple of years of the demise of mandatory evaluations, few students realized narratives were an option or even knew what they were)—and an instructor is not obligated to grant the student's request. [Guidelines: see: https://senate.ucsc.edu/committees/cep-committee-on-educational-policy/policies-guidelines/undergraduate-education-policies/NESguidelinesoct2010.pdf.

4. Lincoln Taiz joined the biology board as a professor of molecular, cell, and developmental biology in 1973. He is a fellow of the American Society of Plant Biologists.

5, See: Jim Burns, "Academic Senate Endorses Written Evaluations," *UCSC Currents*, November 27, 2000. http://www1.ucsc.edu/currents/00-01/11-20/narratives.html.

Illustrations

Figure 1. Illustrating Nature Poster. Science Illustration Exhibit, 1991. Courtesy Special Collections, University Library, University of California, Santa Cruz. UA 60: UCSC Poster Collection: ua060_017_0045.

Figure 2. Illustrating Nature Poster. Science Illustration Exhibit, 1997. Courtesy Special Collections, University Library, University of California, Santa Cruz. UA 60: UCSC Poster Collection: ua060_017_0046.

Figure 3. Digital Arts and New Media Graduate Program Exhibit, 2010. Photo by Jim MacKenzie. Campus Photo Archive. Communications and Marketing Department, UCSC. Copyright UC Regents.

Chapter 29

"In the Spirit of the Early Campus"

Inventing and Reinventing Interdisciplinarity

The world is a complicated ecosystem and it doesn't fit a discipline. You can't just go and publish a paper in your field and get your promotion, if you want to keep the planet functioning.

—Raymond Dasmann

Jim Clifford: When Hayden White and I arrived in history of consciousness, in 1978, it was the moment of so-called "reorganization," when the special, educational role of the colleges was abolished and they were turned into social and residential units. The incoming chancellor, Robert Sinsheimer, represented the new order. And so, by association, did we. I didn't know anything about this at the time, and I had no coherent sense of what the college experiment was. But I was excited by a wide-open field of interdisciplinary work—an ethos of the place that had been part of the college experiment and that has survived the colleges, at least did for a long time—and it's still there, I think.

Hayden White was the new fearless leader. His hiring, without a search, had been worked out and negotiated at higher levels and there was no question about that. He represented a new beginning. No self-respecting university anywhere would ever set up a department called the history of

consciousness. I mean, that would just be unthinkable. The fact that such a department emerged at UCSC is a Santa Cruz story. It's in some ways a fluke, or a very specific result of the history of disciplines at UCSC. The weak boards of study eventually were promoted to departments. And by then history of consciousness had full-time FTEs, so we just went up on the tide with all the rest. It could not have happened anywhere else.

People felt an ambivalence about history of consciousness. A lot of people felt, well, an interdisciplinary PhD program? This has to be irresponsible, because in a PhD you really have to know something profoundly. And in interdisciplinary work you must always, by definition, be superficial. So you would have people saying that we should only be accepting students who already had a PhD, who already had depth in some area. Histcon could only be, what, a second PhD? You couldn't do serious interdisciplinary work until you had a PhD? But all knowledge is interconnected, and you have to do interdisciplinary work if you're really following an idea out. You can't say, well, "Wait until you've grown up." That's not going to happen. Knowledge doesn't neatly fit in disciplinary boxes.

Hayden White: The beauty of history of consciousness was that people could project onto it anything they wanted. You had these bright students. They wanted to develop themselves, have their own views, work out their own philosophies of life, do experimental work. I'm very proud of the people that have come out of our program. They're all people with social conscience, and they're teaching. I've kept up with a number of them. They have an impact.

Jim Clifford: Of course, we were never a conservative, professionalized department. I think it was in the second year I was here that we offered a graduate seminar taught by Norman O. Brown on *Finnegan's Wake*, where the final project for all the students in the course was to perform a wake. They did it all night long in the theater arts complex: it was songs, it was drinking, it was dance, it was film, it was improvisation. There was a mock funeral where Brown himself was carried on stage in a coffin. It went on and on. The event expressed Nobby's idea that *Finnegan's Wake* was an oral text. It was a text that was not really meant to be read. Or at least it had to be read aloud, and once you start reading it aloud how can you not sing it? And since it's got all this dance-hall popular culture stuff running through it, all that had to be performed, not read. So students didn't write papers. Their final projects were performances at this all-night event.

Nobby dragooned other people in to do things. Because he knew I could play the guitar and sing, I had to work up a song that James Joyce had written, a pacifist song he'd composed during

World War I while he was living in Switzerland sitting out the war. The song was about an ordinary Irish guy named Mr. Dooley who saw right through the wartime jingoism, the militarism and the hypocrisy of leaders who were casually slaughtering Europe's young men.

Hayden White: I was never interested in producing a specialist, or a professional. I was interested in producing intellectuals, not just academic scholars, because intellectuals can have an impact on the larger world in a way than an academic scholar cannot.

Jim Clifford: I discovered that the students were remarkable. Histcon was attracting risk-takers who didn't belong in the disciplines. Some were diamonds in the rough; others self-directed, genuine intellectuals; others artists and political activists. Gildas Hamel, who's a lecturer in the history department here now, was a history of consciousness grad student. The program was made for Gildas. He was trying to do something original and hard that he couldn't do anywhere else. He wanted to do a thesis on what people ate, how they dressed, all about daily life in the Palestine of Jesus Christ, and in a most concrete and specific, ethnographic, materialist kind of fashion. There was no program of history, or religious studies, that would allow him to do that, but somehow he cobbled together enough faculty here to support him. And he had the drive and the deep scholarship—he acquired the languages—to do this amazing work of scholarship. Gildas is the kind of a completely unique student who was attracted to the program and found the space he needed.

Sharon Traweek was another. She's now a professor of anthropology at UCLA. Sharon was doing an ethnography of particle physicists at SLAC, the Stanford Linear Accelerator, a big atom smasher up at Stanford. Her work had to do with physicists

Figure 1

Hayden White, 1980

Photo by Carol Foote

and their relation to technology, to detectors—how they jury-rigged these things. It was about men and machines and masculinism and notions of time, a whole lot of things. Where could you do that? Gregory Bateson had encouraged her. He was gone when Hayden and I arrived, and we had to help her do this. She had the drive and the interest to carry it through. Ethnographies of scientific institutions are now rather common in science studies. But Sharon was working before such work was recognizable. In history of consciousness, she could do it.

Hayden White: I became a feminist through the influence of Donna Haraway and a number of the older women graduate students I met here: Susan Foster, Sharon Traweek, and Teresa de Lauretis. That's why it was very easy for me, when they proposed hiring Angela Davis, to go to bat. I'd known Angela at UCLA in the antiwar movement.

I invited a lot of famous people like Derrida and Foucault and so forth to come lecture. And that was an advantage, because these were people I knew and they would come and for very little pay, stay two or three days, and give lectures. And so history of consciousness became a kind of intellectual focus center here at the campus.

Jim Clifford: We needed a PhD that looked like a PhD, one that would be serviceable when students went looking for a job in academia. It had to be enough like a regular PhD for them to get a job. But, of course, it was history of consciousness, so it also had to be innovative. It had to be different, too. This was a difficult line that had to be walked—between being viable in the world of disciplines and also doing cutting-edge, innovative, and even reckless interdisciplinary work.

Donna Haraway: I think history of consciousness students as a whole, as a body of people,

understand living with contradiction, making choices, without necessarily turning the other choices into something an enemy does—an intellectual enemy, or a political enemy. They are better at living with contradiction than most of the folks I know coming through other kinds of graduate programs that are also good, because of the way histcon is set up around work, and not around bodies of knowledge.

Jim Clifford: Beginning in the eighties and especially in the nineties, histcon was the most diverse graduate program in the entire UC system. It won a campus award for its diversity. Over half of the grad students that I directed to the PhD were from underrepresented communities of color. We had a volatile and remarkable mix of students. The whole emphasis on race and ethnicity, which was a dominant, not 'the' dominant, but 'a' dominant element in histcon during the nineties, has since then been supplanted by other perspectives. The emergence of science studies in some of its new forms, including interspecies research, is just one of the approaches to emerge in the new millennium.

In the late 1990s, up until about 2006, history of consciousness was an extremely successful PhD program. In saying that, I'm invoking the standard institutional measures of success in a graduate program. The EKG, if I can put it this way, of a successful PhD program would be: A: that it's extremely competitive in its admissions. We were the most competitive or one of the most competitive grad programs in the university. B: The students move expeditiously to the degree. With such limited support, the PhD took time. But we moved students through. Histcon always graduated every year six, seven, eight PhDs, even as we admitted seven, eight or nine, something like that. And C: outcomes. Do the students get good jobs or postdocs? There our statistics were really

Figure 2

Donna Haraway with Cayenne, 2006

Photo by Rusten Hogness

extraordinarily good, much better than any other department in the humanities except perhaps the program in linguistics, and probably better than almost any program in the university. I know this because I was chair for the last external review and I had to do the statistics for where, over last ten years, all the graduates had gone. More than 90 percent of them were in tenure-track positions or good postdocs. That's astonishingly high. If you looked at any history department of that period you would find at best 50 percent in that category, probably less. Well, this sounds like bragging, but this is how it was.

Around 2000 and 2005, we had a couple of external reviews, and each of them was very unambiguous about history of consciousness being an extraordinarily successful program and a kind of beacon. They used language like that, hyperbolic language: a kind of beacon throughout the country and the rest of the world for innovative, interdisciplinary scholarship. Histcon was a famous program and a vibrant program and a big program.

Helene Moglen: When I came in 1978, both the writing faculty and the language faculty, except for a few faculty in Cowell, Stevenson, and Oakes, were sitting in little dark offices in basements in buildings around the campus. They had no college affiliation and they had no status. And very few of them, of course, had security of employment. When I came as dean of humanities, I met with Don Rothman and Carol Freeman—who were already very important to their colleges: Oakes and Cowell. It was clear that this was an incredible writing program and that they had a vision for writing that was well beyond remedial writing.

I was always very interested in the teaching of writing. I love to teach writing. Among other things, it's literacy education in far-reaching ways. So when reorganization happened, as dean of humanities I insisted that there be a writing person in every college who would be centrally involved with the core course and who would work with the provost and would be available to work with other faculty in the core course. That person was given some release time for doing that work. They were fellows of the colleges and all of the writing faculty had college affiliations.

The program blossomed. Don Rothman was magical. Carol Freeman built the program as well. She was a genius at getting done what needed to be done. She hired Roz Spafford, who was wonderful and who started the Re-entry Women's Writing Program, which was vital to that population.[1] And they hired a group of writing faculty who were totally committed to writing.

Gwendolyn Morgan, Student: As a re-entry student, I reached out to Roz Spafford because she was my writing faculty person. I stayed with her throughout my time as a student, because I took several classes with her. She was my faculty adviser on my thesis. I reached out to her because there were other re-entry women in her classes. And there were older women, which helped me to get over this fear of writing. It really is a fear. It's a blockage that you have to get over, and learn how to write in academia. But it was a re-entry class for all of us. Some of us were up here writing and some of us were here, and some of us were at the bottom. But she made us all feel special. She used to come to class and tell us, 'I get sick every time I start teaching.' It made me feel like, boy, she's human! Sometimes I didn't want to go to class, because I didn't think I'd spent enough time on this paper, and she would have us doing this journaling. I thought that was the worst thing in the world, to put my thoughts down on paper in this little book. Oh, I resisted. And do you know what I do to this day? I journal.

Figure 3

Roz Spafford, 1986

Photo by Shmuel Thaler

Dan Haifley, Student: Roz Spafford was a writing advisor and was a faculty advisor for me. I learned a lot from her. She's the one who told me I needed to keep a journal of my community organizing.

Helene Moglen: The reviews of the Writing Program were extraordinary. It was one of the most distinguished writing programs in the country. The faculty's commitment to writing was not just about freshman writing and was certainly not just remedial. They were teaching all kinds of writing and they were active in all the colleges. Several of the writing instructors became provosts. Roz Spafford was the provost at Merrill with her husband, economist John Isbister, and later at College Eight. Carol Freeman was a provost at Cowell College. On this campus, the writing faculty had real status. They had a place. They had the room to be entrepreneurial in the development of their program. They were well respected. That was not true on many campuses across the country. But unfortunately, the program has been chipped away at and chipped away at. When the campus funds were cut back, the money for writing was also cut back. This was a very special program at UCSC. I think it's unfortunate that the university has not supported it better in recent years.

Jim Pepper, Professor: There's a lot of suspicion in the academic world about interdisciplinary studies. In environmental studies, students learned how to cross disciplinary boundaries without sacrificing the rigor in their thinking. We succeeded by crafting the curriculum in the way in which we did, where students took courses in the natural sciences and the social sciences and the humanities, and where they worked on projects with students with other disciplinary emphases, and where they took courses from faculty from two or more disciplines that provided them with an unusual skill set in this world. They weren't intellectually predisposed to not explore other areas, because they felt comfortable moving beyond the narrow confines of a specific discipline, or even a specific interest. And that's how the world works. The world does not run by the academic departments. It's a much richer tapestry of ideas and ideologies and practices. This program at Santa Cruz prepared them very well to sally forth into the challenges of the real world.

Steve Gliessman: My wife, Roberta Jaffe,[2] and I went to Costa Rica because a couple of graduate students from environmental studies had already started to come down and do homestays, starting in 1999. They had taken the agroecology class and were interested. We went to Agua Buena, the community I'd lived in in the early seventies, and still had connections with. The people we knew there helped us set up a program where kids could come and live with a family for ten weeks and work with a coffee cooperative, a six-hundred-member cooperative. The kids came down and started to get to know what was going on there, and what the issues were. It was just at the beginning of the coffee crisis, and they were beginning to come back with these horrendous stories of collapse in markets, and people struggling to survive.

We decided to go down there and see for ourselves what was going on. We heard this story of struggle, and the desire of the co-op to do something different, to work with our students on projects that would help the community, and everybody working hard. From there, we went to El Salvador, where environmental studies graduate student Ernesto Méndez was doing his study, and went up to the communities he was working with, and heard about their struggles in the coffee crisis, and how, though their little coffee plantations were preserving biodiversity, they needed some way to sell their coffee at a better price so that they could keep doing that.

Then we came up to Veracruz, Mexico, to the city of Huatusco, and went to see Carlos Guadarrama-Zugasti and Laura Trujillo, my two students from Mexico that did their PhDs, some of the first ones in our program here. They are working in communities that are struggling to maintain their livelihoods in the face of the coffee crisis. By the time we'd gotten to that last stop, we kept saying, "Here're all these independent, sort of isolated projects and communities that are struggling to do kind of the same thing. What could we do to link them, to network them, to make them stronger, and at the same help them help themselves?"

And that's where the idea for Community Agroecology Network [CAN] came from, as in networking these communities, using agroecology as the linkage between them, but in community. So Community Agroecology Network was born. That was 2002. Well, the coffee crisis had really hit by that time, and a couple of our students who had gone down for homestays in Costa Rica were coming back with packages of coffee that the families they were staying with had prepared, to sell directly to their friends and family in order to send money back down. I've always been bothered, to say the least, by how the middlemen get in between the consumer and the producer. I saw the same thing happening in the coffee industry. It didn't make sense to me that producers got paid so little and consumers paid so much.

And out of that idea came the idea for: let's connect the two. Let's find a way to develop an alternative market structure. We started thinking, well, why not a global farmers' market? Isn't there a way we can get coffee that's roasted and packaged directly up here? We first had to work with the community, asking them, well, can you guys roast your own coffee? Can you bag it? Can you maintain quality? Can you get it here? How do you do it? Well, let's try the mail. And the mail

worked. All the details had to be worked out in order to make all that happen. This was something they had never, ever done. One of the farmers and a coffee exporter from Costa Rica who was working with the community, they came up and spent a week with us. We went to the Santa Cruz Coffee Roasting Company, and we talked around on campus, and they figured out, "Yes, we think we can do it."

At the end of '03 we started our first sales of coffee direct from the community. The student movement in sustainability picked this up, and helped us motivate the campus to shift its food-service coffee over to CAN. The bulk coffee, that sale of a large amount, four or five hundred pounds a month, makes an incredible difference for the communities we're working with.

Then there's the whole research focus that CAN researchers do. We have a three-pronged approach. There's the alternative market development; the education component with the interns, students in the communities working with this stuff and gaining that experience as undergraduates. And then there's the research piece, the participatory action research model in agroecology, where we work with the community in many aspects to help introduce stronger elements of sustainability in what they do. It's linking livelihoods, and conservation, and alternative market development all together in a research mode. CAN is run 80 percent with student work.

Sam Farr: When I was in Congress, I had a staff member who had me meeting with coffee growers on coffee issues. UCSC got involved because Steve Gliessman was teaching a course; his graduate students were going down to Central America and trying to help the coffee growers upgrade their skills, and at the same time develop direct marketing, where you could buy coffee from the grower in El Salvador, Nicaragua, Guatemala, and so on, Costa Rica. So this new idea of direct marketing was happening right here in my backyard.

Michael Cowan: UCSC was advertised as a university that valued interdisciplinary work. The goal of American studies—which was influenced by my previous experience at Santa Cruz, particularly in Merrill, my concerns with ethnic studies, my concern with the global studies interests of Merrill—was to have a major which would negotiate what we called a series of creative tensions: that is an emphasis on the local, on using local case studies, local and regional, and the national and the global, the international.

American studies, from the very start, was dedicated as a program to building bridges, making connections. Its goal was to bring together a variety of disciplinary perspectives and methods to examine problems that cut across conventional disciplinary boundaries. We wanted to meld perspectives from the humanities, broadly construed to include the arts and the social sciences. We wanted to examine what brought individuals and groups of people together, as well as what kept them apart, to look at what divided and united them within the framework of a nation, within the framework of a larger world. We were looking at political barriers and links, economic barriers and links, social and cultural barriers and links, ideological barriers and links. We wanted to examine conflict; it was a very important part of the American studies movement of the seventies nationally. We wanted to not just look at issues around consensus and commonality; we wanted to see those things that were genuinely being contested. But we were also looking for ways in which common causes could be found across those lines.

I think American studies, in an important respect, was trying to be a paradigmatic liberal arts major. You might argue that we were one of the last general education majors, the way we were

trying to bring things together, bring people with a variety of expertise, testing and pressing our individual boundaries and asking students to do the same thing.

Scott Morgensen, Student: I came to the Department of Anthropology at UCSC because I graduated from Berkeley with a B.A. in cultural anthropology, and I wanted to enter a program that had taken stock of the critiques of colonialism in anthropology and actually done something with them. The story that anthropology, as an intellectual enterprise and a form of research, was linked to colonial histories had become obvious to everyone around the discipline, maybe even more so to people who weren't in it. But it was harder to see how people were going to build graduate programs that could say, "Okay, we'll admit students if they're integrating these critiques into how they conduct their research and their identities as anthropologists."

The remarkable thing about UC Santa Cruz when I arrived was the interdisciplinary conversation on these topics occurring across campus. I studied with professors in the departments of history of consciousness, women's studies, history, sociology, community studies, and literature, as well as my home department. I also got connected to graduate students, post-graduate fellows, and undergrad activists who were interested in creating research that was engaged in social change, particularly anti-colonial activism.

Jim Clifford: Cultural studies has always had the reputation of being a leveling discipline, of undermining the prestige of so-called high culture. The whole category of the popular becomes something that one really takes seriously, in the same way that one might take seriously a Shakespeare play or a poem by Auden. That's cultural studies. It has its problems, but it also had at that time and still does have an enormous excitement and radical potential

The Center for Cultural Studies was the result of a systemwide initiative from the president of the University of California to encourage and subsidize humanities research.[3] That was an unprecedented occurrence. Someone got to him and pointed out that the University of California—which was in one of its flush periods, financially—that the University of California had given and was giving to the sciences and the social sciences all sorts of research support, and that they had never given anything to the humanities.

Some funds came to UCSC and to all of the campuses. It was prorated by campus size, but it was a decent little chunk for us. So, UCSC started out with maybe a hundred and ten thousand dollars. What we did was to found a research center. This was a time when centers were beginning to be developed on a number of campuses. The one nearest to us, and the best known, was the Stanford Humanities Center. It was already a successful operation. The institutionalization of interdisciplinary humanities work was taking place on many campuses. And we decided—the "we" in question was primarily the dean at the time, Michael Cowan—Michael was a very collaborative and consultative dean. He talked to a lot of people. He talked to Hayden. He talked to me. He talked to whomever he could talk to. The proviso from the president was, "Do something for interdisciplinary research in the humanities." So we decided to create a center. We were one of, I think, only three campuses at that time that used the money this way.

I was tapped to be the director. We decided on the name Center for Cultural Studies, rather than Center for the Humanities. In my mind, that was a very important strategic choice. At Santa Cruz we were proud of our interdisciplinary approach.

Murray Baumgarten: We launched the Dickens Project in 1981.[4] It became clear to me that there were other colleagues here, including John Jordan, who were interested in Victorian fiction or Victorian poetry.[5] Charles Hitch, the former assistant secretary of defense, got the job of being president of the University of California. Hitch said that the campuses were competing with each other, rather than collaborating, so he put forward a fund for intercampus collaboration. I had met Ed Eigner, who taught at UC Riverside. Right away, we came up with a range of things. Ed said, "Let's have a graduate-student conference as part of this summertime public program on campus, where the graduate students who worked in the summer with the faculty and the general public get to present their papers, and these will probably be the first papers they present, as scholars." We talked about making sure that the faculty could lecture, but the graduate students would teach the novels for the general course. We wanted to make sure that they did not teach them with their colleague from their campus, that graduate students had an experience which got them out of being prisoners of their department.

Jim Clifford: One thing that was very important to me was that it was not only interdisciplinary within the humanities; it was interdivisional. That meant that this would be a center that, while it would be open to humanists doing crossover work, would also be open to social scientists, and to people in the arts and the historical and the theoretical arts. In the social sciences, anthropology of course, but also qualitative sociology and political theory would be the most immediately accessible elements. These had to be not visitors, but integral to the mix. We felt that cultural studies could break down the divisional borders that were hardening in Santa Cruz after reorganization, in the wake of the demotion of the colleges.

Figure 4

Dickens Project Conference at Kresge College
(August 1-7, 1983); Murray Baumgarten (left)

Photo by Don Fukuda

Murray Baumgarten: We created this network where people would come and lecture, and talk, and meet each other. I kept saying, "This has got to be not just a conference, but a scientific laboratory. And we need to use that model." The scientific model means that just as people do all kinds of things in a lab, they also go and visit each other's labs and learn from each other, so that this couldn't be just a standard conference. And it's developed in that way. It's got major research lectures. It's got a general course that's open to the public.

I was inspired with this idea because I was someone who could have gone into science, natural science, but instead went to Berkeley for English literature. What I experienced in Berkeley was that the difference between my experience as an English-department scholar, in training, as a graduate student, and my colleagues in the social sciences and the natural sciences was the notion of a laboratory and the notion of a center. I said, "Why can't *we* do this? We're doing something just as important." So I tried to use that model, and every once in a while things would come up, and we would reiterate what made us the equal of a scientific laboratory.

We put on the Dickens Universe conference in the summer. I remember someone from New Jersey who said, "My whole life, I've been used to being cold in the winter and hot in the summer, and here I am in the summer in Santa Cruz and I'm cold." People love the climate and the possibilities. John Jordan has this thing about "the fog is your friend. Then it won't be too warm in the middle of the day." At one point, we had these bagpipers. There would be fog in the morning. The bagpipers would be rehearsing, practicing, but they would all go far away from each other, and they'd be hidden in the fog. You'd walk from the dining hall and hear the bagpipes in the fog.

People lived together, ate together, talked about Dickens, sang songs together late at night, drank beer late at night. I think the model could be used with other areas of study in the humanities, no question about it.

Jim Clifford: The whole college background and the interdisciplinary traditions of UCSC had been to transgress the border between the way a sociologist and a historically minded scholar might think about society. If there were differences, they were differences that were the sites of conversation, the sites of mutual stimulation. They were not separate territories around which borders needed to be sustained. So I think that our decision was in the spirit of the early campus with its radical lack of interest in both disciplinary and divisional borders.

Ray Dasmann: The world is a complicated ecosystem. It doesn't fit a discipline. You have to come at it from different angles. You have to consider the people there and how they're reacting. And you have to look at the wildlife and the vegetation and the oceans and they don't lend themselves to disciplinary approaches. The disciplinary approach is important in having your facts straight, in knowing what's going on in this area or that area, but that doesn't lead you to a solution to these problems. You've got to have the whole spectrum of human knowledge applied to the problems that we face almost on a daily basis now—from global warming, to the breakdown of the ozone layer, to the state of the world's fisheries, the future of whales, the survival of endangered species on land, to the spread of deserts. You can't just go and publish a paper in your field and get your promotion, if you want to keep the planet functioning. You have to get into the politics, sociology, and economics to begin to accomplish things. Interdisciplinary, definitely.

Endnotes

1. Roz Spafford was a mentor for generations of UCSC students and a beloved colleague to two of the editors of this book. Spafford graduated from UCSC's Merrill College in 1971, having majored in community studies and done fieldwork with the United Farm Workers. After graduate work in creative writing at San Francisco State University, she returned to UCSC in 1978 as a faculty member in the campus writing program. She served as chair of the program in the early 2000s. Spafford was also a key negotiator for the University Council-American Federation of Teachers (UC-AFT) union, which (among other achievements) made it possible for lecturers employed by the University of California to teach indefinitely at half time or more and to receive health and retirement benefits, giving them some degree of professional and financial stability. In 2004, she became provost of College Eight and coordinator of UCSC's Journalism Program. A published poet and novelist, Spafford also wrote book reviews and a column of media and cultural criticism for local and regional newspapers. She currently writes and works as a writing instructor in Canada.

2. Roberta (Robbie) Jaffe was deeply involved in the United Farm Workers (UFW) movement during her college years. Jaffe first came to the Santa Cruz area with her then-husband, Jerry Kay. In 1976, Jaffe helped start the first farmers' market in Santa Cruz County, at Live Oak School, and later co-founded a school garden at Green Acres School in Live Oak. This was the genesis of the Life Lab Science Program, which grew into a groundbreaking nonprofit organization that works with schools throughout the United States to develop school gardens and curriculum for teaching science and nutrition. See her oral history at: https://escholarship.org/uc/item/3p67k9nr. In 2001, Robbie Jaffe and her husband Steve Gliessman started the Community Agroecology Network (CAN). CAN's goal is to help a network of rural, primarily coffee-growing communities in Mexico and Central America develop self-sufficiency and sustainable growing practices. CAN markets coffee directly to individuals, institutions, and markets in the United States. See: http://canunite.org/.

3. For over thirty years, the Center for Cultural Studies has organized an ensemble of research clusters, conferences, workshops, visiting scholars, publications, film series, and a Resident Scholars Program, which fosters a broad range of research in the rapidly evolving field of cultural studies. The Center for Cultural Studies is now part of the interdisciplinary Humanities Institute. See: https://thi.ucsc.edu/about-us/

4. The Dickens Project is a multi-campus research consortium headquartered at UCSC. It consists of over forty-five colleges and universities from across the United States and overseas. The Project's mission is to promote research on the life, work, and times of Charles Dickens, and to bring the results of this research before both a scholarly audience and the general public. See: https://dickens.ucsc.edu/about/index.html.

5. John Jordan came to UCSC in 1968 as a faculty member in the literature board. He was a founding director (with Murray Baumgarten) of The Dickens Project, and has directed the project since 1986.

Illustrations

Figure 1. Hayden White. 1980. Photo by Carol Foote. Courtesy Special Collections, University Library, University of California, Santa Cruz. MS 259: Carol Foote photographs of the University of California, Santa Cruz: ms0259_neg_bk4_80-01_29.tiff.

Figure 2. Donna Haraway, 2006. Photo by Ruston Hogness. Courtesy of Donna Haraway.

Figure 3. Roz Spafford, Writing Program, 1986. Photo by Shmuel Thaler. Courtesy Special Collections, University Library, University of California, Santa Cruz. UA 50: UCSC Photography Services: ua0050_neg_0275-4045f_12.tif.

Figure 4. Dickens Project Conference at Kresge College (August 1-7, 1983). Photo by Don Fukuda. Courtesy Special Collections, University Library, University of California, Santa Cruz. UA 50: UCSC Photography Services. ua0050_neg_0119-0738d_22a.

Chapter 30

Often Invisible, Underpaid, and Overworked: Staff and Lecturers

If you think of the campus as a world, and you think of Atlas holding the world on his shoulder, the staff really carry the campus.

—Julia Armstrong-Zwart

Carrying the Campus:
Staff

Julia Armstrong-Zwart: "Don't work harder, work smarter." That's baloney. There's an irreducible amount of workload and only so many hours that you have available. If you have to get to everything, you may not get to everything as thoroughly as you would have in the past. The staff here, by and large, are some of the most committed workers I have ever met. They care about the institution as much, and maybe in some cases more, than the faculty, certainly more than a lot of students do. They're here longer, in many cases. If you think of the campus as a world, and you think of Atlas holding the world on his shoulder, the staff carry the campus in a fundamental way. I'm not sure that the campus appreciates that as much as we should.

Page Smith: I had a series of very bright, and somewhat rather intense women as my administrative assistants. They really wanted support and direction and help from me. I had in my mind as an administrative assistant a sort of efficient, rather retiring person, a kind of mother figure.

Arlyn Osborne, Assistant Director, Women's Center: The board assistants were trying to get recognized for the level of skill required for the work they did—advising of students, curriculum, writing, organizing, doing travel, searches—all of this stuff was on their plate. And at one point Teresa Ronsse from the linguistics board put together this reading that she and some other board assistants did. She came and talked with us about it, too. So the Women's Center sponsored this big meeting. Wendy Mink and others were very involved in this. We were at Classroom Unit II. It wasn't very full, but it was a meeting on women's issues. I remember

Figure 1

Faculty Support Staff, 1965

Photo by Vester Dick

Julia Armstrong was there, and the man who was the head of Personnel.

Teresa and this other woman got up, and they read back and forth, line by line, the job description for a painter on campus and a board assistant. Then, at the end, they read the pay. And it was like, I don't know, a thousand or fifteen hundred a month more for the painter than for the board assistant. There was no one in that room who could say that the level of skill required, the amount of training, the level of work was higher for a painter than for a board assistant. It was very clear. And someone in the room had given the statistics for how many women were in one position and how many men were in the other. Clearly, it was a gender issue.

I remember the head of Personnel standing up and going, "But you don't understand. We classed it this way because he is a technician. That is *very* intricate knowledge you need in order to deal with the hazardous materials." And it was like dead silence in the room. Because we had just read the number of computer programs, the level of curriculum understanding, the level of advising that was done—all of that. It was just mind-blowing.

Julia Armstrong stood up and said that this is really being looked at, and Willeen McQuitta, Director of Staff Human Resources looked very thoughtful. They looked again at the classification system, and looked at those positions, and they did get re-classed. The painter may also have been re-classed at the same time. I don't know. This classification system was set up shortly after World War II. It was a very ancient system, and it was based on getting women out of the men's jobs as they returned from the war, and into certain positions. It had all the biases of the 1950s in it. Everyone recognized that at the time, and yet people seemed helpless to figure out how to change this system that had so many biases.

Carolyn Martin Shaw: The heart of Kresge College was Betsy Wootten.[1] Betsy was the office manager for the college. She had a chair right by her desk, and we would all come by and sit there, and she'd just, I don't know, *smile*, and you just started talking; you'd just go on and on and on about whatever was going on in your mind. I got to know her well. She's just a couple of years younger than I am and had worked at the university a little bit longer than I did. And she had another assistant, Shelley Starr, who became a lawyer later on, but while she was working as a secretary, she complained to me about women faculty. She said women faculty would come in and give her work to do, and very apologetically say, "I'm sorry to give you this shit work." Wootten and Starr were livid. They'd say, "My work is important. Why are you doing that?" I ended up getting together the secretaries and the women faculty in the Red Room—one of the meeting rooms at Kresge—to sit and talk about respecting the labor of the secretaries. I think it improved. At least, the language improved, and the women faculty began to understand a little bit about the honor that these women had, the kind of professionalism they brought to their work.

John Lynch: Cowell staffer Angie Christmann is an incredible person. If a history of Cowell College is written, she'd deserve a chapter all of her own, and probably the longest chapter. She really was Cowell College for several generations of students. She carried the torch and carried the ball. She managed to keep up enthusiasm and worked with students effectively, kept them involved in planning, even though they didn't have the kind of financial support that was available previously. Always, every year, it was cut-cut-cut. Sometimes it felt like, would you prefer for your left hand or your right hand to be cut off? Difficult and painful choices had to be made. But she kept the thing going and

The University and its Workers

University Professional and Technical Employees presents:

Staff Rights and UC Budget Cuts

with

Pete Goodman
Outgoing Vice President—UPTE California, and

Teresa Ronsse
Pay Equity Now

Mr. Goodman will talk about issues facing staff during the present budget crisis, and Ms. Ronsse will bring us up to date on the pay equity movement.

Theresa Ronsse

12 noon—1pm
Tuesday April 23
Stevenson Fireside Lounge

Pete Goodman

UPTE and the Community Studies Board present:

University of California Labor History: The Modern Period

with

Pete Goodman

Mr. Goodman has been active for many years in California state labor organizations, including the California State Employees Association, AFSCME, and now UPTE. He recently retired as a machinist with the UCLA Physics Department. He   will discuss some of the organizing strategies, successes and setbacks of UC staff from World War II to the present.

2—4pm
Tuesday April 23
Merrill Baobab Room

Figure 2

University Professional and Technical Employees (UPTE) flyer, 1990s

gave Cowell students a strong sense of identity. Any lack of faculty involvement at Cowell, Angie made up for with her enterprise.

The role of staff probably in any university is underestimated, but at a place like UCSC, which had so many irons in the fire and things going at cross-purposes, staff had to be flexible and very willing and very committed to students.

Herman Blake: Oakes didn't make the abrupt demarcations between staff and faculty that characterized other parts of the university. We saw them as all a part of a whole.

Gwen Lacy, Staff, Oakes College: One of the best things Herman did was to have retreats for the staff. Everybody would go off together for a day, usually to a woodsy or camp-type setting. Our first retreats were coordinated by a counselor, or a lecturer in peer counseling who was on the faculty. We participated in group communication exercises and peer counseling techniques. Most of the staff was not used to that sort of thing, and there were times when it created some sense of discomfort or worry, but I think it was basically a good idea. It did help us to learn to work together and to care about one another, somewhat as in a family relationship. We became closer in understanding and developed better communication.

Herman has given us the opportunity to participate in Oakes classes, particularly the core course, and to go to extension classes or training sessions given by outside consultants. I attended a semester-long management program at another university. Other staff have taken courses for credit. These opportunities, discussion, and informal exchanges have helped us all to develop understanding of ways we might support our minority and nontraditional students. Staff in other units have, for the most part, not had these opportunities.

Ray Charland, Counselor at Oakes: I felt intimidated by Herman. We used to have some wonderful staff retreats. We'd go off campus for them at least once a quarter. We'd get everybody sharing on how things were going; what was going well in their job, and what difficulties they were having. Somehow in one of them it came out that a lot of people on the staff were intimidated, were afraid of Herman. Herman was amazed. I don't know why he should have been amazed, but he was. He comes on strong. He is a big man. He is very charismatic, a very strong presence. He used to wear dark glasses. You couldn't see his eyes. He could see you but you couldn't see him.

Poor Herman. You know, he's such a sweet man. He said, "Good Lord, I can't believe this." One of the people of the staff who was facilitating (it was a psychiatrist) pointed out that it's natural for people to see an authority figure in a parent role and to transfer a lot of feelings they have towards parents to this person. Herman changed his glasses. He wears very slightly tinted glasses now. You can see his eyes and it makes a big difference. Part of that came out of that retreat. That was quite a day. I'll never forget. Herman just sat there saying, "My word. I can't believe this. I had no idea. Why didn't you people tell me?" And we said, "Well Herman, it's because we were afraid of you."

But Oakes staff people feel lucky to be working in a job that allows them to address issues of importance to them. One of my commitments is to make this world a safer and better place for all people to live in. What I'm doing here at Oakes is a step in that direction. I make a contribution to the planet. That may sound grandiose, but I really feel that. That's one of the exciting things about working for someone like Herman who enunciates a clear vision.

Karl Pister: I made it a special point to meet the non-academic staff. I spent time down in Campus Facilities and talked to the custodians. I talked to the shop people. I got out and really learned. Because—and I said this at the first Academic Senate meeting that I attended here—I said, "The students come and go quickly. The faculty come and go and they don't pay much attention to what's going on on the campus, unless something doesn't work. Then they complain about it. But the staff are absolutely the glue, the coherence of a campus, that keep it going." I made that statement and I sincerely believed it. As a dean, I learned that. I've often said to people, "I could never sit all day long and work at a typewriter, or I could never sit all day long and sort mail. I admire and appreciate the work that everyone does. No one of us can do it alone. You have to have a team. I respect your position in that team." Like, I remember seeing Manny Mendoza, who is now our head custodian. I ran across him down at the Barn, and I said, "Gee, you know, I've only been here a short time, but your buildings are cleaner than the buildings at Berkeley." As a result, I've always gotten a Christmas card from the custodians. It really touches me.

Robert Stevens: The people I was most impressed with during the Loma Prieta Earthquake were the staff. The faculty were not heavily involved in the earthquake, except for the provosts, who did a remarkably good job. Essentially the people who bore the brunt of it, who worked day and night, were the staff. We have a command center, and within a few minutes of the earthquake I was up at the command center in the firehouse. I was impressed that people came back to work. Some of the fire people knew their own homes had been destroyed, but they stayed on duty. The medical services stayed on duty. The Marriott [food-service] staff did a wonderful job in the college dining

halls. What amazed me most of all were the janitors, many of whom were from Watsonville, many of them Hispanic. Although their families were often turned out of their homes, they stayed on duty to get things working right. I was really impressed with that. So the first thing I think in my mind is how grateful I am to the staff and to the administrators who were involved.

Michael Warren: I've always been of the view that if a faculty member is missing, it doesn't matter particularly. But if a staff member is missing, everybody suffers. The staff played an immense role in the success of UCSC. I can think of people on this campus whom I regard as quite extraordinary staff members, people of real intelligence, imagination, integrity. They are the people who've sustained the university, who often have a finely tuned view of what the role of the university because they don't see it from the vested-interest position of faculty.

Arlyn Osborne: Women's studies board assistant and later department manager Nicolette Czarrunchick and I were in very similar positions for many years, in that we were both assistants who had a lot of responsibility, did a lot of work, and yet we weren't the lead people, at least not in the eyes of the university.

Jim Clifford: None of what was co-constructed in history of consciousness could have happened without the work of department managers Billie Harris and later Sheila Peuse.[2] When I arrived at UCSC, their job was called board assistant, and it became department manager. Billie was there to greet me. As the program grew, Sheila was hired as assistant and took over when she retired. Those two held the program together. They were the glue—not just practical and administrative—but also social and, well, moral. Billie and Sheila dealt with so many student needs, problems that were practical and personal. That required a lot of institutional knowledge. Also, wisdom and discretion, all sorts of things that we, the faculty, couldn't touch, that made the program work and feel like home.

They tried not to intervene directly in academic affairs, but they gave us faculty good advice when we needed it. I'll never forget one day Billie asking me, casually, "How's your seminar going?" I said something like: "Oh, fine. Everyone seems to like it." And Billie said: "Well, a student was in here yesterday, in tears—"

Arlyn Osborne: I loved working with Nicolette. She was someone who, in spite of dealing with the difficult, time-demanding work of a board assistant, would always stay calm. She meditated. I would say, "How do you stay so calm, Nicolette? I mean, all this is going on, this uproar and everything, and everything has to be done last minute. You have this search going on. These readings are happening. That's happening. All this stuff is happening at the same time. Everything is, like dropping in your lap at once. And yet you just keep plugging along and walking very calmly." And she said, "I meditate, and I try to think about the importance in the long run." So we often would have our own talks, too, about being in the kind of position we were in, and how to empower students, how to empower other staff.

Gwendolyn Morgan, Staff: At my first job on the campus, there were some homophobic comments. I would never, ever admit that I was even bisexual. It was a clerical position in the campus housing office. I just couldn't believe some of the things that I heard. I heard some of the comments, and I said to myself, well, I need a job. I'm just going to lay low because I needed a job. I had to pay my rent and survive until I was ready to move on. I kept my personal life to myself. I would come up

to San Francisco every once in a while and check out the books and the videos at Good Vibrations. I'd take a bus up and have a good time, kind of let my hair loose.

De Clarke: I was the first female staffer who had ever walked into a technical job at Lick Observatory on Mount Hamilton in the 1980s. I got harassed at first. I worked for a year as a telescope technician. My reputation preceded me. When I drove up there to take the job, the first day, every guy who worked there was out front of the shop waiting for me to show up. It was like *Blazing Saddles.* I felt like the black sheriff arriving in town. It was scary. I was young. I was anxious about the job, and I found these guys very intimidating. Big tough working-class guys, and they were clearly not real friendly. I think that they had heard I was a lesbian and they'd all come to see the freak arrive. I had the David Bowie haircut and I was something way out of their cultural understanding.

I was the youngest person on the mountain at the time. I was twenty-one years old. These guys were Vietnam vets, and guys older than that. I was only the second woman in the whole history of Mount Hamilton to hold a technical position. The only woman who had held a technical position before that was the wife of one of astronomers, who had a degree in her own right. That was Mary Stone, Remington Stone's wife, who had a degree in molecular biology. Later, for very understandable reasons, she took off and pursued her own career.

I was the first woman in an all-male workplace, in a sense. The women on the mountain had only ever been domestic workers, and cooks at the café, and minded the gift shop, stuff like that. So these guys were not happy about this, having this girl trying to do a man's job! I sort of brazened it through this welcoming committee, thinking, this is really strange. I remember going to the apartment that was assigned to me, and running a really hot bath and sitting in it and thinking, I want to go home! I want to turn around and run—and having to talk myself out of wanting to turn around and run. Something about walking into a situation where—you're out. Your reputation, true or false, exaggerated or accurate, has gone before you. You can't fake it. You can't duck and cover and assimilate. You have burned your bridges. Retreat looked like a real viable option for about an hour there. Then I guess stubbornness took over and I decided to tough it out and defy these guys.

I'm still the only woman in an all-male shop, basically, after all these years. And this is one of these things that makes me roll on the floor laughing when people talk about post-feminist reality. If this is post-feminism, why am I still, twenty years later, the only woman in an all-male technical shop? I'm a software engineer, which is a line of work in which women have made significant inroads, far more than in mechanical engineering or machine work. But still, we get very few qualified female applicants in my line of work.

Gwendolyn Morgan: After moving over from Housing, I went over to Affirmative Action, and coordinated the Diversity Education Program, which brought me out as an individual. I didn't realize how creative I could be until I started coordinating that program. It was a program for staff on campus, and my job was to get staff to come out and talk about staff issues. We had Culture Talks. The program put me in touch with a lot of people on campus. There were not only women. There were various programs on campus, and we did programs together to educate the campus about the various cultures that make up diversity. It gave me the opportunity to reach out to the Native Americans, to the Asian/Pacific Islander group, the African-American group, the Chicano/Latino group. It heightened my awareness that there is a lot of diversity on the campus. A lot of it was hidden, but there was a lot of diversity.

Scott Brookie: I've always felt like I could be my gay self here. In the first few years, I worked in the social sciences division. A friend of mine reminded me at a party last Saturday night, he used to work there, too. He said, "Remember those early staff meetings? I'd come in the room and it was this very serious, straight-laced staff meeting, and you'd just tell me to sit on your lap, and I'd sit on your lap for the whole meeting. That's just who we were, you know? It was not a touchy-feely meeting or anything like that, but we were out-there. We were just out-there as gay men."

At one point, in the social sciences division people had a really hard time getting along with each other, and as a consequence, they were always bringing in these psychologists and consultants to try to make us work better together and work out our issues and what-have-you. At one of these go-arounds, we were being asked to say something interesting about our past, and I remember saying that I had always wanted to start the union of gay auto mechanics. As a teenager, I'd always wanted to do that, because I was sure that I was the only gay guy who was a teenager who worked on cars. There could be a group of us and it'd be so unusual and so interesting to have all these gay men in their overalls working on cars. That would be fun. So I said that to that group.

I was out-there, and I was always putting it out. I was one of the first people to put my partner, Andrew Purchin, in the campus phone directory as my spouse. As soon as they started offering to put your spouse in the campus directory, I tested it by sending in a man's name. No problem. One year they took it out, and I was all ready to march on the chancellor's office and it turned out I hadn't turned in the form on time. Oops.

Deborah Abbott, Director of the Lionel Cantú Queer Resource Center: I had spent many years working in nonprofit health care organizations, but ironically, had no health insurance. One of the personal appeals about working at the university was that I would finally have health insurance. As a woman with a disability who was getting older, I realized I really needed to take care of myself in that way.

I stepped into this space that houses the Lionel Cantú Resource Center and thought, oh my God, what a beautiful building! Cathedral ceilings, floor-to-ceiling glass windows looking out over the redwoods. This space has a colorful history. It had been a recreation room, the Kosher Co-op. It's been a pottery studio and a dance studio. When I was a student here in the 1970s, there was a fireplace in the middle of the room. I came here for poetry readings. I had a sense that there was a lot of affection for the place. But it was also sorely neglected and very shabby. I had my work cut out for me. I had a three-quarter time position, a very small budget and no staff. I was not daunted. I came from a good working-class family, who taught me about squeezing blood out of the proverbial turnip. I have an aunt who literally still hangs her tea bags on the line to dry to re-use them. I believe they hired the right person.

Dave Kirk, Library Media Center Staff: I never disguised who I was or what I was. I was an employer of students, and I always told the ones who were going to work for me, "I hope you don't mind working for a gay person," and they said, "Oh, no, fine." So nobody ever turned down a job working for me because I told them, "I don't want talk behind my back, or anything else. I'm telling you that here's what the situation is, and I may get a phone call and have to talk to a gay parent or a parent of gays or something." Being out, as such, never affected my work. I just did my work. There was work to do and I did it, did it with a gay flair.

In February a year ago, I received the Outstanding Staff Award of the year from the UCSC Alumni Association. I would say that besides having survived twenty-nine years at the university, the work that I have done for the university for itself has always been the big payoff to me. I've loved doing what I did, and the ultimate goal for my work at the university was doing the best I could, and making our campus better than any of the others in what we had, and what we did with our film archive and video archive.

Deborah Abbott: One of the biggest challenges is how to keep from getting overwhelmed and burned out by the volume of demands. It's been a struggle to add more staff. Our budget is painfully small. There is so much work to do. All of these fabulous ideas get generated but we've got to pace ourselves, do a good job with what we can, and not expand beyond our capacity.

Richard Vasquez, EOP Counselor: As an educator in EOP, I only called in one day: not sick; I just called because I needed a day off from work because I couldn't give young people *that day* a sense of hope. So I stayed home. That's only one day in all my years at EOP, almost thirty years work at EOP, I did that.

Rosie Cabrera, Director of El Centro Resource Center: Counselor Katia Panas understood the history of the campus. She knew all the characters, how to work in white worlds. She was very much into the arts, and so it was not unique for her to be in social settings with the chancellor or the vice chancellor, deans. I remember one time asking her, "How do you do it? How is it that you can be in the same room or eat across a table from someone that you know has made a decision to cut a program?" She reminded me that it's not about her; it's about what she embodies for the constituency. If that meant that social capital and that political capital would be able to translate into something for students later, she was going to do that. She made it work.

Students in the early, early days of the campus took over the chancellor's office. The campus was calling in the National Guard. The National Guard was outside the university; the students had been inside for days, and the institution was going to use violence against the students. So Katia Panas and Pedro Castillo—Pedro was young faculty at the time—negotiated with both the students and the administration. This was negotiated positively and students were not hurt.

When things would happen in the community, you could always count on her. She was never a clock watcher. If you needed her after hours, she was there. If shit came down in the community and mediation was needed, she was there.

Beatriz Lopez-Flores, Director, Women's Center: Working long hours was not a problem for me. But think about it—I didn't have children. I didn't have plants. I only had a dog. No, I got my energy from people. When I went to Nicaragua, because I was the Women's Center director, I made it a point to meet all the top-notch people I would never have had such intimacy with. I'm still friends with Gloria Steinem, with Dolores Huerta. Dolores Huerta is in her seventies and what burnout is there? For me, it was never a job. For me, it was always about social change. And it was always about keeping myself alert, entertained, intellectually stimulated.

Ekua Omosupe, Student: Financial aid representative Liz Martin-Garcia is a wonderful woman.[3]

She took really good care to see that I had what I needed to get through. The testimony is that she does that for all students, that she is faithful and true, and really knows her job and what is available, even when you don't know. She will find what you need. I love her. My heart swells just thinking about her and what she did.

Rosie Cabrera: Sophía García-Robles was central to providing financial aid advice and intervening on issues that were impacting students' finances and retention at the university. Sophía gave so much—she would come in to work, do all her files, whatever it took. I can't even tell you how many weekends. In many respects, Sophia was fearless. She was very fearless in how she would engage political issues. At one point, when there was a movement to bring people together to figure out fundraising for undocumented students, she was the first to sign up to come to the dinner at the chancellor's house. It was one of those dinners of explaining what the situation is and then the students were asked to tell their stories. A few of them had incredible stories. I think she sensed: it's not right for us to hear this and not do something about this. The chancellor started to wind things up. And she just got up. She just got up and she said, "I don't know about the rest of you but I'm willing to put three hundred dollars down right now. What are you willing to do?" You couldn't be there and not give money. It's how she held us accountable.[4]

David Kliger, Dean of Natural Sciences Division: I established a staff scholarship fund. I realized that we had programs for university students and we had all these staff who were working hard, but couldn't afford to have their children go to the school that they were supporting. I thought that was terrible. So we developed a scholarship fund specifically for staff within the division.

Tchad Sanger, Academic Advisor, Stevenson College: My most recent project has been the establishment of the Jay Walker Memorial Scholarship. For my last birthday, family and friends kept asking me what I wanted. I came up with the idea that I wanted to start a scholarship for GLBTI [Gay, Lesbian, Bisexual, Transgender, Intersex] Stevenson students. Instead of giving me a gift, I wanted my friends and family to contribute to sending someone through school. If forty people gave twenty-five dollars, that's a thousand to the fund; if one hundred, that's 2,500 dollars.

I decided to name it after Jay Walker. Jay Walker was the director of admissions when I first came to Santa Cruz. When I came out, he was one of the few out gay male administrators on campus that I knew of. People have asked if I knew him well, and I can honestly say that I never met him. But, just knowing he was here and out was really important to us at the time. Important whispers that, "Jay Walker's gay" often circulated in excited groups, like we could make it too.

He was HIV-positive, and died before I could meet him. He was really involved on campus, at Merrill College, and loved it a lot. Jay was a HIV-positive, black, gay man who loved UCSC and I can think of nobody else I would like the scholarship to be named after.

It's perfect. It keeps his memory alive. He keeps helping people who never had the opportunity to meet him.

Karl Pister: The faculty is not only uninterested in doing the work that has to be done by staff, they are typically totally unequipped to do the work the staff has to do. There's a complementarity of staff and faculty and staff and academic administrators that is not well understood and appreciated by many people but is absolutely vital to the survival of the institution. The continuity of the place rests on the continuity of senior staff. The day-to-day operation of the campus depends on staff almost entirely. And, for better or for worse, the quality of the campus operation is affected, right down to the most junior, entry-level person on the staff. If the gatekeepers, that's what we'll call them, the people that answer the telephone, the people that meet students across the desk, if they don't do their jobs well and don't feel that they are part of the whole operation, this place doesn't work right. They can kill the organization. The only way to try to make that work right is to do whatever you can to convey to the most junior person, whether it's greeting people across the desk or answering a phone, you have to keep reinforcing them and valuing them and validating what they are doing. I would never think of going by my receptionist at night or in the morning without saying good morning, or at night without greeting them and taking the time to say, thanks for handling these complicated calls that come in, or, you know, I really appreciate what you are doing, I could never do your job. Just so simple—but we tend to forget those things.

Tchad Sanger: The university needs to start recognizing staff and part of that is pay. I can't go through another 25 percent housing increase with a 2 percent wage increase. I can't! The math does not add up. My loyalties are with Santa Cruz and it is my second home. But the university could lose me because I'm not going to get my meager 2 percent wage increase.

Rosie Cabrera: Santa Cruz is a high-cost area to live for staff. We're in this quandary. We don't get recognized as a high-cost area, so you don't get the added differential that UC San Francisco, or places that are designated as high-cost areas, get. The days of young people starting here and staying as long as I have and being able to see an

Figure 3

Jay Walker, Associate Director of Admissions
(left); Joe Allen, Director of Admissions, 1987

Photo by UCSC Photography Services

evolution of their career, I think, are passé. It just ain't gonna happen.

Tchad Sanger: I started getting involved in trans issues and rights for staff.[5] We wanted to talk about things happening at Santa Cruz, things like trans discrimination and health care. We wanted to make sure that our vice chancellors and chancellors were aware. We had a reception for the new chancellor, M.R.C. Greenwood. We brought her to the GLBTQ center. I was so nervous introducing her. That was one of her first experiences at Santa Cruz. We wanted to make sure that she knew what was on our plate. We had talked about the meeting and what we wanted to bring up. The big things for me were gender inclusion in the non-discrimination statement, continuation of health care benefits, and equal access to Family Student Housing. At this meeting we said we wanted gender inclusion in the non-discrimination statement; we want your support on domestic partner benefits.

We had medical benefits. We had the medical for GLBT staff and faculty, but there were still no retirement or pension benefits for partners. We made these demands and we thought that we could do a local UC Santa Cruz non-discrimination clause for trans and intersex people. But when it was brought up to UC General Counsel, it ended up that intersex, because it's illegal to discriminate based on sex, is protected by the university non-discrimination statement, but gender or gender identity is not. They are not protected. So we said we want them protected. And that's where we got into this dialogue with General Counsel, who said, "Well, you don't have to protect them." We said, "But we are saying to you that we would like that." So it stirred up this hornet's nest.

I brought these to the University-systemwide group as well. And all of a sudden, we are having a meeting with the Office of the President,

saying, "We want gender and gender identity to be included in the non-discrimination statement. And we want health care." Then it exploded. I was just working off of what I thought was right. It's wrong for someone who is transitioning to lose their job just because they are transitioning. I want to make sure that these people are protected.

Antoinette Gonzalez, Undergraduate Advisor: I am a steward of CUE. Stewards are people who help work through grievances. Grievances are just a formal word to take care of complaints that staff have, and complaints that break the contract. A contract contains written language that the administration, that your supervisor, that your work environment, has to abide by. And if you don't know the contract, if you're not aware of your own rights, you get walked over, especially when there is a push. You have to work faster. There's a speed-up, but the resources are not increasing. With student growth, do you see staff growth? No. There's a hiring freeze. It's impacting the load on everybody.

Julia Armstrong-Zwart: There was a period in the early 1990s when we were getting draconian budget cuts which the campus had to absorb. When the money came back, however, and the campus was reallocating resources, we didn't go back and remedy the cuts that taken place on the administrative side. They were never, ever completely restored. There's a tendency when money comes back again—well, your priority still is the academic mission of the institution. I think (and I think staff would agree) that the workload of staff over the years has increased to a point where I know that some staff feel that they're not able to do their jobs in the way that they would like to, simply because there's so much that they now they have to handle. Where you would have had two people doing something; then you had one and a half; and now you have one.

Ronnie Gruhn: In the early days, it wasn't just faculty. It was faculty and staff. We were all in it together, trying to make this place work. In the early days, the staff was part of everything. The staff was wonderfully dedicated to making this place work. They cared about the place. They were friends with us and we were friends with them. Now the staff is underpaid, underappreciated, hates the place. Most people want to retire as soon as possible.

Antoinette Gonzalez: In my experience as staff, I have seen the dark side of the higher education institution. I've seen the business side. I've seen a very disappointing side. As a student, I had visions of UCSC and its uniqueness. As staff, I've seen the major blocks. I've seen administrators who really don't give a damn about the students, who really don't give a damn about staff, who really don't give a damn about anything else, other than pushing that project, or pushing a particular thing that may be the new thing for UCSC.

So things like being part of CUE [UCSC's union for clerical workers] are pretty important for me. For staff of color, there is a high flight. People are leaving because of the racism, because of the hostile environment in different units, because of the undermining of so many people who may be creative. Creativity is a strength, but it can be seen as a threat.

It's so ironic. I mean, how can an environment so about learning not give a damn about its workers? How can it talk about creating a learning space, when the people who are creating that learning space are under conditions that are abusive? I'm talking not just about clerical workers, but about custodians who have to speed up their work so they can clean.

Herman Blake: People whose names I don't know, I never met, were important, like the women who cleaned the common parts of the residence halls. Most of them were Latinas. We'd say to the students, "This is like your *abuela*. You treat them with respect." I guess it was maintenance supervisor Lowell Burton who got to those women, and those women understood that the students had to go to school. So, the students would say, "You can't lay in your bed in the morning because the housekeeper will come by and the first question they'll ask is, 'Why aren't you in class?'" Well, you can't say, "I don't have class," because then they'll say, "Why aren't you in the library?" And our point was, every person who touched a student had the capacity to teach in some way. So, here's the cleaning woman saying, "Why aren't you in class?"

Lowell Burton, Maintenance Supervisor, Oakes College: My ethnic background is Anglo, German. I grew up in Santa Cruz. We had a black community on the west side of town. My first wife lived up there with her family. She was Filipino and her father lived out in Davenport and he was a farmworker, so I had a lot of exposure to things on that level. We never had a lot of money, so we were always poor. I never really had the best of anything. I worked pretty early in life. I traveled the world. I shrimped in South America. I did all kinds of things.

I came back in the early seventies. I was running a furniture company out in Live Oak, manufacturing furniture. I married a woman; we had a child. Her father worked here in UCSC for Campus Facilities and he told me about an opening at one of the colleges. I came up here and applied. I came in 1976 to Oakes College as a maintenance worker in the fall when we opened. But there were people who worked three, four, five years in advance. There were core black women who were working diligently for years before the college was built. There were people who were involved, who had a dream, like Martin Luther King had a dream.

I integrated my maintenance work with personal relationships with the provost, preceptors, taking time to pick up people in the airport and bring them back, people like Alex Haley, people who visited the college. Taking Herman back and forth to the airport. He went to Daufuskie a lot, to South Carolina, to the islands where he came from. I'd pick him up late at night in the UC truck and we'd come back and talk and stuff. We shared a lot of time together. He taught me a lot. He made me listen and look. I was part of something bigger in my life that I have never been involved with. This was a huge experiment.

And things were just busy. It was moving one hundred miles an hour. I couldn't keep up with it all. I couldn't keep up with what was happening. It mean, it was fun; it was hard. You know, when a kid would sleep in a shower and flooded a whole three floors of the apartment building, we're pulling carpets all night.

I retired in at age sixty, in 1994, The senior building maintenance supervisors were called. We had known for a long time that there was gonna be a move to centralize housing and maintenance on campus. It wasn't to save money. It was to finally get the colleges under a central control. The maintenance money, everything would be controlled, eventually. So this was coming about and we all got together, all of us senior maintenance supervisors from all of the colleges. We were fighting it. We felt that the colleges need to fight more. The colleges were being disassembled academically. The wind was sort of taken out of the colleges.

And finally, that meeting, that day they announced that it would no longer be the way it was anymore. Housing would be in control of maintenance. I'm too outspoken. It was thirty years of having my boss right there and we'd go and work out a problem and we'd know what to do and everything. I couldn't picture this new system. They wanted me to take three colleges. I didn't want all that. My home was Oakes College. So I walked out of the meeting. Everyone looked at me. All the maintenance people and half the other people that were there said, 'What are you going to do?" I said, "I'm gonna retire because I won't put up with this nonsense." I wrote a letter to Jean-Marie Scott and I told them what I think about their corporate model. They didn't save any money. They just took away the heart of things.

I've touched everything here. Everything I have touched. There's a story behind everything here. It's not that I made it, or built it. It's just that somewhere along the line, I've touched it.

Orin Martin, Manager, Alan Chadwick Garden: Yes, we're all pedaling as fast as you possibly can. I'm not complaining. I used to joke, "Well, if I'm awake I'm working. So what's the deal?" I don't know, I just consider that I'm lucky to be able to do this, so I'm not complaining. But we're very stretched, especially people who work indoors in administrative positions, more and more as the bureaucracy of the university has grown. I don't think I could handle it if I had to be in those positions. But yet, you want to offer stuff for the students because they're so hungry for it.

What keeps me up at night? The awesomeness of being responsible for such a biologically active entity like the Garden—keeping it alive and thriving, and soil conservation, and all that sort of stuff. People think you're great and you walk on water and all that stuff, after a while, but the responsibility of trying to be a good instructor, I mean, it's a never-ending, kind of pushing-a-rock-up-the-hill type of thing. And just really being honest with yourself about (and I'm speaking personally now, because I've been doing this for more than thirty years)—are you giving an adequate effort on a daily basis? And the answer is, of course, not. You can't. But wrestling with that sometimes wakes you up at night.

I'll be real frank, I've given my life to the Garden and it's pretty much wrecked my body physically. So there are physical things that wake me up. I have degenerated vertebrae, herniated discs, etc. I'm developing, I think, what are hip and knee problems, maybe towards the realm of replacement down the road, stuff like that. The physicality of the work over thirty years wakes me up at night. The good thing is that the work is often so intellectually and physically exhausting that you fall asleep pretty easily.

Rosa Plaza, Director of Orientation: I love UCSC and have no problems supporting the mission of UCSC. I owe who I am to the experience that I had here. Any institution is going to have its issues: just like family. Things need to get looked at and worked on. You're not gonna hit utopia anywhere, but this is a really good place. I have a lot of respect for what UCSC is and where we are going.

Kathie Olsen, Assistant Director, Women's Center: One of the things we did at the Women's Center was at Christmas time we had a big show of works by women of the *staff* of UCSC, no faculty allowed. We put out a call saying, "If you have something that you do, whether it's knitting hats, or painting, or whatever, this is your chance to be professionally shown. We're going to mount a professional exhibit." We did it at Cardiff House, issued formal invitations, and gave each artist who showed her stuff carte blanche to invite her family and whoever else to come. We had wine and cheese and made it fancy and mounted the stuff beautifully and put up good signage and made it a real exhibit.

People loved it! All day, and all into the night, that house was jammed. People were all over the porches, all over the yard. People were thrilled—and surprised. The faculty members and the administrators who came were totally blown away to see this other side of the people they'd been working with. They didn't know that these women were doing all these things. Women who were poets, we put their poetry up on the wall.

There were all kinds of things we did. We had a masseuse come for three days in a row. Any woman on staff could call and make an appointment to come and have a massage.

Julia Armstrong-Zwart: I can remember one time, this was years and years and years ago, when faculty were talking about how low faculty salaries were, and compared to some of the other campuses we did have lower salaries. But I can remember saying, "You do realize that more than 50 percent of the staff make considerably less than an entering assistant professor. They live in this community and their expenses are the same—electricity, food, housing. These things, they don't change. Everybody has to pay for these things. They have to get around. They have to pay for gas. All of those things." It was like, whoa, a light bulb went on.

"The Most Oppressed of Instructors": Lecturers

Mike Rotkin, Coordinator, Community Studies Field Program: Chancellor McHenry knew me by name: "Mike, it's not right for us to hire people who are getting graduate degrees from our own campus. So how would you feel about being a lecturer?" I said, "What's a lecturer?"[6] He said, "Well, you start off at about the same pay as a first-step assistant professor, a little lower. But they will make a lot more than you over their career. They'll make maybe almost twice as much as you. You will teach eight classes a year instead of five" (or whatever the number was at the time) "and you have no publishing requirements. We don't expect you to publish. We want you to be a teacher." Took me about twenty seconds to say, "Thank you. I'll take that job. I'll be very happy."

I was not really planning a career in academia, but I got this job. Well, far out! I can be a lecturer. I can teach, which I love doing. I was required to teach eight classes per year for the first couple of years I taught. I taught nine.

I had no more security than any other lecturer would have. I was the first person in the UC system, actually, when we got the new union contract for Unit 18, the lecturer contract—the first one to actually go through a post-six-year review to get one of these continuing appointments.[7] They were not called "continuing" at that time; they were called "post-six" appointments, and they were three-year contracts, after which you'd have a brand-new review, just as serious as the six-year review, in your ninth year, your twelfth year, your fifteenth and every three years thereafter.

So I had that status, which gave me some protection during the three-year period, but no guarantee of a job after three years. And had trouble when I refinanced my home, because the university was still listing me as a casual employee when I went for a bank loan—even though I wasn't

thinking of myself as "casual" after having worked for the university for several decades. When we finally got the continuing appointment approved through the union struggle, then they changed all the continuing appointees to—they were called, I think, "permanent," or, I forget the term for it, but no longer "casual" employees of the university.

But my PhD was helpful to me also, I think, in a number of situations where being a "doctor" makes a difference to people. In general, to my students, to others, it never mattered. Frankly, most students at UCSC and I think throughout the UC system don't understand the difference between lecturers and professors, and often called me Professor Rotkin. I made a point of correcting them every time it happened, because to me, there's a political issue going on, about the fact that we have a group of second-class faculty, who are not senate members and don't have the protections of tenure.

Elba Sánchez, Spanish for Spanish Speakers Program: Lecturers in the University of California hierarchy are the most oppressed of instructors. We have a different perspective because we're looking at things from the bottom up and they're looking at things from the top down. And so they can hardly see us. "What, lecturers? You mean they're down there somewhere? Oh, okay. Let's give them another class to teach."

Our Spanish for Spanish Speakers program costs were really cheap for what UCSC was getting. I don't think they appreciate what they were getting or even understand what they were getting. Because you consider the salaries of two lecturers—I found an old check stub of mine, where I was earning, I think it was $36,000 a year as a lecturer when I first started. I'm thinking, that's damn cheap, honey.

NO PEANUTS BAKE SALE

LECTURERS
NEED A
CONTRACT

UC-AFT

Tired of working for Peanuts !!

To dramatize the pitiful treatment of Lecturers
in the UC system, we are holding a BAKE SALE

THURSDAY MARCH 28, 2002
Bay Tree Bookstore
10 am - 3 pm

The University has been stonewalling on contract
negotiations for nearly two years.
Come have a cookie and see what you can do to help!
Proceeds to form an emergency fund for Lecturers.

remove 03-29-02

Figure 4

University Council - American
Federation of Teachers (UC-AFT
organizing flyer, 2002

The stress started to be too much. I started getting really sick. And that's when, towards the end, like around '94, I started thinking, it's either your health or your baby [Spanish for Spanish Speakers]. You're going to have to start really thinking about this because it's getting to you and this is not good. You have to decide what you're going to do. So I had to give up the baby. I figured, well, I did what I could in the almost fifteen years that we kept the program afloat.

Rosie Cabrera: I can't even tell you how profound Elba's role was on this campus. Elba was kind of marginalized. She was not always treated or viewed as faculty. She was a lecturer, with that kind of status distinction. Spanish for Spanish Speakers was not seen as an academic department. But Elba was a kick-ass. Elba wouldn't stand for that shit, so she constantly engaged the faculty and constantly legitimized my role as director of El Centro with students.

Norman Locks, Lecturer (later professor): The hardest thing as a lecturer there was that each year maybe I'd get a one-year contract; maybe I'd get a two-year contract. They'd say, "Well, you can't teach longer than this." Then they'd say, "Well, we're renewing it." At first, you couldn't teach more than four years; then it wasn't any more than six years. So the first six years were rocky because I didn't have any sense of whether I was going to be able to continue here. Every couple of years it was one thing or another. And then was the "eye of the needle."

Jenny Keller, Lecturer: In science illustration most of us were all part-time lecturers, devoted to hundreds of students. We were paid as course-by-course lecturers, which is not very much.

Don Rothman, Lecturer: Despite not being on the tenure track, I have always been accepted at Oakes College as a regular faculty member, not an adjunct, and not seen as somehow of less importance. I've been on all the important committees; I've taken leadership in the college. Probably, the biggest difference has been my role in the college, compared to the role that the other writing teachers have been allowed to play in their colleges. I think that there's more of a traditional hierarchy that exists in the other colleges. At Oakes, those people who want to bring energy into the college, and who want to work, are accepted as equals. I've always been accepted as an equal, despite the fact that I'm a lecturer in writing and that I don't have a board of studies.

Carol Freeman, Chair of the Writing Program: Don Rothman got Security of Employment first, in 1983. And then a couple years later, I did. And in the very first search for SOEs, we had been approved to fill one or two positions, and Roz Spafford got one of the positions, and then Elizabeth Abrams got the other. So we then had four SOEs, which is unique in the UC system.

The Lecturer with Security of Employment position originally—and this is forty years ago—had been awarded to lecturers who'd been around a long time and people decided they wanted to keep them, and so they were given that position. Then things changed, and it became that a lecturer position could not automatically turn into a lecturer with security of employment. So if you were going to make that transition, what you had to do is have the *position approved* and then the lecturer in question might apply for the SOE position. You'd have to do a national search for it.

One of the things that kept coming up over and over, and with increasing frequency with the UCSC administration, was that, well, the Writing Program really needs ladder [tenure-track]

Figure 5

Marge Frantz, 1997

Photo by Don Harris

faculty. And it became an interesting debate, in which we kept deciding, no, we don't need a ladder faculty member. We did a lot of research into the question, and one of the main differences with a ladder faculty member who does research is that they teach very little. That's the typical arrangement, is to have somebody who's the ladder faculty member, and then the rest of the writing people are all down below. Well, by the time you get a really reduced course load, and the requirements to do research, you then have to hire some kind of a lecturer or somebody to do a lot of the administrative nitty-gritty. There are many wonderful people in the UC system who are ladder-rank faculty who direct writing programs, but basically, we thought that there was no real benefit to bringing in a ladder faculty member.

Arlyn Osborne: American studies and women's studies lecturer Marge Frantz was on committees over and over and over again, and always looking at the practical—"let's not forget the working-class women; let's not forget the staff"—even though it's difficult to do staff issues. There wasn't funding for staff programming. She often came up with the ways. Marge also had the most amazing contacts with people. When we wanted to bring a speaker, she often was friends with them, or knew someone who was a friend. Students would connect with her. We waited for the times when she would do her radical women classes, *Radical Women of the Sixties*, and talk about them. Then we often would have associated discussions at the Women's Center, or show films: *Berkeley in the Sixties*,[8] or *Seeing Red*.[9] Marge was in that. Students would see Marge in the film, and then they would meet her, and they were like, "Oh, she's really approachable." She was kind of an entrée for a lot of students, especially re-entry women, to see the women faculty.

And Marge was a lecturer, not tenure-track faculty, which, was always hard for me, because the level of work she did was often faculty level. But she chose to be there, on the front lines. She had gone back to school to get her graduate degree. She was very wise and very accessible, I think to the point of exhaustion. How many times did she threaten to retire? I think she was in her early eighties when I left. She just kept coming back: one more class. She loves students. They often wanted to make Marge their advisor, and that was difficult, because she had so many people she worked with, but she was a lecturer. She kind of became an *ex officio*, or whatever you call it, advisor, for so many students. I don't know how she managed to pull all of that off, because it was a tremendous amount of work and time that she put into things.

Donna Haraway: Marge Frantz is my model in life. That's who I want to be when I grow up. Because Marge is the person who always reminds everybody that if you are in this for a lifetime, you need each other. You need each other's extremes. People like me, who are probably all too ready to find the complexities, need the people who insist on the point beyond which you can't compromise. Marge is always the person who reminds us to open up to our extremes. And I'm the person who always reminds our movements to open up to what you're not sure of. I actually think they come from the same kind of instinct. I think that's why we've liked each other so much. But Marge is overwhelmingly the teacher-activist. And I'm overwhelmingly the teacher-scholar. I'll show up at the demonstrations and so forth. But I have not worked as an activist in building the organizations and doing what it takes to sustain them. Marge has. And I think we need each other.

Endnotes

1. Betsy Wootten came to UCSC in 1971 and supervised Kresge College's Faculty Services. In nominating Wootten for the Outstanding Staff Award she received in 2001, Helene Moglen wrote that Wootten was the "friend and confidant of students, faculty and staff, their first point of contact and their appeal of last resort." In her letter nominating Wootten for that award, then-writing lecturer Sarah Rabkin (one of the editors of this book) noted that Wootten's office had become "absolutely the heart of the college." See: http://www1.ucsc.edu/currents/01-02/11-05/awards.html.

2. After twenty years of service, Sheila Peuse retired in 2008.

3. Liz Martin-Garcia is a financial aid advisor who counseled generations of UCSC students.

4. Sophia Garcia-Robles died on November 5, 2010, after a car accident. During her twenty-seven years at UCSC she served as a financial aid adviser and mentor, and was a tireless advocate for low income and immigrant students.

5. For information on rights for trans students see: https://queer.ucsc.edu/resources/trans.html. For resources for staff see the Title IX office at: https://titleix.ucsc.edu/. The Title IX Office is committed to fostering a campus climate in which members of the UCSC community are protected from all forms of sex discrimination, including sexual harassment, sexual violence, and gender-based harassment and discrimination. UC's Health Plans cover a wide range of benefits, including hormonal therapy and gender reassignment surgery. See Fact Sheet on Transgender Health Benefits: https://ucnet.universityofcalifornia.edu/forms/pdf/transgender-health-benefits-fact-sheet.pdf..

6. Lecturers are faculty members, but not (unless they are Lecturers with Security of Employment, which is very rare) entitled to membership in the Academic Senate. They are hired and paid to teach, not to do research—though many lecturers pursue research, service and creative projects on their own time.

7. This refers to the "post-six-year" review introduced by the UC-AFT contract for lecturers. A lecturer whose teaching record, as established by this rigorous and multifaceted performance review, shows a high level of excellence after six years' accumulated employment credit becomes a continuing employee, entitled to teach indefinitely without annual rehiring reviews, as long as the department sees an ongoing need for the courses taught by that lecturer.

8. Mark Kitchell, Stephen Most, Susan Griffin, Stephen Lighthill, and Veronica Selver, *Berkeley in the Sixties* (New York, NY: First Run Features, 2002).

9. *Seeing Red*. Directed by Jim Klein and Julia Reichert, 1983.

Illustrations

Figure 1. Faculty support staff: Sally Alderson, front desk; (left to right:) Lee Beeby, Helene Beaver, Shirley Beyer, Pat Patnode, and Patti Von Bargen. 1965. Photo by Vester Dick. Courtesy Special Collections, University Library, University of California, Santa Cruz. MS 90: Gordon R. Sinclair papers, 1957-1979: ms0090_pho_65_1793_69.tif.

Figure 2. University Professional and Technical Employees union flyer. Courtesy Special Collections, University Library, University of California, Santa Cruz. UA 70: UCSC Ephemera Collection: ua070-0015.

Figure 3. Staff appreciation day at the East Field: 1987. Jay Walker, Associate Director of Admissions (left) with Joe Allen, Director of Admissions. Courtesy Special Collections, University Library, University of California, Santa Cruz. UA 50: UCSC Photography Services: ua0050_neg_0414-0000g_09.

Figure 4. University Council-American Federation of Teachers organizing flyer. Courtesy Special Collections, University Library, University of California, Santa Cruz. UA 70: UCSC Ephemera Collection: ua070-0017.

Figure 5. Marge Frantz. Photo by Don Harris, UCSC Photography Services, 1997. Courtesy Special Collections, University Library, University of California, Santa Cruz. UA 50: UCSC Photography Services: ua0050_neg_0097-2470b_20.tif.

Chapter 31

Still Pioneering

A New Experiment in College Nine and College Ten

I think Multicultural Weekend is the reason why I stayed in Santa Cruz. After that, I knew that I had potential. I knew that I, as a human being, like every human being, have something to offer, and a purpose in life.

—David Solano

Dean McHenry: I think preserving UCSC's creativity and experimental philosophy depends a lot on the launching of new colleges. If the new colleges each year come in challenging old assumptions, bringing people who are the sons of the wild jackass,[1] in academic terms, wanting to try things, the place will have a pioneering flavor for a long time to come.

David Solano, Student: I'm from Los Angeles. It's chaotic. No one else in my family has ever gone to college, so it's a huge transition for me, and it was really hard to adapt in Santa Cruz because it's very different from L.A. All of my four years in high school, I lived in Pico Union. And even when I lived in East Hollywood, I was surrounded by a lot of Latinx folks. So, I was very surrounded with my culture and I was in a bubble, especially in high school, living in Pico Union, because—I mean, they recently started calling it Little Central America. That's because there's a huge population of Salvadorans, Guatemalans, Hondurans, and

Mexicans as well. So, I went to a high school that was 96, 97 percent Latino. Everyone who was in my school looked like me. We had similar experiences, similar struggles, and we understood each other. It was easy to help each other out and be each other's support system, because we were aware and we knew what exactly was happening in our communities. We had conversations in high school about white supremacy, privilege, and oppression.

UCSC gave you an option to apply to the colleges that you would want to be affiliated with. I read through their themes. I was very interested in College Ten because the themes that represent College Ten were already themes that I was working with in my community. So, I was like, oh, I'll take this to another level. Let's see what it is to work with social justice and community at Santa Cruz.

Katherine Le, Student: I found the ten-college system to be quite fascinating. I imagined it almost

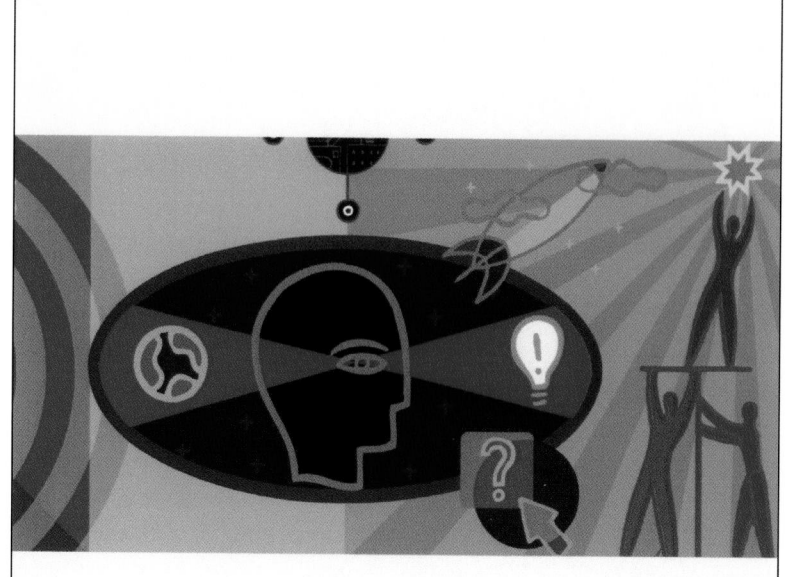

Figure 1

College Nine and College Ten
dedication program cover, 2003

as if it was a Hogwarts-style college, where you had your own affiliation. And whichever theme or area of educational interest that you enjoyed, you would pick the college for that. I really liked the idea of an international, global perspective at College Nine. Traveling is something that is embedded in my family, whether it be from their immigrant story traveling over, or to the travels that my family has done together. Being able to seek different perspectives on a global level was something that greatly appealed to me.

M.R.C. Greenwood: The two new colleges, College Nine and College Ten,[2] had been proposed and they had essentially been affirmed.[3] UCSC was prepared to build them when Karl Pister was chancellor, and, in fact, started building them. But when I got there, the university had to back off of the project because of shortfall funding. Also, the enrollment had taken a dip, and we weren't sure that we could support the facility. After I came, we started getting hit hard with the increased enrollment pressure of Tidal Wave II, and it turned out that there were several millions of dollars sunk in the ground already. All the utility and water lines were in the ground, and a lot of the leveling of the ground was already done. But then UCSC had not been able to move forward on those colleges.

There were two issues that needed to be resolved. One was that we were going to need the housing, because we were being asked to grow and take more students. And then, there was the issue that we needed to develop the programs for the two colleges. Some of that had been worked out, but not thoroughly. So we had to do two things. One was to revitalize the programmatic planning for the two colleges, which we did by putting together faculty committees and deciding what the themes of the colleges would be. And Student Affairs and the dean of undergraduate affairs did

their bit of figuring out what services were going to be in the colleges. The work of Deana Slater and a couple of others to be the lead Student Affairs officers in charge was critical.

Deana Slater: When I started at Merrill as a college administrative officer, there was one college administrative officer for each college. All of the colleges had their own staff and their own structure and they were autonomous in many ways. When Colleges Nine and Ten were opened, there was this idea that there could be one college administrative officer for both colleges. I was drawn to the colleges because of their themes, because College Nine's International and Global Perspectives, and College Ten's Social Justice and Community were a perfect combination of my interests.

Some of my colleagues thought, well, that's a big shift, to do two colleges for one position, instead of just one. Vice Chancellor Francisco Hernandez[4] thought I might be interested. I think most of my colleagues were like, "I don't think so. That's just one person doing two colleges. That's too much." And I thought, no, this could work, because I'd worked at San Diego and the scale was about the same as what was proposed for Nine and Ten. At UCSD, we had three thousand students, and that's about the same as what was projected for the two colleges starting here. I had a lot of confidence because of my understanding of the college system at UCSD and UCSC, and the dynamic themes of these two colleges were so interrelated. So, I applied for the job and I got it.

I was excited about this idea of connecting the colleges again with the academic side of the house. I felt that these themes of the colleges would have much more depth and richness, with the opportunity to combine the resident/student life side with an academic side much more vibrantly, if they were connected. In fact, that's precisely where my passion lay: with the intentional partnering of these important components of the student experience. Student Affairs professionals can do a lot with experiential, hands-on learning with students, but it is more powerful when we can combine it with faculty who share a similar vision and have their own academic expertise. I knew that we would be affiliated with the social sciences division. I knew that we would have these themes. And I knew what the scale of the college would look like.

M.R.C. Greenwood: Then we had the actual construction issues. And that resulted in us building the college backwards [housing first], because we had an approved design, and regental approval to build the apartments as part of the college. It isn't the way you would normally do it. But we had to move fairly quickly.

Deana Slater: The apartments had already broken ground. I remember a photo opportunity commemorating that moment. We were out there with students with hard hats on. They were taking a picture of us and the apartments were just getting finished. They completed the apartments at Colleges Nine and Ten before the residence halls were completed.

When I was selected, I went to visit with Marty Chemers, who was the dean of the social sciences division.[5] He was so generous and flexible with his outlook. He had been approached: "What do you think about this college affiliation?" And his attitude was, "Why not? Let's give it a shot." That type of attitude was so refreshing. We had flexibility to try things a little bit differently. In fact, it was supported here. Marty was open to new ideas.

So, what I came up with was this idea of: how about having one provost for two colleges, instead of a provost for each college? I wanted there to be staff that had developed community around these themes with unified leadership. I didn't want to be doing half time with one provost, and trying to

follow their vision half time with another provost. But rather, the provost and I could work really closely together and combine our visions for how we thought the themes could be implemented.

So, Marty is like, "Great idea, let's have one provost." He was completely open to it. My goal was to bring these themes to life in a way that we hadn't quite been able to do at other colleges, simply because they were no longer affiliated with an academic division. This was a new opportunity to re-envision the colleges.

I thought we could use some salary savings-from hiring only one provost to create a director of cocurricular programs. At that point, there was funding for one associate college administrative officer [ACAO] for College Nine and another associate college administrative officer for College Ten. So, I used the funding for the ACAO for one of those positions, combined with some of the provost's-salary savings, to create a director of cocurricular programs. After getting the clearance to launch this new model, we were able to create a cocurricular unit and start hiring staff. We hired Wendy Baxter, who is fabulous, and is still here as the director of the cocurricular program.

Wendy Baxter, Academic and CoCurricular Programs: We have an Activities and Programs office and the "CoCo" [CoCurricular Program] that works with College Nine and College Ten.[6] Cocurricular programs are programs that are complementary to a student's academic program. Almost all of our cocurricular programming is related to our themes. The philosophy is that students in college learn both inside and outside of the classroom, and that both learning platforms are important to their development. It's based on the belief of developing the whole student.

M.R.C. Greenwood: As we got more and more into academic planning, we realized how constrained our resources were going to be.

And also, something that was, and I think still is, a big issue for Santa Cruz—the core courses and the undergraduate advising of the colleges were becoming increasingly disconnected from the full-time, ladder-line faculty. We were getting into a situation where the part-time faculty and some well-qualified instructional faculty were basically handling the first year or so of the curriculum. The advising in the colleges was not well connected with the major advising. The divisions were beginning to divorce themselves from undergraduate education, particularly at the general education level. That's a real problem. When the faculty get in the colleges, they love it. But you've got to find a way to get them into the colleges. So, a lot of things were discussed. One was more of an alliance, so that a dean of a division would feel that they also had responsibility for the success of the colleges, so that they would put their best faculty forward as provosts, and they would be interested in the quality of education.

Deana Slater: There is a lot of synergy when you are reporting to a division. When we've asked faculty to come to be guest lecturers in our classes, or the core course, there's a lot of enthusiasm. It's usually because the topic reflects their own research and their interests. They're interested in possibly getting some undergraduates interested in their work. What makes our colleges unique is this opportunity to put both the provost's vision and my vision together, and then work closely with our staff to articulate and leverage that vision, and to harness their skills and energy. The way our colleges are organized is an ideal model that really does contribute to student learning both in and out of the classroom.

Structurally, it's one reason why the colleges have been able to have so many robust programs. The themes have driven our ability to share a common vision and develop ongoing sustained programs that engage students all four years. Our structure—having one provost and one CAO [College Administrative Officer] reporting to the social sciences division—has allowed us to create these unique and robust colleges. I would say every single staff member would be able to tell you how central these themes are to their work, and how it guides them in their program development and interaction with students. We got this permission to structure things differently and we didn't spend any more money.

M.R.C. Greenwood: Before College Nine and College Ten, colleges were devolving into student affairs and a core course that some thought had not been reviewed in a very long time. It had become one of the third rails of politics at UCSC. One was either for or against the colleges. That is not a very productive discussion. The colleges as they currently exist are not the colleges Dean McHenry imagined. He would have been horrified that the core courses were being taught primarily by faculty who didn't have permanent status at the institution. And, on the other hand, without divisional buy-in to the colleges, some of your most vital faculty were unwilling to participate, because they didn't see it as a priority for their division. So the idea was to try to repair that with some experiments.

That's why College Nine and Ten being associated with the social sciences division was an experiment. The provost there reported to divisional dean Marty Chemers. He was both an associate dean of social sciences and the provost. I think that was a very important discussion: what can we *really* do with these colleges? We made some progress, at least made people talk about the

670 SEEDS OF SOMETHING DIFFERENT

colleges again, in a nonconfrontational way. There certainly were people who felt we were trying to undermine the colleges. That was not what we were trying to do. I was trying to strengthen the colleges.

Deana Slater: For this model of divisionalization to succeed with other UCSC colleges, a lot would depend on the other academic deans, and their interest and support of these type of affiliations. There are some natural partnerships. For example, Porter's affiliation with the arts division would totally makes sense, as would Cowell with humanities, Crown with the physical and biological sciences, etc. I strongly believe College Nine and College Ten provide a good model that elevates both academics' interest and the student-life program.

The social sciences division is the biggest division, with the most undergraduates on campus. Our college themes are very clearly related to the work that's already valued and taking place in the social sciences division. Other colleges may not have themes that perfectly align with various divisions. I had a very supportive dean when we began this affiliation. That was an important key to its success.

I think there was some notion from others that there may be competition for resources between the academic division and the colleges, if the colleges reported to a division. However, if it could work, if each college could report to a division and reorganize their student affairs side to support a cocurricular unit, the university would come much closer to our original goal of creating vibrant living-learning centers with a strong emphasis on academic initiatives, as well as the potential for more effectively leveraging interdisciplinary activities.

Wendy Baxter: I worked with three students and we did a dialogue class on Israel-Palestine. The three co-facilitators were—one was Palestinian; one was Jewish American; and one was what is called, when talking about that, sort of "unaffiliated," so no perceived or assigned affiliation through their identities. We developed the curriculum together and they did a great job facilitating that class. And given the climate on campus with that, we attended the class as well, me and [CoCurricular Programs Coordinator] Erin Ramsden.

M.R.C. Greenwood: The other thing was to put research opportunities in the colleges. You do that in the colleges, instead of over in some other hall someplace. You begin an intellectual dialogue in the colleges, not just in the core course, but with some more faculty members. You make research money available, and some of it is for undergraduates to do research out of those centers. So you are constantly keeping at least a moderately sized group of students actively involved with faculty members in research, so that students are always engaged in the institutions. The Center for Justice, Tolerance, and Community (CJTC) was a good example of that.[7] You can offer extra things in the colleges, some speakers. CJTC, for example, ran a couple of dynamite seminar series. The one I remember was the Palestinian-Israeli dialogue.

Wendy Baxter: We didn't prioritize anyone getting into the class. We aimed for a balance of perspectives, and committed to providing an environment where productive communication across difference could happen. People had to agree to communication guidelines to be in the class, and it was successful. I'm very familiar with conversations around that topic, so we knew, this is how it's got to be. I knew how important it was to provide this, for our own safety, but also because we need to talk about these problems. It's really important to talk about them. And if we can't talk about them productively halfway around the earth, then how can we expect anyone to talk about them productively anywhere?

We've done debates and roundtables on affirmative action; the most recent one was on climate change. We've done marriage equality two different times. We've done animals in research—all kinds of different topics. Military recruitment on campuses.

With UCSC's reputation as being very left-leaning and stuff, in the early years it was very hard to get conservative voices to agree to come. I remember writing to Ward and he really wanted to talk to us: "How are you going to provide me this? How are you going to promise this?" We have very clear guidelines for those programs, audience expectations. We have free-speech stuff posted everywhere. We set up a temporary designated free-speech zone. We don't allow people to leaflet inside the venue. And then, at the Ward Connerly event, someone stood up with a sign they had somehow smuggled in; in the front row, they were protesting him. My colleague, Jose Olivas, moved the person away, and talked to them, and reminded them of the agreements that are posted at the entrance. They could stay without the sign, if they stayed seated, or they could leave.

Donna Haraway: What does activism mean? Look, the US public when surveyed these days [in 2007], most recently, 45 percent of the US public does not "believe" in Darwinian evolution. We belong to a culture that is *extremely* religious. It's complicated! And we have *got* to talk to those folks. We have got to give up our self-certainties around secularism. It doesn't work. We have got to get what the world looks like without giving up. We've got to learn how to argue. We've got to learn how to talk. We've got to learn how to hear, politically.

Khalen Hudson, Student: College Nine and College Ten offer a student-taught course every winter quarter. College Nine's is around the College Nine theme of global international perspectives. College Ten's is around the social justice theme. The class I taught, the theme was educational inequity. I did the College Ten class because I like change.

Wendy Baxter: We have classes where one of the staff members works with student instructors, and then the student instructors produce lesson plans, under close supervision, and facilitate the actual classes. So, we have one for College Nine: Global Action, and one for College Ten: Social Justice Issues. We develop those student teachers and teach them how to make lesson plans, provide resources.

That's a super-powerful model. Students take that class. They see their instructor: a student. Students learn things from other students that they can't learn intergenerationally. It's a really different kind of learning, not that there isn't a really great place for intergenerational learning as well. But it's very powerful, what they can learn from their peers.

Khalen Hudson: I got really close to the advisor of the cocurricular program. Her name is Wendy Baxter. She's cool. She's the advisor of the College Ten class, the student class. So, she reached out to me. She was like, "You should really apply. I think you should do it." So, I applied and I got it.

I'd never taught in a setting like that. You teach it with a co-teacher. The class is two units to take and it's five units for us to teach. So, you have to assign two assignments, basically, for the quarter. And when we assigned the assignments,

Figure 2

College Nine street view, 2017

Photo by Carolyn Lagattuta

the students actually did them, and did them really well. We were super surprised. They take us seriously as figures and teachers. The class was really good learning experience for us to learn as a teacher. Big props to all the teachers out there, because they deal with a lot of stuff.

Each week had a theme. One week was Islamophobia. One week would be police brutality. One week was food justice. One week was educational inequity. And basically, the class, we like to make the rubber meet the road. So, in our class of social justice—this year the theme was educational inequity—so we reached out to this school called Gault Elementary School in Santa Cruz. They teach many undocumented students and children. A lot of their parents are migrant workers. We asked, "What do you guys need?" And they were like, "Oh, we need books for our library." We ended up raising around two thousand dollars for the school's library. We got to go meet with them and meet the kids. It was really cool.

Yeah, the class was fun to teach. It was fun to learn about things that you don't know as much about, but you have to know about them when you teach. But it was also just cool, being vulnerable in the class. And a lot of your students also teach you some stuff, too.

We had a wide range of knowledge in the class. A lot of our people in our class, they surprised us. They were more "woke" than we thought. Stories speak volumes. A lot of people like to tell stories, but a lot of people don't like to actually listen to the stories that people tell. But in our class, stories were very personal; first-hand accounts were very important. I'd be sharing stories about my blackness and stuff. Other people would share stories about their interaction with the black community, or their interactions within their community. It was a nice growing experience, learning about ourselves with each other.

Wendy Baxter: I see our student leaders norm advanced cultural dexterity and respect. They normalize talking, having conversations about difference, across difference, in a way that gives me goosebumps right now, talking about it, because it's so powerful. Where do we get those models in our world? I don't think many people learn those skills. And they really, really learn, develop, and then normalize those.

I also co-teach *Expressive Arts for Social Justice*. People learn different media, different principles about art making—visual art making, movement, word. They are working on all these different projects: visual lexicons and their sketchbooks. They're doing these things they've never done before, working with the elements of art to create meaning, and to give a visual language to their life experience, and their dreams and passions and traumas. Their final project—we have parameters as to how much energy and work would go into it, but we leave the topic totally up to them. We help them refine that, deepen that topic, and figure out different ways they could express that.

At the end of the quarter, we set up a pop-up gallery, because we also don't have a gallery space. We have Namaste Lounge, which has one wall. Namaste becomes an art gallery for the day. That room is full of powerful truth-telling and passion. We have folks addressing migrant farmworkers; folks working with their experience of living in a world based on rape culture; people talking about the silencing and the cultural encasement of their queer identities. Twenty students and this room brimming with exceptionally beautiful works of art with really powerful messages.

Deana Slater: When Wendy first came over to our colleges to think about developing this cocurricular unit, we took a walk on West Cliff Drive. We were thinking about exciting possible ways to bring these themes to life for our students. Wendy said, "Well, we could do this conference, where we could have students identify social justice issues that really resonate with them." She was talking about how students might grow and learn and become more involved, and have an opportunity to engage with faculty.

Then it was so gratifying to watch how Wendy turned this germ of an idea into such a great program for our students and the campus. It's a hands-on opportunity to build a conference and learn more about social justice issues. Students do the leading.

Wendy Baxter: Practical Activism started as a germ of an idea.[8] Deana remembers we were walking on West Cliff and I was telling her this idea. It goes back to the norming of student engagement, and valuing social justice issues, and respecting difference on every level. I imagined this fall program, a big conference where there were lots of students involved in creating it, where first-year students would come, and right off at the beginning of their academic career see, "Wow, here's all these issues. First of all, I'm learning about all these issues. But look at these cool students who are organizing all this."[9]

So that first year, spring of 2003, we pulled together a handful of students: "Who is interested? Who wants to join us?" At that point, there was a lot of talk about student retention after their first year. I thought, well, students need to feel like they belong, and if they haven't found that belonging in the first year, then they're not going to come back. They are at higher risk of not coming back. So I thought, if we started planning in spring and they'd made this commitment, then that would bring them back, potentially. At that time, I didn't know how powerful Practical Activism would become. It was just all these ideas. We called it "The Conference." That was one of

our first jobs: to get a title. The students brainstormed and we came up with that.

David Solano: Practical Activism is a day-long conference that I helped organize. It has ten workshops and they're all social justice-oriented, related. This past year, we had a topic on transphobia, mental health, queerness and mental health, undocumented students, Islamophobia. Different topics like that. Very burning issues and recent stuff that is happening. The purpose of it is to make sure that as we bring in these resources, as we bring in people who have knowledge on these topics, to make sure that their message is being sent out to our audience, and giving them the tools on how to get involved and what they can do to get involved in the community, and wherever they are, how they can be a part of the movement.

And then, we usually have a keynote speaker and a spoken-word artist. Every year it's been a very unique experience, with our keynote speakers and spoken-word artists. They bring passion and valuable thoughts and advice that awakens our urge to go on out and improve the communities we are a part of. A lot of the feedback that we get is very positive and I was very happy. It's a rewarding feeling, because it impacts a lot of people positively. People look forward to attending the year after. We have booths that have other topics that we couldn't really cover within the ten main workshops. We try to cover as much as we can, recent issues that are happening. And as the years go by, there're always issues going on, or new topics that are on the news. We try to do the best we can to inform people, make people more aware of their surroundings.

Wendy Baxter: Practical Activism is like a machine. It starts in spring and we have to move along; we have to get these people working together. We have to choose topics for the workshops.

And we don't just have the workshops. We also have the hands-on activities, what we call Special Sessions. They are activism booths, learning centers. We have tabling orgs there. We have publicity and everything that we have to do. Outreach. And we have all the logistics, and the food, and the sustainability piece.

The skills people get and bring to Practical Activism are amazing. It's happened more than once where someone is at a job interview and they say, "Now tell us more about Practical Activism—" So they go on. And then at the end the interviewer says, "You know, I was a Practical Activism planner." That always makes me choke up.

Someone interviewed me about what we were doing. They were interviewing people who were doing activism development work with students. They said they hadn't really heard of anything exactly like this. The closest thing they'd heard about was at some university in Arizona. Someone contacted us: "Can we come? We are thinking of doing something similar." "Of course, you can come—and let me know how I can help."

Sometimes students will write and say, "Hey, I'm using tons of materials from when I planned Practical Activism with you," in whatever year. "And I'm doing a conference for Queer Youth," or "I'm doing—" I don't know if there's something at other colleges that has this level of longevity and sustenance. One student came from South Africa, just here to our colleges, and she went to Practical Activism as an attendee. And when she got back to her home university, she wrote a big article about it. She said, "We should do something like this here."

Deana Slater: We also have these weekend retreats that we modeled on the Developmental Model of Intercultural Sensitivity. I started a weekend retreat model like this at UCSD, then brought it

to Merrill, and we then brought it here. We have the Intercultural Community Weekend retreat for College Nine, and the Multicultural Community Weekend retreat for College Ten. Students go off campus, and spend time through various activities exploring our themes, and getting to know one another more deeply. I've heard several students say that the weekend helped to retain them, or that they made some great friends and so on. So that's the first-year opportunity.

David Solano: I was homesick. I was dealing with so much that quarter. And my friends weren't really fully there for me. It was very weird. It was such a weird year with my friends. So, I decided to go to a Multicultural Weekend, just to see how it was.[10] I heard a lot of great things about it from my first-year roommate. I was like, fine, I'll go.

And I went. And, oh my God, it's a space for you to let out everything that you carry inside of you. It was another therapy session, kind of, in a way. We talked about identities. In high school, we would have these conversations, but I'd never really experienced it. Now I was experiencing them. It was a different way of having these conversations about privilege and oppression, and different aspects of my identity that played a role in the way society sees me, what they expect of me.

One activity we did was "crossing the line." They made us all form a line and the activity was based on statements. If that statement applied to you, you had to step over the line, and turn around and see the people who didn't cross the line. So, let's say, for example, "If you are from a low-income home, step forward." And everyone would move forward and turn around to those who didn't cross the line. All these facts were stated, facts that were very relatable, and facts that you lived through. It was a moment where you're just like yeah, I've gone through this, and I totally forgot that I went through this. I haven't had the chance to let it out. It was a very intense and emotional activity. It was a space to share your experiences, what is going on with you, and where you're at in society, and what can you do after the experience.

I had thought of dropping out my second year. And after sharing my experiences, I never felt so motivated in my life. I felt like something was eating me up for several years. I felt like I tossed that out. Yeah, it was very life-changing, very eye-opening. It motivated me to stay in school. I think Multicultural Weekend is the reason why I stayed in Santa Cruz. Because after that, I knew that I had potential. I knew that I, as a human being, like every human being, has something to offer, and a purpose in life. Everyone plays a role in this society. Seeing so many people on the same page from different backgrounds and identities, motivated me to do the work, get involved, keep on with my major.

The next year I applied to lead Multicultural Weekend. It was a different experience being a part of it and leading it. But it still had the same effect, because I did talk a lot about the things that were overwhelming me the previous year. My dad passed away; that year it was very fresh. So, I guess I still carried a lot of my father and how his death affects me. I talked a lot about that. You're given a space to voice anything that's making you feel sad or angry. People would just share. People's perspectives change a lot in the way they see themselves, and I think it's mostly in a positive way. So, the person that I am now, the way I see life now, is because of Multicultural Weekend, a very, very deep retreat.

Deana Slater: We have centered a lot of our work at College Nine around the Developmental Model of Intercultural Communication, based on work by Milton Bennet and Michael Page. It basically says that that people move through stages, from the early stages of Denial of Difference to the later stage of Adaptation, where people are able to move seamlessly between different cultures. So, our goal at College Nine is to help students raise awareness of these differences and provide them knowledge skills and tools to move along this continuum.

We wanted students to think about how one might become a global citizen. What does it mean to contribute to the world? What are your own cultural biases? Those are the issues that we want people to look at, both as an individual, but also as a person from the United States, regardless of your own ethnic background, or whether you're a first-generation student, or hold a lot of other rich identities. How do you relate as a person from the United States, when you go to a different continent, and an entirely different place, and then interact with others? At that point, our identities are reframed and become even more complex and interesting. I don't think one can become a global citizen without really understanding issues of equity and social justice, and what that means across the globe.

Wendy Baxter: We started doing mural painting. Most of them are student murals.[11] There are two murals done by our student group CREATE, which is Cultural Resources to Educate and Empower. That's a support group for students of color, for support and mentorship and retention. So, one of them is the Where is Waldo type of imagery, saying, "Where are the people of color at UCSC?" That was done—I forget the exact year, but 2004, approximately. We had an unveiling and a conversation. It received a lot of attention. Some white students were super offended by it. Some really important conversations came up around it. It was vandalized a few times. And over time, students of color were like, "What is *this* about?" So, it was really interesting. Great conversations.

Figure 3

College Nine tenth anniversary program poster, 2011

The murals at College Nine and College Ten have a great history.

Katherine Le: Something that really impacted my time during my first year was an alternative spring break trip that was offered through College Nine. It allowed students from College Nine and Ten, and students beyond who were interested, to spend spring break on the UCSC campus. And during the day we would go to Watsonville, to volunteer at Second Harvest Food Bank,[12] to work with Digital Nest, a program that helps students in the area access technology resources,[13] and to see what migrant and farmworker and undocumented families go through. Santa Cruz County is very multifaceted, and stepping out of Santa Cruz is also important, too, to realize that hey, there's a network and community that expands beyond just us.

And being able to have a little potluck in a farmworker's house in Watsonville with other UCSC students and listen to her story as an undocumented farmworker, and get involved with the community of Watsonville and hold a clothing drive for migrant and farmworker families in this community, really showed that UCSC does have resources that allow students to become connected to the community. The campus does have a heart when it comes to reaching out to underserved populations that extend beyond just us and beyond just our community here.

M.R.C. Greenwood: And so College Nine and Ten got put in place. I loved opening two new colleges. It was such a wonderful experience. And Clark Kerr—before he died he came to visit the campus. The emeriti had invited him to talk. So I asked him, "Would you like to go see the new colleges?" He said, "Oh—" I said, "Come on, Clark. Let me take you up and show you what we're doing." College Nine was there. The buildings were there. It was coming together. College Ten was still rising. The dining hall was beginning to look like a real dining hall, but it was still clearly a construction site.

So I took him up, and there was some kind of a backhoe or something, and we got out of the car and we sort of walked in between the colleges. And these tears formed in his eyes. He said, "You know, you're still pioneering." I said, "Yes, we still are. We are still building a story, and UC Santa Cruz is an extraordinary institution. It's unlike most public universities. And that's at least, in part, your doing." Sure, we haven't kept the image, all of the pieces that Dean McHenry imagined, but some very critical core components which make us distinctly different are still here, and one of them is the colleges. So he was pleased. It was very touching.

Endnotes

1. Dean McHenry worked with the Upton Sinclair campaign in the 1930s and also (unsuccessfully) ran for Congress in 1952. He also authored many books on political science. It is therefore not surprising that McHenry used this term "Sons of the Wild Jackass." According to the US Senate's website on the Senate's "Art and History": "In 1929 Republican senator George Moses of New Hampshire referred to a group of western progressives as the 'Sons of the Wild Jackass.' At the time, the Senate was embroiled in a contentious debate over the proposed Smoot-Hawley protective tariff, which pitted senators from eastern manufacturing states, sometimes called the Regular Republicans, against Progressive Republicans from the midwestern and western agrarian states. Into this volatile situation stepped George Moses—the Senate's witty but caustic president pro tem. On November 7, 1929, Moses addressed a group of New England manufacturers and voiced his frustration with the independent-minded progressives. 'The sons of the wild jackass now control the Senate,' he complained, accusing the western senators of undermining the efforts of the dedicated old guard. By the next day, his comment was headline news in cities across the nation. Moses' denunciation of his progressive colleagues further inflamed a long-standing rift between the eastern political establishment and the western insurgency." https://www.senate.gov/artandhistory/history/minute/Sons_of_the_Wild_Jackass.htm.

2. College Nine opened its doors in fall quarter of 2000, College Ten in fall of 2002.

3. The genesis of the vision for UC Santa Cruz's newest colleges, College Nine and College Ten, dates back to the 1988 *Long Range Development Plan* (LRDP), which responded both to faculty members who argued that the social sciences division needed academic space in the campus core, and to demographic studies that demonstrated that UCSC would be experiencing rising student enrollments and would need to house more students on campus. The 1988 LRDP thus called for planning two new colleges that would integrate academic and residential facilities. Fast forward to May of 1999, when, under the chancellorship of M.R.C. Greenwood and the vice chancellorship of Francisco Hernandez, The Colleges Nine and Ten Planning Advisory Committee issued a report entitled "Opening College IX and X." Among the report's recommendations were that these two colleges should "continue the tradition of the current UCSC colleges, concentrating upon community life and student affairs," while "being centers of interdisciplinary curricula and courses, intellectual stimulation, research, conferences, and student projects." The proposal was for these colleges to

be affiliated with the social sciences division, as per the 1988 LRDP. The report's authors stated, "We have come to believe that the opening of Colleges IX and X represents a major new opportunity for UC Santa Cruz [that would build] upon the successes and learning from the failures of the past. While we can learn from some parts of the McHenry model, we cannot return to it. It has been rejected by the campus." Instead they called for a third model, which they dubbed "the Greenwood Model," of how colleges could function at UCSC going forward. This model builds on the post-reorganization college focus on community life and student affairs and "engages faculty members and students in a way that the current colleges do not." The writers argued that the existing eight UCSC colleges should not necessarily adopt the Greenwood Model, arguing instead that the two models could exist side by side. College Nine and College Ten, like Rachel Carson College, has no live-in provost and no provost's house.

4. Francisco Hernandez served as vice chancellor for student affairs from 1994 to 2006, when he left to become the vice chancellor for students at the University of Hawaii at Manoa. At UCSC, Hernandez developed a strategic plan for student services, and implemented the plan during a period of significant student enrollment increases.

5. Martin Chemers arrived at UC Santa Cruz in 1995 as dean of social sciences and professor of psychology. During his tenure as dean, the College Nine and College Ten complex was completed, and, with Chemers's leadership, was organized to integrate the themes of the colleges with the academic strengths of the social sciences division. Chemers also initiated the Center for Justice, Tolerance, and Community, supported the development of the Center for Global, International and Regional Studies, and oversaw the creation of seventeen new academic programs, including the PhD in education; several multidisciplinary and interdisciplinary programs. In April of 2004, after Chancellor M.R.C. Greenwood left UCSC to take the position of provost and senior vice president of the UC system, Chemers was appointed acting chancellor of UCSC, a position he held until the arrival of Chancellor Denice Denton in February of 2005.

6. See https://collegenine.ucsc.edu/cocurricular/coco/index.html.

7. The Center for Justice, Tolerance, and Community (CJTC) began in 2000 and was affiliated with College Nine. It closed in 2010 because of budget cuts to the UC system.

8. The annual Practical Activism Conference began in

2003. This day-long conference is led and organized by students from College Nine, College Ten, and Oakes College, with the guidance of Wendy Baxter, Director of Academic and Cocurricular Programs at College Nine and College Ten. According to the conference's website: https://practicalactivism.ucsc.edu/about/index.html: "The previous Practical Activism Conferences have been highly successful venues for education, activism, and networking. Several keynote speakers have been featured including Angela Davis, Zahra Billoo, the Molotov Mouths, Daniel 'Nane' Alejandrez, Boots Riley, Bettina Aptheker, Aaronette White, Darrick Smith, and Eden Silva Jequinto. Through the years of Practical Activism, over 150 workshops have been implemented, covering such diverse topics as art and activism, the criminal justice system, global gender issues, voting injustices, diversity in education, immigration, military, UC involvement with nuclear bombs, UC tuition hikes, sexual assault, homelessness, and student movements."

9. UCSC also hosts another day-long conference about organizing: Earth Summit, the annual environmental forum, now (2018) in its sixteenth year. Earth Summit is organized by the Student Environmental Center.

10. Multicultural Weekend is a retreat held annually in Winter Quarter for students who want to gain leadership skills and deepen their awareness of College Ten's theme of Social Justice and Community through interactive exercises and small-group discussions.

11. For a digital gallery of photographs of the murals at College Nine and College Ten see: https://collegenine.ucsc.edu/getinvolved/murals/index.html.

12. Founded in 1972, Second Harvest Food Bank Santa Cruz County was the first food bank in California and is the second oldest in the nation.

13. Digital NEST (Nurturing Entrepreneurial Skills with Technology) is dedicated to providing equal access to technology and resources to young people in underserved communities.

Illustrations

Figure 1. College Nine and College Ten Dedication Program. 2003. Courtesy Special Collections, University Library, University of California, Santa Cruz. UA 70: UCSC Ephemera Collection: ua070-0064.

Figure 2. College Nine Street View, 2017. Photo by Carolyn Lagattuta. Campus Photo Archive. Communications and Marketing Department, UCSC. Copyright UC Regents.

Figure 3. College Nine Tenth Year Anniversary Program poster. 2011. Courtesy Special Collections, University Library, University of California, Santa Cruz. UA 109: College Nine and Ten Administrative Records: ua109_001_0001.

Chapter 32

"Wounds from Glass Ceilings"
The Brief and Tragic Tenure of Chancellor Denice Denton

I looked around the room and the table was almost full. There was only one empty seat. It was next to Denice. So I went and sat down next to Denice. I remember thinking that it was so weird in such a crowded room that no one wanted to sit next to the chancellor.

—George Blumenthal

Michael Cowan: I enjoyed working with M.R.C. Greenwood. She was a vivid personality, a whirlwind. She really moved through the landscape. She was very sociable, easy in all sorts of crowds. She was quite creative and was constantly looking for new ways of solving problems. She pushed very hard, and some people don't like to be pushed very hard. But I think she did a series of very important things for the university, and she was around long enough to really make a difference. I think she really revved up the campus's commitment to and ability to go after significant fundraising.

M.R.C. Greenwood went to the Office of the President,[1] and Marty Chemers was moved up in the role as acting chancellor. Marine scientist Margaret Delaney came in as interim provost and EVC.[2] Then a search was started for a chancellor, which resulted in the arrival of Denice Denton.

San Jose Mercury News: The University of California regents Tuesday named Denice Dee Denton, the openly gay dean of the University of Washington's College of Engineering, to lead the University of California, Santa Cruz as its ninth chancellor.

University officials said they don't know for sure if Denton is the first openly gay chancellor in the ten-campus system. But if she is, it would be just the latest first for her. In 1996, Denton became the first woman in the nation to lead an engineering college at a major university, coming to UW from a faculty position in electrical and computer engineering at the University of Wisconsin, Madison.[3]

Chronicle of Higher Education: Karl S. Pister, a former dean of engineering at the University of California at Berkeley and former chancellor of

Chancellor Denice Denton, 2005

Photo by Jim MacKenzie

Campus Photo Archive

Santa Cruz, first met Ms. Denton while she was at MIT. Mr. Pister, who was at Berkeley at the time, was attending an engineering conference in Washington. He says the attendees were mostly deans, and exclusively "white male, except Denice." He spotted her at a dinner. "Nobody talked to Denice," he says, who was "sitting over there in the corner."[4]

San Jose Mercury News: At UW in Seattle, she worked to boost the number of female and minority students and faculty in a large and established engineering school with 10 departments and 225 faculty. [5]

UCSC News Center: Denice D. Denton will be invested as the ninth chancellor of the University of California, Santa Cruz, in an afternoon ceremony on Friday, November 4, 2005. The investiture ceremony will follow a two-day academic symposium that reflects Chancellor Denton's commitment to have the campus focus on academic priorities in lieu of a formal inauguration. The "Achieving Excellence Through Diversity" symposium launches three days of investiture activities that also include the annual Scholarships Benefit Dinner.[6]

San Jose Mercury News: Among the current crop of UC chancellors, Denton, 45, will be the youngest. She will start in February, and hopes that her partner of seven years, Gretchen Kalonji, also an engineering professor, will get a job at a UC campus.[7]

Denice Denton, Chancellor: It is a true honor for me to be here today. I pledge my dedicated and passionate commitment to doing everything humanly possible to advance our great university. I am very grateful for the support I've received from my family, academic

mentors, and many friends over the years. I want to acknowledge especially my partner, Gretchen Kalonji, the Director of International Strategy Development at UCOP, who is in the audience today. My mother, Carolyn, who was a single mom supporting three kids as a high school math teacher, also served as a great role model, as have many others in my life, to whom I want to express my deepest gratitude.[8]

George Blumenthal: Denice was one of those people who, when she spoke to an audience, she liked to do audience participation. She'd ask questions of the audience. It is a real skill. That was really very much her style. At her inauguration, it was a refreshing kind of approach.

David Kliger: Chancellor Denton was a brilliant person. She had tremendous rapport with students. She had a real vision for the campus. She had empathy for students and for staff.

Denice Denton: Were the leaders who envisioned the ninth University of California campus with us today—Clark Kerr and Dean McHenry—I believe they would see their dream of creating a unique environment for teaching and learning well on the way to being fulfilled—and fulfilled beyond their ambitious expectations. As President Kerr said in his memoir *The Gold and the Blue,* "Santa Cruz challenged the multiversity model head on. The Santa Cruz Dream was a wonderful dream."[9]

I have been told by those who knew him that founding UC Santa Cruz Chancellor Dean McHenry often recounted the goal of creating an uncommon undergraduate education, rivaling the finest liberal arts colleges, within a great research university. Now, forty years later, the UCSC colleges are undergoing a renaissance. Today, our students not only thrive in an atmosphere of "pursuing truth in the company of friends," as distilled in the motto of UCSC's first college, Cowell, but they are also engaged with our faculty in scholarly activities that are changing the world for the better.

By blurring the boundaries between disciplines and breaking the administrative barriers that typically characterize academic organizations, UC Santa Cruz has escaped the stratification—and stultification—that can occur when thinking is "silo-ed" and research is limited to the scope of a single discipline. Instead, with a propensity for interdisciplinarity that is uniquely spawned by the nimbleness of youth and inclination to explore frontiers that emerge at the borders of disciplines, UC Santa Cruz has truly earned its reputation for "thinking at the edge." Not content with "thinking at the edge," let's accept the challenge to "lead at the edge," to build on our past accomplishments as we continue to make a difference in a society that today is rife with challenges affecting everyone on the planet.

Dean McHenry became the first UC Santa Cruz chancellor during a time that also was characterized by great opportunity as well as nation-shaking controversy. Some of you in the audience participated in the Free Speech Movement, in the controversy over the war in Vietnam, in the women's liberation movement, in the civil rights movement, and other examples that characterize the mid-1960s and early 70s. Today, we again find ourselves in a world that daily greets great discoveries but also beholds constant conflict. Even more so than forty years ago, UC Santa Cruz is poised to address these challenges in ways that no other great university can do. [10]

David Kliger: One of the things that Chancellor Denton and I spent a lot of time on in our first year was working very hard to increase the wages for the lowest-paid workers on campus. It was a struggle because not all campuses wanted to do that. It was a fight with Office of the President to allow us to do that. But ultimately we were successful to increase the wages of the lowest paid workers.

Jim Burns: In some painful ways, it almost seemed as if Denice Denton's tenure on our campus started to unravel pretty early—around the time of her appointment. One of her early challenges was the appointment that the Office of the President made for her partner. Partner hires like that had certainly occurred in relationships that were heterosexual. So my impression at the time was that she and her partner were not being treated very fairly by reporters and the public when concerns first surfaced about UC hiring her partner for another job. At least to me, it seemed that the reaction was in part based on the fact that Chancellor Denton and her partner were in a public homosexual relationship. I also had the impression that the Office of the President was not very prepared to speak supportively of the partner hire. Far be it from me to weigh in about whether the chancellor's partner was qualified for the job that she was given as director of international strategy. What I do remember thinking at the time was that perhaps UCOP could have done a better job preparing for the partner-hire announcement.

George Blumenthal: [At the Office of the President] I met Gretchen Kalonji, Denice's partner. They were talking to her about coming to the UC Office of the President, which she did do, to take a position to encourage international cooperation among the UC campuses with various programs abroad. So when Gretchen came to visit, I went to lunch with her. We had a very, very nice lunch. I liked Gretchen a lot. I thought she was interesting and well-traveled. I think she spoke Chinese, so we went to a Chinese dim sum restaurant and she ordered in Chinese. I found her very, very interesting. Unusual, but interesting and likable.

San Francisco Chronicle, Gretchen Kalonji, a professor of materials science at University of Washington in Seattle and an expert in international education, has been hired as director of international strategy development in the UC Office of the President in Oakland. She will also receive a tenured professorial appointment at one of the UC campuses—possibly UC Santa Cruz. According to UC President Robert Dynes, Kalonji's hiring was part of the recruitment package offered to her partner of seven years, Denice Dee Denton, an engineer who was appointed last December as the new chancellor of UC Santa Cruz. Denton will start in February and will receive a salary of $275,000 and a moving allowance of $68,750. In addition to Kalonji's $192,000 annual salary, UC will provide her with the usual faculty housing assistance allowance of up to $50,000 to help with her transition to California and UC and pay her moving expenses.

Her qualifications have not been questioned, but some observers wonder whether UC should be creating new management positions at a time when it is struggling with a budget crisis and is laying off workers, cutting student services and increasing student fees. One employee union official didn't mince words. "It makes me sick," said Mary Higgins, an administrative assistant at UCSF and statewide president of UC's clerical union, which did not get a raise this year. "It is a violation of the public trust and it is just more of the same. It is just like it is a total corrupt corporate enterprise."[11]

Jim Burns: I recall having a pretty urgent phone conversation with the Office of the President at the time, a call in which they were asking for help in explaining this challenge. Obviously, because Denice was going to be our chancellor, the UCSC people on that call really wanted to help. The partner hire had already been covered in kind of a crude way by the *San Francisco Chronicle*, which, in a sensationalistic headline referred to her partner as a "lesbian lover." During the phone call, I offered to help support Denice because we were getting some local and regional attention for the story. Toward that end, I asked to see a job description, and the UCOP people on the call—much to my dismay at the time—reported that they didn't have one, which only seemed to reinforce the notion that this was a job that wasn't really needed and that it had only been created for Chancellor Denton's partner.

David Kliger: Frankly, she became chancellor too early in her career. She wasn't sufficiently experienced in administration, particularly the part of the administration where you have to have a thick skin and realize that people are going to criticize you as the chancellor, and the criticism is of your position, not you. So that was a major issue.

Nüz, *Metro Santa Cruz:* It's worth noting that Denton's predecessor, M.R.C. Greenwood, never had around-the clock police escort, but perhaps that's because she wasn't plagued by scandal until after her departure from campus, unlike Denton, whose problems began the minute she assumed her $275,000 a year post—a job she began, ironically enough, on Valentine's Day '05.

So, yeah, maybe Denton is afraid that revelations that her partner Gretchen Kalonji was hired for $192,000 a year for a new management position with UC and had been granted $50,000 for moving expenses would get the goat of some downsized/underpaid UCSC worker. Or that she'd be blamed for a Pentagon spying scandal,[12] or that homophobes would harass her after *Sentinel*

Managing Editor Don Miller named her part of a "powerful coterie of lesbians."[13]

Or maybe she decided she needed to be guarded after someone threw a sign through her window during the Tent U affair last spring, or after a UCSC student (who now works as *Metro Santa Cruz's* editorial assistant) wrote a *City on a Hill* column in which she threatened to park her car on Denton's lawn. Certainly, Denton's über-obsession with security would explain why she moved her office from the McHenry Building to the Kerr Building, whose second floor was ripped out in the process, to install, as our highly placed source informs us, a lockdown area for Denton's office with cameras every three feet—a set-up that must have cost thousands of dollars.[14]

George Blumenthal: I was a member of the Senate Executive Committee. They used to have these meetings at eight o'clock in the morning. I'm not real good at getting here at eight in the morning. So I remember stumbling into this meeting at like 8:15 and being shocked because everyone was there. I looked around the room and the table was almost full. There was only one empty seat. It was next to Denice. So I went and sat down next to Denice. I remember thinking that it was so weird in such a crowded room that no one wanted to sit next to the chancellor. I didn't know what that meant.

I was hearing hints, but I wasn't paying much attention to them, that there were problems. I'd heard about the weird trip up into the Sierras where Denice had suddenly found herself driving in the Sierras and had no idea how she had gotten there. I knew that she had missed some senate meetings. I didn't know she was sick. People tended to interpret it as lack of interest rather than illness, but in fact it was probably illness.

David Kliger: But the main issue was that I think she had some mental illness problems resulting from some other health problems. That caused huge problems within the administration. There was a lot of fear. The first week she came in, she fired a number of people in her office. She was always threatening people around her. So I had to go to all of the senior administrators and tell them, "If you have any bad news, you don't go to Chancellor Denton. You come to me and I give her the bad news." I felt I couldn't afford to lose the rest of the administration, and so I needed to protect them from what was happening.

George Blumenthal: I went to Los Angeles for a meeting of the Long Range Guidance Team, which was a group of regents and others who were put together to think about the future of the university.

I attended the regents' dinner (as a former faculty representative) and was sitting, I think, between one of the regents and, I think, the director of the Los Alamos National Labs. I was heavily engaged in dinner conversation when all of a sudden Denice Denton came over to me and said, "I have to talk to you urgently."

So, of course, I got up from dinner. It was a huge room, and we went off to the side of the room and had a really weird conversation. It was 98 percent her talking. I don't know that she actually poked me in the chest during the conversation, but I do remember that she kept getting inside of my space. It felt like she was poking me in the chest, in an emotional sense.

She wanted to talk to me about the students at Santa Cruz and how the students were becoming unmanageable. She said there were ninjas that had gone to one of the colleges and broken the locks on the dormitories and done substantial damage. By ninjas, I gather she meant students wearing masks.

She'd had the incident at her house where somebody had thrown some kind of barrier through one of the bedroom windows at her house. She wanted to talk to me because it was the responsibility of the faculty to keep the students in order.

The only thing I think I said at one point was, "Well, you know, the campus is remarkably safe as campuses go. We have the lowest crime rate against people of any of the UC campuses."

She said, "That's irrelevant." She just went on. She kept talking and talking and talking. It was a rant, basically. The overarching theme was that the students are out of control, and the faculty are going to have to step up in this situation. It was really, really strange. I kept looking over at my table, trying to figure out how I could get back. Finally she said, "Okay, I'll let you go now." So I happily went back to my table and resumed my, by this time very cold, dinner. I was really shaken by this experience.

Chronicle of Higher Education: The 16 months Ms. Denton had spent as chancellor at Santa Cruz had shaken her deeply, with confidence-rattling criticism coming from all directions on everything from her commitment to diversity to her personal appearance. Her ebullient personality went into remission. Ms. Denton had even begun to fear for her safety. Some of her friends wonder if she had a thick enough skin to withstand such an onslaught, given her rapid rise in higher education as an administrator, in which she skipped several traditional steps.

But the job stress was not the only problem plaguing Ms. Denton last summer. Her relationship with Ms. Kalonji was on the rocks. She was also suffering from health problems related to an ovarian cyst that had recently been removed, a thyroid condition, and the onset of menopause. Thyroid dysfunction may contribute to depression, but Ms. Mabee believes the biggest contributor to Ms. Denton's deteriorating mental health was Zoloft, an antidepressant that had been prescribed for her daughter. She was also taking the sleeping aid Ambien.

George Blumenthal: As Denice tried to pull people into her own form of paranoia, she had people staying over at University House because she was afraid to be there alone. And her partner Gretchen never spent the night at University House. Denice was afraid, so she invited several members of the administration to spend extended periods with her at University House.

Jim Burns: Those were very difficult times for UC as a whole, a fact that probably didn't help Chancellor Denton. The president at the time, Robert Dynes—rightly or wrongly — had been pulled into a lot of media coverage about UC executive compensation. In short, it would probably be fair to say that the extensive negative coverage that UC was getting about any number of budget challenges—and the blowback that was having on our own campus back then—may not have helped Chancellor Denton.

Dave Kliger: The budget cuts were the biggest budget cuts that the university ever suffered from. Getting the campus through that time was difficult.

San Francisco Chronicle: The Bureau of State Audits reported Tuesday that the University of California's compensation practices are rife with problems, ranging from bookkeeping errors to policy violations involving millions of dollars in extra compensation. The 137-page audit found that UC administrators sometimes circumvented the university's compensation policies, resulting in questionable forms of compensation and improper payments. In addition, the auditors confirmed that UC has failed to consistently disclose executives' full compensation to its governing Board of Regents as required by university policy. State Auditor Elaine Howle said much of the money at issue comes from student fees and state appropriations. The state auditor said the audit shows the need for stricter oversight and greater transparency in the 10-campus university system.[15]

David Kliger: It wasn't all Chancellor Denton herself—the campus and the community were very unkind to her. They attacked her mercilessly. Maybe if she was in a more stable mental state, or if she was more experienced in just letting those things go and not taking them personally, it wouldn't have been so bad. But the combination of all of those things and people trying to take advantage of her and attacking her, made it intolerable for her and for the people around her.

George Blumenthal: As the year drew to a close, graduation was upon us. That year the graduate degree speaker was Steve Hawley, the astronaut. Steve got his PhD here and he was a former student of mine, and I was pretty close to Steve while he was here. So a few weeks before graduation, I got a note inviting me to a dinner with Steve at the chancellor's house, University House, which I accepted and RSVP'd for. Then, like the day before this event, this dinner, I got a note saying the dinner had been moved from University House to University Center. I didn't give it a whole lot of thought. Well, it turns out, unbeknownst to me, this was the period when Denice had checked herself into a mental hospital, and therefore she couldn't participate in the event. Dave [Kliger] was going to be in charge.

So I showed up for this dinner. I got there early and Dave was the only other person there. So Dave took me aside and started talking about

the obligations of the EVC to inform the president about the chancellor when there were issues with the chancellor's performance and stability. Dave told me that he had consulted with campus counsel about what he could or couldn't pass along to President Dynes and that campus counsel had advised him that there were privacy concerns and that he couldn't violate those privacy concerns.

I remember my reaction was: "bullshit." It seemed to me that the president had a right to know what was going on with one of his chancellors, that it was important that relevant information go forward. If her behavior, even if she was ill, if that impeded her ability to be chancellor, the president had every right to know about it.

Jim Burns: Unfortunately, we all know how that chapter of UCSC's history ended. It was a Saturday in June 2006. In the months leading up, there had been enough media challenges to make me feel like I needed to be tethered to my cell phone all the time. But on that particular Saturday morning—I don't think it ever happened before or after—I managed to leave the house for a few hours without my phone. At the time, my brother Tom and I had moved our then-elderly parents to Santa Cruz, and part of my ritual was to spend Saturday morning each week visiting with them. I'd managed to leave the cell phone at home that particular morning while visiting Mom and Dad. When I got home, I found a large note that our daughter Monica, who was staying with us that summer, had left for me. The note left a phone number for me to call. It had a campus prefix, but it wasn't a number I recognized. But in her note to me, Monica had helpfully added, sort of as a postscript, "And it sounds urgent."

So I dialed the number, not knowing who would pick up. It was Dave Kliger, who was the executive vice chancellor at the time. His words to me were very to the point. He just said, "Jim, Chancellor Denton has died."

Dave Kliger didn't go into detail about what happened, and I think I was stunned enough to not immediately ask for details. Dave essentially told me, "She's died, and you're needed at Kerr Hall immediately." That was the extent of the conversation. I headed up to Kerr Hall for what would easily become the most difficult day of my work life, or at least the most stressful.

I drove to Kerr Hall. My mind was racing, in part because I realized that in my shock at the news I had not asked Dave about the circumstances surrounding Chancellor Denton's death.

By the time I got to Kerr Hall, I also realized that I didn't even have a key to get into the building, and because it was Saturday, that could be a problem. By the time I arrived, probably around 2:00 that afternoon, there were a number of campus leaders already gathered on the second floor, including Bill Ladusaw, who I think at the time was the head of undergraduate education for the campus.[16] Fortunately, I had Bill's number in my phone; I reached him, and he came down immediately to let me in. My first question of him was, "How did Chancellor Denton die?" He informed me that she had committed suicide and that it had happened in a somewhat public way in San Francisco.

George Blumenthal: I took my daughter back east for a week to look at colleges. I got a call from UC Academic Senate executive director Maria Bertero-Barceló, telling me that Denice had killed herself. And immediately thereafter I got a call from Dave telling me the same thing. I was shocked that this could happen, that anyone would do this.

SFGate: UC Santa Cruz Chancellor Denice Denton, apparently despondent over work and

personal issues, died Saturday after she jumped from the roof of a 42-story San Francisco apartment building, police said. Denton had been on medical leave from the university since June 15 and was expected to return to work this week, said UC Santa Cruz spokesman Jim Burns.[17]

Jim Burns: I began to consider how the campus might communicate this fact. I didn't have to ponder that question for long. That's because very quickly, I learned that the story had already broken on the *SFGate* web site, and that the early story contained quite a number of details about the chancellor's suicide. In other words, in all likelihood, I would not be doing a lot of proactive communication. I would be fielding media calls, and I did that—pretty nonstop—until the phone stopped ringing shortly before midnight.

I was very impressed by how Dave and the other campus leaders who gathered in Kerr that Saturday responded. Everyone was in shock, but people were as calm and collected as could be hoped for—figuring out who had to be called, how the campus would be informed, and ultimately what I would say to reporters. From my perspective, the first order of business was to help Dave with a message that he could send out to the entire campus community and a statement we could make available to reporters. He was absolutely terrific that day. Under real duress, he was thoughtful, sensitive, and just everything you would want your leader to be like in the most difficult of circumstances. That's who Dave is, and it was very helpful that particular day.

San Jose Mercury News: The medical examiner's report suggests Denton spent her last few hours in deep despair. Investigators said her mother, Carolyn Mabee, told them Denton was "acting completely irrationally" after leaving Langley Porter Psychiatric Hospital, where she had been seeking treatment for depression, and thought the police had been chasing her. She also told them her daughter "had been suffering from depression and was under severe stress related directly to her job and her personal relationship with her partner," the report said. Citing privacy issues, UC officials refused to comment on Denton's medical history or say when they learned of her illness. She had taken a medical leave nine days before her death.[18]

Jim Burns: The media attention focused more on what Chancellor Denton's last few weeks had been like on campus. Very understandably, reporters wanted to know: Had she been around? Had she seemed distraught? The fact of the matter is she had left the campus some number of days prior to her death, and people had noticed that she had not participated in the commencement activities that had just occurred. She was obviously feeling a lot of stress—I suspect some of it was personal, and some of it was related to her tenure at Santa Cruz. For example, there had been a protest that she had experienced pretty traumatically. As I recall, she and a few other administrators had been surrounded by protestors while already in a car, or while attempting to get into one on campus. There'd been significant vandalism at University House.

It felt like I did close to 100 media interviews, or at least had that many media interactions that day, though I'm sure it was far fewer than that. The interviews began almost the minute I got to Kerr and continued pretty nonstop until I left the building at about 11:00 that night. TV crews, understandably, came to Kerr Hall that night, and I'd go outside and talk with each crew, trying to find the words to describe such devastating news.

Over the course of my many years on campus, I had been through a lot of difficult communication challenges—but I didn't feel at all prepared for that one. When I finally exhaled enough after

the last call was returned the night of her death, probably at about 11:00 or 11:30, I decided I could just go home and try to get some sleep. I remember walking to my truck, which was parked near Kerr Hall, and literally just sitting in it and weeping. It had been one of those days I knew I would never forget.

David Kliger: When she committed suicide, that put the whole campus in a crisis, and we needed to both find a replacement chancellor and also figure out how to heal the campus from that process.

Jim Burns: In the days and weeks that followed, I think that the campus did an amazing job responding to such a very, very difficult tragedy. People in University Relations, working with campus leadership, very quickly realized that it made sense to have a campus memorial that honored Chancellor Denton. So within days, that was planned and executed, and I have to say, executed beautifully. The memorial itself was an amazingly beautiful tribute to Chancellor Denton. President Dynes came to campus for it. It was very well done, and I think greatly helped the campus process the loss a little bit more successfully. You can only hope that it left Chancellor Denton's survivors with as good a feeling as was possible during this most painful and difficult time for them.

San Jose Mercury News: Karl Pister had known Denton since she was a graduate student two decades ago at the Massachusetts Institute of Technology. Both were engineering deans when they came to UC-Santa Cruz. Pister had been dean of engineering at UC-Berkeley, and Denton at the University of Washington. "Being a dean is a totally different job than being a chancellor," he said. "I had 40 years in the UC system, and that made a huge difference. Unfortunately, Denice came into the system without that experience, and that presented a lot of problems for her." Pister said he was scheduled to have breakfast with Denton several weeks ago. But like many of her appointments this month, she canceled without explanation. "Her death is a total shock," he said. "I was fairly close to her. I had no idea she suffered from acute depression, as she obviously did. I'm sorry she didn't get the help that she needed."[19]

San Jose Mercury News: Sixteen months ago, when Denton started as chancellor, she seemed like a perfect fit. If any community would welcome this openly gay academic who overcame discrimination from her earliest days in a small Texas town, who became nationally renowned for her commitment to women in science and social justice, surely it would be the progressive seaside town of Santa Cruz. Instead, she told friends, "I'm under constant siege."

She arrived at the university already trailed by controversy and, during her short tenure, endured unrelenting attacks. In the first week of June alone, just before she left, student protesters barricaded her car and a political cartoon in a local weekly paper depicted her with stubble on her chin.

"It wasn't any single story or any single cartoon, but it was a continuing, rolling, unending set of stories and set of cartoons; it was the continuing everyday assault," said Carol Tomlinson-Keasey, the chancellor of UC-Merced, who kept in frequent contact with Denton in her final weeks. "She was under a great deal of stress," Tomlinson-Keasey said. "I felt she was troubled. I felt she needed some time away. I never felt she was going to kill herself."

When a new chancellor arrives in Santa Cruz, the community very nearly holds its breath. In this city of 55,000, the chancellor carries more prestige than the mayor or state legislators. Some of Denton's predecessors at the 41-year-old institution had earned iconic status in town. The most

recent, M.R.C. Greenwood, was considered by many to be brilliant, accomplished, and charismatic. Many credit Greenwood with retaining the university's reputation in liberal arts while also earning it a name as a powerful research institution, "the UC of Silicon Valley." Denton, 46, had all the credentials of a promising successor.[20]

Dave Kliger: During Chancellor Denton's tenure, she devoted herself to strengthening UC Santa Cruz. Those of us who worked closely with Denice valued her intelligence, humor, and commitment to the ideals of diversity and higher education.[21]

M.R.C. Greenwood and Anne Peterson, *San Jose Mercury News:* On June 24, The University of California and her community of friends experienced one of the most painful, unimaginable of tragedies—the horrible and public suicide of one of the nation's most prominent scientists and supporters of women's rights in science, Denice Denton, a woman of courage, integrity, and quality.[22]

Dave Kliger: She led this campus with clear statements of the importance of education in transforming lives and in creating opportunities for all. She herself had lived that experience, rising from modest means to achieve with distinction at every stage in her life.[23]

M.R.C. Greenwood and Anne Peterson: [Denice Denton] was a national and international leader for women, and in particular, for women scientists. She was a role model for girls and young women and an inspiration to many aspiring scientists. She did not hesitate to "speak truth" or to spend time counseling and encouraging colleagues beginning their careers. She had very high professional standards and did not believe that diversity was the enemy of quality. She demonstrated that everywhere that she served. Her colleagues admired and respected her and at times wished we had her passion and strength, while slogging through the detritus of the entrenched "old boys" networks that continue to permeate the highest level of academe.[24]

George Blumenthal: At the memorial for Chancellor Denton, I met four women who were deans of engineering. They had all been mentored by Denice. They had come out to show their respect. Denice must have done some really amazing work to induce them to come out and show their respect in that way.

Jim Burns: Chancellor Denton's death was and still is very sad. She came here amid great fanfare. By all appearances, she had been a very successful engineering dean at the University of Washington. Yet, after less than 1 1/2 years here, she was gone.

M.R.C. Greenwood and Anne Peterson: This was a woman who made unconventional choices from an early age and was not afraid to defend herself and surmount adversity. Denice was also an excellent engineer. She succeeded in gaining a doctorate in engineering when very few women felt comfortable or wanted in the field. Denice was also gay and took the courageous step when beginning her tenure at UC Santa Cruz to make that clear. In San Francisco and Santa Cruz—both locales where gay rights have seen widespread support—her honesty was sadly often met with hostility and even threats. She deserved better, and met this unexpected response with dignity but sadness.[25]

Jim Burns: By most yardsticks, Chancellor Denton had had an amazing career, was fearless while tackling difficult social justice issues, including difficult issues having to do with women's and civil rights. It said something about her that she insisted that her inauguration focus on the need to have the university be more reflective of the people that it represented. A chancellorship that started with great promise had ended so suddenly and so painfully.

M.R.C. Greenwood and Anne Peterson: We will never know what led her to that fateful moment on the roof of the Paramount apartments in San Francisco, but we can be sure that rampant speculation will follow. Some will try to deny that the harsh male-dominated environment faced by many female leaders at the highest levels of academic and corporate America contributed to her ultimate decision. Some will speculate that the lack of support she received from the UC leadership was the cause. Others may claim that it was all personality motivated. It doesn't really matter. In the end, we have lost a colleague who was badly treated both by the institution that hired her and by the seemingly insatiable appetites of the media. Perhaps the most plausible speculation is that those who break through the glass ceiling may be wounded—even destroyed—by the shards.[26]

Endnotes

1. M.R.C. Greenwood was appointed provost and senior vice president of academic affairs, the second highest post in the UC system, during a special meeting of the Regents of the University of California on February 23, 2004: https://news.ucsc.edu/2004/02/455.html.

2. Ocean sciences professor Margaret (Peggy) Delaney came to UCSC in 1983. After serving as chair of the Academic Senate, she was appointed in 2004 to serve as Interim Campus Provost and Executive Vice Chancellor. Widely published in her field of paleoceanography and a frequent speaker at international conferences, Delaney is a member of American Geophysical Union, the Association for Women Geoscientists, the Geochemical Society, and the Oceanography Society, among other professional organizations.

3. Becky Bartindale and Ken McLaughlin, "Regents Name New Chancellor for University of California, Santa Cruz," *San Jose Mercury News*, December 15, 2004.

4. Paul Fain, "Too Much, Too Fast," *The Chronicle of Higher Education*, January 19, 2007.

5. Becky Bartindale and Ken McLaughlin, "Regents Name New Chancellor for University of California, Santa Cruz," *San Jose Mercury News*, December 15, 2004.

6. Jim Burns, "Denice D. Denton to be invested as UCSC's ninth chancellor on Friday, November 4," UCSC News Center. October 26, 2005: https://news.ucsc.edu/2005/10/771.html.

7. Becky Bartindale and Ken McLaughlin, "Regents Name New Chancellor for University of California, Santa Cruz," *San Jose Mercury News*, December 15, 2004.

8. Denice Dee Denton, "The Inaugural Address of Denice D. Denton, Ninth Chancellor of the University of California, Santa Cruz, November 4, 2005." (University of California, Santa Cruz, 2006.) Available in UCSC Library Special Collections.

9. The Regional History Project was unable to conduct an oral history with Chancellor Denice Denton due to her unexpected and tragic death. This chapter is pieced together from oral histories with other campus figures, newspaper articles of the time, and other primary documents.

10. Denice Dee Denton, "The Inaugural Address of Denice D. Denton."

11. Tanya Schevitz, "UC Hires Partner of Chancellor, Creates $192,000 Post for Santa Cruz Chief's Lesbian Lover," *San Francisco Chronicle*, January 20, 2005.

12. UCSC Students Against War, "UC Students Demand Answers about Spying Scandal," January 25, 2006. https://www.indybay.org/newsitems/2006/01/25/17980511.php.

13. This comment by Don Miller (quoted by Nüz in the *Metro Santa Cruz* newspaper) was in an editorial about the investigation of M.R.C. Greenwood over two potential conflicts of interest that had arisen while she was chancellor. Miller said, "It also adds fuel to the fire of complaints by faculty and students of a highly paid 'elite' at UC and to the whisper campaign that what is seen by some as a powerful coterie of lesbians has gained power and influence within the UC system." [Don Miller, "Strange days and ancient forebodings," *Santa Cruz Sentinel*, November 5, 2005]. After many community members wrote outraged letters about Miller's article, he issued a retraction. The investigation of Greenwood for conflict of interest while she was provost of the UC system is beyond the scope of this book, but interested readers can find more at Todd Wallack and Tanya Schevitz, "No. 2 Official at UC Quits Suddenly / University Probes Possibility of Favoritism in Hiring of Friend and Son of Provost," SFGate, Saturday, November 5, 2005. In 2005, the University of California found that Greenwood had violated its conflict-of-interest rules related to a management position created for a colleague, Lynda Goff, with whom she co-owned a rental property. The university found no evidence of improper conduct in a second allegation that Greenwood influenced a position held by her son at UC Merced, concluding no pattern of impropriety or ethics violations in regard to both matters, which were thoroughly investigated. The university accepted Greenwood's resignation from the position and affirmed her return to the tenured professorship she had formerly held at the University of California, Davis: https://en.wikipedia.org/wiki/M._R._C._Greenwood.

14. Nuz, "Credible Threats," *Metro Santa Cruz*, January 18-24, 2006. http://www.metroactive.com/papers/cruz/01.18.06/nuz-0603.html.

15. Tanya Schevitz, Todd Wallack, "Auditor Blasts UC's Pay Practices / University Routinely Violates Own Policies for Compensating Highest-paid Employees," *San Francisco Chronicle*, May 3, 2006: https://www.sfgate.com/education/article/Auditor-blasts-UC-s-pay-practices-University-2519099.php.

16. William Ladusaw came to UC Santa Cruz in 1984 as

a professor of linguistics. Ladusaw has served as provost of Cowell College, vice provost and dean of undergraduate education, and dean of humanities.

17. Cecilia M. Vega and Jaxon VanDerbeken, "UC Santa Cruz Chancellor Jumps to her Death in S.F.," June 24, 2006. https://www.sfgate.com/news/article/UC-Santa-Cruz-chancellor-jumps-to-her-death-in-2517073.php.

18. Mary Ann Ostrom, "Depression darkened educator's last days: UC Chancellor Left Hospital, Killed Self," *San Jose Mercury News*, November 4, 2006.

19. Paul Rogers, Kimra McPherson, and Leslie Griffy, "Spotlight Troubled UCSC Leader: Peers Say Denton Struggled to Cope with Higher Profile," *San Jose Mercury News*, June 26, 2006.

20. Julia Prodis Sulek, "A Feeling of 'Siege," *San Jose Mercury News*, July 2, 2006.

21. https://www.sfgate.com/news/article/UC-Santa-Cruz-chancellor-jumps-to-her-death-in-2517073.php.

22. "Let Denton's Legacy Be An End to Wounds from Glass Ceilings," *San Jose Mercury News*, Sunday, July 2, 2006.

23. https://www.sfgate.com/news/article/UC-Santa-Cruz-chancellor-jumps-to-her-death-in-2517073.php.

24. "Let Denton's Legacy Be An End to Wounds from Glass Ceilings," *San Jose Mercury News*.

25. "Let Denton's Legacy Be An End to Wounds from Glass Ceilings," *San Jose Mercury News*.

26. "Let Denton's Legacy Be An End to Wounds from Glass Ceilings," *San Jose Mercury News*.

Illustrations

Figure 1. Chancellor Denice Denton, 2005. Photo: Jim MacKenzie. Campus Photo Archive. Communications and Marketing Department, UCSC. Copyright UC Regents.

Figure 2. Autumn near the base of campus, 2012. Photo by Doug Niven. Campus Photo Archive. Communications and Marketing Department, UCSC. Copyright UC Regents.

Figure 3. Bridge between Science Hill and College Nine and College Ten. Photo by Carolyn Lagattuta. Campus Photo Archive. Communications and Marketing Department, UCSC. Copyright UC Regents.

Figure 2

Autumn near the base of campus, UCSC, 2012

Photo by Doug Niven

Campus Photo Archive

Figure 3

Bridge between Science Hill and
College Nine and College Ten

Photo by Carolyn Lagattuta

Chapter 33

"To Steady the Ship"

An Acting Chancellor in a Time of Instability

I still remember my first official day. I had some extra time and I literally drove around campus. I drove the whole loop a couple of times. I'm thinking, "All of this is mine." I was in in awe. It just didn't seem quite right that little old me would be in charge of this vast organization and this vast chunk of land and all that it entails.

—George Blumenthal

Bringing the Campus Together:
George Blumenthal Becomes UCSC's First "Homegrown" Chancellor

San Jose Mercury News: George Blumenthal, a professor of astronomy and astrophysics, was appointed acting chancellor of the University of California, Santa Cruz on Friday, weeks after the apparent suicide of former chancellor Denice Denton.

Blumenthal, 60, has been a member of the UC-Santa Cruz faculty since 1972, and has served as chair of the UC systemwide Academic Senate and faculty representative to the Board of Regents. University faculty lauded the appointment of the 34-year professor as a step toward helping the campus heal after Denton's death on June 24.

Administrators, faculty and students said Blumenthal will face great challenges as the campus recovers from that tragedy and attempts to move ahead with aggressive expansion plans and smooth recent tensions with the surrounding region. But they agreed that Blumenthal was the best candidate to move the university forward at this point. A national search for a permanent replacement will begin this summer.

"The campus has some healing to do, and we all need to come to grips with our feelings, with the death of Chancellor Denton," Blumenthal said. "I see it as my job to bring the campus together." Blumenthal said he would do his best to carry on Denton's legacy, including fighting for diversity and excellence at the university.[1]

Jim Burns: George Blumenthal was the perfect person to succeed Chancellor Denton. He is a high-quality person who has exceedingly deep campus roots. Having been on campus himself for more than thirty years at the time, he knew this place. He was someone people trusted to steady the ship.

David Kliger: I had worked with George Blumenthal earlier because he was department chair when I was dean. Then he became chair of the senate here, and then chair of the systemwide senate. [After Denton died] Rory Hume, Provost and Executive Vice president, Academic and Health Affairs in the Office of the President talked to me. I told him I would think about who would be a good acting chancellor. The first person I thought of was George because this campus really needed support from the Office of the President to get through this period and they needed somebody that they knew well. So, I called George and said, "I want to tell Rory that you're the person. Would you do it?"

George Blumenthal: Dave Kliger is one of the unsung heroes of the campus. I think if we step back and think about what Dave did after he was appointed EVC and Denice was chancellor, it was clear that Dave was doing most of the work of the chancellor, in addition to the work of the EVC, and he was doing it without complaining. I believe Dave deserves an enormous amount of credit and a medal for his contributions to the campus during a very, very trying period.

President Bob Dynes offered me the job as acting chancellor. I still remember my first official day. I had some extra time and I just literally drove around campus. I drove the west side of the campus and then drove the whole loop a couple of times. I'm thinking, all of this is mine. I was in in awe. It just didn't seem quite right that little old me would be in charge of this vast organization and this vast chunk of land and all that it entails.

Associate Vice Chancellor for Public Affairs and Communications Liz Irwin took me downtown to some photographer who took a gazillion pictures. I had to bring jackets and different ties. Oh, my God. To me, it was awful doing things like that. I really didn't like it. But I did it.

Ed Landesman: I would have never guessed that George would be chancellor when he first came to the campus, at Oakes College. Not that he wasn't capable, but often you visualize certain people as being on track for future roles, and in particular, as a chancellor. I always saw George as a scientist dedicated to research and teaching. I learned later of his work and leadership in the Academic Senate and his continual contributions to the campus and to the university, which made him an excellent candidate for chancellor.

George Blumenthal: Frankly, the whole campus was remarkably accepting of me. I wondered whether the fact that I didn't have administrative experience would cause people to be worried, or the fact that I was a scientist might be something that some parts of campus would be leery of. I could think of lots of reasons why I wouldn't be so well accepted. It was quite astonishing to me how accepted I was. People in town, politicians, community members—everyone was so very, very nice to me. I think, in part, people were looking for someone they could feel good about being in the position. But I felt welcomed in this role, by virtually every constituency.

Michael Cowan: The campus united behind George, who was our first homegrown chancellor.[2] We were producing leaders out of our own ranks.

George Blumenthal: I realized I needed a message for the campus. I needed to acknowledge Denice's death in a way that was respectful to her memory, and yet allowed us to move on. So, I adopted a message of talking about the upward trajectory of the campus, and wanting to continue that upward trajectory.

But it was clear there were psychological burdens [from Denton's suicide]. So, I consulted with Dave Kliger, and we agreed to bring in an organizational psychologist to work primarily with the senior management team and the deans to assess the psychological burdens on people here. She met with everybody in the senior management group, including me, and tried to assess what the scars were, what the injuries were, what the PTSD was.

She found that there were some people who needed some help, and she encouraged them to get help. Eventually the psychologist had a joint meeting where people talked collectively about their feelings about Denice and the suicide. There were people in that meeting who were crying, months after the event.

Michael Cowan: Denice Denton's tragic loss meant a situation where you suddenly had a chancellor coming in and two years later is gone. But unlike other times when we've had a quick turnover, it was not something that was seen as a product of an ungovernable campus, but just a tragic accident.

George Blumenthal: I'd been the senate chair and I'd been here a long time, but I wasn't well known throughout the campus. So, I thought it was really important that I go out and visit everything, so that everybody, faculty and staff and students could have, if they wanted to, a chance to meet the new acting chancellor. I didn't think I had any magic formulas, but I'm a pretty WYSIWYG person—what you see is what you get. I think that

comes across, whether or not that is my intention. I thought it was important that people understood that I was there, I was present, and would remain present, especially since Denice was perceived as not having remained present. It was important for people to feel that there wasn't a vacuum up on top.

So, I went everywhere on campus. I pretty much gave the same speech. I always started out with my silly joke about sometimes talking too long. I told the story of how students can evaluate you when you teach a class. I said I once taught a course in general relativity and a student in the class wrote in her evaluation that if she had only two hours left to live, she'd like to spend them in my class. And everyone kind of titters a little bit. Then the second line was, "Because every hour in your class feels like an eternity." It's kind of a self-effacing joke and it put people at ease. So, I used it a lot. I told it so many times I got embarrassed and could never tell it again. But I think people felt a lot more comfortable, seeing me around and seeing my presence.

"A Lot of Anger":
The 2005 Long Range Development Plan and the Road to a Settlement

Dave Kliger: George had the right personality to work with the city. In fact, not only was it his personality, but he had been longtime friends with Santa Cruz Mayor Cynthia Mathews. Personal relationships really help.

George Blumenthal: Cynthia is an old friend. I stayed with Bill and Cynthia when I first got to Santa Cruz. She was then on the city council. I think Cynthia was pleased that I became acting chancellor. She knew I understood what some of the town-gown relationship issues were. Cynthia's smart enough to know that there were not going to be any silver bullets that were going to solve it in one fell swoop. And it was made even more awkward by the then-status of the Long Range Development Plan.

Frank Zwart: We had been at a point in enrollment growth where the campus understood it was time to plan another long range development plan and look fifteen or twenty years into the future. A Strategic Futures Committee [was formed] and looked at four enrollment scenarios. One was no growth at all. The next one was some modest growth, or growth based on some minor tweak of numbers. The top end was 25,000. The Strategic Futures Committee's final report said that while enrollment growth could probably justify the highest number, there are lots of reasons why we shouldn't do that number. We probably wouldn't get the resources that we would need to develop the campus. It would have a big impact on the physical setting and on the community.

George Blumenthal: The LRDP was broiling. A lot of anger.

Frank Zwart: The city said, "We run up into problems in three areas—water, transportation and housing—when we get to a certain enrollment level and then things start to break down."

George Blumenthal: I thought I would at least visit the city council and see whether or not I could tamp down the anger. I made a point of going alone. The city council people were impressed that I'd come. I think they were not used to chancellors coming down and visiting them like that, especially alone. I was trying to indicate to them that I understood their issues. I might not agree with them, but I at least understood them. I think that they had some serious and legitimate issues, but I also thought there was a mandate for the university to continue to grow; that the city had agreed to host a much larger university, and the regents, in reliance on that commitment, had built a campus in Santa Cruz. They may not like it anymore, but it still is a commitment that the city made.

They would argue that you can only do what you can do, and if there're limits on resources like housing or water, there are limits. You can't make water out of nothing: until we have alchemy that can convert dirt to water, there's only so much you can do.

We had a nice conversation. But they basically said to me, boy, if this had happened a year ago, this would have been great. But it's probably too late. The 2005 LRDP was nearing its end and we were on a collision pathway.

Frank Zwart: The Strategic Futures Committee had done a series of drawings that illustrated various kinds of relationships between the campus

Figure 1

Interim Chancellor George
Blumenthal and Santa Cruz Mayor
Cynthia Mathews, 2006

Photo by Matt Fitt

and the surrounding community. There was one that showed the major transportation routes to and from the campus. Transportation and Parking Services has data on where student populations are heavy. So, they had a plan that showed in various densities of red, red fading to pink to almost nothing, the concentrations of student population, mostly around the city of Santa Cruz and south. I always thought of it as the map with the rash because of the choice of red making it look like some kind of skin inflammation, which is, I'm afraid, often the way often that the community thinks of our student population.

George Blumenthal: Things were not going well with the city. But at least people were willing to talk to each other, and they knew that I wasn't going to be the enemy.

At a certain point, Vice Chancellor of Business and Administrative Services Tom Vani suggested that what I might want to do, since the LRDP had come in at 21,000, that maybe if I lowered it to the environmentally preferred option of 19,500, maybe that would buy peace. So, I agreed to do that.

At the regents meeting in September 2006 about the LRDP all of the officials from the city of Santa Cruz and the county of Santa Cruz were there—Ryan Coonerty, Cynthia Mathews—the whole gang. They all testified about what a terrible thing this plan was.

Then the time came when I had to present the item for the regents to certify the environmental impact report for the Long Range Development Plan. My presentation was fine. I did whatever I was prepped to do. Then we opened it up for questions. One set of questions came from Regent Fred Ruiz, who took me to task for having lowered the number from 21,000 to 19,500. He said that the state of California and the regents of the university had invested in Santa Cruz and they deserved

a return on that investment. It was unconscionable that I was lowering that estimate.

Frank Zwart: George did a very good job of answering that question, simply saying, "There are lots of reasons. This is a delicate balance. Growing that fast would be a challenge, and it would be an undue burden on the local community, and that's an important part of the planning effort."

George Blumenthal: I talked to Regent Ruiz after the meeting. I knew Fred quite well. It turned out he did that to help me because in the audience were all the officials from Santa Cruz. So, he was playing to that crowd. Oh, and they were furious. The Santa Cruz folks just couldn't believe it that I was attacked for having lowered this number. He was trying to send them a message by doing that.

Frank Zwart: I think one of the real advantages that the campus had there is that George has been in town since 1972. So, he was not seen as somebody coming in from the outside.

George Blumenthal: I remember talking afterwards to Cynthia and others from the city. They were livid. They felt their concerns were dismissed—which, largely, they were. The 2005 Long Range Development Plan was approved strongly by the regents. Of course, it was going to face lawsuits, which we knew.

Relatively early on, I had had a meeting with CLUE [the Coalition for Limiting University Expansion]. I'd asked for the meeting, and they came to see me, and they were nice; everyone was very polite. But basically, their message was: if you ever think you're going to get us to agree to university expansion—forget it.

Frank Zwart: Under the regulatory structure of CEQA [the California Environmental Quality Act], within thirty-five days of the regents' action, the regents found themselves sued by the city, by the county, and by a local group of slow or, I would say no-growth advocates, CLUE. Essentially it argued that the university's environmental analysis was defective (that's typically the basis of a CEQA lawsuit), and needed to be re-done.

George Blumenthal: Meanwhile, the city of Santa Cruz decided to put on the ballot Measures I and J, which were intended to limit university expansion by denying water access to the upper campus, which is where we wanted to expand for the LRDP. Of course, it became a political issue, and of course the university could not actively oppose these measures. I didn't particularly want to, because I figured they would just pass, so why should we expend our energy there? They passed overwhelmingly.

But we did sue the city. We argued that they had not done an environmental impact report on Measures I and J. So, we sued them on a CEQA lawsuit, and we won. That invalidated the city's vote on Measures I and J. But the city then did their CEQA analysis, and they passed it as legislation rather than as a voter initiative. I and J became the law of the city.

There were lots of people suing us, lots of opposition to university expansion. The city provides the water for the campus, but the county has an interest as well, and in fact Coolidge Drive is a county road. And then of course CLUE and the various organizations up the hill—the Bonny Doon organization, the Cave Gulch organization—they all jumped on with their own lawsuits. And Mardi Wormhoudt got involved with CLUE and the CLUE lawsuit. So, we had lots of opposition. Unfortunately for the campus, the lawsuits were filed, quite legitimately, in Santa Cruz, to be

heard by a judge elected by the local population. So, this went to Judge Burdick, who was regarded as a pretty good judge.

Frank Zwart: This was a process that wound up taking about seven months. Judge Burdick heard arguments from both sides, read written pleadings from both sides, and in his decision determined that the bulk of the university's EIR met CEQA standards and was adequate and appropriate, and therefore rejected a lot of the lawsuit, and in fact rejected a lot of the lawsuit from CLUE because they had said that the environmental analysis on the North Campus, for example, was insufficient, and he felt that it was sufficient, so that the university did not need to redo it.

But the judge said that in three areas of particular concern to the city and county the analysis hadn't been adequate. The three areas were water; transportation and traffic; and housing for students. He said, "The university is going to have to go back and do those over again." Judge Burdick also said, "This is a case that cries out for discussion and resolution short of a verdict. I urge you to take on mediation. I can recommend some mediators." Well, I'd had enough experience with the court system, mostly in construction-law sorts of things in my career, that I knew that a judge's suggestion is hard to ignore.

So, the parties, through their respective attorneys, agreed on a mediator, Lester Levy, who was trained as an attorney. He had done some pretty tricky mediations. So, he started a process.

George Blumenthal: At first I thought this was an impossible task, to get to an agreement. But Levy said, "Let's keep trying," and he kept trying to bite off little pieces at a time. As I watched him operate, and he was really good, it was clear that part of the strategy is just keep the conversations going.

Frank Zwart: This had to have been a tough job, in large part because it wasn't just the university and the city. There had actually been three appellants in this action: the city, the county, and CLUE, and then nine individual citizens filing things together. And there was a big overlap between CLUE and the nine citizens.

George Blumenthal: We held a bunch of meetings in a big conference room here in Kerr Hall. We had a lot of meetings. Thirty meetings—it might have been of that order.

Frank Zwart: Typically, a meeting would include some period of time in which the mediator and all the parties would be together in the same room. These meetings could get fairly large. Then he would want to break the parties up to hold individual discussions with them, and push a little further, and make suggestions, and do shuttle diplomacy. So that meant we needed to have four rooms available—one for the university, one for each of the three other parties, and then one big enough for everybody to get together.

George Blumenthal: I've got to admit, I was skeptical that this was going to lead anywhere. But my skepticism was wrong. Lester did a fantastic job. He didn't try to do everything in one fell swoop. He tried to find the issues on which we might be able to get to an agreement, and to build off of those. When things started getting acrimonious, he would find a way to deflect the conversation into a different direction. He was very skilled. There were times we would have private conversations with him, from both sides, and he was very careful to make sure that he was available to both of us at the same time.

The university's position was, "Well, wait a second here. While there is a relationship between enrollment and impact for water, for housing, for transportation, that may vary from subcategory to subcategory. We're willing to talk about the impacts, but we really need to look at the impacts in that area, rather than just a magic number."

Some of those meetings were painful for me, because for a period of time I had a very stiff neck. I had some issue with my neck, so it was literally painful for me to sit in those meetings. One meeting went on till 2:00 a.m. The meetings were remarkably congenial. There was no shouting or banging, no histrionics.

One day it was the day of March Madness, basketball. People were really upset that they were going to miss the finals of March Madness. We were breaking up into groups and I said to the group that if they wanted they could come into my office and watch March Madness on the TV. So, they did.

Frank Zwart: They were off watching the game, as the other parties were meeting with the mediator. Those little things humanized the whole process.

Ultimately, the parties hammered out a detailed settlement that was signed and authorized by the regents, by the city council, by the board of supervisors, and by the members of the public who had sued us. The 2005 LRDP had said we would house 50 percent of our undergraduates and 20 percent of our graduate students. The Settlement Agreement said we would make housing available for 67 percent of all of our new students after an enrollment threshold of 15,000. And we would also make payments to the city water department using the same formula that the city charges regular customers. There are provisions in California water law under which a water district can declare a water moratorium or develop plans to reduce water use. We said we would follow those requirements, and we would cooperate with the city on all of those.

George Blumenthal: I promised that we would do everything possible to conserve water. Today this campus uses as much water as we used when we had half as many students as we currently do. We've far exceeded the city's water conservation goals, and far exceeded what the city has been able to do in terms of water conservation. When I became chancellor, we were using 6 percent of the city's water, and today we're *still* using 6 percent of the city's water. That's a period of almost thirty years. That's a testament to the work that our staff have done in terms of finding ways to save water, like doing less landscaping with water; putting new fixtures everywhere on campus; putting meters all over campus.

Frank Zwart: We also said that if we did not provide enough housing, then we would limit our enrollment growth, which was something that the city and the county very much wanted.

George Blumenthal: The rental market in Santa Cruz was not yet nearly anything like it is today [in 2019]. But Ryan Coonerty's thinking was: if we house people on campus, then they're not driving to campus. And if they're using water on campus, it's a lot better than using water in the city because we're so much more efficient than the city of Santa Cruz. So, having more people on campus guarantees that we will be more efficient with water. They wanted 100 percent of students housed on campus, but that wasn't anywhere near realistic. We agreed ultimately to housing two-thirds of new students and that was a stretch. We already had the second-highest-cost for campus housing in the UC system. We were housing a higher percentage of students than all but one other public university in California. The only other public university that housed a higher percentage of students was the California Maritime Academy.

Frank Zwart: We also made a significant up-front payment to the city for transportation improvements on routes that would serve the campus, intersection improvements and the like. That was something that they delighted in.

George Blumenthal: We measure car trips to campus, so we know how many car trips there are. We came to an agreement with the city on the number of trips. I did it, knowing that I don't control what people do in terms of driving to campus, but I do control, to some extent, how frequently we have bus transportation to the campus, through the support of the Santa Cruz Metropolitan Transit. And I do control the number of parking lots on campus. In my thirteen years of chancellorship, we have not built new parking on campus. I felt like, if they can't park it up here, they won't drive it up here.

Frank Zwart: Increasingly, it's a very standard model on campuses, even on much simpler, flatter, more conventional sites than Santa Cruz, to move parking to the perimeter rather than building parking spaces so everybody can park right next to their office. Because pretty soon, if you drive and park right next to it, you've got the Capitola Mall. That's not what anybody wants to see on a college campus, particularly not on this college campus.

George Blumenthal: Our great hope was bus rapid transit. We've tried to increase bus service. The campus accounts for half of all ridership in the *county* of Santa Cruz. Right now, [in 2019] the number of car trips is the same as it was when the campus was two-thirds of our current size. Traffic in town is worse, but that isn't because people are driving up to campus. There're more companies in Santa Cruz, more people living here, and therefore traffic has increased, largely due to things that are completely outside the university's purview. It's easy to blame it on the university, but that's not the reality.

Manaiya Scott: Last year (2016) Transportation and Parking Services said they added more buses, but I couldn't tell the difference. I've had people tell me, "I miss three buses because they're all full." Sometimes I leave forty minutes before class just so I can catch the bus. Or sometimes I walk. I beat the loop shuttle bus sometimes. I can walk from Stevenson all the way to Rachel Carson and my friends will come to the dining hall ten to fifteen minutes later.

The car traffic is horrible. We have more people on campus, and people have more cars. We really don't have the capacity that we are supposed to be having for people. You want to explore and go off campus and stuff like that, and go to Capitola, which can be almost an hour bus ride, depending on the traffic. But I'm so over it. I don't have a car. The bus—it's a three-hour trip [round trip] to go downtown. We get there, we shop, we eat, and then spend an hour getting back to campus. It's a hassle. So, unless you need to go get some laundry detergent, some stuff that you need, I really don't go off campus.

Mike Rotkin: In 2008, Chancellor Blumenthal agreed to resolve eleven lawsuits with the city of Santa Cruz through an agreement that they would pay their fair share of water costs and other things. The chancellor basically gave the city more power to have input in what's going on than any campus has ever had in UC history. Most cities don't have the ability that the city of Santa Cruz has to get university money to improve traffic intersections, water improvements, and a bunch of other stuff that the university claims it has no obligation for.

Frank Zwart: These mechanisms were all put in place, and the agreement was announced. It was

signed. There was a lot of good publicity and good feeling. I have to give an enormous amount of credit to George Blumenthal, who wanted to make a deal, and to then-mayor, Ryan Coonerty. He wanted to make a deal, but he wasn't going to do it just for the sake of a deal. And they held firm. George and Ryan got everybody pointed in the right direction.

One of the things that was set up through this settlement agreement was regular meetings of university and city staff to move this forward, and to report regularly to the public, to the city council, the board of supervisors, and to the court about how things had been going. The feedback I've been getting has been entirely positive—that the city is as committed as the university is to making all of this work.

George Blumenthal: We have been doing these settlement agreement meetings ever since 2008. Prior to this settlement agreement, there was a complete lack of trust between the city and the university. When M.R.C. Greenwood was chancellor, we used to have these formal meetings of her and the city council, but they were just for show. It's like Nixon going to China and dealing with Mao. They were show meetings.

Frank Zwart: There was a time in the mid-seventies where the university got vilified. It's taken forever to get the university and the city out of that mindset. There were things that the university did that make it understandable. There was a period of stiff-arming about not paying the local community. But as finances have become stretched for municipalities across the state, I think there is more sensitivity on the part of the campus.

As all of this was playing out, I went to a conference of university architects that was jointly hosted by the University of Cincinnati and Miami University, which is in Oxford, Ohio. We were walking around town. It's much smaller than Santa Cruz. And yet, as we were walking up and down the main street, I saw a public works truck parked there, and on the side of the truck was painted: "City of Oxford, Ohio. Home of Miami University." I thought, now that's something to aspire to, where the university's presence is boasted about by the city.

Michael Cowan: We have had a significant growth element in the community, but the same community has now grown up to enough size that they provide a set of resources—shopping, cultural, others—that are valuable for the campus. We are going to have a Warriors [basketball] franchise. I think that will be the first big venue, outside of an outdoor venue, that the area has. Whether that's good or bad depends on one's sports views. Nevertheless, that wouldn't have happened if the city hadn't been the size it is, and had a population that it could grow into.

Frank Zwart: There's no question that the university has shaped what Santa Cruz is. Would those of us living in Santa Cruz have as wide a choice of movie screens to see, or as wide a selection of restaurants to eat at—I mean, it's just little things like that—or bookstores, if it weren't for the university? It is a symbiotic relationship.

Jim Burns: There seemed to be a renewed appreciation within the city of the value of having a University of California within its midst.

George Blumenthal: I believed that I was not likely to become the permanent chancellor. I didn't know from day one that I wanted to even try for permanent chancellor. It wasn't clear to me I'd like this job. And even if I liked it, I knew they were doing a search. At the best, I could assume

that I would be interviewed. I might have one chance in six of being chosen as the chancellor. So that's kind of how I ranked my chances, a 16 percent chance to be chancellor. That means most likely not. So, I figured, look, I enjoyed being senate chair for a year. I'll enjoy being acting chancellor for a year. I'm going to damn well enjoy it, and do what I think I want to do. I'm not going to worry about whether or not it will position me for the chancellor position.

So, one of the things I decided to do from the beginning was be very outspoken. UCSC was historically underfunded, relative to most of the other UC campuses. We were in the worst of all possible worlds, relative to the weighted formula, by the way allocations had been done across the UC system.

The Fight for State Money: Rebenching

David Kliger: In the early years of the campus, there was a process where you got a certain amount of money for lower-division undergraduates, more money for upper-division undergraduates, more money yet for beginning graduate students, and more yet for advanced graduate students. There was a lot more funds per graduate student than undergraduate. In spite of that, the campus made the decision that we were going to emphasize undergraduate education. So, at a time where you got more money for graduate students, we emphasized undergraduates.

Dean McHenry: A lot of Santa Cruz's problem [in 1969] lies in University Hall, in the University-wide administration, and that's the thing I'm beginning to work on now. We got damn few new faculty positions. But the new campuses should have the lion's share of them, and they didn't get the lion's share this last time, because the state-wide administration allocated many of the new positions to the old campuses on the grounds that they were getting more graduate students. If this goes on another year, I think we're going to have a major crisis. If I can't convince President Charles Hitch, I'll have to fight it out in the open. Resignation is a possibility. I'll do everything I can inside, and if I can't lick it, and conditions are intolerable, I think a resignation is the best way to call attention to it. I haven't ever threatened this, you understand. I don't like people who go around threatening to resign.

It seems to me that the small campuses ought not to be forced to adjust to the faculty-student ratio so drastically; they could be weaned gradually. This is a real starvation diet this year. This last time, the allocation in February, Berkeley and UCLA, which are already maybe 65 to 70 percent

tenure-track faculty, got the same level of appointments that *we* did, and we need full professors desperately, and Irvine does, too. Our tenure-track faculty are 25 or 30 percent; we're about half their level or less. They go on getting richer, and we go on getting poorer. It's not right.

David Kliger: Much later, the University of California decided that they were going to do the budget differently. They weren't any longer going to weight students. You got the same amount of money for students at any level. So, there was a certain amount of state money that goes into every new student, regardless of whether they were an undergraduate or a graduate student. Even though graduate students generally cost more than undergraduates, the decision was made to do it this way.

But at about the same time, UCSC decided we needed to grow our graduate programs. In terms of the goals of the campus, prestige of the campus, it was the right decision. But budgetarily, it meant that there were difficulties.

Now, that wouldn't be so bad, except that when UC decided to change the way it did budgeting they said, "We're changing the way we're doing budgeting from this day forward. Up until this point the base is the base is the base. So, whatever money you get total, is what you get. As you add more students, you get incrementally more money." Well, because of the emphasis on graduate enrollments earlier on other campuses, but undergraduate enrollments here, the campus got a lot less total state money per student than other campuses.

George Blumenthal: President Mark Yudof instituted budget meetings with the chancellors. We'd prepare all these gazillions of tables and financial sheets. He rarely showed much interest in the Santa Cruz presentation, though I heard that a couple of other campuses faced detailed scrutiny. We'd go through our presentations. He'd ask very few questions. He was not that interested or concerned. We were below his radar in terms of what he was going to worry about. But he still met with us, just as he did with all of the campuses.

Well, at this budget meeting, I was showing him how we had made deep cuts in our budget, like 30 percent cuts in administration and 30 percent cuts in academic support, but only like 10 or 15 percent cuts in our academic programs. That's how we had balanced our budget under those extreme circumstances [as the recession was starting].[3]

And he said, "Yeah, yeah, yeah. Good, good, good." I said, "Well, wait a minute, Mark. Don't just say that. This is important. I just want to emphasize to you that I have not cut across the board. If I did across-the-board cuts, you'd fire me because you'd argue that I wasn't exercising discretion, which I should be doing as the leader of the campus. But these are definitely not across-the-board cuts. We've cut as little as possible into the academic mission of the university."

He said, "Oh, yeah. That's very good. I'm glad you did."

And I said, "Well, you'd fire me otherwise."

He said, "Well, maybe not. But we'd have a talk if you hadn't done that."

So, I said, "So you'd have that expectation of me, that I would exercise judgment and try to do the reasonable thing, rather than mindlessly cutting across the board?"

And he said, "Yeah."

I said, "So why can't I have that same expectation of you?"

When I said that to him, he understood exactly what I was saying. I was referring to a discussion we'd had many times about mindlessly sticking with a funding formula for the campuses whose origins no one even remembered. He visibly winced. And he said, "Okay, you've convinced me. We'll do it. We will convene a group to look at changing the benchmarks for the university state budget. And we'll start that right away."

David Kliger: Part of the discrepancy in budgeting between different campuses was this graduate-versus-undergraduate issue. But there were all kinds of special deals that were made for each of the campuses. Nobody knew how we got here, but they could see that there was a large discrepancy. The Office of the President acknowledged that this was a problem.

Obviously, the campuses that were most influential were the campuses that had the most dollars and could scream the loudest in terms of not changing the system. Berkeley and UCLA were the big ones. This was a large amount of money. If UCSC were to get the amount of state funds that was the average for UC, not even the same as Berkeley and UCLA, but just the average, it would be an additional thirty million dollars a year for the campus. The committee said, "We have to look at how we fund each of the campuses." That's when it started being called rebenching.

George Blumenthal: So Yudof appointed a rebenching committee. I was on it. It became a question of coming up with principles. Every student should count the same, no matter what their field is. We shouldn't be allocating different amounts depending upon what majors or graduate programs people are in. It should be independent of campus, in order to avoid treating some campuses to richer funding formulas and others to poorer ones. We should just have one formula that worked for everyone.

I think the consensus of the committee was that there was a need to do weighting again. My preference would have been not to weight students, but I have to admit it does cost a lot more to educate a medical student or a graduate student. At least as a matter of principle, we were prepared to accept that and that this would be basically how money would be distributed from the state throughout the system.

Eventually the committee finished our work and came up with a rebenching plan. We agreed that we needed to implement it in a way that would harm no campus, so we would only implement it as a way of distributing extra resources that come to the system from the state. When the state gave us more money, we would use that more money to try to get to the final state of a fully rebenched university.

We knew the recession wouldn't last forever. And so, the idea was a six-year plan to rebench, so that at the end of the six years, all of the money at UC would be distributed to the campuses in a way that was consistent with rebenching. A couple of years ago we reached that benchmark. We're now fully rebenched.

It was transformative for the campus. We ended up with enough money to hire one hundred new faculty. But we didn't really get to hire those hundred faculty members because of the budget cuts [that came in 2009 due to the Great Recession]. Then we were getting more money from rebenching, but our budget was being cut.

So even though we got more money, we were using that money to fill holes.

But now that the budget has largely recovered, rebenching has been a major advantage for the campus. We've hired many more faculty as a result of the money we've gotten from rebenching. And we've used the money for other things as well: TAs, for example. We've used it to support graduate education. That wouldn't have been possible without rebenching. The campus has been in much, much better shape because of rebenching. It's been a huge boon to the campus. But it hasn't been the kind of boon that made us suddenly rich and well-to-do. It was the kind of boon that avoided a disaster.

From Acting to Permanent
George Blumenthal Becomes UCSC's Tenth Chancellor

UCSC News: Acting on the recommendation of President Robert C. Dynes, the UC Board of Regents appointed Blumenthal the tenth chancellor of UC Santa Cruz during the board's meeting in Davis. The selection culminates a five-month, nationwide search that attracted more than 550 prospective candidates.[4]

George Blumenthal: So, I got the call. I got this job offer to be chancellor. Then they finally got around in the regents meeting to making my appointment. Kelly and I had a press conference together. I was proud. It was nice to be with her at a press conference. One thing that really annoyed me was when I was finally appointed permanent chancellor, one member of the staff here who was fairly senior in University Relations, said to me, "Oh, this is wonderful. We're so happy that you were appointed. Now Kelly can quit her job and spend full-time on campus." My reaction was, have you met me? Have you met my wife?[5] I just couldn't believe that somebody would say that to me. It was so completely divorced from reality.

So, given that I was appointed chancellor, I had to be inaugurated. And God, what a big megillah that was. It turned out, mine was the last of the big inaugurations. After that, because of budget cuts, they scaled them way back.

I wasn't exactly looking forward to having a big megillah to celebrate me. I was quite prepared to believe that this was for the campus rather than for me, but nevertheless, there was no question that I was the center of attention. So, it wasn't an easy thing for me to think about. As we started to plan for it, we did all the right things. We put together a committee. They kept asking me, "Well, what do you want?" Like I knew what the hell I wanted? I

wanted to get through this. My goal was not to make a fool of myself.

But it was an interesting experience. We finally decided that the venue would be the East Field. We set it up as kind of a prelude to graduation so that a lot of people could attend. It was a very big deal on the campus and probably one of our largest inaugurations because it wasn't limited by a building the way so many of the other ones had been.

I was certainly surprised by the turnout, which was very, very large. We did have demonstrations there. AFSME [the American Federation of State, County, and Municipal Employees, UC's largest employee union] decided to demonstrate. So again, I had to go through practices of what to do if people were trying to interrupt the speech, which they did. The interrupters were far away, so their volume wasn't that high. The theory is, you just talk right through it. You ignore it as if it isn't happening. And that's what I did.

I remember that the talks were very, very nice, very, very supportive. Ryan Coonerty gave a talk from the city. I think he said, "We've declared this George Blumenthal Day."

City on a Hill Press: Acting Chancellor George Blumenthal is not a businessman. He previously served as department chair of astronomy and astrophysics, and has been an astronomy and astrophysics professor for over thirty years. He is first and foremost an educator.

We at *City on a Hill Press* (CHP) would like to voice our support for Blumenthal in his candidacy for permanent chancellor. He has made a concerted effort to reach out to individual members of the UCSC community by making personalized video messages for the student body and encouraging students to let their opinions be heard. In these messages, Chancellor Blumenthal encourages every student to come to his office hours or make an appointment with him to voice opinions or simply introduce themselves. He is doing exactly what every chancellor should be doing: opening up lines of communication.

Judging by the communication blocks and various poor decisions made by chancellors in the past, there has been a great leap of improvement of the state of our university. Former UCSC Chancellor Denice Denton dealt with various criticisms about inappropriate use of UCSC money (Creating a $200, 000 position for her life partner, making a $30,000 dog run for her canines, etc.). UCSC Chancellor Greenwood was questioned for compensation practices during her time as chancellor. At the time, certain UC employees were apparently receiving funds (wage increases, special bonuses, etc.) from a pool of hidden UC money. Blumenthal still maintains a relatively clean record.

On an environmental note, what is nearly every UCSC community member (tree hugger or not) adamantly against? Expansion. What was one of the first actions that Chancellor Blumenthal took once in his position of power? A rejection of the UC Regents' expansion proposal.

Chancellor Blumenthal possesses qualities that CHP admires. At the UC Regents' protest on October 18, 2006, Chancellor Blumenthal served as mediator between regents and students. When asked about his choice for the support of the student population, the chancellor told CHP, "I want to be able to hear students' oppositions so that I can take those concerns to the regents."

Admittedly, no chancellor is perfect. Some have viewed Blumenthal as a politician. But we ask you—any administrator who has never once let politics affect the decision making process: cast the first paperweight.[6]

Figure 2

Chancellor George Blumenthal, 2010

Photo by Jim MacKenzie

Endnotes

1. James Hohmann, "UCSC names interim chief: Longtime Professor Takes on Job of Campus Healing," *San Jose Mercury News*. July 15, 2006.

2. Martin (Marty) Chemers served as acting chancellor of UCSC from 2004-2005, after the depature of Chancellor Greenwood and before the appointment of Chancellor Denice Denton. Chemers was also "homegrown" in that he had arrived at UC Santa Cruz in 1995 as dean of social sciences and professor of psychology.

3. According to the Federal Reserve, "The Great Recession began in December 2007 and ended in June 2009, which makes it the longest recession since World War II. Beyond its duration, the Great Recession was notably severe in several respects. Real gross domestic product (GDP) fell 4.3 percent from its peak in 2007Q4 to its trough in 2009Q2, the largest decline in the postwar era (based on data as of October 2013). The unemployment rate, which was 5 percent in December 2007, rose to 9.5 percent in June 2009, and peaked at 10 percent in October 2009." See Robert Rich, Federal Reserve Bank of New York, at https://www.federalreservehistory.org/essays/great_recession_of_200709.

4. UCSC News: September 19, 2007.

5. George Blumenthal is married to UC Hastings Professor of Law Kelly Weisberg.

5. Editorial, *City on a Hill Press*, March 15, 2017.

Illustrations

Figure 1. Interim Chancellor George Blumenthal and Santa Cruz Mayor Cynthia Mathews, 2006. Photo by Matt Fitt. Campus Photo Archive, Communications and Marketing Department, UCSC. Copyright UC Regents.

Figure 2. Chancellor George Blumenthal. 2010. Photo by Jim MacKenzie. Campus Photo Archive. Communications and Marketing Department, UCSC. Copyright UC Regents.

Chapter 34

Endings and Beginnings in a Time of Austerity

Universities are living, breathing institutions.

—George Blumenthal

Community Studies:
Deep Cuts and Balancing the Budget

George Blumenthal: [In 2007-2009] we were in one of the darkest periods in our history: the Great Recession. The state cut funding for UC deeply. The decrease in state funding was equal to the total state funding for Santa Cruz, Santa Barbara, and UCLA. That was one year of budget cuts to UC. And yes, there was a tuition increase, but it didn't come close to making up for those deep cuts.

So we had to make very deep cuts on campus. At Santa Cruz, we basically balanced our budget every year. No matter how painful, no matter how horrible, we balanced our budget. Part of it is we didn't have a lot of other sources of revenue that we could use to make up for the difference. We didn't have a lot of donor money. We didn't have a lot of nonresident tuition. We didn't have any of the things that some of the other campuses used to buffer. We also didn't have the level of reserves that some of the campuses had. We did have enough reserves we could have waded through

things for a couple of years. But it seemed imprudent to not just bite the bullet, as bad as it is, balance the budget.

David Kliger: We took different approaches for the budget cuts. In the first year of the budget cuts we said, okay, there are certain areas that we need to protect. Things like academic programs need to be protected to the extent that we can, and health and safety issues needed to be protected—that sort of thing. So we assigned smaller cuts to academic divisions, bigger cuts to support divisions. The second year of the cuts, the cuts were of sufficient magnitude and we had already taken so many cuts in the academic support divisions, the business and administration divisions, that it didn't seem possible to protect the academic divisions as much as we had the year before. We looked at specific functions and impacts to those functions, and had a budget group working with the senate to say, okay, what would be the biggest negative impact of budget cuts, and try to assign cuts to those areas where it would do the least harm. I think we did a pretty good job in figuring out how can we take the cuts with the least harm to the campus.

George Blumenthal: And now we come to community studies. Budget cuts were here. All of the divisions were taking big budget cuts, and everybody had to think about how they were doing it.

Mike Rotkin: Dean of Social Sciences Sheldon Kamieniecki had a very real budget cut facing him. The dean was not making it up; he was not lying about it, as some people accused him of. He had several hundreds of thousands of dollars he had to cut out of his budget.

He had various choices in front of him. He might have done a 10 percent across-the-board cut to the entire division, which was being contemplated. He had an advisory body of one representative from each of the eight departments in the social science division who had recommended across-the-board cuts. He had already made earlier cuts to his own staff within the divisional office, and was not willing to make any more cuts there. He had already cut field programs, he felt, pretty much to the bone.

He made the decision to basically terminate the community studies program. He came to a community studies department meeting and announced it boldly: that was what he was going to do. He didn't hide the ball; he was very direct. We were shocked. We had no warning that that was what was about to happen. He was coming to, you know, "talk" with us about things in the division—budget issues in the division. And he said, "I'm going to cut community studies. I have some other cuts to make, but that's where I'm going to save most of my money."

George Blumenthal: I kind of overheard a conversation between Sheldon and Dave about community studies. So I said to Sheldon, "So what are you talking about with community studies? He said, I'm thinking of closing them down. I said, "Wow, really?" He said yeah.

Mike Rotkin: Dean Kamieniecki said, "I can imagine a social science division without a community studies department. I can't imagine one without an economics or a psychology department." He had traditional programs that had been in academia since the fifties or earlier, and we were kind of a unique program. He didn't explain why he might cut us and not, say, environmental studies, which hadn't been around in the fifties. Perhaps that's his field; maybe that's something he didn't want to cut. Or Latino and Latin American studies, another example of a non-traditional or interdisciplinary department that he decided not to make major cuts in.

George Blumenthal: I went back to my office and pulled up on the computer—it's what I always do when a program is in trouble—I pulled up their most recent review because we do external reviews of every program on campus on a regular basis. Their most recent one actually had been quite recent. In fact, I think it may have been one of the motivations for Sheldon. Like most reviews, it was generally quite positive. It talked about the many good things that community studies does. But there were two things in there that really struck me. One was, it was clear that the department had a serious problem with regard to their field program. The external review argued that it was completely unrelated to the courses that students take, and this disjuncture between their field studies and course work was a serious issue within community studies.

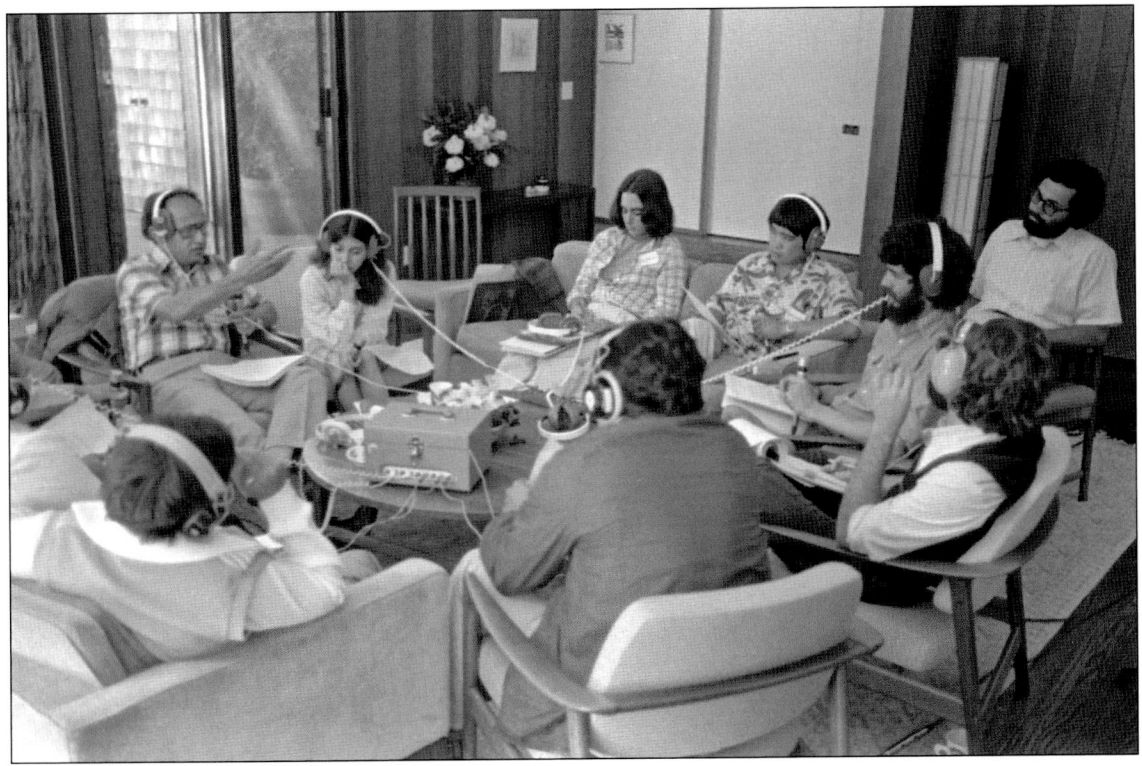

Figure 1

Bill Friedland (left) and community studies students working as lettuce harvest researchers, listening to an audio recording, 1978

Photo by UCSC Photography Services

Figure 2

Community Studies 131 poster, 1986

Jim Burns: As I recall, there was a declining number of faculty in the actual department, due to budget cuts, and allegiance to the field study program by the faculty who remained seemed to be in decline.

Mike Rotkin: The dean gave us a speech about how, in difficult times, you destroy an institution by just indiscriminately cutting across the board—which I don't disagree with in principle—and that therefore he would be better off to concentrate on what we do well and what's important. Community studies was neither done well nor important, in his point of view. The dean didn't like the community studies program. He'd expressed doubts about it right from the time he was hired.

We had had lots of deans who were hired and didn't understand what we were about. We'd meet with them and show them past external reviews, bring them up to speed, educate them. Most eventually decided this was an amazing program, that it was a feather in their cap to have it in their division—a cutting-edge program in the social science field, and something that they should be proud of and should see as something important to what made Santa Cruz unique as a campus. This dean didn't buy that, didn't share that view, thought it was wrong.

Santa Cruz Sentinel: The Community Studies Department at UC Santa Cruz, a popular program that to many is a symbol of the university itself, faces the fate that the many conservative pundits who mock it have long sought. In the wake of the ongoing recession, university officials have proposed cutting the department's undergraduate administrative staff, thus eliminating it from campus as of July 1. The news was delivered Wednesday by Sheldon Kamieniecki, dean of social sciences, to department staff. While conservative commentators like Gary Fouse and David

Horowitz have called the Community Studies Department "the outline of a political agenda," local nonprofits said they will be devastated by the closure; each year hundreds of students volunteer locally as part of the department's curriculum.[1]

Good Times: Forty years ago, at what was then a small, up-and-coming public university, a man by the name of Bill Friedland founded the Community Studies Department. It has since become a trademark of the school, UC Santa Cruz, and synonymous with its liberal atmosphere. Often the target of conservative critics—some may remember right-wing author David Horowitz dubbing Community Studies a "training ground for political activism" in his explanation of why UCSC was the "most un-American school in the country"—the community studies program offers an interdisciplinary education in community organizing and action and sends each student on a six-month field study in their area of focus. Faculty estimates that its undergraduates have done more than 2.5 million hours of community service.[2]

Santa Cruz Sentinel: The department's graduates can be found on the staffs of many local nonprofits like the Santa Cruz AIDS Project, Community Action Board and Barrios Unidos. Its volunteers can be found inside the doors of many more worldwide, as students work part time with local groups and serve six-month "field studies" that involve volunteering full time at nonprofits of their choice anywhere on the globe. The department has inspired similar programs at University of Maryland and University of Massachusetts.

"We don't have a football team, we don't have a business school, we don't have civil engineering. What we have are huge numbers of interns that serve social programs in this community," said Mike Rotkin, the department's field studies coordinator and a Santa Cruz councilman. "The university wants to cut the one thing that actually provides a service to the citizens of Santa Cruz."[3]

Mike Rotkin: Our students, who were very well trained in organizing, got up on their hind legs when they found out that the program was being challenged by the dean. We had 3000 members of Facebook join a Friends of Community Studies within a week after the dean's announcement. We had, before we were finished, about two hundred letters from famous people, including Marshall Ganz, who had been the director of organizing for the United Farm Workers and became, now, a professor of organizing at Harvard University. Letters from congressmembers; letters from the governor; letters from all over the place about how this was a model program that needed to be defended and supported. Letters from all of the nonprofit executive directors in Santa Cruz and elsewhere around the state of California and the country. Strong, supportive letters. Letters from parents of students who had graduated. Letters from people we'd sent graduate students to.

George Blumenthal: The other thing that they said in the external review that caught my eye was that they pointed out that UC Santa Cruz was a campus that had aspirations to be among the elite research universities of the country, but that it was unclear whether a program like community studies could survive or even thrive within a university with such aspirations—the implication being that they were not a program that was going to get us to elite status. There it was in the review. And I'm thinking, what chancellor, reading that, is going to be supportive?

Mike Rotkin: Community studies was supported and appreciated by the executive vice chancellor, Alison Galloway, who was a former professor from the anthropology department. Unlike some other

EVCs that did not much like our program because it wasn't a science program, she was a supporter of the program—and the chancellor, George Blumenthal, had frankly mentioned it in every speech he ever gave in the city of Santa Cruz, something I know from wearing my mayor's hat, as something wonderful the university was doing for the local community. So we had passive support, but nonetheless support, from the chancellor and the executive vice chancellor, who constantly told us, "Let's find some way to save this program; we think it's a great program," but were not willing, for whatever reason, to instruct the dean that he must save this program. Both of them had the ability to do so; neither of them ever did that.

George Blumenthal: That wouldn't have been enough for me to go out saying, "Go kill that program!" But given that Sheldon was already heading down that road, it was enough to convince me that I wasn't going to spend my energy to defend them. So I let this process move along. I neither endorsed it, nor did I oppose it.

Bill Friedland: By the 2012-13 academic year, the community studies faculty had been reduced to a single FTE professor and a single senior lecturer; the department was terminated.

Jim Burns: Did the division make the right call with community studies? I am not in the best position to say; but it was obviously pretty heartbreaking for a lot of people who'd seen that program and had admired the uniqueness of the program, to see it cut that way.

Bill Friedland: Oakes College agreed to take what was left of the program and to continue it in reduced circumstances for a limited number of undergraduates. Thus, after some forty-plus years of successfully operating a program that generated thousands of alumni who built socially active field study and a high degree of academic exposure that had been acknowledged as turning out undergraduates producing academic work at the master's level, the academic legitimacy of departmental organization was wiped out.

George Blumenthal: Alison Galloway came to me [after the community studies department had been dissolved] and said, "Oakes College would like to run a community studies program. Do you have any objection?" I liked the idea. I endorse it, because I liked the idea of having the colleges more involved in the academic mission of the university. I didn't think they should run the major departments, or anything like that, but at that point I started to think of community studies as kind of an offshoot, or an idiosyncratic program, that might thrive in a college. So that's why we started to do it there. I don't think it ever grew to the size that it had before, but at least it exists.

Jim Burns: I think people were heartened, when, through Oakes College, community studies was restored. I suspect the current program is different than the original program was in its heyday, but hopefully it was revived in a way that is meaningful to students and financially sustainable.

Helene Moglen: Community studies is now being relegated, with very little funding, to the colleges, in order to meet a service requirement for undergraduates that was initiated by the faculty at the very time that community studies was being disestablished by the administration. So the administration is now looking to the colleges to provide ways for undergraduates to get these service credits, but they're eliminating the institutionalized ways in which such work could coherently take place. It's just bizarre.

Mike Rotkin: The faculty that came here [in the early years] came at a time when everything was up for grabs in higher education. And whatever you think about the sixties, the people that had been undergraduates and graduate students while that was going on were now becoming professors. That's the kind of people UCSC hired. They wanted people who were interdisciplinary, who wanted to come to a place that didn't have grades, and were not about sorting students, and who didn't imagine their job as being a researcher, and that undergraduates were a pain in the butt. These were people who wanted to be teachers, that were less interested in publishing stuff in the proper journals. Not that they didn't have research goals or intellectual interests, but they were going to bring the three-part mission of the university [teaching, research, and service] back into some reality.

That's who was getting hired here, in every discipline. It wasn't just about the humanities or social sciences. That's who they brought here as math teachers, as physics teachers. These were people who had been active in the student movement—particularly because they were hiring people from the elite and Ivy League colleges, where, frankly, the student movement was more active than it was in working-class colleges. Not that there wasn't some student movement there in the sixties. But where were there big, well-known rebellions? Columbia. Harvard. Cornell University. Brown. Dartmouth. These were places where students were up in arms. The University of Chicago, University of Michigan—those were the grad students that UCSC was looking for in every field. And Berkeley—not to leave out the other places—UCLA and everywhere else. That's who they hired as faculty—not because of their activism per se, but because they were people who understood where education was going, and were interested in interdisciplinary, alternative ways of approaching education, who were not so wedded to the discipline of physics that they wouldn't be interested in what was going on in biology at the same time. Or so much interested in literature that they wouldn't care about landscape architecture. And that's why they would be willing to hire somebody like a Bill Friedland, who came with an idea of an interdisciplinary program for undergraduate students, with experiential aspects to it.

As more and more people around the world began to change, and UCSC became an outlier and an anomaly, people were hired from the same places they were being hired from before, but now were not so sure that the university's going to be a different kind of place. There was retrenchment back to graduate studies, back to disciplinary studies, back to publishing yourself in the right place, to increased expectations of publication on the part of faculty, so there's not time to put the time into your undergraduate students that you might have been hoping to put in there, because you had better get published or you're not going to get tenure, or you're not going to get the merit increases that you expect in terms of salary.

And so, you watch a slow erosion. You can't have an alternative educational system in one university, and expect that somehow eventually you're not going to be swallowed up. That's what's been going on at UCSC. It's not surprising, and it's sad, and it's unfortunate.

George Blumenthal: Public universities have a hard time dealing with the issue of not just creating, but also eliminating programs. We have eliminated very few programs over the years. We don't have good criteria. When we do try to cut programs they often become big causes célèbres. At Santa Cruz, community studies kind of played that role.

Figure 3

Shakespeare Santa Cruz program, 1985

Cutting a Beloved Institution:
Shakespeare Santa Cruz

David Kliger: One of the big things that the campus has never been very successful at is, even though we've said it over and over again for each of these budget cuts, is that we have to stop doing some things. People really don't like to do that. Everybody thinks what they're doing is very important. And that's a good thing. If people didn't think what they were doing was important, they wouldn't be doing a good job.

Jim Burns: Shakespeare Santa Cruz was an absolutely beloved institution — and had been almost since the day it was co-launched way back in the mid-1980s by Audrey Stanley on the academic side, and Karen Sinsheimer, the chancellor's spouse, on the administrative and support side.

Karen Sinsheimer: Chancellor Sinsheimer had given seed money for the first two years. We tried to match the fund but didn't quite measure up. The third year we had a deficit and I remember going with great trepidation to the chancellor's budget meeting where the committee was considering funding Shakespeare. I went as chair of the board, and I stated, "I am not going to run another deficit. I am here to ask if we could carry over the deficit and raise enough money at the same time to get ourselves into the black." It was extremely important to the festival—and to me—that this not be perceived as "the chancellor's wife's little pet project." I wanted them to know that we would be accountable and I promised that if they would fund us for a third year, we would get ourselves on a stable financial footing.

At the next board meeting, I told the group, "I cannot be president if we are not going to seriously commit do doing the fundraising we need to do

to make ourselves financially sound." It was one of the hardest meetings I've ever led, but it started us on a new level of professional commitment. We launched a serious fundraising campaign. We operate under the UCSC Foundation, so we are able to accept charitable contributions. The advantages of being part of the university far outweighed being a stand-alone nonprofit.

Audrey Stanley: Unfortunately, the cost of tickets doesn't cover the cost of the expenses. In the past, we've had support from the university to help this. And they've taken also the losses, which amounts to quite a lot over the thirty-two years, as you can imagine. But they don't have the money to do that anymore.

Karen Sinsheimer: We've had to break some new ground with some foundations, such as the Packard Foundation and the Cultural Council, which initially would not give to "state-supported" institutions. We were able to make the case successfully that the percentage of our budget that came from the university was less than one-third of the festival's total cost. We also made the case that this was a town-gown enterprise, community-based but on the hill and community-sponsored, with the university providing facilities and infrastructure as well as accounting and other services.

I needed to learn how to ask people for money. I couldn't be shy about it because the consequences—not meeting our budget commitment—were even more painful. So I called up a donor in Watsonville. He said, "Who is this?" So I told him who I was and what I was calling about. "I'm an old blue [UC alum]. I helped bring that place (UCSC) here. I sure get mad at it, I'm really mad at that place." But he continued, "For Shakespeare, huh? I'll give you a hundred dollars." So I got off the phone and he began to support Shakespeare. We knew we had to raise the money to keep going.

George Blumenthal: Over the years, I attended a number of Shakespeare Santa Cruz productions, long before I was chancellor. I really appreciated some of their productions. I remember liking, for example, Danny Scheie's productions when he was artistic director. He was innovative and exciting.

After I became chancellor, my first interaction with Shakespeare Santa Cruz was a reception at University House. At that event, I took the opportunity to make a number of Shakespearian puns. Shakespeare Santa Cruz was an important part of the culture and history of the campus. I was happy to move them forward.

Every year the Sinsheimers would come up during the summer to attend Shakespeare Santa Cruz. Kelly and I developed this tradition of hosting them at University House and often they would have extended family with them. So we'd either have a lunch or we'd have a picnic, or we would do something to break bread, and then go to a play together. It was a great annual event, and it was a great opportunity to see the Sinsheimers, who I had enormous respect for.

And over the years, I did get heavily involved in fundraising for Shakespeare. I met a number of donors, took part in several fundraising events. I greatly appreciated Shakespeare Santa Cruz— what it brought to the campus, what it brought to the community, how it related the community to the campus.

Jim Burns: But the challenge with Shakespeare Santa Cruz was the company's ongoing and increasing budget deficit.

Michael Warren: Since the mid nineties, Shakespeare Santa Cruz has been in a constant budget crisis. This has altered ways in which plays have been done. But we've had some beautiful productions. The company has maintained respect for the text, a kind of striving for intelligent imagination in performance that is totally laudable and often quite unusual.

George Blumenthal: Everything was just fine, except for the fact that Shakespeare began to run deficits. Dave Kliger, when he was EVC, was upset by that. Dave liked people to keep within their budget, kind of an elementary thing to have as an expectation. He couldn't find a way to get a handle on keeping them within their budget. Part of it was the spending cycle. Shakespeare Santa Cruz tended to spend a lot of money at the beginning of the year and then do a lot of fundraising at the end of the fiscal year. So it was basically a model of lots of money going out, and then lots of money coming in, and hope against hope that the two balance. And often it wasn't balancing, at least by the time I became chancellor. They would not raise enough money to make up for their costs.

We tried a number of things. We really tried to engage the board in oversight of the operations, with limited success. There were a few board chairs, particularly near the end, who tried hard to be responsible and responsive to this need. But my sense was that the board itself was not particularly interested. They were more interested in what the costumes were going to be than they were in making sure that the budget balanced. There was also an absence of budgetary caution and the ability to make changes.

Audrey Stanley: A lot of people assume that the university allows us to perform these plays freely, but we do pay for rental of rehearsal and performance space.

Figure 4

Shakespeare Santa Cruz program. 1997 festival season.
Autographed by actor and director Paul Whitworth

George Blumenthal: Another issue was the level of student involvement in Shakespeare Santa Cruz. Yes, there were students involved in a variety of ways; students got great experience working with Shakespeare Santa Cruz. But the number of students who were getting that experience was relatively small, considering the amount that the campus was spending on Shakespeare.

Michael Warren: There has for thirty-something years been this endless conversation: how can we fold Shakespeare Santa Cruz more into the educational enterprise? Well, it's folded in rather well-through the interns who take part in Shakespeare Santa Cruz in the summer—and there are a large number of them. I have interns—I say intern dramaturges. It's a wonderful education for them. During the year, Shakespeare Santa co-sponsors with theater arts the holiday show. Then it also works on Shakespeare To Go, which takes a one-hour version of a Shakespeare play into the schools.

There is always that nagging feeling that there ought to be some way to tie this together better. But Shakespeare Santa Cruz runs on a staff of only about six or seven people. It is an extraordinary organization for a community of this size to have. It is an extraordinary organization for a UC campus to sponsor. We're still, I think, the only UC campus that has a summer Shakespeare festival company on board.

We bring in Equity actors. We bring in high-class performers. We bring in high-class directors and designers. It's the real thing. I go to Ashland [Oregon Shakespeare Festival] regularly. I sometimes go to Cal Shakes. And though our performances are often not as consistent in acting quality, because we've got interns on stage with Equity actors, I perceive an integrity in our work which I think is admirable, that I don't always see elsewhere.

George Blumenthal: When they started running deficits, one issue that came up repeatedly was whether or not we could use fewer equity actors and use more students in the productions. What we were told was no, that in fact, the union had already made a big accommodation to the campus by allowing us to use fewer equity actors than was required by union rules, and that we couldn't push that exception any further.

Parabasis: [According to an article in the *Santa Cruz Sentinel*] Shakespeare Santa Cruz's financial woes predate both Yager's tenure at the Arts Division and Barricelli's at Shakespeare Santa Cruz. Ticket sales alone have never been able to sustain the budget of the company, which has, for its entire history, made it an artistic standard to use Equity actors in its productions.

You would never know reading this article that there isn't a single nonprofit theater in America for whom "ticket sales" have "been able to sustain the budget of the company." Instead, you get the implication that if only management were willing to make a cut rate product using non-Union labor (those union actors, after all, being so greedy), Shakespeare Santa Cruz would still be alive today. This kind of stuff—even when obviously unintentional—just ends up perpetuating the poisonous anti-labor conventional wisdom that underlines most conversations about the business of theater, from Broadway ticket prices to showcase code reform.[4]

Jim Burns: Chancellor Blumenthal and EVC Galloway concluded that something had to be done. And the arts dean, David Yager, was certainly of that mindset. There were costs that were coming right out of his division, impacting UCSC programs and UCSC students.

George Blumenthal: During the great recession, the deficit ballooned. It was much more difficult to raise money. Things got tighter and tighter and the pressure increased to find areas we could cut that, like Shakespeare Santa Cruz, live away from the center of our core mission. Dave Kliger believed we should just cut the cord. I remember having many meetings to talk about ways we could move forward. I didn't want to go there. I really, really didn't want to go there. I recognized the symbolic importance of Shakespeare Santa Cruz to the campus and to the community. I was just hoping against hope that we could find a way through all of this.

The poor old arts division had to oversee Shakespeare and didn't have the kind of infrastructure that they needed in order to do it. The dean of the arts was furious at me for not taking more decisive action about Shakespeare Santa Cruz. He wanted it out of the arts division. He didn't care whether we killed it or kept it alive, but he wanted nothing to do with it. I can understand exactly how he felt. I was very sympathetic to his feelings, but I really was reluctant to do it.

But I finally threatened to close down Shakespeare Santa Cruz. The chair of their board came to me and said, "How about we do a big, national internet fundraising campaign?" I said, "Fine. If you can raise," I forget what I said, "three hundred thousand dollars, I'll change my mind and we'll keep it open."

Audrey Stanley: People often come to the rescue of certain areas of the campus. Maybe there's somebody out there who perhaps would do this for Shakespeare Santa Cruz.

San Jose Mercury News: Once more unto the breach, dear friends, once more. Shakespeare Santa Cruz may not be staging "Henry V" this summer, but that rallying cry perfectly captures the mood behind the scenes at the beloved 28-year-old festival, which is facing a do-or-die season.

"It's a make-or-break this summer for us," says Artistic Director Marco Barricelli. "We are doing everything we can to get people out here, but ticket sales are slow, and if we don't break even, we might not make it." The festival, dubbed one of the 10 most influential Shakespeare festivals in the country by *USA Today*, has been a critically acclaimed local treasure almost from the beginning, but it has always struggled to make ends meet, too. Just last winter it narrowly escaped the jaws of death by raising $416,417 in a 10-day emergency campaign, but if the company can't balance its budget this summer, it faces peril once more.

"What's going on in the economy nationally, here in California and in the UC system has really been a perfect storm for Shakespeare Santa Cruz," Barricelli says. He hastens to add that he does not blame the university, which in years past underwrote the theater's losses but hasn't been able to do so since the economy turned sour. "UC is not the bad guy here; they are in dire straits. All the arguments about art and philosophy and enlightenment are off the table right now. They need to see the numbers. If we can't balance the budget, we can't go forward."[5]

Audrey Stanley: Well, it's always touch and go. It has been touch and go from the start. People don't realize how close to being closed we have been. There will have to be changes. We've conformed to our budget but the ticket sales haven't covered the rest of it.

George Blumenthal: So they did this campaign and they raised something like four hundred thousand dollars. I kept my promise. We kept it going. And that was all to the good, at least for that year.

The problem was that the money that was raised in that desperation effort wasn't sustainable. It didn't get raised again next year. They got contributions from all over the country, which was impressive. But it was not a permanent fix. And I found them unwilling to change their operations. At one point I said, "Well, why don't you just suspend for a year? Don't offer it for a year. Spend two years fundraising until you get the money to do it." That was completely unacceptable to them.

I decided maybe the way to do it is to get my office involved and offer matching funds. So I got some money together and I offered matching funds for contributions to Shakespeare. I wanted to show chancelloral support. I think we used up all the matching funds, so that was a successful effort.

But nevertheless, the deficits continued. I think over a ten-year period, we were giving them, I forget exactly how much, 100, 150K a year as a part of our budget. We just allocated it to them. But then on top of that, they were running on average $400,000 deficits every year—much, much bigger than their annual allocation from the campus.

Jim Burns: So, campus leaders made the very difficult decision that they were not going to support this anymore, which in effect ended our sponsorship of Shakespeare Santa Cruz.

George Blumenthal: So this was now a few years later, after the initial threat to close them down. It was going on and getting worse. For me, the issue was, on the one hand, this was a strong, symbolic activity for the campus, high profile, good for town/gown relationships, ties us together with the community. And there was some benefit to students. But against that was four hundred thousand dollars a year, when budgets were still tight. Alison Galloway by then was provost and David

Yager was dean. Alison wanted it closed down. She was tired of dealing with it and frustrated. David was not prepared to defend it. It was not one of his priorities for the arts.

Eventually I felt like I had to make a decision. After ten years of consistent deficits, I didn't feel I could justify this. This was taking instructors out of classrooms in order to hire equity actors to do something on campus. Of course, ending it was very controversial. People felt this was the stupidest thing a chancellor could possibly do. And maybe it was. But I feel this intense sense of responsibility to the academic mission of the university. That's what I'm here for. And this was taking money out of the academic mission of the university, to the tune of four hundred thousand dollars a year, which, particularly in those days, was a big deal. We didn't have excess money to play around with. This was just around the time that rebenching was starting to kick in. We did not have money.

Good Times: For the past three decades, Shakespeare's robust and witty dialogue could be heard echoing throughout The Sinsheimer-Stanley Festival Glen outdoor theater at UC Santa Cruz on any given summer evening. Amidst food-scattered picnic blankets, the community sat rapt by the onstage antics of "A Midsummer Night's Dream" or the drama of "Romeo and Juliet."

But on August 26, 2013, UC Santa Cruz announced that, due to worsening budget challenges to the university and the professional repertory company being deeply in debt, Shakespeare Santa Cruz would be forced to end its 32-year run.

George Blumenthal: So, of course it caused a huge reaction among the supporters of Shakespeare, who found that this was a horrible thing for us to have done. I felt terrible. Karen Sinsheimer was remarkably understanding of the dilemma. I felt terrible for her to be doing this. So we talked about it. I was struck by how supportive she was about that decision. I don't think she liked the decision. But she wasn't angry about it. But of course, many other people were angry. I received a lot of angry communications over that Shakespeare decision.

Good Times: Giles Henderson, a UC Santa Cruz junior and intern with Shakespeare Santa Cruz (SSC), says that the campus' affiliation with the nationally renowned theatre company was the core reason he chose the university. "Having Shakespeare Santa Cruz being a part of UCSC was a major draw for me as a theatre arts student. In fact," he says, "it was the deciding factor."

There is a contradiction in the university's decision, according to Carey Perloff, Artistic Director of the American Conservatory Theater, which is based in San Francisco. In an open letter to UCSC Chancellor George Blumenthal, she wrote, "You yourself, Chancellor Blumenthal, have written eloquently of the need to protect funding for medical research in an era of financial cutbacks. Do you not see that professional theater is a critical component not only of humanistic research but of the maintenance of an ancient and crucially important tradition? You are justly proud of your engineering and genetics departments, which engage in an active way with the latest developments in their respective fields. Yet you question the value of a paltry investment in superb classical theater that not only binds UCSC to its broader community but keeps a rich level of humanistic dialogue alive over generations."[6]

Jim Burns: It was an especially thorny issue to communicate. In the days and weeks leading up to the Shakespeare Santa Cruz announcement, I had many phone conversations with the Office of Planning and Budget about the organization's precise budget predicament with the campus. We put together a press release and everyone agreed on what the facts were as best we could. In that case, and in most cases, I thought it best to just call a reporter, or call multiple reporters, and say, "Here is what is happening."

Good Times: The seemingly sudden decision unleashed a backlash of shock and outrage in a community that deeply values the arts. "Members of our community said, 'This can't happen,'" says Aimee Zygmonski, the former managing and marketing director for SSC. People said, 'There's no way that there can't be a Shakespeare Festival in Santa Cruz.'"

This outpouring of dismay triggered ideas among Shakespeare Santa Cruz board members and the rest of the company—ideas about how to preserve the tradition of Shakespeare Santa Cruz, yet maintain the autonomy of an independent theater company no longer under the thumb of the university system.

George Blumenthal: But this cut was the basis for the beginnings of Santa Cruz Shakespeare. I thought that they wouldn't survive for more than a couple of years. But they have, and they've thrived.

Good Times: A newly formed nonprofit theater company—led by longtime SSC veterans Marco Barricelli and Mike Ryan, and a star-studded Advisory Board, including *Star Trek: The Next Generation's* Sir Patrick Stewart and Academy Award-winning actress Olympia Dukakis—launched a massive fundraising effort in December 2013 to bring Shakespeare back to Santa Cruz. Over the course of just two months, the fundraising goal was met and then vastly exceeded.[7]

George Blumenthal: I give them huge credit. I try to be as supportive as I can be to Santa Cruz Shakespeare. Almost from day one, I supported their fundraising. I even transferred an endowment from UCSC to the Santa Cruz Foundation to be used for Santa Cruz Shakespeare. That endowment was given to the campus to support Shakespeare Santa Cruz. It seemed to me that if Shakespeare Santa Cruz no longer existed, what was the more ethical thing for me to do, to try to put it into something else at theater arts, or to try to support the successor to Shakespeare Santa Cruz? I was not obliged to do that, but I felt it was the right thing to do, and most consistent with the wishes of the donors.

Jim Burns: I was heartened to learn several months later that the campus had been able to reach an agreement with the new organization, Santa Cruz Shakespeare, to continue to use the glen.

George Blumenthal: We rented the glen to them for two or three years. They just continued here, like they always did, but under different management.

Jim Burns: And then [after I retired] I was sad to read that that wasn't going to be more than a Band-Aid fix, and that the organization was going to move its productions off campus.

George Blumenthal: There were two issues that came up with the glen. One issue was that we kept hearing from theater arts that they wanted to be able to use the glen for some graduate programs, so there was potential there for a conflict. But in truth, that conflict hadn't yet become ripe.

The other and much more difficult issue had to do with the Americans with Disabilities Act [ADA]. The glen is not ADA-compliant and at a certain point, I came to know that. So you would think, naively, that okay, so the glen isn't compliant because it's got the slopes and the dirt and all that stuff. So we had to put in ramps and whatever? That can't be that big a deal. It really isn't that big a deal to put in ramps and stuff. The problem is, when you have an area of the campus and it's ADA out-of-compliance and you bring it into compliance, you have to bring the whole area into compliance, which meant that we also had to redo the restrooms. It was a much bigger scope than just putting a few ramps by the seats in the glen. If it was just the ramps by the seats in the glen, we're talking, I don't know, thirty, forty thousand dollars, and that's not enough of a big deal to worry about. On the other hand, we did cost out what it would take to redo the glen and bring it fully up to ADA compliance, and it was well over a million dollars.

SFGate: Santa Cruz Shakespeare's new venue, the Grove at DeLaveaga Park, was planned, funded and built in just over a year. You have to climb hills and traverse a golf course to get there, but you're rewarded with rustic elegance: a spare stage nestled within a eucalyptus grove. The fog starts roaring in well before curtain, coursing through the cones of light emitted by the lighting instruments; that's the perfect effect for the opening moments of "Hamlet," the second show in the company's summer season. This "Hamlet" marks an impressive rebound for the company, which has weathered two huge struggles in recent years.[8]

George Blumenthal: I'm very pleased that Santa Cruz Shakespeare has continued to thrive. They put on plays much as they did when they were associated with the university. I have been and continue to be supportive of their continuation, even though I will always be known as the chancellor who killed Shakespeare Santa Cruz.

"Universities are Living Institutions":
Old Traditions and New Starts in the 21st Century

George Blumenthal: Universities are living, breathing institutions. One of the ways that we've thrived is the ability to start new things in exciting fields. Biomolecular engineering: who'd have thunk it. Twenty years ago, I'm not sure I would have known what those words meant. Latin American/Latino studies? When I was a student, we would never have imagined a department like that, much less a PhD program. We've built some wonderful things.

Patricia Zavella: We wanted to have a doctoral program in Latin American and Latino Studies (LALS). We have what we're calling a disciplinary spine, which means that students not only take our core courses and our graduate courses in LALS, but they also have to take some courses in another discipline that helps them build them expertise in particular methodologies—ethnography or survey research, whatever—so that when they graduate then they can go on the market not only in interdisciplinary programs, but in disciplinary searches. We're very mindful that this is new and people are going to go, "A PhD in LALS? What does that mean?" So we're trying to think ahead of what our students might be facing.

Susy Zepeda, Student: I remember coming here and learning about the Chicano/Latino Research Center and the Latin American and Latino Studies Program and being so blown away, so impressed by what was happening. It felt like a magnet— like, this is where I want to be for graduate school!

Olga Nájera-Ramírez: I remember when LALS became a department, one of the things that the social science dean wanted me to do was to decide,

well, do you want to stay in anthropology in your own home discipline, or do you want to move over to help create the department with your FTE? I was troubled because I thought, well, I like anthropology and I feel like anthropology needs a Chicana to represent the courses. Why do I have to make a choice? Before I wasn't getting anything and now they want me in both. I didn't want to do a fifty-fifty. I always heard that was not a good idea, for promotions and stuff.

So we designed a structure, where there were going to be the full faculty that were the FTE's, and then there were going to be the affiliate faculty, which they always have, what they call the "below the line" appointments. And we created a middle category called "participating faculty." These were faculty who wanted to be a little more hands-on than just affiliates, but didn't have to be at every single meeting. So we designed this middle category of people who were more inclined to participate, but not as fully as an FTE, like we didn't get voting rights. But we would be at the meetings and things like that. So that category was designed and we're still using it.

Jim Clifford: UCSC does have roots in the original vision of interdisciplinarity, even if it that strand doesn't pass through the colleges anymore. There is still something distinctive about the part of UCSC I've been involved in, where collaborative work can cross borders that in other universities would be very difficult to cross.

Donna Haraway: Feminist studies is reinventing itself, both in a disciplined way and in this kind of body-of-work way, at the same time. And its new transnational feminist theory graduate program could be dynamite.

Helene Moglen: Feminist studies now has a graduate program and a strong reputation.

Jess Whatcott: I'm currently a fourth-year graduate student here at UC Santa Cruz in the politics department. They have a special program here, the equivalent of a minor for undergrads, what's called a designated emphasis. So, I have designated emphases in feminist studies and critical race and ethnic studies. I heard about UC Santa Cruz because I'm a huge fan of Angela Davis. I've read all of her work on prisons. I knew that she was professor emeritus here, and looked into it, and then began to realize that many other people whose work I admired, including Donna Haraway, Neferti Tadiar, Gloria Anzaldúa—some folks who are not with us at UCSC anymore, or not with us on this plane anymore—had taught here or been grad students here. So, it seemed like a really rich intellectual space.

I've taken some brilliant classes from people who've introduced me to new works and totally blown my mind. Amazing speakers come through here all the time. I've gotten to see almost everyone on my academic bucket list. I've grown intellectually. One of the first classes I took here was from Bettina Aptheker in the feminist studies department. I took her feminist pedagogies class. Bettina is a very approachable person. She didn't intimidate me like a lot of other famous feminist academics.

George Blumenthal: One of the things I'm most proud of is doubling the number of endowed chairs. When I became acting chancellor, we had fewer endowed chairs than UC Merced had the day it opened. We might have had eighteen or

nineteen. So doubling the number of endowed chairs was a big deal.

UCSC News Center: UC Santa Cruz has established an endowed chair to honor the person most responsible for the thriving Jewish Studies program that exists on the campus today. Over 150 donors have committed a combined total of $977,130 to establish the new Murray Baumgarten Endowed Chair in Jewish Studies in the Center for Jewish Studies, located in the UC Santa Cruz Institute for Humanities Research. The purpose of the chair is to promote research, teaching, and public outreach activities in the area of Jewish Studies.[9]

Murray Baumgarten: We are the first campus in Northern California, among the UCs, to have a Jewish studies major. One of the things that makes us different from other Jewish studies programs is that other Jewish studies programs often have a normative view of what the great achievements of Judaism are, and mostly in modern times they stick with, shall I say, German and Eastern European Jewish culture. By looking at it internationally, we have a much broader reach. There's more interesting stuff going on, including in the United States. We're not making judgments or being normative.

We have this great course that I helped to encourage Lecturer in Music Avi Tchamni to do and, before him, Lecturer in Music Francesco Spagnolo, who was teaching music for us, called *The Music of the Jews from the Lands of Islam*. And that's not what one thinks of when one thinks of the classic stuff in Jewish culture. But I have an interest in music, and music is often forgotten in the arts. I'm interested in dance and choreography. When I was editing the journal *Judaism: A Journal of Jewish Life and Thought*, a friend wrote a wonderful piece about Jewish choreographers. There have been many, many of them in the history of modern dance; Anna Sokolow, for example, comes to mind.

In many places, Holocaust studies has all the glamour, so people say that's the only thing students want to study. Well, it's such a huge moment, a rupture, a watershed in Western history. And to have the Jews be at the center of it is something that brings attention to this. It's also a way of studying what World War II really was about. And, as a friend has said, as long as we study about World War II, there won't be a World War III, right? At least that's the hope.

Holocaust studies are now also outside of Jewish studies and have morphed into genocide studies. And that's been, again, a recent phenomenon since we've started to teach it. There was an interest in it right from the beginning, but now we have so many more genocides to study.

Most of the students in the classes are not Jewish. Judaism is a very important civilization. The history of this civilization has many pathways and they were all very important. People are exploring them. I was recently in Miami at a conference. I went to the synagogue, and people were saying Kaddish [the Jewish prayer of mourning] at the end, as you do, in honor of those who had died, and the rabbi—you read the list of people, and the rabbi stood up and he said, "Sid Caesar [the comedian]." He had just died, so people were saying Kaddish. I stood up and said Kaddish for Sid Caesar. There seems to me an important aspect of Jewish culture and Jewish civilization. We have a course in Jewish comedy. It's a different way of responding to the world that is still very, very engaging and attractive to people, and they want to study the past and think about it as we head to the future.

Donna Haraway: UCSC was set up with an interdisciplinary approach, with the boards of studies rather than disciplines. Of course, it has become significantly more disciplinized as we go. But as we have become more heavily disciplinized, we've also been inventing—again part of the larger ecology—new kinds of interdisciplinarity. I think one of the really good examples of that would be biomolecular engineering, which is a new kind of interdisciplinarity of a highly creative kind that I have deep interest in, and so do a number of other people in feminist theory. I think also of the ties in cognitive sciences between philosophy, linguistics, and psychology that science studies, including feminist science studies, has major interest in. There are several faculty around this campus, including Professor Karen Barad, with deep ties in science studies, and several graduate students working with various of us. And we just put in an NSF proposal this summer for a graduate training grant to make our work with graduate students more coherent, and maybe eventually form a formal graduate group.

And, of course we have the vibrant interdisciplinarity of cultural studies at UCSC. There are all kinds of new interdisciplinarities exhibited in real social forms on this campus, as well as in forms of publishing and public life. I think sometimes we don't see that all over the campus new kinds of conversations are being invented in stabilized and social forms—sometimes departments, sometimes programs, sometimes just research clusters, sometimes reading groups, sometimes with funding, sometimes not. We pay too much attention to the forms of organization that we don't do anymore, sometimes, and don't recognize what we *are* doing.

Leta Miller: We're moving in some really interesting new directions. Much more movement toward multiculturalism, and not only in terms of the faculty members themselves, but in terms of the topics that are studied, the topics of seminars, the lectures for our colloquium series. Both

Figures 5 and 6

Top: "Ms. Blue" whale skeleton at night, Seymour Marine Discovery Center

Left: Swell shark egg case, also known as a "Mermaid's Purse," containing a shark embryo. Seymour Marine Discovery Center

Photos by Elizabeth Van Dyke

the PhD and the Doctor of Musical Arts (DMA) have helped that trend because one of the tracks of the DMA is in world music composition, which involves using musics from other cultures mixed with Western culture in terms of compositional style; and also the PhD is founded on cultural musicology. So that has led to the hiring on our faculty of more ethnomusicologists. So, for example, there is Tanya Merchant, who works in Uzbekistani music and also plays the bassoon, and has a degree from a major conservatory, Curtis, in bassoon. And then there is our latest hire, Nicol Hammond, who works in South African music and in popular music but also has done choral directing. We're bringing these people in who are multivalent. This collaboration and this crossing of subdisciplines is important. It's characteristic of UCSC and the spirit of UCSC.

Gary Griggs: My dream had always been to expand the marine lab to what we're now calling the Coastal Sciences Campus and opportunities for collaboration and interaction. We raised almost seven million dollars to build the Center for Ocean Health. Then some faculty in areas that encompassed coastal and marine science said, "You know, if we had our students down there and our labs and we had internet connection maybe we could teach a few classes, we might all move down there." It was great. It turns out half of EEB [Ecology and Evolutionary Biology] decided to go along with that and they've never been happier. But that changed from this little dusty outpost of a few people working and a few sea lions, to a working lab. I see ten thousand school children come through the Seymour Center every year and people are now working with the NMFS [National Marine Fisheries Service] Lab, USGS [United States Geological Survey], and in the Center for Ocean Health. I was the chair of the committee that planned this building and followed through

with it. It's this wonderful feeling every day when you come in. It's like wow, it's here and people are appreciating it because we did it. I walk down today and I see these people, I don't know who they are, they don't know who I am—it's like, "It's okay. It's for you."

Norman Locks: Who designs the dioramas at the Monterey Bay Aquarium? Who designs the dioramas at Seymour Marine Discovery Center? What is that interface? That's applied design. It isn't what artists do, per se. But what artists do filters down. My former photography students are in music, and in performance, in theater, film, arts, curating. Because art is an abstract. It's about creativity. It's about imagination. And it's about applying ideas to making something. So they end up everywhere. In city planning, architecture. The arts are a root form for things aesthetic.

The Campaign for UC Santa Cruz: UC Santa Cruz is a global leader in marine science and environmental studies, which gives us expertise on both land and sea as we tackle the pressing issues of Coastal Sustainability. Our Coastal Science campus is perched on the edge of Monterey Bay, giving us immediate access to remarkable biodiversity; our research into the critical issues of sustainable agriculture is anchored in our 30-acre organic farm and garden.[10]

Jim Burns: I've always thought that the peregrine falcon effort—launched by local veterinarian James Roush and the late—and beloved—UCSC biologist Ken Norris and continued by Brian Walton and later by Glenn Stewart—was a truly amazing accomplishment. At the time those people were getting involved, the peregrine falcon population was down to single digits in terms of known falcons that existed in California. The peregrine was very, very close to being extinct as

Figure 7

Predatory Bird Research Group report cover

a species. Through our researchers' great work, twenty or twenty-five years later the peregrine was delisted as an endangered species.

Predatory Bird Research Group: Formed in 1975, the UC Santa Cruz Predatory Bird Research Group worked under state and federal permits along with cooperation from the Pacific States Peregrine Falcon Recovery Team to save the Peregrine Falcon from the brink of a pesticide-mediated extinction. Our pioneering work led to the Peregrine's removal from the federal list of endangered species in 1999 and from California's list of endangered species in 2009.

The Santa Cruz Predatory Bird Research Group also led or initiated successful breeding and release efforts for Elf Owls, Aplomado Falcons, Harris's Hawks, and Bald Eagles. We also undertook significant studies of Prairie Falcons, Bald Eagle migrations, Goshawks, and Golden Eagles. In all, more than forty years of conservation biology have been funded primarily by private sector gifts and grants and supported by a robust volunteer effort. Our mission is to use the example of the Peregrine Falcon recovery as an inspiration for tackling today's environmental challenges, and to involve students and citizen scientists in monitoring the current status of predatory birds in California.[11]

Norman Locks: Ken Norris's work with the Natural Reserve System was very important to me. So I take my photography classes out to the field, to the UC Reserve System, to get them out of the classroom, looking at the thing with them, so that we can have common experience in relationship to a place.

Two and a half weeks ago we were at McLaughlin Reserve up by Lake Berryessa, north of Lake Berryessa. Next quarter we're going to the Mojave. Fall quarter I was at Big Sur, Big Creek.

UCSC Natural Reserve System: Our sites ring the Monterey Bay, and along the National Marine Sanctuary that extends up the entire coastline, from the Golden Gate at San Francisco south to Big Sur. The wide range of habitats, from fog-enshrouded redwood forest to maritime chaparral, provide an unparalleled natural laboratory for marine and terrestrial research and serve as study sites for university scientists and students.

The UC Santa Cruz Campus Natural Reserve is separated into parcels that span undeveloped areas of the UCSC Campus. Norris and his students dedicated years of research, surveying and classifying the natural resources in order to provide UCSC with an on-campus collection of, in Norris' own words, "outdoor laboratories" or "classrooms without walls" which add to the importance and uniqueness of the campus. His memory continues to be honored today at the Kenneth S. Norris Center for Natural History on UCSC Campus.

Jenny Keller: I am on the executive steering committee for the Natural History Field Quarter. The Field Quarter has inspired such incredible loyalty. When we had the first reunion, the forty-year reunion in 2012, there were over five hundred participants. It was not only the biggest event that was at the Alumni Weekend at UCSC that year, but the biggest one they've ever had. And it was all for a single class. It wasn't for a major, or something like that. UCSC was astonished that there's this body of people out there who care this much about this one course. And fortunately, from there, with incredible amounts of effort, especially, I would say, on the part of Chris Lay, and Larry Ford, and Jenny Anderson, the Packard Foundation bestowed a grant of two million dollars to support the perpetuation of the Field Quarter and the creation of the Norris Center. That work was done by

Figure 8

Bobcat crossing the UCSC bike path, 2008

Photo by Lee Jaffe

people who cared that much about this particular enterprise and its uniqueness and its power.

Chris Lay and I worked together quite a bit on the [Norris Center] museum itself. I said, "You know what you need? You need some big landscapes of California, and I think you need me to paint them." I was very pleased later that Karen Holl said, "I can't imagine the museum without those paintings now." My vision is that while you're indoors they give you a sense of the outdoors, and of California, the natural history that Ken Norris's course was all about.

We chose the Mojave Desert because that was near and dear to Ken's heart, as were so many places. But you can't think of Ken Norris and the Field Quarter without thinking of the Mojave Desert. So, there's a big one of the Mojave Desert. There's also Mono Lake and there's the Big Creek Reserve.

Norman Locks: But it's not just nature. When we go to the Mojave Desert we're not just looking at the natural environment. We're looking at mining; we're looking at the dunes; and we're looking for snakes. We're finding metal shards and looking at the ranch. The Mojave Reserve was a ranch also. You're looking at ranch artifacts. You're looking at petroglyphs. You're looking at the mining that's going on. You're looking at the waste. We're making trips down to abandoned buildings. We're going down to Joshua Tree National Park. The Mojave Desert Reserve is right in the middle of a very rich cultural environment, of which the students know very little. They've never been to the desert before. So the Natural Reserve System is a location that allows us to put ourselves in the center of a set of experiences that are vital in the total teaching experience. We take different cameras. We take films.

But it's really culture that's the thing that they're encountering. There was a period when we'd drive over to the Colorado River and we'd go swimming. Or we'd go to Las Vegas, and the kids wanted to spend the night in Las Vegas. And so some pulled off and went to Las Vegas. So it's culture. Artists, photographers are interested in the bigger picture rather than simply the natural history. You're in a kind of a natural history environment, but the natural history is mining and ranching and gambling and recluses. You can have meth labs. I mean, what is it that we are encountering when we move through those places?

Frank Zwart: Science has always been extremely strong at UC Santa Cruz. It was overlooked or eclipsed by the countercultural publicity.

David Kliger: In 2011, we were ranked number one in impact. In other words, if you looked at the number of citations per publication, we were ranked number one in the world. We didn't have as many publications as some of the larger research universities. But the research that we were doing was being recognized with citations.

George Blumenthal: Genomics was growing substantially. We were doing more and more stem cell research.

UCSC Genomics Institute: We will openly and responsibly share what we learn and create. We are a public institution dedicated to creating a healthier world.[12]

Victor Garcia-Zepeda: I was able to get a position as a program assistant with the Genomics Institute. Being within the Human Genome Project, conducted by Dr. David Haussler, is exciting. When I first got hired there, I was really excited to meet him and learn a little bit more about the project itself. Being a program assistant there

Figure 9

DNA Day, 2018

Photo by Carolyn Lagattuta

has given me the opportunity to talk to people involved with the project. And now they're moving forward with their bigger initiative; moving forward with big data has been something that they're working with now for the past four, six years. They've gotten a lot more funding. They've really come a long way from what genetics used to be, and genomics, really delving into this idea of: what does it mean for diversity and how does it affect people who are not necessarily from the white middle class. What does it means to have all these intersectional identities and cultural backgrounds that shape the person? How does genetics play a role in the future of genetic diversity?

There was a project that we did last year and we're going to do again this year—the BD2K, Big Data to Knowledge project. We had a few students come in from different universities: one from the University of Puerto Rico; a few from the University of Louisiana, Baton Rouge; some from CSU Monterey; some UCSC students. The main focus is to pair some of these students with labs within the Genomics Institute. Some were paired with the Haussler Lab, some with the Josh Stuart Lab; some with the Treehouse Childhood Cancer Initiative Lab; some with the Shapiro Lab.

Another project that I work with closely within the Genomics Institute is on DNA Day, which is coming up on April 25th. That is the celebration of the discovery of the double helix, and also, the completion of the Human Genome Project. We partner up with the NHGRI to celebrate this day. It's almost like a fair. We have student organizations come in. We have WISE, which is Women in Science and Engineering; we have a few other organizations of students of minority background in the science and technology and engineering and mathematics majors. And we have some other organizations that come in from the resource centers.

The main focus is to explain and showcase the diversity that exists within our campus, and also in the STEM majors, and the diversity that is our whole community. We celebrate the accomplishments that these students have made. They showcase their research, too, through the Research Mentor Internship program. Students who have been awarded this award present their research that deals with something in the genetics field.

Hayden White: The sciences have to have a graduate dimension or they can't keep up. That's not true of the humanities and the soft social sciences. The really radical transformation that occurred in the universities is the moment at which one stopped seeing the university with the college as its central task of kind of a finishing school for the education of the well-rounded person who then might choose to go into medicine or law or the sciences. The research university, once it's set up, it has its obligations with the corporate world, the military-industrial complex, the government, and it has contracts with them and its research agenda is set by these contracts. So there's a conflict between the desire to teach, make well-rounded citizens and professional researchers. And that's the function of the graduate programs in the sciences—it's to produce other researchers, more researchers. It's not concerned with the development of the person.

David Kliger: We started a new department of environmental toxicology. I helped start the Institute for Geophysics and Planetary Physics. We developed an ocean sciences PhD program. We now have pretty strong material science programs in physics, in chemistry, and engineering.

We built a lot of buildings. We developed Earth and Marine Sciences, Interdisciplinary Sciences, the Physical Sciences Building, the Center for Ocean Health, the Seymour Marine Discovery

Center, the Center for Adaptive Optics, and the new Biomedical Sciences Building. That's a lot of buildings.

Lou Fackler, Founding Campus Engineer: If you saw Science Hill with only three buildings, you'd think it was a beautiful place to have a picnic. Redwood trees, gorgeous. It was wonderful in the early days of the campus. Now it is buildings and asphalt. But we all knew it was going to be like that, just like Berkeley. And that is probably more like Berkeley than any other part of the campus, because it's high density, which is okay. You have to do that for science. You have to do it for economies of scale. They're taller buildings.

The current campus leaders have built a lot of buildings. They certainly have helped the campus build an academic reputation in the science fields. They are world famous and I'm happy with that. At one time people said that all we were doing at UCSC was basket weaving. You remember those days? I'm pleased with the way the campus is going. You know, it's not the nice friendly place it was, but we all knew it wasn't going to be in forty years. It's more like Berkeley, big departments and all, and people can't really know each other as well and can't do things because it's too big.

Michael Cowan: Today, we are much larger, but we do seem small. In many different campus locations, we cultivate the attention to individual development, to human-scale interaction, to collaboration. That's what's happening on Science Hill in the labs and in the research groups.

George Blumenthal: UCSC is the hotbed of astronomy. I think it is a good thing for the campus to have some programs that are truly the outstanding programs in the world.

UCSC News Center: The transformation of the Science and Engineering Library will start later this year using a $5 million grant to kickstart the initiative. "The library—a repository of knowledge—remains fundamental to the mission of our university, yet it must evolve to meet the needs of today's world of inquiry," Chancellor George Blumenthal said. "This grant helps to launch an important reimagining of our Science and Engineering Library that will ensure its central place in our campus for the decades to come."

The top floor of the Science and Engineering Library will be named in honor of Sandra M. Faber, professor emerita of astronomy and astrophysics at UC Santa Cruz. Faber's work has helped establish many of the foundational principles underlying the modern understanding of the universe on the largest scales. Faber, who received the National Medal of Science in 2013, is renowned for her contributions to the understanding of dark matter, galaxy formation, and the large-scale structure of the universe.[13]

Santa Cruz Sentinel: A UC Santa Cruz professor President Barack Obama deemed "one of the world's foremost experts in the evolution of the universe" was honored Friday with one of the nation's highest science awards. "Sandra Moore Faber had a passion for astronomy from the very beginning," Obama said at a ceremony held at the White House. "But when she visited one of our nation's top observatories as a grad student, they didn't have a dorm for female astronomers, so Sandra ended up sleeping on the sofa in the caretaker's cottage. Luckily, that didn't stop her," he said, before shaking Faber's hand and hanging the medal around her neck.

Faber, a professor of astronomy and astrophysics, was honored for her contributions to scientific progress in understanding the history and structure of the universe. She was among

12 eminent researchers presented with the 2011 National Medal of Science Friday ceremony, along with 11 inventors honored with the National Medal of Technology and Innovation. The two awards are the highest honors the U.S. government bestows upon scientists, engineers and inventors.[14]

UCSC News Center: In the latest analysis (2017) of the world's top universities published by Times Higher Education (THE), UC Santa Cruz ranked third in research influence as measured by the number of times its faculty's published work is cited by scholars around the world.

Published as part of the THE World University Rankings 2018, the analysis measured overall research influence based on the average number of citations per paper, using a database of almost 62 million citations to more than 12.4 million research publications published over five years, from 2012 to 2016.

With a citation score of 99.9, UC Santa Cruz is tied for third place with Stanford University. St. George's University of London and the Massachusetts Institute of Technology were tied for first. UC Berkeley ranked just behind UCSC and Stanford with a citation score of 99.8.

George Blumenthal: You know: game design? Come on, get real! Who would have ever done something like that? We've built some wonderful new things.

Good Times: While the repetitiveness of regular physical therapy can come to feel like a chore, using a game to engage people in that therapy can spark a new excitement in them, says Sri Kurniawan, a computational media professor at UCSC. This type of game falls under a broader category known as "serious games," or games designed with a primary purpose other than entertainment. While the games may still be entertaining, that playfulness engages the player in ultimately achieving some other goal. Serious games are also designed to guide users through workplace training, educate them on social and political issues, and help them improve their health and well-being.

Students will be learning how to develop the next generations of such projects in the new UCSC master's program on serious games launching this fall. The program joins one graduate-level and two undergraduate-level game-design programs already offered by UCSC, which are ranked among the top in the country by the *Princeton Review.* The new serious games graduate program is the first of its kind in the U.S.[15]

Leta Miller: If the music department can forge more relationships with other departments outside of the arts division, I think that that would be an area to explore. There's been talk between music and engineering, for example, because the engineering school started this gaming program. Games have to have music. And some graduates from music schools are writing music for games, which is good employment for them. And that program requires the students to take courses in the arts.

Jim Clifford: I may be a provincial, but I've taught at Yale and University College London, the École des Hautes Études in Paris, and in Berlin. When I go to other universities, people are more boxed in. The freedom and the permission that I've enjoyed and that I still feel in the air at UCSC just isn't there.

Endnotes

1. Elizabeth Limbach, "On The Chopping Block? All eyes await the fate of UCSC's Community Studies Program," *Good Times*, April 14, 2009.

2. Elizabeth Limbach, "On The Chopping Block? All eyes await the fate of UCSC's Community Studies Program," *Good Times*, April 14, 2009.

3. Genevieve Bookwalter, "Budget ax to fall on UCSC"s popular and controversial Community Studies department," *Santa Cruz Sentinel*, April 7, 2009.

4. Isaac Butler, "What Killed Shakespeare Santa Cruz?" *Parabasis* (Blog) https://parabasis.typepad.com/blog/2013/08/what-killed-shakespeare-santa-cruz-1.html.

5. Karen DeSouza, "Santa Cruz Shakespeare back with winning 'Merry Wives,'" *San Jose Mercury News*, July 18, 2014.

6. Joel Hersh, "Therein Lies the Rub: UC Santa Cruz students, locals speak out on the closure of Shakespeare Santa Cruz," *Good Times*, September 10, 2013.

6. Leslie Patrick, "On With the Show," *Good Times*, February 19, 2014.

8. Lily Janiak, "A promising 3rd act for Santa Cruz Shakespeare," *SFGate*, Sunday, July 31, 2016.

9. Scott Rappaport, "UC Santa Cruz launches Murray Baumgarten Endowed Chair in Jewish Studies." *UCSC News Center*, January 23, 2017.

10. The Campaign for UC Santa Cruz was a large fundraising initiative that took place between 2013 and 2017 which raised 335 million dollars for the campus. The website for the campaign is a succinct statement about the campus's priorities and directions in this era. See: http://campaign.ucsc.edu/priorities/initiatives/coastal/.

11. See the Predatory Bird Research Group website at: https://pbrg.pbsci.ucsc.edu/page1.html.

12. UCSC Genomics Institute Mission Statement: https://ucscgenomics.soe.ucsc.edu/about/our-mission/.

13. Scott Hernandez-Jason, "Grant to transform upper floor of Science and Engineering Library," *UCSC News Center*, March 8, 2018.

14. Jessica Pasko, "Obama honors UCSC"s Sandra Faber with nation"s top science award," *Santa Cruz Sentinel*, February 1, 2013.

15. Alisha Green, UCSC Debuts 'Serious Games' Master's Degree *Good Times,* March 5, 2019.

Illustrations

Figure 1. William "Bill" Friedland (left) and community studies students working as lettuce harvest researchers, listening to an audio recording, 1978. Courtesy Special Collections, University Library, University of California, Santa Cruz. UCSC Photography Services: UA 50: ua0050_neg_sc7721_12.

Figure 2. Community Studies 131. *Community Organizing: Theory and Practice* course taught by Mike Rotkin. 1986. Courtesy Special Collections, University Library, University of California, Santa Cruz. UA 70: UCSC Ephemera Collection. ua070-0117.

Figure 3. Shakespeare Santa Cruz Program, 1985. "As You Like It," "Hamlet," "Rosencrantz and Guildenstern are Dead." Courtesy Special Collections, University Library, University of California, Santa Cruz. UA41: Shakespeare Santa Cruz records: Production files: ua_0041_gra_0005.

Figure 4. Shakespeare Santa Cruz. Summer 1997 season poster. Courtesy Special Collections, University Library, University of California, Santa Cruz. UA41 Shakespeare Santa Cruz records: Production files: ua_0041_gra_0022.

Figure 5. "Ms. Blue" Whale Skeleton at Night. Seymour Marine Discovery Center. October 15, 2015. Photo courtesy of Elizabeth Van Dyke.

Figure 6. This swell shark egg case, also known as a "Mermaid's Purse," contains a shark embryo. Seymour Marine Discovery Center, November 22, 2015. Photo courtesy of Elizabeth Van Dyke.

Figure 7. Predatory Bird Research Group report cover. Courtesy Special Collections, University Library, University of California, Santa Cruz. UA70: UCSC Ephemera Collection: ua070_0091.

Figure 8. Bobcat crossing the UCSC Bike Path. 2008. Photo by Lee Jaffe.

Figure 9. DNA Day, 2018 Photo by Carolyn Lagattuta. Campus Photo Archive. Communications and Marketing Department, UCSC. Copyright UC Regents.

Chapter 35

The Continuing Story of Protest at UCSC

I think that this is the beginning of a long struggle.

—Bettina Aptheker

"What, then do the protestors want?"

UCLA Newsroom: Colleges and universities across the U.S. experienced an increase in student activism over the past year [2016], as students protested rising college costs and hostile racial climates on their campuses. The survey of 141,189 full-time, first-year students from around the U.S. found that interest in political and civic engagement has reached the highest levels since the study began 50 years ago. Nearly 1 in 10 incoming first-year students expects to participate in student protests while in college.[1]

Time magazine: These figures were the highest the survey had recorded since it began in 1967—encompassing the eras of the military draft, the Kent State shootings, the anti-apartheid movement and the protests against the war in Iraq.

Yet for all its force, ubiquity and urgency—and for all the significance it could have in the coming years and decades—the year's groundswell has managed only to baffle the broader public. This year's campus protest, and the movement that has supported it, has no Bob Dylan as its bard, it has no Ramparts as its house organ. And, perhaps more crucially, no Vietnam War dividing the nation. The civil rights movement thriving now, Black Lives Matter, has galvanized supporters nationwide but has focused primarily on police homicides, which is to say that it does not immediately present itself as an issue in college life. What, then, do the protesters want?[2]

Jim Burns: The character of protest changed in the thirty years I was at UCSC, from being focused on a particular topic, like regents divesting from South African holdings, to being very unfocused at times. It almost seemed as if anything that an individual protestor wanted on the group's list of "demands" could be added. The campus could be given a list that included items that you would expect to be there, but the list would also include a lot of other demands that seemed completely unrelated to that particular protest.

Protesting the Regents' Visit Redux:
Students Occupy the Humanities Building (2006)

George Blumenthal: As luck would have it, that first year when I was acting chancellor, the regents had a visit scheduled in Santa Cruz. They visited three campuses a year. The main part of the meeting was going to be held at the brand-new, just-opened Humanities Lecture Hall. And then, we were going to have everyone come over to University Center and have a big dinner with members of the community. That was the theory.

Riseup.net: On Wednesday, October 18, 2006 hundreds of students and workers at UC Santa Cruz marched on a gathering of the UC Regents, using a variety of tactics to forestall, disrupt, and eventually lock-down a "public comment period," which they called a "farce." The action was an attempt to highlight the undemocratic, unaccountable, and illegitimate nature of the regents, asserting the need to democratize the UC system, while demanding that the university fix a score of core problems before considering expansion.[3]

George Blumenthal: Then we got word that there was going to be a big student demonstration with the regents on campus. The demonstration was going to start at the graduate plaza. So I decided to go over to the graduate plaza and talk to the students, thinking that maybe reasoning would help alleviate some of the stresses of that visit. I wasn't treated badly, but I was largely ignored.

Riseup.net: The action started with a rally at the Bay Tree Plaza, before marching up to the new Humanities Building at Cowell College. There, a community speak-out was held for a good period of time before more direct action was taken.[4]

George Blumenthal: Then I had to get over to the regents meeting at the Humanities Building. Well, sure enough, there was a big demonstration and a march over to the Humanities Building. And as part of the demonstration, a decision was made by the students to basically lock the regents in the building. They closed off the entrances and exits, so you couldn't get in or out of the Humanities Lecture Hall.

So, we held this meeting with the regents and some members of the community inside, and the demonstrators outside marching around the building shouting, but with the doors blockaded so that you couldn't open the doors. Associate Chancellor Ashish Sahni was outside the building. We were in communications with Ashish and the police who were outside. But there weren't anywhere near enough police to control the crowd.

Riseup.net: Then, what was supposed to only have been a thirty-minute "public comment period" turned into a three-hour standoff, as protesters, after a failed attempt to prevent the regents' entry to the building, eventually encircled the area, blocking all five exits. As protest tactics escalated and the police became increasingly angry and frustrated with their inability to control some of the protesters, they targeted three activists, took them to the ground, and dragged them inside the building.[5]

George Blumenthal: At a certain point, some of the police who were inside the building tried to go out to clear the entrances. There was a big melee and at the end of that melee, they retreated back in the building, having used their mace. And they brought with them one of the students who

Figure 1

Angela Davis speaking in support of
Alette, a UCSC student suspended
for three years for protesting a visit
to the Santa Cruz campus by the
UC Regents on October 18, 2006

Photo by Wes Modes, 2006

had, they said, attacked a police officer and bitten the police officer. She was screaming. So now we had all the regents in there, plus this screaming student.

Rise-up.net: As students struggled to prevent the abduction of their friends, they were met with a barrage of batons and pepper-spray sent forth from the retreating officers. With the police inside and all doors closed, the stunned crowd sat dazed while a few students assisted those who were hit by the cops and their pepper-spray.[6]

George Blumenthal: Some of the regents, particularly one of them, Judy Hopkinson, really wanted to go outside to meet with the students. Ashish and I had a bunch of backs and forths about that. Finally, he agreed that if they would guarantee that she would be treated safely and allowed back into the building when she was done talking to them, then we could make it happen. They refused. So, I was put in the position of having to tell Judy that she couldn't go outside to meet with the students, that they wouldn't agree to the conditions that we had set for that to happen. We couldn't leave until they brought in some extra police, I think from the city or wherever, to help clear the exits so that we could safely get people out.

Riseup.net: While thirty recently-arrived riot-cops geared up in a nearby parking lot, the community got together to talk about how to get out of this situation. After a long period of negotiations involving students, workers, faculty members and the administration, a deal was finally made.[7]

George Blumenthal: The last thing I wanted was for somebody to get hurt. A couple of the community members tried to leave. One of them

got spit on, and another one got pushed, kind of assaulted as he left. It was a very, very bad situation and we were in there for many hours. And here I am—I'm the brand-new chancellor.

Riseup.net: First, a student and a faculty member would be allowed into the building to ensure that the three students detained inside were okay. Then, the students, who had agreed to the deal by a group consensus process, were to not cross a specific line and allow all the regents and police to go out a back door into their university-supplied buses. Finally, the three detained students would be cited and then they, and the two sent in to check on them, would be released.[8]

George Blumenthal: They had many agendas. The regents are just so good a target. So, it was one of these lists, an all-encompassing list. I don't think students have ever learned that if they had one thing, they might actually have a shot. But once you put together a whole list, because every student group wants to have their key issue on the list, no one takes that seriously.

So, we finally got out of there, went to the dinner. I remember my shirt was soaking wet, because I was so nervous. How had I represented the campus in a situation like this? It was so embarrassing. And there were, for this visit, I think five or six of the appointed regents, plus the alumni. I did give my remarks. People were very nice and relaxed. I was surprised at how little fallout there was. It ended up being not as big a deal as it looked like at first. But certainly, it was not my choice for how to begin. By the way, that visit was the last regents visit ever done to any campus. Where they would do these three times a year, they just stopped doing them after Santa Cruz. I guess having done us, there was no need to ever do any more.

The Biomedical Building and the Tree-Sit (2007-2008)

George Blumenthal: We had rapidly growing work in biomedical sciences, in genomics and stem cell research. This was a flourishing area of the campus, from a research point of view. We were getting lots of money. And in addition, we had an extremely popular health sciences major for students wanting to go into medicine, dentistry, veterinary medicine. It was a major that required students to take Medical Spanish as a part of their curriculum and to do an internship in an underserved community around the Santa Cruz area. It was overwhelmingly popular with students and we couldn't expand it because we didn't have the lab space to be able to offer that major to as many students as wanted it. So, there was no question that the Biomedical Building was a building whose time had come for the campus.

But then, we had the tree-sit. The tree-sit was completely unexpected. We had no advance warning. Basically, a bunch of tree-sitters showed up on campus [to protest the planned cutting down of redwood trees on the building site]. They started to climb the trees. This happened, I think, at night. Somebody called the police, so the campus police came. And there were far more demonstrators there than there were police. So, they called for help. I think there were safety issues for the police. I heard about a police officer that was wrapped up in some mesh and was momentarily at risk of injury.

So, they called for police backup, brought in backup from the city and county police.

Jim Burns: That first day, the campus strategy seemed to be to surround the trees, in an effort to keep others from joining the people who had already scaled them. So, we had our own police attempt to do that. I also think we brought in

police assistance from elsewhere in the Santa Cruz community, and we put temporary plastic fencing around the trees, with the idea that we would be able to isolate the people in the trees, which would help us get them out and end the protest.

George Blumenthal: And that was problematic because city and county—well, the city's pretty good, but the county police had not been trained to work on a university campus. I know one person described to me the Robocop that showed up dressed for combat in Vietnam, just about, as a result. Of course, that didn't go over very well in the campus community. On the other hand, I think police safety is important, and it's important that police be able to call for backup. But the bottom line is, it was a mess the day they showed up. We had officers in trouble. They had to call for support. It was bad.

Jim Burns: Well, it was a good-faith attempt at responding to a kind of protest that I don't believe we had anticipated. The people who were supportive of the tree-sitters tried very hard to break through the police lines; a scuffle with police ensued, and the result was nothing short of mayhem. The protestors would probably say that the police were overzealous in their efforts to secure the site that day. The police would probably say that they were just trying to do a job, and that the protestors had initiated the violence. I was on site, and at least from my perspective, the police were in a pretty tough spot. They tried to resist the protestors' attempts to break through the barriers. Suffice it to say, some really horrific video footage of the protest aired on TV throughout the Monterey Bay and San Francisco Bay regions,

Figure 2

November 8, 2007 cover of *City on a Hill Press*, Tree-sitters protest construction of Biomedical Building

creating even more interest in the protest than it might have otherwise had.

There was a point of real combustion when the protestors tried to get past a police line in order to get food and supplies to the people up in the trees. The protestors pushed; the police officers defended themselves and tried to protect the line they had established. Before I knew it, there were TV cameras swarming all over the site, prompting me to organize and give an unscheduled press briefing on the site, with six or seven TV cameras pointing at me and a very tense protest occurring nearby. I tried to explain what the university was planning to build on the site, why it mattered, and why the protest had become physical. Obviously, most of the questions that day focused on the campus's decision to have police involved, and how successful or unsuccessful that had been. Little did I or anyone else know at the time that the tree-sit, the occupation of those trees, would receive fairly constant publicity for the next thirteen months.

Stop UCSC Expansion: Every morning, current and former UCSC students and caring community members awake to watch the sunrise from sturdy wooden platforms secured sixty feet up Coast Redwood trees on Science Hill. The trees were slated to be the first destroyed as part of the University's plans to decimate 120 acres of forest, but the presence of these tree-sitters has brought those plans to a halt.[9]

David Kliger: It was never clear what the protest was about. There were a group of students who wanted to stop the Biomedical Building because they were against animal research; there was another group that wanted to stop the Long Range Development Plan. There were probably a dozen different reasons, and when you talked to the students, nobody wanted to take responsibility for the group as a whole. It was very difficult

to sit down and come to a resolution. If you don't know what the group wants, it's hard to respond.

Stop UCSC Expansion: This summer, the city council and the county of Santa Cruz settled their lawsuit with the University over the issues of water, traffic and housing. The settlement shows where the University's priorities are. After a long history of attention to undergraduate education, UCSC is shifting its focus to more lucrative graduate studies particularly in the area of biomedicine and engineering, departments that private companies are anxious to fund and control. Opportunities for undergraduate research are quickly vanishing.[10]

City on a Hill Press: Not all of the protesters see the issue through green-tinted glasses. College Nine fourth-year Brenda, who did not want to give her last name, sees it with the critical mindset of a tuition-paying student trying to get her money's worth from the UC system. "I'm worried about the students more than the trees. I love the trees, but I'm worried about compromising the education here," Brenda said. "The class sizes will get bigger, and the buses are already so busy. And it's only going to get worse. I'm worried that the education will go down because they passed this plan."[11]

George Blumenthal: The trees in question were on the construction site, which is on Science Hill. The trees were redwood trees. And the tree-sitters, who turned out not to be students, but rather professional tree-sitters, set up what I could only call an extensive network of ropes amongst the trees. So, they nestled up there at sixty feet. They had a network of ropes that allowed them to travel between trees. They had ropes that allowed them to communicate things to the ground. They had ropes to climb up and down the trees. No individual stayed up there for the whole time, so they constantly relieved their ranks.

Stop UCSC Expansion: Three clusters of redwoods have been inhabited since November 7, 2007, when over 500 students, alumni, and community members rallied in opposition to the University's plans. Other tree-sits have been added, using the same technique of carefully securing pre-built platforms to several redwoods without harming the trees. Tree-sitters continued their vigil through police attacks, winter storms with [strong] winds and the long days of summer.[12]

George Blumenthal: That tree-sit ultimately went on for a year. There were only a couple of dozen redwoods there. The great irony is, there weren't that many trees. A couple dozen redwoods. And the other irony is that we would have happily replanted anything. These weren't even original redwoods. The campus site was essentially clear-cut after the San Francisco Earthquake to get the wood to rebuild San Francisco, so there's essentially no first-generation trees on the campus. And if there are, there're only a few of them up in the north campus. We don't have the original redwood forest anymore. All of the trees at Santa Cruz are about 100, 110 years old. That's why they're all mostly the same size.

David Kliger: We did not stop [the tree-sit], because we were not in the position to start the building. I didn't want to be in the position where we did something major, got these people out of the trees, and then could not start building anyway.

George Blumenthal: You need a take permit from Cal Fire, California Forestry to cut down the redwood trees. We didn't have the take permit. I had

a million people that kept saying to me, "Here's a mechanism. Put up fences so they can't be resupplied. Starve them out. Do this or do that." Lots of people had lots of good ideas, which were more difficult to do than people thought might be possible. But even if they were possible, it seemed to me pointless. Even if we got everybody out of the trees, if we didn't have the take permit, then we'd have to leave the trees there and they might come back. If they were smart, they'd figure out when we got the take permit and then come back.

So, it just seemed to me, the right thing to do was to leave them in the trees, which was no small matter. I remember there was a senate meeting where some of the faculty more supportive of the tree-sitters were arguing that we should not have called out the police the first day, and that we should be more supportive of these people who are saving these trees, and our students. Of course, these weren't our students. So far as I'm aware throughout the entire year of the tree-sit, I think there was only one UCSC student who joined the tree-sitters in the trees. So, it was hardly a student movement, at least in terms of them doing it, although there were students supporting them. There was strong student support for them.

David Kliger: A lot of the faculty on Science Hill were very upset that we let this go on too long. Faculty on other parts of the campus were upset because we were being mean to these people. Everybody was upset about one thing or another.

George Blumenthal: There was a senate meeting where there was a lot of anger at the administration for not being more supportive of the tree-sitters. Then somebody in chemistry got up and said, "Those tree-sitters are right next to my lab and my office, and they're throwing feces at the window of my office. I don't think that that's something I can, or the senate should be supportive of."

And the person said that they resented the fact that their colleagues would support that kind of action. It really changed the conversation.

One of the awkward issues was how are the tree-sitters supplied and replaced. And oh, man, we went through a lot of issues there. They certainly were supplied by mostly students. They had places on campus where they could rest between their shifts. I kind of knew where that was. But we never caught anyone in the act, so we couldn't do anything. We didn't exercise search warrants, or anything like that to force the issue.

On the other hand, it was awkward having them there. It was very distracting for people on Science Hill. And when we held events nearby, for example in Engineering, the tree-sitters would be screaming at us as we held graduation. So, this was not a pleasant experience to have, and yet we kind of reached a point of equilibrium with them. Life went on with the tree-sitters there.

David Kliger: There was a filmmaker from Europe who wanted to film these people. So, they had gone up in one of the trees, even though there were signs posted everywhere that this was illegal, no trespassing and that sort of thing.

George Blumenthal: The filmmaker had climbed up into one of the trees to interview one of the tree-sitters. Dave Kliger encountered him when he came down. The guy was explaining to Dave what he had been doing. Then he realized he'd forgotten his film in the tree. So, he asked Dave for permission to go back up in the tree.

David Kliger: We assured them that we were not going to arrest them if they went and did this, but we were not going to sanction this either.

George Blumenthal: They did an extensive interview with one of the tree-sitters, who went by the name Owl. When the video came out, I looked at the video on the web with great anticipation of what wonderful insights I might learn. I learned a little bit about professional tree-sitting. Owl was happy to demonstrate how he moved between trees. And they had absolutely brand-new, state-of-the-art equipment. It was quite impressive. It takes a certain amount of bravery to sleep in a tree. And expertise, because you really, really don't want to fall out.

But when it came to the philosophy of the tree-sit, I kind of watched that in wonderment. My reaction when I was done watching the interview was that he and I live in a different universe. I couldn't even begin to understand what the hell he was all about.

Jim Burns: Occasionally there were individuals apprehended at the site. Maybe it was a single protestor who would come down from the tree after his or her shift ended. I also remember that there was a faculty member who was approached by police because he was out there providing food that could be sent up the trees to the protestors.

George Blumenthal: One day I get a call from the chief of police. He was really upset because they had just arrested a faculty member who was supplying food to the tree-sitters. He said, "We have him down at the station. We're not sure what to do with him." I said, "Well, what's the big deal?" He said, "This is a faculty member." I said, "So, what's the big deal? How would you treat him if it was a student, or if you didn't even know who it was?" He said, "Well, we'd arrest them and book them." I said, "So? Why would you treat him differently?" We had put a "No Trespassing" sign up. And since the tree-sit was itself illegal, it was aiding and abetting an illegal activity. My attitude was it didn't matter if it was a faculty member.

Jim Burns: I think it would be fair to say that that particular protest created a lot of stress for the faculty, staff, and students who, because of their work or studies, needed to spend a lot of time in that area of Science Hill. And it also created a lot of understandable stress within the senior administration about the best way of coping with or ending the protest.

George Blumenthal: It was clear that this couldn't go on forever. We needed to develop a plan. We decided to look at UC Berkeley and see what they were going to do. They had tree-sitters too, protesting an expansion of Memorial Stadium. Berkeley had developed a plan which was absolutely insane. Their plan was to bring in some guy who hires himself out to crawl up trees, grab protestors, and bring them down. I swear to you, I'm not making this up. They were going to hire this guy to go clear out their tree-sitters.

Meanwhile, back at the ranch, we have a company that trims trees on the campus. Somebody did a raid on their Watsonville yard and damaged several of their trucks. They were furious, so they decided to work with us. They developed a plan which made a lot more sense to me, of getting tree-sitters down by going up to a tree and building a scaffolding up the tree, sort of a round scaffolding up around the tree. And then when you get up high enough, to have one of the tree people go up with a sheriff or a police officer to arrest whomever's in the tree and bring them down. So that was our plan. We decided to be nice. We shared the plan with Berkeley and we told them that we thought their plan was wacko. Berkeley adopted our plan, and even hired the tree company that we were using to enact their

plan. Eventually Berkeley did bring down their tree-sitters using that approach.

But I didn't want to do anything until we had a tree-take permit from California Forestry. When we knew it was about to come through, the question was how to proceed.

Jim Burns: In the end, the tree-sit reached its conclusion very quietly in the early morning hours of a December day in 2008—again, a long thirteen months after it started.

George Blumenthal: I had not been interested in mediation or discussions with the tree-sitters. From everything I'd heard, there was no reasonable thing that we could do that would end that tree-sit, other than agree not to build Biomed, and that was nonnegotiable. But we made a deal with the tree-sitters that we would enter into mediation. They would have their agents, and we would bring in a formal mediator and see if we could get to a solution. We both agreed that if we broke off negotiations, the university would not clear out the tree-sitters within the first twenty-four hours.

I'm going to just admit to you up front, I agreed to all of this because of the twenty-four-hour rule. I wanted to give them notice of twenty-four hours, without giving them notice of twenty-four hours. But who knows? Maybe the mediation would work.

So we brought in these mediators. They went and talked to the tree-sitters. And then they came and talked to me. It was almost hilarious to talk to them because they came to meet me in my office. I said, "All right, so you've talked to the tree-sitters. What do they want?" They said, "We don't want to tell you." I said, "What do you mean, you don't want to tell me? We're supposed to be mediating this." They said, "No, we don't want to tell you because you're going to laugh us out of the office."

Basically it was the kitchen sink. It was the kitchen sink of radical causes. Everything under the sun. There was nothing there you could grab onto and say, well we could do this little piece.

So we waited until we had the permit firmly in hand and then we announced that mediation was going nowhere, and therefore we were ending the conversation. And we made up this plan where the police would come in.

Carolyn Martin Shaw: The university called in police from everywhere. When I'm going into College Nine, I park by the fire station. All the police were there. I had no idea what was going on. My brother had been killed by a policeman. I saw all those police cars: Berkeley was there; Scotts Valley was there; Santa Cruz was there. I walk in, and I asked Shelly Errington, "What's going on?" And she showed me a cartoon. It's a cartoon from the civil rights movement, and it's one of the girls going into an elementary school, a black girl, with all these buses and guns and people. And Shelly says, "There's some kid up a tree—and this is what they do: they bring in all this ammunition for it." I felt the university was hunkering down, was getting into a kind of bunker-like mentality. They wanted to fight the students, no matter what.

Dave Kliger: It came down to the wire, where we were going to have to arrest them. We had a large contingent of police that were prepared to do this.

Jim Burns: After an incredible amount of logistical and law-enforcement planning, and a lot of communications planning, the tree-sit was about to be over. With everything in place, the campus quickly erected fences to keep other protestors out and climbed the trees to bring the tree-sitters down.

Dave Kliger It turned out that the night before we were going to go in, they got the word, and even though they said that they wanted a confrontation, they were almost all gone by the time people got there. There was one person who clearly didn't get the message, and he was arrested.

George Blumenthal: He was scared to death because he didn't really know what he was in for. He had not climbed one of the main trees with the main infrastructure for keeping him there. He was terrified all night that he'd fall out of the tree. So in a way, he almost welcomed us when we came to get him out. He was not a professional tree-sitter. And so we got him out.

Jim Burns: By that time, I think there was one lonely protestor left in the trees, and he came down without incident. It was someone we were familiar with, but not someone with a campus affiliation.

David Kliger: But everybody else was gone, and as soon as we went in there and saw that they were gone, then the clearing started, so they wouldn't go back up in the trees after the police left.

George Blumenthal: And then literally it took them an hour to cut down every single tree and reduce it to pulp. So that was it. The tree-sit was over. We now had the money. We could move forward to building Biomed. It turned out to be a great building. Wonderful work takes place there. It's been a huge boon to the campus.

Frank Zwart: We were able to start construction on the Biomedical Building. It's transformed the face of the campus.

Figure 2

Sign warning pedestrians about tree-sitters above them, 2007

Photo by Alex Nelson

Jim Burns: The longest protest in campus history concluded very quietly, and I think everyone breathed a real sigh of relief that we didn't have to arrest a large number of people, or re-create the conflict that had defined the first day of that particular protest, thirteen long months earlier.

Carolyn Martin Shaw: There are ways to think about how do you lessen the impact of the tree-sit without having the police come. I presented a resolution in the Academic Senate to say we should censure the administration. I have to tell you: to prepare for this, I went to yoga meditation class the night before. I had my little mantra I was going to say in the back of my mind. I had several people speak in favor of the resolution that I'd presented—Don Rothman, I remember, especially, and Shelly Errington, and I think Loisa Nygaard did.

But about thirty scientists got up, and they were so emotional, so upset. I'm glad I had done my meditation before I went, because I would have had a hard time getting through that. They were talking about how horrible this tree-sit was, and how they had been mistreated because of people sitting in the trees. I had a little PowerPoint presentation where I tried to separate out the issues and say, "The tree-sit is over here, and these are the issues I'm trying to talk about over there," but they just couldn't hear it.

I was trying to say, "How do we handle demonstrations on this campus? When is it that we want to call in the police? Why do we call in the police so frequently on this campus?" But it wasn't heard. The head of the student union was there, and he must have been very moved by what happened, because at the next senate meeting when he spoke, he called on the faculty members to be less emotional, and to listen to issues better.

I was profoundly disappointed in the university. I don't know. What is it that I expect? I expect there are some free-speech issues that are involved: that the university will get used to student demonstrations (it's not like they're new!), that they will have a reasonable response to them. I don't expect that students will be able to do everything they want, and disrupt things at all times. But I also don't expect that there will be policemen brought onto campus any time something goes wrong.

Protesting a 32 Percent Tuition Increase:
Students Occupy Kerr Hall, November 2009

SFGate: Students across the UC system mounted protests and occupied buildings in response to the 32 percent tuition increase approved by university regents on Thursday. Students enraged with the decision said the university system is turning its back on underprivileged students in a move that will tear at campus diversity.

UC President Mark Yudof recommended the increase to close a $535 million budget gap that has forced the system to lay off 2,000 workers, impose faculty furloughs and reduce class offerings. The tuition increase, the eighth since 2002, will bring the annual cost for classes over $10,000 for the first time.[13]

Jim Burns: On our campus, the fee protests morphed into building occupations. Many protests over the years had taken place inside campus buildings. But these "occupations" were branded differently by the protestors, and it seemed like the idea was to completely take over and shut down the building.

George Blumenthal: You can imagine how the students felt about that tuition increase. It came to the regents at a regents' meeting at UCLA. I was at the regents' meeting, and while I was at the meeting, that's when the Kerr Hall occupation happened.

IndyBay: On Wednesday, November 18th, 2009, over five hundred students gathered at the Quarry Plaza and marched to the base of campus. After holding a general assembly at the base of campus, the students decided to trek back up to campus and occupy a space. At 3:45pm students occupied the Kresge Town Hall. The students stayed the night and planned for a general assembly the next day.[14]

Jim Burns: And then on a Thursday in November, Kerr Hall was occupied by students and others for a protest that didn't end until the following Sunday. There are always side issues that come up in these protests—the growth of the university; class size—but what was driving this particular one was the cost of education, and quite understandably, the impact that was having on students and the impact that was having on access.

Samantha Caballero: People are taking on tremendous amounts of debt. Almost everybody I know is in at least like ten thousand dollars' worth of debt. That means that pretty much everybody I know that is going to college is starting their adult lives in the hole.

City on a Hill Press: UCSC Radical Student Union hosted a rally in front of occupied Kerr Hall Thursday night. Nearly 200 people showed up, including news stations and UCSC classes. At the rally, speakers addressed the fiscal state of the UC and the importance of action. "Students have an extremely strong moral position right now; most sane people know that what is happening is wrong," said [a student named] Jacobson.[15]

George Blumenthal: Demonstrators came in screaming and yelling and beating sticks on walls. I think some of them were masked. They made a lot of noise, and they scared a lot of people in the building who didn't know what was happening. A lot of staff locked their doors, so they were locked in their offices, or in their spaces. The students

Figure 3

Sign from occupation of Kerr Hall, 2009.

Photo by Wes Modes

quickly took over the building and decided not to let people leave.

David Kliger: A large number of students rushed into the building, really traumatized a lot of the staff there.

IndyBay: [The students occupying Kerr Hall] created a list of demands and around 5:00 p.m. provided the demands to the Executive Vice-Chancellor David S. Kliger.

City on a Hill Press: After the list was dictated to Kliger, he shook the hand of the student who read the list aloud. "Kliger took it gracefully. He listened to every demand," said Matthew Palm, who worked as a moderator between occupiers and administrators. Items on their list of demands were voted on using a democratic process; each student raised a hand for the ideas they supported. "We actually know what democracy looks like," said an individual who spoke at the Kresge Town Hall occupation, which happened moments before the Kerr Hall occupation took place.[16]

George Blumenthal: I believe Dave was a hero. Dave talked to the students, negotiated with the students, and basically told them that it was unacceptable for them to not let people leave the building—that that raised this issue to a completely different level. That's false imprisonment. That's a crime; that's a felony. He persuaded them to let people leave. Some people did leave—and just like a captain leaving a sinking ship—I think Dave was the last person to leave Kerr Hall.

San Jose Mercury News: The campus has closed Kerr Hall due to safety concerns, and students are also occupying Kresge Town Hall. Students reportedly stayed overnight in both locations. No arrests have been reported, though administrators are now considering other punishment.[17]

George Blumenthal: When I came back from the regents' meeting at UCLA, we were in standoff mode. Kerr Hall was occupied. The doors were barricaded. We had a little idea of what was going on inside the building at first, because there are cameras around. Eventually the students got wise and started taping over the cameras. So there was an interesting technological standoff. The students posted blogs about what they were doing, taking over the building—so we cut off internet to the building. They found that there was one internet connection that didn't get cut off, and so they used that. It was an interesting point-counterpoint over the next few days as we matched technological wits with the students. To some extent, they won those battles. The occupation lasted several days. We attempted to negotiate with them, but frankly got nowhere in terms of their non-negotiable lists of demands.

Jim Burns: Whatever one thinks about how the protests against tuition hikes played out, I think people could understand why people were concerned about the increases and about what was becoming of a system of public higher education that was designed to be affordable and accessible.

Carl Eadler, Student: It's daunting looking at how much people have to pay back, especially with the average income for a job for a college graduate straight out of school.

George Blumenthal: We all met for several days down at the base of campus, in our emergency operations room; that became the headquarters of the campus. Our police chief was a very competent guy. So we made plans. As the negotiations basically went nowhere, we got increasingly concerned. We knew there was damage in the building, and that it was only going to get worse. There was a safety issue because they had blocked the entrances. So it wasn't just a question of just waiting them out. We felt it was dangerous.

Jim Burns: By that Sunday, it would be fair to say that patience was wearing a little thin with administrators. There was a sense within the administration that it would be important to have the building open for business again early in the following week.

George Blumenthal: I made the decision that we were going to have to go in there and clear the building. We made sure we had enough police to do that. We brought a bunch of police to campus. We brought a bunch of paddy wagons. It was a clear signal to the students that the end is near.

David Kliger: We made it clear that they were going to have to leave. We also made it clear to them that there was an exit and they could exit the building and not be arrested. Or they could stay in the building and they would be arrested.

George Blumenthal: Crowds gathered around Kerr Hall. People were straining to see what was about to happen.

Jim Burns: When the police showed up, they told the protestors they were about to be arrested and the seventy people who were in the building voluntarily left. It ended pretty darn quickly.

Bettina Aptheker: I co-led the Free Speech Movement [at UC Berkeley] in the mid-sixties. The similarity was that we had also taken over

an administration building. But in our case, there were over a thousand students and they actually proceeded with arrests. So 815 students were arrested at that time.

I'm very grateful that this morning we were able to work out a situation where the students left of their own accord and were not arrested. I think they did beautifully. They exemplified nonviolent passive resistance and made a very important point. I also want to say that I am very grateful to Dave Kliger, the provost here. I was on the phone with him, back and forth, and he was on the phone with the police commander. I think through our mutual efforts in those critical moments we were able to avoid what could have been a very unfortunate situation.[18]

David Kliger: They were actually filmed as they were leaving, so we could identify who was there, but they left the building and nobody was arrested.

City on a Hill Press: The sixty-six hour occupation of Kerr Hall came to a peaceful end early Sunday morning at 8:00 a.m. The seventy students inside the building chanted "Solidarity forever, education makes us strong," while sitting in the lobby, with their view obstructed by the refrigerator they had used to barricade the door. With batons and a dog unit on scene, police pushed back the main crowd outside.

"A mass student movement still needs to be built," said Chris Connery, a literature professor. "We are still at the early stages of that."

Students and administrators negotiated until late last night, discussing seven finalized demands pitched by the organizers. Present in the negotiations were four students, two faculty members and approximately two administrators.

The demands included amnesty for those arrested at previous protests, a commitment to keep resource centers like Engaging Eduacation and the Women's Resource Center open, and a cap on the rent at Family Student Housing to keep it affordable. None of the demands were met, but the final demand to guarantee funding for "graduate students who have lost TA-ships and undergraduates who have lost work-study positions" was considered.

"The fight for public education, that can be our generation's battle," said Steve Hoffman. "I'm proud to be among those fighting for public education."[19]

SFGate: Dozens of student protesters who took over a UC Santa Cruz administrative building after a systemwide tuition increase were removed Sunday morning when police officers in riot gear ordered them to exit the building or face arrest. No arrests were made, and university officials said the operation concluded peacefully. But videos provided by some of the 70 or so protesters show a tense scene, with officers pushing their way through a wall of students chanting "We are peaceful, what about you?" to reach the entrance of Kerr Hall.[20]

George Blumenthal: Then we came in, and we were horrified. The students had said, "Oh, let us clean up. Give us some mops and soap, and we'll clean up after ourselves." But, the issues weren't mop-and-soap; the issues were damage.

David Kliger: They really trashed the place.

Jim Burns: A lot of senseless destruction occurred within the building. Most of it occurred in the conference room that was a meeting hub for the Chancellor's Office. That room was the audiovisual hub for the building. The system's wires were ripped out of the walls.

George Blumenthal: The furniture was on its side; all the wires had been pulled out of everything. "Spaghetti" is the only word I can use to describe it. It was awful. This wasn't mops and brushes. Somebody had pried open the elevators, so they weren't operational. All around the building there were things that were destroyed. They'd broken the locks of the security doors. The graduate division had been broken into. There were staff offices, particularly on the third and fourth floor, where locks were broken. One staff member had the pictures of her children defaced. Another staff member told me that she had brought some presents, some candy, for her children, and she left in such a hurry, she left the wrapped packages on her desk, and they were torn apart and eaten. What I heard about was how they felt: the fear from the yelling; the terror of having screaming people running down the halls and not knowing what it means.

Jim Burns: The destruction of university property seemed unnecessary at best, especially for a protest that was about how much it was costing for students to go to school there and about the university's budget priorities.

George Blumenthal: The costs of the repairs of the building were extensive, in the hundreds of thousands of dollars. That doesn't even include the cost of the police—because we have to pay for those police—as well as the cost of lost operations, etcetera, etcetera. The cost was well over a million dollars, in terms of the cost to the campus ultimately.

David Kliger: One of the things that I did was call in several leaders of the faculty immediately when we had access to the building, and I said, "I want you to tour the building with me." They saw the destruction that had taken place and they were appalled.

George Blumenthal: Not long thereafter was our first senate meeting after the occupation. That senate meeting had a lot of harsh criticism of our response to the Kerr Hall takeover. I remember one faculty member getting up and saying—this is almost a direct quote—the staff of the university should not be afraid of our own students. I remember standing there while this person went on about that, knowing that I couldn't respond to it. But I was so pleased when a couple of faculty members responded, who basically said they had been at a meeting in the building, in the senate office, when the occupation happened, and they were terrified by what was happening. And so, they could certainly understand how staff would feel that way, because that was their reaction. I thought that was so effective to hear that from other faculty members.

David Kliger: It's another thing that the faculty never really realized, that there are staff who are still traumatized. After the whole thing was over, we brought in a psychologist to talk to the staff to try to get resolution for them.

George Blumenthal: Some faculty believed we should have negotiated this, and given into the protestors' demands. I don't remember what their demands were. I simply have had so many demands from so many students over the years, I don't remember them. It is rare that I get a set of demands where seriously we could do something, that's even can-do.

Jim Burns: With the Kerr occupation, there was a very long list of demands, including rolling back tuition to levels that had occurred ten or fifteen years earlier, something that obviously, the campus administration, even if it wanted to do, couldn't do.

David Kliger: For most of the students, there were no consequences. That's partly because we did not do a good job in identifying exactly who was there at different times. But there were consequences for a number of students, where we not only could clearly show that they were involved in some of the destruction, but that they also had been involved in some earlier protests where there had been destruction, so we could show a pattern. But for most of the students not much happened to them.

George Blumenthal: I decided that it was appropriate to bring disciplinary proceedings against those students who had occupied the building, and to demand that those students partially compensate the university for the damage that they had done. The nature of the violation that they had committed was such that the student code of conduct didn't guarantee them a full hearing as a result of what they did. We weren't expelling them. We were simply demanding that they repay the university something of the order of a thousand dollars each, which, of course, they didn't want to do. A lot of faculty took up the cry that this was an inhibition of free speech, to threaten students with a bill which might force them to leave school if they couldn't pay for the bill.

American Civil Liberties Union: The ACLU of Northern California sent a letter today to the Chancellor and Chair of the Academic Senate at UC Santa Cruz, criticizing the University's use of restitution as a penalty for students alleged to have participated in protests in November 2009.[21]

George Blumenthal: But it seemed to me that if we were really going to charge them a thousand dollars in compensation, that's serious enough that they should have a full hearing. I used my chancelloral discretion to put that into place.

David Kliger: But later, after the whole thing was over, some of those same faculty who I had taken to see the destruction in the building insisted that there was not a lot of damage, and we shouldn't make the students pay. They wanted no consequences.

George Blumenthal: Meanwhile, a group of members of the Academic Senate decided to call a special meeting of the senate in Kresge Town Hall. What a memorable meeting. This meeting didn't feel like a representative group of UC Santa Cruz faculty. It was those who had called the meeting and their friends, etcetera. There was probably a hundred people in the room. I was up there for somewhere between an hour and a half and two hours answering questions. I told myself near the beginning that under no circumstances was I to look at my watch. I had an event I was supposed to go to, but I was not going to look at my watch because that conveys a message. I cannot tell you how many times in that meeting I really had this urge to look at my watch, and I just wouldn't do it.

But that was a good thing to concentrate on, because the meeting made me progressively angrier and angrier. Some of the questions and comments were fair and good. But the discussion got progressively more aggressive, and progressively nastier. It was ramping up. Finally, a member of the faculty asked me a question about the fact that in a subsequent demonstration at Kerr Hall, after the occupation, that we had police presence at that demonstration, even though the demonstration was peaceful, and that

it was not only inappropriate, but almost Nazi-like in its character for us to have a "police state" that inhibits free speech of our students.

I got angry. I didn't blow up. I don't blow up publicly. But I remember vividly how I answered her. I reminded her that after we moved back into Kerr Hall, I had walked around the building and I had spoken with staff in every office. I described to her some of the reactions I'd heard from staff about their fear, some of the reactions they had when masked people occupied the building. I stopped and looked at her, and said, "How would you feel if somebody defaced the pictures of your children? I know how I would feel about that." I said, "You know, you can say that we're Nazis, or a police state, for having police there, but I, as a chancellor, have a responsibility to the staff members who work at Kerr Hall to provide them some level of security—particularly because of the time proximity to the occupation—to feel that they are protected, and that they are safe in their environment. Every staff member and every faculty member on this campus has an intrinsic right to feel safe in the workplace. If that means that I need to bring out police to monitor demonstrations at Kerr Hall, then by god, that's what I'm going to do. And if you feel otherwise, go ahead and say so, but I want you to explain your position to the staff who work in Kerr Hall."

American Civil Liberties Union: The ACLU letter cites due process concerns, criticizing the University for subjecting students to a $944 fine without a hearing and without proof of individual responsibility for claimed damage. The letter also criticizes the University's failure to provide students who are being granted a hearing for other forms of discipline with specific factual allegations of misconduct and a description of the evidence the University has of their alleged misconduct.[22]

Letter from a Group of UCSC Faculty to Chancellor Blumenthal: We write as faculty alarmed by the University's disciplinary actions regarding the November 19-22 activities in and around Kerr Hall, We worry that the implementation of the student judicial procedure in these cases violates constitutional due process and basic principles of fairness. These disciplinary actions also create a chilling effect on political dissent in the campus community.[23]

David Kliger: I was really disappointed in some of the faculty who, even when they saw the evidence directly, could not acknowledge that there should be consequences. My point to them is: this is an educational institution. What is it that you're trying to teach students, that you can be destructive and that there are no consequences to being destructive? Or do you want to teach them that you're responsible for your actions and when you do something wrong you have to pay a price for it?

Jim Burns: That particular protest did receive lots of coverage. I remember being in touch with the *New York Times* and other national media. But the coverage of the tuition increase was pretty diluted by other issues—in this case, the destruction of the building. In my mind, that was unfortunate, as the negative impact that increasing fees was having on the quality of and access to public higher education was a very legitimate issue to protest.

Bettina Aptheker: I think that this is the beginning of a long struggle, most of which will be based in Sacramento and with the regents. And it has to do with the terrible inequities and corruption in how the budget in California is decided. I think we have a long hard road ahead of us.[24]

Figure 5

Mural, College Nine and Ten

Photo by Irene Reti, 2017

Endnotes

1. UCLA Newsroom, "College students' commitment to activism, political and civic engagement reach all-time highs." Feburary 10, 2016. http://newsroom.ucla.edu/releases/college-students-commitment-to-activism-political-and-civic-engagement-reach-all-time-highs.

2. Jack Dickey, "The Revolution on America's Campuses," *Time* magazine, May 31, 2016.

3. Bradley, "Weeping Wednesday: A Protest Against the UC Regents," October 22, 2006. Santa Cruz Indymedia - Independent Media Center for the Monterey Bay. https://www.indybay.org/newsitems/2006/10/22/18322376.php?show_comments=1.

4. Bradley, "Weeping Wednesday..."

5. Bradley, "Weeping Wednesday..."

6. Bradley, "Weeping Wednesday..."

7. Bradley, "Weeping Wednesday..."

8. Bradley, "Weeping Wednesday..."

9. This excerpt is from the website for Stop UCSC Expansion, a local activist group (student and nonstudent) which organized against development at UCSC. See: https://stopucsc.wordpress.com/.

10. Stop UCSC Expansion.

11. Aliyah Kovner, "The First Anniversary of the Tree Sit," *City on a Hill Press*, November 13, 2008.

12. Stop UCSC Expansion.

13. Alejandro Martínez-Cabrera and Joe Garofoli, "UC Santa Cruz protest ends in tense scene," *SFGate.* November 23, 2009.

14. "UCSC expands occupations," November 19, 2009. Santa Cruz Indymedia - Independent Media Center for the Monterey Bay: https://www.indybay.org/newsitems/2009/11/19/18629337.php.

15. "Occupants Expand Movement," *City on a Hill Press*, November 20, 2009.

16. "Over 150 Students Occupy Kerr Hall," *City on a Hill Press*, November 19, 2009.

17. *San Jose Mercury News*, November 20, 2009.

18. "Bettina Aptheker's reaction to Kerr Hall occupation at UCSC": https://vimeo.com/7805368.

19. "Over 150 Students Occupy Kerr Hall," *City on a Hill Press*, November 19, 2009.

20. Alejandro Martínez-Cabrera and Joe Garofoli, "UC Santa Cruz protest ends in tense scene," *SFGate.* November 23, 2009.

21. ACLU Raises Constitutional Concerns Regarding UCSC Judicial Process, by Occupy CA." April 27, 2010. Santa Cruz County Santa Cruz Indymedia - Independent Media Center for the Monterey Bay. https://www.indybay.org/newsitems/2010/04/27/18645893.php?show_comments=1.

22. "ACLU Raises Constitutional Concerns Regarding UCSC Judicial Process, by Occupy CA." April 27, 2010. Santa Cruz County Santa Cruz Indymedia - Independent Media Center for the Monterey Bay. https://www.indybay.org/newsitems/2010/04/27/18645893.php?show_comments=1.

23. "Over 100 UCSC Faculty Sign Letter Protesting Campus Judiciary Process by Checking Education." April 22, 2010. https://www.indybay.org/newsitems/2010/04/22/18645395.php.

24. "Bettina Aptheker's reaction to Kerr Hall occupation at UCSC": https://vimeo.com/7805368.

Illustrations

Figure 1. Angela Davis speaking in support of Alette, a UCSC student suspended for three years for protesting a visit to the Santa Cruz campus by the UC Regents on October 18, 2006. Photo by Wes Modes, 2006.

Figure 2. Cover of *City on a Hill Press*, Tree-Sitters protest construction of Biomedical Building. November 8, 2007.

Figure 3. Sign warning pedestrians about the tree-sitters above them, 2007. Photo by Alex Nelson.

Figure 4. Sign from occupation of Kerr Hall, 2009. Photo courtesy of Wes Modes.

Figure 5. Mural at College Nine and College Ten. 2017. Photo by Irene Reti.

Chapter 36

What We Value Now

UCSC at Fifty

Who is this university made for?

—Manaiya Scott

The Colleges Still Exist: The Foundational Structure of UCSC

Campaign for UC Santa Cruz: All UC Santa Cruz students are part of both a prestigious university and a college—one of ten communities that provide an academic home, residential life, and social connection. The college structure is designed to combine the intimacy of a small, liberal arts college with the depth and rigor of a major research university.[1]

George Blumenthal: I knew we couldn't escape the historical background that we came from, or the historic changes. The issue of the colleges is a Santa Cruz issue which is been burned into the psyche of individuals with history on this campus, in both positive and negative ways. I have seen faculty who feel strongly about the colleges one way or the other. Some had bad experiences that they can't escape from and which will forever affect their views of the colleges at Santa Cruz. Some had wonderful experiences and long for the day when they could recreate those wonderful experiences. The colleges are one issue which I really

do believe is burned into people's psyches and difficult to escape. It's also burned into the psyches of our alumni, to varying degrees, depending upon when they graduated.

So, there's no question that the colleges were explosive. When I was inaugurated, I made some comments in my inauguration speech about the colleges. I think that was the highest applause line, by far. Of all the things I said—I said a million things—that was the one that generated the most response.

Samantha Caballero: People have pride in their college. People from Merrill are like, "Yeah, I'm a part of Merrill and we have MAC [Merrill Activities Council]. We have all of these things that make us Merrill. I'm a Merrillite and that is my identity." And Stevenson: "I'm a Stevensonian. And we have the Path to a Greener Stevenson. House 3 is where I threw up and that is my place. And I have all of these memories." And I guess in Kresge: "Kresge is my place and I'm a Kresgean.

This is where we do Pride. And this is where I constructed a really big dreamcatcher and hung it off of Building 3." People seem to build community and bonds based on what college community they're in.

Louis Odiase: When I was a student employee at OPERS, I came up with the idea of the Battle of the Colleges. It's a campus-wide event. At certain sports events throughout the year, fans can come to the event and can earn points for their college. You get one set of points for attendance, one set of points for how interactive and loud you are during the game, and then one set of points for a halftime contest. During the time outs, we'd go around, say like, "Okay, let's hear Cowell! Let's hear Oakes!"

Khalen Hudson: My first impression of College Nine was orientation. I was just like, these people here are hella crazy. When you move into College Nine, they have this big pride on making people feel welcome. They're also screaming at you. I guess that's their definition of feeling welcome. They're like, "Yeah! Hurrah! Welcome!" and all this stuff. It's nice, but it's also a little overwhelming. But it takes the edge away because they're being stupid, so things are less serious. My first impression was just like, I'm going to be here for four years. And I'm in the forest. I didn't really know what to think of it. It's just such a different place from home. But eventually this ended up becoming my home, too. The people that I met made the transition seem pretty seamless.

Tommy Herz: I'm at Cowell. Cowell has a rep for being more social. Partying, in a way. But definitely a social kind of vibe; everybody is very out-there. I think Cowell's the best college, but you could easily go up to someone at Porter and they will say Porter is the best one, or you can talk

to my friend Evan, and he'll say Oakes is the best one. But I'm happy with my choice.

Louis Odiase: I remember when I first seen Oakes on Destination Higher Education. I did not think I was going to live there. I seen Oakes, the actual wood buildings. And I was like whoa, that is not me. That is not me. I'd rather live in an actual concrete building because I don't know what's inside there, like are there lizards going all across, lizards running across the hallways? I do not want lizards waking up next to me.

Then, a friend told me actually Oakes was the most diverse. I thought oh, that definitely helps out a lot. I wanted to see people that were just like me, other minority students. Because the African American population on this campus, I think is around 2 to 3 percent, I'm most likely not going to see a lot of African American students around campus. So, I thought, why not be in a place where maybe more of them are and other minority students? And it was extremely diverse: African American, Hispanic, Asian, white; I even met a few Native Americans.

People were saying this campus is predominantly white, which it is. But when I finally seen that there was a place for minority students, I was like, that's beautiful. I've always loved Oakes because of that reason.

Oakes has its little family. We have our little small community. Because like a lot of people don't come to Oakes. It's on the outskirts of campus. So, if you do want to go to Oakes, you usually have a reason.

When I come to the outer campus, it's not like I have a problem. I make friends easily. I have no problem with any race. I make friends regardless. If you're a cool person, you're fine. But it's comforting to know there are people like you. And then when you come to the outer campus, it's fine

Figure 1

Reading on the Porter Wave (otherwise known as The Squiggle, and earlier in UCSC's history as the Flying IUD)

Photo by Carolyn Lagattuta, 2009. Sculpture by Kenny Farrell

because you know you have your community back at home.

Sofia Johnston: During my spring break in high school, we drove up here, visited the campus. We started in order. We saw Stevenson and Cowell. Then we went to Crown and Merrill. We drove by Nine and Ten; we didn't really look at those. We saw Kresge, Porter, walked down to Rachel Carson, and then Oakes. The more colleges we saw, the more I was warming up to Santa Cruz. Oakes just happened to be our last college. I really liked the architecture. A lot of people hate that about Oakes. They hate how it looks like a cabin in the woods with the wood shingles. But for some reason, I really liked that. We were walking through the apartment area and I saw students had put pictures in their windows. Some of them were popular memes at the time that I liked, or just pictures I recognized. So, I was like okay, this is cool. Oakes was my top choice. I've never regretted that decision at all. I've loved every second I've been at Oakes. It felt a lot like a family. Everyone was welcome there.

Samantha Caballero: There are people in Kresge that are really alternative and what you would call hippies. But generally, most people are pretty open minded. I mean, you do have to have occasional conversations with white people who walk around with dreads and talk to them about cultural appropriation. So, I'm not saying that it's a paradise of thought. But I think generally people who choose Kresge tend to be more open minded.

George Blumenthal: We have preserved a lot of the foundational structure of UCSC. The colleges still exist; it's a crucial part of the student experience. To the extent that the colleges have unique programs that they can offer, that means that they're contributing to the innovations of the

campus. I don't see that as inconsistent with our being a research university.

Michael Cowan: The coming of fraternities and sororities to the campus was seen as a betrayal of the college system. But you have to ask why the students decided that they wanted that as a point of interaction and identification. Were there things that the colleges weren't doing, or couldn't do, that were creating some gaps in what the students wanted? There were several task forces to consider that question: were the fraternities and sororities antithetical to the Santa Cruz system? Are they going to hurt the colleges? The fact is the fraternities and sororities emerged for a variety of reasons, one of which is that students off campus wanted to have convenient, congenial cadres with them. Also, the colleges weren't focused on upper-division students. The colleges, for all their great strengths, were not serving certain social and cultural needs.

George Blumenthal: When I became chancellor, one of my goals was to increase the roles of the colleges without impinging on the prerogatives of the departments, which sounds like a difficult challenge, and of course it is. I wanted to encourage the colleges to develop new ideas and think about new ways that they can contribute to students' success. In a way, I thought of it as let a thousand flowers bloom. We didn't have to have cookie cutter colleges. They didn't all have to be the same. I did think it was important that all the colleges had a core course because I think that's a feature of the UCSC experience, but beyond that there was a lot of freedom. I thought we should even be supportive financially if colleges had ideas that they wanted to pursue and provide support for doing that.

Victor Garcia-Zepeda: I took the Merrill core course. One of the books that resonated with me was *Dreaming in Cuban*. It was a story of a family immigrating to a new country. I felt connected to the generational gap and how, though they had come through a similar struggle, the daughter and the mother—how different their lives were.

Sareil Brookins: In Stevenson Core Course, we started reading Malcom X, Gloria Anzaldúa, Martin Luther King—all these writers of color. And I was like, wow, core is cool. I had the greatest instructor. But I was the only black student. My blackness was always questioned and asked about and looked at.

Sofia Johnston: I remember my first Oakes core class. Oakes' core theme is Communicating Diversity for a Just Society. The class is focused on people of color as a group that has been marginalized and systematically oppressed. It gave me a vocabulary to describe stuff I didn't know I had experienced. I remember that class being so eye-opening, and making me feel like yeah, Santa Cruz is awesome. And my first few weeks I found out who else was queer and who I could be friends with. I didn't have too many queer friends in high school.

Carol Freeman: The colleges offered a place where faculty would have colleagues and be connected to something in the university that was bigger than an isolated composition program. I worry now that not as many Writing Program people are being located, in meaningful ways, in the colleges, beyond the people who are the core course instructors, or the college writing coordinators.

George Blumenthal: When I became chancellor, I was aware that many faculty had not affiliated with colleges. Part of the problem was that the provosts didn't want us to be mandatory about this. They wanted to attract faculty, rather than be receivers of forced faculty commitments, which I can understand. I was unable to build an agreement that we could just put in place, a policy that we could just do. So, I backed off.

Helene Moglen: You've had the absolute abandonment of most colleges as significant academic entities. Cowell and Stevenson may remain presences to some extent. They may still have some faculty presence. Otherwise it seems to me, as I understand it, the colleges are without a faculty presence, and they are certainly without a curricular presence, except for the core courses, which are mostly not taught by regular faculty.

George Blumenthal: The provosts have put in a great deal of effort to recruit faculty to their colleges. They have receptions. They encourage new faculty to come. The amount of work that a faculty member needs to do in a college depends upon their level of commitment. Some colleges have explicit requirements. I don't know if they still do it, but in Cowell College, for example, the commitment that was expected of all faculty members was attending one College Night a month, which I thought was not unreasonable.

I think all faculty should be in colleges, period. The college faculty have a responsibility because the college faculty are actually a Faculty with a capital F, which has a very special meaning within the University of California. It means that they have a self-governance responsibility. The college Faculty with a capital F are essentially a committee of the Academic Senate. So, I think they have a responsibility to the academic mission of the college, and oversight of that mission. My sense is that some colleges exercise that very well and some don't.

Figure 2

Rachel Carson College at night

Photo by Chian Tu, 2011

Helene Moglen: The colleges have no authority, no status, few resources, and most of them no faculty! They simply provide office space. You go over to Kresge College. It is dead. That college that I enlivened, brought people over to—there isn't even a faculty services office, because there is nobody there to serve. It's all been moved to the Humanities Building and to the Social Sciences Buildings.

George Blumenthal: Part of me wanted to provide opportunity. Part of me wanted to do no harm and do nothing that would make it more difficult for the colleges to succeed. Some colleges ended up doing some very interesting things. College Eight (and this was still while they were Eight), put in place a three-quarter environmental course. They had faculty from all five academic divisions teaching in this three-quarter course about the environment. I don't think all three quarters were required of their students. They found a way to do something innovative.

The idea for naming [College Eight] Rachel Carson College I think originated with Ronnie Lipschutz, who was the provost. As soon as I heard about it, I thought it was a fantastic idea. I decided to do a scientific poll. So, I walked outside. I collared the first ten students that I could find and I asked each of them if they knew who Rachel Carson was. Nine of the ten did not.

Manaiya Scott: I read *Silent Spring*. I know where the name Rachel Carson College comes from. We finally have a college named after a woman. That's really cool.

George Blumenthal: We had a naming ceremony. It was the first naming in thirty years. It was one of my favorite events as chancellor, this naming event. It was meaningful to be able to name a college, and to name a college in a way that carried so much meaning. I'm very proud of it. When I go out on my road trip each year to speak to admitted students, I try to explain the colleges and give examples. The example I used this year is Rachel Carson College because I so love the name.

Rosie Cabrera: It saddens me to see where the colleges are at now. You've got to go through all gyrations to have a community meeting that's a facilitated dialogue. We don't have those anymore. We've lost something as a result of that. The role of the residential people is totally different. They're more disciplinarians and they're not programmers like we were.

Victor Garcia-Zepeda: There was this lunch that the undocumented students were invited to with all the provosts and some faculty. At the time, I didn't know Elizabeth Abrams, the provost for Merrill. I was sitting at the table with Faye Crosby, Cowell's provost. She seems very approachable. And then she introduced me to Elizabeth because she had asked me, "Oh, what college are you going to be at?" I told her, "Merrill." And she's like, "Oh, the Merrill provost is here." So, she introduced me to Elizabeth. I was very intimidated by Elizabeth, for some reason. I didn't really connect with her at that moment. I felt like okay, she gave me her business card and she said hi. All right. I don't think I'll ever talk to her. But now it's funny, because now I'm really close to Elizabeth. She's been a great mentor.

Murray Baumgarten: I think that we may be in a situation now where enough alumni have graduated, and are putting pressure on the university to revive the role of the colleges and to expand it in terms of academic matters, not just social and living arrangements. I welcome that. The future is hard to predict, full of surprises.

"When you say 'narrative evaluations,' what exactly do you mean?"

Academic Senate Executive Committee: In 2000, UCSC adopted a revised student evaluation system that added mandatory letter grades (previously optional) to the existing performance evaluation system. It has now been ten years since that modification. Across the divisions, conversations have been occurring that consider the size and scope of written performance evaluations. It is evident from these many discussions that there is much of value in this assessment method and that for some courses and instructors, written performance evaluations are closely integrated into the pedagogical framework. Campus-wide discussions also reveal that for some courses narrative evaluations do not add value to the learning experience nor help create a meaningful record of student performance. Support for, as well as opposition to, the current system is, at best, only loosely correlated with course size, or upper-division versus lower-division. The appropriate and meaningful use of narrative evaluations is contingent upon the degree to which the instructor incorporated the end-of-term assessment into the overall pedagogical approach. After carefully hearing the concerns of students, alumni, teaching faculty and staff, the Senate Executive Committee now puts forward a change to the regulations that makes undergraduate narrative evaluations instructor-optional.[2]

Jess Whatcott: The way it was communicated to me is that if a student wants a narrative evaluation, they have to request one. I haven't had a student request one from me.

Committee on Educational Policy: In 2010, the UCSC faculty voted to make narrative evaluations optional.[3]

Louis Odiase: When you say narrative evaluations, what exactly do you mean? I have not seen the narrative evaluations. I've not seen them. I've never actually heard of them. Maybe I haven't run into the right professor that's done it yet.

Sareil Brookins: How do you—yeah, they don't do that. How do I make sure they do that? Because I want narrative evaluations.

UCSC Academic Senate Regulations: Each instructor teaching a credit-granting course has the option to prepare a written evaluation for any student in the instructor's class. The narrative evaluation must evaluate the quality and characteristics of the student's performance in the class. A student may request the evaluation, but the faculty is not obligated to write them.[4]

Rosa Melero: I've never received a narrative evaluation. That would be helpful, but I've never received one. I think our classes just got way too big. Although some of them—twenty students doesn't seem like a lot. I feel like the professor could do it.

Sabina Wildman: I have never received in my time at UC Santa Cruz any kind of written grading thing—unfortunately—that would be great. I think that grades do not help learning, as much as knowing about what specifically that grade stands for. It's just a letter. How can that help anyone?

Khalen Hudson: I've never been evaluated. It's always the test.

Figure 3

Student with narrative
evaluations, 1970

Photo by UCSC Photography
Services

A Future in Online Education?

Murray Baumgarten: The course Peter Kenez and I taught on the Holocaust was UCSC's first MOOC—massive open online course. The UC Santa Cruz Faculty Association was concerned that MOOCs were going to take over and destroy faculty positions. Well, there's very little evidence that that's really happening, because it's such a different format, but there is very good evidence that there's more student engagement.

Helene Moglen: The university administration has signed a contract with Coursera without any consultation with the senate. I just saw the contract today. I would say this is a very dangerous situation for the senate. The one area in which the senate has plenary power in the institution is curriculum. What does it mean for the university administration to sign a contract with Coursera without senate consultation?

The future of education in online education, that's very dubious. Yeah, it's very good that students around the world, people who want to take courses around the world, who can't afford it, who have no access—it's good. It looks like everybody wins but what happens to privacy? What happens to forms of education that we have most valued? Everybody wins, but a number of the major players lose. So, this is a discussion that is going to have to happen on this campus, as it will on campuses across the country. What I see is that faculty don't begin, the senate does not begin to understand what it is losing and the way it would be contributing, not just to the increasing mediocrity of education, but much worse.

George Blumenthal: A few years ago, in certain quarters, online education was regarded by many as the future. It was going to change the way colleges and universities worked and classrooms

would be obsolete. Now there have been enough online courses that there is significant research on online education. And that research shows that in certain populations it is not an end all, be all. Particularly for first generation and minority populations, the hands-on meeting with people is really important, particularly in the early years of their education. In some courses, online education can work to some degree, particularly courses that are very formulaic, math for example, but in other courses, like history, it's not quite the same thing, where you're really trying to get people to think independently, or think in different ways about an issue. I'm not saying there can't be good history online courses, but I am saying that the student experience is different.

Relatively early on in this online debate, I decided that if this was going to be the future of education, I should know more about it. I decided to take an online course. So I took an online course in artificial intelligence from Udacity. The idea was that maybe I'd learn something. I don't mean I don't know anything about artificial intelligence, but I thought it would be interesting, and even though it was a technical course, I'm technically capable, so I could do this.

So I took this course. I did learn a lot of things. But it was hard for me to motivate myself to do this and I'm a pretty motivated person. If it's hard for me, I can't imagine what it would be for a student. It was hard sometimes for me to go sit at that computer. And while I learned a lot, I didn't find it all that interesting and stimulating.

Certainly, the thing that I think is so crucial in undergraduate education—namely the ability of an instructor to inspire a student, to take a student and make them really interested, so interested they want to pursue the subject further—didn't come across to me in the online course. Part of that had to be a lack of human interaction. If I were a student and I needed that course to graduate, or if I needed that course to get into my major and I couldn't get it a different way, I would certainly do the online course. But that isn't something I would be happy about having as a significant part of my curriculum.

So what about today? Well, we have been advancing online education. The UC system has a series of systemwide courses that can be taken by any student at any UC campus. Santa Cruz produced the calculus sequence. It's a really good series of courses that was produced in the math department here. We've been talking with a few other UC campuses about jointly developing an online undergraduate program.

But I still don't think that that's a substitute for a residential college. UC Santa Cruz has residential colleges. We call them residential colleges for a reason. Seventy percent of our students do undergraduate research with faculty. The idea that we're going to replace all of that with an online program is, to me, kind of crazy. I don't think that that's likely to happen anytime soon.

Helene Moglen: Online education is part of a larger picture of decline.

Murray Baumgarten: I remember a conversation with Chancellor Sinsheimer, where he said, "Many of our colleagues are very upset about being part of this industrial participation in the military economy, but none of them are giving up their computers." Or we should add now smartphones, or any of those other things. Now that's all given way to globalization. We're much more intertwined.

Michael Warren: I always spent 9:00 a.m. to 6:00 p.m. in my office. But in my last years of teaching here, there were fewer and fewer faculty on campus. People worked from home. People relate now more to somebody on the East Coast than to the person sitting in the office next to theirs. It's that curious aspect of globalization. We are all interconnected, except to the person next door.

Murray Baumgarten: The Holocaust course reaches people across fifty-nine countries. In some ways, it fits with the university's call for public service. Many people say it's like publishing a book rather than teaching a class in the usual way.

UCSC News Center: UC Santa Cruz has launched a new online course open to the public through the Coursera platform. Titled *Feminism and Social Justice*, it is an adaptation of a popular course taught on campus for nearly a decade by Distinguished Professor of Feminist Studies Bettina Aptheker. The condensed, four-lecture course critically examines three significant post World War II movements for social justice in the United States from feminist perspectives—considering how participants in these movements thought about race, gender, and class; how they organized; and what progressive changes may have resulted from their efforts.

Murray Baumgarten: Online education does have the potential to change what university education is about, but Santa Cruz had some of that as part of its mission from the beginning, to make this a place where student learning was central, not just teacher presentation.[5]

More People are Coming:
Growth, Cost, and Housing Crises at UCSC Today

Samantha Caballero: It boggles my mind. I look at rent [in other parts of the country] and I'm like wow, that place is a thousand dollars a month? That's not too bad. If I went to a place like Montana, I could get a house for a thousand dollars a month. Just for me. Overall, going to this university requires that you have a lot of money. Even if you're not rich, you have to find a way to make it work, or else you're going to get kicked off.

Victor Garcia-Zepeda: I worked in the housing office as a student assistant. Sometimes students think, "Oh, the administration's not worried about it." Or that the housing office, they don't care, either. They really do. It does affect their work as well. I remember Lindsay, who was my supervisor there—she would be stressed out about knowing that there were going to be a lot more students coming in.

I don't think it's in anyone's interest to be devious and be like, yeah, let's put in more students even though we don't have the space for it. It's a problem that we have with the space that we're in. We have to find a way to work with it. It is frustrating, and it is difficult. I wish there was an easy answer to it, where it's like yeah, we just magically get a whole bunch of new buildings, or a whole bunch of dormitories. But unfortunately, it doesn't work that way.

I'm working on a project with Cynthia Chase, the current mayor right now, and with University Relations, Howard Heevner. We're trying to develop this project where we're going to be discussing some of these key issues like housing, the water situation, and some of the other regulations, and how the city, the UCSC community, and just the people of the community itself within the city can all work together to bridge the gap between miscommunication between all these groups, how we can work together to provide a sustainable, equitable, and community-driven city. Housing was one of the big issues that we brought up. This city is growing at a fast pace, in part because of the students, but also because of the high growth in jobs that's been happening. I wish I had the answers to all these questions and I wish I could do something about it now, versus in the long run.

No Place Like Home: Santa Cruz is the least-affordable small city in the US. It is also the city with the highest rate of homelessness in the nation. 60 percent of Santa Cruz residents are renters, with the median rent pushing past $3,000 per month. Santa Cruz faces a full-blown housing crisis: Its many facets—extreme rent burdens, precarious living situations, widespread displacement and homelessness—have enormous impacts on the community.

UC Santa Cruz provides on-campus housing for 53 percent of its over 16,000 undergrads, the highest for any of the ten University of California campuses. Nonetheless, this pushes the remainder into the local rental market. The influx of students into town in the midst of a housing crisis affects both students and residents. On the one hand, it increases competition for affordable units for all renters. On the other, it creates added stresses for students. Financial aid packages decrease if students live off campus, limiting income that can go towards rent. Residents often complain about having students as neighbors, and many landlords to refuse to rent to them. Those landlords that do often charge well above market rate. As a result, students often live three or four to a single bedroom in the few units available to them. Besides overcrowding, the shortage also leads to informal, precarious, and unsafe housing situations—including students living in garages, sheds, and vehicles. It also causes extreme rent burdens, leading many students to become food insecure to cover rent. All of this takes a toll on students' academic performance, as well as their physical and emotional health.[6]

Manaiya Scott: In Rachel Carson College [College Eight], they converted the doubles into triples. My first year, the lounges in Oakes were quads. Now they're quints. They're five people in one room.

Samantha Caballero: We just can't build enough housing to house as many students that want to come here. The level that we're growing at is not possible, but we're still trying to do it, and that's why we have so many problems. I know people who live in houses that have mold problems. I know people who live in places where their landlords are slumlords and they don't repair the things that they have to because they know that if [the current tenants] get fed up and they can't live there anymore, somebody else is going to take the spot.

And I think it's a shame that the lounges in the dorms are gone [having been converted into bedrooms] because lounges are ways that people who live in the dorms can go and just hang out with each other and study. Now there aren't spots to do that, so it's harder to bond with each other.

Tommy Herz: We had a lounge. I was at Cowell College in Adams House, Room 217, and we had a lounge on one of the other floors and that lounge was kind of the thing that brought everybody in my house together. The majority of my friends are from that house, are from the people I lived with, just because of that lounge. I attribute that to the power of that space to bring everybody together.

Manaiya Scott: I've heard some horror stories about housing. Sometimes we let homeless students in to take showers in the dorms because they have nowhere to go. I've met people who sleep in the Metro Station and then catch the bus in the morning. People are doubling up when they're not supposed to, but that's because that's all people have. Living rooms are converted into bedrooms, because that's all we have.

Victor Garcia-Zepeda: All of my friends keep asking me if there's going to be an open space at my house once I leave. And unfortunately, there's not, so I have to tell them that. It's hard, because I know they're struggling to find a place. I don't know what to do. There's so many students and so little space. And then the regulations, as far as where you can live and how you can live and the living situation. Some landlords might not allow for more than, let's say, four people in a house that could fit maybe like seven or eight people.

Jess Whatcott: I commute from the East Bay to UCSC. I didn't necessarily want to, but I couldn't afford the rent in Santa Cruz. I have a dog and so I can't live on campus [in graduate student housing]. So I've been personally affected by the housing crisis, and I've heard from many students, especially international students, who are really being gouged by the rent around here, and who are living in unzoned places, or who are doubling up, or living with a bunch of other students. I know a ton of students that commute from the East Bay, because I carpool with them. People are driving really long distances to get here.

The campus's solution is to build; is to do a public/private partnership. They're going to get bids from private companies to build more dorms on campus. I'm opposed to privatization, so it's not my first choice. But I understand that there really may not be another option because of the debt ceiling situation. The university can't take on any more debt.

Victor Garcia-Zepeda: I think next year there's even more students coming in. We have a lack of space, so it's something that affects everyone. If you're in a space where you have overcrowding, it's going to affect your education, because you're going to be stressed out about that. And then it's going to affect your mental health, which then can affect your physical health. It keeps leading to more and more problems. The solution would be, let's build more buildings and more residential spaces. But then there're so many old restrictions that were put in place where there are certain places where you can't build. You can't build above the trees now. Luckily, the trees have grown a lot more, so maybe they can still build up.

George Blumenthal: One of the reasons I've been such a strong advocate for Student Housing West [in 2019] is because I think it is a model for building housing that might allow us to be able to commit to housing all new students on campus. When the public-private partnership became a viable option, suddenly I realized that this could be a model for how we could build a lot of housing on campus successfully, and therefore we could theoretically commit to housing all new students on campus.

City on a Hill Press: Student Housing West (SHW) is set and ready to begin major construction, which will have major impacts for the Santa Cruz community. On April 1, the UC Board of Regents approved the proposed SHW, a construction project aiming to provide additional campus housing to students, Chancellor George Blumenthal said in a campus-wide email. SHW will consist of developing 13 acres of land at the Heller Site and about 17 acres of land at the Hagar site. SHW will

replace Family Student Housing and construct on the East Meadow. The goal of SHW is to create an additional 3,072 on-campus beds and 140 housing units.

UC Santa Cruz Vice President of Internal Affairs of the Student Union Assembly Citlalli Aquino supports the SHW initiative. "With over 100 houseless students in the city, it is absurd for there to be so much open space on campus—like the East Meadow—and leave it unused," Aquino said.

Not everyone is supportive of the SHW development. The most prominent opponent of SHW is the East Meadow Action Committee (EMAC), a coalition of UCSC alumni, faculty, staff, students and community members. EMAC opposes the planned development of the campus's East Meadow and advocates for alternative sites.[7]

East Meadow Action Committee: The open meadows are central to UCSC's world-renowned design aesthetic. This proposal overturns a fifty-year tradition of environmentally-conscious planning. We support more, better, and more affordable student housing and improved childcare facilities on campus. There are other places to build them that do not overturn UCSC's proudest traditions.[8]

Frank Zwart: I served as UCSC's campus architect and associate vice chancellor for physical planning and construction from 1988 to 2010, a period during which the requirement for each campus to prepare a Physical Design Framework [PhDF]. I was the principal author of UCSC's Framework, which was presented to and accepted by the regents in March 2010. The PhDF identifies the campus' planning principles and objectives for design of the physical environment; how the PhDF relates to the campus LRDP; and how objectives will be integrated into project planning and design. The PhDF is a comprehensive document with both visual and textual elements and includes key planning requirements such as density parameters, sustainability guidelines, circulation guidelines, vistas and sightlines, physical connections to the adjacent community, and design guidelines.

At the Hagar Drive site, the Student Housing West project would build 140 apartments, a childcare center, and about 150 parking spaces at the southern edge of a major meadow, contrary to [Physical Design] Framework guidelines that call for the campus to maintain the continuity and visual "sweep" of the meadow landscape across the lower campus and to maintain the lower campus meadows as a buffer between central campus development and the city of Santa Cruz, continuing the role of campus lands as an important element in the city's greenbelt. Furthermore, it does so without taking a careful look at the surrounding context so necessary for such an important and sensitive site. As former Executive Vice Chancellor Alison Galloway put it in her comment letter on the original Draft EIR, "the proposed project makes poor use of a prime location on campus, capturing neither the density nor the views that this site warrants. If such a project is to be considered, it should be part of a much larger and comprehensive approach to the probable eventual development of all the meadows."

In my twenty-two years as campus architect, no building project ever aroused such vehement and fervent opposition, particularly from alumni, faculty and emeriti faculty, supporters, major donors, and other friends of the campus; I know that you have heard from a number of them. Those of us who love the campus—and here I write as someone with over fifty years affiliation with UCSC: a proud member of its Class of 1971, the third class to enter—are convinced that the campus can do better.[9]

Manaiya Scott: And it's not only housing—it's the resources. It's increasing enrollment, but not increasing financial aid, not increasing tutoring services, not being able to increase funding to different areas. It's maxing out all of the supplies that we already have to ensure that more people are coming.

Carl Eadler: We have a lot of students here on campus who are on food stamps.

Victor Garcia-Zepeda: Yes, there's been times where it's like okay, do I want to eat, or do I want to pay rent? It's a serious decision that I've made. And sometimes I have to pay that rent.

I worked for the dean of students on a project called the Care Closet. I think now Slug Support is the title for it. It's to help students in financial strife to get access to basic necessities. Being a student who actually was affected by these things, I did take advantage of the program itself, too. So, I've had to navigate through different outlets to find the funds that I need or the help that I needed, whether that was going to the food pantry, going to some food closet, going to free events. I love going to free events because there's always food. I've noticed that's the main reason why a lot of students go to events is for the food and the entertainment.

Tommy Herz: In a perfect world, you wouldn't need money to do things. I mean, of course that's a long shot, and impossible. But it's really a shame that college is so incredibly expensive that you have to essentially dictate how you obtain the knowledge that you will use in your future by your bank account. I'm not exactly educated on how our money is used and what exactly the university needs and all that, but I do know it sucks.

Sareil Brookins: It is overall really expensive, no matter who you are. My first mistake was first quarter, first year, going to Literary Guillotine [bookstore for textbooks]—that shit's expensive. I was like, "What is a reader? Why is it sixty bucks? Why is this little thirteen-chapter book so much money?" I am very frugal. I've always been frugal since forever. I mean, I'm a yard sale, thrift store, hand-me-down girl. All my life, we shared hand-me-downs. This shirt, hand me down. Six bucks, this hat. I'm reaching out for free things. I was trained like that by my mom. I've been going to yard sales and being really cheap since then. I realize that it's really expensive here, but they also give a lot of aid, in my opinion, here. But it also depends on how much money you make.

Manaiya Scott: If you know anything about UC history, in 2012 they did a big protest to get the tuition hikes frozen for five years. In 2017, they were unfrozen, in spring quarter. The UC Student Association Conference gets together during August. All the UCs come together, talk about different campaigns they want to do for the year. SUA puts it on, the Student Union Assembly, the student government for the UC Santa Cruz campus.

Tuition is expensive. I'm like, I got the Cal Grant. I got some money, got some scholarships but how am I going to guarantee I'm going to be here for four years? Don't plan for your first two years and then not have a plan for your junior and senior year, which a lot of people do. My problem was going to be tuition. I [recently] heard something about Pell Grants are being snatched. That's how we pay for things a lot of times—Cal Grant, Pell Grants—that's how we pay for tuition.

Victor Garcia-Zepeda: I think one of the most important things is to ask for help and not to be shy about it. You should take advantage of the resources that you have on campus and really seek out those resources. It might not be easy. Sometimes I had to explain my situation in one day to five different offices, five different people. It was frustrating, but at least I felt like something was getting done. And you have to be on top of things. Sometimes you're the one that has to be a little more adamant about things and advocating for yourself.

Definitely, I would have to say if you have the opportunity to use some of the resources, do. I have some friends who have that stigma from back home of, that's a bad thing to use welfare or food stamps. That's not something that's looked highly at, so they choose not to, even though they're struggling. But you are a student right now and you do need to be eating. If not, then it's going to affect everything else. You have to be able to be healthy in order to learn, and you're going to be distracted if your stomach's growling. If you are the person that has access to these resources, then help others.

Samantha Caballero: There are people who have parents willing to pay their rent or tuition. But even in families where the parents can afford it, that means that they had to take out a second mortgage. I've seen people who identify as being middle class being heavily affected by the cost. Because some people will only be offered loans and some people will not be offered any financial aid. And their parents just don't have the capability of paying for it. That doesn't mean that they shouldn't also get access to university. I want to see more services be applied to people who fall under that bracket. I know that Financial Aid does a middle-class scholarship and they do have the Blue and Gold.[10] But having more help beyond that would be good.

Khalen Hudson: Everyone hates financial aid. Everyone hates the Financial Aid office. Taking out loans was just something that I knew that I was going to have to do. And when I lived off campus, that was also crazy, because of rent. So I applied to be an RA.

But there's resources on campus that I just figured out. If Financial Aid is messing with you, or if you've exhausted all your financial aid and still need stuff, then people are there for you on campus. Like the dean's office, they loan out computers for free. If students have exhausted all their financial aid and they still can't afford to pay, they can apply for funds to buy their school supplies, or have their books paid for the quarter. Or just help with food for the quarter. I also know a lot of people that are on food stamps.

So, yeah, there are ways of making it work, but it's a struggle for a lot of people. For some people, it's not a struggle at all. It's like, wow, you really have no cares in the world and that must be great. But we can't always just be going out every weekend, because I'm poor.

Manaiya Scott: Who is this university made for? I'm low income. It was made for people who are wealthier, who can afford these things. I think we pay thirty-three fees right now for different parts of our Student Life and Campus Life. And the overcrowding of UCSC is impacting everyone, even the dining halls. The lines, especially for Rachel Carson College, the lines are ridiculous. And in the dining hall, the food quality is just getting worse and worse. They do burger bars, quick stuff, because that's what they can do in the amount of time that they have.

Khalen Hudson: Especially being an RA, with the residents, it comes up across a lot. Things that they will say, like, "Oh, yeah, this weekend I did this, this, and this." They'll be buying shoes every weekend. And I'm just like how? How? Please, tell me how. So, it's just weird. It shows up mostly in, I would say, clothes. This is the era of online shopping. When people are getting packages all the time, it's just like, how are you affording to get these packages all the time? It's a different reality than mine.

Victor Garcia-Zepeda: I remember meeting the financial aid advisor, Liz Martin-Garcia. She has been a great friend to this day. I almost consider her my second mom. She's helped me out a lot. I think that she is great and I feel like a lot of the other AB 540 students would say the same thing—she's a great resource and a great person that's always advocating for us within the Financial Aid office. She understands where we come from and our struggles. We all have such different stories.

At my high school, there were a few other undocumented students. And really the resources offered here, and then hearing their experiences at their universities or their colleges, and how they were struggling—I wish that a lot of the resources that were available to us here at UC Santa Cruz were available to them, too. I remember some of them saying that they were sleeping in their cars, or having to go and like pretty much sleep at the campus, in the libraries or something, because they didn't have access to some of the resources that we have here.

Out-of-State Students:
A New Source of Campus Funding

Mike Rotkin: For a long time, the Office of the President received all tuition and all state funding, and then decided how to distribute it, by a secret formula, to the campuses—in which the vast majority of the resources go to the two flagship campuses, Berkeley and UCLA; much lesser amounts to smaller campuses. Santa Cruz and Riverside get screwed completely, particularly because they have fewer graduate programs, which are the coin of the realm.

George Blumenthal: Our students pay tuition. I'd always assumed that the tuition went to the campus. But in fact, for many years when our students paid tuition, the tuition went to the Office of the President, which then distributed it back to the campuses. The Office of the President felt under no obligation to distribute tuition income back to the campus from which it was generated. They distributed it in a very different way, so that at the end of the day in Santa Cruz, we were getting back about 67 cents for every dollar our students paid in tuition. I felt that if students pay more, they should get more. The Office of the President argued that no, the only reason we do tuition increases is because the state doesn't increase state support, the state has fallen short of their state support obligations, and therefore we should distribute the tuition money in the same way that we distribute state support money, which before rebenching was inequitably distributed.

UC Santa Cruz was way below the UC average in terms of dollars per student. We're talking about 30-40 percent below the UC average.

Before 2011-12, campuses did not get to keep their nonresident [out-of-state] tuition.[11] It was distributed across the system. [Due to pressure from Blumenthal and others, this was changed.] Now the UC campuses basically get to keep all the tuition they collect. It's like you get to eat what you catch. I thought that was a good thing, because I was so concerned about the resident tuition issue.

But the motivations for the campuses suddenly became very, very different. And since this was happening at a time of severe financial crunch for the state, the response of campuses like Berkeley and UCLA and, to some extent, San Diego was, "Oh my goodness, let's just crank up the number of nonresident students, collect nonresident tuition, and that will be great for us." They raised their percentages of undergraduate nonresidents to the low to mid 20 percent levels. And they collected a lot of money by doing so.

Mike Rotkin: So, for example, at Berkeley this past semester, almost a third of their incoming class came from outside of the state of California, to raise a lot of money. Now the campuses have a direct economic benefit from taking outside students, who bring more money with them.

George Blumenthal: When I became chancellor Santa Cruz's nonresident undergraduate student population was about 1.5 percent. We were down at that level when Berkeley was at 23 percent. So, you could argue that I, as chancellor, should have turned up that crank faster than I did. But things change slowly. If we were Berkeley, we could turn that dial and get it to respond quickly. But we aren't Berkeley. We're Santa Cruz. We don't have the international or national reputation that a Berkeley or a UCLA has.

But we did decide to respond. I remember for years saying, "We've got to increase our number. It makes no sense. I said, "We've got to get to 10 percent. And then once we get to 10 percent, we should have a discussion about how high we want to go." That was my constant mantra on the subject.

I certainly would argue that at the 1 or 2 percent level, even if there was no money involved, we were too low. Our students deserve a more international student body that they can interact with.

Sareil Brookins: Stop lying about "We care about diversity." I feel like that's like a code word. I feel like what they include in diversity is just bringing a ton of international students who are usually of the same racial background. It's not really bringing diversity. It's just bringing folks for money. They're getting their money. I want more involvement in retaining students of color, black students, undocumented.

George Blumenthal: I'm not above admitting that getting extra money is a good thing. Of course, you can ask the question: how much is too much, and are campuses like UCLA and Berkeley overextending? They would argue, with some justification, that their nonresident student population actually supports California residents, that but for those students, they wouldn't be able to take the same number of California students that they do. In fact, financially, one nonresident student basically pays the extra money that we need for two resident students.

So, this issue started burbling more and more. We slowly started raising our nonresident student numbers. The numbers coming in for next year [2019-20] are something like 11 percent. I have not initiated a campus discussion about whether 10 percent is enough, or how far we should go, because I'm now convinced that there's no question we need to go further. We can't be competitive with the other campuses if we stay at 10 percent. It just isn't realistic. We're talking about a chunk of money. There's a case to be made that nonresidents

make it possible to educate as many Californians as we do.

Figure 4

Rally for public education poster, Circa 2015

"You've Got to Put Out a Number":
Mapping UCSC for 2040

George Blumenthal: President Mark Yudof's sense of humor was a little wry at times. He basically called UCSC the communist campus. We were weird and leftist, and that's all he knew. But I think, over time, our image has changed. There's a greater recognition of excellence at the campus. We're not the kooky campus anymore. We're not the campus that's so different, you always have to think of us as an asterisk. But we are a campus having growth issues. And I think from the standpoint of UC President Janet Napolitano, who is a president who's very pro-growth, that's the biggest problem with Santa Cruz.

Frank Zwart: If you go to campuses of about this size and look at the kind of student facilities that they have and the kind of plazas that they have—they are big, big spaces. Short of clear-cutting a bunch of redwoods, there just isn't that kind of real estate around in the developed area of the Santa Cruz campus, to develop those kinds of spaces. One of the things that makes the campus such a pleasant environment to occupy is that the scale of things is not overwhelming.

We've done things fairly modestly scaled. They fit in very well with the redwoods. If we look at some of our recent science buildings—the Physical Sciences Building or the new Engineering 2 Building—it's not uncommon on university campuses to see buildings two and three times that size, built all at once. And those are really tough buildings to site and to do sensitively. So one of the things that has saved this campus, that's made the campus so nice, is that relative scale.

George Blumenthal: So, you know, having lived through an LRDP, naturally I was chomping at the bit to start a new one. (Or, as I've told some people, I was this luckiest chancellor in the world who gets to do two of them, not just one.) But the time was coming. We are approaching the limit of the 2005 LRDP, which covers campus planning until 2020.

Frank Zwart: As the student population grows, particularly if they want to centralize facilities, the temptation is going to be there to make these great big spaces. The initial concept of the campus was to spread things out and break it into smaller, more manageable chunks. I hope the campus, administratively, can figure out a way to keep that happening, so that the physical development of the campus is in keeping with its physical setting.

George Blumenthal: So we need a new LRDP. I didn't want to be dragged kicking and screaming to do it. I felt like we really needed to do this in a way that avoids the worst mistakes of last time. One of the advantages of having me involved in last time and this time is that at least I know the worst mistakes. Of course, what I think is the worst mistake may not be what everyone else thinks is the worst mistake. But all I can do is my best.

One mistake that was made last time was the lack of involvement of the faculty and of the Academic Senate. So I appointed two co-chairs of the LRDP committee, Literature Professor Kim Lau, who's the chair of the senate, and Vice Chancellor of Business and Administrative Services Sarah Latham, who really does need to be involved in the leadership of the LRDP.

The second thing I wanted to do was have early communications with the community. So we formed a Community Advisory Group. We wanted broad representation of various organizations in the community, government, and private organizations. We decided we would invite the organizations to send their representative and let them choose. It isn't just opponents of university growth that are on this group. It's more diverse than that, although it's dominated by opponents of university growth. They've been meeting regularly. It's an effort on our part to reach out to the community, so that they get some input in early days, if not all of the input that they would like—they would like to be able to determine what we do and that can't happen—but we certainly can hear their concerns and try to mitigate them to whatever extent that we can.

So I put out there an enrollment planning figure of 28,000. The blood pressure throughout the county went up dramatically when I announced that figure.

Santa Cruz Sentinel: UC Santa Cruz is preparing to grow its student body by more than 50 percent—some 10,000 students—by the year 2040, Chancellor George Blumenthal announced Friday. Planning for a student body of 28,000 students in the next two decades would aim to meet rising demand among an applicant pool that surged to record-setting levels in the fall at UCSC and systemwide. At present, about 18,000 students are enrolled at the campus. Expanding the campus's student body, and particularly its graduate programs, would also allow the campus to take a more prominent role as a research institution, which Blumenthal described as a key part of his vision for the campus's future.[12]

George Blumenthal: It's a planning figure. You've got to put out a number. You can't plan to no number. I put it out as a 2040 plan. We're talking about twenty years, so it had to be a large number.

The university is going to get pressure to grow. We just need to figure out how to grow, and whether or not it can grow in an environmentally appropriate way. We do need to be sensitive to the needs of the community. But let's see if we can do it. Let's see what happens.

The enrollment figure of 27,500 was in the original agreement between the city and the university, as well as stated in the first two LRDPs of the campus. The city was well aware of that number at the time that they agreed to the 27,500. And it was the number in our first two LRDP's, so it isn't a number that I just made up out of thin air.

Santa Cruz Sentinel: "The notion that we're going to cap enrollment and live with a capped enrollment is simply not realistic in the world we live in," Blumenthal said a news meeting Thursday. "I think it's a pipe dream, because the demand for the UC education is increasing by leaps and bounds." Enrollment at UCSC is currently capped at 19,500 by a 2008 settlement between the campus and the city of Santa Cruz. The settlement, which brought an end to litigation by the city, county and citizen groups, also required UCSC to house two-thirds of new students on campus.

George Blumenthal: Having said that, I did make it up out of thin air. I didn't choose that number because it was based upon the LRDPs, otherwise I would have made it 27,500 rather than 28,000. The reason I chose that number was because if we project the amount of growth that we've been experiencing forward to 2040, that's about where we would end up. It's a projection of what I think is likely to be the demand, given the growth of California.

I want to structure the LRDP in a phased approach, so that it isn't just one fell swoop going from 19,500 to 28,000. There are benchmarks along the way, where a certain infrastructure needs to be built, certain mitigations need to happen. If those benchmarks are met, then growth can continue. But if those benchmarks are not met, then growth has to be stopped until you can meet the benchmark. There are members of the community who applaud the benchmark but don't applaud the numbers. And you can't keep everyone happy.

We have 10 percent graduate students; we have a lot of pressure to get that number up to 15 percent. I think we ought to do it, for a whole bunch of reasons. But if Berkeley and Davis and Irvine are at 25 to 30 percent graduate students, I don't think we should go there. I think we should do our 15 percent, take a deep breath, and say "We are still a university committed to undergraduate students." I don't see us going further. I'm not even 100 percent convinced that we need to go even to 15 percent. In the long run, we need to think carefully about what our goal is in that regard. We need to remain an undergraduate-focused campus. The colleges bring quality to our institution. They bring a meaningful experience for students. They're an important part of who we are. I don't know that we have the physical space to grow within existing colleges. I think we will have to add one or two colleges. I love that image of Clark Kerr's, of "seeming small while growing large." I still believe in that image, particularly for freshmen and sophomores. But I don't think we're going to build a lot of new colleges; It's going to be very limited; the financing just isn't there.

We accomplish a lot by growing. One of the things we accomplish is that we can erase our mistakes. Another thing we can accomplish is we can be creative in wonderful new ways. So growth is, in that way, very good.

But growth can't be forever. A lot of people would like us to cap our enrollments and not grow anymore. I hope that we don't go that far, because I don't think the campus is ready for steady state yet. But our next chancellor is going to have to prepare the campus for a steady-state world. Because even if we decide we'll grow to 28,000, and even if we do it, eventually there's a limit. And as a culture, we need to understand what that limit means. Part of that is kind of a relentless willingness to re-imagine ourselves, which means sometimes eliminating things that we're doing. There will always be oxen gored when you eliminate stuff that you're doing. But sometimes you can rebuild, from that, much better things going forward.

Figure 5

Path to the Bookstore, 2011

Photo by Irene Reti

"The Original Authority on Questioning Authority":

Values, Fundraising, and the Future of Public Higher Education

Jim Burns: When I started working at UC Santa Cruz, our office was called the Public Information Office. The name was reflective of an era when there was tremendous state support for the UC system, for the CSU system, and for the community college system in California. Having the campus function as transparently as possible seemed in keeping with that kind of taxpayer support. I loved the simplicity of the office's original name: the Public Information Office. In fact, when I began working at UCSC in 1984, our office functioned more like a university news office. We wrote press releases, put them in envelopes, and mailed them to reporters. It would be fair to say that we spent little time using such terms as "marketing" or "issues management."

George Blumenthal: I came in as chancellor and I realized immediately that there needed to be a cultural shift on the campus. Fundraising was not something that we, as a campus, thought about. I visited all of the departments twice. The first time I went around to the departments, one of my messages was that we were going to have to do fundraising in a big way. I remember one of the departments; I think it was histcon, somebody there said, "Aw, come on. We've heard this from other chancellors before about how they were going to raise money for us and they never did." I said, "Yeah and I'm not going to either. All I'm going to do is facilitate your raising money for yourself."

I was trying to convey a message that we would do fundraising. It would be a big part of what we do, and that everybody had a responsibility and had a role to play. The second time I went around and visited departments, I found some had not changed, but some had. There were development committees within some departments.

We put in place training for faculty and administrators to learn how to make asks. We put in place some courses. The final exam was you had to go make an ask. All of the deans took the class. A whole bunch of faculty did. I got positive feedback from faculty about the class. That was a part of my thinking about culture change on the campus. I wanted some ambassadors. I would have been willing to pay for training for every faculty member on campus, but every faculty member wasn't willing to do that.

Jim Burns: Initially, there was some tension within the office about the fact that the operation was transitioning away from just being an old-fashioned university news office. And, truth be told, in the old days the word "marketing" carried some negative baggage. It may have made people think that we were going to be promoting UCSC in a way that was less straightforward and less honest.

But I thought it was a false choice. I had a terrific colleague in our office who helped me understand why. She reinforced the notion that any marketing we did about UCSC—if it was to be successful—had to be based on reality: what the campus was authentically about, what its values were, and what it had actually accomplished.

George Blumenthal: UC Santa Cruz has several challenges to raising money. Some of our early alums became quite wealthy, but we probably have a higher percentage of alumni who went into public service, and you don't get wealthy in public service. I think we currently have something like 110,000 to 120,000 alums. And the median age of our alums is about thirty-five. Enrollment has gone up so sharply over more recent years, so most of our alums are recent alums. If you looked at

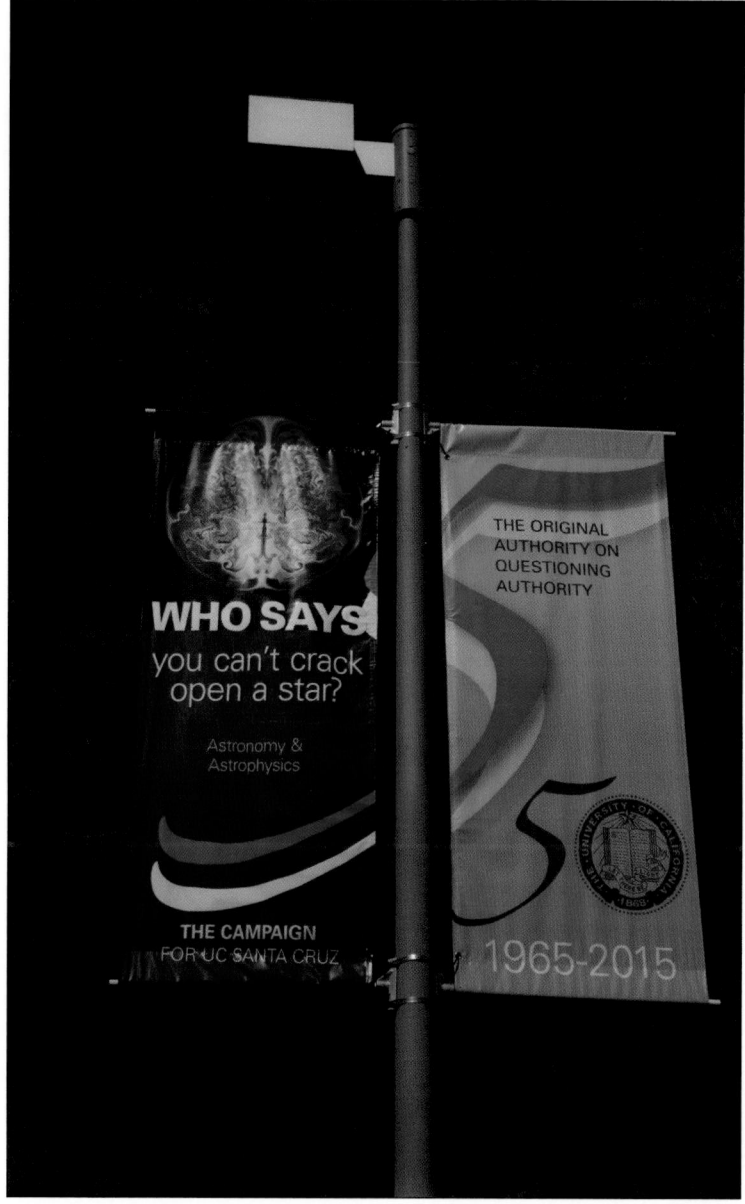

Figure 6

Banner for the Campaign for
UC Santa Cruz, 2015

Photo by Irene Reti

Berkeley, for example—I'm guessing the average age of their alums is probably fifty-five—a big difference in terms of where they are in their careers in terms of donor capacity.

Another barrier to fundraising is many people feel as though they gave at the office. "I pay taxes, so therefore why should I have to pay twice for a university?" I understand that. On the other hand, part of the message is how little we get from the state anymore.

Lastly, when I became chancellor and I looked at our fundraising operation: oh, my God. It was almost entirely directed at the town of Santa Cruz. My reaction was, we have squeezed every drop of blood out of that particular turnip. It makes no sense to put additional resources into fundraising in Santa Cruz. We need to expand to San Francisco, to Silicon Valley, and to Los Angeles. So, we've put people in Los Angeles and in Silicon Valley and in San Francisco. We have decent fundraising operations in those locations, and now in others as well. I started going to New York and developing relationships with some of our New York alums.

Michael Cowan: We have to go after more private funding in an increasingly competitive market. As public institutions as a whole—public radio or universities and colleges, or nonprofit organizations—compete for these same resources in tight economic times, it's a challenge.

Jim Burns: A lot of times people think of marketing as a clever tagline or something that you can build a brand around. In the world of computing, for example, Apple has done a terrific job of marketing itself. I think for years their tagline was: "Think different." Consumers understood that Apple's advertising was indeed accurate. Their products really were different. Obviously, the company has been wildly successful because their products have been great. But their marketing also helped because it reinforced what was authentically true about the company.

George Blumenthal: Even when I was acting chancellor, I knew we had to do a fundraising campaign, but I couldn't do it as the acting chancellor. But as soon as I was appointed, literally the day I was appointed chancellor, I immediately realized, this is the first day of the campaign. I knew this is something we had to do as a campus.

I went around to websites of other universities and looked at their campaigns. Stanford's campaign had a fancy name that basically said, well we're going to raise a lot of money and we're going to get a scholarship for students and do other good stuff. I think that is the difference between an organization like Stanford, that does fundraising by just sneezing, and us. They don't have to do anything and money rolls out of the pockets of their donors. We have to do everything exactly right and offend no one. We have a much higher bar.

We brought in one of the standard firms to do a campaign assessment. They came back and said that they thought we could do a campaign of 250 million dollars if we push it. And so, I, having heard that, made a decision to do a 300-million-dollar campaign. The campaign themes included support for the Institute of Arts and Sciences; the Genomics Institute; coastal sustainability; student support, among other goals.

I met with alumni all around the country. I did a lot of traveling, meeting with every single conceivable group of alumni or potential donors to alert them to the campaigns, and to show some enthusiasm for the campaign. Of course, some people gave a lot of pushback: "Why aren't the colleges mentioned in the campaign explicitly? Why are two of the three programs science, and even the other one, arts and sciences, is half science?" I got a lot of pushback on that. Most people were pretty receptive. But whenever you have a bunch of Santa Cruz alums in the room, you're always going to get some level of skepticism and pushback.

We needed to bring in an advertising firm. Sheldon Kamieniecki in social sciences had brought in an alum, Larry Rowan, who owns a business called Fly Communications in New York City, that does advertising. Larry feels a deep affiliation with the campus. So we decided to bring in Fly Communications and see what they could do. Larry presented some ideas to us. He had four potential campaigns that he could offer. He told me later that there was one that he thought was, by far and away, the best one and he thought there was zero chance we would accept it. That was "The original authority on questioning authority." He thought it would be just too edgy, way too edgy. But I loved it. Alison Galloway loved it. I figured if Alison loved it and I loved it, that was it.

Jim Burns: There has been a recent push to have the campus use "The Original Authority on Questioning Authority" tagline or theme. As with most things in communications, there were people on campus who liked that approach and others who really didn't. Personally, I think it certainly spoke to an essence of the campus that is true, and I think that is the reason that George Blumenthal and Alison Galloway selected it as the theme they wanted associated with the recent fundraising campaign.

George Blumenthal: I've heard all kinds of criticisms of that theme. A lot of the criticism I heard was that it's not literally true. We weren't the original authority. Campaigns don't have to be literally true. I heard all the pushback, but I still loved it. To me, this theme isn't about protest. To me, this is about innovation, about creating new

fields of study. This is about doing things in ways that are different than everyone else.

Ronnie Gruhn: I have a very angry, saddened view. The purpose of this campus—to provide something that the other campuses are not providing, and do it in a different way—has essentially been erased. The fact that it hasn't been erased is essentially only left in the rhetoric of this campus. I can hardly stand hearing the rhetoric from the administration: how we're unique, and what we're doing, and we're distinctive. "No matter how bad the budget situation goes," says the chancellor, "We're sticking to our values." Excuse me. Almost all the Santa Cruz "values" have eroded. It makes me livid.

George Blumenthal: I don't buy the notion that we've lost the vision at UCSC. Things have changed. We don't have narrative evaluations; we do have grades. That was a reaction to the times; it was a reaction to changes in faculty sentiment. It may have been inevitable, even though I actually regret those changes myself. If it wasn't going to happen then, it would have happened a few years later. Not everything can remain exactly the same as it was. You move on and try to maintain those things that you really think bring quality.

Jim Burns: A terrific spirit is still very much alive here. I think it has to do, probably, with the fact that we were born to be a little bit different. We're located in the community of Santa Cruz, which is a little bit different. We have this absolutely amazing setting for a place, which fosters lots of creativity. And we're still pretty darn young, just now turning fifty. Yet we're doing amazing things. Are we the same as we were in the early years of the campus? Absolutely not. And I don't think we'd want to be.

Khalen Hudson: It's a pretty chill campus overall. And the whole model, the authority on questioning authority. That's like, whatever. It does resonate with me just a little bit, though—the way I've seen my bosses at College Nine and my teachers approach their work. Especially my bosses, they're really cool people, and they're always willing to grow and they're always willing to learn.

Jim Burns: It's true that we are not the same place we were twenty-five years ago, when the place was smaller and budgets were more plentiful. But I still think that there's a uniqueness about this place, even at our current scale, and even with our current budget challenges, and even with our current class size, that makes us just a little bit different— and different in a very positive way. I guess that's a wordy way of saying that I think that the "Original Authority on Questioning Authority" theme or tagline is still true.

Sabina Wildman: Touring campus, we walked through the Humanities Building. My mom kept on telling me, "They care about humanities here. See, they built this new building." She was really trying to say, "No, they're not only going to do math and science here. And there are some psychology people here who are kind of big." I was thinking of doing psychology.

But what really got me was when I saw "Angela Davis" written on one of the name tags for one of the offices. And I was like, what?! I had no idea she taught here. I did a project on her in third grade. I love her! You have no idea how much I love her. So, I was really excited about that. I was like, okay, if she's a professor, I'm already here. That means that there's activism still on campus.

And a big part of what I liked about Santa Cruz also, is that at least historically, there's this idea that students are really active. A lot of it is in hippie culture, but I think a lot of it was the whole slogan of the authority on questioning authority. That's something that definitely resonates with me.

Helene Moglen: The rhetoric of the administration makes me crazy. I hear it as a kind of propaganda from which the university emerges as a kind of Potemkin Village.

50th Anniversary website: Breakthroughs aren't achieved by adhering to the status quo. And for fifty years, UC Santa Cruz has been blazing a trail of bold, progressive, fearless inquiry. We aren't stopping now.[13]

Jim Burns: Maybe the tagline's critics were saying it's a reasonable way to express who we were and not who we are now. I understand where they are coming from, but I'm not sure I agree with them.

George Blumenthal: The campus as created by Dean McHenry—take a snapshot of it in 1968, or whatever—I don't believe that that model of a campus could possibly have survived the evolution that we've seen in state-funded universities over the years. It could survive in Cambridge, England, or Oxford, England, because of the level of funding that they get at Cambridge and Oxford, because of their eliteness. But I don't think it ever could have survived in California, unless the system had decided that they were going to fund Santa Cruz at a much higher rate than they funded the other campuses. And frankly, I think that, had they made that decision and Clark Kerr said, "I really want Santa Cruz to succeed in the original vision; I'm going to give them much richer funding than anybody else, so that they can do this"—I know the politics of the world enough to know that might survive Clark Kerr, and it might even survive his successor; it wouldn't have survived till today.

Jim Burns: UC Santa Cruz, while it's significantly larger and therefore inherently less personal than it used to be, is still a place where imagining the possible is valued. It was a campus where the word "interdisciplinary" was almost invented. What that meant for people at UC Santa Cruz was an understanding that very transformative knowledge was often found at the edge or intersection of disciplines. Some of the most interesting work that has come out of UCSC has involved multiple disciplines approaching the same problems from different perspectives. I do think that this was done to a greater extent at UC Santa Cruz, and still is. Some of that has to do with our heritage, that we were created to be a different place. Some of that probably has to do with our scale, that as a major research university we're still relatively small. And maybe some of that has to do with the fact that things are done a little less formally here than other places. Some of that probably has to do with our age, that our departments have not existed for one hundred years, and perhaps are more flexible in how they evolve.

George Blumenthal: Ultimately, we finished the campaign six months early. We raised three hundred and thirty-five million dollars. So, we exceeded our goal. And the year or two since then our fundraising has been more than double what it was before the campaign. We had some really strong donors that we developed. Our alumni became much more supportive. And we got a lot of small donations as well.

You could ask the question: Is fundraising going to be the way we extricate ourselves from the dilemma of declining state support for higher education? I think the answer is no. It's just a numbers game. We now get, roughly speaking,

in terms of our core mission of teaching and research, 40 percent of our funding from the state and 60 percent from tuition. We're no longer state supported; we're state augmented. Our tuition is already higher than we feel comfortable with in a public university. Politically, there's very little appetite for increasing tuition more. So, when we look at the gap—how much we need to fully fund the university without overcharging students—that gap is much greater than we would ever be able to make up by fundraising. We're way short.

Helene Moglen: The classes are larger. The TAs have been cut back. The numbers of students that teaching assistants serve have increased many times over. The writing faculty has been cut way back. Many faculty are massively overworked, massively demoralized.

Ronnie Gruhn: This campus, I think, will become just one of the weak sisters in the UC system.

George Blumenthal: Compare Berkeley to Stanford, and compare what they do and how they raise money for it. Stanford has a huge endowment. Their pay-out on their endowment on a per-student, or per-faculty, basis is quite significant. They do have huge tuition. Yes, they discount it for many students, but they still collect more money per student in tuition, by far, than the University of California does. So, they have those huge benefits, and then on top of that, they have one of the top fundraising profiles in the world. Compare that to Berkeley, where tuition can't go up; it's pretty puny. We don't get that much money from the state, far, far less than Stanford on a per-student, or per-faculty basis. So, it just isn't realistic for Berkeley to make up the difference and be competitive with Stanford based upon fundraising. Berkeley is competitive with Stanford, but Berkeley is competitive with

Stanford because they do what Stanford does on half the money that Stanford has to spend.

I just gave a talk in Berkeley on the future of public higher education. I think that the answer ultimately has to lie with the federal government. It's not going to happen during the Trump administration or even the next administration, but we need to think long term about what the funding model for higher education is. Right now, in the United States, 70 percent of all bachelor's degrees are given by public universities. In addition, the United States has dropped from number one in the world, in terms of the percentage of twenty-five to thirty-five year olds who have a four-year college degree, to now number seventeen in the world. And part of that has been the decline in funding for public higher education.

Hayden White: There are changes in the university, transforming it into a kind of corporate bottom-line, run by managers rather than by educators. Its function is no longer primarily educational; it's training, training of people in research techniques, training people to be surgeons, or training people to be lawyers. Its purpose is no longer cultivation. It's certification.

Ronnie Gruhn: In the twenty-first century education is going to have to revolutionize for it to be meaningful. How to educate undergraduates and how to use faculty effectively has to be fundamentally rethought.

George Blumenthal: The federal government funds higher education only through Pell Grants, through student loans, through research grants, and through a few very specialized programs like Hispanic Serving Institution money. They do not do not provide much in the way of general support for higher education in the states. That all comes from the states, and the states are not a reliable source of funding for higher education. States have cut their budgets. Most states are like California and are not allowed to carry a debt. They have to balance the budget every year; they are subject to the ups and downs of the economy. The federal government doesn't have to do that. Ultimately, if we are to have successful higher education in this country, the federal government is going to have to play a much bigger role.

Manaiya Scott: Going to college, being eighteen, being an adult, is a big transition. Being a student leader at this time is quite hard. I know a lot of people who wear many hats. People, myself included, feel like we have to be everywhere and everyone. That's exhausting. Sometimes I forget that this is just a stage; I'm going to graduate and I'm going to move on. Sometimes, it feels like the end of the world, like I have to do stuff right now. Change is a process, right? But if X, Y, and Z can't get done, then what happens in ten years? Tuition hikes—I'm not blaming anyone or anything, but it's just like, history is going to come back to you, right? Some of the things that have made me who I am—it's not going to be the same thing for my nieces and nephew growing up.

George Blumenthal: We are on a slippery sliding slope and unless something changes I think it will just go downhill.

Katherine Le: I am in Student Lobby Corps; I am in a legislative assistant position; and I am the lead for the Fund the UC campaign, a longstanding campaign under the UC Student Association that focuses on reform for Proposition 13 and focuses on the cost of rising tuition on UC campuses. I recently organized an event called Tuition Talks here, where I invited previous Mayor Mike Rotkin; UCSA President Ralph Washington, Jr.; and Interim Vice Provost of Student Success Jay

Padgett to talk about the issues from a student, administrative, and faculty perspective.

During spring break, I was a delegation leader for the Student Lobby Conference, which is held in Sacramento. We brought a delegation of approximately twenty-four UCSC students. It was a free trip for students to learn how to lobby representatives on bills that affected UC students. Monday was reserved to meet with the representatives at the Capitol, which was an engaging experience, because many of the students had never lobbied or met representatives before.

I also work with the External Affairs Office; we push for local, state, and federal advocacy. Recently, UCSC students went to Washington, D.C. on a federal lobbying trip. Although it was tiring, the work that the team has put in has been amazing. It was my first time ever going to Washington, D.C. The experience of walking in those congressional buildings, and meeting with those representatives, feeling that excited but nervous feeling in my stomach before I went into the offices of these representatives—who were just people, too, you know, fighting for a cause— made me feel like I had agency. It made me feel like hey, I do have a space to stand up for UCSC students. Through student government, I am able to not only propel the voices of other students, but propel my own voice as well.

There are more black folks than white folks in Washington, DC. They're in the 40 percent ranges. And Washington, D.C. is, I believe, 3 or 4 percent Asian, and then like 3, 4 percent Mexican and Latinx folks. So, something quite astonishing that I saw when I came to Washington, D.C. was that there was very little representation in these congressional buildings.

Manaiya Scott: What were they doing in the sixties and seventies that we're doing now? What has really changed through history? Fifty years later, where are we at? I feel like people think, "Oh, you're going to do great. You're involved in college and you're going to get a job." But it's not the same anymore. In the sixties and seventies, you could guarantee yourself a career path. Now, you're hopping everywhere just to make sure you can pay your bills. Some of the alumni come back and they're like, "Oh yeah, I'm writing a book." But we don't have secure jobs anymore. And why is that? The EPA just got slashed. Don't be so quick to judge us as "Millennials," as people like to put us into the category of.

Katherine Le: I was the only Asian Pacific Islander woman in the building, of congressional staff, of anybody working in the buildings. There was an extreme lack of diversity. And what was really jarring was that many of the folks behind the food and service counters were people of color and everybody outside of those food counters were not. I remember sitting there and being like, wow, I'm one of the only people of color in this room right now. That's reflective of our governmental system and its lack of diversity in terms of representing constituents and representing America as a whole.

Seeing that made me feel even more empowered to be there and to be a student of color representing UCSC. That motivates me to create relationships back at UCSC, to improve diversity and push for intersectional change on campus, and to listen to other stories.

Figure 7

Seeds. Santa Cruz Women's March, 2018

Photo by Irene Reti

55

Endnotes

1. See: http://campaign.ucsc.edu/priorities/student-experience/colleges/.

2. For documents related to the history of the narrative evaluation system at UC Santa Cruz see: https://senate.ucsc.edu/archives/Past%20Issues/narrative-evaluations/index.html.

3. See Committee on Educational Policy Advisory Guidelines on Writing Undergraduate Performance (Narrative) Evaluations, October 2010. https://senate.ucsc.edu/committees/cep-committee-on-educational-policy/policies-guidelines/undergraduate-education-policies/NESguidelinesoct2010.pdf.

4. https://senate.ucsc.edu/manual/santacruz-division-manual/part-two-regulations/section-three-ug-program/chapter-nine-grades-eval-records/index.html.

5. Scott Rappaport, "UC Santa Cruz launches online 'Feminism and Social Justice' course with Bettina Aptheker," UCSC News Center: March 7, 2019.

6. "No Place Like Home is a community-initiated, student-engaged research project on the affordable housing crisis in Santa Cruz County. Based at UC Santa Cruz, the project grew out of two ongoing research initiatives: Critical Sustainabilities, led by Miriam Greenberg, and Working for Dignity, led by Steve McKay." See: https://noplacelikehome.ucsc.edu/en/makings-of-a-crisis/.

7. Julia Barragan, "Student Housing West Approved," *City on a Hill Press*, April 19, 2019.

8. "The East Meadow Action Committee (EMAC) is a group of University of California, Santa Cruz (UCSC) faculty, students, alumni, staff, and concerned community members that organized to prevent development on the East Meadow, north and east of the intersection of Hagar and Coolidge Drive on the UCSC campus." https://www.eastmeadowaction.org/.

9. "Letter to Regents from Frank Zwart (3/24/19)." Available on the East Meadow Action Committee website: https://www.eastmeadowaction.org.

10. See Blue and Gold Opportunity Plan: "UC's Blue and Gold Opportunity Plan will ensure that you will not have to pay UC's systemwide tuition and fees out of your own pocket if you are a California resident whose total family income is less than $80,000 a year and you qualify for financial aid." http://admission.universityofcalifornia.edu/paying-for-uc/glossary/blue-and-gold/index.html.

11. See the 2010 report "University of California Funding Streams Proposal," which includes a study of nonresident tuition at: https://blink.ucsd.edu/_files/finance-tab/cbo/FundingStreamsUCProposal.pdf.

12. Nicholas Ibarra, "UCSC planning for 10,000 more students by 2040," *Santa Cruz Sentinel*, January 12, 2018.

13. http://50years.ucsc.edu/thenext50/.

Illustrations

Figure 1. Reading on the Porter Wave (otherwise known as the Squiggle, and earlier in UCSC's history as the Flying IUD). Photo by Carolyn Lagattuta, 2009. Sculpture by Kenny Farrell. Campus Photo Archive. Communications and Marketing Department, UCSC. Copyright UC Regents.

Figure 2. Rachel Carson College at Night, 2011. Photo by Chian Tu. Campus Photo Archive. Communications and Marketing Department, UCSC. Copyright UC Regents.

Figure 3. Student with narrative evaluations. 1970. Courtesy Special Collections, University Library, University of California Santa Cruz. UCSC Photography Services: UA 50: ua0050_neg_06639_17.tiff.

Figure 4. Rally for Public Education posterSee, Circa 2015. Courtesy Special Collections, University Library, University of California, Santa Cruz. UA98: Women of Color Research Cluster Records: ua098_007_0001.

Figure 5. Path to the bookstore. 2011. Photo by Irene Reti. 2010.

Figure 6. Banner for the Campaign for UC Santa Cruz. 2015. Photo by Irene Reti.

Figure 7. Seeds. Santa Cruz Women's March 2018. Photo by Irene Reti.

Chapter 37

Transforming Fear

The 2016 Election, Reaction, and Resistance

People seem to realize shitty stuff is going on in America. America's not the greatest place everyone thought it was.

—Khalen Hudson

"You Knew Something Was Wrong": The 2016 Election and UCSC

Sareil Brookins: Oh. Trump. Leading up to the actual election, I was always calling my dad, getting really worried. Because I was like, oh, there's so much shit happening in the world. Here, there was a student—there were rocks thrown at the back of her head while she was walking in the quarry, or something like that. There were a lot more occurrences of hate crimes. During the election season before Trump got elected, my first quarter, somebody tore down the Black Lives Matter poster on my neighbor's door.[1] Tore it, and then left it on the floor. Erased their white board, erased my white board. I have no idea why, because I didn't do anything. And also, somebody tore down the Rosa Parks poster.[2] So the RAs are completely stressed out. Like why do people hate us? Somebody had the N-word with the ER in their Wi-Fi name[3] in R.PAATH [Rosa Parks African American Theme Housing.][4]

And then all we get is a freaking email, "Stevenson is a very diverse community. Be aware of that." We get mass emails, like, "Oh my gosh, don't hit Hank the turkey. Don't hit Hank. Oh my goodness, please be careful of this turkey," who attacks cars.[5] Hank is the turkey that lives in Stevenson with like a family of freaking twenty. And he will attack your tires and jump on the hood of your cars and just be a little boss and sit there. And he literally was like rolled under somebody's wheel and everybody freaked out. He's totally fine. But we got a mass email. Or we get mass emails about, "Oh, somebody's bike was stolen. Please be on the lookout for this." But then, when all that shit happened in R.PAATH, where was the support?

And when it came down to that election day, boy, it was wild.

Carl Eadler: I was here in fall 2012, when Obama got reelected. I remember that night pretty clearly. And I was here on campus the night that Trump won the election. Those were two very different nights on this liberal campus.

Sareil Brookins: Everybody was hoping Hillary Clinton would win. But then when she didn't, everybody, thousands came to the quarry.

Katherine Le: Right after the election results were announced, students gathered in the quarry and protested.

Sareil Brookins: And even that was a problem, because it was just a whole bunch of white students up there speaking. When somebody who wasn't white would try to go up there, it was always cut off early. They weren't given the megaphone. There were some very loud verbal arguments that happened that night. A lot of people were showing their true colors. Like, "Yeah, I'm one of those people who voted for Trump. And he won. So now I'm going to yell it out loud, because I'm proud."

Samantha Caballero: I heard lots of people outside. I joined them. It wasn't a student-organized event. It wasn't like Gay Pride, where we've had this planned out. All these people were upset. We just wanted to go outside and be upset together.

It was powerful and moving. There were literally thousands of people. And the Quarry Plaza—there are pictures, too—where it's completely filled.

Louis Odiase: The day after Trump was elected, at Oakes, at least in Biko House,[6] a lot of people were crying. People did not come out of their rooms. A lot of people are immigrants and they're scared about what's going to happen. Or African Americans, they're like, "What's he going to do now?"

Sareil Brookins: That next day was very gloomy. You knew something was wrong. Everybody was talking about it. Some people were not talking at all. A lot of people were overwhelmed. I was comforting people—I had no idea who they were—because they were screaming and crying and having panic attacks. And it's like, "Yo, my parents are undocumented immigrants. Yo, I'm undocumented." And I'm just like, "I don't want to lie to you and say everything's going to be okay because I'm not that kind of person."

Sofia Johnston: So many of us were so heartbroken, and so in disbelief, and so worried about what would not only happen to us, but what would happen to our family. There was a lot of heavy emotion for the next couple of days. But a lot of us were just in a moment. We need time right now to mourn. Tomorrow we'll march. Tomorrow we'll do our activism. But right now, we need our space to mourn and be together as a community before we can start resisting.

Khalen Hudson: I was mad, but then I talked to my dad on the phone. And he was just like, "Hey, it is what it is. As black people, there's really nothing different. Another racist white guy's in the office. Like, hurray." And I was like, "You know? You're kind of right."

People were out there really protesting Donald Trump. And we were just like, "He's president. This is not going to get him impeached." I'm really logical, so it takes away a lot of my emotions. But I was just like, "We should be protesting about the electoral college[7] and not Donald Trump. Because it is what it is."

When he got elected, I was like, yes, he's probably going to do some horrible things, but we don't really know that yet. So, we can only react when shit starts happening. I'm really a big proponent of don't worry until you really have to, because that's bad for health and stuff. So, I was pretty calm through that whole process. I was looking out for other people and just telling them, "He's not president yet; we still have all these days left with Obama."

Louis Odiase: I guess the thing that's really keeping me comforted is, you know, this happened; there's no going back. The worst thing you can do is just keep on saying, "How did this happen?" It already happened. So just hope for the best, keep on living my life. Hopefully things don't go too bad.

Khalen Hudson: I had a meeting with my supervisor that day. She was also crying. She was really sad. And I was telling her, "Being in the black community, our people have not stopped dying. Our people have not got out of poverty. And we've always been getting the shit-end of the stick." And I was just like, "What's unique about this election, is now everyone is experiencing what we have been for this whole time. We've been out here protesting, but our voices have never been heard. But now that everyone's rights are getting attacked, now everyone all of a sudden is just on this train, like oh my gosh, what's going to happen to us?" And I'm like, welcome to our world.

People seem to realize shitty stuff is going on in America. America's not the greatest place everyone thought it was.

Samantha Caballero: The election of Donald Trump is strangely vindicating. For years, people at this campus have said there are people out there who are racist. There are people out there who hate immigrants and want them gone. There are people who are really angry. We are being marginalized. And a lot of people were like, "Oh, no, you're just exaggerating, that doesn't really happen." So now that a lot of those officials are in positions of power, people are like, "Okay, maybe all of you angry college students are right. Maybe you didn't just like think that up by yourself."

Katherine Le: The election results have caused a lot of unrest, especially within the marginalized communities of UCSC: students of color, LGBTQ-plus students. Now, more than ever, we need to stay in solidarity with one another.

Sabina Wildman: The Muslim Student Association is a really strong place of love on campus. Like, the nicest people ever. To have that ability to come together on campus is really, really great and powerful, especially in a time like this when you see people who are part of your community being pushed around, or violated, or demonized. And then, also feel really safe with each other. I think a lot of us, especially a lot of Hijabis who I know, are worried about walking around on campus. So just kind of being there for each other. Like oh, I'll walk with you. Just hit me up.

David Solano: When I saw the protest on campus the night of the election, I felt a sense of unity because I knew that there were a lot of us that felt the same way. UC Santa Cruz is a little bit more open-minded than a few other spaces, not entirely liberal, as people claim it is, but a little more open-minded. This election was very controversial and scary. For me, it did bring a lot of fear, not only for myself, but for my family back at home, and my friends and their families.

Samantha Caballero: When Trump was elected, the whole week was really sad. I don't think I'd ever seen my Facebook feed be so sad. I'd never seen so many students just openly crying. I think that happened for a lot of different reasons. I think the one that hits the closest to home for me is that

Figure 1

Women's March, Santa Cruz, 2017

Photo by Irene Reti

Trump had a lot of comments about people who were undocumented and he continues to have this image that people who are undocumented need to leave, and people who are immigrants, especially Muslim people are not Americans. And there are a lot of those students on this campus and in the United States but at UCSC, there were a lot of demonstrations happening because we don't agree with that. We don't want that. That's not our version of America.

George Blumenthal: One of Trump's first efforts was to eliminate DACA. He was prevented from doing that by a series of court cases, some of which were initiated by UC and by UC President Janet Napolitano.

Jess Whatcott: Napolitano has, surprisingly, mobilized many resources in support of undocumented students.[8] If undocumented students have any legal trouble, the university will provide them with an attorney. Our chancellor is very supportive of this, although he said he didn't want to be arrested, when I asked him how far he would go. But he is very supportive of undocumented students. And even our police chief. As president of the Graduate Students Association, I also go to the Police Advisory Board meetings. The police chief at UCSC is taking a pretty proactive line to protect undocumented students.

George Blumenthal: Napolitano was the one who came up with DACA for the Obama administration. Those court cases have been quite successful so far. But from the standpoint of our DACA students, successful though they may have been, they've got to be feeling really vulnerable. DACA has survived in court cases because the Trump administration didn't follow appropriate procedures in terms of eliminating DACA. But at the end of the day, DACA was created by the president, and

DACA can be eliminated by the president, if they go through the right procedures and safeguards. So it is a rearguard action to preserve DACA. That's all we're fighting when we go to court.

Even though we have so far saved DACA, that doesn't affect new students who are not eligible for DACA. So the longer DACA remains, the more it becomes the safeguard only for older students that have been in the system. You can't become a new DACA student; you can just renew your old DACA status based upon the court cases. So, de facto, DACA is disappearing as a safeguard. And that leads us back to where we were in the pre-DACA days, when students on campus felt unbelievably vulnerable. And although we've always said that we would not help federal agents or ICE come onto campus and round up students who didn't have visas or appropriate documentation—we've had to reiterate that many times—it still provides limited assurances to our students who are not documented, because it only takes once for them. They are very much at risk. And they feel very much at risk.

Jess Whatcott: People are very concerned and want to protect undocumented students against the Trump administration's war against them. The campus administration made it clear that they're not going to stand in front of an ICE officer to protect a student. That's not going to happen. But they have put in place a lot of legal support for students. They do want to make our campus safe for those students. They're doing the best that they can.

George Blumenthal: And for those students who cannot become DACA students, we can't even give them the kind of financial aid necessarily that we were able to put together for DACA students. So the situation is getting worse, rather than getting better. Many of these students, particularly DACA students, have been in the country for many years. Many of them are scared to death of being deported to countries where they don't even speak the language, in some cases. It's a human tragedy.

Rosie Cabrera: As long as I can remember, we have had undocumented students. They have been called different names. AB 540 did not exist until 2001.[9] We have had students who, as a result of the immigration laws and their own histories of how they have arrived to the US, either had started the process of becoming a resident, or did not have "papers." The legal battle around diversity, bilingual education in California, and within the national front has been difficult, and that is a whole history lesson, including Propositions 187, 227, and 209. Mingle this with the ramifications of immigration issues and an increasing population that was undocumented, and the University of California and universities across the nation became a mess in dealing with the financial needs of our undocumented students.

Santa Cruz had done well with the students that we now call undocumented students. The money had been there, because the state of California didn't prohibit the funds from being used and UC didn't prohibit the solicitation of scholarship monies for this constituency group. Maybe we had between eighteen to twenty undocumented students, not too many more than that. Esperanza Nee, who was the director of Financial Aid (at the time), did all the fundraising for that group to cover their total cost of tuition.

Then the door closed. The regents said, "Nothing. No monies can be given to students that are undocumented." It was the political climate. You couldn't fundraise. At that point, the vice chancellor of student affairs didn't even want us to say the words "undocumented students" out loud. We couldn't put anything in an email. It was like this aura of, if anybody finds out that you're

even talking to someone, you can end up in jail. I mean, it was really bad.

When we started organizing at El Centro [Chicanx Latinx Resource Center],[10] the students wanted to have a forum, an educational forum. I was like, oh, my god. I was censoring their flyer. "Oh, my god, we've got to be careful." Without even realizing, I was censoring. So I worked with the students and then invited our alumni to the forum. That was the first time that people started to self-disclose. All of a sudden, things started emerging. Students Informing Now [SIN] started.

Students Informing Now (S.I.N.): On a cold and wet Friday night in January of 2006, thirteen of us gathered together in a small room on campus at the University of California, Santa Cruz. It was a combination of a need to survive and a feeling of hopelessness that brought us all together for a future of joined hopefulness. We were all first-year undergraduate students who had grown up in California, attended and graduated from California public schools, and gained admission to UCSC. Some of us were born in the US, but many of us had migrated here as young children, and a few were considered undocumented. There we were at the same university with different histories and backgrounds, but tonight we had gathered with one goal in mind. The goal, if oversimplified, sounds something like this: to create an organization in support of AB 540 students, labeled by this nation as illegal aliens. AB 540, or the California nonresident tuition exemption, allows any student, including undocumented immigrants, to be exempt from paying nonresident tuition at public colleges and universities in California if they can show that they have successfully attended a high school in California for at least three years and successfully graduated or obtained a G.E.D. Not all AB 540 students are undocumented immigrants; approximately two-thirds of AB 540 students are US-born citizens who temporarily left the state and would be required to pay out-of-state tuition if it were not for this legislation. For the purpose of this article, however, AB 540 student refers to an undocumented immigrant student. We use this term because it reflects the language used within S.I.N. Little did we know that we were about to kick off a new chapter in our communities, our schools, and our own lives.

On that cold Friday night in January, we gathered together for a six-hour meeting to solidify our purpose as a new student organization called Students Informing Now (S.I.N.). Inspired by Paulo Freire's philosophy of popular education, we used an activity called "the flower" to develop our organizational mission and vision statement. The activity was prepared by one of our founding members, Metztonalli, and it used the analogy of a flower to represent our new organization: the roots, the stem, its center, the petals, the sun and the wind that also contribute to the growth of the flower. The center of the flower represented our organization, Students Informing Now. As a visual, the acronym S.I.N. was written at the center of our flower. The roots represented the social-economic factors that influence our lives. The stem represented the things that support and transmit nutrients needed for the flower to grow. The petals that surrounded the center represented our values. Our first activity in that meeting was to create this flower together by writing in the specifics for each part of the flower. This was our first step in using the tools of popular education in S.I.N.[11]

Yolanda Venegas, Lecturer: In 2006, I began working in the EOP office. There were a lot of crises. We were moving from one mini-crisis to another, every day. Undocumented students didn't have housing, didn't have funding, so students were always on the verge of leaving. The university was not acknowledging that it had a pretty good number of undocumented students. It was a very different time. If I had a student who was having an issue and I had to talk to people in Financial Aid, I literally had to walk over there and talk to one of my colleagues because I didn't feel comfortable sending an email, or calling even.

And frankly, what changed all that was the SINistas, who founded the organization Students Informing Now, five or six people, and we had a few of them working at EOP. They were relentless in terms of saying, "Okay, we need to do this. We need to do that." They knew exactly what needed to be done.

Within a span of less than five years, they transformed the campus. They were doing everything. They would do performances using the guerilla theater tactics, plays that the campus community went to. They had teach-ins for faculty. They put together workshops. They had a radio show that was intended to educate Santa Cruz; everybody and anybody could listen. They moved the whole campus. It was a multi-pronged approach using the methods of popular education.

Pablo Reguerín, Director of EOP: In my role as EOP director, I work in the area of student success, focusing on educational equity. Our program is a direct descendant of the civil rights movement. EOP programs didn't exist prior to the civil rights movement. I like to remind our team members, and staff, and students that we stand on the shoulders of the struggle of the civil rights movement and all those who fought for broadening the access to higher education.

My students have probably been my best teachers, in terms of how to work with students, in terms of listening. I remember a young man who couldn't pay tuition anymore. He was not welcome at his home anymore, back home. That was partially rooted in his sexual orientation, how he identified. He got to a point where he had run out of money. He had had scholarships that had run out. He needed a few more quarters to graduate, maybe three at most. And he just didn't leave. He was no longer on the books. He was couch surfing, and he made friends, and he kept going to class. A quarter into it, a second quarter, he was still going to class.

I said, "Why are you doing this? Do you realize you're not going to get credit?" I remember him telling me, he said, "What are my options? I can go back home, be homeless, maybe live in a warehouse, or seek some shelter. Being a student here, at least I'm learning. It's easier to be homeless here as a student."

I've seen so many undocumented students and families who had basically their education and hope, and that's it. They counted on people finding an exception, getting them their textbooks, piece-by-piece stitching together their survival, and their ability to study, and just be a student here. We still have a lot of issues on this campus around educational equity. Currently our under-enrollment of American Indians and African American students is unacceptable. Our students of color are graduating at the same rate as other students, but it's still too low.

This work at EOP has been, in the words of Paulo Freire, "an act of love."[12] This work has been about courage. It's been about fighting injustice. There is so much strength, and persistence, and humanity demonstrated by these students, in the face of such unjust and inhumane treatment. They are still coming to say, "I want to be here. I want to study. I want to contribute to society." It leaves me no place other than to be empowered to figure out solutions, to use my influence, everything that I can on every student case. They've taught me to be creative, to be resourceful, and to not accept any lack of success. Nothing has been as inspiring,

as powerful, as the lessons that I've learned from students, from their stories and their families.

Richard Vasquez: I live in Watsonville. I am retired from UCSC and I'm also an alum. Now, I have a moral and social responsibility to be there for the undocumented students and their struggle, because it's a human rights issue. I am seventy years old. We need to work across generations. That's not happening. I'm tired of participating in organizations where there are a bunch of viejos, my age, or ten years older. Where're the young people? When I say "young," I am talking twenty or thirty. We need them at the table. This is going to be their generation, their world. What do they need from us? We have an organization here in Santa Cruz County: we call ourselves Dreamweavers. We are working with UCSC students, but also students across the county—high school students from Watsonville to Santa Cruz. We're working with UCSC students, in terms of housing, financial aid. We are trying to raise money. So, for example, on May the seventh, we'll be having a fundraiser at Cowell College, where Dolores Huerta will be coming.[13] She is the keynote speaker for the Chicano/Latino convocation that night. We have been asked to donate one hundred dollars for Dream students. So, I put my money where my mouth is. Gotta walk the talk. And I'll be bringing a young person from Watsonville High School with me.

Victor Garcia-Zepeda: Here at UCSC, we have a very cohesive community and we like to help each other out. That's inspiring for other students who are thinking about going to UCSC. I think that it's a great school in the sense of community. Maybe that should be our motto now.

"There is Still More Work to Be Done"

David Solano: There's this whole stigma against millennials. It's like, "Oh, millennials, they're so bad. I hate them." Why do you hate them? "They're always creating chaos, blah, blah, blah." Whatever. It's like nada chaos. But people of my age, or around that age range, are not being scared any more of voicing out. There's not only white people protesting, it's people from different intersectionalities—black folks, Latinx folks, queer folks, people with disabilities—everyone coming together and voicing out their thoughts and fears.

Rosa Melero, Student: We needed to make the Disability Resource Center (DRC) more visible, make students with disabilities feel more comfortable.[14] Our program is dedicated to making UCSC a more welcoming and inclusive place for students with disabilities. The DRC is not very well known and often people don't come looking for it unless they have a disability. And even then, sometimes people don't come looking for it, because they're shy about having a disability.

There's a stigma around having disabilities on campus. There's this feeling that if someone goes to the Disability Resource Center, there's something wrong with them, when it's not that at all. It's just that you might need another way of doing something, like getting around. And people who have depression or anxiety, which is a large part of our population at the DRC—there's such a stigma around that. People, when they find out that someone has like depression or bipolar disorder or something, change their attitudes around those people. No wonder those people don't want to come and receive help. People believe they're going to be judged if they come, when in reality, we're in no place to judge you. In fact, you should be proud of coming to get help for your disability. You should be proud of standing up for yourself.

Sabina Wildman: I'm mixed race and I'm also of mixed religious background. My dad grew up Protestant Christian; my mom grew up Sunni Muslim. So, coming to Santa Cruz, I was like, wow, there are some Muslim students. I know, because there's some hijabis. That's pretty cool because growing up, I didn't really see that many.

So, coming here, I met some people—I would go to programs and events that I'd find out through student government-related things. There was a whole week, I think the Women's Center put on, probably with MSA [the Muslim Students Association]—this movie with different women talking about their life stories, and why they wear hijabs and what it means to them. I found hope and happiness and comfort. And community.

Sareil Brookins: I came here for Destination Higher Education [DHE], part of Student-Initiated Outreach weekend.[15] It blew my mind. It completely, I guess you'd say, woke me up. You hear the term "woke" or, "she's so woke," or really conscious. That was one of the turning points of my life in terms of, like, okay, okay, I'm black.

When I went, what changed my whole mindset was they had this group come in. They simulated what it would have been like to have been African [and captured by slave traders.] We were blindfolded, basically, and went into a room holding each other's shoulders. All you had were your ears and your nose to smell things. They made a simulation of what it would have been like to be African, to have been stripped away from everybody [and sold into slavery]. It was scary because it was pitch black, and they had music. They had vivid descriptions of what you were doing at that moment. There were people crying, in tears. I had this realization that I needed to look into who I am, and pay my respects to the folks that sacrificed themselves, or were forced to, for people like myself and other students.

Sabina Wildman: As time moved on, I've gotten really involved, especially in MSA and activism. We're always about bringing people together. That's a powerful thing, spiritually, and socially and culturally. We have social events and invite people in. It's never only for Muslim folks. A lot of Americans have never met someone who's Muslim. People need to meet Muslims so they break those stereotypes.

Sareil Brookins: Here at UCSC, there is the African American Resource and Cultural Center.[16] There's the ATAT, the African American Theater Arts Troupe,[17] there's BSU, Black Students United. BMA, Black Man Alliance. ABS, African Black Student Alliance. There's NSBE for black engineers. There's ASU for African Student Union.[18] There's EOP for low-income, first-generation students. There's the DRC [Disability Resource Center]. There were all these places where I felt supported. They told us about protests that they had, actions that they had. And I was just like: is this college? Is this what college is about? I was really excited and couldn't wait till I'd come here.

And a big, big part of why I came here was because we got a tour of R.PAATH, which is the Rosa Parks African American Theme House in Stevenson, the most white college. And I was like, wow, they really need us here. It was nice to walk into a place and see people who look like you.

Khalen Hudson: I'm the only black student graduating this year, I think, in the chemistry field. Last year, a couple graduated. And the year before that, a couple graduated. So, they were like my "mentors." And they were always super smart, in labs, in their studies, really doing it.

It's also cool that I'm a black scientist. I would like to, when I leave, later on in life do something for black people in the STEM [Science, Technology, Engineering & Mathematics] field, just so they have resources. Because it's hard when you're at this school and you see no one. That's why you only have your friends in the STEM field, which is really cool, because we're such a close little community. It's just like, "Oh, you're really doing neuroscience." And then like, "You're really doing chemistry. And it's good shit, man. Good shit." So, it's really nice and affirming to know the people here. We have no black faculty in the sciences at this school. It was pretty hard. So, it would be nice to give back to my community that way.

Louis Odiase: I'm in Oakes College. I'm an RA for the Biko House. I'm originally from Antioch, California, which is in the East Bay area, forty minutes north of Oakland. I went to a predominantly black high school, African American. In high school, we never talked about social justice issues, or anything political.

I'm Nigerian. And my parents, of course, they're Nigerian, too. Education is a huge thing in the house. Like straight As, everything. If you don't, it's like whoa, who are you, you're not a part of this family. So, I had to be in one of those top tiers in school.

I think the biggest reason that made me come here was Destination Higher Education [DHE], which is for high school seniors. They bring high school students here, minority students, bring them here, give them a tour around the school for three days. And they show them different things about this campus. And I started seeing like wow, this could be possible, a great place to go. Mainly the people I ran into were friendly.

Figure 2

Rosa Parks African American
Theme House, (R.PAATH)
Stevenson College, 2018

Photographer unknown

Sareil Brookins: But the town of Santa Cruz, it's hella white. There's certain parts where you go and there are Latinx.[19] And I love that. But downtown, it's not always that comfortable. I've had friends kicked out of stores because they were talking too loud. And it wasn't a library. These were black students. They asked why and they don't give them answers: "Just get out of my store."

Sabina Wildman: Downtown Santa Cruz is white-dominated. And it's kind of strange because you have all this Silicon Valley and hipster stuff going on. Then you also have the hippie culture—there's some of that left. Some of that's a little problematic in certain ways. But you also have a huge population of Latinx, undocumented and basically low socioeconomic status income folks. So, there's a huge array of the demographics of Santa Cruz. And then Santa Cruz also includes Watsonville, which a lot of people are not in touch with, or don't even know.

Sareil Brookins: There was a student who I'm a mentor for in R.PAATH and they are Nigerian. They're darker skinned. And they were walking with a friend of theirs who's Afro-Latinx. This is like Ocean Street or something. A car of two white men drove up next to them and called them "fucking [N-word]" and then drove off. This was on that student's birthday, and that was their first time going off campus. This was a first-year student. So I was like, damn. That sucks. I was so angry, I was just like, what? I can't control this city. I think this town is really weird, if I'm honest. I'm really careful when I'm in the city. I'm not just like, oh, yeah, carefree.

Victor Garcia-Zepeda: I've visited a lot of Latino neighborhoods within Santa Cruz. The conversations I've had, learning about their struggles and their worries got me a little bit closer to that community. Then a lot of these communities were talked about in my classes, like Beach Flats. Some of the indigenous populations of Oaxaca—there's a high density of them here. How is that these people of indigenous background, and also these Latino communities, are able to function and live in these predominantly white neighborhoods?

Sabina Wildman: We're involved in some local masjid [mosque], and sometimes we'll go there. There's Jumu'ah every Friday, which is Friday prayers, similar to how Christian people pray on Sundays. We have recently been working to get a prayer space on campus. The dining halls have been serving more halal food. I don't know if that's just recently, or if we've been asking for that, but that's pretty cool. Last year, Ramadan was during finals week. You fast during the day, sunrise to sunset. The dining halls close at certain times and they don't open until certain times. So, we were trying to get boxes to take out the food and sometimes it was a lot of discussing and trying to explain this is a religious holiday. Then there'd be a line of people behind you and you'd be like okay, I feel so bad, I'm just going to grab a snack and sneak it out and leave, for the morning, for Suhoor [the pre-dawn meal eaten during the month of Ramadan]. You can take like one piece or something. So that's why we were trying to get boxes to be able to eat early in the morning for Suhoor, for the food that you eat before you fast during the day. And especially during finals week, you want to make sure you have that energy. It's those little things that people don't really think about.

I worked with MSA to do the first protest against President Trump's first Muslim ban this winter quarter.[20] There was a huge turnout and it was very supportive. It was great to see the UC Santa Cruz community feel so connected to each other—who came out to that protest, and so strong in our voices and in people power.

Wendy Baxter: This year has been defined by moments where many of the students we work with felt personally threatened and attacked, by either the shooting at the Pulse Nightclub[21] or results of the election. As an older person I can look back and know that yeah, this is a horrific political time in my experience and for my identities and the identities of people that I care a lot about. But we have had these moments before and will have them again, probably. I know we will get through. But many students, like with the Pulse Nightclub, felt personally attacked and threatened, which I totally understand. They don't have years of knowing that most people are good people. So, we try and teach self-care and hope, provide hope.

Sabina Wildman: I think a lot of times, if you're just watching the news, or reading the news, or doing whatever, it gets really like, oh, I'm helpless, I can't do anything about it. But you realize that you can all come together to create those kind of spaces and have your voices heard. When you chant, and go around campus and rally each other up, and have the signs that you're able to say what you want to say, you are heard.

Samantha Caballero: I'm happy to go to a place where people are united in not agreeing with the values of the Trump administration. I know that if I wanted to be really critical about this presidency, I wouldn't be seen as being un-American.

Khalen Hudson: I had a Trump supporter on my floor. That was interesting, to say the least. He was just like, "Yeah, I'm a Trump supporter." And I was just like, "Why?" And he was just, "Because my grandpa worked for him," or something. His grandpa was involved with him somehow business-wise and he really respected the fact that he was such a good businessman. And I was just like, "How can you overlook all the other stuff?" And basically, he didn't understand; he was this white kid from Boston, so he was raised pretty conservatively. So, he just didn't understand. He just didn't understand.

Wendy Baxter: It's hard. Most of the students that I work closely with were feeling threatened. Like, "I can't believe there are people who hate us that much, hate *me* and my identity." It felt really personal. So, all of us—not just at the CoCo [CoCurricular Center], but all of us at Nine and Ten—are reaching out to try to provide hope and nurturance and longitudinal perspective, from those of us who are a different generation than our students. In this election time, in this political climate, it's my responsibility to listen to all people, even people who support Trump. They support him for a reason, and whether I agree with the reasons or resonate with the reasons, it's important to talk to those folks and make sure they feel included in our community.

Khalen Hudson: A lot of people are more open to learn about differences. A lot of stuff, especially transgender rights and stuff like that, is coming up. And a lot of people don't know the difference between sex and gender, or the difference between all the different types of sexualities and stuff like that. So, education is happening, and I think it's pretty good. All you can do is just educate and hope that it resonates with them.

Samantha Caballero: Something that I've especially tried to work on is to avoid using call-out culture. What I mean by that is that, especially when I started here, if somebody would say something that was problematic, or something wasn't considerate, people would just call them out and call them a bad person, blah, blah, blah. What I've been trying to learn is even if I don't share the same opinions as somebody else, I think that I should still respect their right to having opinions and other people should respect their rights. I think there is a line to that. The line is that once it starts infringing upon other people's rights, then I can't be okay with it.

George Blumenthal: I'm concerned about some of the symbolic issues and symbolic changes that have emanated and become pervasive in society as a result of the Trump administration. The idea of false news is anti-intellectual. His administration has provided a divisiveness in society which affects us all. There aren't that many Trump supporters at UCSC, but we're not isolated from the rest of society. And the lack of tolerance in the administration and in Washington, D.C., for other viewpoints, I believe, has translated onto the campus. I think that people of the left and people of the right have developed an unwillingness to tolerate opposing views, even, or to hear opposing views. That has become much more acute of late. It has also become quite noticeable, at least to me, that there's a tendency to Satanize those how have views other than your own. Most people are not satans. Most people are well-meaning people wanting to do right. And yet they find themselves Satanized by those holding different views, which I find deeply disturbing.

Pavel Machotka: There will be such challenges ahead. Suppose the political climate becomes so fearful that we commit 50,000 soldiers to Syria, limit the civic freedoms of certain groups (or even all of us), and tighten all forms of surveillance. We're going to see, I think even in the University of California as a whole, not specifically UCSC,

a restriction on academic freedom, of thought and of expression. Acts such as the creation of new Manzanars may not take place, but others, responsive to new fears, may. America is likely to overreact with fear and simplistic solutions, and I hope the university is not infected by them, or by the climate that inspires them.

David Solano: There is still more work to be done on campus. I think a lot of the movements we do now are so that someday people won't have to go through this anymore. That's going to take a long time, a very long time, hundreds of years, maybe thousands, I don't know. But it's a start. It will create a bigger impact someday.

What I've learned here at UC Santa Cruz is passion in working with people and making sure people don't have so much fear. And if they have fear, to transform that fear into something else, whether it be in forms of activism, expression through art, I don't know, just something, whatever they like to do. We are in a different time, and in a time where we have the ability to fight back.

Endnotes

1. Black Lives Matter (BLM) is an international activist movement rooted in the African American community. The movement has organized against police brutality, racial profiling, a racist criminal justice system, and other forms of systemic racism.

2. Rosa Parks was an activist in the civil rights movement, best known for her pivotal role in the Montgomery Bus Boycott in 1955.

3. Brookins' emphasis of the N-word ending with "ER" is as opposed to the n-word ending with "A" is meaningful. The latter is more casual, friendly, the way the word is reclaimed and used by some in the black community. "ER" implies a severe pronunciation, more of like a racist white person-Bull Connor-George Wallace kind of pronunciation.

4. R.PAATH—Rosa Parks African American Theme Housing—is a student-initiated living-learning space located at Stevenson College. It houses students whose interests span historical, present-day, and future experiences of predominantly African American, Black, and Caribbean peoples.

5. The population of non-domesticated turkeys in California has increased dramatically in the past decade. A quarter of a million of these "wild" turkeys (naturalized from wild turkeys imported from Texas and released in California in the 1960s through the 1990s as part of a California state government-sponsored recreational hunting program) are now roaming across the state. This increase is also visible at UCSC, where it is now not uncommon to encounter turkeys in campus parking lots and on roads. For the most part, the turkeys are not aggressive. See Dan White, "Turkey Tale: How the Big Birds Have Pecked Their Way Into Campus Legend," *UCSC News*, November 20, 2017. https://news.ucsc.edu/2017/11/tough-turkeys-on-campus.html.

6. Biko House is part of Multicultural Theme Housing at Oakes College. It is named after Bantu anti-apartheid activist Stephen Biko.

7. Donald Trump won the Electoral College, 306 votes to Hillary Clinton's 232, but lost the popular vote by over 2.5 million votes. According to the *New York Times*: "Presidential electors—and particularly Republican electors, who are bound by tradition and often state law to support Mr. Trump—were inundated with phone calls, emails and even threats demanding that they vote for someone else. Leaders of groups that were lobbying the electors had privately believed they had a chance to persuade enough Republican electors to defect, denying him an Electoral College majority and throwing the election to the House of Representatives." See Richard Pérez-Peña, "Donald Trump Completes Final Lap, Electoral College, to White House," December 19, 2016. https://www.nytimes.com/2016/12/19/us/politics/electoral-college-vote.html. This effort was not ultimately successful but the debate over the electoral college continues. See: https://www.npr.org/2016/11/06/500660424/how-the-electoral-college-works-and-why-you-don-t-want-to-think-about-it.

8. Janet Napolitano became the 20th president of the University of California on September 30, 2013. Napolitano had served as Secretary of Homeland Security from 2009 to 2013, which is why Whatcott is expressing surprise at her support for undocumented students. Napolitano introduced the Undocumented Students Initiative, which provides UC campuses with funding to address undocumented students' unique needs through a range of support services, including academic and personal counseling, financial aid and legal advising. See: http://undoc.universityofcalifornia.edu/.

9. California's Assembly Bill 540 was signed into law by Governor Gray Davis on October 12, 2001, allowing access to in-state tuition rates for undocumented and other eligible students at California's public colleges and universities. The law allows students who attended high school in California, among other eligibility requirements, to pay in-state tuition fees instead of out-of-state tuition at California's public institutions of higher education, including the University of California, California State University, and California Community colleges. The law has been important in the pursuit of college accessibility for undocumented students in California.

10. "The Chicano Latino Resource Center was established in 1995 as a response to the educational needs of Chicanx Latinx students at the University of California, Santa Cruz. Better known as "EL CENTRO" by students and staff, the Center serves as a hub of organized activity and resources that support student transition, retention, graduation and academic advancement." https://elcentro.ucsc.edu/.

11. S.I.N. Collective, "Students Informing Now (S.I.N.) Challenge to the Racial State in California without shame, SIN Vergüenza," *Educational Foundations*, Winter-Spring 2007.

12. Paolo Freire wrote "Education is an act of love, and thus an act of courage," in *Education for Critical Consciousness* (Bloomsbury Publishing, 1974) 781-784.

13. Dolores Huerta spoke at UCSC's 10th Annual César Chávez Convocation on May 7, 2013.

14. For more on the Disability Resource Center's mission see https://drc.ucsc.edu/about/about-us/index.html.

15. "The Black Student Union's (formerly known as the African/Black Student Alliance) program, Destination Higher Education (DHE), introduces newly admitted students to the Afrikan/Black/Caribbean community and student life on the UC Santa Cruz campus. DHE provides personal, social, and academic workshops that focus on the Black Experience at UC Santa Cruz and are presented by Afrikan/Black/Caribbean students at UC Santa Cruz. In addition, the weekend features critical dialogue, workshops and interactive activities focused around community issues as well as current events." See: https://admissions.ucsc.edu/visit/sio/index.html.

16. The African American Resource and Cultural Center was the first ethnic resource center at UCSC. It provides a wide range of support, resources, and programs for students from the African diaspora at UCSC. See: https://aarcc.ucsc.edu/about/index.html.

17. The UCSC African American Theater Arts Troupe began in 1991 and continues today. See: http://artsites.ucsc.edu/aatat/04/about.html.

18. For more on African American student organizations see: https://aarcc.ucsc.edu/student-life/student-orgs.html.

19. Latinx is the gender-neutral alternative to Latino and Latina. This term aims to move beyond gender binaries.

20. "Executive Order 13769, titled Protecting the Nation from Foreign Terrorist Entry into the United States, often referred to as the Muslim ban or the travel ban, was issued by President Donald Trump. It lowered the number of refugees to be admitted into the United States in 2017 to 50,000, suspended the US Refugee Admissions Program (USRAP) for 120 days, suspended the entry of Syrian refugees indefinitely, directed some cabinet secretaries to suspend entry of those whose (primarily Muslim) countries do not meet adjudication standards under US immigration law for 90 days, and included exceptions on a case-by-case basis. The signing of the order provoked widespread condemnation and protests and resulted in legal intervention against the enforcement of the order with some calling it a 'Muslim ban' because Trump had previously called for temporarily banning Muslims from America soon after the 2015 San Bernardino terrorist attack, and because all of the affected countries had a Muslim majority." https://en.wikipedia.org/wiki/Executive_order.

21. On June 12, 2016, forty-nine people were killed and fifty-eight others wounded in a terrorist attack/hate crime inside Pulse, a gay nightclub in Orlando, Florida.

Illustrations

Figure 1. Women's March, Santa Cruz, 2017. Photo by Irene Reti.

Figure 2. Rosa Parks African American Theme House, Stevenson College. 2018. Photographer unknown.

Coda

Bookworm Banana Slug Weather Vane by West
Coast Weather Vanes

Photo by Matt Fitt

Bridge to Hahn, 2018

Photo by Irene Reti

Chapter 38

"For Times We Can't Imagine"

Clark Kerr: UCSC comes out as probably the most successful of the many experiments tried in the United States in the sixties, which was a decade of a lot of experiments in higher education. Most of them failed and were lost without trace. There's been a tendency to, as with all other reform campuses, revert to the standard pattern, standard mold. But Santa Cruz is going to be better off trying to figure out its own personality and not try just to imitate other existing personalities.

Dean McHenry and I played the initial role. What a wonderful evening it was when the campus was first opened, and the new students were here in their enthusiasm. It was also a little sad, because we'd had the dream and the dream was born, but as soon as it was born it belonged to other people. It had been our dream, and had now become the reality. But the reality belonged to the new faculty members, as they were brought in, to the new students, as they came, and to the new administrators.

One has to reconcile oneself to separation from one's dream and to recognize that others are going to see things in different ways than you did, and make changes. That's their business and their right. And however well or ill you think you bent that twig when you planted the tree, that twig gets subjected to sun and wind and shadows. It may

grow, has a right to grow, must grow in other ways than, to some extent, then you dreamt.[1]

Byron Stookey: California was the first state to really come to grips, in the twentieth century, with the fact that higher education of the public must be planned. Its text and rationale was the Master Plan for Higher Education in California, published in 1960. The Santa Cruz design is aimed at making education powerful and alive for people. The question is, "Can it work? Can the house—and the cliché is too right to avoid—be made a home?" I expect that it can. But not without difficulty. And the difficulty stems from the fact that the University seems not wholly ready to take the creative risks operationally that the architects of the Santa Cruz campus have undertaken theoretically. The Santa Cruz campus, if it is to be a human institution true to its design, must give rise to passion, irrationality, vision, and eccentricity. At Harvard, despite all its appearance of conservatism, these qualities do have a place. In the University of California, despite all its progressiveness, it may be that, as yet, they do not. The Santa Cruz campus is an experiment. It must therefore be unusually clear about its aims. And understanding them it must take the initiative in developing means of evaluation. At the same time, however, the University must have the courage to welcome, as faculty, people who may bring to a

Figure 1

Robert Jorgensen, Executive Assistant to Dean of Social Sciences (in front of a banner with an Ansel Adams quote) fields questions on campus growth, 1991

venture that is unconventional the unconventional vision it requires. And the University must allow that vision to operate, and be tested in ways that are consequential. These are the challenges that Santa Cruz and the University have begun to face: to establish an institution which, though massive and public, offers live and powerful education.[2]

Robert Sinsheimer: If you go back to the original description of the campus, it is a lot of rhetoric and not a lot of plan. But if you really believe that rhetoric—and this is really curious—it's not a UC campus; UCSC doesn't belong in the University of California under the California Master Plan. Yet, who were the people that made the California Master Plan? Kerr and McHenry. In fact, there are quotes where Kerr and McHenry point out that the Master Plan hangs together; you can't start making exceptions here and there, that's it's an integrated whole; and it only works as an integrated whole. Here they were, setting out to make UCSC a major exception, and apparently quite unconscious of the fact, or quite willing to overlook it. UCSC breaks the spirit of the Master Plan, which they themselves invented. You remember Al Capp's cartoons, those little figures that always had a dark cloud over them? It's sort of like that with this campus. It was to be primarily an undergraduate campus. That's not part of the UC system. It was out of place; it didn't fit, either in the UC system or in the Master Plan. It's had to struggle with that ever since.

Solomon's House: Santa Cruz was created as a reform within the University of California system, but that reform did not end with the opening of a new campus. Rather, we hope, it has begun there. Cowell College was meant to function as an inspiration for change in the academic world. If the faculty and the administration ever become content with Cowell as it is, Cowell College and

Santa Cruz as a whole will be nothing more than ordinary.[3]

Michael James, Student: I graduated in 1975, so it's been almost forty years since I started here. UCSC has sort of devolved. It was an alternative school of the nine campuses when it opened. Dean McHenry, who is not any educational radical, was part of the movement inside the university to open the academy to consider different kinds of ways to do higher education. UC Santa Cruz, Antioch—different schools in the country at that time, Evergreen as well—were experimenting in higher education that was more interdisciplinary and grounded in reality. The remnant of that vision still exists in Santa Cruz, but it's much more homogenous now. It's much more UC. The eclectic element that Dean McHenry had, and people like Herman Blake had—a lot of that is gone. You see elements of that. You see that in women's studies, queer studies.

But when you win a victory over discrimination and become part of the culture, there is both a loss and a gain. The gain is that you gain some equity. The loss is that edge that got you there is compromised, to some extent. A lot of students of color may go through Oakes now but Oakes has a different meaning for this generation of students of color. In one sense, you win the victories of overcoming racism and class bias by getting into the institution, but what the institution will do is say, "Now you are a part of what we do. You are no longer a part of what you came here to do." Jimmy Baldwin[4] always said, "Why would you want to get a room in a house on fire?" In neoliberalism and globalization, what does the university mean to poor people and people of color? We manage to get some educational equity, but what does it mean to be equal in an institution that reproduces the 1 percent?

At a particular time, there were enough convergences of different political and institutional forces that made something possible. It's hard for us to sustain the public aspect of the public university. It gets more and more difficult, and that's a constant struggle that people of color have. You almost have to be affluent to go to a four-year university these days.

I've been involved with popular education and advancing the work of Brazilian educator and philosopher Paulo Freire with communities of color for the last forty years. So I've made some choices to do social movement work inside institutions and outside of it. That's the legacy I've inherited from people like Ralph Guzmán and Herman Blake and all those guys.

There are a number of obstacles: the obstacles of globalization; the obstacles of attacks on affirmative action; the obstacles of nonprofit work being underresourced; the obstacles of diminishing opportunities for people of color, in the context of globalization. While we're earning and fighting and gaining equity at certain levels of society in the job market and institutional life, at the same time, we're in a tumultuous period, in terms of global neoliberalism; fluctuation; so much migration.

I think what's good about working with students now is that you are already accustomed to complexity and you're not intimidated by it. In my generation, things were more binary—with capitalism/communism, black/white, and US/Not US, Third World. We were the last generation of people who functioned with binaries as a way of understanding reality. I think this generation finds binaries like that less useful, and to me that's a success.

Glenn Willson: This, I think, is the tragedy—that Santa Cruz started with a whole group of people who had great integrity about what they were trying to do, who didn't want to introduce low standards for their own sake. They didn't want people to smoke pot as part of life. They didn't set up the place in order that there should be no self-discipline or collective discipline, no manners or anything of the sort. They didn't set the place up intending that it would be wracked by demonstrations and would chase the governor off the campus! All that hit us after we'd started.

If we ask, "What would have happened if it had started in 1956," when there was no Vietnam War, when the racial thing hadn't blown up in the States, none of these great outside forces we somehow picked up, the whole story would have been completely different. The thing that really does madden me, what infuriates me, is the statements that have been made several times in these last few years by people, even on the campus here, that Santa Cruz was a sort of crazy joke, that it never had any decent standards, and that the whole thing was a total failure. It is grossly untrue. You've only got to look at the academic records of this place, and the kind of students we got and what they achieved. If we'd all been such knaves and fools, not a single student would have come out with a decent degree.

Page Smith: My regrets are that gradually, year after year, the faculty participated less and less in the life of the college. I blame that largely on the competition from the boards. The real mistake was in not having the gumption to make the colleges the whole show. I don't know that we could have under the circumstances. There were many things working the other way, but the (lack of) resolution to really make it a collegiate arrangement, and to have the boards function in a much more limited and informal way even than they did, was the principal failure.

One of the things that was constantly in Chancellor Dean McHenry's mind was how to

Figure 2

Restored Hay Barn, Cowell Limeworks Historic District, 2018

Photo by Carolyn Lagattuta

make this campus both innovative and prestigious. I think you can't. That was trying to carry water on both shoulders. I don't blame him for that. I just think that made inevitable the colleges' decline. I certainly didn't fight against it. I accepted that as a proposition. I think our subsequent history makes very clear that, with all our concern with so-called innovations, we weren't ready to go the last mile. That that was a very serious mistake.

I don't think the boards and the colleges can peacefully co-exist. The nation can't exist half slave and half free. We could have gone the whole hog and not had boards of study. I think, in retrospect, we should have. If Dean McHenry had not been so preoccupied with our social rating, our standing in the eyes of the outside world, that could have been done, and Kerr might have backed him up. We would have been infinitely better off for that.

We were often frightened by our own temerity. We were trying something that, by the standards of the University of California, was quite unorthodox. We were constantly being reminded of the need to achieve respectability in certain areas, in order to be allowed to be experimental in others. I think, in retrospect, that without any question, we should have grasped the nettle firmly. The notion of college autonomy, which I certainly didn't fight for or propose at the beginning, was in fact essential.

And if suddenly, I were sitting down with lots of people now to talk about creating a university in Santa Cruz—having the experience and knowing what I do now—I would want it in the town itself. I don't blame anybody for not thinking of that in 1960. That would have been rather novel and probably dismissed as an inappropriate notion, but I feel very strongly that that's where the university belongs—right in the town. That's hard to say in view of the beauty of the campus site, but I believe that the physical distance of the university from the town represents the intellectual and psychological distance of the scholarly community from the practical world, which is bad for both.

Paul Niebanck: If we were to try to become a small-scale Berkeley—that is, yielding to the traditional structure entirely—we would be engaging in a losing operation. If we were to engage, for example, in a graded system here—A, B, C—or whatever, or if we were to eliminate the colleges, or if we were to make student life in many ways more routine than it is, less oriented to the individual, it would all be self-defeating. What I would like to see is the colleges be enhanced and that we retain all of these other supporting elements that give Santa Cruz its vitality and uniqueness. We have to operate from strength and we have plenty of strength. We cannot say, "We're going to outdo our competitors in their terms." We have to say, "We are something distinct, if you like what we are." Over the long run, I have to believe that the health of the society depends on units like UCSC, not on what we call the traditional forms. We will survive and be a vital element in American education.

George Von der Muhll: Was UCSC to be known primarily to the outside world as an excellent and innovative set of colleges, or as a respectable, but middle-rank university? In principle, Kerr and McHenry had contended that such issues posited a false dichotomy: UCSC would grow big but still seem small because of its colleges. But over time, that saying began to lose credibility.

The University of California said that, as one of its campuses, UCSC was a university, and that its standards for tenure, its rate of expansion, and the national and international attention given to its research findings should be determinative of its character. On the other hand, the institutional innovations that seemed to the outside world to give UCSC its character seemed to say that it was

Figure 3

Sinsheimer Labs and Science Hill, 1990

Photo by Joel Levick

aspiring to be a Swarthmore in the woods. I don't see how they could have hoped to break the hold of these conflicting expectations.

UC Santa Cruz has established itself as a respectable and respected campus of the University of California, blessed with its unmatched sylvan setting, and is to this day a most agreeable place in which to pursue teaching and research of high quality. Despite occasional protest demonstrations incited by the high costs of a college education even at a publicly supported university, its students seem generally appreciative of their surroundings and their classes, and the administrative staffs have maintained, from its earliest days, intangible qualities of personal concern and responsiveness that mark them off from the disgruntled placeholders of large and impersonal corporate bodies. Taken together, these are qualities that provide daily reminders of the potential privileges of membership in an American academic community.

But the founders of this campus brought with them a more ambitious agenda. They presented UC Santa Cruz to the world as an antidote to the desiccation and fragmentation of university education throughout this country and abroad. And the world listened. Journalists, novelists, and philosophers came to observe the regeneration of the human spirit, not only in its classrooms, but in its ancillary farm, gardens, and arboretum, its rejection of big-time commercial sports in favor of lifelong athletic skills, its celebration of continuous innovation and experimentation in its college-centered communities, and search for truth in the company of friends. Santa Cruz asked to be judged less by its immediate achievements than by its self-presentation as a model that challenged even such conventionally successful and prestigious institutions as Berkeley, Stanford, and Harvard.

That is a role that UCSC can no longer plausibly claim, nor does it seek to do so. There were some crucial decisions and critical turning points that removed it from consideration in this light. But seeking to account for this trajectory by spotlighting the internal dilemmas of its design and its vulnerability to external pressures tends to raise, perhaps too forcefully, the question of why such worldly and experienced figures as Clark Kerr and Dean McHenry had ever embarked on a venture so likely to fail, and even more, why they should have thought that its distinguishing features could last amid the turbulent currents of American society.

Hindsight, as has often been remarked, embodies twenty-twenty vision. I think we can be grateful that Kerr and McHenry lacked a clear understanding of just how much of a risky experiment their long-held dream of a campus really was, and how many of the crucial factors in the demise of their model were simply beyond the control of the founders. At any rate, that's why I, somewhat sadly, conclude that this campus isn't what the founders really wanted it to be. But it certainly is not a place that I myself have ever regretted coming to. For many people, it gave them a degree of freedom which they could never have found on another campus.

Michael Cowan: I think the campus has never been as different as it may have wanted to think of itself as being. The rhetoric of difference was probably overstated rhetorically, in the early years. It wasn't that we weren't, in some respects, different. But we could argue that any campus is different in various ways. A lot of the things we argued were innovative weren't—even in the context of public universities and even within the UC system—particularly innovative.

For example, the concern with undergraduate teaching. We place a great deal of concern on that. But I know colleagues at Davis and Berkeley and Irvine and San Diego and the other campuses who are equally dedicated, excellent teachers, who spend a lot of time thinking about undergraduates, even while they are working with graduate students. I have, over the years, worked with quite a few graduate students, in literature, and history of consciousness, and some other programs. I've had great experience with them, and it's never seemed to me that my work with them has conflicted with my work with undergraduates. In fact, the graduate students have been extraordinarily important resources in working with undergraduates. So I've really enjoyed that. For me, the discussions that have had to do with that kind of dichotomy have never played themselves out. I think that's true of the natural scientists too, when you think about the research teams that pulled graduate and undergraduate students together. Those kinds of differences, those kinds of innovations have been overstated.

We were helped by being a part of the UC system. We were helped through our crisis in the 1970s because we had a salary base that was set by the UC system. We had resources coming to us that were resources coming to the UC system. And so we were helped in very significant ways, even when sectors of the campus wanted to argue that we had gone our own way and we were independent of the system. We still are different, as various other campuses are different. I'm proud of those differences, but I don't think they should be overemphasized.

Karl Pister: UC is embedded in this group of major research universities in the United States who have their own culture. That culture was set following World War II after the decision of the federal mission agencies[5] to take over the support of graduate research, particularly in the sciences and engineering. The evolution of science was also influenced through Vannevar Bush's mission and ideal of "science, the endless frontier" statement that led to the establishment of the National Science Foundation.[6] This put tremendous emphasis on disciplinary loyalty and the importance of research. That made a major shift in the daily life of faculty members on every campus that aspired to be, or had become, a research university.

So the system grew. It wasn't handed down on a tablet. As a young faculty member at Berkeley, I typically taught three lecture courses per semester. I had, at most, one graduate student at a time. I got tenure at Berkeley, never having written a grant proposal. I had no sponsored research when I got tenure. That's the way it was in the early 1950s, or even the late 1950s.

One of the things that radically changed this, in addition to the Vannevar Bush Report and the emergence of the National Science Foundation, was entirely beyond our control. It was the launching of Sputnik. That totally changed the nature of our universities. The Space Race, the Cold War—created a national unity of purpose that substituted for the national purpose to win World War II, and now we had to win the Space Race and the Cold War.

Now, ironically, we are at a stage in history where those things have disappeared, and we don't seem to be able to find a national purpose that can be translated into a new job for our universities. Economic competitiveness, or the global economy, are much more amorphous. There's not an enemy to fight.

Pavel Machotka: I cannot conceive of another experiment such as UCSC. It was backed up by an enormous optimism in California, in the early 1960s; by the desire to give everybody a public university education, under Clark Kerr; by a Supreme Court presided by a former governor of California, Earl Warren, which turned out to be very liberal. An extraordinary time. Nobody [now in the summer of 2016] seems to be thinking, or saying publicly, that a broadly educated citizenry would be desirable, let alone useful. Have you ever read such a headline in the newspaper, or anywhere else? No. It's all quite concrete, not necessarily all wrong, but certainly limited by that sense that we now have to defend ourselves. We have no room left for imagination. If somebody said, "Here's ten million dollars to found a university. If you find the buildings I'll give you ten million dollars and you're going to try to produce a hundred scholars in the humanities in the next ten years," who would take them up on it? The level of imagination, given all the constraints, fiscal and military and so on, is very low. No, I don't see anything happening in the next fifty years, really.

But then, my vision is equally cloudy about the future of American democracy and its government. There are some dangerous signals and possibly very serious ones.

John Lynch: I seem to have lost the battle that education should become more social and cooperative, less competitive and individualistic. We're going through a much more competitive and individualistic phase in literary studies, and in the university in general. I hope the more communitarian concept of education will not be lost forever.

Education is a living thing. As a teacher, Socrates was a "midwife" of ideas, not a storage jar of information. A midwife assists in the birthing process, enabling life to come about and continue on its own. It is a major breakthrough if you can communicate that concept of education.

Michael Warren: The coherence, the social homogeneity, of the early days cannot be reproduced, nor should it be. Cowell College was very white. Stevenson College was very white. There were African American students here; they were a very conspicuous minority. I can remember my own, in a sense, innocence in relation to the pronunciation of the name of one my students, who was Hispanic. I realize that now, and it was just simply absence of familiarity. What I can talk about now sentimentally is something about the retrograde state of American society at that time. So I'm guilty of praising, in some sense, something that needed to be changed. But Cowell in the very early days, with Herman Blake here organizing the Cowell outreach program on Daufuskie Island in South Carolina— the seeds of that change were there.

Norman Locks: My classes in the last four years have been some of the most dynamic I've had for the diversity in the classes. People are out and open, and you have people of multiple races. There's so much gender diversity now. The quality of education, and the sharing of information among students, and the acceptance of others, is incredibly high. It's enriching. It helps people recognize their experiences more clearly in relationship to the artwork that they're making.

Early on, UCSC seemed to be very homogenous. Everybody came from the same place and everybody had the same experiences. Now, it's obvious that that's not true. And if that's not true, then we have different stories to tell.

Michael Warren: When I came to the campus, there were only about two or three women in the literature department. There was that homogeneity. Everybody read the same books because everybody came from similar backgrounds. There were people coming, I'm sure, from some poverty. Financial aid was not developed to quite the same extent at that time. There was no writing program on campus. Every college used to find out who of its students had not satisfied the Subject A writing requirement, and then arrange a course for them. We would appoint one person to teach the Subject-A students.[7]

Now, there is this large composition program, because so many students need it. This is a whole question of educational backgrounds, but it's also about the way in which the university has gone out and attracted a far broader body of students. There's a far broader ethnic range. There's a difference in levels of preparation within all ethnicities. That's very different. Homogeneity made it all easier. It was a different world. Any person of my age has to recognize the degree to which they grew up in an incredibly homogeneous society. Therefore the question of recognition and understanding of what goes into racial diversity is something we've had to learn.

Yolanda Venegas: Especially for first or second-year students, it's overwhelming, this huge institution. I want them to know that it's their university, and if they feel like there is something that needs to be changed, they can change it.

Robert Imada: Students of color on this campus feel the lack of diversity on this campus every day. In my classes, I am one of five people of color, and the only Asian. We feel marginalization and tokenization constantly. Even on the broad level, it's easy to only identify by what you're personally affected by. It shuts you out from other people's needs sometimes. So I had to talk to people and say, I can cover queer issues on this campus. At the Hate Bias Forum I talked about the hate crime that had happened recently in Santa Barbara, where a gay man was burned to death, and talked about intersections of racism and homophobia, and some examples of queer hate. When I spoke, I talked about how I am sick of white queer folks saying that "we" need to stand in solidarity with people of color because racism is hate just like homophobia. And queers of color are always sitting in the room going, "You bastards. We're here. We're queer, too. We are part of this community!" We are constantly

having to point that out. People of color do the same thing. Many people of color leaders I see on the news say, "If you're black, you need to stand up for people who are gay or lesbian, and if you are gay or lesbian and you see that a black person is being made fun of, you need to stand up." I say, okay, well I guess I'll stand up for myself! Gay is seen as white. I am not sure how people see me on this campus. I'm only here for four years. I'm a small piece of history.

Sareil Brookins: The first time I set foot here, I was like, where are the black people? I honestly cannot remember if I saw anybody else outside of the Destination Higher Education program, other than the mentors and the RAs that I had. I definitely noticed, this is a PWI, "predominantly white institution." So, my first impression was, I'm not going to see a lot of me here.

But that gave me all the more reason to come here and try to make some change, and live in R.PAATH. Honestly, the only reason I'm in Stevenson is because that's where R.PAATH was, is. It's House 7. Being there was great. It was like chocolate city. And then I walk out and I'm like, oh, I live in the chocolate-chip house in a vanilla shake. That was the best analogy I could come up with: we are the one chocolate chip in the vanilla swirl.

Something I do, especially now, in spring specifically, when they have like Spring Spotlight, I always, if I see a black student or a group of black students touring, or a group of Latinx students, students of color in a group, coming from a low-income area: I always go to them. I don't care if I have class. I will stop. I tell them about all the resource centers. I tell them about all the organizations, all of the retention programs. I just lay it down and then I leave.

The other day I was walking up toward Science Hill from Kresge. There was a group of elementary school students. They were all black. I wanted to cry. I was like, oh my gosh, black children! Like children in general, they're so happy and smiling and carefree. That was very therapeutic. I was like, wow, I just feel warm and fuzzy inside. I feel like the Grinch just getting his feelings back. I was like, wow, there is humanity. There's hope! Just seeing children smiling and people who look like me.

Julia Armstrong-Zwart: One way to make the campus a welcoming environment would be to understand that people who are different from you want to keep their difference. Women don't want to stop being women; people of color don't want to hang their ethnicity at the gates in order to come in. We don't want to be honorary white males. We want access to the richness, the resources that the university provides, and we're willing to compete in a fair way.

We, as women; we, as people of color, shouldn't automatically assume that we don't belong here. There's a real sense among students of color that the hook, the hook is going to come and they're going to be gone.

We're here because this is our place. We're here because this where we belong. The people who are from the dominant culture need to understand that it is our place, too. We haven't been invited into their home—you know, that sense of who's the owner and who's the guest or interloper. Those are concepts that need to be eradicated. The campus has gone a long way towards achieving that, but there's still a feeling of being here on sufferance. You were invited in and you need to be respectful because you're in somebody else's house. You don't start rearranging the furniture in somebody else's house. You do it in your own house. And certainly, that's what we were doing.

All of a sudden the influx of women and minorities occurred, and we came in and started saying, "We don't like that wallpaper. We're going to put new drapes up. That's an uncomfortable couch. We're not going to sit on that couch." I imagine that for many white males it was exactly as if somebody had come into their house and started doing that. Others said, "You're right. It's an ugly couch. It's an uncomfortable couch. Let's throw it out and get something that we both can sit on." So it's the willingness of everybody to work together to create a house that is comfortable for us all.

Olga Nájera-Ramírez: Los Mejicas is probably the largest university folklorico group in California now, not just in the UC system. We're the largest and we're the oldest. Some of the dance groups dwindle and die. UC Berkeley, right now, does not have a dance group. It died. I think one of the reasons that Mejicas is able to thrive is because, now that it's offered as a class, it's always visible. But it remains a student-run, student-directed group. We're marrying the best of both worlds. There's institutional support, but it's still thriving in the hands of the students and they pass on the baton.

We did a folklorico summit this year for the first time, and it was hosted by UC Riverside. People look at Los Mejicas as a model that they want to emulate. It's really nice that it's reached that status. It's not because the dancing is perfect. At university groups, it's never going to be perfect, because generations graduate, people move on. They go to graduate school or follow a career. So our membership is always rotating. But it's a very good company. It's a good place to learn. It's a good support environment. It's good community building. It's open to people of all backgrounds. It's open to people who've never danced. You can't ask more than that from a group. This year [2013] we're winning the Diversity Award at UC Santa Cruz. The celebration is next week, so I'm really excited. It took us forty-one years, but we did it.

We are about building community and supporting each other on campus. For the spring concert, families come to watch the students. The younger generations say, "I want to be up there." And the parents say, "Yeah, we're going to have our kids come up and go to UCSC."

Rosa Plaza: EOP has so many resources now, and they protect and advocate for students like the AB 540 population. They don't just say, "We are going to help you," but they go out of their way to make sure that students are healthy, to make sure students are eating, to make sure students have enough money to pay their tuition, and to make sure they have a job if they need it. As director of orientation, I support that. I work closely with EOP's staff. We help them with their Bridge Program and with the AB 540 extended orientation. We help them with staff support sometimes.

I love UCSC. I owe who I am to the experience that I had here. Any institution is going to have its issues, just like family. Things need to get looked at and worked on. You're not gonna hit utopia anywhere, but this is a really good place. I have a lot of respect for what UCSC is, and where we are going.

Jess Whatcott: I heard about UC Santa Cruz because I'm a huge fan of Angela Davis. I've read all of her work on prisons. And not only do I value everything that she's contributed to the field of critical prison studies, but I appreciate her wisdom about community organizing, and being in solidarity with people. That's why I first heard about UC Santa Cruz. When I was considering applying, I knew that she was professor emeritus here, and then began to realize that many other people whose work I admired, including Donna Haraway, Neferti Tadiar, Gloria Anzaldúa, had taught here, or been grad students here.

Carl Eadler, Student: There are sixteen thousand different stories going on for the undergraduates. There are sixteen thousand different conceptions of what UCSC means. And while there may be a couple of common themes that run between them, there is no one identity on campus. An amalgamation of a whole bunch of different identities come together for this four years in this one place. It's interesting to see things evolve over time. Everything is temporary. We're in a juxtaposition of these twenty thousand people on this campus. Not only will this time not exist again, these moments won't exist again. But the campus is more than just this place, and it's more than just this university, and it's more than just these buildings, these trees and these fields. What does it mean to be a UCSC student? What does it mean to be here right now, at this time?

Murray Baumgarten: In the early years, there were a whole bunch of people who said, "We should not grow any more. Pull up the drawbridge." I always thought of them as deep, dyed-in-the-wool conservatives, because they were conserving their privilege of having gotten here, and had no sense of the responsibility of the state of California to educate Californians all over the state and even here in this beautiful location. I'm very pleased that we've grown. I think we now are at the point where we can do interesting things as a public university of 18,000 students. Maybe we'll grow even more in the next few years. You can't be a public university of less size than that and do the range of things that we want.

I think that we may also be in a situation now where enough alumni have graduated, and they are putting pressure on the university to revive the role of the colleges and to expand it in terms of academic matters, not just social and living arrangements. We'll see how that plays out. I welcome that. The future is hard to predict, full of surprises.

John Daly: My original hope was that Santa Cruz would grow into a very desirable upper-middle-class community with a great university, and have the recreation of the Boardwalk, and then maybe a couple of hotels down in the beach area, where we would have conventions. We don't get any of that. We had more conventions of business and clubs in the 1950s than we get today, fifty years later.

And we have so much more traffic going up the west side to the university, coming around from River Street, around the bend and up High Street to the university. These no-growth people don't want to have any of these national stores in. We don't have a department store in downtown Santa Cruz. Ours are out on 41st Avenue in Capitola now. But in downtown Santa Cruz we have little shops selling beads, and lots of eating places. It really hasn't developed into any kind of a central, affluent community.

Just go over the hill ten miles, fifteen miles. Los Gatos has a gorgeous downtown. Gorgeous, with beautiful stores—outstandingly beautiful stores. We don't have any of those here. For example, one of the most popular franchises now is In-N-Out Burger. Everybody loves In-N-Out Burger, especially older people. And we don't have In-N-Out Burger in Santa Cruz County. It boggles the mind because they usually build them close to university campuses. But we don't have one in Santa Cruz. Ooh. Amazing. And so, the no-growth people have really overall kept this town squashed down.

But the campus, beyond teaching students, also brings prestige to itself and the community. I must say, UCSC has done quite a good job in that, especially in astronomy and in some of the sciences. And now in engineering. It could have done a lot more. And remember, as McHenry said, we were going to have an engineering school, which we finally got just six to eight years ago.

Before the university, Santa Cruz was a little beach town. The university has brought great cultural benefit to the community. It's increased the level of education and knowledge among the citizens. Without the university, and with no new industry (with more than ten employees) the town would be very poor. Or it would be a bedroom community for San Jose—something that people used to abhor, the thought of that. Well, we still are kind of the bedroom for Silicon Valley. But without the university, this town would be pretty hard up for income.

Carl Eadler: Kresge has a night hike that they do at the beginning of the year during orientation where everybody gets a glow stick necklace, or bracelet. We all go hike up into the woods and tell some Kresge history mixed with some weird rituals. We talk about how Kresge seceded [symbolically] in the nineties. Kresge tried to secede from the university. They wouldn't let you pass into Kresge unless you had a Kresge passport. This is the story that I've been told. You could get a passport if you were a resident of Kresge, or if you had a class in Kresge. But otherwise, people weren't allowed to cross into Kresge. It was kind of a statement of Kresge not really totally agreeing with the rest of the university and the way things were going, in terms of how UCSC wanted to expand and some of the decisions they were making. When we go up to the water tanks up on the fire roads in the undeveloped upper campus, we tell new students about how Kresge's been a very free and independent place for the last forty years.

Wendy Chapkis: I can't think of a better place to have gone to school as an undergraduate, or as a graduate student. With my interests, my personality, it was a glorious match. I fear that UCSC is rapidly undoing many of the elements that made it the kind of place I was glad to be as an undergraduate and a graduate student. The institution of grades and the incredible pressure on junior faculty to produce and be super scholars has come at the expense of doing small seminar classes, and having lots of direct contact with students. When I taught 120 people in my *Queer Politics* class, I had never taken a class at UCSC that was bigger than twenty or twenty-five students. This was a shock to me, that those kinds of classes even existed. There are more and more classes now that are lecture classes, and graduate students are expected to do all of the actual teaching in the seminar sections.

But there was a moment before that, when faculty actually lived on campus, when core course teachers and preceptors were senior faculty. There was a different model of education that wasn't about grades. It was a time when the political climate created constant links between what you were doing in the classroom, the theory you were learning, and what you were living. There was a tremendous excitement around sexual politics, gender politics, race politics, class politics and international justice. That is still here, but it is threatened by the increasing professionalization of UCSC, mainstreaming it as an institution.

Nancy Stoller: The thing that I find a little bit frustrating and distressing is that there's a conservatizing trend that often takes place as things are institutionalized. The more recent hires on our campus don't seem to have a sense of the history of the relationship between their positions in academia and the community struggles that have made them possible. There is a benefit to institutionalization, which is that people get to study and develop and become scholars and expand their teaching and research range into these areas. The negative side is that the political edge can be lost,

and the emphasis on theory loses what I'd call its critical edge, which has to do with addressing issues of social justice, of activism. That edge gets lost, and is replaced by academic elitism. I think it has been lost some on this campus.

Sareil Brookins: Now that I'm a student, I've done a lot of questioning of why am I here? Why am I studying this stuff? Why am I not out there doing the actions, the activism I want to be doing? It's true we need to do readings, because we need to understand what's going on. We need to have better ways of looking at things, and theorizing, and we need to learn from wonderful people who have written about these things. Yes. I totally feel that. But at some point, we can't all just be sitting here. What good is that knowledge if you're not putting it to practice?

I'm always thinking, what are people going to think when they look back on this time that we're in right now? What am I going to think? What is the next generation going to think about us? Wow, were we just laying around while the 45th [Donald Trump] was president?

Helene Moglen: What is the great liberal arts education that we are offering students now? I see many of the things that I've worked very hard to enable disappearing.

M.R.C. Greenwood: The dilemma that all public universities are facing is a disinvestment by most states in higher education. When that happens, you have two choices to make. One choice is that you just degrade the quality. You don't raise the tuition. You just say, "Well, we're going to do less with less." So your classes get bigger. You offer less of them. People can't get through in four and a half years. And pretty soon, the faculty wakes up to the fact that they have a heavier teaching load than the kinds of institutions they want to be in.

So when the next phone call comes, they start thinking about leaving.

Once you go over that cliff, you're over it. It's very hard to get back up on it. So you have to constantly say, we've got to maintain the quality. And if we have to maintain the quality, what does that mean? Well, one of the things that this functionally means is that we have to have a higher tuition and higher aid. The discounted price for students who are in the bottom third of financial need, for most of them it's essentially transparent. They might be working a couple of hours more, but their financial aid package is covered. They're still not paying that much more. It's really the middle-class families and the graduate students who are getting hurt, because there is not enough financial support there.

The academic programs the colleges are offering are not what was planned originally in the Dean McHenry days. What he really wanted was a coalition of independent colleges, all of which would be a complete academic environment—the antidote to the megauniversity. Sure, if you get funded at an 11:1 student-faculty ratio, like selective liberal arts colleges, we could probably do a pretty good job of that. But we don't get that level of funding. Nonetheless, what we still have are very good cocurricular and learning environments.

We have to figure out what would bring faculty back into the colleges in a different way. My view is that what brings faculty anywhere is the opportunity to interact with each other and with students over serious intellectual issues. So I feel that, rather than trying to argue over this core course or whatever, we ought to be putting research units into the colleges, so that there's a group of faculty that want to be there, that are going to be there. That's what we tried to do with Colleges Nine and Ten.

One of the original tenets was to make higher education as inexpensive as possible, and that it is a public good for states to subsidize higher education to ensure that they have an educated citizenry, so they can be economically competitive, create wealth in the state, and make it possible to have a good life in California. That was the enlightened view of the late 1960s and 1970s, when the Master Plan was coming into its early stage of fruition. People believed that an educated populace was in the state's best interest.

One of UC's Nobel Laureates just recently wrote a paper showing that the amount the state gets back for the investment that they make in an undergraduate or graduate degree, in taxes that that individual pays above and beyond what they would pay if they had only a high school education, is way more than the dollars that the state invested. You have to look at investing in higher education as a wealth-creating strategy. That may be a little crass for some academics. But it's really true.

It's also true that if we don't educate this next generation with the same enthusiasm that we did earlier beneficiaries of the Master Plan, we will regret it. It bothers me a great deal that we supported the Master Plan when the major beneficiaries of the Master Plan were traditional Caucasian students, even though many of them were the first in their families to go to college. California public higher education has always been an entry route for people who didn't come from an educated family. But now, when we're facing demographics that are substantially different, we don't have the same commitment. I think it will be fatal for the state if it persists to its logical, obvious outcome, which is that the university will be a pretty expensive place to attend, even though we may have very good financial aid. It will not be seen as within the grasp of a significant part of this new demographic. And in the final analysis, that will be very hard on the university, because we will be seen as not serving the population that the legislature cares about.

George Blumenthal: And then there are policy issues that face the campus from Washington. A few months after Trump was elected, a few months after Betsy DeVos was confirmed by the senate as Secretary of Education by one vote, there was a meeting of the presidents of Association of Public Land Grant Universities. Betsy DeVos came and gave a talk which didn't say much that was new or interesting.

But then they opened it up for questions. I asked her a question. I first reminded her that in the United States, 70 percent of all bachelor's degrees are granted at public universities and that twenty-five years ago, the United States was number one in the world in the percentage of twenty-five to thirty-five year olds with bachelor's degrees. Today we had fallen to number seventeen in the world. I said, "My question is, does this decline in our position with regard to higher education concern you at all, as the secretary of education, in terms of the future of American competitiveness?"

And her answer, which I can almost quote in its entirety, was, "No, I'm not at all concerned because as long as we remain innovative and entrepreneurial, we will do just fine." That answer had a big effect on me.

It's clear that the Trump administration, or Secretary of Education Betsy DeVos in particular, is going to get tougher on student loans with regard to alternative repayment methods, as well as relief from student loans for those who want to do public service. I think also they're going to be more liberal on student loans for for-profit colleges, which I also am opposed to because this is just feeding money from the federal government into the private sector without necessarily benefiting students. If this were accompanied by an upgrade to the oversight of private, for-profit

colleges, I would think about it a little bit differently, maybe. But that's not the case. It's really private sector *uber alles*.

The Trump administration has also had a real influence on scientific research. They've tried to do significant cuts in funding for research for agencies like the National Science Foundation, Department of Energy; NASA; NIH, maybe a little bit less so, but certainly including NIH. Fortunately, Congress has not yet gone along with that. My fear is that if we end up in a recession that the Trump administration will succeed in making significant cuts to those agencies. I think that's potentially one of the most long-term serious things that they could be doing.

The Trump administration has caused a lot of fear that data will be not preserved on environmental or climate issues. I also worry that the Trump administration is preventing federal scientists from doing fair and accurate assessments of climate change because of their ideological belief that climate change, if it exists at all, is not due to human intervention. I think that is a strong conclusion not based on evidence—the evidence is very strongly suggestive of a connection to human beings causing climate change. And of course Mr. Trump believes that although he doesn't have a scientific education, his intuition is so strong, it's enough to make him a good scientist, as he said in one recent interview. So we shall see.

Finally, the president has created fear among an ever-increasing group of very legitimate members of our community. That contributes to the climate on campus and a sense of fear on campus. I've sensed that for non-resident students who are coming in on legitimate visas, the United States does not feel welcoming anymore in quite the same way that as a country we used to feel. If you're from China, now you're coming into a country that you're in a trade war with. If you're from Mexico or Canada, then there're all these trade issues between Mexico and Canada and the US. It's not that students care about trade, but they do care about being dehumanized, which is what happens when you're in a conflict. So I think all of it is really unfortunate in terms of universites in general, or our campus in particular, being able to reach out and be seen as a truly international campus.

Rosie Cabrera: The institution has to make decisions about how it changes its culture, so that the mentoring Santa Cruz says it's all about truly happens, and structures are in place to make the mentoring happen. So, how does the institution change its culture, so that what the students want and need is acknowledged and worked through? Our students are very resilient. If you have good people around mentoring you, people can develop. Or it can shortchange them. They don't get what they want; they're constantly doubting their ability, and not engaging.

Probably for 95 percent of those students that I engage with—and I engage with a lot of people—their community and their families are everything to them. So how do you affirm that what you're learning here has a relationship to that? It's about being civic minded. It's about understanding we have a role to voice what is important to us. We have a responsibility to use this education to benefit others and to understand we're part of the privileged.

I don't think we should be apologetic that one of the underlying values of most of the faculty here is social responsibility. We don't play it up like we should. It's where the creativity and the new thinking, the new problem solving comes from.

The African American Resource Center was started in the late eighties. And then there were no other ethnic centers until 1995, with the Chicano/Latino Resource Center. Then after that was the Asian American Pacific Islander Resource Center

that emerged out of the Proposition 209 take-over of Hahn Student Services.[8] It was years after that that the American Indian Resource Center became a reality.[9] The Women's Center existed back in 1985, '86. The GLBTI Resource Center, that was a whole student-initiated effort out of Merrill College, with queer students demanding programming and space.

Santa Cruz is growing up. We're growing up, and we still have issues around the diversity effort. Diversity is not front and center, so when the finances wane, then that's the first thing that goes. I think that it's going to require of everybody a recognition that race matters, that we have a charge. We have a charge, and we're responsible for future generations.

There are so many powerful people that have gone through this institution and are doing incredible things. And is it recognized, in terms of the community contribution, the contributions to California, the contributions to scholarship? It's profound. I know that history will be written, because there's no stopping it now. There's no turning back. The color of this place is permanently going to be changed.

Patricia Zavella: I've had three different job offers where I've had to think very seriously and practically: do I go or do I stay? Every single time, I decided to stay. What sustains me is the Santa Cruz mission. This is a university that values undergraduate teaching. I spent a semester at the University of Michigan, and I remember at a cocktail party overhearing a faculty member brag that he had just received tenure, even though his teaching evaluations were terrible. And I was just like, how can you hold your head up? That is not something to brag about. That's just weird.

But at Santa Cruz, I've served on the Committee for Academic Personnel, so I get to review faculty files. And we have some great researchers; we have some great instructors. The mission of Santa Cruz is something that I believe in. And diversity—I think that gets taken seriously here. Maybe not as much as it *could* be, maybe we need more resources, but people have a commitment to that core value. So that's part of what sustains me. In the Chicana Feminisms Cluster we all had a little moment where we disclosed how we got to Santa Cruz. It turned out that for a bunch of us this was our dream job.

I've always had really good students in community studies, and in Latin American and Latino studies. I love my students—they're smart and they have an interesting perspective on things. I learn from my students. I especially like working with graduate students; I feel like we're in a co-seminar where we're sharing with one another. It's really vibrant intellectually.

I love the beauty of Santa Cruz. I love the lefty politics of the city of Santa Cruz. This is a good place to live. And then, I have all these great colleagues and projects. A lot of times work is very stressful and you don't have a lot of contact with folks, but you know people are there, and you can reach out. And occasionally, we *do* get to get together, and commiserate and share and celebrate. That's an important part of being here. I hear of colleagues who are in universities where they are the only women of color, or they feel like nobody takes them seriously. I've been there, so I can totally understand that, and I feel very lucky to be here.

John Dizikes: What now sets UCSC apart from the rest? Very little. It is a very conventional American university. The former students whose children are thinking of coming here talk to me fairly often: "What's it like? Should we send our daughter or son?" I say to them, "It's not the place it was when you were here, for better or for worse." It's a place where there are still many very fine instructors, many people who work very hard. It is a place where a student who wants to learn can learn an enormous amount. But that's the case in any college, anywhere. Students who want to learn will learn.

Sometime in the next ten, fifteen, twenty years, a group of faculty and administrators are going to get together, whatever the situation is in the nation, and they'll say, "My God, I just had a really brilliant idea. There are these colleges, these architectural, distinct things. We could develop something here that would be very different and very interesting." And maybe there will be a time when they want to come back and develop that. Of course, it's too early to say. Kenneth Thimann used to say, "A hundred years: there's no point in saying anything about a university unless it's been around for a hundred years." Five hundred is a very Cambridge and Oxford thing to say. Harvard isn't yet four hundred years old.

Is there a possibility that UCSC could be refashioned in a very different way? Yes, of course, there's always that possibility. I think it is, however, the more an institution remains a traditional one, it's harder to break out, bring in new people, or reinvigorate the people who are there. But students might lead the way. Students might, at a certain point, five, ten, twenty, thirty years from now, say, "My God, I don't want just that. I want something else." Then who knows what would come out of it. Helene Moglen used to say, "Our architecture is our future, our destiny. We can't escape the fact that we're not built like a conventional university." And this is why I say sometime somebody will say, "Hey, what a brilliant idea, there are these colleges. Let's do something with them."

Nobody predicted the sixties in '58 or '59, believe me. In reaction to the dismal and bland and suffocating fifties, many people in the sixties wanted to explore something else. So, who knows?

Maybe the period of austerity will lead people to say, "Look, if we're paying this much money, and it's this difficult and the rest of it, we ought to at least get something more out of our undergraduate experience, not just what goes on everyplace else." Who knows? And then maybe the regents and the university administration would have to listen to that. Maybe they'll decide to make it entirely an undergraduate campus. There's always been talk of that. I don't know what would happen to the faculty here who want to do graduate work, but suppose they decided they would, over a period, migrate and this would just be—well, who knows what could come out of that? That's not beyond the realm of imagination.

Katherine Le: We've always been activists here. We've always been pressuring for students to have their voices heard. And we have seen changes, in terms of creating demands for more access to resources for students of color, and supporting the Ethnic Resource Center, fighting for the Disability Resource Center, fighting for the Critical Race and Ethnic Studies major.[10] These are all things that are built into the robust activist history of UC Santa Cruz.

The fight doesn't stop. Even coming into college in the 2015-2016 school year, where UCSC has so many more resources than when it was founded in 1965, work still has to be done. Especially with this new Trump administration in the White House, more now than ever, I think we need to protect our students and make sure that our public higher education system is as inclusive as it can be.

A majority of my family are Vietnam War refugees and immigrants. There were many anti-Vietnam War protests and movements on the UCSC campus in the early years. Many students were involved in this. My family was in the process of fleeing the Vietnam War during this very time. During the fall of Saigon in 1975, was when my mother came over. During the Vietnam War, my mom was being born and bombs were bursting from the skies. While this was happening, UCSC students were protesting against the war.

These narratives are all intertwined.

Herman Blake: Oakes paved the way, broke the path for those students who were in the elementary and secondary schools, who ultimately made up the population in California. When I was at UCSC last year, the whole place looked like Oakes.[11] The whole place. They're all over the place: Asians, Latinos—to a lesser extent African Americans—but they're all over the place.

My dreams for Oakes College are more than fulfilled. Far beyond anything I ever expected—far beyond anything I ever expected. Dreams fulfilled. We used to say to the students, "When you get to the table, think about who's not there." And they developed these kinds of interests for gay students, which I think was an important development; more attention given to women; more attention given to students with disabilities. Not 'disabled students,' but students with disabilities. A constantly inclusive environment, which, I think, spills over to the campus, by virtue of its continued enrollment of people from diverse backgrounds, as a result of the changing demography. So I'd say those dreams have been fulfilled, and more than fulfilled. That emphasis on undergraduate education and excellence, *excellence* in undergraduate education, is an important part of being able to sustain the Santa Cruz mission. We didn't ask people to drop high expectations. We raised them, but we broadened them.

Lowell Burton: I spent half of my adult life here. It's a beautiful place. I'd come to work every day and park in the lot and walk in. Morning and nighttime were totally different. When they put the bridge in, I'd leave here at night and walk

Figure 4

Oakes College, the bridge, 1990

Photo by Joel Levick

across to the dorms—where in the world can you see a view like the one from the Oakes bridge staring out towards the ocean? I don't know if you have ever been on that bridge at four or five or six o'clock and looked out over there. I've got a couple of bucks looking at me, and there's hawks flying, and that water, and there's the smell of that ocean. I can hear students in the dorms.

In the morning, it's so quiet [whispers]. There a mountain lion running around. Everything is crispy. I've got a whole family of quail running by my leg, and I've got deer, so many deer I can't get by them, and I got raccoons chasing me. I got all this going on. I got the smells of the garden. I might walk down there and look over the playing field, and I'll see deer and more deer and I look and say, my God. Herman was right. This has to be utopia.

But I've looked through the windows of classroom Oakes 104. There's this second floor and it goes up in the ceiling and all these big windows. It's a historical thing. Oakes 104 was made for Ed Carrillo. He was a world-renowned muralist, and he was also a faculty member at UCSC. They built that studio for him in the construction of Oakes College, as an art studio to bring art to Oakes College. That was set up according to his needs, the lighting and everything. He was a Latino figure in the community, so students were taking his courses. He did a lot of murals. We displayed them in the Learning Center. We hung them on the walls outside on mural ropes. We had a lot of involvement in art, science, and math—Don Rothman and the California Writing Project and all the things Don was involved with in the community. And there's community studies, looking at everything as a whole, as a package.

All of that has become more homogenized. It's just a college now. The notion was to create a community here. To create a real community requires a lot of different things. It's a great big pie. And

in an academic community, it's even more difficult. If you're going to classes, and eating, and doing everything together in this environment, it requires toughness from staff, faculty, and students.

Anyway, that's what that room Oakes 104 was for. I look back and laugh at it because no one will ever know. No one will ever remember Ed Carrillo, one of the most prominent Latino artists, muralists in the country. Does anyone know he was here?

This is *something* out here: Oakes College. It's more than just the window, the building, or the tree. What was this community here? What were these people doing? Who was Herman Blake, a big black guy with a beard walking around; what was this hippie, Don Rothman, doing down here? What was this about? It's important. It's important to understand what these people, who are no longer around, went through for UCSC students to be here.

Pedro Castillo: The times have changed. But one thing that I still see in our students is that they want an education. They are interested in these subjects that deal with race, ethnicity, class, gender, sexuality. They're still very much involved in working off campus, on campus. They still have a social consciousness. It's different than the sixties. It's a different time. Some of them are career-centered. They want to go to law school, but not necessarily to work for a big firm. They might want to work for a firm that works with undocumented immigrants, let's say, something like that. They're still open to doing things that are not traditional. I still think our students are very different from the Berkeley or UCLA students, who are more career-centered. Our students want a career; they want to work. They want to make a living, to pay their debts and not live at home. But we have one of the highest number of students that go into the

Peace Corps. We still have the highest number of students that do Education Abroad.

We still have nontraditional students. They're very much interested in social justice. They have an awareness of who they are, and what they want to do, and how they want to change things. Maybe that's why I never wanted to leave Santa Cruz. The students were terrific.

Steve Gliessman: Things are collapsing around us, it feels like sometimes, in terms of the quality of the environment we live in and its ability to support us. It's phenomenal. The evidence just keeps mounting, too. What I always talk about is, rather than studying what's going to happen with global climate change, we need to be making different choices about how we live, in order to reverse the process. But it's fascinating to me that to promote or advocate change in, say, transportation systems, or the way food is grown, to really advocate for it, is considered activism, and not something that we as academics should be engaged in. But our students want to do more than that, because they, almost better than we, sense the urgency of it.

Donna Haraway: UCSC is more like a species assemblage. It's certainly not an organism, or even a super-organism. It's more like an ecological assemblage. I think universities are like edge areas in ecology where different habitat assemblages intermix, like ecotones, where all of the species are, in a sense, outside their comfort zone. They are outside of their normative comfort zone, but they can still make a living well enough to be there. But new things are happening in these ecotones. Their livings aren't being made in quite the same way that they are at their centers of distribution, their population centers. In ecotones, things are happening that can't happen in the comfort zone of any of the species in question. So I think of universities as ecotones more than as organisms.

Borderlands are ecotones. A borderland, as Gloria Anzaldúa thought of, as she invented or re-invented that term, *was* this place where nobody was in their comfort zone. It was a real geographic place, but it was also a place of pain, of invention, of fantasy, hope, of possibility, of defeat. A borderland was a place of breaking and building. It was a place where no one could be the same. There was no way you could inhabit a borderland and be who you were before. You didn't know what that was going to mean. And you couldn't really control it.

So if you relate that to the biological metaphor of an ecotone, you see how these are actually contact zones. I am thinking of Mary Pratt's *Imperial Eyes*[12] and the way she invented this term "contact zone" for thinking about colonial studies and post-colonial studies, where peoples, and ways of living, and technologies, and ways of doing the world, are forcibly brought together in relations of serious inequality, but which do not take the simple shape of dominator and dominated, or victim and oppressor. It does not take a binary shape, even though inequality of relations of power define the zone, as they do borderlands, as they do ecotones. As they do universities.

So I'm interested in these sorts of naming practices, these ways of inhabiting—ecotones, borderlands, cyborgs, zones of implosion, science fictional worlds—where you are required to be dead literal, you are required to be precise, analytically good, unforgivingly technically right, and flaming imaginative at the same time, if you're going to get it. And, of course, you can't do that. Nobody can do that. And so your breakdowns (this is what phenomenologists in the history of philosophy taught us best) are your most precious moments, because a breakdown is where the normalizing fails. The possibility of something else emerges through breakdown.

M.R.C. Greenwood: I was trying very hard when I was at UCSC to both accommodate the continuing slow-growth restraint that the campus was going to have as it faced its future, and to find ways to give release valves so that the campus would not get locked into a small, less-than-fully-fleshed-out research university that could not grow, and couldn't change, and therefore was going to struggle constantly. That's why I was trying to craft a situation where we could grow relatively modestly at UC Santa Cruz, but we could develop professional schools, in Silicon Valley, if necessary. Obviously, for a lot of reasons, I would have preferred to develop them here. But I didn't want to leave the campus to be a large liberal-arts undergraduate institution, with 10 percent graduate students, and only one professional school, and no opportunities to expand because of the controlled growth environment. I saw the opportunities, both in Fort Ord in Monterey and over the hill in Silicon Valley, as our major possibilities.

If you're going to be forever constrained, what are the institution's further options? Do you simply accept that fate, knowing then that the other campuses will go marching down other paths and they'll have a different life, and this one will be really, perhaps good at what it does, but it won't be doing much else? My personal view was we would start losing faculty when that happened, when people began to understand that there were going to be no new professional schools, there was not going to be any real growth in graduate education, that our building program had come to a standstill because our student population was not changing. When that began to dawn on people, we'd start losing people and it would take us a decade or more to catch up. There are some people who think they'd like that, but there's no funding mechanism currently in the University of California, and there never has been one, that would allow Santa Cruz to be different.

The only other option would be if we found a very generous donor who wanted, effectively, to name the campus and provide a really serious major endowment for us that would allow us to have funds to work with, like a private institution. I haven't seen that happen yet. I'm sure any chancellor would welcome someone walking in the door and saying, "How about if I gave you a billion dollars."

One of the things I said when I was at Santa Cruz was that you have to respect your roots, but you can't be afraid to flower. And you can't be afraid that the plant will look a little different as it grows. If somebody had been willing to provide enough money to keep a ten-to-one [student-faculty] ratio, we probably could have maintained some of the things we did in the first ten years. But nobody is going to give that to a public university today. You just have to be the best you can be, and still be distinctive. And be proud of *that*. And don't worry about the fact that, gee, it would have been great if we could have had everything that we had forty years ago. We've got some things we didn't have forty years ago, like a fabulous research program.

Frank Zwart: One of the great things about the campus is its immediate emotional impact on first-time visitors. The first time people set foot here they can't believe it's a college campus. I had Italian relatives visiting, their first trip to the United States, and they were visiting me in Santa Cruz. I took them up to the campus. We were walking through the redwoods. They were looking up, and spinning around because they'd never seen anything like it. That moment captured me. I think lots of people coming here for the first time experience that.

People think the campus is easy to understand because it has such an immediate impact, when in truth, as both a physical setting and an academic institution, it's a place that's very slow to reveal itself. It takes a while to understand it. I was thinking, as I was driving up to the campus this morning, going through an area of developed campus by Cowell and Stevenson Colleges and the Humanities Building, and then looking up and seeing College Nine in the distance, and then driving through a wooded area—this is not a campus where you can get a sense of the whole by standing in any one place, or by taking a simple walk. It's a campus that reveals itself to you over time. That's true both institutionally and physically.

The way that we developed the campus means that as you move through it you have surprises of—well, I didn't expect to find *that* here." It's like Dante moving through the Inferno and the Purgatorio and the Paradiso; there are discoveries at every step of the way that say something about his life.

Physical movement through the campus can be a metaphor for the intellectual development that occurs here, for a student, or for a faculty member—where you follow a particular trail and you find something unexpected or delightful, or you follow a more routine trail and you find something you hadn't thought of before. This is a campus that you need to wander around to get to know, for it to have its full impact on you.

The original, 1963 Long Range Development Plan is a wonderful document to read. It's extraordinarily well written, much better written than most planning documents today. There's a poetic sense to much of its language. And it's clear that the people who planned the campus were moved by the physical setting, which is a not uncommon reaction, and they managed to put it in this document that affected the early days of the campus.

I think that's part of what makes that first Long Range Development Plan so fantastic, is that the approach to designing buildings here has to start from this incredible, incredible site. It doesn't start from a grid, like Manhattan. It doesn't start with a sense of a particular kind of architecture, like Mr. Jefferson's lawn at the University of Virginia. Every site is unique. Every site is specific. And whatever we do in the way of buildings here has to respond to the power of that landscape.

Todd Newberry: We seem to have had failures of nerve, failures of imagination, failures of support, failures of purpose. A lot of us who came at the start have had, not only a career-long commitment to UCSC, but really a love affair with the place. With its failures, its cavings-in to ordinariness, to what we hoped to try to do better, we are bound to feel profoundly disconcerted, dismayed, dis-something, discouraged sometimes. I don't think that Chancellor Sinsheimer is right in talking about nostalgia for an era that never was. He wasn't here. I was here. It happened here.

But we faltered. We let other people trivialize it. They trivialize what they don't know anything about. William Everson used to give a course called *Birth of a Poet*. Everyone smiles when they think about *Birth of a Poet*. But I was there, and it produced some fine young poets. His evaluations of his students were kind of dopey. So what? What has that to do with the quality of the class, of the experience students had in it? *Birth of a Poet* is always being trashed, as you know, one of these loopy Santa Cruz things by people who weren't here—it is deeply unjust. There was a *Newsweek* article some years ago that was such a bunch of cheap shots by people who weren't here. So vulgar!

The untended garden reverts to what was there before. Maybe the lifetime of a great educational experiment like Santa Cruz, or Black Mountain— maybe it is a decade or so, not much more. Then, the thrill quelled, they diminish to a kind of ordinariness. I think that is what the campus has become, kind of ordinary.

We had to raise ourselves from infancy and we blew it. We lost the spirit. Karl Lamb once captured our timidity in what some of us called Lamb's Dictum: that the more UC Santa Cruz tries to be like UC Berkeley the more it ends up like UC Santa Barbara. That exposes part of the problem. And we've been chronically unfortunate in our central administration, in our leaders after Dean and Page Smith. Our chancellors and vice chancellors, with rare exceptions since McHenry's first five years, have not connected spiritually with their faculty, nor cared to. It's become distant and dysfunctional. My view, admittedly, dates back to the days when Dean McHenry, living in Pasatiempo, would come across me hitching a ride to work and would pick me up. That did create a bond! Here at UCSC we once had our voices heard and honored, one by one, our voices of UCSC experience—or at least our voices of passionate commitment.

Has this originally experimental campus succeeded or failed? If I had to choose, if I had to choose one verb or the other, I would have to say it's failed. But in a way, failure is built into an educational experiment, and this was an educational experiment. I think that failure is the normal outcome of educational experiments. And that's why there will be another someday. One of the unique strengths of our campus, though—one that won't be repeated, it seems—is its beauty. To go home down by the east pasture at the end of the day is still one of the great exhilarations after thirty years. To look out over that bay—what a redemption!

Gary Griggs: Walking around campus, everybody's wired up. We're out here in this beautiful redwood forest. They're either talking on the phone, or they're listening to music. There are no birds. There's no wind in the trees. They're all wired.

Rosa Melero: I chose Santa Cruz because it had an ocean. I like being in the trees. I feel like I'm in a treehouse all the time.

Khalen Hudson: I really like nature. So I was, like, this looks like something totally different. It's nice to come up here and not have smog in the air. And nice to see trees. I saw a deer for the first time. I'm like, oh, shit, it's a deer!

I knew I wanted to go somewhere in Northern California and I don't really like crowded city life. I liked how chill the campus was, and how isolated it was on the hill, so I could just get away from people and stay on campus. UCSC is one of its kind, especially in the UC system. I don't feel there's anywhere else where there's so much accessibility to so many quiet places in nature. Especially in College Nine, we are, literally, the top of campus. There's nothing beyond our colleges but forest and trails. It's pretty cool. I walk out of my room, go up the hill, and I'm in the forest.

Jim Clifford: We have slipped, or introduced, a university of now seventeen thousand students into a redwood forest, among rugged knolls and deep ravines, on the edge of a great meadow, overlooking a fantastic bay. And we haven't screwed it up.

Of course, if you build a university you're going to disturb nature. It was never pure nature anyway. The redwoods are all second growth, and Cowell Ranch was a site of industrial production, lime works of a major scale. But that said, we haven't screwed it up. Of course, we've knocked down a few trees. There are certain buildings that some people don't like, and other people don't like others. There're always one or two things that irritate you. But for me, there's nothing really horrible on this campus. The sense of beauty, the sense of magic, the sense of a special place has come through. There's been some real restraint. We went from a few thousand students to seventeen thousand students, without adding a single new road of any size. That's amazing. There's one basic loop: that's it. Earlier plans had that loop turning into a four-lane road. That has been resisted. The founding commitment to not build in the Great Meadow has been respected.

Narratives of decline are endemic at UC Santa Cruz. People felt the place was being ruined almost from the beginning. We all have a story about how something essential that was lost—whether it was the colleges, or the narrative evaluations, or Elfland, or histcon, or God knows what. There's truth in all of these stories. I'm certainly not one of those who thinks the campus should just get with the twenty-first century program: onward and upward with making a research campus that looks like every other corporately organized campus around the country. I do think that the special-ness, the radical difference of UCSC, is in danger of being lost. Much of it has been destroyed. We need to defend what's left.

And if there's one thing that's left that's special, that in some way secretes the spirit—the founding spirit, maybe—if there's one thing that really is left and that we haven't yet ruined, it's the campus itself. You can't come here and not feel you're in a special place.

I've brought people to UCSC and they all just say, "Wow!" You take them across those bridges and you go through that wonderful dreamlike alternation between being deep down in the forest and then suddenly the curtain parts, and you're high up on a hill, looking out over a vast expanse of water. This is a place unlike anywhere else. Or you go wandering down into a ravine, losing sight of the university in the great trees and underbrush, and then suddenly above you—a big building, maybe the library. It's astonishing. An experience.

UCSC remains a place apart, a place that holds somehow inside it the seeds of something: the seeds of something different, something new, something radical. It's a kind of spatial reminder of a vision and of a project. It's still something to live up to. Maybe I'm just whistling in the neolib-eral wind, but I think there's something essential, and something that could be reborn and made new in a place like this.

So I want to help deepen a consciousness of the campus. Not in an aesthetic or nostalgic way—you know, "this beautiful thing that we have"—but seeing it as something generative. That would be the trick. The whole discourse of beauty seems to me not the place to go. Everyone says, "Oh, it's so beautiful. How majestic the red-woods are." If we could figure out language that didn't fall into cliché but could talk about the alternation of spaces that you find on this campus: the many paths through it and the affect, the emo-tional responses it can evoke. But first, you have to notice it. Of course, if you work here, you're busy getting from place A to place B in your rat race and you don't even see the place.

Yet we've all had the experience of driving home, maybe it's six p.m.—the sun is going down, shedding its oblique light across the Great Meadow, revealing all its textures and con-tours, and you can see all the way out to Moss Landing and beyond to the mountains of Big Sur. You think, "Wait a minute." You stop your car, pull over, and say to yourself, "This is not wall-paper. This is real." I sometimes feel that way on the bridges that go across the ravines, or really throughout the campus. That's something that we need to have language for, to think about.

The early architects and landscape planners understood how the campus should be built. It's a lot more than those stories of Dean McHenry forbidding the cutting down of redwood trees without his permission. That story is true, it seems.

But there were some very important visionaries, especially the great landscape architect Thomas Church, who need to be recognized. Church's plan and spatial philosophy was formative and it has been sustained over the years. I'm thinking of the key decision not to put the whole campus out in the meadow, but to occupy the transition zone, using big trees and uneven land as, in effect, architectural partners. Don't try to compete with the redwoods; they'll always win. That was Church's perspective. A certain modesty and lightness of touch in architecture's relations with the land and its creatures.

I'm grasping, struggling for a thread of continuity that isn't just a relation to the past, but is a continuity with the ongoing site that is generative, that comes out of the past, through me and the present and into a future. A future which isn't one of conformity—not a matter of building yet another 'great university' that is basically out of a cookie cutter. No.

So, a resistance to conformity—something of that spirit that I absorbed during my career here. The permission that this place gives to wander, to get lost, to innovate, to cross boundaries, to transgress: that's something we need to be able to name and carry forward in new ways. It's a sense that, even in a corporate university, there can be local niches where unique forms of life can persist. Mutant forms, perhaps, seeds. Things like histcon, those kind of ad hoc, improvised forms of research collaboration that the greater humanities have been good at doing, and must continue to be good at doing. We need to find ways to name and recognize them, to support them in modest, but real, ways. You can do a lot with the right spirit and the right commitment and flexibility. That's something we can bring forward from the early spirit of the campus. That spirit was, in many ways pretty crazy, weird enough to found a program called history of consciousness! We need to find ways of talking about how to make that new.

"The pursuit of truth in the company of friends." Something of that spirit will come forward, and it will take new shapes. Maybe it'll be online—I don't know—something like a wiki, or all the other emerging forms that people like me find so confusing.

I see this as UCSC's legacy, a kind of open politics of the possible. It's a legacy of the sixties, as Fredric Jameson put it, "without apology" and without nostalgia. Something fundamentally rebellious, perverse, romantic, critical—for times we can't imagine.

Endnotes

1. Clark Kerr, "The Santa Cruz Dream" Number 1. Occasional Papers of Adlai E. Stevenson College, (University of California Santa Cruz, Santa Cruz, CA, 1988).

2. Byron Stookey, "Starting from Scratch: Santa Cruz," *The Harvard Review*, vol.3 n.1, Winter 1964.

3. *Solomon's House: A Self-Conscious History of Cowell College*, 128.

4. James Baldwin (1924-1987) was an African American novelist, essayist, playwright, poet, and social critic, and one of America's foremost writers about race, gender, class, and sexuality.

5. Mission agencies are federal agencies that support research as a means to securing the national defense, addressing national energy challenges, ensuring an efficacious transportation system, etc. This is in contrast to pure-sciences agencies such as the National Science Foundation.

6. Vannevar Bush (1890-1974) was one of the primary architects of what has come to be known as the military-industrial complex. During World War II, he became the first chairman of the Office of Scientific Research and Development, organizing research by American scientists and engineers. The system of funding and research through the military provided the economic support for the Manhattan Project. These wartime activities were further institutionalized during the Cold War and resulted in the shift from industry to government funding of large-scale scientific research, or "big science," in American universities.

7. Subject A was the name of the exam administered annually to high-school seniors who had been admitted to UC campuses. Warren is referring here to students who entered UCSC not having passed the exam, and therefore needing additional writing instruction to prepare them to pass it during their first year of college.

8. The Asian American Pacific Islander Resource Center helps students developing leadership, builds a stronger sense of community on campus, and links students to community service opportunities.

9. The American Indian Resouce Center is dedicated to supporting the needs of American Indian students and increasing Native visibility on campus by advocating for student-centered programs, cultural events, and tools for academic success and well being. The center serves as a vital link between American Indian students, the university, and tribal communities.

10. Critical Race and Ethnic Studies (CRES) is a BA program that "seeks an understanding of 'the public' and 'the common good' as centrally constituted by racial and ethnic formations." Doctoral students can also pursue an emphasis in CRES alongside their degree program in another field.

11. See "Rediscover: Herman Blake and Don Rothman - UCSC Reunion Weekend 2012." https://youtu.be/bsDW_M-NdtY.

12. Mary Louise Pratt, *Imperial Eyes: Travel Writing and Transculturation*. (London and New York: Routledge. 1992).

Illustrations

Figure 1. Robert Jorgensen, Executive Assistant to dean of social sciences (in front of a banner with an Ansel Adams quote from his Charter Address in 1965) fields questions on campus growth at a student teach-in regarding College Nine and College Ten, at McHenry Library. 1991. Courtesy Special Collections, University Library, University of California, Santa Cruz. University of California, Santa Cruz: Campus History Slides: 91DH266_A.tiff.

Figure 2. In 2015, the campus restored the 150-year-old Cowell Ranch Hay Barn near the entrance of campus. On March 21, 2015, a group of twenty professional timberframers, joined by fifty community volunteers, worked together to raise the frame of the new barn, using mortise and tenon joinery to assemble the massive Douglas fir and redwood timbers. The barn has been one of the key buildings in the Cowell Lime Works Historic District, and now serves as the headquarters for the Center for Agroecology and Sustainable Food Systems (CASFS). Photo by Carolyn Lagattuta. Campus Photo Archive. Communications and Marketing Department, UCSC. Copyright UC Regents.

Figure 3. Sinsheimer Labs and Science Hill, 1990. Photo by Joel Levick. Courtesy Special Collections, University Library, University of California, Santa Cruz. 1990. UA 22: Twenty-Fifth Anniversary Photography Project.

Figure 4. Oakes College, the bridge. Photo by Joel Levick. Courtesy Special Collections, University Library, University of California, Santa Cruz. 1990. UA 22: Twenty-Fifth Anniversary Photography Project: ua0022_pho_002.

Figure 5. View of Monterey Bay. 2019. Photo by Irene Reti.

Figure 5

View of Monterey Bay, 2019

Photo by Irene Reti

Appendices

Tree shadows near McHenry
Library, 2016

Photo by Irene Reti

Opening day of Santa Cruz
Wharf, 1914

Courtesy Special Collections,
MS 427: Santa Cruz Historical
Photographs Collection

Timeline

1791

The Santa Cruz Mission is founded, one of twenty-one Franciscan missions (with associated military outposts) established in Alta California between 1769 and 1833 to convert the Indigenous population and extend Spain's political control of the region.

1821

California becomes part of Mexico after the Mexican War of Independence.

1849

The California Gold Rush brings a population wave.

1850s

California becomes the nation's thirty-first state, with Santa Cruz County among its original twenty-seven counties. Over the ensuing decades, the state of California promotes policies that lead to the harassment, dispossession, and murder of Indigenous peoples. After generations of Spanish, Mexican, and then American control, most land in California (including Santa Cruz County) is held by settlers.

Commercial logging begins in the Santa Cruz Mountains when the Gold Rush brings thousands of people to San Francisco, stimulating a building boom. By 1890, most old-growth redwoods have been felled.

1853

Isaac Davis and Albion Jordan begin quarrying and making lime on what will become UCSC campus land. Jordan builds a farmhouse, which will later be known as Cardiff House.

1865

Henry Cowell, a wealthy industrialist who originally came to California for the Gold Rush, purchases half ownership in Davis and Jordan's lime production company and moves to what becomes known as the Cowell Home Ranch.

1866

Santa Cruz is incorporated under California state law.

1868

The University of California is founded.

1902

Through the efforts of conservationists, including several women, Big Basin Redwoods State Park (California's first state park), is created to protect old-growth redwood trees.

1907

Santa Cruz Beach Boardwalk is founded. With logging and other extractive industries fading, Santa Cruz begins to remake itself as the "Playground of the West."

1932

Dean McHenry rooms with Clark Kerr at Stanford University.

1954

The American War in Vietnam begins.

1956

The Cowell Foundation is established through the bequest of S. H. Cowell, who died in 1955.

The University of California decides to open three new UC campuses, including one on California's Central Coast.

1957

Dean McHenry chairs a study of potential new UC campuses.

1958

The Board of Supervisors of Santa Cruz County unanimously passes a resolution requesting that the regents "give favorable consideration to the establishment of a University of California campus in the county of Santa Cruz."

Clark Kerr is appointed president of the University of California.

1959
Consultants hired by the regents recommend a site in the Almaden Valley for a UC campus. Regents vote for the Almaden site.

Edmund G. (Pat) Brown is elected governor of California.

1960
Survey team led by Dean McHenry develops the California Master Plan for Higher Education of 1960.

Regents reconsider their Almaden Valley site-preference decision. In July, they visit Almaden Valley and Cowell Ranch for firsthand comparison. By December, the regents have changed their minds and vote in favor of the Cowell Ranch site.

1961
The Board of Trustees of the Cowell Foundation offers UC three parcels of the Cowell Ranch, totaling 2,000 acres, at below-market price, and then grants back $920,000 (nearly all) of the parcel price to UCSC for the building of Cowell College and the Cowell Health Center. In December, after negotiation with the city and county of Santa Cruz, the purchase of the Cowell Ranch parcels for UCSC is complete.

Dean McHenry is appointed UCSC's first chancellor.

1962
California voters pass Proposition 1A, a $270 million bond issue to support construction and/or improvement of the state's higher-education facilities. This funding is critical for UC Santa Cruz.

Regents approve selection of architect John Carl Warnecke to work with the Campus Planning Committee on a UCSC Long Range Development Plan (LRDP). Thomas Church is hired as consulting landscape architect.

Ansel Adams becomes UCSC's first official photographer.

1963
UCSC opens planning offices at Cabrillo College, with a tiny pool of pioneering staff.

UCSC's first LRDP is approved in September by the regents. It projects that UCSC will grow to 27,500 students by 1990, have twenty colleges and ten professional schools, and house at least 50 percent of its student body on or near campus.

President John F. Kennedy is assassinated.

1964
Page Smith is hired as first provost of Cowell College. Founding-faculty recruitment accelerates.

The Free Speech Movement organizes protests at UC Berkeley.

The US Congress passes the Civil Rights Act.

Construction begins at UC Santa Cruz.

UC Santa Cruz officially dedicated.

UCSC offices move to four historic Cowell Ranch buildings on the campus site.

1965
UC Santa Cruz opens for fall quarter with 652 students in Cowell College, which is still under construction. Most students are housed in trailers on the East Field.

1966
Cowell College construction is completed.

Stevenson College opens, with Charles Page as founding provost.

The systemwide UC Academic Senate approves UCSC's experimental pass/fail grading system with narrative evaluations.

Lick Observatory moves its physical offices to UCSC from UC Berkeley, the administrative transfer having taken place on paper in 1965.

1967
Ronald Reagan becomes governor of California.

Governor Ronald Reagan fires UC President Clark Kerr, just eighteen months after UCSC's opening. In the first mass demonstration at UCSC, 900 UCSC students protest his firing.

Alan Chadwick breaks ground for what becomes the Chadwick Garden.

Crown College opens with Kenneth Thimann as founding provost.

1968
Charles Hitch becomes president of UC. Hitch implements a weighted formula for allocating funds to UC campuses, which gives more to campuses for graduate students. Chancellor Dean McHenry opposes this plan, which penalizes UCSC for its focus on undergraduate education and represents a major financial blow to the campus's future.

Governor Ronald Reagan imposes student registration fees, so that for the first time, California residents are charged to attend UC.

In October, a regents' meeting (including Governor Reagan) at Crown College is stormed by more than 1,000 students demanding the establishment of a college named for Malcolm X, university support for the United Farm Workers Union's grape boycott, and the removal of limits on the number of times a guest lecturer may appear during a quarter (a rule that had been aimed at keeping Eldridge Cleaver, the Black Panthers Minister of Information, from speaking on campus).

Merrill College opens. Paul Seabury, the college's first provost, is replaced after his first year by Philip Bell.

Plans for a school of engineering at UCSC are shelved after the Terman Report, issued by the California Council for Higher Education, advises the UC Regents not to open more engineering schools.

Robert Kennedy is assassinated.

Martin Luther King, Junior is assassinated.

Richard Nixon is elected president.

1969
UCSC Academic Senate approves development of an ethnic studies college, which becomes Oakes College.

President Richard Nixon authorizes secret bombing of Cambodia, which leads to widespread protests.

Governor Ronald Reagan and the regents attempt to bar Angela Davis from teaching at any California public university because of her political beliefs. Students, including UCSC students protest, and Davis is reinstated.

People's Park protest in Berkeley.

UCSC commencement is taken over by antiwar demonstrations.

College Five (later renamed Porter College) opens, with James Hall as founding provost.

1970
Student strikes are held in May at UCSC and across the United States in protest against the Vietnam War. Four Kent State University students are killed and nine are injured when members of the Ohio National Guard open fire on student protestors. UCSC students burn draft cards in Quarry Plaza, take over Central Services, and shut down Highway 1 in front of Fort Ord, at the time a US Army post.

UCSC 'desegregates' (by gender) the dorms, with men and women inhabiting separate floors within each building.

Whole Earth Restaurant opens.

Banana Slug is conceived as a mascot for the UCSC men's volleyball team by team member Dave Van Cleve.

1970-1973
After a series of grisly murders, Santa Cruz is dubbed "Murder Capital of the World." This, among other factors, contributes to a decline in applications to the campus, culminating in what becomes known as "the enrollment crisis."

1971
Voting age is lowered from twenty-one to eighteen, giving college students the right to vote and changing local politics.

Kresge College opens with Robert Edgar as founding provost.

1972
Oakes College opens with Herman Blake as founding provost.

College Eight opens in Kerr Hall with Paul Niebanck as founding provost.

Donald and Marion Younger donate oceanfront property, which becomes Long Marine Laboratory.

UCSC students participate in United Farm Workers grape boycott.

Chancellor McHenry revises enrollment ceiling to 7500 by 1980 and a final enrollment of 12,500 (instead of 27,500).

1973
Page Smith retires from his faculty position in protest after Paul Lee is denied tenure, feeling this decision represents a betrayal of the original UCSC vision.

American war in Vietnam ends.

1974
Dean McHenry retires.

After the Watergate scandal, President Nixon resigns from office.

Regents deny a $1.5 million request to fund the building of College Eight (later called Rachel Carson College).

Mark Christensen is appointed UCSC's second chancellor.

Undergraduate enrollment reaches 5,000 students.

Gary Patton is elected to the Santa Cruz County Board of Supervisors—a victory made possible in large part by UCSC student support, signaling a major leftward shift in city and county politics.

1975
The Gay and Lesbian Alliance (GALA) is established as UCSC's first official gay and lesbian organization.

Jerry Brown becomes governor of California.

1976
Chancellor Christensen resigns in January under pressure amid deep campus conflict. Angus Taylor becomes acting chancellor of UCSC and the campus's third chancellor overall.

Ground is broken for the Long Marine Laboratory, which later expands into the Coastal Science Campus.

UCSC undergraduate enrollment decreases by 200 students, intensifying the debate about the campus' stability and future.

1977
Robert Sinsheimer becomes UCSC's fourth chancellor.

The enrollment crisis worsens as freshman applications to UCSC drop to 20 percent of what they were in 1971.

In May more than 1,000 anti-apartheid demonstrators occupy the Central Services building, resulting in 401 arrests.

1978
Chancellor Sinsheimer presents his controversial "Reorganization" plan.

White UC Davis medical-school applicant Allan Bakke prevails against the UC regents in a landmark US Supreme Court case. The Court's decision invalidates racial quotas in academic admissions processes, but establishes affirmative action in general as constitutional.

California's voters pass Proposition 13, reducing property tax rates on homes, businesses and farms and freezing them at the 1976 assessed value level. The measure cuts billions of dollars in state education funding overnight.

1979
First wave of progressives is elected to Santa Cruz City Council.

UCSC students join widespread protests against Diablo Canyon Nuclear Power Plant near San Luis Obispo, California.

The Berkeley Redirect Program, established to stem the enrollment crisis, admits students to UCSC for two years with a promised transfer to UC Berkeley at the beginning of the junior year.

1980
Ronald Reagan is elected president.

For the first time, UC requires state-resident as well as nonresident undergraduate students to pay tuition.

The United States enters a deep recession that lasts until 1982.

1981
Native American (Cahuilla) lecturer Ed Castillo is denied tenure. Students hold a protest hunger strike from April 20 to April 25 and an all-night sit-in at McHenry Library.

Shakespeare Santa Cruz is founded.

The Dickens Project is founded at UCSC as a UC-wide intercampus research group.

College Five is renamed Porter College.

Graduate student enrollment reaches 500 students.

UCSC's Academic Senate approves a letter-grade option in upper-division courses as supplement to narrative evaluations.

1982
Community studies professor Nancy Shaw (Stoller) is denied tenure, engendering student protest and a legal battle.

UCSC students protest UC involvement in nuclear weapons research at Lawrence Livermore National Laboratory.

1983
The regents amend UC's non-discrimination policy to include sexual orientation.

George Deukmejian becomes governor of California.

1984
UCSC's Martin Luther King, Jr., Memorial Convocation is founded.

1985
The UCSC Women's Center is founded in the historic Cardiff House.

Chancellor Robert Sinsheimer convenes a group of eminent UCSC biologists to propose a project to determine the complete DNA sequence of the human genome. This develops into the Human Genome Project.

The SUA (Student Union Assembly) is founded to place students in a stronger bargaining position with the administration.

1986
Large anti-apartheid protests are held at UCSC. During a meeting at UC Santa Cruz, the regents vote to divest from South African investments by the end of the 1980s.

Banana Slug becomes UCSC's official mascot.

UCSC enrollment crisis ends with a large influx of freshmen. Enrollment stands at 8,409.

A building site on the west side of campus is approved for College Eight.

The Baskin Center for Computer Engineering and Information Sciences is dedicated in a newly remodeled two-story wing of the Applied Sciences Building.

1987
Robert Sinsheimer retires in July.

Robert Stevens is appointed UCSC's fifth chancellor.

1988
Plans are approved for construction of Colleges Nine and Ten.

"Asian Food Affair" controversy ignites on campus.

1989
UC Regents approve the campus's 1988 Long Range Development Plan. The plan and its environmental impact report are based on a projected campus population of 12,000 undergraduates and 3,000 graduate students by 2005.

The Loma Prieta Earthquake (7.1 on the Richter Scale) occurs at 5:04 p.m. on October 17, 1989, creating widespread damage in the San Francisco and Monterey Bay Areas and taking several lives in Santa Cruz County.

George H.W. Bush takes office as president of the United States and serves one term.

1990
Enrollment reaches 10,000 undergraduates.

African American Student Resource Center is founded.

The United States enters a recession that lasts about eight months.

UCSC offers a Voluntary Early Retirement Incentive Program (VERIP) to faculty and staff as a way of obtaining salary savings, leading to the retirement of many prominent early campus figures.

1991
Robert Stevens resigns; Karl Pister becomes interim chancellor and UCSC's sixth chancellor.

Forty-two people are arrested in daylong demonstrations on the site where construction of Colleges 9 and 10 is beginning, an area known as Elfland.

Plans for constructing the Music Building and Meyer Drive Extension are met with protest.

Pete Wilson becomes governor of California.

Anita Hill becomes a national figure when she testifies that US Supreme Court nominee Clarence Thomas (who was her supervisor at the United States Department of Education and the Equal Employment Opportunity Commission) sexually harassed her.

Persian Gulf War begins with a massive US-led air invasion known as Operation Desert Storm.

Communism collapses in the Soviet Union.

1992
Riots in Los Angeles County flare after a jury acquits four white officers of the Los Angeles Police Department of the use of excessive force in the arrest and beating of African American man Rodney King.

1993
Rita Walker becomes UCSC's first Title IX Officer.

Bill Clinton is elected president of the United States.

1994
California passes Proposition 187 (also known as the Save Our State (SOS) initiative) to establish a state-run citizenship screening system and prohibit undocumented immigrants from using health care, public education, and other social services in the state of California.

1995
Regents pass Standing Policy 1 (SP1) and Standing Policy 2 (SP2), prohibiting "preferential treatment" on

the basis of race, ethnicity, sex, and national origin in admissions, employment, and contracting.

El Centro (Chicano Latino Resource Center) is founded.

1996
After Karl Pister retires, M.R.C. Greenwood becomes UCSC's seventh chancellor.

After major debate and controversy, Proposition 209 ends affirmative action in the state of California. Students occupy Hahn Student Services for twelve hours in protest.

1997
UCSC adopts the standard terminology of "departments" in lieu of the original "boards of studies."

Lesbian, Gay, Bisexual Community and Resource Center is founded (later known as the GLBTI Resource Center); in 2002 renamed the Lionel Cantú Queer Center in honor of a beloved faculty member in sociology.

UCSC's School of Engineering, endowed by Jack Baskin, is founded decades after plans for such a school were originally laid.

1999
The Asian American/Pacific Islander Resource Center is founded.

Gray Davis becomes governor of California.

Enrollment reaches 10,000 undergraduates.

2000
Academic Senate votes to replace the letter-grade option with mandatory letter grades alongside the existing narrative evaluation system. The move, and its departure from the original campus vision, is greeted with controversy.

College Nine is founded, with Campbell Leaper as founding provost.

On June 22, UCSC and the other members of the International Human Genome Project consortium complete the first working draft of the human genome assembly, ensuring free public access to the genome and the information it contains through the Human Genome Browser.

2001
On September 11, militants associated with Al-Qaeda hijack jets in a series of suicide attacks on New York City, Pennsylvania, and the Pentagon, killing nearly 3,000 people and causing widespread destruction.

United States invades Afghanistan, launching a long-term war.

State legislature passes AB 540, or the California nonresident tuition exemption, which allows any student, including undocumented immigrants, to become exempt from paying non-resident tuition at public colleges and universities in California if they can show that they have successfully attended a high school in California for at least three years and successfully graduated or obtained a G.E.D.

George W. Bush is elected president of the United States and will serve two terms.

2002
College Ten is founded. Provost Campbell Leaper oversees both College Nine and College Ten.

2003
United States invades Iraq and topples Saddam Hussein, launching an eight-year war. Students protest the war at UCSC and across the world.

Arnold Schwarzenegger becomes governor of California.

UCSC's American Indian Resource Center founded.

2004
First annual Cesar Chavez Convocation.

Martin Chemers becomes UCSC's acting chancellor, and eighth chancellor overall, after M.R.C. Greenwood leaves UCSC to become Provost and

Senior Vice President for Academic Affairs at the UC Office of the President.

2005

Denice Denton is appointed UCSC's ninth chancellor.

Student organize Tent University protests in response to rising costs of education.

2006

Regents certify UCSC's 2005 Long Range Development Plan, which caps enrollment at 19,500 students.

Chancellor Denice Denton commits suicide in San Francisco, stunning the UCSC community. George Blumenthal becomes acting chancellor.

2007

George Blumenthal is appointed UCSC's tenth chancellor by the regents.

Tree-sitters protest over the planned construction of the Biomedical Research Facility building; protests last into 2008.

2008

Undergraduate enrollment reaches 15,000.

A nationwide Great Recession generates a devastating budget crisis.

UCSC and the city of Santa Cruz sign 2008 Comprehensive Settlement Agreement.

Barack Obama is elected president.

2009

Students occupy Kerr Hall for three days, partially in protest of a 32 percent increase in tuition.

2010

In part due to concern about faculty workloads, the Academic Senate votes to make narrative evaluations optional.

UC tuition has effectively doubled over the past decade.

2011

Occupy Movement organizes protests against economic and social inequality around the world, including at UCSC and in the town of Santa Cruz.

Jerry Brown becomes governor of California for a second time.

2012

UCSC is designated a Hispanic Serving Institution by the US Department of Education, with more than 25 percent of the campus's undergraduate students identifying as Chicano/Latino (Latinx). This qualifies the campus for special federal funding.

2013

UCSC ceases financial support for Shakespeare Santa Cruz, which reconstitutes itself as Santa Cruz Shakespeare.

2016

College Eight is renamed Rachel Carson College.

Donald Trump is elected president of the United States.

2017

Total enrollment for fall 2017 reaches 19,457.

2019

Gavin Newsom becomes governor of California.

Chancellor George Blumenthal retires.

Cynthia K. Larive is chosen as the new chancellor of UCSC.

UCSC gains acceptance into the Association of American Universities. The association, founded in 1900, has 65 members, including six other UCs, flagship public universities such as Ohio State University, land-grant universities like Purdue University, and private institutions, such as Harvard.

Bibliography and Selected Resources

Selected Books

Arnett, Jeff, ed., *An Unnatural History of UCSC*. Second Edition, Santa Cruz: UC Santa Cruz, Bay Tree Bookstore, 2008.

Banham, Reyner and Taina Rikala. *The First 20 Years: Two Decades of Building at UCSC*. Santa Cruz, CA: UC Santa Cruz, 1987. Available at UCSC Library Special Collections.

Bassett, Patricia Dorsey. *A Study of the College System at the University of California, Santa Cruz*, 1990. (Unpublished). Available at UCSC Library Special Collections.

Calciano, Elizabeth Spedding and Ray Collett. *The Campus Guide: A Tour of the Natural Environment and Points of Historical Interest, University of California, Santa Cruz*. Santa Cruz, CA: UC Santa Cruz, 1973. Available at UCSC Library Special Collections.

Clifford, James. *In the Ecotone: The UC Santa Cruz Campus*. Photographs and Text by James Clifford. 2015. Available at the Bay Tree Bookstore and the UCSC Library.

Collective Museum Collection: University of California, Santa Cruz. Public Doors and Windows. Santa Cruz, CA: UC Santa Cruz Institute of the Arts and Sciences. 2014.

Cowell College. *Solomon's House: A Self-Conscious History of Cowell College*. Santa Cruz, CA: UC Santa Cruz. By the members of the Cowell History Workshop 144G, 1970.

Doyle, William. *UC Santa Cruz: 1960-1991: Campus Origin, and Early Program and Facility Development in the Sciences with Special Emphasis on Marine Sciences*. Raleigh, North Carolina: Lulu.com, 2011.

Doyle, William. *The Origin of UC Santa Cruz: 1957-1961, Activities Resulting in the Selection and Purchase of the Cowell Home Ranch, Santa Cruz County, California*. Raleigh, North Carolina: Lulu.com, 2014.

Duke, Alex. *Importing Oxbridge: English Residential Colleges and American Universities*. Includes chapter on UC Santa Cruz: "The University of California, Santa Cruz: 'The City on a Hill.'" New Haven, CT: Yale University Press, 1996.

Grant, Gerald and David Riesman. *The Perpetual Dream: Reform and Experiment in the American College*. Includes chapter "Communal Expressives: Kresge College at Santa Cruz," and "The Cluster Colleges at Santa Cruz." Chicago, IL: The University of Chicago Press, 1978.

Haff, Tonya, Martha T. Brown and W. Breck Tyler, eds. *The Natural History of the UC Santa Cruz Campus*. Second Edition, Santa Cruz, CA: UC Santa Cruz Environmental Studies Department, 2008.

Jones, Richard M. and Barbara Leigh Smith. *Against the Current: Reform and Experimentation in Higher Education*. Includes Chapter 5: George Von der Muhll, "The University of California, Santa Cruz: Institutionalizing Eden in a Changing World." Cambridge, MA: Schenkman Publishing, 1984.

Kerr, Clark (with the assistance of Marian L. Gade and Maureen Kawaoka). *The Gold and the Blue: A Personal Memoir of the University of California 1949-1967* (Vol. 1 Academic Triumphs; Vol. 2 Political Turmoil). Berkeley: University of California Press, 2001, 2003.

Noreña, Carlos G. *The Rise and Demise of the UC Santa Cruz Colleges*. Berkeley: Berkeley Public Policy Press, Institute of Governmental Studies, University of California, Berkeley, 2004.

Rizzo, Martin Adam. "No Somos Animales: Indigenous Survival and Perseverance in 19th Century Santa Cruz, California," (2016). PhD Dissertation in History, UC Santa Cruz. Available on the University of California Escholarship: https://escholarship.org/uc/item/72n1q0vz.

Schwartz, Christian. *Fungi of the UCSC Redwoods*. UCSC Natural Reserves, 2017. One of several field guides in the UCSC Campus Natural Reserve Field

Guide Series, including *Spiders of UC Santa Cruz*; *Plants of UC Santa Cruz*; *Birds of UC Santa Cruz*; and *The Curious Observer's Guide to Slime Molds of UC Santa Cruz*.

Sinsheimer, Robert L. *The Strands of a Life: The Science of DNA and the Art of Education.* Berkeley: University of California Press, 1994.

Warrick, Sheridan, ed. *The Natural History of the UC Santa Cruz Campus.* First Edition, Santa Cruz, California, Environmental Field Program, 1982.

Selected Periodicals, Articles, Papers

Adams, Ansel. "Thoughts on the University of California, Santa Cruz Campus," March 30, 1967, UCSC Library Special Collections.

Adams, William. "Getting Real: Santa Cruz and the Crisis of Liberal Education." *Change: The Magazine of Higher Learning* 16 (4) 1984: 18-27.

Church, Thomas. "Random Notes on the Site. A memo written to Jack Wagstaff and John Carl Warnecke," 1962. Available in UCSC Library Special Collections.

Fischer, John. "The Easy Chair: A Different Kind of Campus. The Experiment at Santa Cruz." *Harper Magazine,* Spring 1969.

Garret, James L. "Santa Cruz After One Year," *Saturday Review* 50, January 21, 1967.

Giles, Ray. "Growing Pains at UC Santa Cruz," *California Higher Education*, October 1982.

Hamilton, Francis. "The 'Small College' Concept Takes Shape at UC Santa Cruz: Newest UC Santa Cruz Campus Bucks the Trend in Education," *San Francisco News Call Bulletin.* January 22, 1964.

Kamen, David A. "The New Santa Cruz Campus: An Idyllic Experiment," *The Daily Californian Weekly Magazine*, March 6, 1966.

Korman, Seymour, "Santa Cruz: Revolt Against Assembly-Line Academics." *Chicago Tribune Magazine*, July 24, 1966.

Lamb, Karl A. "Seeking the Essence of Oxford," *American Oxonian*, April 1964.

Lictenstein, Grace. "Should You Move to Santa Cruz? A Tough Look at a 'Feminist Utopia'," *Ms* Magazine, December 1983.

McHenry, Dean E. "Small College Program for a Large University," *College and University Business*, July 1964.

Moll, Richard. "A Flower Child Grows Up: Responding to Changing Times at UC Santa Cruz," *Case Currents*. November/December 1983.

Seidenbaum, Art. "Santa Cruz: Doubts in the Garden," *Los Angeles Times West* magazine, March 30, 1969.

Stookey, Byron. "Starting from Scratch: Santa Cruz," *The Harvard Review*, vol.3 n.1, Winter 1964.

Trombley, William. "Santa Cruz Emerges as the 'Place to Go'," *Los Angeles Times*, January 16, 1966.

Villet, Barbara. "An Old Idea Flowers Anew at Santa Cruz," *LIFE* magazine, May 8, 1970.

Warnecke, John Carl. "Another View of the History of a Campus," *American Institute of Architecture Journal*, vol. 69:2, 1980.

Waters, Christina. "UCSC Founders Evaluate their Creation on its 25th Anniversary," *Pacific*, 13-36, 1990.

Oral Histories

All of the oral histories conducted by the Regional History Project and excerpted in this book are available in searchable full text (PDF) (some are also available in audio format) through the University of California's escholarship site: https://escholarship.org/uc/rhp.

Cowell College Oral History Project, 2013. Interviews conducted by students in a Cowell College class. Transcripts available in UCSC Library Special Collections: LD781.S52 C69 2013.

Oakes College Oral History Project, 2013, 2014. Interviews conducted by students in an Oakes College class. Transcripts available in UCSC Library Special Collections: LD781.S52 O25.

Digital Resources

UCSC Library Digital Collections—Campus History: Photographs and Maps. This collection includes digitized photographs, maps, and architectural drawings documenting the historical development, culture and social environment of the University of California, Santa Cruz. See: https://n2t.net/ark:38305/flv123xf.

UCSC Digital Collections online: Includes the Santa Cruz Historical Photograph Collection. This collection contains hundreds of images of Santa Cruz County from the nineteenth century to the present day: https://digitalcollections.library.ucsc.edu/.

UCSC Library Campus History—Publications: This collection includes publications from the early years of the university produced by UC Santa Cruz students, staff members and departments, as well as local press publications such as the *Santa Cruz Sentinel* that focus on the university. See: https://n2t.net/ark:/38305/flq81c7k.

Online Exhibits

Digital Exhibit: "Look'n M' Face and Hear M' Story": An Online Exhibit about Professor J. Herman Blake. Curated by Regional History Project Director, Irene Reti: http://exhibits.library.ucsc.edu/exhibits/show/j--herman-blake.

Digital Exhibit: "Chancellor Dean McHenry, the Political Mastermind behind UC Santa Cruz." Curated by Regional History Director Irene Reti: http://exhibits.library.ucsc.edu/exhibits/show/chancellor-dean-mchenry--the-p.

Digital Exhibit: "An Uncommon Place." Curated by emeriti professors James Clifford, Michael Cowan, Virginia Jansen, and emeritus campus architect Frank Zwart for the 50th Anniversary of UCSC: http://exhibits.library.ucsc.edu/exhibits/show/an-uncommon-place.

Digital Exhibit: "History of the UCSC Quarry and the Cowell Ranch." Curated by UCSC graduate student Christine Turk for UCSC Physical Planning and Construction: https://quarryamphitheater.library.ucsc.edu/exhibits/show/home.

Digital Exhibit: "Reading Nature, Observing Science: Examining Material Practices in the Lick Observatory Archives and Kenneth S. Norris Papers." Curated by CART [Center for Archival Research and Training] fellows Alex Moore, Christine Turk, and Danielle Crawford: http://scalar.usc.edu/works/reading-nature/cover.

Digital Exhibit: "Women of Color Research Cluster Film Festival." Curated by UCSC Library CART fellow Alina Ivette Fernandez: http://exhibits.library.ucsc.edu/exhibits/show/woc-research-cluster/the-women-of-color-in-conflict.

Digital Exhibit: "Raymond F. Dasmann, UCSC Environmental Studies professor." Curated by UCSC Library CART fellow Maggie Wander: http://exhibits.library.ucsc.edu/neatline/show/raymond-dasmann.

Digital Exhibit:. "Shakespeare Santa Cruz." Curated by UCSC Library CART fellows Megan Martenyi, LuLing Osofsky, and Alex Ullman: http://exhibits.library.ucsc.edu/exhibits/show/ssc/ssc-home.

Digital Exhibit: "Jean Langenheim: 90 Years of Learning and Discovery." Curated by Special Collections Archivist Kate Dundon: http://exhibits.library.ucsc.edu/exhibits/show/jeanlangenheim.

UC History Timeline: https://150.universityofcalifornia.edu/.

Historical Films

UC Santa Cruz: Audacious and Academic from the Start: https://www.youtube.com/watch?v=o4VSyCQDOC8.

Fiat Fifty: To celebrate fifty years since the founding of UC Santa Cruz, pioneer faculty and staff look back on the early years of the campus: https://www.youtube.com/watch?v=TJCCrT1Eb_c&t=8s.

UC Santa Cruz Farm and Garden 50th Anniversary: https://www.youtube.com/watch?v=rF4GbmOBDZc.

KRON News Historical Footage of the Whole Earth Restaurant from November 17, 1971.Bay Area TV News Archive-San Francisco State University: https://diva.sfsu.edu/collections/sfbatv/bundles/227866.

Historical footage (Eyewitness News) of Loma Prieta Earthquake. Bay Area TV News Archive-San Francisco State University: https://diva.sfsu.edu/collections/sfbatv/bundles/231159.

UCSC Library Special Collections site on the Internet Archive: Several rare short historical films about UCSC are online and can be viewed in streaming format at https://archive.org/details/ucsantacruz. The original films are also available in Special Collections.

Archival Materials in Special Collections

University Archives: Special Collections & Archives has been collecting UCSC history since even before the campus opened its doors; the collections on the history of the university are ever expanding. Interested researchers see: https://guides.library.ucsc.edu/aboutspeccoll/universityarchives for a guide to University Archives and consult with Special Collections staff.

For many more resources see the Seeds of Something Different website, the companion to this printed book, which contains digitized archival images and documents not found in these volumes, as well as audio clips of oral histories, links to archives, and other resources:

https://exhibits.library.ucsc.edu/exhibits/show/seeds

About the Narrators*

Deborah (Deb) Abbott majored in biology and creative writing in the 1970s; from 1997 to 2015 she directed the campus's Lionel Cantú Queer Center. Abbott was interviewed in 2002 as part of the Out in the Redwoods series.

Robert (Bob) Adams arrived at UCSC (Merrill College) in 1967. A professor of economics, he also served as acting dean of social sciences and coordinator of fiscal and academic planning at the time of his oral history, which was conducted in 1976.

Rahne Alexander was an undergraduate student in the mid- to late 1990s. She was interviewed in 2002 as part of the Out in the Redwoods series.

Frank Andrews came to UCSC (College Eight) in 1967. He taught in the chemistry board for four decades and served as a resident preceptor at Crown College for five years. When his oral history was recorded in 2014, eight years after his retirement, Andrews was still offering two courses annually (not for chemistry, but for Crown and Merrill Colleges) focusing on the psychology of personal growth. Andrews spearheaded the publication of *Teacher on the Hill*, a campus newsletter of "faculty conversations about teaching and learning at UCSC."

David Anthony came to UCSC (Oakes College) in 1988 as a professor of African history, later serving as provost of Oakes College from 1996-2002. Anthony's 2013 oral history was one in a series of student-conducted interviews focusing on Oakes College history.

Julia Armstrong-Zwart was hired in 1981 as special assistant to the chancellor for matters of informal grievance and affirmative action, and served as UCSC's first ombudsman. In 1983, she assumed the additional position of assistant academic vice chancellor for faculty relations. She also served as assistant chancellor for human resources, with responsibility for the offices of Academic Human Resources, EEO/Affirmative Action, Labor Relations, Staff Human Resources, and Title IX. Her oral history was conducted in 2013.

Lorenzo Asisara (Awaswas tribe) was baptized at the Santa Cruz Mission in about 1819. Asisara was interviewed three times: twice in 1877 by Hubert Howe Bancroft's historian, Thomas Savage, and once in 1890 by E. L Williams. Native American scholar and former UCSC professor Ed Castillo first published his narrative in 1989. Asisara is one of only three Indigenous individuals who lived in the California missions, and who left their testimonies of their experiences.

Murray Baumgarten arrived at (Stevenson College) UCSC in 1966 as a professor of literature. He served as the first chair of the Modern Society and Social Thought major, offered through Stevenson College, and cofounded The Dickens Project. Baumgarten was interviewed in 2014.

Wendy Baxter graduated from Porter College in art in 1984; since 2000 she has directed the Academic and Cocurricular Programs Office (The CoCo) at College Nine and College Ten. Baxter was interviewed in 2017.

Ciel Benedetto came to UCSC in 1974 and graduated in women's studies. Benedetto has held several staff positions at UCSC, including assistant director for equal employment opportunity in the Office of Diversity, Equity and Inclusion. She was interviewed in 2000.

Michael Bergazzi was a lifetime resident of Santa Cruz County who spent the years between 1901 and 1922 working in almost every phase of redwood lumbering, both in the mills and in the woods. He was interviewed in 1964.

Harry Berger, Jr., was a founding faculty member in literature affiliated with Cowell College. He was interviewed in 2013.

J. Herman Blake was recruited in 1966 by Founding Chancellor Dean McHenry to teach sociology at Cowell College. The first African American to join the faculty, he remained at UCSC for eighteen years. Blake founded UCSC's seventh college, Oakes, and served as its first provost. Blake was interviewed in 2013.

Frank Blaisdell was born in 1888 and lived in Santa Cruz until his death in 1972. He worked as a postal carrier from 1904 until 1949. Blaisdell was interviewed in 1967.

George Blumenthal was UCSC's 10th chancellor. He joined the campus in 1972 (Oakes College) as a faculty member in astronomy and astrophysics. He served as chair of the UC Academic Senate (2004-05), was the faculty representative to the UC Regents (2003-05), and chaired the UC Santa Cruz division of the Academic Senate (2001-03). Blumenthal was named chancellor on September 19, 2007, after serving as acting chancellor for fourteen months; he retired in June 2019. His oral history was conducted in 2018 and 2019.

Rita Bottoms began working at the UCSC Library in 1965 as a reference librarian. She directed the library's Special Collections for thirty-seven years. Bottoms was interviewed in 2003.

Teresa Antonia Broccoli was a literature major at UCSC in the early 1990s. This excerpt is from a narrative she contributed to the Out in the Redwoods project in 2002.

---

*Some excerpts in this book are from published material; these are attributed in the endnotes to each chapter. These capsule biographies are for oral sources only.

Lori Brooke was a College Five student in the 1970s. Her interview was part of a series on UCSC history conducted by students at Cowell College in 2013.

Scott Brookie came to UCSC in 1974 as a Stevenson College student and later worked in a variety of campus staff positions; he has served as the Arts Division's computing director for many years. He was interviewed in 2002 as part of the Out in the Redwoods series.

Sareil Brookins was a student at Stevenson College in the late 2010s, serving as a residential mentor in the Rosa Parks African American Theme House. She majored in psychology and critical race and ethnic studies. She was interviewed as part of the Student Interviews 2017 series.

Shannon Brownlee came to UCSC as an undergraduate in 1974. After taking Ken Norris's *Natural History of California* field class in 1975, she went on to study under Norris's direction, and graduated in biology in 1979. She then joined Norris's research team in Hawaii, studying spinner dolphins from 1979 until 1982, and earned her M.S. in Marine Science from UCSC. Brownlee was interviewed in 1998 as part of the series of oral histories about Ken Norris.

Ellen Marie Bulf arrived at UCSC in 1965 and majored in sociology. She was affiliated with Stevenson College. Bulf was interviewed in 1967 as part of a series of student interviews.

Jim Burns arrived at UC Santa Cruz in 1984, hired by the Public Information Office as publications editor, and later became public affairs director. He was interviewed in 2015.

Lowell Burton was senior building maintenance supervisor at Oakes College from the early seventies until his retirement in 2004. He was interviewed as part of a series of oral histories conducted by Oakes College students in 2013.

Samantha Caballero graduated in 2017 from Kresge College and was interviewed in 2017 as part of the Student Interviews series.

Rosalee (Rosie) Cabrera directed El Centro, UC Santa Cruz's Chicano/Latino Resource Center, and served as counselor and academic coordinator at the campus's Educational Opportunity Program. Cabrera was interviewed in 2012.

Elizabeth Spedding Calciano was the founding director of the Regional History Project from 1963 to 1974. She was interviewed in 2016.

George Cardiff was a longtime Santa Cruz resident who moved to the area in the 1890s. For forty years, Cardiff worked closely with the Henry Cowell Lime and Cement Company at the Cowell Ranch, in various roles ranging from bookkeeper to caretaker. He was interviewed in 1965.

Pedro Castillo came to UCSC (Merrill College) in 1976 as part of the history board. Castillo was also an early affiliate of the American studies program and served as its chair in 1984. In 1990, Castillo and literature professor Norma Klahn cofounded UCSC's Chicano/Latino Research Center (CLRC). From 2002 to 2008, Castillo served as provost of Oakes College. He was interviewed in 2013.

Ann Caudle majored in art, graduating in 1971. She was invited by science communication program director John Wilkes to join UCSC's science illustration faculty in 1986, and shortly afterward became program director. Caudle was interviewed in 2017.

Wendy Chapkis studied politics and sociology at UCSC from 1973 to 1977, did graduate work on campus in sociology from 1985 to 1995, and served as a lecturer in women's studies, politics, and other departments in the 1990s and early 2000s. Chapkis was interviewed in 2002 as part of the Out in the Redwoods GLBT series.

Ray Charland was a psychological counselor at Oakes College. He was interviewed in 1982 as part of a series of oral histories focusing on Oakes College.

Valerie Jean Chase graduated from College Five in politics in 1981. From 1985 to 2016, she worked in a variety of campus staff jobs, culminating in a position as the assistant college administrative officer (ACAO) at Merrill/Crown Colleges. Chase organized UCSC's American Indian graduation, as well as many other American Indian programs and events. She was interviewed in 2002 as part of the Out in the Redwoods series.

Mark Christensen was appointed UCSC's second chancellor in 1974 and served until January 1976. Prior to his appointment as chancellor of UCSC at the age of forty-five, Christensen had served as vice chancellor at UC Berkeley. A member of the Berkeley faculty since 1959, Christensen returned to Berkeley after he left UCSC, as a professor of geology and geophysics, focusing on renewable energy resources. He retired in 1994 and died in 2003.

Angie Christmann worked for thirty-five years in the Cowell College Programs/Student Activities Office. Since retirement, she has managed the Cowell Archives Project. Christmann was interviewed by a student in 2013 as part of an oral history course at Cowell College.

Donald T. Clark was the first of founding chancellor Dean E. McHenry's academic appointees at UCSC, arriving in September 1962 as the founding university librarian. He retired from UCSC in 1973. Clark was interviewed between January 1984 and January 1986. He died in 1993.

D.A. (De) Clarke was a student at Kresge College from 1975 to 1979, graduating with a degree in linguistics. She worked for Lick Observatory in a variety of positions from 1980 until her retirement as a software engineer in 2008. She was interviewed in 2002 as part of the Out in the Redwoods series.

James (Jim) Clifford came to UCSC (Oakes College) in 1978 as a professor in the history of consciousness board. He also founded UCSC's Center for Cultural Studies. Clifford was interviewed in 2012.

Jim Cochran came to UC Santa Cruz in the late 1960s as an undergraduate student at Merrill College. He was interviewed in 2007 as part of the Cultivating a Movement series.

Neal Coonerty and his wife, Candy, bought Bookshop Santa Cruz in 1973. Coonerty served on the Santa Cruz City Council from 1990 to 1994, including a 1993 term as the city's mayor. In the 2000s he served two terms on the Santa Cruz County Board of Supervisors. He was interviewed in 2011.

Sheila Coonerty was a member of UCSC's pioneering class. Coonerty was interviewed in 2013 by participants in an Oakes College oral history class.

Kathy Cowan worked as a staff member for University Relations. She was interviewed as part of a series of oral histories on Oakes College in 1982.

Michael Cowan arrived at UCSC (Merrill College) in 1969 as an associate professor of community studies and literature. By the time he retired in 2004, Cowan had filled a variety of campus leadership positions, including two years as Merrill College provost, from 1978 to 1979; six years as dean of the division of humanities, from 1983 to 1989; and multiple terms as chair of the departments of literature and American studies. He was interviewed in 2012.

Roberto Crespi came to UCSC (Crown College) in 1970 as a professor of Latin American literature; he joined Oakes College. Crespi was interviewed in 1982 as part of a series of interviews on Oakes College. He died in 1992.

John Daly moved to Santa Cruz in 1953 and set up a downtown optometry practice. He served one term as a city councilman, from 1959 to 1963, including a stint as mayor from 1961 to 1962. During his four years in city government, Daly helped promote a series of key growth projects in the community, including the new UCSC campus. He was interviewed in 2012.

Raymond F. Dasmann (College Eight) joined UCSC's environmental studies faculty in 1977 as a professor of ecology. Dasmann was interviewed in 1999; he died in 2002.

Jessica Delgado was a student in politics at UCSC from 1992 to 1995. She was interviewed in 2002 as part of the Out in the Redwoods series.

William (Bill) Dickinson was a student in the pioneer class at Cowell College, graduating in 1968. He founded the Page and Eloise Smith Scholastic Society, which provides scholarships and mentoring for UCSC students who grew up as foster children, orphans, or wards of the court. He was interviewed in 2002 as part of the Out in the Redwoods series.

John Dizikes came to UCSC (Cowell College) in 1965 as a member of the founding faculty. In his ensuing thirty-five-year career, he was a professor of history, a professor and co-founder of American studies, provost of Cowell College, and chair of the Council of Provosts. Dikizes was interviewed in 2011; he died in 2018.

G. William (Bill) Domhoff arrived at UCSC (Cowell College) in the fall of 1965 as an assistant professor in the psychology board. He later also became a professor of sociology. He was interviewed in 2013.

Allan J. (Lan) Dyson was appointed UCSC's University Librarian in August 1979 and retired in July 2003. He was interviewed in 2004.

Carl Eadler triple-majored in mathematics, computer science, and network and digital technology, with a minor in STEM education. He was affiliated with Kresge College. Eadler was interviewed in 2017, his graduation year, as part of the Student Interviews series.

Marsha Ehrenberg transferred to UCSC from Reed College in 1967. She was affiliated with Cowell College and studied literature. Ehrenberg was interviewed in 1967 as part of the Student Interviews series.

John Ellis arrived at UC Santa Cruz (Crown College) in 1966 as a professor of German literature. His 1976 interview was part of a series on the Chancellor Christensen era.

Richard Fernau transferred to UCSC in 1966 as philosophy major affiliated with Cowell College. Now an architect, he designed the renovation of UCSC's 150-year-old Cowell Ranch Hay Barn, which was completed in 2015. Fernau was interviewed in 1969 as part of the Student Interviews series.

F. Louis (Lou) Fackler was UCSC's founding campus engineer. The campus's eleventh employee, he began work in January of 1963. He became director of Campus Facilities in August 1975 and retired in October 1990. At the time of his retirement he had been promoted to the position of associate vice chancellor for facilities and services. Fackler was interviewed in 2012 and died in 2013.

Michael Farney transferred to UCSC in 1965; he affiliated with Cowell College but lived off campus. He was one of UCSC's first physical sciences majors. Farney was interviewed in 1967 as part of the Student Interviews series.

Sam Farr represented California's Central Coast in the United States House of Representatives for twenty-three years, until his retirement from office in 2016. He also served six years as a member of the Monterey County Board of Supervisors and twelve years in the California State Assembly. Farr was interviewed in 2016-17.

Lawrence (Larry) Ford graduated from UCSC in 1978 with a double major in biology and environmental studies. He worked closely with Ken Norris from 1977 to 1984 as instructor for the *Natural History Field Quarter*, as coordinator for the Environmental Field Program, and as manager of the Landels-Hill Big Creek Reserve. He was interviewed in 1998 as part of the Ken Norris series.

Marge Frantz came to UCSC in 1973 as a history of consciousness graduate student, receiving her PhD in 1984. First as a teaching assistant in 1973 and then as a lecturer beginning in 1976, she taught a range of courses for the American studies and women's studies departments. Frantz was interviewed in 2004 as part of a series about the Women's Center. She died in 2015.

Carol Freeman arrived at UCSC (Cowell College) in 1974; she was the founding coordinator and eventually chair of the Campus Writing Program. Freeman taught writing at UCSC for thirty-four years, obtaining Senior Lecturer status with security of employment. She served in many capacities on the campus Academic Senate, including three years as chair of the Committee on Committees, six years as chair of the Committee on Educational Policy (CEP), and two years on the systemwide CEP. In 1992, she became the first female provost of Cowell College, a position she held until 1997. Freeman was interviewed in 2012 and died in 2019.

Mike Fresco was a member of the pioneering class at Cowell College, graduating with a degree in biology in 1969. He was interviewed in 1967 as part of the Student Interviews series.

William (Bill) Friedland was hired as a professor in 1969 (Merrill College) to establish a major in community studies. He was interviewed in 2012, and died in 2018 at age 94.

Tim Galarneau transferred to UCSC in 2002, graduating in psychology and community studies with an emphasis in agroecology and social justice. Galarneau was interviewed in 2008 as part of the Cultivating a Movement series.

Victor Garcia-Zepeda majored in community studies and sociology with a focus in public health. A Merrill College student, he was active in Merrill student government. He also worked as a program assistant for UCSC's Human Genomics Institute. Garcia-Zepeda was interviewed in 2017, his graduation year, as part of the Student Interviews series.

Lyn Garling was the apprentice coordinator for the UC Santa Cruz Agroecology Program (Farm and Garden) from 1984 to 1992. Garling was interviewed in 2007 as part of the Cultivating a Movement series.

Steve Garvin was a theater arts student at UCSC in the late 1980s. He was interviewed in 1990 as part of the Loma Prieta Earthquake series.

James (Jim) Gill joined the Oakes College faculty in 1972 and taught earth sciences at UCSC for almost four decades. He also served as dean of graduate studies. Gill was interviewed in 1982 as part of a series of interviews about Oakes College.

Stephen (Steve) Gliessman came to UCSC (College Eight) as a professor of environmental studies in 1980. He was the founding director of the Agroecology Program (now the Center for Agroecology and Sustainable Food Systems). He taught the *Natural History Field Quarter* and founded the Program in Community and Agroecology (PICA), an experiential living/learning program. Gliessman was interviewed twice: once in 1999 about his teaching with Ken Norris and again in 2007 as part of the Cultivating a Movement oral history series.

Antoinette Gonzalez was a UCSC student in the 1990s and later worked on campus as an undergraduate advisor. Gonzalez was interviewed in 2002 as part of the Out in the Redwoods series.

Allan Jamie Goodman transferred to UCSC and Stevenson College from UC Riverside. He graduated in 1969. A government major, he was interviewed as part of the Student Interviews series in 1967.

Drew Goodman graduated from UCSC in environmental studies in 1983. Goodman was interviewed in 2009 as part of the Cultivating a Movement series.

Greg Graalfs graduated from Cowell College in 1976 with an individual major in The Art of the Book. Graalfs conducted a series of oral histories on the Cowell Press in 2005.

M.R.C. ("Marcie") Greenwood was appointed UCSC's seventh chancellor in July 1996 and served until April 2004. She had previously chaired the department of biology and directed the Undergraduate Research Summer Institute at Vassar College; in 1989, she was hired by UC Davis, where she held positions as a professor of nutrition and internal medicine, dean of graduate studies, and later vice provost for academic outreach. From November 1993 to May 1995, Greenwood served as associate director for science in the White House Office of Science and Technology Policy under President Bill Clinton. She was interviewed in 2004-2005.

Gary Griggs came to UCSC (College Eight) in 1968 as a member of the earth sciences faculty. He served as chair of earth sciences from 1981 to 1984 and associate dean of natural sciences from 1991 to 1994; he directed the Institute of Marine Sciences and Long Marine Laboratory from 1991 until 2017. He was interviewed in 2011-2012.

Isebill (Ronnie) Gruhn arrived at UC Santa Cruz (Stevenson College) in 1969 as a member of the politics board. One of very few tenured women during UCSC's early days and one of the first to serve as a high-level administrator, Gruhn was also the first female dean of social sciences (1981-1983) and the first female academic vice chancellor (acting) (1987-1989). She was interviewed in 2013.

Dan Haifley transferred to Kresge College in 1977 and graduated in economics in 1979. He was interviewed in 2012.

Brett Hall was a student at Crown College and worked at the Arboretum, graduating in biology in 1975. He started on the Arboretum staff in October 1975 and became garden manager in 1976. He is now manager of the Arboretum's California Native Plant program. Hall was interviewed in 2007 as part of a series of interviews on the Arboretum.

Conn Hallinan began teaching as a lecturer (Oakes College) in the Campus Writing Program in 1982. He oversaw the campus journalism program beginning in 1988. He served from 2001 to 2004 as Kresge College provost and retired from UCSC in 2004. Hallinan was interviewed as part of a 2013 series of student oral histories focusing on Oakes College.

Donna Haraway came to UCSC (Oakes College) in 1980 as a professor in history of consciousness. Her position in feminist theory was probably the first of its kind in the country. She was interviewed in 2007.

Dan Harder achieved a distinguished career in international botanical research before serving as executive director of the UCSC Arboretum from 2001 to 2009. His oral history was conducted in 2007 as part of a series of interviews on the Arboretum.

Rachel Harwood arrived at Kresge College in 1976 and graduated in the early 1980s. Her degree is in women's studies and history. She was interviewed in 2002 as part of the Out in the Redwoods series.

Catherine (Kate) Howells came to UCSC as a member of the pioneering class at Cowell College in 1965 and majored in history. She was interviewed in 1969 as part of the Student Interviews series.

Khalen Hudson majored in chemistry and biochemistry and graduated in 2017. An active member of the College Nine community, he served as a resident assistant for three years and as a mentor resident assistant. He was interviewed in 2017 as part of the Student Interviews series.

Allen Hunter came to UCSC in 1967 as a transfer student in history affiliated with Cowell College. He was interviewed in 1967 as part of the Student Interviews series.

Harold (Hal) Hyde, a fifth-generation Santa Cruz County resident, contributed to the creation of institutions ranging from UCSC and Cabrillo College to the Community Foundation and the Cultural Council of Santa Cruz County. Founding chancellor Dean McHenry hired Hyde in 1964 as vice chancellor of business and finance, a position that entailed responsibility for initiating all nonacademic aspects of the new campus. After leaving UCSC in 1975, Hyde continued to serve the campus as the first president of the Arboretum Associates and as a trustee of the UC Santa Cruz Foundation. He remains an active supporter of the campus at the time of this writing. Hyde was interviewed in 2002.

Robert Imada attended UCSC from 1998 to 2002. Imada was interviewed in 2002 as part of the Out in the Redwoods series.

John Isbister came to UCSC in the late 1960s as part of Merrill College and the economics board. He served from 1984 to 1999 as provost of Merrill College. Isbister left UCSC in 2006 to return to his native Canada and teach at Laurentian University.

Rik Isensee graduated from Porter College in 1972 and was interviewed in 2002 as part of the Out in the Redwoods series, in a "Living History Circle" group interview.

Michael James was a student at Merrill College from 1970 to 1975. He was interviewed in 2013 as part of an oral history series conducted by students in an Oakes College course.

Aaron Johnson was a studio arts major in the early 1980s and studied at the Cowell Press. He was interviewed in 2005 as part of a series of interviews on the Cowell Press.

Stephen (Steve) Kaffka came to UC Santa Cruz as a philosophy student in 1967 and began volunteering in Alan Chadwick's Student Garden Project. He worked side by side with Chadwick, becoming the Garden's student president in 1968. After Chadwick left the campus, Kaffka managed the UCSC Farm. Kaffka was interviewed in 2007 as part of the Cultivating a Movement series.

Amy Katzenstein-Escobar majored in community studies in the mid-1970s. She was interviewed in 2007 as part of the Cultivating a Movement series.

Jennifer (Jenny) Keller studied art and science illustration at UCSC in the early 1980s. Together with UCSC alumna Ann Caudle, she has built, administered and taught in the Science Illustration Certificate Program since helping to establish it in the 1980s under the auspices of UCSC's Graduate Program in Science Communication. Keller was interviewed in 2017.

Clark Kerr was the twelfth president of the University of California, serving in that position from 1958 to 1967, during which period he initiated, promoted, and oversaw UC's greatest era of expansion. Among his major contributions to the UC system was his conception of UCSC as an experimental research university built around small residential colleges, with an emphasis on undergraduate education, close faculty-student interaction, and human-scale community life. Kerr was interviewed in 1987; he died in 2003.

Elaine Kihara came to UCSC in 1988 to serve as the assistant to Oakes College provost Victor Rocha; she worked as the Oakes College academic preceptor for more than twenty years. Kihara was interviewed in 2013 as part of a series of student oral histories on Oakes College.

Tom Killion was a student at Cowell College from 1971 to 1975, majoring in history. Introduced to fine book printing by William Everson and Jack Stauffacher at the Cowell Press, he went on to an eminent career as a woodcut artist. He was interviewed in 2004 as part of the Cowell Press oral history series.

Alison Kim attended UCSC from 1985 to 1989. She co-edited and co-published *Between the Lines: A Pacific/Asian Lesbian Anthology* in 1987. She was interviewed in 2002 as part of the Out in the Redwoods GLBT series.

Katie King arrived at Cowell College in 1970. She earned a joint BA in literature and anthropology in 1975 and a PhD in the history of consciousness in 1987. She was interviewed in 2018.

David Kirk served on the UCSC staff from 1972 to 2001, first at the Office of Instructional Services and then with the Media Services Department of the University Library. He was a founder of the campus's Gay and Lesbian Alliance (GALA). Kirk was interviewed in 2002 as part of the Out in the Redwoods series.

Stephen Klein came to UCSC (Cowell) in 1968 as a student and graduated in 1972. He is a librarian and gay activist. He was interviewed in 2002 as part of the Out in the Redwoods series.

David Kliger arrived at UC Santa Cruz In 1971 as a chemistry professor and an affiliate of Kresge College. He served the campus in a variety of administrative capacities: as chair of chemistry from 1985 to 1988, as chair of the Academic Senate from 1988 to 1990, as dean of the division of natural sciences (now physical and biological sciences) from 1990-2005, and finally as campus provost/executive vice chancellor from 2005 to 2010. He was interviewed in 2011.

Reggie Knox attended UCSC in the late 1980s, majoring in earth sciences and community studies. Knox was interviewed in 2008 as part of the Cultivating a Movement series.

Ernest T. (Bud) Kretschmer was a notable philanthropist in the Santa Cruz music community. Kretschmer was interviewed in 1992 and 2000. He died in 2009 at age 94.

Gwen Lacy was an administrative assistant at Oakes during the college's early years. She was interviewed in 1982 as part of a series of interviews about Oakes College.

John Laird came to Stevenson College at UCSC in 1968, majoring in politics, and graduated in 1972. In 1983 he was elected mayor of Santa Cruz, becoming the first openly gay mayor in the United States; in 2002, he was elected to the California State Legislature as one of the first openly gay men in the State Assembly. Laird spent eight years as the state's natural resources secretary under Governor Jerry Brown; as of this writing, he is running for election to the California State Senate's 17th District seat in 2020. He was interviewed in 2002

as part of the Out in the Redwoods GLBT oral history series.

Cynthia Cliff Lance came to UCSC in 1965. A Stevenson College student, she graduated in biology in 1969. She was interviewed in 1969 as part of the Student Interviews series.

Ed Landesman taught mathematics from 1966 to 1994. He served on numerous Academic Senate committees, became UCSC's first associate academic vice chancellor for undergraduate education, and served as provost and senior preceptor for academic affairs at Crown College. Landesman was interviewed in 2015-2016.

Leo Laporte arrived at UCSC (Cowell College) in 1971 as a professor of earth sciences. He chaired that department from 1972 to 1975 and served as dean of the natural sciences division from 1975 to 1976. He was interviewed in 1994.

Katherine Le majored in politics and legal studies at UCSC and graduated in 2017. The daughter of two Vietnam War refugees, she was active with the campus's Asian American/Pacific Islander Resource Center. As a College Nine student, she served on the college senate, including a term as vice president of internal affairs. Le was interviewed in 2017 for the Student Interviews series.

Burney Le Boeuf arrived at UCSC (Crown College) in 1967 as a member of the psychology faculty and began working with biology professor Richard Peterson on seal and sea lion research. Le Boeuf is now internationally known as a pioneer in the field of marine mammal behavior, focusing on elephant seals at Año Nuevo Island. Le Boeuf has held several administrative positions at UCSC, serving as interim vice chancellor and associate vice chancellor for research and as managing director of the University Affiliated Research Center (UARC). He was interviewed in 1994 and again in 2014.

Jim Leap managed the campus's twenty-five-acre farm from 1990 to 2010. He was interviewed in 2008 as part of the Cultivating a Movement series.

Paul Lee was appointed an assistant professor of philosophy (Crown College) in 1966; in 1967 he brought Alan Chadwick to UCSC to oversee the Student Garden Project. Lee was interviewed in 2001 as part of a series of interviews about the early UCSC Farm and Garden Project.

Diane Lewis joined the anthropology board and Oakes College in 1974. She was interviewed in 2013 as part of a student oral history series at Oakes College. Lewis died in 2015.

Mark Lipson majored in environmental studies in the late 1970s and early 1980s. He was interviewed in 2007 for the Cultivating a Movement series.

Norman Locks came to UCSC (College Five) in 1978 to teach photography. College Five Provost Pavel Machotka hired him to teach courses and manage a darkroom for aesthetic studies, an interdisciplinary major affiliated with College Five.

In 1980, when the major was disbanded as part of Chancellor Robert Sinsheimer's college-system reorganization, Locks was hired as a lecturer in the art department; ten years later that department promoted him to a tenure-track position. Locks was interviewed in 2016.

Carrie Lodge was the granddaughter of Martina Castro Lodge, holder of the Soquel Rancho, the largest Mexican land grant in Santa Cruz County. She was also the descendant of Isidro Castro who came to California as a soldier with the de Anza Party in 1776. Lodge was interviewed in 1965.

Beatriz Lopez-Flores was hired as the Women's Center director in September 1986 and held that position until 1994. She was interviewed in 2005 as part of the Women's Center oral history.

Linda Luder came to UCSC in 1965 as a member of the pioneering class at Cowell College and majored in Medieval history. She was interviewed in 1969 as part of the Student Interviews series.

Evelyn Luluquisen arrived as a student at Cowell College in 1978 and transferred to Oakes the following year. She was interviewed in 2013 as part of a student oral history series at Oakes College.

John Lynch arrived at UCSC (Cowell College) in 1969 as a professor of classics and literature. He helped found the classics program at UCSC. He served as Cowell's provost from 1983 to 1989. Lynch taught at UCSC for thirty-seven years. He was interviewed in 2013.

Pavel Machotka arrived at UC Santa Cruz in 1970, hired by the psychology board and by Provost James Hall of College Five. One of the founders of the interdisciplinary aesthetic studies major, Machotka also served as provost of College Five from 1976 to 1979. Machotka was interviewed in 2015. He died in 2019.

John Marcum was a professor of politics affiliated with Merrill College. Arriving at UCSC in 1969 as a visiting professor, he joined the permanent faculty in 1972. Marcum was provost of Merrill College from 1972 to 1977. Marcum was interviewed in 1976 as part of a series of interviews on the Chancellor Christensen era. He died in 2013.

Jacquelyn Marie was women's studies/reference librarian at the University Library from 1981 to 2001. The excerpts included in the book are from a narrative she contributed to the Out in the Redwoods Project in 2002.

Orin Martin manages the Alan Chadwick Garden. He was interviewed in 2008 as part of the Cultivating a Movement series.

Tera Martin was a graduate student in American studies in the mid-to-late 1990s. She was interviewed in 2013 as part of a series of student interviews on the history of Oakes College.

Carolyn Martin Shaw (earlier known as Carolyn Clark) joined the UCSC faculty in 1972, hired by the anthropology board and Kresge College, where she served as provost from 1991 to 1996. She was interviewed in 2014.

Douglas McClellan arrived at UCSC (College Five) in 1970 and taught on campus until his retirement in 1986. He was a founder of the art board, serving as chair from 1970 to 1975 and again in 1983. McClellan was interviewed in 2014; he died in 2016 at 94.

Daniel (Dan) McFadden came to UCSC in 1973 as an assistant to Chancellor Mark Christensen and continued to work in campus administration through the 1980s. He was interviewed in 1976 as part of a series of interviews on the Christensen era at UCSC.

Dean McHenry was UCSC's founding chancellor, appointed in 1961 by UC president Clark Kerr. He also led the Master Plan Survey of Higher Education for California (1959-1960) and served as the UC systemwide university dean of academic planning under President Clark Kerr (1960 to 1963). McHenry helped Kerr plan the development of three new UC campuses authorized by the Board of Regents; the site-selection process ultimately led to the founding of campuses in Irvine, San Diego, and Santa Cruz. McHenry was interviewed between 1967 and 1969. He retired in 1974 and died in 1998.

Rosa Melero was a student at Porter College majoring in art and anthropology. She was interviewed in 2017, her graduation year, for the Student Interviews series.

Henry Mello was elected to the Santa Cruz County Board of Supervisors in 1966 and to the California State Assembly in 1976; he represented Santa Cruz and San Benito counties for twenty-two years as a California State Senator. Mello was interviewed in 2000; he died in 2004.

Leta Miller arrived at UCSC in 1978 as a part-time lecturer in music; in 1987 she was hired for a tenure-track position. Miller's oral history was conducted in 2015. She is still teaching in 2019.

Helene Moglen was hired at UCSC in the fall of 1978 (Kresge College) as a professor of literature and the dean of humanities, becoming the first female dean in the University of California system. From 1978 to 1983, she also served as provost of Kresge College. Moglen transformed what was then a fledgling student-run women's studies program into a nationally prominent feminist studies department. She founded and directed both the Focused Research Activity in Feminist Studies (1984-1989) and the Institute for Advanced Feminist Research (2003 to 2006); in 1985, she helped found the UCSC Women's Center. Moglen was interviewed in 2004 as part of a series of oral histories focused on the Women's Center and participated in a broader oral history about her UCSC career in 2013. She died in 2018.

Gwendolyn Morgan came to UCSC as a re-entry student in 1989 and graduated in 1991 with a bachelor's degree in classics. Until 2000 she held a variety of campus staff positions, including founder and coordinator of the staff Diversity Education Program. Morgan was interviewed in 2002 as part of the Out in the Redwoods series.

Scott Morgensen was a graduate student in anthropology from 1991 to 2001. Morgensen was interviewed in 2002 as part of the Out in the Redwoods series.

Olga Nájera-Ramírez attended UCSC as an undergraduate student, then returned as a tenured professor. She arrived as a Merrill College student in 1973, danced with the troupe Grupo Folklorico Los Mejicas, and earned a dual degree in history and Latin American studies in 1977. She has taught in the anthropology department since 1989. Nájera-Ramírez is a founder of UCSC's Latin American and Latino studies department and has directed the Chicano/Latino Research Center (CLRC), now called Research Center for the Americas. Since 1996, she has provided faculty advising to Los Mejicas. She was interviewed in 2013.

Michael Nauenberg began his UCSC career in 1966 (Crown College) as a professor of physics. He served as department chair from 1970 to 1972, and again from 1983 to 1985. He was instrumental in developing both Stevenson and Crown Colleges, but in 1973 shifted his focus to building a physics graduate program. He also founded and served as the director of UCSC's Institute of Nonlinear Sciences. Nauenberg was interviewed in 1994 and died in 2019.

Jim Nelson came to UCSC in 1967 as a transfer student in literature and became a protégé of Alan Chadwick at the Student Garden. Nelson was interviewed in 2008 as part of the Cultivating a Movement series.

Todd Newberry arrived at UCSC (Cowell College) in 1965 as a founding faculty member in biology. He was interviewed in 1994.

Paul Niebanck came to UCSC (College Eight) in 1973 as a professor of environmental planning and was the founding provost of College Eight. Niebanck was interviewed in 1976 as part of a series of oral histories focusing on the Chancellor Christensen era at UCSC.

Ramona Noriega attended UCSC in the late 1980s, majoring in community studies and living at Student Family Housing. Noriega was interviewed in 1990 as part of a series of interviews on the Loma Prieta Earthquake.

Kenneth (Ken) Norris came to UCSC (College Eight) in 1972 as a professor of natural history in the environmental studies board, retiring in 1990. Norris helped establish the Center for Coastal Marine Studies (now the Institute of Marine Sciences) and the Long Marine Laboratory, the University of California Natural Reserve System, and the *Natural History Field Quarter* course. Norris was interviewed in 1998, which

was also the year of his death.

Phyllis Norris is a biologist who came to UCSC in 1972 with her husband, Ken Norris. Norris has been a key volunteer at the UCSC Arboretum and also at the UCSC Farm. She was interviewed by the Regional History Project in 2001 about the UCSC Farm and Garden and again in 2003 and 2007 about the Arboretum.

Robert Norris, Ken Norris's brother, was a professor of geology at UC Santa Barbara. Norris oversaw several of UC's Natural Reserve System sites, and was his brother's colleague throughout their professional lives. Norris was interviewed in 1998 as part of the Ken Norris series; he died in 2012.

Louis Odiase studied economics at UCSC, where he was a resident assistant in Oakes College's Biko House. He volunteered for Destination Higher Education, an outreach program that introduces newly admitted students to the Afrikan/Black/Caribbean community and student life on the UC Santa Cruz campus. Odiase was interviewed in 2017, his graduation year, as part of the Student Interviews series.

Kathie Olsen came to UCSC as a re-entry student at Oakes College in 1976, graduating in anthropology. In the fall of 1985, she took a position as the first assistant director of the UCSC Women's Center. Olsen was interviewed in 2005 as part of a series of interviews on the Women's Center.

Glenn Omatsu came to UCSC in 1967; he affiliated with Stevenson College and majored in psychology. He was interviewed in 1969 as part of the Student Interviews oral history series, and again in 2015 as part of a series of oral histories conducted by Cowell College.

Ekua Omosupe was a graduate student from 1985 to 1997, earning her PhD in American literature. Omosupe was interviewed in 2002 as part of the Out in the Redwoods series.

Arlyn Osborne came to UCSC as assistant director of the Women's Center in 1987 and served as interim director twice during her ten years with the Center. Osborne was interviewed in 2005 as part of a series of interviews on the Women's Center.

Nancy Pascal was born and raised in Santa Cruz and came to work in the UCSC registrar's office as a senior clerk typist in 1966, eventually becoming associate registrar. Pascal was interviewed in 2013 as part of a series of oral histories conducted in a Cowell College class.

James (Jim) Pepper was recruited by Richard [Dick] Cooley in 1972 to help develop UCSC's new environmental studies program, in which he taught courses on environmental planning. He taught at UCSC until 1994.

Karl Pister was hired as the campus's sixth chancellor for an interim two-year appointment in August 1991, after the resignation of Chancellor Robert B. Stevens. Prior to his tenure at UCSC, Pister had spent thirty years at UC Berkeley as a faculty member and fifteen years as an academic administrator. In March 1992, Pister was appointed as permanent chancellor, a position he filled until 1996. Pister was interviewed in 1996.

Rosa Martha Plaza was an Oakes College student in the 1990s. She is now director of orientation for the Educational Opportunity Program. She was interviewed in 2013 as part of the Oakes College student oral history series.

Siegfried (Sig) Puknat arrived at UCSC in 1964 as the first full-time non-administrative faculty member hired by the campus. A professor of German and comparative literature, Puknat was affiliated with Crown College. He was interviewed in 1976 as part of an oral history series on the Chancellor Christensen era. He died in 1997.

Pablo G. Reguerin came to UCSC as a student in 1990, graduating in Latino and Latin American studies in 1994. He has since worked as the deputy director of UCSC's Educational Partnership Center and as a senior admissions counselor with the Office of Admissions. He led efforts to reorganize the campus's student services to assist vulnerable student populations. Reguerin currently serves as the associate vice chancellor for student achievement and equity innovation. He was interviewed in 2016.

Felicia Rice graduated from UCSC In 1978 with an independent major in fine printing. She worked with master printers William Everson, Jack Stauffacher, Adrian Wilson, and Sherwood Grover, studying at both the Cowell Press and the Lime Kiln Press. After graduating, she founded Moving Parts Press. She has also taught book arts at Porter College and for the arts division and managed UCSC's Digital Arts and New Media MFA Program, as well as the now-defunct UCSC Extension Visual Communication Program. Rice was interviewed in 2005 for a series of oral histories about the Cowell Press.

Inigo Rose is the younger son of Jasper and Jean Rose. He was interviewed as part of a Rose family history in 2018.

Jasper Rose came to UCSC in 1965 to help Page Smith found Cowell College, where he served as senior preceptor and later as provost. He had studied and taught at King's College, Oxford University, and co-authored an influential book on the Oxford-Cambridge model, *Camford Observed*. A professor of history and art, he taught especially popular classes in art history. Rose left UCSC in 1989 and returned to England to paint. He was interviewed in 2018 and died in 2019.

Jean Rose is a prolific painter of frescos and oils and has exhibited widely. She is married to Jasper Rose and helped create Cowell College. She was interviewed in 2018 as part of a Rose family oral history.

William Rose is a painter and the first son of Jasper Rose and Jean Rose; he grew up at Cowell College. Rose was interviewed as part of a Rose family history in 2018.

Linda Rosewood came to UCSC in 1981 as a junior transfer student at College Eight, graduating in chemistry. She graduated from the Graduate Program in Science Communication in 1986. Rosewood worked on campus as an editor, computer technician, and network analyst until her recent retirement from UCSC. Rosewood was interviewed in 2002 as part of the Out in the Redwoods series, in a "Living History Circle" group interview.

Donald (Don) Rothman came to UCSC and Oakes College in 1973 to teach writing and coordinate a college-based writing-tutoring program; he was one of a small number of faculty members on the campus to hold the position of senior lecturer with security of employment. In 1977 he founded the Central California Writing Project (CCWP), a literacy education think tank for teachers of kindergarten through university, which he directed for twenty-seven years. He retired from UCSC in 2007. He was interviewed in 1982 as part of a series of oral histories done on Oakes College. A broader oral history with Rothman was planned in 2012, but he died just a few days before the interviews were to begin.

Michael (Mike) Rotkin came to Santa Cruz in 1969, initially as an assistant to William Friedland, the founding director of the community studies program. Accepted in the fall of 1969 into the interdisciplinary history of consciousness graduate program, Rotkin began working as a teaching assistant for community studies, where he was hired as a lecturer in 1976 and as coordinator of field studies in 1979. Rotkin has also served as a community organizer, a multi-term Santa Cruz mayor and city councilmember, and a local and statewide leader in the UC-AFT (the union representing lecturers and librarians in the UC system). He was interviewed in 2013 as part of a series on community studies.

Alan Sable (Merrill College) was a faculty member in sociology from 1970 to 1977. In 1971, he became the first UCSC professor to come out to his class as gay. Denied tenure in 1977, he became a psychotherapist in the Bay Area. Sable was interviewed in 2002 as part of the Out in the Redwoods series.

Roger Samuelsen began his professional UC career as coordinator of special projects under UC President Clark Kerr in 1967, when he began working with Ken Norris to develop the fledgling UC Natural Reserve System, dedicated to providing field teaching and research opportunities in a variety of representative California habitats. He was interviewed in 1998 as part of a series of interviews about Ken Norris.

Elba Sánchez earned a BA in Latin American studies as a Merrill College student in the late 1970s. Encouraged by her faculty advisor, Roberto Crespi, she went on to earn a UCSC MA in literature. Crespi hired Sánchez as a tutor in the multidisciplinary Spanish for Spanish Speakers Program. Sánchez spent the next fifteen years teaching in and directing that program. She was interviewed in 2013.

Tchad Sanger was a student from 1989 to 1993, majoring in psychology; since graduating he has worked in campus staff positions, serving as an academic advisor at Stevenson College and now as the campus registrar. He was interviewed in 2002 as part of the Out in the Redwoods series.

Ziesel Saunders was a student at UCSC from 1972 to 1977. She worked as an administrator at Merrill College from 1984 to the late 1990s. She was interviewed as part of the Out in the Redwoods series in 2002.

Peter Scott arrived at UCSC (Stevenson College) in 1966 as a professor of physics. He was interviewed in 1994.

Priscilla (Tilly) Washburn Shaw arrived at UCSC for the opening of Stevenson College, in 1966-67, as a visiting faculty member. In 1967, the literature board hired her as a tenured faculty member. Shaw was interviewed in 2013 and died in 2015.

Marilyn Shea came to UCSC in 1965 as a history major. She later became a Crown student. Shea was interviewed in 1969 as part of the Student Interviews series.

William Shipley (Stevenson College) was a professor of linguistics from 1966 to 1991, founding UCSC's linguistics board and chairing it until 1980. He was interviewed in 2002 for the Out in the Redwoods series. Shipley died in 2011.

Quinton Skinner attended UCSC in the late 1980s and was working downtown at a record store when the Loma Prieta Earthquake hit on October 17, 1989. He was interviewed in 1990 as part of the series of interviews about the quake.

Karen Sinsheimer came to UCSC in 1981 to join her new husband, Robert, who had been hired as the campus's fourth chancellor in 1977. A former executive secretary at Caltech and 20th Century Fox, with a background in arts curating and photography, Sinsheimer took on leadership roles at UCSC and in the local community, including many years with Shakespeare Santa Cruz as founding board president. She also advocated at the systemwide level for the recognition of the role and contributions of UC chancellors' spouses. Sinsheimer was interviewed in 1990; she died in 2015.

Robert Sinsheimer became UCSC's fourth chancellor in June 1977 and held that position until 1987. He had previously served as chair of the division of biology at Caltech. Sinsheimer was the first UCSC chancellor to come from outside the UC system. He was interviewed in 1990-91, and died in 2017 at the age of ninety-seven.

Valerie Simmons came to UCSC in 1982 as director of the campus's Equal Employment Opportunity/Affirmative Action Office, a position she held for seventeen years. She was interviewed in 2013 as part of an oral history project undertaken by students in an Oakes College class.

Heidi Skolnik came to UCSC in the early 1970s at the age of nineteen to volunteer in the Student Garden Project. When the project expanded to include a farm near the base of campus, Skolnik and a group of student and non-student workers who called themselves "The Home Farmers" took up residence in teepees on the land. Skolnik was interviewed in 2007 as part of the Cultivating a Movement series.

Deana Slater came to UCSC in 1997 as College Administrative Officer (CAO) of Merrill College. She helped plan Colleges Nine and Ten and became the CAO for those colleges. Slater was interviewed in 2017 as part of a series documenting the history of Colleges Nine and Ten. She retired in 2019.

Page Smith joined the UCSC faculty in 1964 as a history professor and the founding provost of Cowell College. During the campus's first decade, he promoted a number of institutional innovations, including the narrative evaluation system. Smith resigned from UCSC in 1973 after his colleague and friend Paul Lee, a professor of religious studies, was denied tenure. He was interviewed in 1974 and died in 1995.

Russell Smith came to UCSC in 1965 as a member of the pioneering class at Cowell College. He later transferred to Stevenson College. Smith majored in government. He was interviewed in 1969 as part of the Student Interviews series.

Shane Snowdon became director of the UCSC Women's Center in 1995 and served in that position until 1999. Snowdon was interviewed in 2004 for a series of oral histories about the Women's Center.

David Solano majored in psychology. His extensive involvement in the College Ten community included working as a resident assistant and helping organize the college's annual Practical Activism conference. He was interviewed in 2017, his graduation year, as part of the Student Interviews series.

Ruth Solomon arrived at UCSC in 1970 (College Five) as a professor in the theater arts board. She created a visionary program that synthesized dance and theater. She also founded UCSC's Summer Dance Theater Institute, coordinating that program from 1972 until 1980. Solomon was interviewed in 2014.

Audrey Stanley (Stevenson College) came to UCSC in 1969 as a professor of theater arts. She was the founding artistic director of Shakespeare Santa Cruz. Stanley was interviewed in 2013.

Jack Stauffacher established his Greenwood Press in 1934 and moved it to San Francisco after World War II. In the 1970s, Stauffacher taught book-arts classes at Cowell College centered on what later became the Cowell Press. Stauffacher was interviewed in 2004 as part of an oral history on the Cowell Press. He died in 2017 at age ninety-six.

Robert Stevens was appointed the campus's fifth chancellor in July 1987, serving until July 1991. Born in England in 1933, Stevens was educated at Oxford and Yale. A law professor at

Yale from 1959 to 1976, he served as provost and professor of law and history at Tulane University from 1976 to 1978. He then became the president of Haverford College, holding that position until he came to UCSC. Stevens was interviewed in 1991.

Nancy Stoller (Shaw) arrived at UCSC (Oakes College) in 1973 as a professor of community studies. She was denied tenure in 1982 and contested the decision; prevailing in 1987 after a protracted legal and political battle, she returned to teach at UCSC. She was interviewed in 2002 as part of the Out in the Redwoods series.

Susan Sward came to UCSC in 1965 as a member of the pioneering class at Cowell College, majoring in psychology. Sward was interviewed in 1967 as part of the Student Interviews series.

Sean Swezey came to UCSC's Center for Agroecology and Sustainable Food Systems (CASFS) in the late 1980s as a researcher working with Steve Gliessman. He was interviewed in 2008 as part of the Cultivating a Movement series.

John Taub came to UCSC as a student in 1965 and was affiliated first with Cowell College, then later Crown and Merrill. He majored in psychology. Taub was interviewed in 1969 as part of the Student Interviews series.

Angus Taylor was appointed the campus's third chancellor in February 1976. Prior to his appointment, Taylor served in the UC systemwide administration as vice president for academic affairs from 1965 to 1970, and as university provost from 1970 to 1975. Taylor was interviewed in 1997; he died in 1999.

Kenneth Thimann was invited in 1965 by founding chancellor Dean E. McHenry to head what would become Crown College and to build the science faculty at UCSC. Prior to coming to Santa Cruz, Thimann was an internationally renowned plant physiologist. He was the first member of the National Academy of Sciences to join the UCSC faculty. Thimann was interviewed in 1986; he died in 1997.

David Thomas (Stevenson College) was a professor of politics at UCSC from 1966 to 2000. Thomas was interviewed in 2002 as part of the Out in the Redwoods series.

Don Usner earned his B.A. in biology and environmental studies in 1980. A student in the *Natural History Field Quarter* in 1980, he served as a TA for Field Quarter in 1984 and 1985. He was the caretaker at the Landels-Hill Big Creek Reserve from 1982-1986. Usner was interviewed as part of the Ken Norris series in 1998.

Richard Vasquez came to UCSC in 1972 as a student at Oakes College. An academic advisor for the Educational Opportunity Program for many years, he now co-chairs the UCSC Latino Alumni Network. Vasquez was interviewed in 2013 as part of a series of oral histories conducted by students in a Cowell College class.

Yolanda Venegas taught writing for UC Santa Cruz's Educational Opportunity Program Faculty Mentor Program from 2006 to 2009. In 2010, she became EOP's Faculty Mentor Program Director and coordinated pre-graduate programs and AB 540 student campus resources. Venegas also taught for UCSC's Writing Program and the Merrill College core course. She was interviewed in 2016.

George Von der Muhll arrived at UCSC (College Five) in 1969 as a professor of politics. He was acting provost of College Five at the time of his first oral history in 1976. He was interviewed again in 2014, and died in 2016.

Michael Warren (Cowell College) came to UCSC in 1968 as a professor of literature. He was interviewed in 2012.

Jess Whatcott was a graduate student in politics with a designated emphasis in feminist studies and critical race and ethnic studies. She served as president of the Graduate Student Association (GSA). Whatcott was interviewed in 2017, during her fourth year of graduate study, as part of the Student Interviews series.

Hayden White came to UCSC in 1978 (Oakes College) as a professor and chair of the history of consciousness graduate program. White was interviewed in 2012; he died in 2018.

Albert Whitford directed the Lick Observatory on Mt. Hamilton from 1959 to 1968. Whitford was interviewed in 1995; he died in 2002.

Sabina Wildman majored in sociology as a Crown College student in the late 2010s. She was active in the Muslim Student Association and other student activist organizations. She was interviewed in 2017, during her sophomore year, as part of the Student Interviews series.

John Wilkes transferred to UCSC from City College of San Francisco, ultimately completing his BA, MA, and PhD in literature at the Santa Cruz campus. Wilkes served from 1981 to 2006 as the founding director of the Graduate Program in Science Communication and was affiliated with Crown College. He was interviewed in 2014-15.

Carter Wilson (Merrill College) was a professor of community studies from 1972 to 2002. He was interviewed as part of the Out in the Redwoods series in 2002.

Glenn Willson (Stevenson College) came to UCSC in 1965. He served as provost of Stevenson College from 1967 to 1975; he also chaired the Academic Senate and held the title of vice-chancellor for college and student affairs. He left UCSC in 1975 to continue his career in England. He was interviewed in 1989.

Nancy Wolfberg transferred to UCSC from UC Berkeley in 1965 as a member of the pioneering class at Cowell College, majoring in history. She was interviewed in 1969 as part of the Student Interviews series.

Adalbert Wolff immigrated to the US from Germany in 1911. Between 1911 and 1926 he held a variety of jobs, including as a timekeeper (keeping payroll records) for the Henry Cowell Company's Santa Cruz ranch. He was interviewed in 1971.

Patricia Zavella is an anthropologist hired in 1983 to teach in UCSC's community studies program; she later transferred to the Latin American and Latino studies department. Zavella directed the campus's Chicano and Latino Research Center from 1999 to 2003 and was a founder of both the BA and PhD programs in the Latin American and Latino studies department. She has also served as UCSC's representative to the UC Committee on Latino Research. She was interviewed in 2013.

Susy Zepeda was born and raised in Los Angeles, California to Mexican immigrant parents. Zepeda earned her PhD in sociology from UC Santa Cruz in 2012, with a designated emphasis in feminist studies and Latin American and Latino studies. She worked as an interviewer for the Regional History Project on the Latinx oral history series. Zepeda is is currently an assistant professor in the Department of Chicana and Chicano Studies at UC Davis.

Frank Zwart arrived at UCSC as a Cowell College student in 1967, graduating in mathematics. After completing graduate work in architecture, he returned to UCSC in 1985 as a staff architect and project manager, beginning a career that spanned the tenures of seven UCSC chancellors. Zwart became campus architect in 1988 and directed UCSC's Office of Physical Planning and Construction until his retirement in April 2010. From 1999 until 2010, he also was associate vice chancellor for physical planning and construction. Zwart was interviewed in 2010.

Margaret Zweiback came to UCSC in 1965 as a member of the pioneering class at Cowell College. She later transferred to Stevenson and ultimately graduated from Merrill. She majored in government. Zweiback was interviewed in 1969 as part of the Student Interviews series.

Lamp, UCSC

Photo by Krikor Andonian,
Campus Photo Archive, 2000s

About the Photographers

Ansel Adams (1902-1984) was an American landscape photographer and environmentalist known for his images of the American West. Between 1962 and 1968 he photographed the land, building sites, and early activities of the UCSC campus: https://oac.cdlib.org/findaid/ark:/13030/c8ns0z6m/.

Krikor Andonian is a lecturer in the Department of Ecology & Evolutionary Biology at UCSC.

Phil Carter is a freelance photographer based in Oakland, California. He received his BA in community studies with a concentration in documentary photography from UCSC. See http://www.pcarterphotography.com/.

Jonathan Chang is a techie who loves photography. See https://www.instagram.com/jonathancphotog/.

Vester Dick (1922-1998) was a press and studio photographer and owner of Vester Dick Photography during his many years in Santa Cruz. Many of his photographs appeared in the *Santa Cruz Sentinel*. See: https://oac.cdlib.org/findaid/ark:/13030/c8sf2xtt/.

Saxon Donnelly created many portrait photos for UC Berkeley.

Matt Fitt's photos have appeared in numerous publications, including the *San Francisco Chronicle, SF Bay Guardian,* and *East Bay Express*. He holds a BA from UCSC. See: https://mattfitt.com/1.

Carol Foote worked as a freelance photographer for the UCSC Public Information Office from 1978 to 1982. Foote also taught photojournalism and news writing for the Science Communication Program. See: https://oac.cdlib.org/findaid/ark:/13030/c8db836n/.

Don Fukuda worked for UCSC Photography Services for many years. His photographs are part of UA50, the UCSC Photography Services Collection.

Don Harris worked for UCSC Photography Services for many years. His photographs are part of UA50, the UCSC Photography Services Collection.

Rusten Hogness is a science writer and host and producer of California Bird Talk.

Lee Jaffe worked as a librarian at UCSC for several decades.

He lives near UCSC and makes many of his wildlife and landscape photos in the Arboretum and Farm. See: https://www.flickr.com/photos/ldjaffe.

Chenyue Jiang was an exchange student in Film and Digital Media at UCSC in 2011.

Steve Kurtz's photography has been featured in *The New York Times, TV Guide, The San Jose Business Journal* and *Monterey Life Magazine*. See: http://www.kurtzphoto.com/.

Carolyn Lagattuta is a professional photographer who lives in the Monterey Bay area. She took photographs for University Relations. See: https://www.stocksy.com/catklein.

Joel Levick is a UCSC alumnus (B.A. Aesthetic Studies, 1972 College Five). Together with Tony Grant and Robert Dawson, he created photographs for UCSC's 25th anniversary in 1990. Leivick is currently the Robert and Ruth Halperin Professor of Photography in the Department of Art and Art History at Stanford University. See: https://oac.cdlib.org/findaid/ark:/13030/c8ns0z6m/.

Alexander Lowry worked as UCSC's first staff photographer, from 1966-1968. During his thirty-year photographic career, Lowry made images of landscapes, wildlife, and people, often for conservation and educational projects. Lowry died in 2010. See: http://www.alexanderlowry.com/.

Jim MacKenzie retired from UCSC after thirty-one years as director of publications, art director of the university magazine, and editorial photographer, He is now an independent art director, publication designer, and photographer. See: https://jimmackenzie.zenfolio.com/.

Wes Modes is a Santa Cruz artist focused on social practice, sculpture, performance, and new media work. He holds a MFA from the Digital Art and New Media program at UCSC. His sculpture, photography, and new media works have appeared in group and solo shows since 1996. His project *A Secret History of American River People* has been exhibited nationally. See: https://modes.io/.

Alex Nelson earned his PhD in computer science from UCSC. He has a particular interest in the banana slug. His interests outside of academics and molluscs include performing on viola, dancing or DJ'ing swing, and dabbling in photography, particularly long-exposure photography. See: http://alumni.soe.ucsc.edu/~ajnelson/.

Andrew Neuhart earned a BA in art from UCSC and is a photographer in Los Angeles area.

Doug Niven is a UCSC systems administrator. He is also a photojournalist who worked in Phnom Penh, Cambodia, for Agence France Presse from 1992-1995. His book *Another Vietnam: Pictures of the War from the Other Side* (National Geographic Press, 2002) is a collection of photos from the Vietnam War as seen through the lens of North Vietnamese photographers.

Alan Nyiri is a photographer and artist living in Poultney, Vermont. In addition to his fine-art landscape and nature images, Nyiri has won acclaim for his architectural studies of some of America's most beautiful campuses. See https://alannyiriphotography.zenfolio.com/.

Steve Rees was a member of the first class to attend Stevenson College, in 1966-67. As photographer for the *Adlai E. Stevenson College Journal*, 1967, he captured images that document the people, places, and events that shaped the experience of his pioneer class. See: https://oac.cdlib.org/findaid/ark:/13030/c8988bbq/.

Irene Reti is the director of the Regional History Project. Reti is also a landscape and nature photographer who particularly loves to photograph the UCSC campus, sandhill cranes in the Central Valley, and the High Sierra. See: https://ireneretiphotography.smugmug.com/.

Jeff Roisman lives in Santa Cruz County and makes images of birds, landscapes, and people. See: https://www.flickr.com/people/47200589@N06/.

Ron Ruby (1932-2003) was a founding member of UCSC's physics faculty. A scholarship for undergraduates was set up in his memory. .

Victor Schiffrin worked for UCSC Photography Services for many years. His photographs are part of UA50, the UCSC Photography Services Collection.

Tina Silverstein is an instructional designer in the Bay Area and an alum of the UCSC Farm apprenticeship program.

Shmuel Thaler has been a staff photographer at the *Santa Cruz Sentinel* since 1987. Thaler's photographs have been published in many newspapers and he has twice been honored with the prestigious National Press Photographers Association's Best of Photojournalism award. In the 1980s Thaler worked for UCSC Photography Services; the images featured here are from that period. See: https://www.shmuelthaler.com/index.

Eric Thiermann is a member of UCSC's pioneering class. He won an Oscar for his documentary film *In the Nuclear Shadow* and founded Impact Creative, a media agency and production company. See: http://www.impactcreative.com/.
Chian Tu graduated from UCSC in accounting in 2015.

Annie Valva is a UCSC alum who has worked as a typographer, digital artist, photographer, and director of technology for PBS.

Elizabeth Van Dyke is a nature photographer who contributes her images to support conservation issues. She served as a board member of the Ventana Wildlife Society involved with recovering California Condors in the wild. She spent most of her technology career in Silicon Valley, while delighting in photo adventure trips to six continents. See: evandyke.com

Wilton Woods served as the photo editor for *National Geographic* photographers Frans Lanting and Kennan Ward. He has also worked for Ziba Photographics (SF), Bay Photo Lab (Santa Cruz, Soquel and Cabrillo, CA), and Pro Camera Rental (SF). See: http://wiltonwoodsmultimedia.blogspot.com/.

Mark Zemelman is a UCSC alum (Crown College) who earned a degree in history during the 1970s. See: https://humanities.ucsc.edu/news-events/gleason/mark-zemelman.html.

Frank Zwart was a student at Cowell College in 1967 and made photographs for Cowell College's yearbook in 1969. Zwart later became the campus architect.

*Thank you also to M.A. Stroud and Mike Kay, for whom the editors could not locate biographical information.

About the Editors

Irene Reti escaped from Los Angeles to UC Santa Cruz in 1978. She fell in love with environmental studies and with the landscape of the campus. Reti earned a BA in environmental studies with a minor in women's studies in 1982. While at UCSC, she first lived at Crown; then at College Five (now Porter College) in housing provided for College Eight students. Finally she moved to and graduated from Kresge College

After a brief stint as a writing tutor, a two-year position working at the Registrar's office publishing the *UCSC Catalog* and *Schedule of Classes*, and another brief appointment as an administrative assistant for the women's studies board, Reti began working at the Regional History Project as a transcriber in 1989. She found a calling in oral history. As the years passed, she branched out into editing and interviewing, and in 2004 became director of the Project. In 2004, she also earned a master's degree in history from UCSC. She has served on the executive council of the Oral History Association and chaired the association's publications committee.

Reti is also a writer and publisher. She founded and ran HerBooks, a feminist press, for many years. She is the author of a memoir, *The Keeper of Memory*, which explores the emotional territory of a child of Holocaust refugees growing up in a house filled with secrets and silence, and *Kabbalah of Stone*, a LGBT novel of Jewish history and magic set in 15th century Spain. When she is not doing oral history or writing, Reti is out photographing landscapes and creating books that weave together her photography and creative writing.

Cameron Vanderscoff lives in New York City, where he is an oral historian, writer, and educator, working with Columbia University, the Apollo Theater, Tina Brown, the Narrative Trust and other projects. He earned an M.A. in oral history from Columbia in 2015, and has consulted widely across the U.S. and over three continents. A musician, he is co-directing a film about the intersection of jazz and veterans' stories in Harlem.

A California native, Cameron has connections to UCSC that run across years and generations. He first came to Santa Cruz as an undergraduate in 2007, where he found a home at Cowell College. He graduated magna cum laude in 2011 with BAs in history and literature (creative writing). While he was a student, Vanderscoff worked at the Page Smith library and as a resident assistant in Cowell and the Village. He delivered his college commencement speech. He soon conducted his first oral history for the Regional History Project, where he found his calling; he has worked with the Project ever since. His link to UCSC is further alloyed by his role as co-founder of the campus-based Okinawa Memories Initiative, and by a world of family ties. His mother and aunt both attended UCSC in the 70s; one cousin was a recent student, and another was an early staff member, imprinting the campus as a collective home for his family. He sees education and historical dialogue as the center of his work.

Sarah Rabkin is a writer, editor, teacher, and oral historian. Her multifarious UCSC connections began during her childhood in the 1960s, with a visit to a family friend who was a literature professor and a fellow of Cowell College. Rabkin returned to the campus in 1978 for a summer-school organic chemistry course, and again in 1983 as a graduate student in science communication and a resident preceptor at Crown College. In 1985 she joined UCSC's writing faculty, teaching classes in composition, expository writing, and journalism. She also led college core-course sections and later taught literature and writing courses for the environmental studies department. After retiring from her faculty position in 2007, Rabkin began working as an interviewer and editor for the UCSC Library's Regional History Project. In addition to her graduate certificate in science communication, she has a bachelor's degree in biology from Harvard University. She is the author and illustrator of *What I Learned at Bug Camp: Essays on Finding a Home in the World* (Juniper Lake Press, 2011).

Northern Flicker and
persimmon fruit,
UCSC Farm, 2014

Photo by Lee Jaffe

Index

Page numbers in *italics* indicate illustrations and captions; n indicates a note.

Students painting, April
1967

Photo by Ansel Adams

Acknowledgements

This book would not have been possible without the synergistic collaboration of many creative individuals. As the director of the Regional History Project, I want to express my deepest thanks to my two co-editors, Sarah Rabkin and Cameron Vanderscoff. It is rare to find colleagues who are not only skilled oral historians, but also gifted and brilliant editors and writers. Furthermore, Cameron and Sarah are generous and kind companions who walked with me into the deep and tangled ravines of UCSC history with humor and fortitude, keeping the faith that we would somehow invent coherent ways to tell the stories of a place we all love.

Another heartfelt thank you goes to Alessia Cecchet, graduate student in film and digital media, who came to the Regional History Project in the summer of 2018 as a Chancellor's Graduate Internship Program recipient, working on the selection and digitization of archival material, and then returned for another fellowship in 2019 to create the companion website for this book. Alessia in many ways served as the visual editor for this entire endeavor, bringing a brilliant sense of history, narrative, and aesthetics to the curation of these materials, as well as marvelous organizational skills.

A huge thank you to my dear friend and longtime collaborator, UCSC alum and former staff member De Clarke, who not only listened to me agonize over this project for five years, but then dove in and proofread this monster while sailing her boat on the wild coast of British Columbia.

We began this endeavor by consulting with a team of UCSC faculty and staff, many of whom had earlier completed oral histories with the Regional History Project. I want to thank Deb Abbott, Harry Berger, De Clarke, Jim Clifford, Michael Cowan, Virginia Jansen, Helene Moglen, Todd Newberry, Linda Rosewood, Hayden White, Michael Warren, Frank Zwart, and Richard Wohlfeiler for their thoughtful responses in this initial phase of the project. Thank you to my colleague and friend, environmental planner and historian Alisa Klaus, for many illuminating lunchtime conversations about UCSC's history, and for reviewing several of the endnotes in this collection. Special thanks to Chancellor George Blumenthal, who devoted extensive time to an in-depth oral history with me in the last year of his chancellorship. Thank you to Tina Silverstein and Clare Henjum for design consultation. Thank you to Chuck Atkinson, Robin Chandler, Carol Christenson, Valerie Jean Chase, Kim Hughes, Linda Hunt, Waverly Lowell, Andy Reti, Shoney Sien, Tina Silverstein, and Elizabeth Van Dyke for wise counsel and support during different phases of this project, and most especially to my extraordinary life partner, Lori Klein, for her unstinting support.

A special thank you to Marina Dundjerski, Susan Lewis, and Will Nagel, my colleagues at UCLA and UC Irvine, who edited and published university history books and generously offered me advice during the inception phase of this project. Thank you also to John Sheehy of Reed College, for his book *Comrades of the Quest*, an oral history of Reed College, which provided inspiration for our project. John was generous with offering advice to another oral historian embarking on an ambitious endeavor. Thank you to Karen Schmidt of the Getty Museum for her production advice and to the folks at Integrated Books International for being the perfect printer to work with on this project.

Gratitude to Jonathan Zimmerman for generously agreeing to write the foreword to this collection and to Cameron Vanderscoff for writing the "Interlude" piece which appears at the end of Volume I.

Appreciation to the photographers for their extraordinary images: Jon Covello (for Vester Dick's photographs); Carol Foote, Lee Jaffe, Carolyn Lagattuta, Joel Levick, Wes Modes, Steve Rees, Jeff Roisman, Tina Silverstein, Shmuel Thaler, Eric Thiermann, Annie Valva, Elizabeth Van Dyke, and Frank Zwart.

The five-year lifespan of this endeavor extended across the tenure of two different heads of UCSC Library's Special Collections and Archives—Elisabeth Remak-Honnef and Teresa Mora, both of whom believed in Regional History's ability to pull off what must have often seemed an utterly insane undertaking, contributing financial resources as well as collegial advice. I want to thank them for having faith in me and my team and for helping in innumerable ways to make this all possible.

Gratitude to former Head of Special Collections and Archives Christine Bunting, whose gifts of mentorship were manifold and whose support of Regional History during the lead-up to the 50th anniversary made it possible for us to interview many of the narrators included in this book. I am especially indebted to my hardworking and meticulous former colleague in Special Collections, Mary De Vries, who served as photo archivist during UCSC's 50th anniversary, creating, organizing, and digitizing an extensive treasure trove of historical photographs of the campus which has greatly enriched this book. Thank you to the University Library's financial wizard, Kim Hughes, who patiently tracked the complex financial aspects of this project and helped me squeeze the turnip on more than one occasion.

Thank you to my amazing team of colleagues in Special Collections for their support as this book came to fruition: Maureen Carey, Kate Dundon, Belinda Egan, Luisa Haddad, Alix Norton, Jessica Pigza, Debra Roussopoulos, and Janet Young. Appreciation to Mathew Simpson and Maureen Carey for their beautiful organization and processing of Dean McHenry's archive, which was a valuable resource for this book. Thank you to Angelika Frebert for her precise and patient help with digitizing archival material for this project and also to Kristy Golubiewski-Davis, Jess Waggoner, Scott Campbell, and Sue Chesley Perry, who facilitated the digitization process and with the development of the companion website. Thank you to Special Collections students Rebecca Rapp and Klytie Xu, for helpful editorial feedback. Thank you to Joop Rubens and Linda Hunt of Library Development for help with outreach.

Finally, thank you to University Librarian Elizabeth Cowell; Associate University Librarian for Planning and Resource Management John Bono; and Associate University Librarian for Collections & Services Kerry Scott for their administrative support of this endeavor.

The Regional History Project is a small but mighty program. In its fifty-seven years there have only been three directors: Elizabeth Spedding Calciano, who founded the project and had the vision to create an oral history program that bridged community and university history; Randall Jarrell, who steered the project from 1974 to 2004 and conducted many extraordinary interviews featured here; and myself (director since 2004). I wish to express my deepest gratitude to both of the former directors for their foresight and labor in documenting both university and community history, and helping to establish what is now one of the oldest oral history programs in the United States. This book partly stands as a tribute to them. Appreciation also to founding university librarian Donald Clark and founding chancellor Dean McHenry for having the chutzpah to establish an oral history program even as they were dreaming up this extraordinary campus between the redwoods and the sea.

Special appreciation to the often unseen and unappreciated transcribers, interviewers, and editors who have worked with the program: staff transcriber and assistant Doris Johnson; contract transcribers Mim Eisenberg and Teresa Bergen; editor Esther Ehrlich; interviewers Tandy Beal, Valerie Jean Chase, Ellen Farmer, Greg Graalfs, Sarah Rabkin, Roseanne Shensa, Nikki Silva, and Cameron Vanderscoff. Over the years, many students and several UCSC staff have worked with Regional History as interviewers and editors and their work too is an enormous contribution to this book. So thank you to Elizabeth Bennett, Teresa Bergen, Regan Brashear, Alana Chazan, Erin Colliau, Sheila Della Ratta, Michelle Espino, ClaireMarie Ghelardi, Patrick Letellier, Leslie Lopez, Andrea Lowgren, Lizzy Gray, Maya Hegege, Jacquelyn Marie, Evelyn Richards, Jonathan Shapiro, Jesse Silva, Yvonne Sherwood, Samantha Williams, and Susy Zepeda.

Much appreciation to Virginia (Ginny) Campbell, who served as secretary to Dean McHenry for many years and who donated funds to UCSC that helped support the publication of this book.

And finally, this book is dedicated to all of the students, staff, and faculty whose labors and visions have brought UC Santa Cruz to life over these past five decades. We are the seeds of something different.

—*Irene Reti, Director, Regional History Project*

Ferns near Hahn
Student Services

Photo by Irene Reti,
2018

Support the Regional History Project
at the UCSC Library's
Special Collections & Archives

Seeds of Something Different was edited and published by the UCSC Library's Regional History Project as a nonprofit endeavor. You can support the collecting of future oral histories by making a tax-deductible gift to the Regional History Fund at the Library online at:

https://tinyurl.com/quagvaj

Thank you for your support!

Sunset, UCSC
Arboretum

Photo by Irene Reti,
2016